W9-AYA-499

Acclaim for Helen Lefkowitz Horowitz's

REREADING SEX

"Horowitz encourages us to reflect upon the continuing relevance of [her subject]. . . . More than a century later, she contends, Americans remain deeply divided over the same issues: contraception, abortion, sex education, pornography, and censorship. *Rereading Sex* turns out to be both a powerfully revisionist history and a compelling story for our times."
> —from the citation naming *Rereading Sex*
> a finalist for the Francis Parkman Prize

"Impressive. . . . An intricate tapestry of nineteenth-century American sexual culture that fully reveals the power and complexity of sexuality and its profound impact on every facet of life."
> —*Booklist* (starred review)

"In letting us eavesdrop on nineteenth-century discussions of sex, Horowitz demonstrates that while the language has certainly changed, many of the arguments have not."   —*Providence Journal*

"In Helen Horowitz's wide-ranging account of the culture wars of the nineteenth century, anxieties that we live with today—about pornography, contraception, abortion, and free expression—turn out to have surprising histories."
> —Linda K. Kerber, author of *No Constitutional Right to Be Ladies*

"Entertaining. . . . The huge number of philosophies and personalities that played a role in the debate, and made a foundation for our current sexual ideas, are brilliantly distilled."   —*The Lafayette Times*

"Moves us beyond the old binary of Victorian lights and shadows, of prudery versus passion, to show the interwoven complexity of our first national conversation about sex."
> —Patricia Cline Cohen, author of *The Murder of Helen Jewett*

Helen Lefkowitz Horowitz

REREADING SEX

Helen Lefkowitz Horowitz is Sydenham Clark Parsons Pro-
fessor of History and Professor of American Studies at
Smith College. She is the author of *The Power and Passion of
M. Carey Thomas* (1994), *Campus Life* (1987), *Alma Mater*
(1984), and *Culture and the City* (1976). She is the recipient of
grants and fellowships from, among others, the Radcliffe
Institute and the American Antiquarian Society. *Rereading
Sex* was a finalist for the Pulitzer Prize, the finalist for the
Francis Parkman Prize, and the winner of the Merle Curti
Prize from the Organization of American Historians. She
has taught at Scripps College and the University of Southern
California. She and her husband, Daniel, live in Northamp-
ton and Cambridge, Massachusetts.

ALSO BY HELEN LEFKOWITZ HOROWITZ

The Power and Passion of M. Carey Thomas

Campus Life

Alma Mater

Culture and the City

Landscape in Sight (editor)

Love Across the Color Line (editor, with Kathy Peiss)

REREADING SEX

REREADING SEX

*Battles over Sexual Knowledge and
Suppression in Nineteenth-Century America*

Helen Lefkowitz Horowitz

Vintage Books

A DIVISION OF RANDOM HOUSE, INC.   NEW YORK

FIRST VINTAGE BOOKS EDITION, OCTOBER 2003

Copyright © 2002 by Helen Lefkowitz Horowitz

All rights reserved under International and Pan-American Copyright Conventions.
Published in the United States by Vintage Books, a division of Random House, Inc.,
New York, and simultaneously in Canada by Random House of Canada
Limited, Toronto. Originally published in hardcover in the United States by
Alfred A. Knopf, a division of Random House, Inc., New York, in 2002.

Vintage and colophon are registered trademarks of Random House, Inc.

The Library of Congress has cataloged the Knopf edition as follows:
Horowitz, Helen Lefkowitz.
Rereading sex : battles over sexual knowledge and suppression in nineteenth-century
America / Helen Lefkowitz Horowitz.
p.   cm.
1. Sex customs—United States—History—19th century.   2. Sexual Ethics—United
States—History—19th century.   I. Title.

HQ18.U5 H673 2002
306.7'0973—dc21 2002019105

Vintage ISBN: 0–375–70186–9

Author photograph © Ben Horowitz

www.vintagebooks.com

Printed in the United States of America

10   9   8   7   6   5   4   3   2   1

To Dan
First, last, always

CONTENTS

Contents

REREADING SEX

I

Introduction

Historians live in both the present and the past, and their work reflects their Janus-like double gaze. In the mid-1990s, I found myself bewildered by forces in the society that seemed to insist on the suppression of straight talk about sex in the public arena when, at the same time, popular culture was rife with sexually explicit lyrics and films. AIDS was taking a terrible toll, but parents and school boards were attempting to prevent schoolchildren from receiving scientific knowledge about sex. As the Internet broke down boundaries to the transmission of information, it opened up a vast universe of sexually arousing and violent images. And yet, after Dr. Joycelyn Elders answered a question following an AIDS conference in which she stated that as a part of human sexuality, masturbation was an appropriate subject in sex education classes, she was forced to resign as surgeon general of the United States. I felt I was living in a baffling sexual culture.

This sense was in my head and heart when I began to think about returning to historical research. I had just completed a biography of M. Carey Thomas, in which I had tried to determine what she had known about sexuality as she came to maturity in the 1870s. I had learned a great deal about my subject but wanted to know more about her era. I began with a seemingly simple question: How did Americans imagine sex in the nineteenth century?

This turned out to have no easy answer, and I started to study the impact of new understandings of the body, especially the reproductive organs and the nervous system, on the conception of desire. I came to ask how sexual knowledge and the questions it posed shaped the ways in which sexual matters were written about and discussed in the public arena. In the process I uncovered the nineteenth century's complex conversation about sex. In reading it, I bumped into efforts, partially successful, to suppress elements of that conversation. I learned also that, from early on, as critics challenged the power of the state to regulate sexual speech, they created a vital counter-tradition opposing censorship.

I had already begun to question the usual way that standard texts treated the history of nineteenth-century sexuality in America. They contained many versions of "Victorian sexuality"—that Americans beginning in the antebellum years had constructed a self that focused on self-control, suppression of sexual urges, and denial of women's sexual feeling. Even writers who in recent years have challenged the hegemony of sexual repression have nonetheless continued to work within a conceptual framework that allows an easily comprehended conflict between expression and restraint. They have not seen what this book demonstrates, the role of the courts. Notions of nineteenth-century Victorian repression emerged in part because the normal routes of historical discovery were distorted by government suppression.

My book contests "Victorian sexuality" at a deeper level than earlier works, and I hope it will lay both the concept and the term to rest. By rereading sex in terms of contending conversations, this study offers a new and more supple way to envision sexual discussion in both past and present. The American polity was split along many lines, economic, religious, and ideological. Among the matters about which Americans disagreed most sharply was sexuality.

I take Americans quarreling about sex as my subject and look at many of them as I track the cultural divides shaping distinct understandings of the body, reproduction, and desire. I focus on the work of some famous Americans, such as Sylvester Graham, Robert Dale Owen, and Anthony Comstock; I also examine that of others, such as Mary Gove and Cephas Brainerd, who are relatively unknown today. As I have read what Americans wrote in the nineteenth century, I have discerned from the welter four primary voices, and I have come to imagine Americans engaged in a complex four-way conversation about sex. In the conversation each side not merely disagreed; each imagined sexuality from a distinct cultural perspective. Each of these four stances shaped the way Americans received and conveyed sexual knowledge. Because it is a metaphor that invokes both structure and background, I have adopted the term "framework" in referring to each of the four sexual cultures. American vernacular sexual culture, the first framework, was based on humoral theory and carried with it an erotic edge. Evangelical Christianity, the second, held a deep distrust of the flesh. In the nineteenth century the third framework emerged, a new consciousness linked to new notions of the body, nerves, health, and the relation of mind and body. At its outer edge, a new sensibility that placed sex at the center of life came into being, creating the fourth framework.

Exploration of the four sexual frameworks in nineteenth-century America begins with vernacular culture. Passed down through the generations and sideways among peers, this framework sustained an earthy acceptance of sex and desire as vital parts of life for men and women. It is best labeled "vernacular" because it was a largely oral tradition outside the literate discourses of religion, science, and law and typically despised by those in power. As it portrayed sex, vernacular sexuality looked back deep into the European past to the medical perception of the body as governed by the four humors—blood, phlegm, yellow bile, and black bile—related to the four states—hot, cold, dry, and moist—with heat and blood as the source of sexual desire. Its gendered forms took different emphases. What can be known about female vernacular sexual culture centered on childbirth and efforts to control fertility. Male vernacular sexuality paid great attention to sexual intercourse between men and women, emphasizing sharp arousal and release. This framework has been the source of bawdy humor in America, many popular terms, and, as literacy spread, numerous sexually arousing texts.

Lying at the base of conscious awareness and corresponding to strong bodily urges, vernacular sexuality retained power throughout the nineteenth century. Although plenty of prescriptive statements from the pulpit and the printed page attempted to shape what Americans thought and felt, they did not fully supplant what seemed to many to be common wisdom. My sense of the power of vernacular culture is one of the reasons why I have chosen the word "framework" instead of the more fashionable word "discourse." In contrast to those who deem that ideas about sexuality are linked seamlessly to sexual practice, I perceive more disjuncture and internal conflict, possibilities allowed by imagining a conversation in which participants expressed competing sexual frameworks and perhaps accepted into their own lives and practice messages from more than one.[2]

Christian ministers were certainly aware of vernacular sexuality, as it was for them a central component of "Old Man Adam." As men such as Lyman Beecher put it, ever since God placed man on earth, he had a tendency to sin. And "Eve," that representative wayward woman, hardly helped.

In the nineteenth century, as revivals spread evangelical Christianity across the nation, ministers waged war against many sins of the flesh. In this second framework, lust became a preeminent deadly sin, its fiery rages threatening both body and spirit. As preachers fought for the souls of sinners, they knew that they had a battle on their hands. Their strength increased through lay efforts to found and support Sunday schools and missionary, Bible, and tract societies. In New England, with its long tradition of communal oversight of moral behavior, the Second Great Awakening unleashed campaigns against alcohol, prostitution, slavery, stimulating food and drink, desecration of the Sabbath, and obscene images and words.

By the 1830s, evangelical Christians were not alone in their verbal efforts to shape sexual feeling and behavior. As freethinkers such as Frances Wright and Robert Dale Owen demanded a new approach to sexual questions, a vast conversation about sex began. Basing their philosophy on the Enlightenment's credo "Let there be light," radicals such as Owen valued frank, open discussion of sexual matters. Owen wrote and published the first book on birth control in the United States. Encouraged by the example and hospitality of freethinkers, Charles Knowlton added his scientifically grounded book on contraception. Owen and Knowlton created a new literature of sexuality that, beginning in the 1830s, laid one of the foundations of the third framework. The books and pamphlets took the term "reform physiology" to designate their efforts to describe the reproductive organs and their functions and to prescribe healthful ways of living. Readers of reform physiology included those rural and urban northerners who were successfully seeking ways to limit the size of their families.

Alongside the freethinkers, reformers rooted in the Christian tradition, such as Sylvester Graham, laid the third framework's other foundation. Soon ministers, moralists, doctors, and commentators added their voices and printed words to the conversation. These texts of reform physiology began to displace a conception of sex existing within a body of four humors with new notions of the body, nerves, and the relation of mind and body. Sexual desire, no longer imagined as springing from heated blood, was in mind, originating in messages sent from the brain through the nerves. In turning to health and disease, lecturers and writers focused concern on the nervous system. As they added new notions of romantic love that put feeling and its expression at the center, some found reasons to separate sexual intercourse from conception. Locating sex in mind at a time when poems and fiction centered on heightened emotion emphasized the potential power of imaginative literature and thus its danger. Such ideas constituted the third sexual framework in its early phase.

Although based in an emerging science of the body emphasizing the nerves and health, the third framework was divided from the outset. As its writers explored the relation of sexuality to new notions of the body, mind, and health, they struggled over words and concepts by which the passions and the reproductive organs and their functions could be best understood and explained. In this clash, voices urging restraint and inhibition, such as Graham, were contested by others, such as Knowlton, seeking sexual expression less constrained by traditional morality. Health reformers, for example William A. Alcott and R. T. Trall, preached ways of healthy living, including sexual practices believed conducive to well-being. As some evangelical Christians joined the discussion and adopted the new language of health, they added medical reasons for denying the flesh. Books authored by such writers as Luther V. Bell and Mary Gove proliferated, counseling youth against masturbation and describing a youthful sexual culture that seemed especially worrisome to adults at a time in which more and more boys and girls were leaving home for school and work. These writers were countered by a strong strain of medical common sense and religious free thought in writers such as Frederick Hollick and Edward B. Foote, insisting on the naturalness of the body's sexual appetites and desires.

Moreover, within this large evolving third configuration there was movement and change. Some of those who began with a reawakened evangelical Christianity ended up as enthusiastic about sex as they once were about the Second Coming. Amherst College graduate Orson Squires Fowler, for example, preached phrenology and gradually moved from exhorting his audience to suppress "amativeness," or the reproductive instinct, to celebrating it. Sexual experimentation played an important role in a number of reform and utopian movements of the antebellum years, some of which began within evangelical enthusiasm. John Humphrey Noyes's utopian colony of perfectionists at Oneida, New York, believed in "complex marriage," where each member of the community was a potential sexual partner of every adolescent and adult of the opposite sex. Within the emerging Spiritualist community the notion of spiritual affinity led some to reject their husbands and wives to take new temporal as well as spiritual lovers.

The authors of the third sexual framework attempted to present to a growing middle-class audience the new science of the body, along with prescriptions for living. To the uncertain world of the emerging middle class, many counseled sobriety and habits of order. New canons of middle-class respectability emphasized decorum and bodily control. Unquestionably in the antebellum years there came into being a middle-class awareness of appropriate public behavior that sought to remove overt sexuality from the public arena. A range of evangelically inspired movements before the Civil War added their voices, urging temperance and Sabbath keeping. Writings of the third framework often contribute to this project. I would distinguish, however, between admonitions about public behavior and prescriptions in areas governing private life, as well as between what is written and how it is read.

Much of what others have understood as Victorian sexuality is the play of this verbiage over vernacular sexuality. It is a mistake to see the sexual prescriptions of reform physiology, however, as all of a piece. I emphasize both the varied nature of this writing and the complexity of its hold on the psyche. I agree with Karen Lystra that reform physiology spans a spectrum from sexual restriction to sexual enthusiasm and with Carl Degler that there was a gap between what people did and what the prescriptive literature told them to do.[5] In addition, I think that there was often a cognitive gap between contending sexual frameworks. To me the nature of the human psyche is such that individuals can hold multiple understandings about sex and be divided within themselves. While human complexity may have generated the confusion and guilt apparent in some diaries and letters, it also made possible a realm of freedom that allowed mid-nineteenth-century men and women room to find their own way. In sum, reform physiology was varied and normally had a lighter hold on the psyche than is generally understood.

Moreover, from the beginning through the middle and end, there were countervoices to sexual prescription and messages of restraint. America has had a continuous and lively tradition of free thought that punctures pieties and demands straight speech. Early in the nineteenth century there were those, such as Abner Kneeland, who took frank relish in blasphemy. As the century progressed, freethinkers and materialists such as Charles Knowlton pushed the limits of the sexual conversation, challenging medical orthodoxy and notions of verbal propriety. By midcentury, social movements began to alter the nature of the sexual conversation in the United States, adding the voices of John Humphrey Noyes, women's rights advocates, Spiritualists, Fourierists, and free lovers. By the 1850s, there were those at the far reaches of reform physiology who placed sex at the center of life. Provoked by agitators, including Victoria Woodhull and Ezra Heywood, the fourth framework

8

combined visionary and radical politics with notions of sexual liberty and freedom of expression. Believing that sex lay at the core of being, adherents held that sexual expression in heterosexual intercourse was the most vital facet of life, as important for women as for men. They asserted that because sex was so valuable to the self, it must be freely expressed, that any diversion or repression of sexual urges from their "natural expression" in coition was harmful.

As a historian I study documents, and thus this became a book that focused on certain sexual representations printed and sold to the general public from the late 1820s to the end of the 1870s. Each chapter of the first three sections is freestanding but connected to the larger structure of the book. These chapters are building blocks in which I attempt to re-create the nineteenth century's conversation about sex and sexual representation. When I write of "sexual representation," I typically mean portrayal in writing or through printed visual images. The universe of potential sexual representations is, of course, larger than my purview here and includes the fine arts, drama and staged entertainment, and fashion and body art, among other forms. When I use the phrase "sexual culture," I am referring to the domain of values, beliefs, ideas, attitudes, and expectations about sex. I have adopted the term "sexual conversation" to express my sense that rather than nineteenth-century Americans having a single sexual culture, they had competing ones contending with one another.

As I began this work, my attention was first drawn to writings of reform physiology. An important motive behind understanding the sexual body in the nineteenth century arose from the drive to control reproduction; thus works on birth control emerged as texts important to my research. The need of writers to earn a living meant that words to inform became words to sell. The expanding American economy encouraged words to advertise the sale of products and services. Texts of reform physiology were often classed with those advocating reform of marriage and divorce laws, including ones that the era perceived as promoting free love. As I read these various works and learned about their authors, I came upon legal suppression and began to trace its history.

This led me to texts of a different sort, erotic writing whose explicit intention was to arouse sexual feeling. In a world of buying and selling, some sought to cash in on the public's hungry interest in materials about sex and use of the printed page for both information and sexual arousal. There was a lively, albeit partially hidden, commerce in erotic printed materials, both words and pictures. In contrast to the plethora of works on reform physiology available, little of the erotica circulating in the mid–nineteenth century made its way into the public collections open to inquiring historians. The example of Samuel Pepys was probably followed by many American men. After reading *L'Ecole des filles,* he burned the book so that "it may not stand in the list of books nor among them, to disgrace them if it should be found." Others who were more careless had descendants who cleansed their libraries before donating them or librarians who did so after receiving the books. This has created a deficit or silence that has distorted our understanding of the past. Although some libraries are attempting to redress the balance by acquiring erotic books and prints, many gaps in knowledge remain.[4]

In the face of historical matter that has been deliberately destroyed or hidden, the historian's role is to be a detective. One of the most intriguing elements of my research has been the effort to find and understand the texts of the standard works of nineteenth-century commercial erotica, what I have called the "erotic canon." These books are identified in older reference works and the small body of historical literature devoted to them. I have tried my hardest to locate these texts as they circulated in the United States, relying primarily on court records and newspaper accounts of trials, supplemented by book advertisements and the books and prints themselves. To a certain extent the information that I have gathered has been backlighted by the arrest records, beginning in 1872, of Anthony Comstock, who on occasion commented on the earlier histories of some of the major figures whom he targeted. One of the important contributions of this book is to offer a new trail of authors and printers and sellers of erotica in the United States whose wares were the subject of legal suppression before 1880.

Beginning in midcentury, these books were sold with texts of a sensationalist nature by American authors, works that the era called "racy." Such books and prints were often marketed with works of reform physiology, including those dealing with birth control, free-love tracts, and articles for contraception and abortion. As information about sex and commerce became intertwined, so did the effort to regulate them through prosecution and legislation. The twentieth century has seen the criminalization of contraception and abortion as the primary outcome of obscenity law. In the nineteenth century, however, the attention of much of the public was focused on commercial erotica. What made this writing about sex dangerous in some eyes was its very purpose, its power to arouse its readers. To many in the nineteenth century it was the relation of erotica to masturbation that posed the great peril to readers. The "secret vice" was the central concern of opponents of obscenity. Fearing masturbation, some powerful men emerged from evangelical Christianity, the second framework, to lead the battle against obscenity. They linked commercial erotica to all sexual portrayals and materials and perceived them as too threatening to move freely in the marketplace.

These men were aware of the lively, multivalent conversation about sex in their time. In one sense they participated in it, albeit reactively, seeing its dangers, not its possibilities. Changing sexual knowledge and the issues it raised helped determine the ways in which these critics judged how sexual matters should be written about and discussed in the public arena. The texts of reform physiology shaped censors' thoughts on sex and desire and the power of sexual representation. Certain matters remained constant: young children should be kept innocent, and sexual knowledge posed a special risk to girls, who should remain ignorant about sex until marriage. But one element in their thinking changed.

By midcentury the youth seen to be most in danger were young men, urban lads living in boardinghouses away from their families and working as clerks. They had inherited male vernacular culture and its counters in evangelical Christianity and the texts of physiological reform. In the city they were surrounded by a new "sporting culture" with its many attractions, including printed erotica. In the light of the many changes in urban life, some reformers perceived the new sexually explicit newspapers and the older books and prints as a potential incitement leading young clerks to destructive sexual practices. Conservative men moved to suppress erotica through the courts. In time, a new group of censors emerged from the Young Men's Christian Association to follow in their path and seek to silence additional contributors to the sexual conversation, including reform physiologists writing about contraception or advocating free love.

Their efforts differed from those of other participants in the sexual conversation. Unlike the largely verbal exchanges of unofficial adversaries engaged in an informal war of words, those attempting to suppress what they labeled "obscenity" in the courts undertook a public struggle whose stakes were high—for both the protagonists and the society. Much of what follows examines court cases, important in themselves and as windows into the past. These legal and constitutional conflicts illumine the critical fault lines that rumbled beneath the surface of America's complex nineteenth-century sexual culture.

Those who turned to the courts found an effective and reliable tool. At both federal and state levels the United States had constitutional commitments to freedom of expression. But the nation also had a common-law tradition from England that governed sexual speech. This deeply conservative legal tradition appealed to the established members of society who controlled state courts. In the antebellum years a body of practice in the common law of obscene libel developed in New York courts that enabled prosecutors and judges to silence those whose representations they judged "obscene." During and immediately following the Civil War, as conservative reformers got state and federal legislation to suppress obscene material, they drew on the well-established practices of the New York courts to prosecute and convict violators. Precedent had great power not merely because the court is a tradition-bound institution, but also because in the late nineteenth century it was administered by judges, all men, who were often deeply conservative. My research and writing about the law go against the influential work of advocates and many legal scholars and makes an important new contribution. I discover and elucidate cases dealing with obscenity before the Civil War, link them with common-law theory and practice, demonstrate their connections to the better-known efforts of the 1870s, and establish the deep groove in American legal traditions inimical to free speech and the First Amendment.

In the early part of the story I have to tell, courts were largely concerned with policing the raw edges of vernacular sexuality, particularly the print that sought paying male readers by offering them sexually exciting words and images. At moments, entangled in conflicts over blasphemy, prosecutors and judges moved against those seeking enlightened discussion of new sexual knowledge, but this was infrequent. This changed as a complex process altered perceptions. Understanding all of this requires a dialectical narrative with many elements—changing sexual knowledge and the reconstruction of desire; the impact of evangelical Christianity and its collision with emerging free thought; the emergence of masturbation as a great obsessional fear; the rise in the society of an alternative male subculture that came to own the streets of American cities; the persistence of common-law tradition and courts willing to police obscenity; and the creation of a new ideology that combined visionary and radical politics with notions of sexual liberty and freedom of expression.

As the third framework, that of moral physiology, took hold and new understandings of the nervous system became entwined with a new place, for the imagination, more and more of the sexual conversation began to appear dangerous to conservative eyes. This sense of danger grew as the fourth framework, placing sex at the center of life, emerged from radical social movements. Articulated in representations at the farthest reaches of physiological reform, the fourth framework carried a different power. Born in advocacy, it evoked apprehension that printed word might become deed.

As I have talked about my work with others, many have pointed out to me that judgments about sexual acts underlie efforts to control portrayals, that ultimately it is behavior that is at issue. I am not fully convinced of this—or, more precisely, I am not convinced that the relation between forbidden acts and feared depictions is as direct as my interlocutors assume. Unquestionably, nineteenth-century efforts to suppress representations regarded as obscene are related to efforts to control sexual activity. But complex understandings of who is at risk and of the dangers they face intervened to shape the campaign against obscenity. For much of the nineteenth century the drive to police obscenity sprang from the fear of youthful male masturbation. However, as the fourth framework took shape, increasingly the politics of who was doing the writing came to matter.

Community sanctions that had once served to censor or at least isolate those parts of the conversation about sex deemed off limits seemed insufficient as the society grew more complex. A greater recourse to the law and the courts on the part of those seeking to suppress commercial erotica signaled the change. During the Civil War, sexual license became more visible than before. Scandals that followed in the war's wake linked sexual representation to threats to the social order. The Young Men's Christian Association of New York, formed to offer a moral alternative to urban youth working in the city, led the fight to get state and federal legislation to criminalize words and images about sex. The association greatly expanded the reach of earlier anti-obscenity efforts by including birth control information and materials and advertisements for abortion. A Christian movement to place God in the Constitution turned to the more winnable battle against obscenity. A watchdog materialized in the person of Anthony Comstock, a young clerk determined to root out the commercial erotica sold on the streets.

By the 1870s, culture and politics converged to forge a powerful new coalition eager to rewrite American law governing obscenity and its interpretation by the courts. In 1873 Congress passed the federal act for the "Suppression of Trade in, and Circulation of, Obscene Literature and Articles of Immoral Use," introduced and championed by the New York Y.M.C.A., and created the office of special agent in the United States Post Office with power to confiscate immoral matter in the mails and arrest those sending it. With the office on the books, the postmaster general appointed Anthony Comstock to fill it. The Y.M.C.A. had the Society for the Suppression of Vice incorporated to pursue prosecutions under new state and federal laws and named Comstock its secretary and chief agent. In the fourth section of this book I trace the political and legal story of the 1873 federal statute, a story that includes its antithesis—assertions by the law's opponents of freedom of expression under the Constitution.

Legal suppression, especially after 1873, had a powerful effect on what could be published about sex at the time. Its impact has continued to the present. If there are profound connections between efforts at censorship then and now, it is because many of the same forces are still at work in the culture and polity. At some level I undertook this work to understand the mystifying sexual conversation of the present and the perplexing efforts at suppression of contemporary times. Rereading the past can help bring the present into clearer focus.

Rereading nineteenth-century sexual representations also explains why the nineteenth century itself has been so misunderstood. Law and the courts reinforced the power of one side of the sexual conversation and forced another—its most radical strand—underground. Suppression thereby removed from the public arena valuable materials for individual and collective self-understanding and historical reevaluation. The way that the legal system of the nineteenth century dealt with sexual matters that some judged obscene has thus led later Americans to misread sex in the nineteenth century.

Unquestionably, evangelical Christianity as combined with reform physiology won out in numbers. Hegemony in the United States, however, does not normally mean silencing others, nor does it necessarily require twisting opponents' words out of shape. In the 1870s, it did. The opposition did not disappear, however. Brave writers and lawyers, such as Edward B. Foote, Ezra Heywood, and Thaddeus B. Wakeman, fought openly in the courts, beginning a counter legal tradition that ultimately reshaped the boundaries of freedom of speech. Other opposing elements went underground to await more opportune times.

Telling the story of sexual knowledge and suppression in nineteenth-century America requires two different narratives. I must relate a national story, for part of its subject is the production and diffusion of materials dealing with sex. To recount it requires knowing, as best as can be known, the content of what was written, drawn, and published about sex, and thus made available to Americans. At the same time I need to give a detailed narrative of New York City, because it is there that the principal action took place. As the leading cultural center of the nation, the city had important writers and printmakers, the major printing presses, and the primary distributors of written and visual representations of sexual matters. It was a center of reform agitation about sexual questions, including prostitution and abortion. It had the courts that tried significant cases, and, more important, established the central traditions of court practice dealing with obscene libel.

Perhaps most tellingly, it had the critical social forces to battle obscenity. New York saw the rise of male sporting culture. Within the city a specific movement of conservative reformers emerged to combat it, focusing on the welfare of the young clerk and his reading. The Young Men's Christian Association of New York came into being in the 1850s to offer clerks moral alternatives to commercial entertainment. Confronting printed erotica, it turned to suppression. After the Civil War, as social movements and corruption seemed to link sexual representation to threats to the social order, the New York Y.M.C.A. and its offshoot, the New York Society for the Suppression of Vice, fought for federal and state legislation to curb commercial erotica, birth control information, and advertisements for abortion. Congress passed the Comstock Law in 1873, and Anthony Comstock became a federal agent of the U.S. Post Office. By 1879 a federal appellate court in New York confirmed the constitutionality of the law and the proper action of a lower court in enforcing it. As defendants were prosecuted for obscenity and their lawyers in New York challenged the law, a countertradition came into being. A community of supporters emerged who were committed to keeping free speech alive in an era of suppression. What had begun as a New York struggle became one of our first national culture wars, a battle between those committed to sexual knowledge and those determined to suppress it.

PART I

THE SEXUAL CONVERSATION

2

Vernacular Sexual Culture, Commercial Erotica, and Obscene Libel

Since colonial times Americans have worried about what their neighbors read about sex. Exactly what they did about those worries, however, has changed over time. In 1744, in Northampton, Massachusetts, Jonathan Edwards conducted a formal church inquiry into who was reading a popular compendium of sexual information and what they were doing with that information. By the nineteenth century, criminal courts were deciding the fate of those selling books considered erotic. In 1879, for example, D. M. Bennett was tried in a federal criminal court in New York for selling a free-love tract. A brief look at these two cases, 135 years apart, conveys the distance that this work must travel if it is to explain both the kinds of sexual representations available and the drive to suppress them in nineteenth-century America.

It was a minister's duty in eighteenth-century New England to supervise the morality of the town. *Aristotle's Master-piece,* a guide to reproduction and sexual matters, was one of the most commonly available books dealing with the body in the eighteenth and early nineteenth centuries. Later advertisements of the book suggest that by the nineteenth century it was read both for information about the body and for erotic arousal, and that may have been true in the eighteenth century as well. The book first appeared in English in 1684, and within a year eight copies, presumably printed in England, appeared in the inventory of the Boston bookseller Chiswell. By the mid–eighteenth century, *Aristotle's Master-piece* had made its way beyond the cultural centers of seaport cities, such as Boston, to provincial outposts such as Northampton, a town one hundred miles to the west, where it was widely available.[1]

Worried about his flock, Edwards asked his church to vote for a formal inquiry, and with that vote began to hold meetings at which he gathered testimony. In a letter to a congregant, the wife of Eleazar Hannam, asking her to testify, he wrote that he had heard that two young men in Northampton, lads in their early twenties, were "reading [a book] about women kind, that which wa[s very] unclean to be read; and that they [made] sport of what they read before som[e wo]men kind." Edwards asked Mrs. Hannam to send him testimony of what she knew, stating that it was her duty to do so. He wanted to learn what she knew about the contents of the book itself—was it "about women's having childre[n]"? And he sought information on the way it was read. Did the young men seem "to make sport [and di]version of what was read"? Did they take "occasion from it to run upon the [girls] and the like"?[2]

Edwards's notes of the testimony, written in his hasty scrawl, make it clear that the book was no rarity in Northampton. Witnesses reported to Edwards that it was found in a number of households. Yet, probably because of its open consideration of sexual matters, it was not the kind of book that appeared in household inventories, and in 1744 one did not find it out in plain sight in the hall or parlor. It was a book held privately. In one house it was kept up a chimney; in another, under the lining of a cot. The one exception to its secret nature was found in the testimony of a young woman who stated that she had seen the book "at Dr. Mathers"; this was a significant exception, for it named the respected local physician Samuel Mather.

Why did Edwards not read *Aristotle's Master-piece* himself? In the letter to Mrs. Hannam, he stated that he had already learned that the book in the hands of the young men was "about women kind, that which wa[s very] unclean to be read." The nature of his questions to Mrs. Hannam suggest that Edwards did not think that the book was unclean for women to read, but it was likely that he so regarded it for many men. As he prepared to seek the church inquiry, Edwards had made notes on a scrap of paper. His tiny, crabbed hand is difficult to read, but it reveals a number of biblical references that served a minister as legal precedents served a judge in a court of law. As Edwards prepared to give "Reasons why I think it was not a private affair," but one that called for a church inquiry, he noted the need to call witnesses, confront the offenders face-to-face, and deal with all of them in a group. Behind this was a matter of church doctrine: Edwards believed that he could not administer Communion to those who he felt defiled the injunction in

Leviticus 10:10 to "put difference between holy and unholy, and between unclean and clean." But what was unclean?[3]

The passages in the Bible that Edwards noted include ones that censure "filthy communication out of your mouth" (Colossians 3:8) and "evil communications" (1 Corinthians 15:33). Was Edwards regarding the book itself as such a communication? It is possible. He cited Job 31—"I made a covenant with mine eyes; why then should I think upon a maid?"—which he interpreted as David's meditation. *Aristotle's Master-piece* discussed women's bodies and had illustrations of uncovered women and one showing a fetus in utero. Reading the text and viewing the pictures may have seemed to Edwards the equivalent of David's looking upon the naked Bathsheba, making the book "unclean to be read."

What became clear in the formal inquiry, however, was that the issue more important for Edwards than the reading of the book was the use of the book in the teasing conversations of the young men of Northampton. Most of the biblical references that Edwards cited in his notes denounce lascivious conduct, such as consorting with whores (Proverbs 6:27–28). This is a matter of sexual misbehavior, not of representation. With one exception, the testimony focused on behavior, not on the act of reading. In the exception, a woman recalled a young man saying that he had "sat till mid night reading in 2 of them Books," and that he had added, "dont you think I would sit up

The female body with a fetus in utero. *Aristotle's Compleat Master-piece*, 1741, opposite p. 44. Countway Library of Medicine.

again if I had opportunity." This statement did not lead to further questions, and the matter was dropped. The line of questions elicited much about the way that the book featured in the speech and actions of the young men. One woman testified that several of the young men had been talking about the book "in a private way" and that "when talking about the Book they talked about women and girls and turn about and Looked upon me and said you do not need to be scared we Know as much about ye as you and more too." According to one female witness, at one point the boys "Run upon the Girls at that time boasting how much they Knew about them." They had learned about menstruation, and they bragged that they could tell from the circles around a girl's eyes if it was the time when "the moon Change Girls." Another young woman testified that the boys read the book before her. After that they "Laugh[ed] ready to kill them and catch hold of the Girls and shook 'em." Another fellow asserted that they "knew about Girls—Knew what belonged to Girls as well as Girls themselves." One of the female witnesses stated that one of the fellows, bringing up the "Granny Book," talked "exceeding uncleanly" and "Lasciviously."

At the inquiry, the male youths were not contrite. When called to testify before the church, several demonstrated contempt for the whole proceeding. Witnesses reported statements of angry disrespect for Edwards and the elders: "I don't care a Turd" or "I don't care a Fart for any of them" or "I ben't obliged to wait any longer on their Arses, as I have done." As they waited, the youths played leapfrog, took refreshment at a tavern without being given the "liberty" to leave, and complained that they were being detained from their work. One repeatedly stated, "I won't worship a wig." When questioned, however, he rephrased his words to suggest that he was not angry about the class presumptions of the minister and the committee but rather that he was fearful that the fine clothes of the inquiry committee would intimidate witnesses.[4]

In the face of this disrespect, Edwards's primary concern shifted from the indecency of the young men's behavior to their insubordination. He acted in a manner to affirm the authority of the church to discipline its members. He wrote out similar statements to sign for the three young men he regarded as the most culpable in which they confessed their wrongdoing and sought pardon. In one of the statements Oliver Warner acknowledged that he accepted the testimony of the female witnesses that he uttered "certain very unclean and Lascivious Expressions," although he did not remember doing so. Nonetheless, he appeared "publickly to humble" himself and asked for "forgiveness of God and his People." He promised to be "more watchfull for the future to avoid all Lascivious, vain and Light conversation." The statement of Timothy and Simeon Root sought forgiveness for "Sinfull and foolish Behavior."[5]

In the light of the direction of the inquiry and the public apologies of the guilty, Edwards's question to Mrs. Hannam about whether the book was "unclean to be read" was less about the propriety of the book than its misuse by readers, its relation to lascivious conversation and behavior. While it remains significant that Edwards did not acknowledge reading *Aristotle's Master-piece,* a sign of its inferior standing, he never questioned its open accessibility in a physician's office or the right of a woman, including the respected Mrs. Hannam, to examine it. In his notes preparing for the inquiry, Edwards did recognize that a man's reading it might be a violation of biblical injunction, but he did not dwell upon this. When one man bragged that he had read the book at night for enjoyment, in this eighteenth-century inquiry—unlike the questioning of nineteenth-century writers on physiology—his thoughts, emotions, and possible private practices were never investigated. The focus of the inquiry was elsewhere. The brunt of the responses witnesses made to questions describe the actions of young men in the presence of young women—reading the book aloud to them, talking about it with them, or using it to tease them. Ultimately what was at issue in 1744 was not the possession or the reading of *Aristotle's Master-piece* or its solitary perusal but the "unclean" and "lascivious" speech of young men to women that accompanied it and the disrespect the men showed to the minister and church elders who questioned their behavior.

More than a century later, a federal criminal court in New York held the power to judge matter suspected of being "unclean to be read," but the term was now "obscenity," and the questions for judge and jury involved the distribution of the book and a determination about selected parts of its text. In 1879, Judge Charles L. Benedict, presiding over the federal criminal court for the Southern District of New York, heard the case of D. M. Bennett, indicted for sending *Cupid's Yokes* through the mail. At the trial Judge Benedict was careful not to allow inquiry into Bennett's character or actions. The charge was not that Bennett read material "unclean to be read" or that he ran after women in a teasing fashion. The judge insisted that Bennett's respect or disrespect for authority was not at issue. Nor was reading the work. The pertinent question for the jury in considering Bennett's actions was: Did Bennett put *Cupid's Yokes* in the mail? Nothing was allowed in court about the nature of Bennett's trade in books, his motives, or his state of mind.

What about the work itself? This time there was no Mrs. Hannam to consider the nature of the book. No one was allowed to testify as to its content or meaning. Nor would Judge Benedict allow Bennett's defense to read the entire book to the jury, as a way of placing passages within the context of the work as a whole. The question about the work open for deliberation by the jury was: Were the specific passages in *Cupid's Yokes* marked by the prosecution obscene?

Of course, this left a difficult question: What was obscene? Here Judge Benedict had a ready answer: "It is whether the tendency of the matter is to deprave and corrupt the morals of those whose minds are open to such influences and into whose hands a publication of this sort may fall." The minds Benedict invoked were those of the young, especially young men on their own in the city. What threatened to "deprave and corrupt" those minds were words of erotic content, especially those that might stimulate the impulse to masturbation. Benedict's words came from an English judge's ruling in an English court. When the case came up for appeal, Judge Samuel Blatchford confirmed Benedict's judgments. Blatchford's learned and reasoned appellate opinion, enhanced by his 1882 appointment to the U.S. Supreme Court, was to have standing for the next fifty years.[6]

But unlike the ruling in Edwards's church, Benedict's and Blatchford's decisions were opposed in an equally learned and reasoned manner by leading lawyers for the defense. The brothers Abram and Thaddeus Wakeman represented D. M. Bennett. Although they took on all procedural possibilities for dismissal, they argued the case on the high ground of the Constitution and free speech and the ambiguities inherent in the designation "obscene." The defense stated that the criteria for the crime of obscenity could not be clearly defined but were a matter of mere taste, about which good people could disagree. The federal statute that suppressed obscenity sent through the mails was unconstitutional.

What explains the change from Edwards's church inquiry to Bennett's trial? This is essentially the task of the chapters that follow. Tracking America's nineteenth-century culture war, the battle over sexual representations, requires inquiry into the sexual frameworks as they emerged over time and their relation to the shifting contours of religion and free thought. This, in turn, demands examination of the state of sexual knowledge and the emergence of the literature of physiological reform with its fear of masturbation. The primary battle over sexual representations took place in New York City as it grew to be the nation's cultural capital. In this publishing center, young men living on their own read books and newspapers identified with sporting culture. Some of their elders and peers feared the power of the printed word and image, especially on young men. They sought to suppress the commercial erotica available on the streets and turned to the courts. Ultimately the censors established the national ground rules governing obscenity that Judge Benedict's court upheld and Judge Blatchford confirmed, the 1873 Comstock Law. In turn, those defending Bennett began a crucial countertradition that challenged key elements of the Comstock Law and its enforcement.

Before starting off on the historical journey of this book, however, it is necessary to establish the ground. This requires exploration of three critical and intriguing questions. The first is the book at the center of Jonathan Edwards's church inquiry, *Aristotle's Master-piece,* which turns out to be a significant document allowing access to vernacular sexual culture. What ideas about sex and desire did the book present? Second, even in the eighteenth century *Aristotle's Master-piece* hardly defined the range of printed erotic material available to American readers. Much more was available by the early nineteenth century and forms the second area of scrutiny. What was the commercial erotica out there, and what did it say about sex? Third, prior to the Bennett case of 1879 and the nineteenth-century trials that preceded it stand developments in the common law as it emerged in England and was adopted by the states after the American Revolution. What is the history of the law and early-nineteenth-century court practice governing obscenity? Treatment of vernacular sexuality, commercial erotica, and obscenity in common law provide the necessary foundation for the book to come.

I

Aristotle's Master-piece is an important work, for it provides a means of accessing the understanding of the body and sexual desire held by ordinary men and women in the eighteenth and nineteenth centuries. It is the central document of *vernacular* sexual culture. Using the name of Aristotle largely to give the book authority, it was a text that drew on an eclectic mix of medical lore, including classical sources, seventeenth-century treatises, and popular folklore. The book dates from a time in which there seems to have been little split between the ideas about the body held by scientists and medical men and those believed by common people. Although a written text, *Aristotle's Master-piece* conveyed significant elements of the oral tradition, and while it might have been found in an occasional physician's office, it was never considered part of official culture, sanctioned by those in established positions of authority. The roots of the popular understanding that *Aristotle's Master-piece* expressed went far back into the past. Contested by Christian tradition and later by Enlightenment notions, the ideas of the book continued to be received popular wisdom well into the nineteenth century.[7]

Popular understanding in the seventeenth and eighteenth centuries drew on traditions harking back to ancient Greece. In a body that consisted of solids and fluids, health and well-being came with equilibrium. Important solids were the blood vessels and nerves. Fluids were fungible and transmutable. Four fluids called "humors" were critical to the body: blood, phlegm, yellow bile, and black bile. The humors were related to the four states—hot, cold, dry, and moist—and the four prime elements—fire, air, earth, and water. The pneuma, or vital spirit, was the body's source of heat. Blood, both hot and moist, was related to the element air. Combined with heat, blood was the source of sexual desire.[8]

In this understanding, men are the hotter, drier, and lustier sex; women, the cooler and more moist. Semen is blood turned white because of man's great heat. As explained in *Aristotle's Master-piece,* "Nature has so ordered it, that when the Nerves are fill'd with animal Spirits, and the Arteries with hot and spirituous Blood, the Yard is distended, and becomes erect." The text describes the way that the active force, the man's seed, meets with the passive force, the egg generated by the woman's ovaries, alternately called women's stones or testicles. In coitus the man's seed travels to the ovaries, unites with an egg, and brings it down. As the pseudo-Aristotle puts it, the egg "being impregnated by the most spirituous Part of the Man's seed in the Act of Coition, descends thro' the Oviducts into the womb where it is cherished till it becomes a living Child."[9]

Aristotle's Master-piece carried both information and entertainment, and in the version published in 1741, it has many passages in rhyme. At the end of the section describing the act of generation are found these lines:

> *The purest Blood, we find, if well we heed,*
> *Is in the Testicles turn'd into Seed:*
> *Why by most proper Channels is transmitted*
> *Into the Place by Nature for it fitted.*

What then follows is an important element in vernacular sexuality, the celebration of sexual gratification in coition:

> *With highest Sense of Pleasure to excite*
> *In amorous Combatants the more Delight.*
> *For Nature does in this great Work design*
> *Profit and Pleasure, in one Act to join.*[10]

The book describes the physical source of male sexual pleasure as located in the glans at the end of the penis, "covered with a very thin Membrane, by reason of which it is of a most exquisite Feeling." The foreskin, "by its moving up and down in the Act of Copulation brings Pleasure both to the Man and Woman." Female sexual pleasure is more variously located. The word "womb" was applied to what is today separated into two organs, the uterus and the vagina. The womb's "neck" or "channel," the unnamed vagina, "receives the Man's Yard like a Sheath. . . . That it may be dilated with the more Ease and Pleasure in the Act of Coition, it is sinewy and a little spungy." On both sides of the thighs are veins and arteries needed to supply heat and moisture to the vagina during coition: "because the Neck of the womb requires to be filled with abundance of Spirits, to be dilated thereby, that it may the better take hold of the *Penis;* such Motions requiring great Heat, which being made more intense by the Act of Frication, consumes a great deal of Moisture."[11]

Searching for a female analogue to the penis, *Aristotle's Master-piece* does not find it in the womb or its channel, but in the clitoris. The book follows the one-sex model, as the historian Thomas Laqueur has described the basic conception of sexual anatomy before the nineteenth century. The clitoris is depicted as "a sinewy and hard Part of the Womb, repleat with spungy and black Matter within, in the same manner as the Side-ligaments of the Yard; and indeed resemble it in Form, suffers Erection, and Falling in the same Manner." The clitoris is critically important: "it both stirs up Lust, and gives delight in Copulation." Its variable size explains the degree of women's lust. In this way, women are like men. "The Use and Action of the *Clitoris* in women, is like that of the *Penis,* or Yard in Men; that is, Erection; its extream End being like that of the Glans is in the Men, the Seat of the greatest Pleasure in the Act of Copulation, so is this of the *Clitoris* in Women, and therefore called the Sweetness of Love, and the Fury of Venery." Additionally, what "does greatly delight the Fair-Sex" is the expelling of a humor or fluid.[12]

For all their ardor, however, females are cooler than males. When they are young, girls need all their blood for growth, but once they are mature, they cannot use all the nourishment they digest, and some of their blood becomes superfluous. Once a month, governed by the moon, their bodies release the extra blood in menstruation. The timing of a particular woman's period is linked by her temperament to different phases of the moon: "one of a sanguine Complexion hath her terms in the first quarter, a cholerick in the second, a melancholy in the third; and so in the rest." The female stops menstruating when pregnant because all her blood is needed to nourish the child growing in her womb.[13]

Since regular flows are important to keeping the balance of humors in the body, women should pay great attention to their menses. Women who are pregnant need to be careful. They are apt to run to a doctor if they experience a cessation of the menses, and he may give them "a strong enthartical Potion, which certainly destroys the Conception." This is the only indirect mention in the book of what the twenty-first century calls birth control. What is being suggested is not a contraceptive, but rather a medication to induce abortion.[14]

Although much attention is given to the bodily sources of desire, sexual expression in *Aristotle's Master-piece* is always envisioned in terms of the adult heterosexual relationship defined as marriage. The male perspective predominates. Women's anatomy and desire are etched along the lines of a one-sex model. Imagined sexual acts are male-centered, looking to sharp arousal and release. In preparation for sexual intercourse, the just-married pair should "survey the lovely Beauties of each other" but if there is any deformity, it should be covered by darkness. The man might then recite to his new wife this poem:

> Now my fair Bride, now will I storm the Mint
> Of Love and Joy, and rifle all that's in't.
> Now my infranchis'd Hand on every Side,
> Shall o'er thy naked polish'd Iv'ry slide:
> Freely shall now my longing Eyes behold
> Thy bared Snow, and thy unbraided Gold.
> Nor curtains now, tho' of transparent Lawn,
> Shall be before thy Virgin Treasure drawn:
> I will enjoy the[e] now, my Fairest; come,

> *And fly with me to Love's* Elizium.
> *My Rudder, with thy bold Hand, like a try'd*
> *And skilful Pilot, thou shalt steer; and guide*
> *My Bark in Love's dark Channel, where it shall*
> *Dance, as the bounding Waves do rise and fall;*
> *Whilst my tall Pinnace in the* Cyprian Strait,
> *Ride safe at Anchor, and unlades the Freight.*[15]

Some editions contain suggestions of ways to heat the blood to better pre-pare for coitus. They recommend meat and game, especially when rare—"making the body lively and full of sap." They also recommend shellfish, spicy and salty foods, wines, and certain pungent vegetables to create and intensify desire and promote fertility.[16]

Further evidence of the male perspective comes from some of the max-ims offering advice for women. For instance, virginity if held too long loses its value: "A stale Virgin . . . being looked upon like an old Almanack out of date." The book states that moderation in women is linked to their fertility: "Satiety gluts the Womb." Women enjoy moderation more than excess: "Women rather choose to have a thing well done, than to have it often." Again, drawing on the one-sex model that heightens women's similarity to men, women's sexual pleasure is given a role in conception: "That the greater the Woman's Desire of Copulation is, the more subject she is to con-ceive." Expelling the egg is like male ejaculation; thus reaching orgasm is necessary to conception. As a result, a woman raped against her will cannot conceive.[17]

Copulation is valuable to men, especially the man who uses it "lawfully and moderately," because it "eases and lightens the body, clears the mind, comforts the Head and Senses, and expels melancholy." Sexual intercourse should be moderate. It should not be too seldom, because "the Seed of a Man retain'd above its due time, is converted into some infectious humour." Nor should coitus be too frequent, because "it destroys the sight, dries the body, and impairs the Brain . . . [and] often causes Fevers." Copulation is more pleasurable if less frequent. If used too often, it fails to give delight because "the passages of the Seed is over-large and wide," the seed is too scant, or the ejaculation is not of seed but of blood or other "watry sub-stance, which is not hot, and therefore affords no delight."[18]

Another poem makes explicit the critical assumption of sexual sameness between women and men. After a discussion of "Womens Secrets," or the female reproductive system, it states in regard to women:

> . . . that, tho' they of different Sexes be,
> Yet in the whole they are the same as we:
> For those that have the strictest Searchers been,
> Find Women are but Men turn'd Out side in:
> And Men, if they but cast their Eyes about,
> May find they're Women, with their Inside out.[19]

In keeping with this governing concept, the reciprocality of male and female genitalia is repeatedly considered and emphasized.

The wood engravings in many of the editions of *Aristotle's Master-piece* relate oddly to the text. Two standard illustrations deal with the influence of the astrological signs of the zodiac on the body, bearing out assumptions in the text. One links the parts of the face to the signs. The other, associating parts of the body with the constellations, is intended to indicate the phases of the stars' passage when surgeries or manipulations of the different organs are safe. In addition, there is an effort to show the fetus in utero. The text assumes that couples want children, "the fair Image of themselves," and directs its instruction and entertainment in sexual matters to foster fertility, to "make their mutual Embraces most effectual to that End."[20] Given this, a number of subsequent illustrations are curious, for they represent the opposite of the desired child—"monsters" born covered in fur, children with extra limbs, or twins joined together. To these are joined an example that gives visual expression to the deep-seated racial prejudice of the era, an image of a child of white parents born black.

One illustration has a curious progression, perhaps indicative of the increasingly playful nature of the work, a kind of visual equivalent to the erotic doggerel that later versions contained. The 1700 edition has a rough image of two monsters: a woman whose body is covered with hair accompanied by a small black child. By 1741, on the obverse side of this image is the frontispiece to the book. Here the woman has been transformed into a nude looking much like Botticelli's Venus. The furry tufts over her body are now turned into inoffensive speckles. Accompanied by the child, she visits the philosopher writing in his study. In this guise, she may be more a muse to Aristotle composing the book than a problem to be solved by him.

Aristotle's Master-piece is an important text for discovering vernacular sex-

The hairy woman and black child visit the philosopher. Frontispiece, *Aristotle's Compleat Master-piece*, 1741. Countway Library of Medicine.

ual culture. It contains much information about the ways that the body and reproductive sex were understood. The book gave clear messages about sexual pleasure that resonated long after new texts offered different information and advice. However, it has limits for the historian. Written from the male perspective, it hides the oral culture of women from view. It is resolutely heterosexual, telling nothing about same-sex practices and the emerging culture of sodomites in England and the colonies. Finally, it does not treat the sexual practice that would dominate much of the writing about sex in the nineteenth century, masturbation.[21]

2

It may well have been that *Aristotle's Master-piece,* at least in some of its editions, offered readers erotic stimulation. If so, it had real competition. Commercially available by the early nineteenth century were literary works understood to have the power to arouse male readers. There is nothing new about either bawdy humor or the use of the obscene to shock—both have ancient origins. Similarly, artistic representations of sex are as old as art. What is new in the modern era in Europe and its colonial outposts is a continuous tradition of writing and graphic material specifically intended for a male audience to, as the scholar David Foxon put it, "arouse lust, create sexual fantasies or feed auto-erotic desires." This stream of erotic writing and prints began in sixteenth-century Italy and spread in the seventeenth century to France and England.[22]

Lynn Hunt has described the "demimonde of heretics, freethinkers and libertines" spun off by the scientific revolution and the Enlightenment, men who wrote and engraved erotic works out of conviction and the need for money. Some of their materials tended to be relatively expensive, designed for the elite libertine, but by the second half of the seventeenth century, booksellers were offering sexual representations at prices that professional men, such as Samuel Pepys, could afford. Some of this writing expressed a libertine ideal that combined reason and sexual pleasure, along with a disdain of emotions. At its outer edge, sexual pleasure is advanced as life's only aim. From the outset, printed erotica was opposed by the authorities, who saw it as a threat to the state, linked inextricably to philosophic radicalism, heresy, and political subversion.[23]

A number of works printed and distributed in the eighteenth century formed a set of books well known by some readers that can be best regarded as the erotic canon. Typically illustrated with explicit engravings, these books were one of the desiderata of a gentleman's library: *L'Ecole des filles,* of unknown authorship, Nicholas Chorier's *Dialogues,* Jean Barrin's *Venus in the Cloister,* Gervaise de Latouche's *Histoire de Dom B,* and John Cleland's *Memoirs of a Woman of Pleasure* (also known as *Fanny Hill*). Many of these titles made their way into American collections and by the nineteenth century were joined by *The Lustful Turk, The Confessions of a Young Lady of High Rank,* and others.

These works emerge from an understanding of human sexuality to be found in *Aristotle's Master-piece.* The body is governed by the humors; hot blood becomes sperm; as the cooler sex, women need to be aroused. Yet these works take these notions of vernacular sexual culture in a new direction. A typical work of the erotic canon contains common elements. A girl is introduced to sexual experience by a woman or a man. She becomes sexually active in behavior and in her imagination. In sexual congress, she is both compliant and playful. What seems most valued in these representations is the description of a woman's sexual fire, her feelings of desire, and her experience of overwhelming orgasm. But women are the wayward sex, and a woman's fidelity lasts only so long as a dominating man holds immediate sway over her. Pregnancy is never a consideration, and the need for male fidelity is never stated.[24]

Erotic writing may begin in vernacular culture, but once it develops into a commercially driven enterprise, something new happens. Others have written about the way in which this writing is repetitive and episodic.[25] It is, and for a reason. What it contains is a narrative designed for repeated male sexual arousal. After the stage is set, the female heroine is deflowered. She has a range of sexual encounters in an additive fashion, but each must bring a new and more powerful element to feed male fantasy. Erotic fiction is "successful" if it works its magic on the male reader and its chapters generate the physical arousal necessary for successive male masturbatory experiences. Samuel Pepys, the seventeenth-century English diarist, left an account of reading *L'Ecole des filles*. He read it, became sexually aroused, and masturbated. He intentionally bought a cheap edition of the book so that he could destroy it after taking his enjoyment.[26]

Fanny Hill can be considered as the *ur*-text, at least for erotic writing available to Americans. This 1748 novel by John Cleland of the adventures of a spirited prostitute was well known and had occasioned prosecutions in England. The book moves in typical fashion from Fanny's introduction to sexual relations as a postpubescent girl to a range of sexual adventures with men and women (and, at least in terms of viewing, of men with men), all done in a playful rough-and-tumble fashion. Once initiated, this good-hearted, robust woman enjoys sex in all situations and all positions. In the end she winds up in a love match promising sexual fulfillment and fidelity.

The book crossed the line into obscenity in its graphic depiction in print of sexual acts. What makes the violation both typical and flagrant is that the narrator is a woman, and in describing the acts, she speaks of her own sexual arousal and pleasure. If one were to isolate the point of sexual danger in imaginative works in the nineteenth century, it is here, in a woman's statement of her sexual desire. Generally written by men, such statements and accompanying prints constitute an important target of indictments for obscenity in the early nineteenth century.[27]

With the exception of *Fanny Hill,* France was the major source of writing in this vein for both Great Britain and North America. A small amount of this material has found its way into the Kinsey Library at Indiana University. A striking element of these books is their expensive bindings, pointing to their possession by the rich (and perhaps the reason for their preservation). For example, *Venus en rut,* dated 1790 and likely French, is elegantly bound in deep red leather, with gold tooling on the inside and multicolored marbleized paper. Contained within are prints of playful putti, childlike angelic figures, copulating.

Americans had access to these materials, if they could afford expensive imports. American printers, however, were beginning to supply the less affluent. One piece of evidence in the new republic has comic possibilities. Among the goods that the Worcester master printer Isaiah Thomas, Jr., used to bind many volumes of newspapers and books around 1814 were sheets of blue marbled paper to line the boards. On the reverse side of a batch of these sheets are the printed pages of *Fanny Hill.* As a result, pages from the most notorious erotic work of the age wrap the writings of Cotton Mather and some records of the Massachusetts Court of Common Pleas. Countering the assertion that Isaiah Thomas, father or son, printed the book, a scholar of printing has determined that the specific typeface was in use not by Thomas but by the Boston firm of Munroe and Francis and has suggested that Thomas may have bought the marbled sheets from the firm. One guess is that some Boston journeymen or apprentices printed some sheets, got caught, and, with expensive paper at a premium, their master marbled the unbound sheets to turn them to a productive use.[28]

Even if in this instance a Thomas was not the printer, it is likely that on other occasions the father had printed the book. Isaiah Thomas, Sr., wrote to a bookseller in England in 1786 to purchase a copy of *Fanny Hill* (and was told he might best do so from a ship's captain). In an era without copyright, such a request from a printer may signal that he was seeking a model to pirate. More telling are the records in the firm's account books that point to a Thomas printing of the book. Both Thomases aided former apprentices by setting up their presses in the outreaches of New England and supplying their bookstores. In the 1817 accounting of final stock of Anson Whipple of Walpole, New Hampshire, were 293 copies of *Fanny Hill.* Whipple was the resident partner of Thomas's bookstore in that location. If he printed Whipple's copies of the novel, Thomas was hardly unique in New England. In 1818 a Concord, New Hampshire, bookbinder wrote to complain to his governor about *"Two Large Editions* of a very improper book, with very obscene plates," presumed to be *Fanny Hill*. At least one other edition was circulating in that region in 1815–17, sold by five booksellers or storekeepers. These dealers supplied peddlers who traveled the countryside with books for sale, taking *Fanny Hill* far beyond printing centers.[29]

3

As erotic books and prints circulated in early-nineteenth-century America, persons who found them distasteful or wrong found a means to try and suppress them through the courts. Although in the mid–eighteenth century a

Printed pages of *Memoirs of a Woman of Pleasure*, with blue marbleized paper on the reverse, c. 1810. BDSDS.1810. Courtesy, American Antiquarian Society.

church in a New England town could assume responsibility for policing texts, by the early nineteenth century a worried minister would have turned to the legal system. Americans learned that criminal courts were an appropriate venue for conflicts over sexual representation. At issue in Edwards's church inquiry in Northampton was that young men were reading a book appropriate only for women and, moreover, using it to tease and taunt them about their bodies. Ultimately what was at issue was behavior, the utterance by young men of "certain very unclean and Lascivious Expressions." Prosecutors in the civil courts of the nineteenth century, however, sought indictments not for the behavior that followed the reading of a text or the viewing of images but for their publication, which essentially meant their sale.

Because actions of courts have consequences, they bear a special relation to the sexual conversation of the nineteenth century. The persons who manage the apparatus of the legal system in the United States—the police, judges, juries, legislators, and lawyers—have a complex connection to sexual representation. At one level they participate in the culture's sexual conversations, for in their private capacities they live as sons, brothers, husbands, and fathers. But in court their words take place within an institutional structure derived from England and modified by the actions of legislatures. Here precedents have great power. In matters of obscenity, court judgments do not mirror public opinion but lag long behind it, responding only very slowly to changing standards.[30]

In the nineteenth century, judges, elected to their posts or appointed by holders of political office, represented only a small segment of the population: they were all male, they were relatively affluent, and they were typically well connected. If, as was likely, they came from the ranks of lawyers, they had been educated in the traditions of the law and were sworn to uphold it. Thus by background and perhaps training as well as by the roles they assumed, judges interpreting and applying the law generally represented a deeply conservative element of society. In their private capacities such men wielded significant power. They could discipline their children, wives, and mothers, using material and corporal rewards and punishments. Yet daughters as well as sons turned wayward, wives were not necessarily obedient, mothers turned obstinate, and judges themselves were not necessarily of single mind over matters of sex. Their impulses and desires often conflicted with their principles; their actions might belie their professed beliefs. Church and court records are filled with sexual misdeeds in families of publicly virtu-

ous men of property and influence—and with the actions of their own wayward hearts.[31]

In court such men had an opportunity to impose their will on others
clearly and directly. Not only could they give public expression to what they
understood as community standards, they also had the authority to punish
and the power to give orders to others to execute their will. With a gavel they
kept order in the court, assisted by sergeants at arms who subdued any who
refused to obey. When they imposed a jail sentence, the person convicted
was shackled and led to prison by armed officers of the law. As Robert Cover
has made clear, although at one level the law is a discourse on a par with
other discourses, it has a different weight: "Legal interpretation takes place in
a field of pain and death." When a judge utters an understanding of a text,
"somebody loses his freedom, his property, his children, even his life."[32]

What were the laws under which those brought before the courts were
tried? Until the Civil War, one cannot look for federal statutes against
obscene matter because police powers were understood as belonging to the
states and through them to communities. As Morris L. Ernst and Alan U.
Schwartz have noted, few states had laws against obscene literature and
images before the Civil War. The reason for this is not what these writers
suggested—that there was a general lack of interest in obscenity in this
period—but because such laws were unnecessary. To prosecute obscenity,
states could rely on a century-old common-law tradition, derived from
England. Although legal scholars writing about the antebellum years have
stated that the common law was relied on in civil courts, not criminal ones,
those who applied common law to obscenity cases in the United States in the
nineteenth century did not know that. In dealing with obscenity, American
criminal courts accepted common law.[33]

This discussion and much of what follows goes against the prevailing
wisdom.[34] A good deal of legal scholarship has come out of advocacy. In the
case of obscenity law, lawyer Morris L. Ernst of the American Civil Liberties
Union represented both Mary Ware Dennett, indicted for *The Sex Side of Life*
in 1929, and Random House in its landmark effort to legalize the importation
of *Ulysses* in 1932. *Censorship: The Search for the Obscene* (1964) by Ernst and
Schwartz serves as the standard reference book on the history of literary censorship.[35] In the courtroom Ernst sought to establish the authority of the
First Amendment and the corresponding weakness of efforts to suppress
obscene matter before the 1870s, and he carried these governing themes into

his text.[36] The typical reliance by legal scholars on the printed and bound state compilations in law libraries has supported Ernst's interpretation.

These sources, however, have a built-in distortion. They contain cases that went to appeal at the state level. To take a case to appeal required money and influence that the marginal printers and booksellers charged with obscenity in the first half of the nineteenth century did not have. Learning about their cases requires research of a different nature. As the chapters on the sporting press will illuminate, in the weekly publications that emanated from New York in the early 1840s, with names such as the *Whip* and the *Flash,* editors testified in their columns to their own arrest, which can then be traced through New York City newspapers. New York court records document these arrests and many others for obscene libel.[37]

The English common-law tradition dealing with obscenity in print began in the early eighteenth century. Prior to that time ecclesiastical courts and the secret judicial body of the Crown, the Star Chamber, had exercised oversight. In 1727, when Edmund Curl was prosecuted for publishing *Venus in the Cloister; or the Nun in her Smock,* English courts extended the notion of criminal libel to include obscenity. The attorney general in the Curl case argued that the book, in tending "to corrupt the morals of the King's subjects," is "against the peace of the King." The ruling stated that even without "an actual force," a book had the power to destroy the basis of public order—morality. In part, the extension of libel from personal libel, which involves injurious words directed at a person, to "obscene libel" hung on a verbal trick: the court returned to the Latin *libellus,* meaning "little book."[38]

But even had this opportunity not presented itself, the English courts would have found a way to protect the state against what it perceived as written threats against the Church or against morality and public order. The spread of printing could no longer be contained by the licensing power of the Crown. The rise of literacy and the emergence of the reading public offered publishers and booksellers new opportunities for gain. There was a broad market for erotic literature, and it was published in a range of genres. Edmund Curl had tapped a widespread interest in crime and gained notoriety for his publication of criminal trials, including those for criminal conversation or adultery. The judge made clear that *Venus in the Cloister* threatened religion and public order; given Curl's prodigious output and popularity, a salient element may have been the broad accessibility of his book.

Early in the history of obscene libel, another notable aspect emerged: a charge of obscenity was useful in a political conflict. In 1764 John Wilkes, politician and polemical writer (later one of the principal supporters in England of American independence), was tried in the House of Lords for "publishing an obscene and impious libel entitled an 'Essay on Woman,' " a privately printed erotic burlesque of Alexander Pope's "Essay on Man," complete with mock heading, graphic notes, and explicit illustrations. It is likely that Wilkes had arranged for a printing of twelve copies of this ribald parody of unknown authorship for his libertine friends. After government spies had gotten a proof copy from the printer, the notorious Earl of Sandwich, one of Wilkes's former libertine associates, gave the poem shocking publicity by reading the entire text aloud to the House of Lords. His effort to discredit Wilkes in the eyes of his parliamentary supporters was successful. The real issue was not Wilkes's obscenity but his liberal politics. The Lords' determination that the *Essay* was "a most scandalous, obscene, and impious libel" provided fuel for the more important debate in the House of Commons on the charge that Wilkes's *North Briton No. 45,* a political tract highly critical of the king's ministers, was seditious libel. After Wilkes sought refuge abroad, he was expelled from Parliament and arrested for the printing of the *Essay* and the republishing of *No. 45.* When Wilkes did not return to face trial, he was declared an outlaw by the Court of the King's Bench. Wilkes lived in celebrated exile on the Continent. When he returned, he successfully stood for Parliament and submitted to the Court of the King's Bench in 1768. Cleared of the high crime of outlawry, he was sentenced for his publications, receiving a fine and a twelve-month sentence for the obscene libel. He emerged from prison a popular favorite, in part because he was repeatedly expelled from the House of Commons, and, supported by admirers, he went on to a successful and effective political career.[39]

Prosecution for obscene libel in England was rare until the late eighteenth century. In 1787, King George III issued a proclamation against vice, urging the public to "suppress all loose and licentious prints, books and publications, dispensing poison to the minds of the young and unwary, and to punish the publishers and vendors thereof." While largely ignored in this era of licentious libels, William Wilberforce established the Proclamation Society, dedicated to the enforcement of the king's charge, and several prosecutions for obscene libel followed. In 1802, the Society for the Suppression of Vice was founded to fight against the publication of erotic words and images. It investigated the trade in obscene materials and initiated prosecutions. In the fifteen years that followed, more than thirty prosecutions were successful. It was no longer necessary that a work be found to threaten religion or public order; merely to be judged obscene was enough.

In the eighteenth century, British legal scholars attempted to systematize common law and ground it in principles. The most successful was William Blackstone's *Commentaries on the Laws of England* in the mid–eighteenth century. Because of its comprehensibility and clarity, Blackstone's work had great power in the new United States. Blackstone did not deal with obscenity as such or name it as a crime or misdemeanor. In two sections of his fourth volume, *On Public Wrongs* (1765–69), however, he laid the necessary ground. He made an important distinction in law between a private vice and a public wrong. One can be drunk alone in one's home and, although engaged in sinful behavior, be beyond the reach of the law. However, if one is drunk "publicly, in the face of the world, it's [sic] evil example makes it liable to temporal censures." Blackstone named as high crimes some public wrongs, such as apostasy, which, in his words, strikes "at our national religion." He also named a lower class of crimes of "gross impieties and general immoralities," normally the subject of municipal courts, such as blasphemy, swearing and cursing, and lewdness. The latter, often said to be the result of obscenity, he defined in part as "some grossly scandalous and public indecency."[40]

One could not locate obscene images and words in this category of offense. They belonged among libels, which Blackstone considered "in their largest and most extensive sense" to "signify any writings, pictures, or the like, of an *immoral or illegal tendency.*" The test of "bad tendency"—that words served to "harm the public welfare"—was taken into American law, subjecting those who published words to punishment not only in obscenity cases but also in others such as blasphemy and sedition. In a civil suit involving libel, falsity is necessary to conviction; in a criminal prosecution for libel, the only issue is the tendency "to create animosities, and to disturb the public peace," and the only facts to be considered are "the making or publishing of the book or writing" and whether the matter within be "criminal."[41]

Blackstone insisted that in the punishment of these criminal libels "the *liberty of the press,* properly understood, is by no means infringed or violated." He understood this liberty to consist of freedom from prior restraint, not of "freedom from censure for criminal matter when published." A person has the right to express his thoughts but must take the consequences if that leads to publishing "what is improper, mischievous, or illegal." In a seemingly innocuous statement, Blackstone wrote what became perhaps the

most serious obstacle to free speech in America: "To punish . . . any dangerous or offensive writings, which, when published, shall on a fair and impartial
trial be adjudged of a *pernicious tendency,* is necessary for the preservation of
peace and good order." By Blackstone's lights this ability ironically protects
the press from the censor or the licenser. "So true will it be found, that to
censure the licentiousness, is to maintain the liberty, of the press."[42] Judgments based on "bad tendency" became the bedrock of federal obscenity
convictions after 1872.

Massachusetts went beyond England and, beginning in 1711–12, long
before Blackstone, prohibited obscenity in its codes. This Puritan "city on a
hill" failed to inspire other colonies in the New World. But beginning in 1727
with the ruling in the Curl case, other American colonies could rely on the
establishment of obscene libel in common law. During and after the Revolution, states confirmed their legal systems based on common law, English
statutes not in opposition to their constitutions, and acts of colonial legislatures. In the new republic common law undergirded decisions of state courts
in civil and criminal cases, but from the outset there was opposition to its
application for federal crimes. Although in criminal courts, in contrast to
civil ones, there was far less trust in common law, few states before the Civil
War wrote statutes regarding obscenity. They generally relied on the heritage of common law.

A law based on statute differed in a fundamental way from one based in
common law. The colonies and states passed statutes that were binding on
their people, but they could not be applied retroactively. A ruling in common
law could, however, because, it was argued, "it always existed, and a breach of
it was criminal," even if not clarified at the time the breach was made. Such
reasoning was possible because eighteenth-century legal thinkers understood the work of judges as discovering, not creating, what was believed to
be natural law. Judicial decisions, based on a careful study of those that preceded them, stood as the law governing civil and criminal matters. A central
task of lawyers and jurists was to comprehend the vast body of precedent in
order to argue and decide on the basis of its cumulative guidance.[43]

In the chaotic legal situation that existed in the early nineteenth century,
a range of digests and treatises helped tame the law and make it comprehensible. The basic treatise on obscenity was *The Law of Libel* by Francis Ludlow
Holt, published in many editions in England and the United States in the
early nineteenth century. It built on Blackstone's firm base. Holt gave a statement even stronger than that of Blackstone of the logic of obscene libel or

"libels against morality and the law of nature." Morality or "the law of nature . . . is necessary to society, and society, therefore, must maintain it. This is the reason of the English law in prohibiting and punishing all open and public immoralities, obscene writings, speaking, and exhibitions, the tendency of which is evidently to poison the springs and principles of manners, and disturb the peace and economy of the realm." As had Blackstone, Holt distinguished between private vice and sin, punishable by the Almighty, and public example, which is prosecutable by the state. In notes attached to the various editions, Holt and succeeding English and American lawyers went through the important cases and extracted their central elements. Holt put particular emphasis on the responsibility of publishers and booksellers.[44]

Obscenity as defined in the law is obscene libel, a criminal violation, tried in local criminal courts. For there to be a printed record, easily available for legal research, a case needs to go to appeal. The decisions of appellate judges rendered in state compilations thus have important standing. The first such case dealing with obscenity in American records was heard in the Supreme Court of Pennsylvania in 1815. Jesse Sharpless and others had been found guilty in the Mayor's Court of Philadelphia of the exhibition for money of an obscene picture "representing a man in an obscene, impudent, and indecent posture with a woman." Their counsel presented a scattershot argument, seeking all possible ways to free his clients. The pertinent elements for consideration here are the contention that while Sharpless's act was improper, it did not violate either statute or common law, and that its indecency was private.[45]

Chief Justice William Tilghman denied this defense. That something occurred in private had no bearing. He wrote, "No man is permitted to corrupt the morals of the people. Secret poison cannot be thus disseminated. A slight knowledge of human nature teaches us, 'that while secresy [sic] is affected in a case like the present, public curiosity is more strongly excited thereby, and that those persons who may ignorantly suppose they have had the good fortune of seeing bawdy pictures, will not content themselves with keeping the secret in their own bosoms!' " In terms of precedent, the critical element was Tilghman's determination that what was at issue was a libel, not an act, and his use of Blackstone. The Pennsylvania chief justice grounded his decision in English common law, as interpreted by Blackstone, volume 4. Tilghman stated that the English court clearly established in the Curl case that "*an indecent book* is indictable," and went on to extrapolate to the case before him: "A picture tends to excite lust as strongly as a writing;

and the *shewing* of a picture, is as much a *publication,* as the *selling* of a book." That the picture was placed in a private room, unadvertised, and shown to only a single person was no defense. "If the privacy of the room was a protection, all the youth of the city might be corrupted by taking them one by one into a chamber, and there inflaming their passions by the exhibition of lascivious pictures." The defendants "exhibited it [the painting] to sundry persons for money; for that in law is a *publication.*" The concurring judge was succinct. What was at issue was "a libel on the morals and government of the state, in the same manner as was done in the case of *Wilkes* for his Essay on Woman."

The phrase "bawdy pictures" is important. What the Pennsylvania court sought to regulate was the "publication" by sale or by exhibition of images of "lascivious pictures" capable of "inflaming" the "passions" of the "youth of the city." In a polity concerned with the protection of social order, the danger to society lay in sexual incitement of the kind well understood by ordinary people who shared vernacular sexual culture. Seeing Sharpless's painting on the wall, with its representation of "a man in an obscene, impudent, and indecent posture with a woman" would "excite lust" in the male viewer. It would heat his blood, and he would seek relief. In 1815, the charge of obscenity was connected with inflaming lust, especially in the young, through an imaginative representation offered to the public for a fee.

Most likely, this is what obscenity meant in Massachusetts in 1819, when Peter Holmes of West Boylston was convicted in the Circuit Court of Common Pleas, sitting in Worcester, for "publishing a lewd and obscene print" in *Fanny Hill,* and additionally for "publishing the same book." As publishing meant selling, it is the act of sale that is documented in court records. Although there were many attempts to suppress the book in England, no known record exists of this effort in America before 1821.[46]

The Peter Holmes case thus came at an important moment in New England. In the half century after the Revolution, elemental literacy became almost universal for men and predominant for women (roughly 80 percent). Simultaneously, new technology brought down the price of printed materials as books, pamphlets, and newspapers became affordable to people eager to read them and an effective distribution system came into being. Commercial networks of bookstores and peddlers put books into the hands of many whose parents and grandparents had never aspired to reading beyond their Bibles. In this period, in places such as the Upper Valley in rural New England, reading became, as historian William Gilmore has put it, "a necessity of life." For this population as well as those gathered in cities elsewhere in the new nation, reading served as "a form of power, as entertainment, as an avenue of escape, as a means of self-improvement, and as a useful tool." As readers ventured far beyond the texts that were sanctioned by Church and community, they gained access to novels and commercial erotica. Changes in literacy, printing, and the book trade made possible the publication of books such as *Fanny Hill* by Peter Holmes and its suppression.[47]

We know little about this case because the appeal was waged on technical grounds. In 1821, the Supreme Court of Massachusetts ruled that because the matter was one of common law, not of statute, the Worcester County Court of Common Pleas had jurisdiction. More significantly in terms of precedent, the court determined that it was not necessary to set in the court record the statements alleged to be obscene or to specify the particulars of prints. It affirmed Holmes's conviction of misdemeanor. Holmes was fined $300 and court costs. By forcing Holmes to post a $500 bond as security against future violations, the court effectively censored him.[48] In its decision an early-nineteenth-century Massachusetts court stated that an eighteenth-century text found in inventories of bookstores and private libraries could not be sold openly.

Much more was to happen to the law of obscenity between the Peter Holmes case in 1819 and the Benedict and Blatchford rulings of 1879. But these changes are intertwined with the story to come and will have to wait as it unfolds. The important point is that by 1819 the legal system had interjected itself into the sexual conversation of the United States. It successfully established that it had the power to set the ground rules for debate and the authority to prosecute, convict, and imprison. Building on this ground, there were, before 1879, additional developments in the law and court practice governing obscenity. These changes came, in part, in response to the transformation of America's sexual conversation that began with the arrival of Frances Wright to these shores and her establishment of the Hall of Science in New York City in 1829.

3

Free Thought, Sexual Knowledge, and Evangelical Christianity

I

On April 26, 1829, Frances Wright and Robert Dale Owen opened the Hall of Science in New York as part of their larger scheme to reform America. The Hall of Science is important as the initial site in America where the first books of reform physiology and birth control were openly distributed. America's first sex instructors were political radicals and infidels who spoke and wrote about the body as acts of defiance. Blasphemy has many guises. In America, one of its most important and creative aspects was that of teaching about the body and its sexual functioning and giving practical information on birth control. Unlike vernacular sexual culture, which was largely conveyed orally, reform physiology—the third sexual framework—took written and printed form from the outset. This chapter traces its original impetus in the work of Frances Wright and Robert Dale Owen.

Both had immigrated to America with revolutionary hopes. Robert Dale Owen was the son of British industrialist and utopian philanthropist Robert Owen. Born in 1800 in Glasgow, he had been well educated by tutors and at the progressive Hofwyl school in Switzerland and influenced by the ideas of the Enlightenment, his father, and Jeremy Bentham. He came to New Harmony, Indiana, to oversee his father's utopian community and became editor of the *New-Harmony Gazette*. Frances Wright, a Scottish heiress and writer, had twice ventured to the United States, in 1819 to see her play *Altorph* produced on the New York stage and in 1824, when she accompanied her friend, the Revolutionary War hero the Marquis de Lafayette. In 1825 she returned to America to found Nashoba, her own utopian experiment outside Memphis, Tennessee. Modeled on some of the older Robert Owen's ideas, it added to collective living an effort to educate slaves in the ways of freedom. By her plan, donated and purchased slaves would work for their freedom under the supervision and tutelage of their white managers. Wright was an intellectual who left the management of her enterprise to others. She traveled abroad, and when she came back to the United States in 1828 she went to New Harmony.[1]

In her lectures across the country she called for a hall of science in each city to serve as a secular center containing museums, libraries, and rooms for teaching. She rented a New York building on Broome Street, near the Bowery, that had been the Ebenezer Baptist Church. This was perfect, for Wright imagined her halls of science as free thought's equivalent of churches. The New York Hall of Science welcomed freethinkers and workers to full-day programs on Sunday that included gymnastic classes for children, evening addresses, and scientific lectures—physiology among them. The building included an auditorium with a seating capacity of more than 1,200, and Wright's own lectures attracted full houses. Among the thousands who came was the young son of a Brooklyn carpenter, Walt Whitman. He later recalled Frances Wright as "one of the sweetest of sweet memories: we all loved her, fell down before her; her very appearance seemed to enthrall us."[2]

In addition to its weekly Sunday program, the hall was intended as a daily social and intellectual center for freethinkers and working-class radicals. It offered the important service of a free medical dispensary for the laboring community, open every day. The building housed the office of the *Free Enquirer,* a weekly newspaper edited by Wright and Owen. It also had a library and bookstore in the front of the building, conspicuously open on Sunday. Prominently placed in the bookstore's windows were works by the radical Thomas Paine, the poet Percy Bysshe Shelley, and the political philosopher William Godwin. Some of these books came from available stock, but some were issued under the imprint of Wright & Owen. They were joined in the bookstore by a controversial work by the British freethinker Richard Carlile, first printed in 1826.[3] Carlile's *Every Woman's Book* was the first text published in England that gave clear, unambiguous directions for birth control, or, as it was euphemistically stated, instructions for married persons on limiting the number of their children. In late October

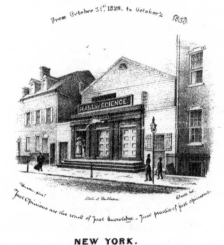

"Hall of Science, Office of the Free Enquirer," published by Wright & Owen, c. 1830, lithography by Pendleton, C. Burton, A. J. Davis. © Collection of The New-York Historical Society, negative #16602.

1830 Robert Dale Owen announced to the readers of the *Free Enquirer* that he had written a book, and in early 1831 his *Moral Physiology; or, a Brief and Plain Treatise on the Population Question* appeared. It was the first book written and printed in the United States that discussed contraception and gave practical guidance.

The Hall of Science was located across the street from Tract House, the headquarters of the New York Tract Society. Like the Hall of Science, Tract House also represented the new, in this case the evangelical Christian movement sweeping across the country. This confrontation between the free enquirers and awakened Christianity in the late 1820s and early 1830s helps situate the second sexual framework specifically. The Second Great Awakening, which had begun around 1790, reached a new phase in the 1820s, as the fires of revival again blazed. Prominent evangelicals restated earlier Christian notions of sexuality with new intensity, and sinful lust became a chief way of comprehending sexual desire.

As Americans turned to religion, the number of professing Baptists, Presbyterians, and Methodists multiplied manyfold. In an intensely studied county in upstate New York, church membership reached roughly 25 to 30 percent in the antebellum decades, in line with the national figures in 1850. As more people declared themselves Christian, the nature of their commitment changed. Those experiencing saving grace believed that not only could they save themselves, they could save the world. Allied with the churches were Sunday schools, missionary and Bible societies, and the tract societies that were attempting to use the expanding power of print to publish Bibles and religious pamphlets in cheap bulk editions and to distribute them widely. The New York Tract Society, founded in 1827 as an urban missionary auxiliary of its parent American Tract Society, had as members Presbyterian, Congregationalist, and Dutch Reform laymen.[4]

These prominent businessmen engaged in highly personal efforts. Arthur Tappan distributed tracts to the warehouses and piers of the lower East River; William Dodge was one of those responsible for steamboats. Beginning in 1829, when the society decided to distribute materials systematically throughout the city, each member took sixty families, visiting each once a month to give out tracts and advise on religious life. As freethinkers waited for a lecture at the Hall of Science, from across the street came evangelicals to pass out tracts. The free-enquirers taunted the tractarians, as they did all Christians, with invitations to debate.[5]

Stirring the Tract Society's members was Charles Grandison Finney, who came to New York in the fall of 1829 at its initiation and whipped up the spirit of revival continuously until the spring of 1830. Lewis Tappan agreed to buy Finney a theater for his revivals and worked out an agreement for him to be the minister of the Second Free Presbyterian Church. The tractarians' goal of religious conversion intensified, and tract distributors prayed with the visited families. As the tract men engaged in a range of good works in the city, they fought for stricter Sunday Sabbath observance and temperance. Inspired by Finney, some, such as the Tappan brothers, turned to freedom for southern slaves. Within a few years the tractarians would seek to reform prostitutes. For such men, free thought was anathema. It threatened to unleash the floodgates of lust-driven sin. The reform physiology of the freethinkers was a threat to the presumed sexual ignorance of children, a critical pillar of sexual restraint. Birth control was a special danger, for it removed the fear of pregnancy, believed to be necessary for the protection of female virginity.[6]

At the outset the tractarians realized something that the freethinkers did not. Changes in the production of paper and in printing technology had greatly reduced the costs of publishing, making it possible to offer printed materials at low cost to a wide public. Evangelicals were among the first to take advantage of this development. Ignited by the power of the Word to save souls, their associations pioneered in the newest machines and techniques of printing and forms of organization and distribution. In the process they helped to revolutionize publishing and advance literacy in America. The Tract House had small religious pamphlets mass-produced on inexpensive paper and gave them away.[7]

In their bookstore Wright and Owen may have tried to appeal to the common man and woman, but the price of books in the Hall of Science win-

The First Home of the American Tract Society, at the Corner of Nassau and Spruce Streets, lithograph, n.d. © Museum of the City of New York.

dow was too high for ordinary people to afford. For example, a highly skilled printer could hardly buy a book that took more than 10 percent of his weekly wage of $11. Wright and Owen quickly responded to the challenge of Tract House, and beginning in 1830 produced their own set of popular tracts, which were extracts from the *Free Enquirer*. In pamphlets that ran from four to twenty pages, they publicized their views on a wide range of subjects and responded to their rivals across the street. Suddenly there was an explosion of print that broadcast conflicting ideas and values.[8]

2

Beginning this story with Frances Wright is a reminder that two deep inequities inform all the words that follow—black slavery and women's subordination. By 1828 the last northern state had ended the enslavement of African Americans, but in the South the institution was gaining strength with southwestern settlement. Some had imagined that as eastern plantation land was exhausted, slavery would die out because it was unprofitable. But growing demand in what became the cotton kingdom of the lower South made the traffic in slaves a source of revenue in the East and forcibly drew two million black souls to the lower and middle South. In the narrative about sexual representation and censorship that follows, only a fraction of the printed material examined explicitly engaged race. Yet all of it implicitly did, for, unless specified, the described bodies with their reproductive organs and functions were imagined as white. Occasionally, as will be considered subsequently, sexual relations across the color line, real or imagined, prompted discussion. When they did, the words were always controversial and often designed to incite opposition.

Women often got equal or even predominant billing in nineteenth-century sexual discourses, but their prominence on the page did not reflect their position in society. Women lived, worked, and loved in a political and legal system of inequality. Although citizens, women were denied many of the fundamental rights and responsibilities of citizenship. They could not vote or be elected to office. They could not serve on juries, or be lawyers or judges. A critical element was couverture, inherited from the common law, in which a woman's legal identity was covered by that of her husband. Not only did women lose legal personhood with marriage, they were also barred from the opportunities afforded men for education and training for occupations. They were excluded from apprenticeships that allowed entry into the

Frances Wright, painting by Henry Inman, c. 1824.
© Collection of The New-York Historical Society,
negative #38842.

crafts. Women who entered fields such as printing generally did so as wives and widows. They could not receive training for the learned professions, except irregularly, and entry was typically blocked. And women, as a rule, did not speak in public to mixed audiences.[9]

What made Fanny Wright both loved and hated was that she defied some of the most deeply held conventions of gender and race. She took to the lecture circuit, speaking in Cincinnati, New Orleans, Baltimore, and Boston. In New York she attracted great crowds at Masonic Hall and the Park Theater. Purchasing an ownership interest in the *New-Harmony Gazette* from Robert Dale Owen, in 1829 Wright left New Harmony for New York and a large country house on the banks of the East River five miles outside the city. She gathered other Owenites, including Robert Dale Owen and Josiah War-ren, who had left New Harmony following its dissolution. From this site out-side the city she and Owen printed their weekly paper, renamed the *Free Enquirer,* for one thousand paying subscribers.

Wright's and Owen's editorial partnership, lasting until 1830, was a vital one, critical to an understanding of the public discussion of sexuality in America. The *Free Enquirer* was fundamentally concerned with posing alter-natives to private property, religion, and marriage. Emphasizing free thought, it broadened the topic of marriage to explore the tyranny of custom and morality for women. Included in their wide-ranging calls for reform were attempts made by Wright and Owen to help readers understand the unnatural restrictions that the culture placed on women. Church, literature, and fashion distorted the way that women were seen and saw themselves. Wright focused on education, and Owen wrote on the need for women's emancipation and the liberalization of divorce laws.[10]

In critical ways Wright, Owen, and the American free enquirers attempted to bring some of the radical ideas of the Enlightenment into American discussions of sex. To understand what they were advocating and the broader context of sexual culture requires considering the impact of the Enlightenment on notions of the body. In the late eighteenth and early nineteenth centuries, Americans' reception of the new thought emanating from England and France was complex, for on this side of the Atlantic it mixed with religion, irreligion, and deism in complicated ways. But however much Thomas Jefferson of Virginia and Benjamin Rush of Pennsylvania differed on God—or politics, for that matter—they agreed that one must search for natural causes of phenomena in the natural world. The Enlightenment served as an important stimulus to science and medicine. Underlying scientific inquiry was the Lockean belief that all ideas come from sensation or reflection rather than innate knowledge. National boundaries were disregarded as natural philosophers opened important channels of information to communicate their discoveries. Americans studying abroad brought home with them methods and theories of Scottish and French medical practice.

Alongside the Lockean notions was a new understanding of the brain and the nervous system. This had two elements. Whereas in earlier centuries, those concerned with human anatomy had often sited the soul or the seat of consciousness in the heart or chest, by the late seventeenth century they understood its specific location in the body as being the brain. The nerves—often perceived as tiny hollow tubes—emanating from the brain traveled to all parts of the body and were responsible for all perception and knowledge. Inside the nerves flowed the animal spirits, the brain's unique secretion. By the late eighteenth century, the brain was also seen as the location of a distinct organ, the imagination. It controlled the passions, sending impressions to bodily organs, including the sexual ones. And as an organ, the imagination could be healthy or diseased. Such notions underlay psychology, which was beginning to emerge out of philosophy.[11]

Although these new understandings had a powerful impact on the ways that sex was understood, some of this lay in the future. There were limits that the Enlightenment did not breach in bringing scientific light to human reproduction, sex, and desire. Barring the way was the importance that the Enlightenment gave to reason. Sexuality in the eighteenth century was immensely complex. The era saw a new appreciation of sentiment and emotion. Libertinism in France and England unleashed an efflorescence of sexual play in the lives and culture of aristocrats. Subversive writing took the form of the *chronique scandaleuse,* which deliberately used obscenity to attack the monarchy. At the same time that male homosexuals were defining a sodomite culture, writing appeared that placed a new emphasis on male heterosexuality.[12] Despite all this, within natural philosophy the brunt of the effort to understand instinct and passion was to bring both under control. In political theory, the notion of interests and power and the fear of the passions of avarice and ambition led to the devising of a system of checks and balances. In psychology, the instincts and passions of one's animal nature were to be balanced by reason.

Moreover, medical practice had largely left the female body and its reproductive organs to midwifery. This began to change in the eighteenth century, and physicians began to assist in childbirth. Formal medical education came to include obstetrics, and students received training in female anatomy and the use of bloodletting, opium, and forceps in parturition. The English physician William Hunter studied the uterus. However, although empirical science made great inroads into understanding the circulation of blood, the role of the lungs in respiration, and even the relation of the fetus and uterus, it was slow to add the study of sex and conception to its list.[13]

In America the reticence of natural philosophy and medicine about sexuality was broken by freethinkers and advocates for change. Controversy first impelled Frances Wright to speak and write about sex. While she was abroad in 1827, her Nashoba associate James Richardson published his account of life in the colony in Benjamin Lundy's abolitionist newspaper, *The Genius of Universal Emancipation.* Richardson included journal entries disclosing that blacks under his care and that of Frances Wright's sister, Camilla, were subjected to physical discipline, including flogging. One entry concerned the sexual threat faced by a black woman who asked for a lock on her bedroom door. Camilla Wright denied her request on the grounds that true protection lay in her attacker's understanding that sexual relations needed to be "the unconstrained and unrestrained choice of *both* parties." Finally, Richardson declared that he was living with Mam'selle Josephine, the daughter of Nashoba's free black school director. Critics howled that Nashoba promoted promiscuity and miscegenation, that it was, in their terms, a "brothel." Their vituperative attacks forced Fanny Wright to respond.[14]

On Wright's return to the United States in 1828, she began to publish in the *New-Harmony Gazette* a defense of her position. In her most controversial statement, she argued for the interbreeding of races and a new understanding of sexual relations. At Nashoba, she explained, laws governing marriage had no force:

> The marriage law existing without the pale of the Institution, is of no force within that pale. No woman can forfeit her individual rights or independent existence, and no man assert over her any rights or power whatsoever, beyond what he may exercise over her free and voluntary affections; nor, on the other hand, may any woman assert claims to the society or peculiar protection of any individual of the other sex, beyond what mutual inclination dictates and sanctions, while to every individual member of either sex is secured the protection and friendly aid of all.[15]

By the late 1820s, the Shakers had refused to recognize marriage, but they based their position on denial of the flesh, requiring the celibacy of community members. In speaking for Nashoba, Fanny Wright took an opposite course, insisting that expression of sexual feeling was a vital part of life, necessary to human happiness. As she put it, sexual passion is "the strongest and at the same time, if refined by mental cultivation, the noblest of the human passions." It is the basis of "the best joys of our existence" and "the best source of human happiness." In a judgment that echoed *Aristotle's Masterpiece,* Wright stated that sexual passion is as much a part of woman's nature as man's. She considered the independent, childless women of Britain—they were, she wrote, wrongly bound by "unnatural restraints," denying themselves love to avoid "the servitude of matrimony." She pondered the parent looking anxiously at the "dying health of daughters condemned to the unnatural repression of feelings and desires inherent in their very organization and necessary alike to their moral and physical well-being."

Sexual passion, Wright asserted, is a great force: if it is distorted, moral and physical disease follow. Victims of "ignorant laws, ignorant prejudices, ignorant codes of morals," women become prostitutes or prudes and men, rakes. These restraints "condemn one portion of the female sex to vicious excess, another to as vicious restraint, and all to defenceless helplessness and slavery, and generally the whole of the male sex to debasing licentiousness, if not to loathsome brutality." Opposing both public opinion and law, Wright insisted that the true regulator of sexual passion is a person's knowledge of its consequences, not law or custom.

> Let us not teach that virtue consists in the crucifying of the affections and appetites, but in their judicious government. Let us not attach ideas of purity to monastic chastity, impossible to man or woman without consequences fraught with evil, nor ideas of vice to connections formed under the auspices of kind feelings. . . . Let us teach the young mind to reason, and the young heart to feel, and instead of shrouding our bodies, wants, desires, senses, affections and faculties in mystery, let us court enquiry, and show that acquaintance with our own nature can alone guide us to judicious practice, and that in the consequence of human actions, exists the only true test of their virtue or their vice.[16]

The clergy and the press accused Wright of threatening to bring to America the excesses of the French Revolution. In response, she launched into a defense of its heroes, "the virtuous supporters of order, peace, brotherly union, and brotherly love." With sexual knowledge as an ever-important theme, she cried out against those forces that would keep women "hoodwinked and unawakened" so they might better serve and amuse men. The Church was a primary target. She called ministers "hired supporters of error," men who understood that "if the daughters of the present, and mothers of the future generation, were to drink of the living waters of knowledge, their reign would be ended—their occupation gone." Wright appealed to men as well as women. By mentally enslaving women, she told them, men were themselves bound.[17]

In New York, Wright and Owen entered into labor politics. Facing the threat to democracy that the growing division between classes posed, the two focused on educational reform. They advocated a system of boarding schools as the way to equalize opportunity in the next generation. With Wright away on lecture tours, Owen took the lead in this arena, joining the Working Men's movement, composed of journeymen and radicals. The Working Men scored an early success in the 1829 election, but Jacksonian Democrats quickly regained the support of New York workers and future

Robert Dale Owen, sketch from life, in Richard William Leopold, *Robert Dale Owen: A Biography* (Cambridge, Mass.: Harvard University Press, 1940).

victory at the polls. Owen was burned by factional fights and outmaneuvered by conservative forces.[18]

In early 1831 Owen published his *Moral Physiology; or, a Brief and Plain Treatise on the Population Question,* the first American work to offer arguments for limiting births and practical advice on contraception. Many elements conspired to push Owen to write this work. In the public debates surrounding the Working Men's party, Owen was attacked for his public support of Carlile's *Every Woman's Book,* the pioneer British pamphlet advocating and explaining birth control. In the work Carlile had indirectly implicated Owen by asserting that his father was the man responsible for bringing the knowledge of Continental methods of birth control to England. The Typographical Society refused to accept a gift of specimens of English type from Owen because he had sanctioned *Every Woman's Book.* Adoniram Chandler, an evangelical Christian, was the head of this association of master printers in New York. Once a political ally of Owen, he joined the opposition. The Typographical Society's spokesmen condemned Carlile's book as holding out "inducements and facilities for the prostitution of their daughters, sisters, and wives."[19]

Examining Carlile's *Every Woman's Book* sheds light on why it became a useful tool in a political conflict against Owen. Carlile was a champion of free thought and a believer in plain speech. Some of his language recalled *Aristotle's Master-piece*. He stated that women have "the same passions, the same desires" as men. In the well-formed and healthy of both sexes the instinct to reproduce is, he wrote, "as powerful as hunger or thirst or the desire of self-preservation." What is experienced as love "is nothing but this passion." Carlile insisted that women as well as men must satisfy their sexual needs or turn sour. He wrote, "If the proper secretions be not promoted, ripeness is either never accomplished, or, if accomplished, hastened to decay. Those, therefore, who abstain from sexual commerce, are generally useless for the purposes of civil life. They seldom possess either common cheerfulness or gaiety." Without sex, women begin to "droop" around age twenty-five. As their physical form degenerates, they become fidgety and suffer from melancholia and consumption, turning into what the world recognizes as old maids.[20]

Most shocking to the artisanal Christian paterfamilias of New York City must have been Carlile's challenge as a freethinker to the power of the state to regulate marriage. Carlile argued for early marriage, but at the same time he questioned the legitimacy of governmental regulation surrounding it. The reproductive instinct, he argued, cannot be neatly channeled into English law, which in the early nineteenth century ordained marriage for life. According to Carlile, passion is "not constant, but occasional," it "dies with gratification," and it ought neither to "be forced nor shackled." Finally, as he presented his instructions for birth control, Carlile clearly saw their value for the young unmarried woman as well as the married couple seeking to regulate the number of their offspring. Carlile advocated the sponge method, giving instructions to women that prior to intercourse they should insert in the vagina a small sponge, moistened with water, to which a ribbon was attached.[21]

Tarred by association with Carlile, Owen sought to shake free. But he was also dealing with the loss of Fanny Wright. She had left New York in July 1830 to arrange the removal of Nashoba's slave residents to Haiti. On her journey she traveled with William Phiquepal, a Frenchman living in the United States who had been a teacher at New Harmony. Their sexual relationship led to her pregnancy and marriage, and Wright retreated to France to have a child. Bereft at losing his platonic friend and intellectual companion, Owen was left to run their enterprises alone. Perhaps he felt that although he could not save Wright from pregnancy, he could help others.[22]

When he did, two of the central impulses that impelled Wright's thoughts on sex were stilled. In *Moral Physiology*, Owen addressed neither the racial controversy provoked by Nashoba nor the gender inequalities that Wright faced. Rather, he restated many of her positions about sex in language that is both race- and gender-free. Accepting her position that the reproductive instinct is essentially good, Owen wrote, "Controlled by reason and chastened by good feeling, it gives to social intercourse much of its charm and zest." Sexual urges are natural, alike to hunger and thirst, and their satisfaction is a legitimate pleasure. But in addition, the reproductive instinct serves to draw human beings outside themselves and toward others. "It is an instinct that entwines itself around the warmest feelings and best affections of the heart." Although Owen believed that it was possible to repress the reproductive instinct entirely, he saw that effort as misguided and "very mischievous." Celibacy, he wrote, "if it do not give birth of peevishness, or melancholy, or incipient disease, or unnatural practices, at least it almost always freezes and stiffens the character."[23]

As did his Enlightenment mentors, Owen found that the source of morality lay in nature. He cited Benjamin Franklin as his moral guide, saying that chastity is "the regulated and strictly temperate satisfaction, without injury to others, of those desires which are natural to all healthy adult beings." One seeks measure in the reproductive instinct as in all things. Reasonable satisfaction of the instinct is necessary for it to assume the proper proportion. Owen considered the ways in which repression creates problems in the mind. "The imaginations of the young and the passions of the adult," he wrote, "are inflamed by mystery or excited by restraint, and a full half of all the thoughts and intrigues of the world has a direct reference to this single instinct." Because the reproductive instinct cannot be destroyed, it should be wisely regulated with knowledge and a sense of measure.[24]

Owen himself seemed to agree in part with Carlile's critics. In *Moral Physiology*, Owen wrote that, despite his admiration for Carlile's "courage and strength of mind," among the reasons he had not reprinted the Englishman's pamphlet was that he "did not consider its style and tone in good taste." Owen brought to his subject a sensibility more refined than that of the rough-and-tumble Carlile. In the third person Owen gave his own character reference, and it reads like a Methodist primer. Owen asserted that he had never imbibed spirits and was now a vegetarian. Writing of himself, Owen stated, "He never chanced to enter a brothel in his life," nor had he ever associated with a prostitute. He enjoyed the company only of "intellectual and self-respecting" women. He believed that women were men's equal and even men's superior "in generous disinterestedness and moral worth."[25]

Owen insisted that only "libertines and debauchees" would find his book improper. He stated that it offended them because they assumed that "violence and vice are inherent in human nature, and that nothing but laws and ceremonies prevent the world from becoming a vast slaughter-house or a universal brothel." His book was, however, not for "prudes and hypocrites." Owen offered evidence of the emerging canons of middle-class respectability when he chastised his era. He opposed the false modesty of those "who will affect to blush if the ankle is incidentally mentioned in conversation . . . who, at dinner, ask to be helped to the bosom of a duck, lest, by mention of the word breast, . . . [they] call up improper associations." Some of the prudes are hypocrites who hide their own immoral private behavior and "read indecencies" in private and "make appointments only in the dark." Owen stated that he had written his book for ignorant and uncorrupted young men and women, those of warm sympathy who are "yet unlearned alike in the hypocritical conventionalities and the odious vices of pseudo-civilization."[26]

Owen introduced the theory of Thomas Malthus that population always outpaces the food supply. Although he is sometimes linked with the Malthusians, Owen opposed many of the gloomy economist's ideas, looking to economic and social solutions to cure the ills of society. And he fought Malthus's prescription that men and women should prevent overpopulation by waiting until age thirty to marry. Owen saw this as the wrong solution, for he judged that it would increase prostitution, drive men to drink, harm health, and hurt morality. He regarded marriage as an unmixed good: its sole problem was the birth of too many children. "Let us look solely to the situation of married persons," he wrote.

> Is it not notorious, that the families of the married often increase beyond what a regard for the young beings coming into the world, or the happiness of those who give them birth, would dictate? In how many instances does the hard-working father, and more especially the mother, of a poor family, remain slaves throughout their lives, tugging at the oar of incessant labour, toiling to live, and living only to die; when, if their off-spring had been limited to two or three only, they might have enjoyed comfort and comparative affluence![27]

In addition, he argued, there are many women whose physical condition does not allow the birth of children, and for them remaining childless is essential to well-being. For men, the issue of health is different. Here Owen had a specific referent: masturbation. It would be several years until prevailing British medical understandings about masturbation entered fully into American thinking, but Owen was a recent arrival from Scotland and remained part of the transatlantic intellectual community. He partook of British medical judgment that masturbation led to insanity. But as one who sought the social and economic causes of ills, Owen found that the source of the new "disease" of masturbation was delayed heterosexual relations. "For a vice so unnatural as onanism there could be no possible temptation, and therefore no existence, were not men unnaturally and mischievously situated. It first appeared, probably, in monasteries; and has been perpetuated by the more or less anti-social and demoralizing relation in which the sexes stand to each other, in almost all countries." Birth control, enabling early marriage and natural sexual relations at a young age, would wipe out the resort to masturbation in a single generation.[28]

To the great fear of his time that contraception would lead to an increase in prostitution, Owen responded with an examination of socioeconomic conditions. Except for about one case in ten, he argued, prostitution is caused not by the woman's inclination but by the pressure of economic need. Young women are indeed the victims of seduction, but only pregnancy marks them for life, and it can be avoided. Thus he would have the unmarried read his book. Owen also forgave the errant young, who, unlike the "matured and heartless" libertine, whom he despised, were led astray by the "unreasoning—sometimes even generous, imprudence of youthful passion."[29]

Owen anticipated the opposition's argument that any effort to interfere with conception is unnatural. Given his own sympathies for the "natural," this was a potential stumbling block. He countered with an answer worthy of the Enlightenment tradition that he inherited: "I will ask, in reply, whether nature also declares it to be right and proper, that, when the thermometer is at 96, we should drink greedily of cold water, and drop down dead in the streets?" In that instance the same nature that created the desire for cold water also produced the human reason that restrained that desire. In the case of birth control, nature, giving sexual passion to humankind, gives also the power to control its effects.[30]

The birth control method that Owen advocated was coitus interruptus. He had doubts about the efficacy of the sponge method that Carlile proposed in *Every Woman's Book,* although he argued that this approach had the great advantage of placing the power of birth control "where it ought to be, in the hands of the woman." Three married men had told him, however, that it was not a successful method. Whereas Carlile had advocated partial withdrawal, Owen made a case instead for "complete withdrawal, on the part of the man, immediately previous to emission." Introducing coitus interruptus as if it were a new method brought from the Continent, Owen wrote that the French considered their technique "a point of honor," and "all young men learn to make the necessary effort." Owen admitted that complete withdrawal does involve a slight loss of pleasure, but he argued that it is one that a man can become accustomed to. Owen did consider the condom, what he called the "baudruche," describing it as "a covering made of very fine, smooth, and delicately prepared skin," used by the man. He stated that it had been used for at least a century, primarily by elite men as a guard against syphilis. Although it was an infallible method and healthy, he judged it both expensive and objectionable "on the score of cleanliness."[31]

Moral Physiology had a long career in America. Disheartened by the terrible turn in her life, Fanny Wright gave it only muted praise, stating that she hoped it would do "some good" and would be reprinted "at a moment when the world may be less inclined to take fright at common sense than it is now." American audiences did not seem to "take fright," however. By March 1831, Owen's book had gone through two editions and a third was on the way. It was reissued repeatedly in the following decades, occasionally in pirated editions. Its author, however, turned to less controversial pursuits. He married Mary Jane Robinson, the daughter of a New York merchant and a regular attendant at the Hall of Science, and they went abroad. When they returned, they settled in Indiana, where Owen managed his property along capitalist lines and served in the Indiana legislature and the U.S. House of Representatives. An echo of his earlier career as freethinker, radical editor, and author of America's first birth control tract was his successful advocacy of freer divorce laws in the state of Indiana.[32]

3

During these years, evangelical Christian ministers across the country were calling to their flocks to experience saving grace and then to sin no more. To these ministers, Owen and Wright were the Antichrist. Some believed that the best defense was silence: when Frances Wright spoke in

Boston in 1829, a committee of merchants signed a circular requesting the newspapers to take no notice of her. But as Reverend Lyman Beecher watched her make "converts . . . among . . . females of education and refinement—females of respectable standing in society—those who had been the friends and associates" of his own children, he decided to attack. There was, Beecher declared, "a conspiracy in our land against the being of God, and our civil, and social, and religious institutions," and Fanny Wright was a part of it.[33]

Beecher was then the pastor of the Hanover Street Church in Boston. As a student at Yale, he had been transformed by Timothy Dwight, an intractable opponent of the French Revolution. Beecher knew where danger lay and how to recognize it. Characterized by the *Free Enquirer* as a "staunch Presbyterian divine of the old school, bitter enough against all who dwell without the pale of his church," Beecher was actually the prophet of a new evangelical order, a Christianity that sought to change America through spiritual renewal. Beecher, in turn, saw the teachings and practices of Wright and Owen as a revival of "the atheistic conspiracy in France against the being and government of God" responsible for the French Revolution. Recalling not the democratic tradition of Lafayette that Fanny Wright celebrated but the excesses of the Terror, Beecher reminded his audience that the French Assembly "abolished the Sabbath, burnt the Bible, instituted the decade [the ten-day week] and ordained the worship of the goddess of liberty, in the person of a vile woman. . . . The consequences were too terrible to be endured; it converted the most polished nation of Europe into a nation of fiends and furies, and the theatre of voluptuous refinement into a stall of blood." It was this "dreadful experiment" that the political atheists sought to repeat in America.[34]

Beecher wanted his following to know that they confronted not just an attractive woman on the lecture podium but an organized movement of political atheism. The plans of Wright and Owen, he warned, "were avowed in their books, and tracts, and newspapers, and inculcated in their temples of reason, discussed in their weekly meetings, and threatened as an achievement which was near, even at the door." The true danger they posed was not their attempt to charter a college, the near success of their candidates at the New York polls, or their numerical strength; the true danger was their doctrines, which were "poisonous leaven," capable of undermining the "faith and moral principle of the nation." They planned to abolish private property, put children in state nurseries, and destroy the family, Beecher insisted. In the place of Christian marriage, they sought to "substitute the vagrancy of desire, the rage of lust, and the solitude, and disease, and desolation, which follow the footsteps of unregulated nature, exhausted by excess."[35]

Beecher's line of thought is critical to understanding not just the threat that Wright and Owen posed but that of the second sexual framework as well. As Beecher reflected on the French Revolution or sin, his mind immediately turned to sex. In his pulpit he thundered against the temptations of the Devil. Among the deadly sins, lust outstripped the others to take the lead. Its flaming passions put men in peril of the Hell to come.

Beecher had been nurtured in both the Western tradition and Christianity as modified by Puritanism. What did his heritage offer to those attempting to comprehend sexual desire and its expression? A fundamental element of Western understanding of sexuality is the distinction drawn between human beings and other animals. Philosophers and theologians argued that what lifted men above brutes was their minds and souls, which gave them reason and the ability to control their passions. As historian Keith Thomas has put it, "A transcendent God, outside his Creation, symbolized the separation between spirit and nature. Man stood to animal as did heaven to earth, soul to body, culture to nature. There was a total qualitative difference between man and brute." An important part of training and education was learning to subdue the bodily functions and appetites that linked human beings and others in the animal kingdom. Men were valued above women, adults above youth, English above Irish, the civilized above the savage because of their supposed distance from their animal natures, which included distance from "beastlike sexuality." Sexual desire was a powerful reminder of animality and thus was particularly threatening.[36]

At least since Paul, the Church had seen sex as suspect. Within men and women a war waged between the animal and the spiritual. The sexual urges of the body came from the depraved animal nature tied to the Fall. Tempted by Satan, Adam and Eve ate the apple of sexual knowledge and brought sin into the world. Children were thus born in the Original Sin of the first parents. Beginning with the Fall, children were conceived in sin and birthed in the agony of their mothers. As children, boys and girls were to be shielded from the temptations of the Devil. They were to be kept ignorant of sex. A basic element of goodness in the young was sexual purity. The Catholic Church Fathers had stated that although it is better to marry than to burn in Hell, it is better not to marry.

In the long history of Catholicism, the Church moved from denial of the flesh to an acceptance of sexual expression in marriage. As Scholastic unities fractured, the center of moral gravity shifted to the individual conscience. In 1551 the Council of Trent asserted the need for all believers to confess their sins at least once a year. Catholic writers instructing priests in the confessional continued to distinguish between sexual acts that were "natural," leading to procreation, and those regarded as "unnatural," such as masturbation and sodomy. As ordinary men and women participated in confession, they were to examine not only what they had done but how they had felt. Sin consisted not only of wrongful sexual acts but also of unnatural sexual desires and the play of the imagination.[37]

Protestants amended this message to stress its counters: it is not good that man should be alone; people should be fruitful and multiply. Rejecting the celibacy of priests, Martin Luther emphasized sex's naturalness and necessity. Although sex continued to carry the taint of sin for some Calvinists, the Puritans who came to America brought a new acceptance of sexual intercourse. Grounding their theology in the science of their day, Puritan divines insisted on the duty and pleasure of sexual union in marriage. Edward Taylor stated that "the Use of the Marriage Bed" is "founded in mans Nature." For a husband or wife to deny that use "Denies all reliefe in Wedlock unto Human necessity: and sends it for supply unto Beastiality when God gives not the gift of Continency." Yet similar to other Protestants, Puritans worried about sexual excess. As Taylor suggests, all sexual acts outside marriage were forbidden. Even within marriage, sexual ardor should be kept within "measure." It should not be "an inordinate love" that would interfere with the most important relation, that between a man or a woman and God.[38]

As Puritanism softened through the eighteenth century into a liberal Christianity, sexuality became bound up with attitudes toward France. In American consciousness France was firmly linked with sensuousness and the erotic. There had been a growing rapprochement between the two cultures as increasing secularization, a mellowing of Calvinism, and enthusiasm for the ideas of the Enlightenment opened the way to French ideas. After Lafayette joined the American forces during the American Revolutionary War and France supported the patriotic cause, Americans were able to admire and adopt elements of French style, manners, and ideas in the belief that they were thoroughly in keeping with national values.[39]

Americans greeted the French Revolution enthusiastically, seeing its imitation of Republican institutions as a great compliment. Protestants saw the

French Revolution as an embodiment of the Enlightenment and a victory over the Catholic Church and initially tolerated even such gross violations of Christian practice under the Cult of Reason as the abolition of the Sabbath. Such leniency survived the Terror. During the early 1790s, enthusiasts for more radical Enlightenment ideas were given a hearing in America. Thomas Paine joined the French cause; his *Rights of Man,* published in 1791, offered the hope of a world governed by reason, not superstition, overcoming all evils. In *Political Justice,* from 1793, the English radical William Godwin questioned all institutions, putting them to the test of reason and usefulness. Mary Wollstonecraft, an admirer of the French Revolution, explored in 1792 the sources of women's subordination in *Vindication of the Rights of Women* and argued for a rational education for both sexes. Their works were printed and reprinted in America.

France's war with England brought an abrupt end to the general enthusiasm for all things French, and attitudes toward France took on a political cast. The Anglo-French conflict strengthened the hand of English conservatives and gave their ideas a greater resonance in America. Diplomatic embarrassments raised questions in America about France's good faith. French expansion during the Napoleonic era raised fears about the dangers posed by its colonies on this side of the Atlantic. As the emergence of a new national politics in the United States altered the context in which Enlightenment ideas were considered, New England Federalists began to raise the specter of an anti-Christian conspiracy reaching American shores. There had always been forces opposed to both French Catholicism and deism in America, but beginning at the turn of the nineteenth century the voices of Christian opposition took on a new urgency and found broader support. Federalists' antagonism to Jefferson linked his politics to his science and deism and proclaimed them anathema. They broadcast the conspiracy theory that the Illuminati, a special group of Freemasons, and their allies among the *philosophes* had caused the French Revolution and were now seeking to expand their reign. Were they to gain power in America, Yale president Timothy Dwight predicted, Protestant churches would became temples of reason and daughters and wives "would change characters with the bawd and the strumpet," turning the home into a "brothel."[40]

What Dwight's prediction suggests is that combined with reaction against the French Revolution was the fear of unleashed sexual desire. If the desanctification of many aspects of French life allowed the days of the week to be reconfigured, could other institutions and social arrangements be altered? Might sexual expression be divorced from marriage? Dwight's fears were connected to the spread of literacy and print culture. As he saw the danger, enthusiasts for the new revolutionary ideas were forging titles and distributing books "at lowest price, through all classes of men." Ideas could no longer be contained within an elite, but as they spread promiscuously among men, they fueled rebellion. They turned women from duty to self-indulgence and sexual license.[41]

Yet there could be no full swing of the circle back to the beginning. Republican government was a fact, and much of the thinking that underlay it remained fundamental to American political theory. New developments in science could not be denied. In the War of 1812 France returned as an ally. The aesthetic achievements of French arts and letters and French style in consumer goods served as a standard and a temptation.

By the late 1820s, however, new forces were in the wind. Religious enthusiasm reasserted traditional notions about the body and soul that went back deep into the Christian tradition. At revivals, as Americans sat at the anxious bench and declared again the spirit of Christ working within them, Christian notions about human nature and sin resurfaced. If the soul implanted by God was warring with the desires tempted by Satan, then the body was its battleground. This is how Beecher saw the field and why Fanny Wright posed such a threat.[42]

A few years later, Beecher reflected on his conflict with the freethinkers, "In this crusade against virtue and happiness, all that is odious and all that is deadly takes on the specious name of some moral excellence. It is all done under the name of virtue. I have read the tracts of Fanny Wright and Robert Owen, and I felt ashamed, although I was alone. I believe I blushed, though no human eye was upon me. In these productions, there is nothing which men have agreed to call wicked, which is not canonized; and nothing which they have united to call virtuous, which these writings do not ridicule, vilify, and throw mud upon."[43] His words make it clear that the conflict between the evangelical Christians and the freethinkers went deeper than any specifics. Each spoke from within a different frame of reference, and, regarding any particular, each felt quite different emotions. What Beecher revered, his religious enemies in the society, the freethinkers, reviled. The two parties made meaning in the world in radically different terms, and these terms included their understandings of sex and its role in human life.[44]

Lyman Beecher did not have Fanny Wright as his primary target, however. He was after the ordinary sinning mortal. Fundamentally Beecher was seeking the conversion of the unbelieving multitudes. His task was to bring those who were unchurched into the fold. He saw their ways, including their sexual attitudes and practices, as profane and un-Christian. Men were, as he put it, subject to "volcanic passions," hot and violent. This bodily part of men was prey to the Devil's work. Beecher's primary task, as he saw it, was to change men's hearts and in so doing subdue their sinning natures. Coming out of the Second Great Awakening was a call to reorder society and culture in a way that would keep human passions in control.[45]

A DOWNRIGHT GABBLER,
or a goose that deserves to be hissed—

"A Downright Gabbler," caricature of Frances Wright, published by J. Akan, Philadelphia, lithograph, c. 1830–35. © Collection of The New-York Historical Society, negative #43461.

To this project Owen posed a particular threat. When those with a Christian cast of mind thought about his arguments for deliberately limiting births, they returned to the religious question of the morality of sexual intercourse. Clearly God as creator had ordained coition. He had given humans a reproductive system and the instincts to fuel it. But children were the ends that justified the means. Sex designed for any purpose other than to produce offspring held the danger of licentiousness. Related, yet distinct, was anxiety about daughters and wives. When master printer Adoniram Chandler refused Owen's gift of English type, he was drawing on this well of Christian belief.

Owen did not answer Chandler's statement directly, but he did respond to that of William Gibbons, a Hicksite Quaker. Owen replied that his arguments for birth control had mistakenly been turned into an advocacy of "prostitution and unseemly licentiousness." His statements about the naturalness of sex had been twisted out of shape and, in contrast with Owen's high regard for woman, had wrongly identified him with "the profligate axiom, 'that every woman is at heart a rake.' " In the early nineteenth century, religious conservatives smeared free-thought radicals with the red brush of the brothel. Owen tried to explain his own belief that the human heart and "the power of unshackled virtue" could serve best to regulate sexual expression.[46]

At the very outset of the debate over contraception in America, opponents voiced what remained a primary theme for at least fifty years: if given the means for not suffering the consequences of sexual intercourse in pregnancy, women would be more easily seduced by men and would become promiscuous. Trying to understand what lay behind this response is a reminder of the notions of sexuality imbedded deep in Christian tradition. In its interpretation of the Fall, it was Eve who had tempted Adam. Although woman was not seen as more passionate than man, she was perceived as more wanton, for she was less under the control of reason. Without the check of reason over her emotions and instincts, woman was always in danger of going astray.

Patriarchal structure stood in the place of inner strength. The inconstant woman needed to be controlled by the requirement of virginity at marriage and prohibitions against adultery to keep her from submitting to another man's embraces. Aiding this was the physical fact that woman wore the sign of fornication in pregnancy. The fear of being cast out of a father's or husband's house for premarital sex or adultery was a means of governing her actions. Basic to this check was the link between sexual intercourse and pregnancy, a powerful tool to keep woman within the bounds of virtue.

The danger for the sexually awakened girl is the brothel. The aroused female cannot be trusted: she needs to satisfy her lusts. She looks first to a man and, if not protected by marriage, is seduced and abandoned. Pregnant, she has no recourse but the brothel for support and the continued gratification of her desires. The brothel leads her to sexual excess and death. One could argue, as Owen alone did, that birth control allowed an unmarried woman the means to err without such severe consequences. That only inflamed the opposition: to its opponents, contraception offered to women the means to engage in illicit intercourse without penalty, and that was unthinkable.

It was in these terms that Lyman Beecher, on the one hand, and Frances Wright and Robert Dale Owen, on the other, joined in combat in the opening battle in America's first culture war. Admittedly, in these early years the contest was unequally drawn. Had a survey been taken, the freethinkers' camp would have been overwhelmed by that of evangelical religion. But Wright and Owen had much of the future on their side. They might not have understood or accepted many of those who in the next decades entered the debate over sexuality in support of many of their positions. Wright and Owen wrote in the language of the Enlightenment; future writers were to add new understandings from science and religion. Nor would Beecher have agreed with all who would take his position. His forthcoming supporters, too, added new nineteenth-century ways of thinking and touched on matters he believed were better left unstated. Moreover, while Beecher relied on the pulpit and the power of moral suasion, they imagined new ways of fostering virtue and policing vice.

4

Blasphemy, Birth Control, and Obscenity

Lyman Beecher was right in one respect. The ideas of Frances Wright and Robert Dale Owen did go beyond New York to Massachusetts. The words and thoughts proclaimed in the Hall of Science took root in Boston and spread to the western reaches of the commonwealth. As free thought became diffused, it stimulated ideas and language that led to the trial of Abner Kneeland for blasphemy. It also encouraged Charles Knowlton to write and publish *Fruits of Philosophy,* the first book on contraception based on empirical medical science in the United States. This work advanced sexual knowledge and enriched the physiological understandings at the base of the third sexual framework.

I

In 1834, in Boston, two hundred people gathered in Julien Hall at a dinner to celebrate Thomas Paine's birthday. Seating had been limited by the hall's capacity, and at the ball that followed, one hundred more attended. In the freethinking world this anniversary had become the occasion of annual observance. Paine's *Age of Reason* challenged the Bible as a forgery, contrasted its teaching to science, and demonstrated its immorality. Anathema to evangelical Christians, Paine was a hero to English and American radicals and freethinkers, who, beginning in 1818 in London, used the event to laud Paine and demonstrate their strength.[1]

Abner Kneeland organized Boston's Paine celebration. A lecturer, writer, and former minister, he migrated from the Baptist Church to Universalism to free thought and from Gardner, Massachusetts, to New York, where he arrived in 1825. There he was a friend and associate of Robert Dale Owen, who appeared before Kneeland's Broadway Hall congregation. In 1831 Kneeland returned to Boston as paid lecturer to the Society of Free Enquirers and began editing the Boston *Investigator,* a weekly newspaper. The society was committed to the full and open discussion of all questions. Men, women, and children were welcome at its Sunday meetings and Wednesday dances. Kneeland advocated the rights of women in unequivocal terms, supported the labor movement, and put forth his particular form of irreligion. In the December 20, 1833, issue of the *Investigator,* Kneeland reprinted an item clipped from Owen's *Free Enquirer* and learned that Boston was not New York.[2]

In New York one could write and publish this commentary on a quotation from Voltaire: "The Frenchman will ask *why* the Hottentot allow their boys but one testicle,—but that same Frenchman, though he be too stupid to understand the laws of evidence, or too illiterate to apply them to history, firmly believes that Jesus Christ was begotten without any testicles at all." One could also state, as Kneeland did, that philosophy is independent of the clergy, as is morality of the Bible. One could write a statement such as Kneeland's that put freethinking in oppositional terms: "Universalists believe in a god which I do not. . . . Universalists believe in Christ, which I do not."[3] In Boston, these three pieces were the subjects of indictment under the 1782 Massachusetts Act against Blasphemy. At the 1834 Thomas Paine celebration, one of the formal toasts joined to tributes to Jefferson and Adams: "The invidious Laws of Massachusetts against Blasphemy and Witchcraft—May they soon be abolished."[4]

Kneeland's trials have received serious scholarly attention, for although prosecution for word crimes was familiar in nineteenth-century England, he was the only American to serve a sentence for blasphemy.[5] His case is important to this discussion for two direct reasons and one indirect one. Like his counterparts in New York and England, Kneeland employed intentionally shocking words that in the eyes of the prosecutor blended blasphemy with obscenity. Secondly, the critical appellate decision of Massachusetts Chief Justice Lemuel Shaw greatly restricted freedom of expression and would often be cited by future justices. Finally, less directly, Kneeland's position became linked to that of Charles Knowlton, the first American to be tried for publication of contraceptive information.

One element important to the court and to a study of obscenity was the distinction made in the trial regarding the type of publication and nature of the audience. The prosecution contrasted the writings in the books of Hume and Voltaire, "read only by men of literary habits—necessarily a few," and presumably not indictable, with the publication of their words in a newspaper "so widely circulated, so easily read—so coarsely expressed—so industriously spread abroad." It was the widely available, cheap publication that constituted a critical element of Kneeland's offense, as it would in future obscenity trials.[6]

In making its arguments, the prosecution drew on what Blackstone and Holt had written about blasphemous and obscene libel and added an authority that proved powerful in the Kneeland case and many to follow, *A Treatise on the Law of Slander and Libel,* written by British jurist Thomas Starkie. In a polity that valued freedom of the press, Starkie reassured his readers—as had Blackstone and Holt—that the law of libel was essential to a free press, for it protected against abuses. "The liberty of the press and rational freedom of public discussion are the real bolts and bars by which alone deprecators on the religious and political rights of society are to be shut out, and the interest of the community preserved." By Starkie's understanding, the real danger to freedom of expression came not from the courts but from those "who endanger the liberties of all, by abusing the most valuable of their own, for unworthy, base, and venal purposes." Citing Holt and Starkie, the prosecution argued that Kneeland had violated common law, of which Christianity was a part. "The common law is part and parcel of the law of this land. It is recognized in the Constitution of the United States. . . . It is recognized in the Constitution of this Commonwealth." Kneeland's particular violation was of "composing, printing and publishing an impious, obscene and blasphemous libel."[7]

The prosecution won, and Kneeland appealed the verdict. Serving as his own lawyer, he argued that Article XVI of the Massachusetts Declaration of Rights guaranteed his freedom to put forward his opinions on religion, and that the state statute against blasphemy was in violation of this guaranteed freedom. His case ultimately came before the Supreme Court of the Commonwealth of Massachusetts. Chief Justice Lemuel Shaw, a man of great learning and prestige, spoke for the majority of the court in his decision against Kneeland. His statement greatly restricted freedom of the press. Rights that had seemed protected in state constitutions and the federal Constitution under the First Amendment emerged in Shaw's decision as weak reeds. Shaw reinterpreted state protection in the light of Holt and Starkie to mean only that there was no prior censorship. One who sold a writing was criminally responsible if that writing threatened the social order. Constitutional guarantees had less power than the common law as interpreted by British commentators.[8]

Shaw's argument had standing and became an important authority cited by subsequent courts. At the time, however, it was contested by the sole judge of the five-man appellate court who was a Democrat, the Jacksonian Marcus Morton. The Massachusetts statute on blasphemy could be applied constitutionally, Morton argued, only if motive were taken into account. Simple denial of the existence of God did not constitute blasphemy. It "must be blasphemously done," that is, accompanied by malice. "I cannot agree that a man may be punished for wilfully doing what he has a legal right to do." Many prominent Bostonians agreed and circulated a petition to the governor to grant Kneeland a pardon. Ellis Gray Loring drew it up, William Ellery Channing revised it, and its signers included a roster of distinguished men of letters and reformers: George Bancroft, Theodore Parker, Ralph Waldo Emerson, Bronson Alcott, and William Lloyd Garrison.[9]

Political divisions governed the outcome of the appellate ruling as it did all the lower-court rulings in Kneeland's case. In his many trials all the judges who found him guilty were Whigs; those finding him innocent were Democrats. Edward Everett, the governor of the Commonwealth of Massachusetts, was not only a Whig; in the last four elections he had faced the Jacksonian Democrat Marcus Morton. Thus it came as no surprise that the pardon was denied and Kneeland had to serve his sixty days in jail. Although Kneeland was to take refuge in Salubria, Iowa, where he died in 1844, the Boston *Investigator* had a long and useful life.

2

In June 1829, Charles Knowlton, a young physician from western Massachusetts, spoke on physiology at the Hall of Science in New York. At that time he was, as he later put it, "in a fine pickle." He had just gotten out of jail, after having served part of a sentence for human dissection (on a charge that included grave robbing to obtain a cadaver, one of his common pursuits). He could not support his wife and three young children. Known locally as "a deist, infidel, 'bad man,'" he had no patients. And he was consumed by the philosopher's dream: "At length my great end and aim was to astonish the world, and become even far more famous than John Locke ever was."[10]

Knowlton had had only intermittent schooling until he attended Dartmouth Medical School in Hanover, New Hampshire, for two years after apprenticing with several physicians. He married Tabita Stuart at age twenty and by 1828 had three children. Undeterred by the lack of a baccalaureate degree, the young physician chased after the president of Williams College, trying to engage him in philosophic argument. He wrote a learned treatise—*Elements of Modern Materialism*—and published it in 1829 at his own expense. In this deist work, Knowlton rejected all spiritual and psychical concepts, such as soul and conscience, and insisted that human beings feel, think, and know only through the physiological processes of the brain and the nervous system. As he later declared, "A man has no soul, no spirit, no mind, no memory, no imagination—nothing at all within his skull but just a brain." What Knowlton's contemporaries called a self or the personality is solely the result of past sensations. All actions are caused by other actions, including human passions and external stimuli; thus there is no free will. Knowlton's book did not sell.[11]

His debt now increased by printing costs, Knowlton traveled to New York with a trunkload of books, hoping to find buyers of *Elements of Modern Materialism* among freethinking New Yorkers. The Free Press Association gave him an audience for his materialist speculations; at the Hall of Science he gave a lecture on physiology. However, he sold few copies of his books, and he returned to his wife and children with little possibility of getting out of debt. While he was traveling to peddle his own books and others he had gotten in trade, the president of Amherst College had him arrested.[12]

Knowlton's links to the New York freethinkers continued during the period when leadership passed to other hands after Owen's marriage and departure. By May 1832, the Hall of Science was no more, and the building on Broome Street was leased to a minister and restored to its religious purposes. The office of the *Free Enquirer* moved to the establishment of printer Benjamin H. Day. In the edition of the weekly of May 19, 1832, Owen announced to readers of the *Free Enquirer* that Augustus J. Matsell, the young man who had been assisting in the bookstore at the Hall of Science since its beginning, was now the person in charge of bookstore operations. As the store moved to the shops of the successive printers of the paper, George Washington Matsell joined his brother as manager. On October 27, 1833, as the *Free Enquirer* announced that Carlile had been released from prison in

England, its bookstore advertised that it had received copies of Charles Knowlton's *Fruits of Philosophy* and offered them for sale.[13] Copyrighted in Rhode Island in 1831, this miniature book was printed anonymously in 1832 in New York. It is possible that it was printed at the press of the *Free Enquirer*.[14]

Charles Knowlton's *Fruits of Philosophy* is a pathbreaking work, for it attempted to apply science to sexual relations, based on the most advanced writing on women's anatomy and reproduction.[15] The title was no vague euphemism but a statement of the basis of Knowlton's understanding of contraception. Knowlton's philosophy led him away from any sense of the sinfulness of lust to a definition of virtue based on a temperate satisfaction of natural appetites. This required him, as a physician, "to inform mankind of the means of preventing the evils that are liable to arise from gratifying the reproductive instinct." To the traditional insistence of moralists that humanity not engage in sexual relations beyond what is needed for health or off-spring, Knowlton countered, "Mankind *will not* so abstain." Sex and sexuality, he said, must move out of the realm of morality into that of physiology.[16]

Knowlton based his technique on the understanding that male sperm

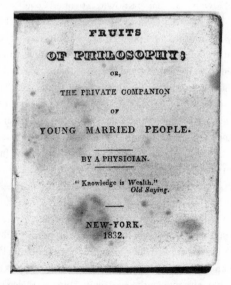

Title page of Charles Knowlton, *Fruits of Philosophy*, first edition, 1832. Courtesy, Lilly Library, Indiana University, Bloomington, Indiana.

fertilizes the female ovum and that one can destroy "the fecundating property of the sperm by *chemical* agents." A woman should use a female syringe in the vagina "immediately after connexion," to apply "a solution of sulphate of zinc, of alum, pearlash, or any salt that acts chemically on the semen, and at the same time produces no unfavorable effect on the female." Women had been douching in this manner for some time to treat various conditions of the uterus and vagina; thus these ingredients were known to be safe and the female syringe was easily and cheaply available at an apothecary. The disadvantage of his method, Knowlton granted, is that a woman has to leave her bed "for a few moments," but its advantages outweigh. It is inexpensive; "it requires no sacrifice of pleasure; it is in the hands of the female; it is to be used after, instead of before connexion, a weighty consideration in its favor, as a moments reflection will convince any one; and last, but not least, it is conducive to cleanliness, and preserves the parts from relaxation and disease."[17]

When Owen wrote his *Moral Physiology*, he chose to cast it in language that removed it from controversies over race and gender. As far as can be known, Knowlton was unaware that such controversies existed. When he turned to the larger social context and made the Malthusian argument, he literally borrowed Owen's language. Knowlton penned Owen's sentence as if it were his own: "In how many instances does the hard-working father, or more especially the mother, of a poor family, remain slaves throughout their lives, tugging at the oar of incessant labor, toiling to live, and living to toil and to die; when if their offspring had been limited to two or three only, they might have enjoyed comfort and comparative affluence!" The prudential need to delay children (and hence marriage) had led to both dissipation and prostitution, on the one hand, and celibacy with its attendant evils on the other. Knowlton engaged most fully when he considered the psychological rather than the social dimensions of sexuality. In writing of his own life, he stated that abstinence is "fraught with many evils. Peevishness, restlessness, vague longings, and instability of character, are among the least of these. The mind is unsettled, and the judgment warped. Even the very instinct which is thus mortified, assumes an undue importance, and occupies a portion of the thoughts which does not of right or nature belong to it; and which, during a life of satisfied affection, it would not obtain."[18]

Like Kneeland, Knowlton learned that Massachusetts was not New York. A Boston pamphlet already expressed deep hostility to Owen's *Moral Physiology*, sold by Kneeland and advertised in the *Investigator*. It stated that Owen and Kneeland had attempted to "vitiate the morals of the rising generation" by giving them a means of engaging in sexual intercourse without enduring the consequences of pregnancy. The result would be the realization of Frances Wright's goal "to turn the world into a universal brothel."[19] A war of words, such as Owen faced in New York, was one thing; resort to the courts, another. After Knowlton published *Fruits of Philosophy*, he faced prosecution under state law. In 1832, a court in Taunton, Massachusetts, fined him $50 for selling his book. Caught at it again in Lowell, Knowlton was arrested a second time and tried in Cambridge; on December 10, 1832, he was sentenced to hard labor for three months. Knowlton's crime was obscenity. Knowlton had not published *Fanny Hill*; but, in the eyes of Massachusetts prosecutors and courts, writing about contraception was deemed obscene.[20] In contrast to Kneeland's trials, much less can be learned about those of Knowlton, as they never reached the appellate level. However, Knowlton was eager to tell his side in print.

Prior to his trial, working in relative obscurity in western Massachusetts, Knowlton had had closer links to the free enquirers of New York City than to those in Boston. This was to change when Abner Kneeland gave his case public notice. Massachusetts papers had subjected Knowlton to a code of silence, with no mention of his book, arrests, or trials. Kneeland broke the code. When he learned of Knowlton's sentence, Kneeland printed in the January 4, 1833, *Investigator* under the title "The Days of Witchcraft Returned" this statement: "A man has received a sentence of three months hard labor in the House of Correction at Cambridge for publishing a book—in other words, for dissemminating knowledge—alias, 'for publishing the idea of destroying the fecundating property of the sperm by chemical agents.' Whenever the authorities try to proscribe the propagation of knowledge by coercive means, it is only the means of disseminating it so much the faster."[21] From this moment, Knowlton's fate was bound up with Kneeland, who was himself soon to be caught in the meshes of the law. It may have been that their association fueled opposition to both of them.

Knowlton replied to the *Investigator* from his jail cell, and Kneeland published the letter the following week. Knowlton wrote that the "slight notice" of his case had given him pleasure, especially since Kneeland regarded his imprisonment as a return of the Salem witch trials. Knowlton relished the opportunity to present his own case. "Yes, in this theoretically free country, I am imprisoned for publishing what I honestly and firmly believe to be the most useful idea that ever entered the brain of a philosopher." Why, when others had published about checks, had he been singled out? He had presented a scientific work, while copies of *Aristotle's Master-piece*—in Knowlton's words, "that dirty, useless thing called 'Aristotle' "—were sold openly. He believed he had been prosecuted because his birth control method required anatomical description to make it understood.

Knowlton described what it had been like for him to appear in court. "I had no trial," he wrote. He had given his lawyer $20 to defend him on the agreement that they would "fight the whole ground over." After waiting for ten days, he had made a journey to Cambridge on short notice. Once he was there, the lawyer advised him to plead guilty. "I told him I was willing to plead guilty to the charge of having sold the book . . . but that I would contend roundly that the book was useful—such as I had a right to sell, that my motives were good, &c." The lawyer assured him that he could make these arguments after the guilty plea. "Yet he afterwards made no attempt to defend the work. He simply said he presumed my motives were good, and gave the Judge a copy of 'Moral Physiology,' a work I had with me, on the same subject as my own, from the pen of one of the most powerful writers in this country," i.e., Robert Dale Owen. Knowlton was confident that the judge did not read it, "for the court immediately adjourned to dinner, and immediately after dinner I was called into court, and without my lawyer changing a word with me, I 'like a sheep dumb before its shearer,' received my sentence." The lawyer then promised to visit Knowlton in prison and plead an alternative sentence of a fine, but, Knowlton complained, "I have not seen him since."[22]

Unable to defend himself in court as he had planned, Knowlton now made his defense in the *Investigator*. He was aware of the argument that "there are many things very good and proper in their place, but quite otherwise out of place." Thus he had taken great care "not to offend the prejudices even of the most inconsiderate and prudish." He had tried to keep control of the book by securing a copyright. He had not advertised it. And he had kept the price at a "respectable price of fifty cents, though it is a very small book." That being stated, Knowlton then launched into arguments justifying his work that he put into later additions. He added a statement that linked him firmly to his new audience of Boston freethinkers: "What proportion of books now in America would escape the flames, if all were to be discarded which some part or class of the community might conjecture to have an immoral tendency?"[23]

While Knowlton remained in jail, his sentence and his letter continued to occasion comment in the *Investigator.* Kneeland clarified that Knowlton had appeared before a single judge in a case without a jury. In one piece Kneeland stated that Knowlton's indictment had charged him with "publishing the *idea* of destroying the fecundating property of the sperm [semen] by chemical agents," but he may not have been looking at the document, only repeating a statement made by Knowlton. Kneeland's real value is not as a source of trial testimony but as Knowlton's warm defender. Kneeland used words that anticipated some of his future encounters with the law: "Let us no longer speak of the Inquisition in Spain. Let us no longer condemn the courts which punished with death those involved in the Salem witchcraft. But let us look to our own times, our own judges, and our own legislators." He erred, however, in one important respect, for he regarded Knowlton as a popularizer of knowledge fully known by a medical elite, rather than as an innovator. In his eyes the crime of which Knowlton was guilty was not of writing a book on contraception but of making "the knowledge too cheap; and that is not the worst of it, he has permitted common people, people who can be benefited by the knowledge to have access to it. It will spoil the trade of the great and the rich." In his view, Knowlton was merely breaking the monopoly of elite physicians.[24]

The Boston *Investigator* became a platform from which Knowlton could now speak to a larger audience. The weekly advertised *Modern Materialism* and sold it in its bookstore, and he used its columns to promote his philosophical speculations. On March 29, 1833, out of jail, Knowlton delivered the first of three Sunday lectures at Julien Hall. Those coming to learn about birth control must have been disappointed, for Knowlton used the opportunity to instruct the freethinking congregation about his philosophical ideas. Kneeland published two of these in a pamphlet and the third, on human happiness, in the *Investigator.* In this last lecture Knowlton argued for the importance of pleasure, including bodily pleasure—"the exercise of BODILY functions"—and against priests for "robbing us of this life, and tickling our ears with another in lieu of it." In an unusual statement, he asserted the importance of equal property and education. His grounds were that equality led people to seek agreeable pleasures, such as reading, not "out of the way enjoyments," such as prostitution.[25]

Knowlton gained attention and needed money. From as far away as Pittsburgh, a "meeting of the friends of the liberty of the Press" sent to the *Investigator* resolutions in support of Knowlton. These explicitly stated his right to publish *Fruits of Philosophy.* The words of esteem must have bolstered his spirits. In addition, the signers stated that they would use their "influence, to make his writings known, in the western country." In a letter to the *Investigator*, Knowlton gratefully acknowledged the $30 that he received at the end of a lecture.[26]

Knowlton attached his name to the second edition of *Fruits of Philosophy*, which Kneeland published in Boston in 1833, and the *Investigator* began to advertise the book on its back pages.[27] With Knowlton one senses the mark of the village inventor. Knowlton had a technique he could not patent, for its advantage was that it was based on household ingredients and commonly available tools. But he could copyright the presentation of his method in print and thereby both coin it and take credit for it. The *Investigator* carried a notice to "Printers, Book-binders and Sellers" that Knowlton vowed to go after those other than Kneeland who printed text or ideas from the book. "I am the sole, true, and lawful Proprietor of said work," Knowlton stated, and he offered a reward of $50 for information about any future violations of his copyright.[28]

The second edition was an important advance over the first because it set out more fully the science underlying Knowlton's birth control method and, anticipating criticism, articulated a justification for its plain language and explicit treatment of sexual matters.[29] To convince readers that his method was effective, Knowlton corrected popular errors and named the reproductive organs, male and female. He stated that he offered his text not to gratify curiosity but "for utility in the broad and truly philosophical sense." The physicians who wrote about eating and drinking failed to offer instruction about sex beyond "some faint allusion." Knowlton asserted that their reticence arose from "the customs, not to say pruderies, of the age." He suggested that it was possible to present "some small work, indicated by its title to be for private perusal . . . with the utmost propriety." Perhaps this explains why this book, as well as the 1832 one, is a miniature. However, neither its size nor its claims to science protected Knowlton from the law.[30]

In the 1833 edition, Knowlton paid close attention to the nature of male semen. Contained within, he wrote, are "seminal animalcules," or sperm. Examined under a microscope, they have "a rounded head and a long tail" and move rapidly. While some writers argued that the animalcule is the beginning of the child, and other writers posited the female ovum, Knowlton understood from biracial children that both must unite to create life. His task was to give instruction on how to keep the two from joining. The syringe method works, he argued, because the chemicals inserted into the

vagina destroy the sperm before it reaches the ovum. "As the seminal animalcules are essential to impregnation, all we have to do is to change the condition, of, or, (if you will,) to *kill* them."[31]

To understand this, the reader needed to comprehend the internal reproductive organs of the female, and thus Knowlton described them. He also
dealt with the nature of female sexual response. As had *Aristotle's Master-
piece,* he named the clitoris as "the principal seat of pleasure," and, in that
way, as analogous to the male penis. Although he accepted that women have
some form of ejaculation, he did not equate it with the expulsion of the egg.
It is, rather, "the result of exalted excitation, analagous to the increased secretion of other organs from increased stimulation," not essential to the fertilization of the ovum. This is important, for women need to know that their
state of sexual excitement bears no relation to becoming pregnant. Women
conceive whether or not they experience sexual pleasure, orgasm, or secretion. Knowlton acknowledged that he was not certain how the sperm
reached the egg, but he accepted the hypothesis of a Philadelphia physician
that there were undetected "absorbent vessels" leading from the vagina to
the ovaries that carried the semen. This mistaken hypothesis did not keep
him from understanding the crucial element, that if any sperm remains alive
in the folds of the vagina, it can potentially reach the ovum, making it necessary not only to wash away the semen with water, but also to kill the sperm
with a chemical agent.[32]

As Knowlton moved from the prevention of pregnancy to discussions of
curing infertility and impotence, he conveyed a full sense of the importance
of sexual desire and its gratification for women and men. He stated that the
reproductive instinct, or "the desire for sexual intercourse," is one of the
strongest drives in humans. "Surely, no instinct commands a greater proportion of our thoughts, or has a greater influence upon our happiness for better
or for worse." Unfortunately, its unhealthy or improper indulgence had
caused misery and led some to regard it as "a low, degrading, and 'carnal'
passion, with which a holy life must ever be at war." As a philosopher, he saw
that inner conflict was not inherent in the satisfaction of the sexual instinct.
"In savage life it *is,* and in wisely organized societies of duly enlightened and
civilized beings it *would be,* a source of tenfold more happiness than misery."
As Knowlton turned to consider women who suffered from a lack of desire
or failure to enjoy pleasure in sexual intercourse, he argued that they needed
treatment just as did impotent men. Referring to loss of desire, he wrote, "All
young people ought to be apprized of the causes of it—causes which in

many instances greatly lessen one's ability of giving and receiving that pleasure which is the root of domestic happiness."[33]

Knowlton was arrested a third time and tried in Greenfield, Massachusetts. This time he published a pamphlet in his own defense. It asked an important question: Is *Fruits of Philosophy* obscene? In his understanding, a book or print that is obscene is one with the power to "excite a particular passion in healthy persons." The writing or drawing must cause sexual arousal. A representation that is "coarse, low, or vulgar" is not necessarily obscene in a legal sense. Because his book was written in medical language, it was exempt. To apply a different standard to obscenity—that a work is of "an immoral tendency"—endangers the society. "Where would be the liberty of our press, if the law were to be so construed as to apply to books which a jury might judge to be of an immoral tendency?" If a jury consisted of those of one belief, those of another might be judged immoral, including "abolitionists and the anti-abolitionists, the Mc & anti-McDowallites, until half the books in the country would be condemned, and their publishers fined or imprisoned. There would be no fixed standard, every thing would depend on ever changing opinions, and circumstances." The argument that discussion of contraceptive techniques by their very nature constituted obscenity had never crossed his mind.[34]

Knowlton believed that the source of his own prosecution, particularly the third one in Greenfield, had been a campaign by Massachusetts ministers against freethinkers. According to Knowlton's narrative, Mason Grosvenor, a new pastor in the small town of Ashfield in western Massachusetts, had returned from a meeting of his ministerial organization, in which "all the publications of the Free Enquirers were laid before them," to wage a campaign against Knowlton and his medical associate, Roswell Shepard. Grosvenor called a meeting in the orthodox church in which he linked "infidelity and licentiousness" and warned against both. Thomas Shepherd, the minister preceding Grosvenor, had, on his marriage, bought *Fruits of Philosophy* from Knowlton and defended him at the meeting. Knowlton wrote that Shepherd "could not say but that the little book might have been written with good motives—and may be useful in some cases." Grosvenor, fired up by religious enthusiasm, brought a declaration to the meeting: "Resolved that we will do all in our power to suppress the circulation of *Fruits of Philosophy*." When Knowlton asked to speak, he was denied on the grounds that he was not a church member. The resolution against him carried without a dissenting vote. Grosvenor then passed around a paper that committed those signing it not to use Knowlton or Shepard as physicians. Not yet satisfied, Grosvenor went to Greenfield after the gathering and got both Knowlton and Shepard indicted.[35]

In this instance, the case came to trial three times. But western Massachusetts juries contained independent thinkers, and twice the Greenfield jury failed to agree on a verdict. With the third trial in August 1835, the two defendants got dismissal of the case, a proceeding known as *nolle prosequi*. Knowlton had previously insisted that his medical practice had not been harmed by the minister's campaign against him. "Well, it so happens," he wrote, "that most of the people in Ashfield, and many in the towns round about, are the strangest folks you ever did see. They will go to just what store they please; employ just what mechanic they have a mind to, and just what doctor. . . . Oh, they are a stiff necked people."[36]

After the early 1830s, Knowlton was let alone and subsequently published many editions of *Fruits of Philosophy*. Although his basic message remained the same, his discussions of the sexual organs and their functions became increasingly explicit in later editions. In the fourth edition of 1839, for example, he attempted to explain to his audience his understanding of sexual response, turning first to men and then to women. He confessed that beyond the increase in blood, he did not know the cause of the male erection: "we know that titillation, as well as certain thoughts, give rise to this congestion or turgesence," but how they do so, "we do not exactly know." It is "the nerves of his genital organs, and I believe principally . . . the nerves of the urethra and glans penis" that give rise to "the pleasurable sensation experienced by the male." The quality of male pleasure depends upon the state of a man's nerves and the thickness of his semen. Knowlton believed that an interval (unspecified) between ejaculations added to seminal thickness and thus to male pleasure; the pause, however, should not last too long. In referring to the male genital organs, he wrote, "During a short abstinence, they acquire increased excitability, just as the brain and muscles do by short periods of rest; but let this abstinence be very long continued, and their share of nervous energy seems to take a different course. The individual will not so frequently *desire*, as if he had been in the habit of enjoying himself at shorter intervals." As he turned to the female, Knowlton repeated his earlier discussions of female sexual response. He added that women's pleasure is not contingent upon the size of the male penis or on the emission of semen. Women's desire and capacity for sexual pleasure are not directly linked to their reproductive lives. In addition, "It is not by any means to be infered that 'amitiveness' [sic] ceases at the 'turn of life,' that is, when the woman ceases to menstruate." Despite his own seeming reliance on the lore of *Aristotle's Master-piece,* Knowlton sought to counter it. Confirming its ubiquity in the culture, Knowlton stated that, as a man of science and a physician, he offered his work as an alternative to the endemic text. He stated that part of the motivation for his book was that the "unprincipled persons" without qualifications who had compiled the Aristotle texts had given readers a "jumble of truth and error, of science and obscenety [sic]."[37]

Although Knowlton did not advocate abortion, he allowed it. In his understanding, the notion that the fetus had life had been the cause of great mischief. Drawing on his philosophic approaches, he argued that in earlier eras, whenever men could not explain something, they had given it a name. Thus "many thingless names were brought into use, which have been great stumbling-blocks in the way to truth." One of the "thingless names" is "life." Knowlton asserted that the fetus, until close to birth, has a merely vegetative existence. It belongs to the female to which it is attached and has no more rights than a tumor. As a physician and scientist, Knowlton believed that "the laws in this country against abortion were never made by physiologists; and I should hardly think by men of humane feelings."[38]

There are additional changes in emphasis in the 1839 edition. Confronting the argument that contraception is "against nature," Knowlton answered in a manner similar to Owen, "Well, what if it is? . . . It is also against nature to cut our nails, our hair, or to shave the beard. What is civilized life but one continual warfare against nature?" As Knowlton shifted the question to whether or not contraception is beneficial to humankind, he added an even stronger statement on the importance of early marriage to prevent prostitution. "Nature will have its course through some channel or other, and to dam the stream or to smother the flame is to furnish no lasting security against floods and fire."[39]

The Greenfield trials were Knowlton's last brush with the law. He remained in Ashfield, developed a thriving medical practice, and became a well-respected contributor to the *Boston Medical and Surgical Journal.* He and his wife, Tabita, had several more children at well-spaced intervals.[40] He never relented from his freethinking ways. In 1845, five years before his death, he spoke to the United Liberals of Franklin County, a group he had helped organize, and rallied them to support "Freedom of speech and of the Press— a grappling of truth and error in fair and open encounter." He urged that his hearers and readers "proclaim to the world, that in mind as in body you will be free."[41]

Fruits of Philosophy in its many editions had great influence in the United States and England. Over the course of the nineteenth century, the number of children in each family fell from roughly seven to three and a half. This falling birthrate, so often attributed to "domestic feminism," had many causes, to be sure, but contemporaries understood the importance of the postcoital douche.[42] William A. Alcott, a leading exponent of sexual restraint in marriage, acknowledged subsequently that, as much as he opposed Knowlton on moral grounds, he knew that the latter's ideas were broadly disseminated. Alcott declared in 1856 that Knowlton's book "had a wide circulation. I have found it in nearly every part of our wide-spread country." About Knowlton's contraceptive system, the spermicidal douche, Alcott noted, "It is in vogue, even now, in many parts of our country, and is highly prized."[43] Knowlton's work, however, contributed to a project larger than birth control. He introduced into the conversation about sexuality new knowledge about the body and sexual desire. In a voice marked by wit and common sense, he encouraged his readers to acknowledge their bodily impulses and to accept sexual pleasure as one of life's gifts. Knowlton was present at the creation of the third sexual framework, and although his perspectives were overshadowed by those who followed him, his message was never lost.

5

The Masturbation Scare
and the Rise of Reform Physiology

In the decades after her departure from the United States in 1830, the name of Fanny Wright was frequently invoked as a warning. When evangelical Christians and political conservatives fought against the introduction of sexual knowledge and contraceptive information by freethinkers and their allies, she stood for the dangerous, promiscuous woman who threatened all good men and true women. The clear lines of opposition, however, soon became fuzzy. New actors appeared in the drama of sexual culture in the decades before the Civil War, and the plot quickly changed. Lecturers and writers offered to their audiences "reform physiology," the phrase they often used for sexual knowledge. They argued that Americans needed to understand the workings of their bodies and reproductive systems in order to avoid a particular danger to life and health: masturbation.

Appealing to the emerging Protestant middle class, Sylvester Graham and his physiological followers found a hearing. Advocates of the water cure chimed in, as did phrenologists, led by O. S. Fowler, and the popular writer Frederick Hollick. All agreed that the present culture was breeding sexual ills. As these reformers focused on the cultural atmosphere, they singled out books and reading as especially dangerous to youth, inciting them to practice what the age called the "secret vice." Dangers lurked in unsuspected places. In contrast to the generally cheerful tone of freethinking discussion, the early words of many reform physiologists were those of warning. When they joined the sexual conversation, the third sexual framework took on a more foreboding cast.

I

Who constituted the audience for writings of physiological reform, the third framework? America had always known "middling folk," those who were neither rich nor poor. But in the nineteenth century the middle class came into being, fed by a number of streams. The Industrial Revolution changed the nature of work. In towns and cities some master craftsmen sank into the army of wage workers while others became businessmen. As these business-men bought and sold, advertised and delivered, managed production and kept accounts, they needed employees who would work with their heads and pens rather than their hands. They took on clerks, often older boys and young men, who aspired to be businessmen and hoped that their salary might set them on the road to independence and success. They drew on the surplus of rural youth drawn to the city. These urban-going lads were green-horns who were a bit rough, perhaps, but literate, capable of working long hours, and used to the discipline of the common school. A more elite stream also fed urban migration. Burgeoning commercial opportunity drew college-educated young men to serve as lawyers. As they grew, cities offered liveli-hood to doctors, writers, architects, and engineers.[1]

Many sought guidance in this society on the move. Parents wanted advice about how to raise their children to succeed, yet keep the values of home. As sons left home for education or employment, parents counseled them and gave them books that urged restraint, control, and mastery. One needed not only to work hard during the day but also to develop habits and manners that demonstrated personal order. One should seek only that leisure consistent with work. Prohibitions against alcohol, gambling, theater, and premarital sex all served to enable youth to retain self-command.[2]

Some information about sex came from the effort to instruct Americans about how to live morally and raise children in the new era. But some came from a different source, from physicians and other writers about the body. They taught sex as a part of physiology. Normally they saw their work as a part of the larger project of health reform. To understand reform physiology requires exploration into the world of medicine in the 1830s and the follow-ing two decades, a time when medical theory and practice were in flux.

Lecture addressed to a middle-class audience of men and women. "A Lecture by James Pollard Espy, Meteorologist, at Clinton Hall," lithograph, 1841. © Museum of the City of New York.

Scientific discoveries had demolished humoral theory. Much discrete knowledge had been gained about the circulation of the blood and about the various organs of the body. The microscope had revealed the minute parts of many tissues and fluids. But in the place of ideas about solids and the governing humors—blood, phlegm, yellow bile, and black bile—of the eighteenth century, there were merely theories and countertheories. In the meantime patients got sick and sought remedies, and women got pregnant. Although the bodily theory underlying treatments had altered, regular physicians—called allopaths by their medical opponents—continued many of their old therapies. They sought to restore balance to the body by getting it to release its impurities through secretions or excretions or by stimulating solid tissues.[3]

Diseases, they thought, were not specific entities with specific causes but sprang from general conditions of the body. When the body was overstimulated or inflamed, it was to be treated by bleeding, purging, or cauterization. Over the course of the nineteenth century, the principal therapeutic strategy shifted. Early physicians concentrated on depletion; later ones attempted to stimulate a weakened system, using drugs such as quinine, iron compounds, and alcoholic beverages. Central to the role of a regular physician was heroic intervention using known therapeutic remedies. Knowledge came from apprenticeship alone or accompanied by formal medical training. Although there was no uniform medical system and individual practices varied, "all regular American physicians drew their treatments from roughly the same armamentarium." Despite the differences in degree, doctors "sought to attain a shared therapeutic objective by exploiting a common arsenal." By the 1840s, some regular physicians were questioning conventional treatments, looking to empirical approaches that involved direct observation and the use of statistics to determine efficacy, but this had relatively little impact on therapeutic practice.[4]

Alternative medical approaches both challenged regular (or allopathic) medicine and began to contribute to it. Thomsonianism, a popular medical movement of the 1830s, submitted the body to herbal remedies, some of great strength. Eclecticism relied on plant substances, but its practitioners were willing to use minerals and vegetable poisons such as opium and digitalis. Both Thomsonians and eclectics believed in broadly educating members of the public—women as well as men—to become their own doctors. Homeopathy, brought to the United States by physicians trained in Germany, was based on a long-held theory that "like cures like," that the best remedies induced in patients the same symptoms as those of the disease. When the vital principle animating the body was paralyzed by disease, the homeopathic physician administered minute doses of substances to restore vitality. More than traditional allopathic practice, homeopathy drew on the capacity of the body to heal itself. Other movements such as hydrotherapy (the water cure), frequently allied with homeopathy, emphasized the body's healing power—the body, that is, whose powers had been protected by right living.[5]

To a significant extent, phrenology undergirded new understandings of the body and alternative therapies. The new science located cognitive, emotional, and sensory capacities in different areas of the brain. In 1832 Americans listened to the lecturer Johann Spurzheim, who traveled to the United States to disseminate the theory of the Viennese physician Franz Joseph Gall that the brain was made up of separate parts, each governing a specific aspect of character. Orson Squire Fowler immediately became converted, as did his Amherst classmate and close friend Henry Ward Beecher. While Beecher floundered and then, for lack of a better option, went into the family business of preaching, Fowler dedicated his life to phrenology. He began by lecturing on the subject and, joined by his brother, Lorenzo; the latter's wife, Lydia; his sister, Charlotte; and her husband, Samuel Robert Wells, created a vast array of enterprises designed to spread phrenological wisdom across the nation. They formed the publishing company Fowler and Wells. The entire

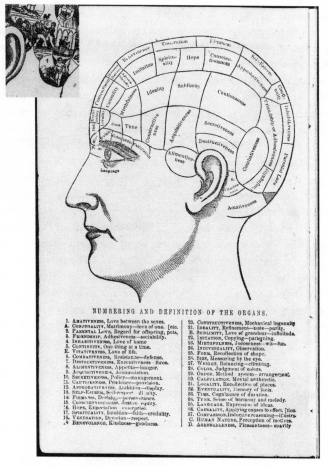

NUMBERING AND DEFINITION OF THE ORGANS.

1. AMATIVENESS, Love between the sexes.
A. CONJUGALITY, Matrimony—love of one. [etc.
2. PARENTAL LOVE, Regard for offspring, pets,
3. FRIENDSHIP, Adhesiveness—sociability.
4. INHABITIVENESS, Love of home
5. CONTINUITY, One thing at a time.
E. VITATIVENESS, Love of life.
6. COMBATIVENESS, Resistance—defense.
7. DESTRUCTIVENESS, Executiveness—force.
8. ALIMENTIVENESS, Appetite—hunger.
9. ACQUISITIVENESS, Accumulation.
10. SECRETIVENESS, Policy—management.
11. CAUTIOUSNESS, Prudence—provision.
12. APPROBATIVENESS, Ambition—display.
13. SELF-ESTEEM, Self-respect—dignity.
14. FIRMNESS, Decision—perseverance.
15. CONSCIENTIOUSNESS, Justice—equity.
16. HOPE, Expectation—enterprise.
17. SPIRITUALITY, Intuition—faith—credulity.
18. VENERATION, Devotion—respect.
19. BENEVOLENCE, Kindness—goodness.

20. CONSTRUCTIVENESS, Mechanical ingenuity
21. IDEALITY, Refinement—taste—purity.
B. SUBLIMITY, Love of grandeur—infinitude.
22. IMITATION, Copying—patterning.
23. MIRTHFULNESS, Jocoseness—wit—fun.
24. INDIVIDUALITY, Observation.
25. FORM, Recollection of shape.
26. SIZE, Measuring by the eye.
27. WEIGHT, Balancing—climbing.
28. COLOR, Judgment of colors.
29. ORDER, Method—system—arrangement.
30. CALCULATION, Mental arithmetic.
31. LOCALITY, Recollection of places.
32. EVENTUALITY, Memory of facts.
33. TIME, Cognizance of duration.
34. TUNE, Sense of harmony and melody.
35. LANGUAGE, Expression of ideas.
36. CAUSALITY, Applying causes to effect. [tion.
37. COMPARISON, Inductive reasoning—illustra-
C. HUMAN NATURE, Perception of motives.
D. AGREEABLENESS, Pleasantness—suavity

Above: The phrenological head. "Numbering and Definition of the Organs," *New Illustrated Self-Instructor in Phrenology and Physiology* (New York: Fowler and Wells, Publishers, 1859), p. vi.

Inset: Phrenology's "Symbolical head," illustrating the attributes of different organs of the brain. Number 1 is "Amativeness, Sexual and connubial love." O. S. and L. N. Fowler, *Illustrated Self-Instructor in Phrenology and Physiology* (New York: Fowler and Wells, Publishers, 1851), p. v. Countway Library of Medicine.

family conducted the Phrenological College, edited and published the *American Phrenological Journal,* and established a major museum in New York City. Orson and Lorenzo Fowler wrote many books that sold widely.[6]

Behind these alternative approaches was a growing belief by Americans that sickness was an evil to be eliminated. Although many agreed that the age was troubled by ill health, they disagreed on treatment and on the medical theories underlying it. Regular medicine was not the established church it became after the Civil War. Thus many contending medical denominations explored alternative approaches to the body and vied for practitioners and believers. Organizations such as the Ladies' Physiological Institute of Boston, founded in 1838, invited lecturers from across the spectrum of medical thought, developed a medical library, and displayed a full model of the female body.[7]

By and large, the writers of reform physiology were medical irregulars. Allopathic physicians wrote normally only for one another in medical journals, but an element that helped define the irregulars was that they were willing to write for a broader audience. In the language of Jacksonian democracy so favored by medical irregulars, writer and lecturer Frederick Hollick argued for the right to disseminate broadly physiological knowledge. "Society," he wrote in 1845, "will no more allow any class to possess all scientific information, than it will allow others to possess all political power, or religious rights." Moreover, the notion that knowledge of the body and the reproductive system is for men only is "preposterous, and tyrannically unjust." Edward Bliss Foote conveyed a sense of the conflict when, in 1858, he wrote in *Medical Common Sense,* "My prayer is that I may prove worthy of Allopathic denunciation."[8]

And denounce they did. Allopaths sought control over their craft by gaining power at the state level to license medical practice and to control medical education, but before the Civil War they were largely unsuccessful. The popularity of their competitors generally overwhelmed their efforts. No one stopped the medical regulars, however, from writing scathing critiques of those who claimed medical knowledge and sought to disseminate it. In 1835 the respected *Boston Medical and Surgical Journal* railed against lectures on health given to a popular audience: "We cannot look with indifference on such itinerant doings—such undignified efforts, alike degrading to the individual and to the profession at large, without feeling that it is more important that female anatomy should be taught minutely in the [medical school] theatre, than that the sex at large require any more insight into the physical condition of themselves, than every intelligent woman already understands." In 1852, defending the new fields of gynecology and obstetrics, Augustus K. Gardner wrote with hostility of all those, especially strongminded women, who stood in the way of the male physician:

> The dark ages seem to be again reviving. Hand in hand with the infinitesimals and the water-wonder-worker, comes the hard-faced midwife, tinctured with both theories. . . . We have lecturers and lecturesses, and female colleges, where the very large and highly intelligent classes are taught how to get children, and especially how not to get them. The Women's Rights Convention cannot see why women should bear children more than men, and while waiting some plan to equalise this matter, they refuse to bear them themselves.[9]

There was, however, no dearth of writers willing to defy Gardner and his allopathic allies. An army of lecturers and writers followed in the wake of Owen and the freethinkers. Antebellum America was a land of opportunity, where writers could print their own words and lecturers could tack up notices, hire halls, and get a hearing. As a result, there was an outpouring of works dealing with the body, the sexual organs, and human emotions. It was hardly a uniform flow. Writers disagreed about many matters, from the way the body worked to the best way to express or control its impulses. As they considered sex, their advice can be laid on a spectrum from restriction to sexual enthusiasm. One must always recall, however, that although reform physiologists helped inform and guide many Americans about sex, they did not uproot the solid core of vernacular sexuality, typically communicated orally, that continued to inform the sexual ideas and practices of their listeners and readers.

2

It was in the context of this body of writing about sex that masturbation emerged in the decades following 1830 as "self-pollution," the "solitary vice," the "secret sin." Why did a private sexual practice—deemed by many at the beginning of the twentieth-first century to be normal, even salutary—cease to be a relatively minor sin, seldom mentioned even in sermons, to become suddenly a terrifying threat to self and society? The answer begins with the medical texts in Europe that linked masturbation to insanity.[10] Sylvester Graham, who profoundly shaped the American literature, believed that masturbation was one way to explain the physical and mental diseases to which the men and women of his country were prey. The creation of asylums for the insane in America before the Civil War seemed to provide scientific support for Graham's arguments, dramatize his fears, and put them on local ground. While these texts offered explanations, they fed anxieties rather than allayed fears.

The curious history of European attitudes toward masturbation before the eighteenth century is only now being discovered. Not only was the gap between vernacular understanding and official condemnation particularly wide, but those who wrote for a general audience often spoke in code because they feared that explicit mention would introduce the young to the practice. Attempts to counter libertinism in the seventeenth century opened the way for a book in 1676 on masturbation, the first known discussion in print intended for readers who were neither physicians nor clergymen. When an anonymous writer in Holland in the early eighteenth century called masturbation "onanism," he used the familiar association of the practice with the sin of Noah's son, who was punished by God with death. He condemned masturbation on the religious and moral grounds that were customary; but, more important, he popularized medical writing that linked masturbation to venereal diseases.[11] Samuel August Tissot, a French physician, wrote the most famous eighteenth-century treatise, summing up the physical and moral harms of masturbation. In the 1766 edition, Tissot claimed that forty ounces of blood were required to make one ounce of semen (one fluid could become another in humoral thinking). Such loss of fluid was the source of physical weakness and debility and contributed to disease. Tissot argued that masturbation was more dangerous than coition because it was unnatural, not necessarily practiced lying down, solitary, and unrefreshed by the fluids and attractiveness of the opposite sex. Tissot's work had great influence in England and America.[12]

In the 1830s, Sylvester Graham brought Tissot's concerns to the attention of many Americans. At the time that freethinkers and the irreligious were turning to Robert Dale Owen and Charles Knowlton, those of an evangelical temperament listened to and read Graham. Lyman Beecher's thunderings against Frances Wright were part of a larger evangelical outpouring that reached a crescendo in the 1820s and 1830s. In the rural areas and small towns of New England and western New York, the fires of reawakened religious faith brought some to reconsider the fires within the body. For some

Christians of his era, Graham was the person who defined sex as the problem of the age and seemed to offer a solution.

In 1832 Graham achieved renown with lectures on the cholera epidemic, published in 1833, that established the link between illness and sexual expression. The son and grandson of Connecticut clergymen, Sylvester Graham prepared for the ministry but turned to temperance reform and the lecture circuit. Unlike many of his coworkers, who focused on morality and the family, Graham explored the relation of alcohol to disease. He studied Benjamin Rush and the French physiologists Xavier Bichat and François J. V. Broussais and through their ideas developed an understanding of alcohol and all stimulants as irritants of the natural system. In keeping with his era's approach to disease not as a discrete entity but as a sign that the body's systems were overtaxed, he determined that the cause of cholera was bad habits. The recent sudden death of canal diggers in Washington, D.C., came to those "who by excessive sensuality, filthiness and pernicious diet, have reduced the vital powers of their organic nerves almost to the line of death." The key to the path of cholera is sexual indulgence: "In every country, the drunken and the lewd have fallen almost by hundreds and by thousands before this terrible destroyer!—We are informed, that out of fourteen hundred lewd women in one street in Paris, thirteen hundred died of cholera! In a single house, sixty of these wretched creatures perished by this disease."[13]

Graham, like his followers, generally did not discuss race or social class explicitly, but these divisions nonetheless hovered over his writings. Canal laborers in Washington, D.C., whether black or white, were the poorest and most exploited of workers. But when Graham turned to those who were wealthy and therefore might have been exempt from the terrible conditions of lower-class workers, the example he gave was from India, a racial other. Graham wanted his readers to know that this colony of the British Empire, ravaged by the disease, was not a temperate, vegetarian society but rather a caldron of sensuality. In describing a Hindu festival Graham moved into high melodrama:

> We see the effeminate lust that inspires the Baboo to bring the first beauties into his house; we see spirits and liquors of all sorts freely indulged in, and terrible tumults excited by their heat; we see excesses of every kind, committed without hesitation, and boys of very tender age, freely allowed to ramble over nights and nights, and spend hours and hours in immoral pursuits:—we witness youth of

fourteen or fifteen years old, indulging to excess in the stupifying and mischievous fumes of tobacco and other drugs; we see goats, rams and buffaloes, savagely butchered, and men rolling on the ground, besmeared with blood and dirt; and at the time when the idols are thrown into the water young men go upon the river with their lewd companions, and revel in all sorts of licentiousness.[14]

When Graham expanded his understanding of the body and its sexual functioning, the body he cared about belonged neither to the canal worker nor to the Indian follower of Hinduism, but to the middle-class white men in his audience. The language that he used was universal, but his mind had more specific referents. Beginning with *A Lecture to Young Men,* first delivered in 1832 and published in 1834, Graham argued that there are two kinds of appetites. Those that enable the individual to survive—hunger and thirst—require constant appeasement. The one that allows the survival of the species—reproduction—demands no necessary exercise or satisfaction. In humans the reproductive organs are not complete until many years after birth. Human beings are unlike animals, driven to reproduce by instinct, healthy because they use their sexual organs only as their natural urges require. Although human beings' sexual organs are under the control of their "rational powers," ironically, the very powers that place humans above "the brute creation" give them the unique ability to harm themselves. Using the masculine gender, Graham wrote, "It is by abusing his organs, and depraving his instinctive appetites, through the devices of his rational powers, that the body of man, has become a living volcano of unclean propensities and passions."[15]

Graham regarded nutrition—eating and digestion—as the most important function of the body and the key to health. What he is remembered for today, the Graham cracker, was an adulterated element of his health crusade to return Americans to whole-grain food. Nutrition and the other vital functions of life, he felt, depend upon the nervous system. Graham theorized that there are two nervous systems that control bodily functions. The nervous system of organic life oversees all the vital organs, including those governing nutrition. The nervous system of animal life controls voluntary motion and the sense organs. The reproductive function is unique in that it engages both nervous systems: the nerves of organic life, attached to the stomach, and the nerves of animal life, tied to the brain. Both systems are connected to the sexual organs in that the organic directs the production of semen and enables the male "to eject it with peculiar convulsions," while "the nerves of animal life," controlling the senses and voluntary motion, enable sexual union. The wrong use of the reproductive organs can harm nerves governing the vital organs, thereby injuring the digestive system. Sex can thus threaten the body's most basic mechanism.[16]

The act of coition creates danger and risk to the body. "The convulsive paroxysms attending venereal indulgence," Graham stated, "are connected with the most intense excitement, and cause the most powerful agitation to the whole system, that it is ever subject to." As Graham continued in a second repetition, he conveyed his sense of awe at the power of sexual intercourse: "The brain, stomach, heart, lungs, liver, skin—and the other organs—feel it sweeping over them, with the tremendous violence of a tornado. The powerfully excited and convulsed heart drives the blood, in fearful congestion, to the principal viscera . . . and this violent paroxysm is generally succeeded by great exhaustion, relaxation, lassitude, and even prostration."[17]

The body should undergo such excitement only a few times in its lifetime. For health's sake Graham urged restraint in marriage and abstinence outside. He campaigned for a series of measures to protect the stomach and to calm the passions. Diet was the most important element. *Aristotle's Masterpiece* saw juicy meat and racy wine as adding heat to the body to contribute to the vigor of sexual embrace; Graham turned to vegetarianism and cold water to cool the body down. His regimen consisted of a diet of unrefined grains and cold water, exercise, the use of straw mattresses instead of feather beds, and loose-fitting clothing. These measures can best be understood as a complex prescription to dampen lust. In contrast to the pseudo-Aristotle, who had couples admire each other's beauty and recite poetry, Graham attempted to discourage mental sources of sexual stimulation. "Lascivious thoughts and imaginations will excite and stimulate the genital organs; cause an increased quantity of blood to flow into them; and augment their secretions and peculiar sensibilities:—and, on the other hand, an excited state of the genital organs, either from the stimulations of semen, or from diseased action in the system, will throw its influence upon the brain, and force lascivious thoughts and imaginations upon the mind." Through this means, "lascivious thoughts" can lead to irritation and debility in the nerves of organic life, causing harm to the vital organs, insanity, and death.[18]

Graham knew that his recommendation for sexual restraint within marriage flew in the face of the body's urges, driven by sexual desire. Here Graham admitted that he did not understand the physical source of what he called "animal spirits—nervous fluid—vital electricity." The best he could do to define and ground sexual desire was to use a metaphor: "something very analogous to electricity or galvanism, diffuses a peculiar and powerful excitement, and sensation, throughout the whole nervous system." Whatever it is, the sex drive is a great force: "the peculiar *excitement* of venereal indulgence, is more diffusive, universal and powerful, than any other to which the sytem [*sic*] is ever subject." It has a profound effect on organs, the nervous system, and health. It has great power over the mind.[19]

Especially in the young, sexual desire can persuade the intellectual and moral faculties, take over the understanding, and force the will to act in opposition to the moral sense. Because of its power, sexual desire is to be feared and contained.

> Hence therefore, SEXUAL DESIRE, cherished by the mind and dwelt on by the imagination, not only increases the excitability and peculiar sensibility of the genital organs themselves, but always throws an influence, equal to the intensity of the affection, over the whole nervous domain. . . . And hence, those LASCIVIOUS DAY-DREAMS, and *amorous reveries,* in which young people too generally,—and especially the idle, and the voluptuous, and the sedentary, and the nervous,—are exceedingly apt to indulge, are often the sources of general debility, effeminacy, disordered functions, and permanent disease, and even premature death without the actual exercise of the genital organs! Indeed! this unchastity of thought— this *adultery of the mind,* is the beginning of immeasurable evil to the human family:—and, while children are regularly trained to it, by all the mistaken fondness of parents, and all the circumstances of civic life, it is but mockery in the ear of Heaven, to deprecate the evil consequences; and folly, little short of fatuity, to attempt to arrest the current of crime that flows from it.[20]

Given Graham's understanding of the body, awe at the power of coitus, and fear of sexual desire, it is understandable why he regarded masturbation in the young as a particular danger. "Onanism," he stated, is "by far the worst form of venereal indulgence." In language that echoed Tissot's, Graham wrote that masturbation, unlike sexual intercourse, has no justification in the species' need to perpetuate itself, and is therefore "wholly unnatural." Moreover, it is "generally commenced very early in life," when bodily organs are still undeveloped. Unlike mature men who start the practice after age twenty-five, children who masturbate begin a practice of excitation that destroys body and mind and leads to early death. Graham was particularly shocked by masturbation in boys before puberty. Aware that boys as young as four were known to masturbate, he first blamed nurses, parents, servants, "and other laboring people of loose morals" for teaching them. He then turned to what he believed was the primary conduit to this illicit sexual knowledge, boys themselves: "It is, however, more frequently communicated from one boy to another."[21]

It turns out that the terrifying aberration is extraordinarily common. "Seven out of ten boys in this country, at the age of twelve, are, at least, acquainted with this debasing practice." They masturbate alone; they masturbate frequently. Graham related confessions by boys who did so as often as three times a night. They also masturbated in the presence of a close friend. As Graham described what he admitted was a common practice, one can only wonder at the dire consequences that he insisted must follow for the male body and soul.[22]

Perhaps that is why the annual reports of Samuel Bayard Woodward, the superintendent of the State Hospital for Lunatics in Worcester, Massachusetts, seemed particularly compelling to contemporaries. When the Worcester hospital opened in 1833, Woodward received 107 inmates who were "so furiously mad, as to be manifestly dangerous to the peace and safety of the community at large." To a hospital designed to give them a place of "comfort and safety" came some convicted murderers. Many had been chained for years. Some of the men had not had a razor or scissors to their faces for more than a decade. A few of the women had long refused to wear any clothing and were described as filthy and obscene.[23]

A liberal Calvinist trained in medicine by his father, Woodward had been a respected doctor in Connecticut. Although he had known insane patients in his practice and had helped found the Hartford Retreat in 1824, he was profoundly shocked by what he saw in 1833. His hospital, he wrote from the outset, was not like others. It housed pauper lunatics and criminals, and most of its inmates had long suffered from mental disease. Woodward believed that most of them were incurable. As he began to write for a medical audience in 1835, he expressed his sense of horror. What confronted him at the hospital were patients masturbating in plain view. In the masturbating insane, he wrote, "the libidinous desires are greatly increased, and the influence of self-restraint cannot be brought sufficiently into action to prevent the constant, daily, and I might say almost hourly recurrence of the practice." As the patient increasingly loses powers of "mind and body . . . the practice is not abandoned. All the remaining energies of animal life seem to be concentrated in these organs, and all the remaining power of gratification left is in the exercise of this no longer secret, but loathsome and beastly habit." What to an early-twenty-first-century psychiatrist might seem like an act of boredom or rebellion or perhaps a symptom of distress, to this early-nineteenth-century physician was clearly the cause of mental disease. In his annual reports and articles, he listed masturbation as the second most important cause of insanity.[24]

To some of Woodward's contemporaries, his words came like a bolt of lightening, illuminating the familiar by a new light. Luther Bell, a physician and the superintendent of McLean Asylum in Boston, wrote that "there are frequently new discoveries of truth in relation to matters immediately before us" that completely change one's understanding of the familiar. Such a discovery came to a well-informed reader of reports of institutions of the insane (perhaps Bell himself), as he saw "for the first time in his life, the word *masturbation*." The reader does not know what the word means, and the dictionary does not avail, so he turns to a friend. When informed that the word "means nothing more nor less than the practice of imitating the act of sexual connection upon the individual's own person, perpetrated with his own hand, he will be lost in amazement and incredulity, that an act so commonly, I may say so universally, known amongst young men as this is, should be connected with insanity to such a frightful extent." Bell, like a multitude of others, wrote his book to warn young men of the evils to body and mind of the practice.[25]

Sylvester Graham's lectures and tracts and the testimony by Woodward and Bell may have established the necessary ground, but the question remains: Why did masturbation loom so large in the antebellum imagination? One potential answer is that masturbation posed a great problem to those coming to believe in the sexual innocence of children and in the naturalness of procreative sex. If children come into the world without sin and nature calls for a healthy sex life centered on sexual intercourse, how is it that children, often at a very young age, engage in nonprocreative sexual practices?

As Woodward moved beyond superintendents' reports and medical journals to write about masturbation for a broader audience, he emphasized both its universality and its deleterious effects on mind and body. He wrote that those who insisted on childhood innocence were "hardly aware how extensively known the habit is with the young, and how early in life it is sometimes practised. I have never conversed with a lad of twelve years of age who did not know all about the practice, and understand the language commonly used to describe it." Luther Bell agreed, testifying that as a doctor with the care of the young, "I never yet have met with the young man, who has not at once apprehended (as his eye and countenance assured me) any indirect and distant allusion to it . . . and comprehended the vulgar colloquial terms employed amongst lads in expressing the idea." These words tell of the pervasiveness of masturbation as a youthful male practice in antebellum America and something of the vernacular sexual culture surrounding it. To twenty-first-century eyes they may be descriptive, but to some readers in the nineteenth century they caused great fear. This fear was assuaged—and fed—by the many works on physiological reform that came to focus on masturbation.[26]

3

Writers of reform literature against masturbation pile case history upon case history in the effort to demonstrate the fatal harm to youth of masturbating. To read these pamphlets and books is to enter a netherworld of dark shadows. Is it a nineteenth-century version of the Salem witch trials in which the finger of accusation points at the stranger and the friend? In this literature, what can be salvaged? Certainly not the relation of cause and effect: masturbation and insanity. The historian can find value, however, in some of the rhetoric of the discussion.

The works generally began by an announcement ritual in which each author proclaims that, moved by a sense of righteous calling, he or she will speak the unspeakable. I know, each states, that public opinion forbids the conveying of sexual knowledge in public lectures or in written form. Normally I respect it. Certainly I understand the responsibility not to harm young minds. However, the evil that I am trying to prevent is so enormous and the forces of society and culture arrayed against me are so great that I must speak out. Anyway, children are already receiving sexual information from the wrong hands. At this point an author typically makes a declarative statement about the widespread sexual experience of children. Then each declares: I must lecture and I must write to save the young. This ritualized bow is curious. In a plethora of texts offering sexual knowledge, there was a

INSANITY.

CONSUMPTION.

ONANISM.

"Masturbation's Consequences," *The Patient's Guide: A Treatise on Diseases of the Sexual Organs,* c. 1860, p. 28. Countway Library of Medicine.

need to acknowledge its opposite, a code of silence about sexual matters. Is this an affirmation of sexual reticence or an effort to win an audience by promising to reveal hidden knowledge?

The cases that writers present of young persons gone astray give narratives that convey how the nineteenth century understood the transmission of sexual knowledge, the creation of sexual desire, and the arousal of uncontrollable lust. There is no way to know if the stories told were true—only that some antebellum Americans believed them to be, that they made sense at the time. They described a world in sharp contrast to a myth of childhood sexual innocence, a world in which youths and adults introduced children to sexual acts and children introduced them to one another.[27]

Samuel Gregory related the "Case of a Mechanic," which he received from a young man living in a country town in Rhode Island: "When *five years old*, a man, or one calling himself such, instructed him in the process of self-abuse." Sometimes teachers of sexual practices were hired men or servants. Sometimes they were impeccably respectable. In 1839, in *Solitary Vice*, Mary Gove gave an example of the statement by a minister's wife about her foster child, a girl of ten. The girl admitted that "she had been practising the vice for a considerable length of time. She named the person who taught her. This individual was an intimate acquaintance of the lady. She also ascertained that this person was taught the sin by another of her intimates!!" Gove quoted a young woman who had masturbated as a child: "I always supposed I contracted this practice instinctively, till recently, a friend who is several years older than myself, informed me that at the age of *four* years she taught me."[28]

Many cases, as they developed, involved the young in acts engaged in alone and in private. But some masturbation involved groups. The mechanic whose story Gregory told above had insisted that not only had the twenty or so boys in the neighborhood masturbated; they had done so together. The mechanic's claims escalated, and he said that the girls as well as boys in his school had joined in: "This social vice took the place of solitary; and when left by themselves during the intermission, the school-room was oftentimes a den of impurity, a juvenile brothel; yet all was conducted with so much concert and secrecy, that neither teacher nor parents feared or suspected evil."[29]

Although in these narratives many boys and girls were introduced to masturbation by childhood companions or adults, there are statements that with the maturation of the male sexual organs a youth required no teaching. Luther Bell stated that a boy's amative "instinct, thus brought into activity, is so energetic" that he finds the way to masturbate without assistance. The youth is easily aroused. The culture around him stimulates him at every turn. Erotic literature and pictures excite his sexual desire. Bell saw danger lurking everywhere. "Every library, public and private, every classic, every print-shop, has something, prose, poetry, or picture, which can be perverted . . . to the base use of exciting the passions, and which is impressed into the service of pollution." As he addressed his readers, he played on their experiences. Many a man, he wrote, will recall with a "blush of shame . . . the volume, the page, the print to which he turned in ardent youth."[30]

In the writing of reformers, the distinction between young children and youths is not carefully drawn. From the content of cases, however, it is clear that the focus of most attention falls on males in the years from puberty through young manhood. The tales they tell have great narrative power. Woodward's writings, in particular, profoundly affected his audience. As he gave case studies of young men and women who had come under his care, Woodward seemed to give scientific confirmation to Sylvester Graham's theories. For example, D., a man twenty years old, had suffered from ill health for a year or more: "He was pale, feeble, nervous—lost his resolution—had no appetite—took to his bed much of the time, and became dull, almost speechless, and wholly abstracted and melancholy." When he came under Woodward's custody, he was "in the most miserable condition conceivable; emaciated, feeble, pallid—had night sweats . . . his heart beat, his head was painful, and he felt no desire, and would make no effort to live."

Woodward suspected that he was masturbating, and found "upon strict inquiry and watching," that his suspicions were "well founded." Woodward confronted D. and told him that his habit was the source of all his suffering. He prescribed total abstinence from masturbation, a simple diet, exercise, and doses of bark and iron. "After a long time he is wholly recovered, and is now a healthy and valuable citizen."[31]

Woodward's cases have some variation and include females as well as males. In some cases the masturbators recover; in others they fail and are reduced to a state of utter degradation. But in one respect they are essentially the same: they involve youths or young adults with great advantages who falter or fail. The model figure is the fair young man of promise who leaves college, comes home, loses his ability to work or concentrate, and becomes irrational, even violent; the female variant is the beautiful young lady wasting away.

The physician can help some of these sufferers. He offers moral exhortation, exemplified in the case of one male patient as a remonstrance designed "to excite in his mind self-respect, and some ambition to be useful and active in life." The doctor suggests the Graham system of plain diet, exercise, hard mattress, and sexual abstinence; and then he adds some mild medicine. In cases where the patient cooperates, the physician is successful. In others, where masturbation has gone on so long that the habit cannot be broken or has led to idiocy, or in cases where the patient refuses to admit to the practice or simply lacks will, the physician is powerless. Thus the reader confronts "a young man of respectability, of good education, of respectable connexions, of fine talents, reduced to a condition of the utmost degradation."[32]

Ultimately, the existence of these narratives suggests that there were dark forces in human beings that defied reason and understanding. As did authors of Gothic fiction, physicians explored the realm of powers that seemed beyond human will. Young men and women with every advantage sickened, became deranged, did evil, died. Woodward's understanding of masturbation made it all comprehensible, unlocking the mystery of mental illness, especially among the young. And, following the course so desired by Americans, Woodward shifted the grounds to a level that allowed ill persons to will themselves into health.

Others added their voices to Woodward's narrative. Bell seconded Woodward, finding the person at risk less among the young farmer or the apprentice than "amongst the youth for whom fortune and circumstance seem to have done the most," the student with the time for solitary pursuits.

Bell saw him to be in greater danger because part of his education, "the culti-vation of his imagination and fancy . . . may perhaps add to his power of depicting to himself imaginary scenes of voluptuous enjoyment and licen-tious opportunity." Bell went on to generalize: "The young man, abandoning his employment, whether of labor or study, returns to his father's house,—loses all his energy and enterprise of mind and body,—hangs about in listless idleness, under the pretence, on his own and his friends' part, of his suffering from poor health. He is not exactly sick . . . but he is dronish, irritable, suspi-cious and unhappy. He may take to his bed, and lay recumbent most of his time; avoids seeing any person, as far as possible." At this point the young man is not seen as insane, "but he is perhaps deemed *love-cracked* or *hypoish.*" One telltale sign is that he "give[s] way to laughter, when by himself." As his disease develops, he may become a monomaniac and later violent.[33]

Parents concerned about their children might look for early signs of the masturbating boy. They should not be misled by appearances, for he might be healthy and robust in the initial stages and even have increased appetite. They should worry if they find him unwilling "to engage in the common, active, exciting plays of boys," if he reads novels or chooses a "sedentary amusement" rather than playing ball or climbing rocks. Reflecting the values of New England, Bell warned against any deviation from what he regarded as normal boyhood. A boy must not loll on chairs or read in bed at night. Bell linked the masturbating boy with an esthetic temperament. In him, "the imagination runs riot; day dreams, fanciful castle-building in the air, involv-ing especially the sensual, usurp the place of the practical, and common sense views of things." Masturbation offered a satisfying explanation to the problems of the deviant from boy culture and to the disturbances of the ado-lescent male.[34]

Because young people could introduce one another to sexual acts, the places where they congregated were particularly dangerous. No boy was safe, but Woodward claimed that there were more hazards for "students, merchant's clerks, printers and shoemakers" than for "those young men who labor at agricultural employments or active mechanical trades." The most dangerous places were schools. Woodward warns, "in our High Schools, Academies and Colleges, the evil is as alarming."[35]

The school as site for masturbation was particularly compelling because it was a gathering place growing to great importance in the culture. As high schools spread and as academies and colleges rose in prestige, parents who felt that they were providing their children with opportunities to advance in the world were unwittingly putting them at risk. In one of Samuel Gregory's cases, a high school teacher confessed that he entered, when he was "comparatively young," a university in New England, and "a gang of corrupt and unprincipled students used to get him into their rooms, lock the door, and absolutely compel him to take part with them in their abominable self-pollutions." In a later edition, Gregory quoted a doctor's statement that in schools and colleges masturbation "can hardly be called a solitary vice. It has become so common that it is indeed a public vice." These statements played into the fears of parents who sent their children away to school with the best of intentions and now found they put them at risk of losing both mind and body.[36]

If the path of the young male masturbator led from college success to home failure, debility, and blasted hopes, what about the girl? In the early texts, the female masturbator is normally a beautiful young lady wasting away. As she fails, she is taken by loving parents to doctors, who dose her and let her blood to no avail. Unlike her male counterpart, however, she seems easily cured by correct information, proper living, and the best restorative of all, marriage. Mary Gove received this confession from a woman: "When very young I became addicted to self pollution, and continued it for several years, but for a merciful Providence that made me a subject of converting grace, and an early marriage, I might now be suffering all its concomitant evils."[37]

Writers did warn girls and women that they could suffer physical harm from masturbation. Comparable to the male list of diseases produced by the practice is Woodward's list of female complaints: "leucorrhoea . . . incontinence of urine, strangury, prolapsus uteri, disease of the clitoris, and many other diseases, both local and general, which have been attributed to other causes." To this the physician Calvin Cutter added consumption, nervous diseases, and heart disease. In his treatment of the criminally insane, Woodward had in his care women "without mind, without delicacy or modesty, constantly harassed by the most ungovernable passion." Yet when he came to individual female cases, these seem quite curable. One young woman of twenty-two, "furious, noisy, filthy, and apparently nearly reduced to idiocy," responded to his antimasturbation admonition immediately and quickly became healthy and "perfectly sane."[38]

With the exception of Mary Gove, discussed below, girls were generally subordinate players in the antebellum drama of masturbation, while center stage was commanded by the blighted male youth. As the literature on sexuality grew and became more diffuse, however, masturbation came to pose a true danger to girls. The young male masturbator turned inward and shunned the opposite sex. The young female experienced a sexual awakening that led her to the opposite sex. For her the path from masturbation was to fornication and prostitution.

Believing that women suffered from "sexual abuse" in a manner different from men, the Grahamite William A. Alcott saw the woman who taught a girl to masturbate as an agent of Satan. Alcott was one of a number of physiological reform writers who argued that women, in his words, "in a natural state—unperverted, unseduced, and healthy," felt no sexual desire until awakened. The marriage bed was the appropriate place for a woman's inauguration into sexual feeling. Masturbation threatened this pattern by prematurely introducing desire in a girl. To Alcott, the woman who instructed a girl served as an agent of her ruin. After initially fulfilling her "diabolical purposes" by inducing desire, the woman then led the girl to a brothel, where she herself was likely an inmate.[39]

Not all writers agreed with Alcott that girls needed a teacher. The physician and health reformer R. T. Trall was convinced that the "morbid sensations" produced by constipation, occurring as they did "in the immediate vicinity of the sexual organs," led young girls to early sexual awareness and masturbation. This and the sexualized culture surrounding young people were all that were needed to lead girls to a practice that Trall believed was destructive to health and well-being.[40]

Beyond masturbation as a key to understanding childhood sexuality and a reminder of the dark forces of human existence, is there a way to understand why it emerged as an obsessive fear for many middle-class parents beginning in the 1830s? Its timing suggests that a dramatic change in American life was the key. As middling folk became middle class, their primary responsibility to their offspring became education, both socialization and formal training. Their real legacy was less the transfer of property than what they left in their children's heads. This was particularly true for the group most involved in generating—and probably reading—the literature dealing with masturbation in these years: white middle-class New Englanders, especially from the area's smaller cities, towns, and farms. Fathers who held land and conveyed it to their sons (and movable possessions to their daughters) could control their young by threatening to withhold their birthrights. Middle-class parents, by contrast, invested in educating their children so that they could succeed in the society through work and marriage.

Yet accompanying the new task of middle-class parents was a deep insecurity. Without the whip of disinheritance, parents retained far less control. Boys and girls could go wrong. They could become wayward artists rather than disciplined workers, they could struggle against or deviate from parents' notions of respectable behavior. If children were away from home in school or working in the city, how could they be kept to home ways and made to conform to home expectations? Parents who tried their hardest and failed needed an explanation. Parents who feared for their children craved ways to assuage that fear. Above all else, the masturbation scare addressed the anxiety about children and their future that was constricting the chests of middle-class parents.[41]

4

Many of the writers on masturbation, including Mary Gove, were followers of Sylvester Graham. In his lectures and writings, Graham argued persuasively that right ways of living—his ways—were conducive to health and longevity. A pioneer in reform physiology, his example prompted others to add their voices to discussions of the body. Of particular interest to this study are those reform physiologists who focused on sexuality or, as the age put it, the reproductive organs and their functions. Graham himself did not live by his rules of health, and, after apologizing to his followers for his gluttony, died at age fifty-six in 1851. Earlier, in 1837, with Graham's encouragement, William A. Alcott had helped form the American Physiological Society to foster information and education about the body and its proper care. The water-cure movement drew on certain of Graham's ideas and prescriptions. Mary Gove, one of its practitioners, emerged as a leading voice in water cure, particularly important to female followers.

In the years that followed Graham's death, Alcott served as the reformer's most articulate spokesman, and his reasonable voice helped promote Grahamite ideas throughout the 1840s and 1850s. But even he had to admit that there was resistance at a popular level to Graham's sexual prescriptions. Rescued from dependence upon patent medicines by his own hand, Alcott spent his adult life fostering a regimen of bodily practices conducive to Christian life. In his extraordinarily prolific career of writing (more than a hundred books and innumerable articles) he seconded Graham's teachings and worked to get instruction into the schools about physiology. His publications over many decades encouraged a water-and-vegetable diet, sensible dress without corsets for women, and sexual restraint. Although he sought to be moderate and reasonable, Alcott was at odds with those who accepted the naturalness of sexual functioning. In arguing the propriety of allowing his *Physiology of Marriage* to be printed in 1856 and thus read by boys, Alcott applied a religious vocabulary in insisting that boys were not ignorant of sexual matters: "Satan already has his emissaries abroad, in various shapes. . . . What is left to the friends of God and humanity . . . is to counteract his plans, by extending the domain of conscience over that part of the Divine Temple which has too often been supposed not to be under law, but to be the creature of blind instinct, in which we are only on a par with the beasts that perish." Marriage, in Alcott's view, should be based not on sexual passion but on companionship and familial devotion. Sexual desire in men, called by Alcott an "instinct" or "appetite," is to be guided by "reason and conscience," not the other way around. (Women are not troubled by it.) Men are not animals: "It is only in the brutes to whom God has denied reason and conscience and science and the light of revelation, that appetite or instinct, is a guide."[42]

As could be anticipated, Alcott advocated a high degree of continence within marriage. He cloaked his view, however, in tones gentler than Graham's. Alcott stated that he was often asked by young men how much sexual intercourse was right. He seemed to hedge, stating that to answer, it was important to know the specific circumstances of the person asking. He then reported that upon inquiring of a physician, he had gotten the response that less than two times a week was best, while a clergyman suggested once a month, the recommendation of Sylvester Graham.

Alcott understood that the suggestion of the "far famed, and very far-hated" Graham had not been popular in the way that Charles Knowlton's instructions for the postcoital douche had been. Alcott's words offer a window on the relation between sexual practices and the ideas generated by writers on sexual matters. Graham's prescription, Alcott admitted, was "so utterly at war with the general habits and feelings of mankind" that it was "almost enough, at the time it was announced, to provoke the cry of, Crucify him. Indeed, I have often thought that while the public odium was ostensibly directed against his anti–fine flour and anti–flesh eating doctrines, it was his anti–sexual indulgence doctrines, in reality, which excited the public hatred and rendered his name a by-word and a reproach."[43]

Despite this popular resistance to Graham, Alcott generated a consequential following among health reformers during his years of lecturing and writing. Collectively they profoundly affected the understanding of the body in the early nineteenth century and redirected the healing arts. They insisted that the way to health was through right living—fresh air, exercise, bathing, vegetarianism, and sexual restraint. They believed that education in Graham's definition of the real demands of the body and his hygienic discipline could restore the afflicted and prevent disease in the future.

Graham's ideas entered into the water cure, or hydropathy, an important route for the dissemination of many of the principles of health reform. Based on the practices of Vincent Priessnitz in Silesia, hydropathy insisted that disease was an aberration of the naturally healthy condition of the body. Internal and external applications of water brought a chronically unhealthy condition to an acute stage through eruptions, such as boils, rashes, sores, or diarrhea, all of which were ways the body had of expelling disease. Depending upon the condition or disease, the patient was wrapped in wet sheets or bundled in dry sheets and plunged into a cold bath, bathed and soaked in toto or in part, or douched. Sufferers went to water-cure establishments or were doctored in their own homes. The therapy was dubious, based on age-old humoral approaches that sought to restore balance to the body by getting it to release its impurities through excretions or secretions, but many Americans found it beneficial. By the late 1840s, there were thirty water-cure establishments in the United States. The *Water-Cure Journal* had a circulation of fifty thousand in 1852.[44]

More important than its therapeutics were hydropathy's instructions in healthful living. These generally followed Graham's dietary and sexual prescriptions. Hydropathy encouraged its adherents to take control of their own well-being, a possibility for those who understood physiology. The movement's leaders became teachers of fundamental principles and hygienic practices. Of critical importance was knowledge of women's reproductive system. Unlike allopathy's sense that the great changes in women's lives— the onset of menstruation, pregnancy, childbirth, and menopause—signaled imbalance and crisis, hydropathy emphasized the naturalness of all phases of women's development.

In 1839 Mary Gove began a long career that brought her into the water-cure movement as speaker, writer, and institution builder. In a later phase her writings stretched to the far reaches of free-love advocacy.[45] Born in New Hampshire in 1810 to a freethinking father and Universalist mother, Mary Gove converted to Quakerism as a girl. After an unhappy marriage, she became a follower of Sylvester Graham, accepting both his physiological sys-

"School Room, Miss Sarah Elizabeth Hollen (mother of donor), a teacher of phonetics, is seen instructing her class," watercolor drawing, c. 1840, gift of Miss E. H. Fairman. © Museum of the City of New York.

tem and his deep anxiety about masturbation. She lectured to women on the body, provoking controversy over propriety that only increased when she began using a mannequin for illustration. Her first printed offering, cited above, was a 1839 book on masturbation, very much in the mode of Sylvester Graham. In 1842 she published *Lectures to Ladies, on Anatomy and Physiology,* a straightforward presentation of skeleton and viscera, with extensive consideration of the digestive and nervous systems. To those who questioned why she "should deviate so far from what is considered the appropriate sphere of woman" to lecture and write on anatomy, Gove answered with the personal testimonial of Graham's impact on her own well-being. Although her book was conventional in many ways, its effort to treat sexual questions was important.[46]

Gove's discussion of the "nervous system" in the 1846 edition contained her judgments about sexual passion and its expression. Her tone in this work is unstable, deriving from the conflict between her commitment to the Graham system and her growing belief in the naturalness of sexual functioning. Although Graham essentially held that total sexual abstinence was the healthiest possibility for the individual, Mary Gove was coming to have different ideas. She quoted an author, later identified as Dr. Francis Condie of Philadelphia, on the value of the "appetite, instinct, or passion which impels us to the propagation of our species." When properly exercised, it increases health, longevity, happiness, and has "a tendency to soften and improve the heart." But it needs careful watching. "Its tendency, in the present artificial state of society, is to premature and excessive development, and to unnatural, excessive, and destructive indulgence."[47]

This is an important statement. Emerging in Gove's work is an assumption that there is a "natural" state of society that lies in contrast to the present one, which is "artificial." In the natural one women are "hardy and robust," but in the artificial one they are often frail. In the natural one a healthy woman finds pregnancy, birth, and nursing "as natural as digestion; and were mankind brought into a natural and healthy state, we have reason to believe that these functions would be attended with little, if any pain." But in the artificial one of the present, often a woman's "nervous system is destroyed."[48] In the natural one sexual expression is in balance and sustains health. In the artificial one women fail and die from weakness and disease. Mary Gove advocated the Graham diet to restore them to health. One of a cadre of women in New England and New York who shared an intense interest in learning about the body and its healthful functioning, Gove had an important impact.[49]

Gove put great emphasis on the natural, a testament to the influence that romanticism was beginning to have on an understanding of the body. Belief in the natural grew stronger in the writings of the later followers of Graham. They shifted from a fear of sexual intercourse to a reverence for it, and it is this that served as the rationale for its limitation. R. T. Trall, who became a major promoter of the water cure, wrote that the misuse of sex led to disease for reasons obvious to "the reflecting mind. . . . The very intensity of the sexual orgasm, when legitimately exercised, is sufficiently evincive that it is not to be promiscuously nor too frequently excited with impunity." Trall did not, however, follow the logical trail of Graham. Rather, he assumed that sexual desire was a part of the healthy person. As he discussed with his audience the health problems that arose from sexual misuse, he not only listed the diseases that induced "a constant and almost restless propensity for sexual commerce"—satyriasis in men and nymphomania in women—he included as well "Loss of Sexual Appetite" as a disease and asserted that "a few years of rest, and a life in conformity with the laws of life, may re-develop the natural sensibility."[50]

5

In discussions of sexual restraint and masturbation, where were the voices of freethinkers? After 1835, Charles Knowlton was no longer in the public eye as he practiced medicine in small-town western Massachusetts and revised *Fruits of Philosophy.* In 1842, he reemerged in print to dissent from his medical colleagues' treatment of nocturnal seminal emissions as pathological symptoms. In an article on "Gonorrhoea Dormientium" in the *Boston Medical and Surgical Journal* in 1842, he wrote that when young men come to him with fears that wet dreams will incapacitate them for marriage, "I make light of it, and laugh a load of melancholy out of them." It was not that he did not take the issue seriously. As he stated, "For good and sufficient reason my thoughts have been directed to the subject of nocturnal seminal emissions for more than twenty years."[51]

Only after his death eight years later did his memoirs, published in this same journal, detail his own painful experience. At age seventeen, he was tormented with the "disease," caused, he surmised, by some combination of "onanism" and digestive troubles. Given medications by ten doctors, he became only more wretched and depressed. His distress over his condition largely incapacitated him for work or companionship. He was one of those "dronish" youths that Luther Bell depicted. Then a local jack-of-all-trades returned to his western Massachusetts town, bringing with him an electrical machine that he insisted could cure the young man. Charles Knowlton moved in with him. "He had no sons, but six daughters, all at home, and all singers, dancers, and adepts in the amusements and pleasures of accomplished and well-educated young women. Many people were about there; and we had checquer-playing, backgammon, chess, music and dancing, more or less, almost every day and evening." Knowlton submitted to jolts from the electricity machine. "It put the 'vital fluid' into me, as I was made to believe." And he fell in love with and married his host's seventeen-year-old daughter.[52]

To the young men in his office, Knowlton did not offer electric shocks or six daughters, but he read to them the statement by a medical authority that nocturnal emissions are the way that the system rids itself of superfluous semen. He told them that their fear that they are "incapacitated for giving and receiving pleasure"—because of the instantaneous nature of their sexual response during sleep—is groundless. To their belief that "it would kill them to marry," the good doctor responded and suggested that, on the contrary, it would be good if they did marry. To his colleagues in 1842 he attempted to offer a medical explanation of what seemed to baffle them. He wrote that the medical term for this condition of young men—"seminal weakness"—is both "erroneous in theory and mischievous in practice." Knowlton argued that it is irritability, not debility, that in alliance with the brain causes emissions. When the male genitals are in "a ticklish, sensitive state," the presence of semen makes an impression that, when carried to the brain, creates a dream. "The imagination now re-acts powerfully and concentratedly . . . upon the irritable genital organs, and thus the emission is speedily produced." For young men who are troubled by this condition, marriage is the answer. Marriage will "soothe their nerves, becalm the whole body and mind, take off the local irritation of seminal repletion, supersede involuntary emissions, about which they have been so much troubled, and finally restore them to perfect health." No moral quandary, no guilt; just the body acting naturally. Of course, what Knowlton offered to the bride of the young man was the knowledge of the reproductive process and the means to prevent pregnancy, another fruit of his materialist philosophy.[53]

Frederick Hollick did not seem to have Knowlton's sense of humor, but he likely offered similar advice. A British follower of Robert Owen, he came to the United States to join New Harmony. In 1845 he published *The Origin of Life: A Popular Treatise on the Philosophy and Physiology of Reproduction*. Although Hollick called himself an M.D., had a consultative practice, and sold contraceptive information and devices, he earned his living primarily as a lecturer on the body and as a writer of books. Like his other texts, *The Origin of Life* offers clear drawings of the male and female sexual organs.[54] It defines each organ, establishes its relation to others in the reproductive system, and describes the process of impregnation as Hollick understood it. This scientific information came with a point of view. Like Robert Dale Owen before him, Hollick argued for the positive value of sexual feeling. Not only is it neither immoral nor injurious, it is the basis of morality and society. Sexual desire is not "merely an *animal,* or *sensual,* impulse." Although it is "certainly connected with a physical function," from it come "the deepest and most sacred, moral, and social interests and obligations! Sexual desire originates the holy feeling of *love,* the great tamer of mere brute passion, and the great sweetener of life."[55]

When he attempted to describe the nature of sexual pleasure, Hollick sought to be physiologically precise. Like Graham, Hollick understood sexual sensibility in terms of the nervous system. "The sexual feeling," he wrote, "like every other physical sensation, results from a specific excitement of the nerves in certain parts of the body. In the male this part is chiefly the glans, on the end of the penis. In females it is either the external lips, the interior of the vagina, or Os Tincae [the mouth of the uterus]; but most usually the clitoris." Hollick continued, "The exciting cause is generally mechanical irritation, by copulation, or otherwise, to which persons are led by an intense desire. This desire is first produced by some unknown sympathy between the brain and sexual organs; afterwards the recollection of former pleasure increases its intensity."[56]

Hollick sounded a great deal like *Aristotle's Master-piece* as he dealt with sexual response. In his discussion of the clitoris, Hollick was equally emphatic about its role in female sexual excitement: "This part appears to be the principal seat of venereal pleasure! In some respects it much resembles the male penis, as it becomes erect and extended when excited." When Hollick turned to discuss the penis, he determined that the glans was the specific element corresponding to the clitoris: the glans is "very sensitive, somewhat resembling the clitoris in females, and, like it, is the principal seat of pleasure. Both the glans and the clitoris are profusely supplied with nerves, to which is owing their extreme sensitiveness."[57]

Hollick was a sexual enthusiast. He believed that as the sexual organs mature, all persons experience sexual feelings, although to varying degrees. He advocated early marriage and regular sexual intercourse, although he did not comment on frequency. He wrote that with the development of sexual organs "it is necessary for the subsequent healthy action of the system that these organs should be duly exercised. If they are not, the whole being will deteriorate. Undue continence, in those properly organized, produces a state of nervous agitation which completely unsettles the mind, disposes the body to various diseases, and makes the disposition irritable and unhappy." Although men always experience sexual feeling in what Hollick calls "connexion," women can be more variable. When they do respond, the mouth of the uterus opens to suck up the semen. Arguing that women do experience sexual feeling "in most cases," Hollick added, "*it ought to be so always. Its absence is very frequently attended with barrenness*, though not always, and it is rarely accompanied by good health and spirits." He referred to his ability in his consulting room to restore patients to sexual desire, but refrained from treatment of the subject in print.[58]

6

Imagining itself as the objective science of the mind, phrenology attempted to stand outside the divide between the Christian Grahamites and the free-thinking enthusiasts. It posited that the cerebellum, at the base of the brain, contained an organ of "amativeness," which was the source of the reproductive instinct or sexual feeling. The shape and size of this organ determined the strength of a person's sex drive. Positioned at the base of the skull above the nape of the neck, it thus stood at the link between the brain and the spinal column, the governing center of the nervous system. Although the cerebellum sent messages to the sexual organs through the nervous system and received messages from them, sex was essentially a matter of mind.

In the 1840s and 1850s, Fowler and his followers presented themselves as sexual teachers to the nation. At one point, in a footnote using the third person, O. S. Fowler gave a reading of his own phrenological makeup: "His Amativeness being only moderate."[59] With this as a recommendation (or perhaps a limitation), Fowler wrote many books on what he politely called "the matrimonial instinct," attempting to apply his knowledge to sexuality, heredity, and domestic relations. His books sold extremely well, most going into as many as forty editions (normally of 1,000 copies each). After an initial book in 1837 designed to prove phrenological doctrines, in 1841 Fowler wrote *Matrimony*, which sold more than 50,000 copies, and continued with *Love and Parentage* and *Amativeness*. His brother, Lorenzo Fowler, also tried his hand, publishing *The Principles of Phrenology and Physiology Applied to Man's Social Relations* and *Marriage: Its History and Ceremonies* in the 1840s.

Despite its efforts to be a neutral science, the early years of phrenology show clear marks of its origins in New England. Its practitioners were children from an evangelical milieu trying to make an accommodation with science and its understanding of human reproduction. They embraced the sexual as "natural," but they did so with fear and hesitation. In the language of a nineteenth-century scientist, O. S. Fowler asserted in *Love and Parentage* the following principle regarding reproduction: "As no department of our nature was made in vain, so this was not created to slumber." This double negative came, however, only after an introduction of three cases of amativeness gone astray.[60]

O. S. Fowler ultimately declared that sexual passion is legitimate, God-given, and appropriate to women as well as men. Nonetheless, he insisted that it be exercised only when spiritual love overrode it. When Lorenzo Fowler attempted to describe love, he stated that "it commences with the physical and when perfected, ends with the spiritual." From the outset the Fowlers offered to their readers a curious mélange. All the conventional virtues abide—men are to be upright, gallant, charming, the protectors of women's virtue, while women are to be beautiful, soft, winning, domestic, and gentle to children. However, these qualities, so identified with

A phrenological examination at Fowler and Wells. "The Candidate of Many Parties," a caricature by H. R. Robinson, 1848, illustrating a phrenological examination. © Collection of The New-York Historical Society, negative #40839.

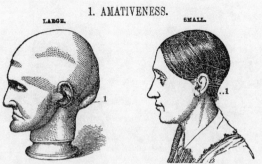

1. AMATIVENESS.

LARGE.   SMALL.

No. 43.—BUST OF AARON BURR.   No. 44.—MISS MODESTY.

SEXUALITY; the LOVE element; attachment to the OPPOSITE SEX; desire to LOVE, BE loved, and MARRY.

Gender stereotypes in action: the bust of Aaron Burr is used to demonstrate large amativeness, while "Miss Modesty" serves for small. *New Illustrated Self-Instructor in Phrenology and Physiology* (New York: Fowler and Wells, Publishers, 1859), p. 75.

nineteenth-century sentimentality, exist because of sexual characteristics. Stated in general terms, those persons with large and active organs of amativeness "are alive to the personal charms and mental accomplishments of the other sex; ardent admirers of their beautiful forms, graceful movements." They are the kind of people who arouse in others friendship and "the passion of love." They are the ones most likely to marry, the ones "capable of the most devoted connubial love." For those who might imagine that this fundamental truth of phrenology applied only to men, O. S. Fowler added at a later point, "Woman's endowment with the sexual passion is admitted. Deprived of it, she would be shorn of every female charm."[61]

When the Fowlers turned to the exercise of the organ of amativeness, however, little separated them from conventional wisdom. Fowler wrote that women's amative organs in the cerebellum were small relative to those of men, thus "Constitutionally, therefore, she is more virtuous and less passionate than man." Within marriage, her more subdued passion should guide the frequency of sexual intercourse. Couples should seek to limit the number of times that they engage in sexual relations. In addition to contributing to health, restraint leads to less sin. Fowler reminded his readers that marriage does not "wipe away the polluting stain. Carnality is carnality, in wedlock as much as out of it." Somehow all this had to fit with Fowler's

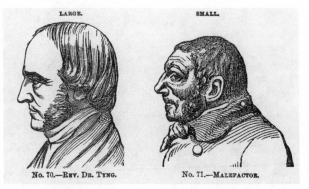

Ethnic stereotypes in action: the head of Reverend Dr. Tyng illustrates large moral sentiments, while the "Malefactor," playing on a hackneyed image of an Irishman, small. *New Illustrated Self-Instructor in Phrenology and Physiology* (New York: Fowler and Wells, Publishers, 1859), p. 116.

major prescription: "To those whose social organs are both large and active, Phrenology says, with all the emphasis of a law of our being,—Marry! Marry soon." Fowler shared the fear that unnecessary delay would lead youth to masturbation. He was clearly a man who hedged his bets.[62]

Given phrenology's concern with carnality in marriage, it is not surprising that in their early years, Fowler and his associates first allied with Sylvester Graham and then with the water-cure movement. Fowler and Wells published water-cure books and journals. The phrenologists advocated many elements of the Graham regimen designed to dampen sexual fires. To prevent the premature development of amativeness, O. S. Fowler counseled that the young should eat a nonstimulating diet of cooling food and drink, take plenty of exercise, and avoid those elements of the culture apt to inflame them: suggestive conversation, theatrical performances, especially dancing, fashionable music, improper prints, and novels.

7

For a number of writers on physiology, the key to Americans' ill health was sex gone awry. The violation of what they deemed healthy sexual life seemed to be at the root of the pervasive mental and physical distress of the era. For example, R. T. Trall announced, "Nor can the individual in any way more rapidly waste his or her vital energies, nor more surely induce nameless diseases and anomalous infirmities, nor more certainly hasten on the period of decrepitude and decline, than by excesses or irregularities in the indulgence of the sexual appetite." Parents should talk to their children about the reproductive system, sexual feelings, and sexual expression—mothers to daughters, fathers to sons. However, parents find this conversation difficult and delay it. They are supported in so doing by the widespread belief that children are best kept innocent by being kept ignorant.[63]

Many of the writers were coming to share a common notion of the hydraulics of sex. They could see a clear link between the images available to the senses; the brain with its powers of imagination and its source as the center of desire; the nervous system connected to the brain, which received and sent messages to all bodily organs; and sexual arousal. Knowlton and the followers of Graham differed mightily on many things, but they saw a link between libidinous images and sexual desire. Because of this, culture mattered to them. Books, lectures, pictures, plays, conversation, and gestures carried import, shaping the way that Americans behaved because they shaped the way they felt.

Many of the books already considered, including parts of many of the books of popular medicine, offered advice to the American public. For example, the phrenologist Andrew Boardman recommended succinctly: "avoidance of lascivious books, plays, dances, and associates."[64] Prescriptive texts have fueled some of the histories of American sexual culture of the nineteenth century, buttressing the common understanding of the era as sexually repressed. Although this view has been called into question, especially in the light of love letters, private correspondence among friends, and a slight bit of survey data, prescription should not be tossed aside, for it has a great deal to say, both intentionally and unintentionally. To use prescriptive literature effectively requires a trick of perception. The reader must see less the new rule being advocated than the way that its maker sees it being violated. When Catharine Beecher tells parents not to let their young children talk at the table, for example, instead of letting her words convey the image of silent children, the reader should imagine what Beecher saw—high-spirited American children in the 1850s talking at the table. Thus when writers set forth the causes of what they see as the sexual ills of their time, readers should attend carefully to the ways that they talk about the culture they are trying to change.

For those who understood sexual intercourse as natural, a corollary was that the product of sexual union, the child, could no longer be seen as born in sin. To Protestants of a more evangelical stamp, a notion of growing in grace was beginning to supplant the sudden change of heart of religious revival. Writers of prescriptive works based on new understandings of the body taught that children are neither innocent nor evil, merely filled with potentialities. They are human beings born with a reproductive system designed to perpetuate the species. Although children's sexual organs are not fully developed, they can be easily stimulated. Young children can experience sexual sensations that arouse their curiosity.

These sensations in children are nurtured in what reformers called the "hot-house" atmosphere of the broader culture. As Trall put it, writing of children in mid-nineteenth-century America, "the sexual propensity is often prematurely and preternaturally developed. Perhaps a majority of the children of civilized society are not exempt from some degree of a forced, unnatural, hot-house cultivation of sexuality, both bodily and mentally." In some reformers' eyes the broader culture of adults was harmful to children. As enthusiastic as he was about the exercise by adults of their sexual natures, Frederick Hollick believed that children became sexually mature too early for their own good. The culture was the culprit. Young people were aroused too early by the sexual atmosphere of the day: "A child cannot walk out, but his eyes and ears are assailed with sights and sounds all bearing on this topic." It is in what they read and what they hear, even from their parents' conversation. "In short, a child very soon discovers that this is the main subject of interest with nearly every person he knows, and consequently it becomes so with him at once."[65]

Aware that the general public was ready to indict the street for its role in contributing to the precocious knowledge of children, some of those who wrote serious texts of popular medicine insisted that children also picked up knowledge in houses and shops. Trall described what he saw around him: "It is hardly possible for children, now-a-days, to associate freely with their seniors in age, without having their plastic minds filled with wanton and libidinous ideas and images." A critical element of this was the "common talk" of ordinary people—their jokes, repartee, anecdotes, and songs. The speech children heard was "based on perverted ideas and depraved images relating to the sexual organs, and to sexual commerce." Trall continued, "Too frequently do men in the middle period of life, married men, and men who are fathers of sons and daughters, indulge, in the field, in the workshop, behind the counter, and even around the family hearth, in a style of lascivious hints, inuendoes, etc., relating to the sexual distinctions, in the presence of young, but not listless nor unobserving children," thus exciting their erotic curiosity.[66]

Children were being further corrupted by books. Whereas history, biography, and the natural sciences could elevate the mind, popular literature of the day threatened to sink it. Trall declared that one of the most pernicious sources of premature knowledge and sexual stimulation was books. He wrote that "obscene novels and fictitious writings, specially addressed to the amative propensity, full of lewd images, impure conceptions, and lust-engendering narratives" were abundant and available to the young. Trall continued his indictment to include even the best publishing houses. They disseminated " 'light literature,' in the shape of trashy romances, exciting seduction stories, narratives of dissolute characters, and fictitious histories of imaginary debauchees, whose deeds of sensuality and depravity are detailed with all the minuteness and circumstantiality that can arrest the attention and inflame the passion of the youthful and susceptible mind." Trall believed that such literature was ruinous to the young because they had not developed the mature judgment of adults, who had brought their passions and imagination under the rule of intellect.[67]

And thus the circumference of the circle was drawn by sexual reformers. It framed a frightening picture for increasing numbers of parents who watched their adolescent children leave home for school or work. These reformers saw the risks that young people faced. Stimulated by their own physical drives, excited by the feverish nature of the culture around them, prodded by associates in shops and colleges, young people were drawn to titillating reading and turned to masturbation. With this act they began a downward course that led them to ruin. The brothel claimed the girls. Boys turned away from the paths of rectitude and ambition to withdraw into solitary pursuits that would take them to the asylum and the grave.

These threatening visions of reform physiologists were powerful in New England, but they had a particular saliency in New York City. There, as early as the 1830s, the new culture of sporting men was emerging. Drawn into its ranks were some of the young clerks who had left their homes in New England and upstate New York to seek opportunity in the city. These young men were enjoying their first taste of freedom, but with it came the danger of license. Prostitutes walked the streets, and newspapers carried advertisements for abortion. On the street there was plenty of reading for sale that could fuel temptation, and conservatives found that the courts offered a potential means of checking it. Worry about the young clerk and the downward spiral into which he could spin helped fuel a growing campaign for the suppression of obscene materials.

PART II

THE NEW YORK SCENE

6

New York and the Emergence of Sporting Culture

When Frederick Hollick observed that the "eyes and ears" of children were being bombarded by sexualized "sights and sounds," he captured the reality of New York streets in the years before the Civil War. Words and images evoking sex were everywhere. New York was a printing center, and the newspaper world quickly became adept at playing scandal as news. Theaters provided arenas for sexual display; blackface minstrels created a freer style. The rough ways of male working-class life encouraged camaraderie and led to disorder. Male sporting culture was emerging on the city's streets, at odds with middle-class respectability. Warnings of city dangers accompanied boys and young men migrating from the country, but some of them found the warnings appealing rather than threatening. Freedom from middle-class constraint was what they wanted. As New York underwent this transformation, it became the place where important conflicts over sexual representation were waged.

In 1836 a beautiful young prostitute was brutally murdered in a high-class New York brothel. A nineteen-year-old male clerk was immediately arrested and charged with the murder, having left his cloak and bludgeoning hatchet at the scene. The trial of Richard Robinson for the murder of Helen Jewett introduced New Yorkers to a new phenomenon. At the trial Robinson's partisans cheered him on, donning what they titled "Frank Rivers caps," in honor of the alias that Robinson had assumed when he entered the house of Rosina Townsend for his regular visits to Jewett. Philip Hone, who attended the trial, reported that Robinson was "surrounded by young men about his own age,

Entertainment on the New York streets. Jerome Thompson, "Street Scenes: Peep Show," 1851. © Museum of the City of New York.

apparently clerks like him," knowledgeable about the interworkings of the brothel.[1]

Robinson, the son of a respected family from Connecticut, was a clerk in the Maiden Lane establishment of Joseph Hoxie, a highly regarded Christian merchant. Young Robinson had come to make his fortune in New York, traveling the route taken by young men before him. What made Robinson the representative of a new age was his freedom. By the 1830s, New York merchants had abandoned the apprentice system that had once supervised youth after hours. Robinson lived in a boardinghouse, and his time away from Hoxie's store was his own. One of the ways he chose to spend it was in Helen Jewett's company at Townsend's bordello. The madam testified in Robinson's trial that he was a regular client, and on the night of the murder he had come to see Jewett in her room at 9:00. At 11:00, Townsend served them a bottle of champagne. At 3:00, she awoke to find Jewett's room on fire and Jewett dead from the blows of a hatchet.

The case excited great attention, fanned by the flames of the new penny journalism, which kept the Jewett story on the front page. Robinson was acquitted, perhaps, as it was later charged, because the jury had been bribed. Press accounts of the trial reveal many intriguing elements about American urban culture in the 1830s—such as the nature of prostitution and its place in the city. Of specific interest here is what the reports disclose about the emerging world of male sporting culture.

These young men—living in boardinghouses and having money to spend—sought enjoyment in the city. They found it in games, such as cock-fighting and bare-knuckle prizefights, liquor, theatrical entertainment, and commercial sex. Their needs and desires became sources of opportunity for those eager to make a buck. Just as boardinghouses emerged to cater to them, so did gambling houses, saloons, theaters, brothels, and a network of printers and distributors of erotic literature. These commercial establishments undergirded what is commonly called male "sporting" culture in the antebellum years.[2]

As these men moved about the city in small packs in the evening, all partook of the fashion of the moment, be it a Frank Rivers cap or a cape or a certain cut of jacket. Their conviviality was loosened with alcohol. And they walked with a certain swagger. These young men were shaping an alternative culture in urban America, that of sporting men. This world celebrated an ideal of leisure devoted to the pursuit of pleasure, as young men defined it. By its ethos, a blade with money to spend could take his enjoyment where he could find it, without thought of consequences or obligations. New York and other cities offered opportunities for blood sports, intoxicating drinks, gambling, and theatrical performances. It was a sociable world in which wealthy associated with poor and old with young, linked by the pursuit of thrills. It valued fancy clothes and jewelry, the outward appearance of gentlemen. A key element of its culture was the dream of unrestricted male heterosexuality. Women were to be instruments of men's pleasure, to be used and discarded freely. Thus, for a sporting man with money to spend, the prostitute was the perfect imagined sexual object. A wife, by contrast, limited a man's sexual and personal freedom.

To describe their own world, the unattached urban men might have used the word "flash." Originally connoting the argot of the underworld, its application was being extended in the early nineteenth century to the pursuits and style of male sporting life, particularly prizefighting, which was illegal at the time. What remains today in the word "flashy" is its link to high-style dress and adornment. In the 1830s, however, the term still carried the edge of risk and danger. It was a code word that gave a positive spin to the culture of the male sporting world in its conflict with the canons of respectability of the emerging middle class.[3] "Sporting" was a useful euphemism for elements of male urban life, for not only did it retain its meaning of recreation and amusement, but in slang it carried from an earlier era the connotation of coition.[4]

The new urban economy and society fundamentally shaped the flash world of sporting men as it emerged in New York City. By 1830 New York was a city of more than 240,000 persons and had supplanted Boston and Philadelphia as the economic capital of the nation. Its economic power quickly translated into cultural strength, as newspaper and book printing attracted authors and artists and theaters multiplied. It seemed to contemporaries to be a city of "lights and shadows," whose extremes of wealth and poverty, of sin and piety, met the eye.

A place where goods were made and sold, New York developed its own distinctive pattern of economic life. It had few great factories because of a lack of waterpower. The city's great advantage was its workers, who had a wide range of skills. It developed small manufactories employing skilled labor in machine and toolmaking and in distilling. Economic changes split apart a once proud artisan class. While a small minority of masters could profit by the new system, the majority lost ground. They found work, but they did not find the status or independence of the master craftsmen of an earlier era. Moreover, as more and more people competed for housing, living conditions deteriorated. In the years between 1800 and 1850, New York's population grew by 750 percent. Into the city came rural migrants from the immediate region and New England, British Protestants, and, especially in the immediate antebellum decades, Germans and Irish.[5]

New York was awash with print in the 1830s as newspapers, pamphlets, and books flooded the market. Unlike other industries in the city, printing adopted machinery and factory methods. Emerging alongside the new technology of printing, the penny press came to broadcast the news. People with causes—evangelical and freethinking—may have been the initiators, but many followed their lead. In a growing but unstable commercial world, writers and printers were eager to find a market and earn a living. With low postal rates, the more than five hundred papers in the country traveled through the national postal system to destinations far beyond their specific locales. By 1833 there were eleven daily newspapers in New York City.[6]

Imagining New York as a composite of urban types. "The New-York Elephant, National Monument to be erected at the top of New City-Hall," caricature, 1859. © Collection of The New-York Historical Society, negative #48542.

In that year Benjamin Day began the *Sun* and founded the penny press. James Gordon Bennett followed with the *Herald* in 1835. Unlike the more expensive papers to which wealthier persons subscribed, the penny dailies were affordable to working people and hawked by the copy on the street. The penny dailies catered to no group, in contrast to their subscription rivals, which were tied to an urban elite. There was from the outset an edge about the penny dailies that governed their tone and content. They were committed to the position that every person had the right to know, and they accused their competitors of having an interest in suppressing knowledge. The editors of the penny press asserted that knowledge was the source of power. They would expose all, tell all, no matter whom they offended. Any form of censorship threatened the diffusion of information. As a result the penny dailies championed—and began to exploit—the freedom to write about sex.

The editors of the penny press filled the papers with the kinds of news that encouraged men and women to purchase papers. Earlier papers had mixed commercial news and items culled from other papers. Day and Bennett realized that they had a commodity to sell and could attract regular purchasers if they filled the papers with local human-interest stories. Sensation caught the ear and eye: "fires, theatrical performances, elephants escaping from circus caravans, women trampled in the street by hogs run amok." Without having the resources to gather international news or reports from the nation's capital, penny daily editors could place reporters at city courts— by 1836 there were nine so employed. The tone of court reporters was often jocular, their goal as much entertainment as information: "New Yorkers soon learned that the penny papers were the best place to read all about how Daniel Sullivan beat and choked his wife to death in a drunken rage or to verify the rumor that the Reverend Joseph Carter had been arrested for rape." From the outset, these accounts of sexual misdeeds included the seduced-and-abandoned stories of prostitutes, such as the November 1833 chronicle in the *Sun* of Mary Hill, a Pennsylvania daughter who had become a Five Points slattern. In "'Turkish Harems,'" Bennett revealed in the *Herald* the private seraglio of a New York merchant through the story of an abducted young woman. Bennett, in particular, "fashioned a distinctively urban journalism of secret immoralities, daring escapes, and dramatic intrusions," and by 1836 the *Herald* could claim a readership of 20,000.[7]

The newspaper world of the 1830s was rough and dangerous. A miscreant might be angered at the publicity given his deeds or feel he was misrepresented in a reporter's narrative. He could take the writer or editor to court in

Young men reading a newspaper. Gabriel Harrison, *California News,* 1850–51. Gilman Paper Company Collection.

a libel suit. Or he might choose to confront his enemy on the streets or in a park. In 1835 William H. Attree, then a police court reporter for the *Transcript,* was stabbed in Sybil's Cave near Hoboken by one member of the Bowery's Chichester gang out to defend the name of another. Bennett was assaulted in his office by Thomas S. Hamblin, the tempestuous actor and theatrical impresario of the Bowery Theatre, as well as beaten in the street by rival newspaper editor James Watson Webb of the *Courier and Enquirer.*

The reporters and editors who created the popular press were undaunted by these threats to their livelihoods and lives. They moved on to carve out a new role, that of the investigative reporter, the detective of the people who went behind the courtroom accounts to ferret out the real story. In an era when police work was limited, the reporter turned detective justified his work as using the power of publicity to capture felons and to deter crime. Helen Jewett's 1836 murder gave James Gordon Bennett a great opportunity. In the ensuing weeks and during the trial, as he gathered clues, sifted evidence, and pronounced judgment, his exhaustive coverage in the *Herald* paradoxically aroused the curiosity it seemingly sought to allay.[8]

Bennett of the *Herald* came to succeed by flexibility and opportunism. His great skill was attack. In his first few years he assaulted "the Catholic Church and the Protestants, Free Love and prudery, the abolitionists and the police, banks, beggars, high society, low society, extremes of fashion, failures in etiquette," and his professional colleagues. Bennett understood the potential of a mixed class readership and sought to bridge the gap between classes and attract advertisers among middle-class businessmen eager to sell. The *Herald* contained mercantile news and serious political reporting along with its police reports. Although it appealed through the "low babble of the street, the theater, and the police court," the *Herald* offered precious information to those in the city seeking knowledge. If its advertisers are any guide, the new penny press attracted both artisanal and middle-class readers.[9]

Bennett's success led the older Knickerbocker elite to attempt a boycott of the *Herald*. In 1840 editors of the more established "sixpenny" papers—the *Courier and Enquirer* and the *Evening Post*—got merchants, clergy, and men of reputation to demand that the public boycott the *Herald* and any merchant advertising in it. They based their demand on the editor's immorality, using epithets such as "obscene vagabond," "profligate adventurer," and "moral pestilence." Bennett seemed to bend with the wind and promised to mind his manners but then went forward to continue many of his editorial practices. As he expanded his coverage and as the established press adopted many of his ways, the two kinds of papers increasingly came to resemble each other. The forces that Bennett represented—those seeking to make money by publishing news about violence, crime, scandal, and sex alongside business and political news—were stronger than those governed by propriety, stronger than any one editor or newspaper.[10]

As Day's *Sun* and Bennett's *Herald* developed greater readership, they took advantage of new technologies allowing for increased production, speed, and economies of scale. The great proprietors built large factorylike establishments for the new cylinder presses powered by steam, fed by stereotype, and worked by large numbers of employees. A hitherto artisanal craft became a major industry, one that paid its skilled workers the relatively high wage of $12 a week. As the major penny presses moved to new locations from the small shops on Ann Street where they had begun, they turned their hand- or foot-powered presses over to job printers. The area at the junction of Nassau and Ann Streets in Ward 2, just below City Hall, became known as the brains of the city. It was a rough-and-tumble world, "a mecca not only for gentlemen of the book trade but for sharpers, gamblers, and fireladdies." On the three blocks of Ann Street much of the popular literature of the day was printed and sold, including materials with an erotic edge.[11]

To the north and east, the Bowery, one of New York's great streets, became a legendary place of entertainment. Along the Bowery and on Chatham Street, a rich and rowdy working-class culture came into being. Young journeymen, workingmen without property, typically lived in boardinghouses. After hours they roamed the neighborhoods for entertainment. Here they came into contact with sailors moving up from the wharves. A range of commercial establishments grew up to cater to their hunger for leisure: "free-and-easies," or saloons, improvised gambling dens, and bawdy houses. Model artist exhibitions, first featured in saloons, later moved onstage at popular venues. In imitation of famous statues or paintings, such

News on the New York skyline. The New York Herald Building, Nassau and Fulton Streets, undated. © Museum of the City of New York.

as "The Three Graces" or "Susannah and the Elders," tableaux vivants presented scantily clad women posed as nudes.[12]

In the eighteenth century, male youths had been controlled by an apprentice system in which a young man was bound over to a master to learn a craft or a trade in exchange for service and obedience to the master, who stood in place of a father. The indenture that William Cowan signed in 1784 when he became an apprentice house carpenter prohibited the young fellow "from fornication, gambling, and other 'sins.' "[13] Burgeoning commerce and industry in nineteenth-century cities both marginalized crafts and ended the apprentice system. As the numbers of journeymen in New York swelled and as the working-class districts expanded to the north, the Bowery emerged by the 1830s as the focus of working-class commercial culture. As historian Sean Wilentz has written, "Here were the groggeries, oyster houses, dance halls, gambling dens, and bordellos that catered to workingmen and adventuresome tourists from around the world." Although workingmen constituted part of the audience in many theaters, the Bowery Theatre with its participatory culture became their own place. Bowery workingmen developed their own distinctive dress and style. Wearing the red shirts of fire companies and the hair at their temples long and greased, they took the nickname "soaplocks." In the 1840s they found a fictional exemplar in Mose, the tough, rowdy, but heroic "Bowery B'hoy," a stock character on the American stage.[14]

These youths frequented theaters in which the minstrel show gradually took form. Blackface performance of many kinds went back well into the eighteenth century in America, but the beginnings of minstrelsy date from the late 1820s, when white singers, dancers, and actors began creating blackface comedy on stage for working-class audiences as entr'acte entertainment. There are many tellings of minstrel origins. One of the most compelling has performers learning their moves at the Catherine Market near Chatham Street as they watched young black roustabouts dance to amuse the crowds, their staccato rhythms and jerky gestures transmuting defiance into entertainment. Watching and learning, whites began to imitate them and went on stage with the pretense that their characters were free blacks, wandering minstrels. These white performers in blackface created stage types and songs. George Washington Dixon introduced the song "Coal Black Rose" in 1829 and followed with the character Zip Coon, the black urban dandy. Such stage acts were wildly popular. Interacting with audiences they sought to please, blackface entertainers developed a series of routines of farcical improvisational comedy, sentimental music, a dash of frontier

Male life in shops and on the streets. Hudson Street, Numbers 2, 3, and 5. © Collection of The New-York Historical Society, negative #16930.

humor in southern dialect, and spirited dancing. It was all carried off with "a vitality, exuberance, and rapid-fire pace previously unknown on the American stage."[15]

Antebellum theaters were not places of quiet order in which a play was passively received by a respectful audience. They offered nightly fare of dramas and variety acts to a rough and rowdy public. Actors faced three distinct groups: the working class of the pit, the middle class and upper class of the boxes, and prostitutes and their clients in the gallery. The action of the audience was as important as that onstage, and lights were kept on so that patrons could see one another and move back and forth to get food and drink. Applause punctuated the performance, along with demands for repetition of choice bits. Disapproval came in the form of hissing, shouted insults, and pelting with food. Audiences had their favorites and their enemies.[16]

Working-class men lived much of their life in groups, such as volunteer fire companies. Fire fighting in New York had been a citizen responsibility from the beginning. By the 1820s and 1830s, its leadership had largely shifted from merchants and master craftsmen to journeymen, especially those in shipbuilding and carpentry. The stations became centers of male communal life, places for popular blood sports. Equipment and regalia offered the symbols of fraternal orders. Companies rivaled one another for first place at fire scenes and for putting out blazes, and street brawls could ensue. In 1836, for example, in Chatham Square, two engine companies attacked a third on the way to a fire. "More than 1,000 people participated in the resulting riot," in which one of the engines was captured, stripped of its decorations, and turned upside down in front of its rival's engine house. As politicians vied for votes, they began to court the "laddies," as the volunteer firemen were called. For some, such as William M. Tweed, service in the companies became a step to political power.[17]

Loose groups of men held together by the need to protect their honor from rivals constituted the gangs that patrolled the streets. Journeymen

Printing close to the minstrel stage. Advertisement for Robert H. Elton, *Ripsnorter Comic Almanac*, 1849, back cover. Courtesy, American Antiquarian Society.

butchers, dressed in their bloody smocks, their day's work accomplished by midmorning, were particularly associated with gangs and drunkenness. Endemic to the city, by the 1830s gangs seemed to become more organized and more violent: "Undomesticated by women, loving drink, and seeking distinction among peers, members valued strength, independence, and devil-may-care audacity." Politicians such as Mike Walsh began to see their potential as muscle men, vote stuffers, and ballot-box stealers. More than any other place, the prizefight ring distilled working-class male life. Working outside the law, saloon owners, gamblers, and fighters created a counterworld to bourgeois respectability that gave form to the manly code of the streets.[18]

All of this happened through the haze of alcohol. Americans of both sexes and all regions and classes drank, especially potent distilled spirits—whisky, rum, gin, and brandy. But some drank more than others and more publicly. The average man drank nearly half a pint of distilled spirits a day; while some drank temperately, one quarter were drinking twelve to twenty-four ounces a day. Liquor punctuated the journeyman's day: "at all times, in and out of the shops, New York's journeymen could be expected to drink." They drank at work, taking breaks during the long day. They drank in their workingmen's saloons and grog shops, where their credit was good and where they could learn about jobs.[19] They drank routinely throughout the day, and they drank for celebrations, bingeing ten to fifteen times a year on such occasions as the Fourth of July and election day. Communal drinking of the early nineteenth century merged into the ideology of free-and-equal men. "All men were equal before the bottle, and no man was allowed to refuse to drink," noted W. J. Rorabaugh. The many absences after a weekend of drink gave "Blue Monday" its name.[20]

Issues both economic and symbolic aroused workingmen in the antebellum decades. As the power of manufacturers increased and as their own standard of living declined, workingmen turned to politics in the 1820s and trade union organization in the 1830s. Led by those in construction, printing, and consumer goods, male workers joined together across ethnic and skill lines. The General Trades' Union turned to strikes as a way to restore power to workers in the shops. Informed by a producers' ethic that asserted the value of labor over capital, they envisioned an artisan republic shaped by the mutuality and interdependence of wage earners, a mutuality, however, that excluded women, unskilled workers, and small masters. Some levels of change were directed inward, and union leaders advocated education and temperance, along with a revisioning of the society. The most dramatic expressions were outward: New York saw a rash of strikes, both disciplined and violent, in the inflationary mid-1830s.[21]

Riots erupted frequently. Incited by newspapers, mobs frequently gathered during elections and often appeared at theaters. Here the enemy was not masters or fellow workers opposed to strikes, but rather objects of symbolic hatred. Brothel riots, often directed against houses where blacks and whites mixed, repeatedly endangered property and persons. In 1834 a series of riots punctuated early July as mobs lashed out against abolitionists and blacks. Mobs attempted to disrupt an abolitionist meeting, ransacked the house of Lewis Tappan and the store of Arthur Tappan, attacked approximately twenty houses of blacks and seven churches in the Five Points neighborhood, and rioted at the Bowery Theatre.[22]

The 1834 riots reveal links between hostility to merchants—especially temperance and abolitionist merchants—racism, and patriotism that are particularly interesting. New England–born silk merchants Lewis and Arthur Tappan had long been hated. It was one thing for craftsmen to advocate temperance to their own workers. It was quite another when moral reformers from the middle and merchant classes sought to change workers' ways. Workers saw the wealthy Tappans as outside meddlers who sought to take away their drink and their Sunday pleasures. By the 1830s, in addition to temperance and Sabbatarianism, the two merchant brothers were advocating freedom for black slaves. White workingmen in New York joined their endemic antiblack racism to a "deep distrust of the small, unskilled black community as a class of supposedly abject dependents." The 1834 theater protest was against the appearance of English actor George Farren, who had supposedly insulted Americans and their flag. Rioters were quieted when the manager "rushed in from the wings to apologize, waving an American flag in each hand and summoning an American singer to perform Zip Coon."[23]

The worst theater riot took place in 1849 at the Astor Place Opera House. The workingmen of the Bowery Theatre held Edwin Forrest in particular regard. When his rival William Charles Macready appeared at the more elite theater in Astor Place, Forrest's adherents were in place in the pit and the gallery. Their hisses escalated to chair throwing: Macready escaped, determined never to appear again. However, urged by a petition of city leaders and protected by police, he returned two days later. The enraged crowd outside the theater grew. The police panicked and shot into the crowd, killing twenty-two. The Astor Place riot has been seen as providing an important cultural marker: in its wake theaters began to target more specific audiences and certain theaters sought the presence of middle-class women. It is important, however, in another sense, as the moment in which the elite no longer accepted the rule of the rioters. Breaking the code that had governed for decades, the mayor sent the police and the militia to defend an actor and his elite patrons.[24]

Gangs, riots, and social disorder had one meaning when all participants were working class and quite another when they included members of the middle class. What the trial of Richard Robinson for the murder of Helen Jewett revealed was the extension of the working-class world of male solidarity and commercialized leisure to the young clerk. However they may have been seen by their family at home or by their employers, young fellows such as Robinson, some in their late teens, were part of a larger group of men

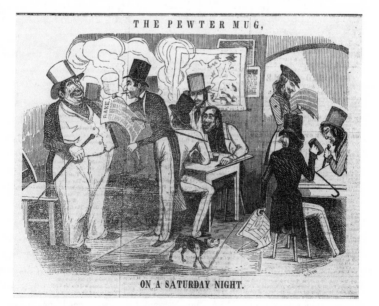

Reading and talking in a saloon. John H. Manning, "The Pewter Mug, on a Saturday Night." *Weekly Rake*, 1, no. 19 (October 22, 1842): 1. Courtesy, American Antiquarian Society.

Sporting life. This masthead is a composite of many images of sporting life by delineator John H. Manning. There are fast horses and buxom women. Two drunks sit in an open carriage, one waving a bottle, the other brandishing a whip. One man serves another a warrant. In one scene, a man in an opera box looks at a woman through binoculars; she, in turn, looks out from her opera box, as does a man in the next box. Above them all a man in a top hat with the word "po-

drinking and whoring alongside members of the working class. Sporting men, dubbed by writer Ned Buntline the "fancy men for the upper ten-thousand," were a heterogeneous group that included wealthy men on the town, college students, and young clerks. Most were single, although some married men joined them. The bachelors were a portion of the large, unmarried male population in American cities, estimated as constituting between 20 and 40 percent of men under age thirty-five.[25] What particularly troubled some observers of sporting life was that among the Bowery "nabobs" were

lice" on it leans on a ledge. In another, a large man reads a copy of *Life in Boston* as another picks his pocket. At the center, a gentleman is sitting on a sofa with two women in reclining postures, reading to them a book with the words "Paul de Kock" on the cover. At the lower left is the devilish Asmodeus. Masthead. Manning, Del[ineator,] and F. E. Worcester. *Life in Boston and the New England Police Gazette*, 2, no. 28 (April 6, 1850): 1. Courtesy, American Antiquarian Society.

young Protestant men from New England and upstate New York, really only boys, frequenting Bowery and Broadway saloons, theaters, gambling dens, boxing rings, and brothels.

They had come to New York for opportunity. Although the growth of mercantile establishments and the rise of manufacturing lessened chances for artisans, these same economic forces created positions for a new group of young men, workers with the pen who wore white collars. New England and upstate New York had many redundant young men, no longer needed on the farm. Trained in the common schools, they were literate. The sons of white Protestant farmers and tradesmen, they spoke the language of their employers and had the manners, at least superficially, of the middle class. Seeking opportunity, young men left villages and towns to come to the city with the hope of rising in the world.[26] They were supposed to be following a clear ideal. They were to work hard at their jobs and gradually learn the business so that they could advance. They were to board in a respectable boardinghouse, take their leisure in the parlors of middle-class houses, go to lectures, read for self-culture, join associations of fellowship and improvement, and attend church on Sunday. In all that they did they were supposed to be practicing habits of self-control and postures of self-command.[27]

Or so they were told by many a minister and advice-book writer. A small cottage industry of writers addressed the dangers that they faced. For example, in his *Lectures to Young Men,* Henry Ward Beecher, a son of Lyman soon to outstrip his father as one of America's most famous preachers, waxed eloquent about the evils to be encountered by a youth making his way in the world. "With his father's blessing, and his mother's tears, the young man departs from home." He is an innocent at a vulnerable moment. He "knows little of life; less of himself. He feels in his bosom the various impulses, wild desires, restless cravings he can hardly tell for what." In his path are elders eager to sway him from the path of virtue. The libertine is ready to guide him to the gaming table and the house of "the strange woman," the inmate of the brothel. Youthful companions are there to lead him astray. Troops of traveling players—minstrels—seek to educate the young from the stage, insisting that religious men have no right to keep them away. And all around are evil books and pictures. "Books are hidden in trunks, concealed in dark holes; pictures are stored in sly portfolios, or trafficked from hand to hand." Many of these evil influences come from abroad. In language that his father could have composed, Henry Ward Beecher wrote, "France, where religion long ago went out smothered in licentiousness, has flooded the world with a species of literature redolent of depravity." In fact, the novels of France and England are collectively "the common-sewers of society, into which drain the concentrated filth of the worst passions, of the worst creatures, of the worst cities." Some of these works, such as Eugène Sue's *Mysteries of Paris,* offer themselves dressed in the mantle of reform, but they are not to be trusted. And behind them are even more dangerous works. "A bookseller in a large city on the Ohio river, on being asked, of what work he sold the most, replied—'of Paul de Kock!'—the literary prince of nastiness."[28]

At moments Henry Ward Beecher seemed to think the apprentice system in which young men boarded with their employer and were governed by his family discipline was still operative. In arguing that elders have a right to determine what is best for youth, he said, "The young men are *ours;* our sons, our brothers, our wards, clerks, or apprentices; they are living in our houses, our stores, our shops, and we are their guardians, and take care of them in health, and watch them in sickness." Beecher failed to notice that this quasi-familial system was long gone. But the young men just come to the city were fully aware of its absence.[29]

Some young clerks, far from feeling unprotected, reveled in a world without masters. Had they wanted the discipline of the Protestant middle class, they might have chosen a smaller city closer to home, where merchants insisted that their employees attend church and where social mobility was clearly linked to professions of faith. But they came to New York, where anonymity was possible. They had disembarked in a world in which—at last!—they were free after hours.[30]

7

Moral Reformers

In 1836 the Helen Jewett murder trial may have caught some New Yorkers off guard, but not the leaders of the Female Moral Reform Society. As women who focused on the prostitute and her clients, the female reformers were no strangers to male sporting culture or to the dangers faced by the young clerk. Writing in the *Advocate of Moral Reform,* a twice-monthly paper, a spokeswoman for the society warned against the saloon, the gambling den, and the brothel, all of which she believed were closely linked. "Remember Robinson and his associates," she wrote. "They stand as monuments—as beacons to warn you to avoid their sins."[1]

Female moral reform was the movement that most explicitly and repeatedly engaged the sexual conversation of its time. The women who supported it had to face these essential questions: Does making knowledge about sexual matters public work for good or harm? Does ignorance protect women or male prerogatives? Its advocates were part of the larger movement of evangelical reform that swept through the Northeast with the Second Great Awakening. As they engaged in their work, they saw the world through the lens of their religious faith.

To be sure, other reforms supported by evangelical Christians bore some relation to the sexual conversation. One of the most powerful grounds for opposing Americans' high consumption of alcohol was how it relaxed men's control of their passions, unbridling their lust. Some reformers used prostitution and the brothel as markers to signify the harm of institutions inimical to freedom. Historian Ronald Walters has written of the way that sexual imagery entered into the abolitionist imagination. Antislavery advocates pictured white masters who held absolute power over black slaves freely indulging their sexual appetites. Thinking in this vein, the South became "one vast brothel," carrying both its pleasures and its dangers. Both abolition and its opposition played on the erotic possibilities of the varieties of what the age called "amalgamation," or sexual intercourse between black and white.[2]

Those opposed to Catholicism transferred absolute power from the plantation to the convent and conjured up images and stories of demonic priests turning nuns and novitiates into their sexual slaves. Such images became the staple of anti-Catholic literature and helped fuel anti-Catholic riots. Drawing on a European tradition of erotic writing surrounding the confessional and situated in places of Catholic enclosure, Maria Monk wrote and published *Awful Disclosures of the Hotel Dieu Nunnery in 1836,* aided by prominent members of the clergy, including Theodore Dwight. The writer, a Canadian unwed mother sheltered by the Montreal convent, told a fantastic brothel tale in which priests substituted for clients and mother superior for brothel madam.[3]

In New York attention came to rivet on actual prostitutes in 1831, when John R. McDowall, a young urban missionary brought to the city by the American Tract Society, issued *The Magdalen Report.* It caused a storm of criticism and touched many a sensitive nerve. Prostitution in New York City was a big business. The port of New York had long provided opportunity for commercialized sex along with its taverns and inns around the docks. By the 1820s, prostitution had spread with the population to all settled parts of Manhattan. Landlords, rich and aspiring alike, leased houses to brothel keepers and madams, aware that they were desirable tenants who could pay. There were an estimated two hundred brothels, as well as uncounted boardinghouses and houses of assignation. The greatest concentrations were in the large tenant districts: Five Points, Water Street, and Corlears Hook. But on the fashionable West Side commercialized sex was keeping pace with the new hotels and the flourishing male institutions, such as Columbia College and the College of Physicians and Surgeons, still at their early-nineteenth-century sites in lower Manhattan below Canal Street.[4]

In 1831 it was the theater that made prostitution particularly visible to many middle-class New Yorkers and visitors to the city. Streetwalkers jostled the crowds along Broadway and the Bowery. Inside the theater, actresses on stage were often confused with courtesans. In the side boxes of the third tier

NEW-YORK by GAS-LIGHT.
Hooking a Victim.

Prostitutes plying their trade. "New-York by Gas-Light: Hooking a Victim," lithograph, Serrell and Perkins, c. 1850. Gift of Karl Schmidt. © Museum of the City of New York.

of even the most respectable theaters, such as the Park, prostitutes were allowed to seek clients. Many entrepreneurial madams located their brothels nearby to service both actors and theater patrons.[5]

McDowall was a ministerial student who had come to the city from Princeton at the behest of Arthur Tappan, Anson G. Phelps, and Thomas Stokes to work in the American Tract Society's New York City missions. McDowall felt a call and did not return to Princeton. His primary concern was the young men of the city whose lives and souls were endangered by prostitutes. In *The Magdalen Report* McDowall expressed his sense that although men are the seducers of women who, abandoned, turn to prostitution, these "women take their revenge an hundred fold." Men seduce virgins, but "bad women multiply the seduction of heedless youth, more rapidly than bad men seduce modest women. A few of these courtesans suffice to corrupt whole cities, and there can be no doubt that some insinuating prostitutes have initiated more young men into these destructive ways, than the most abandoned rakes have debauched virgins during their whole lives." Change must begin with arresting and reclaiming "those wretched females, who are the pest and nuisance of society."[6]

Although McDowall's exposé had plenty of rakes and villains who destroyed the flower of young womanhood, the primary figure in McDowall's account is the male victim. Harlots prey upon youth—"young men, clerks, apprentices, etc." More than half of their clients come from "silly and inexperienced youth" lured by "these infatuating furies, whose syren song lulls conscience to sleep." The youth rob in order to pay for their visits to prostitutes. Each prostitute has three customers a day. McDowall's math leads him to estimate that New York prostitutes have ten million visits a year. Five million dollars alone go for liquor and other extras, in addition to paying for the prostitutes' services. "But what is all this waste of wealth compared with the ruin of the generation of young men, and the destruction of female purity?"[7]

The Magdalen Report estimated that in New York City, with roughly a quarter-million souls, there were ten thousand prostitutes and a large, perhaps equal number of private harlots composed of women in domestic service who met men in houses of assignation. (While this figure is clearly too high, most observers regarded the city's official estimate of 1,438 as far too low.)[8] The women in the report ranged from the girl seduced, abandoned, and forced into a life of prostitution to the experienced, wanton whore to the cold-blooded female brothel owner running a business. The women's economic and social origins differed. At the center of McDowall's portrait was the archetypal country girl of prosperous and pious parents brought to her ruin by a rake. There were also the urban daughter of a poor widow lured to the brothel to work as a maid, kidnapped, drugged, and enslaved; and the wife of a drunken husband forced to prostitute herself to support her children. In addition to these victims, there were the "daughters of the ignorant, depraved and vicious part of our population, trained up without culture of any kind, amidst the contagion of evil example, and [who] enter upon a life of prostitution for the gratification of their unbridled passions, and become harlots altogether by choice."[9]

Throughout his report McDowall hinted that he knew much more than he told. "Indeed enough is in our possession," he wrote, "to cause a thrill of horror to be felt by every virtuous man and women in the community, such as was never produced by any expose of vice which has ever met the public eye. Did not prudence and delicacy forbid the disgusting detail of what has been brought to our knowledge . . . every parent would tremble for the safety of his sons as well as his daughters, and we could a tale disclose which would cause the blood 'to chill within the veins . . .' " Included in his knowledge were the names and addresses of brothels and houses of assignation, some in respectable neighborhoods, behind doors with brass plates. Through the police, informing prostitutes, and the "vigilance" of the society, "we have arrived at very many of the secrets of these nests of abomination, the number of lewd women who reside, or resort to each, the arts and intrigues by which the victims of seduction are procured, as well as the names of scores of the men and boys, who are the seducers of the innocent, or the companions of the polluted."[10]

McDowall's report caused immediate outcries. On August 20, 1831, a group of indignant men met at Tammany Hall and passed resolutions demanding proof of the report and asserting "that we will not rest until these base slanderers be punished." In early September, they met again and adopted resolutions as a people's tribunal that denounced the Magdalen committee as "traitors against their country" who had "forfeited their rights as citizens." In these men's minds, the Magdalen reformers were part of a larger conspiracy formed by the Bible, tract, missionary, and temperance societies. McDowall believed his opposition to be disciples of Frances Wright and the Hall of Science. In language that would have done Lyman Beecher proud, McDowall asserted that the freethinkers were bringing the deistic origins of the French Revolution and its Terror to American shores. More secularly, McDowall announced that their fulminations against him warned of the "smothered volcano that threatens the very existence of the social compact."[11]

There is no evidence that the Tammany audience involved the freethinkers, although the latter certainly opposed McDowall's tractarian supporters across the street. The *Free Enquirer*'s only comment on *The Magdalen Report* was to note that Christian doctrine had not reformed New York men. Who did oppose McDowall? At one point the reformer accused the *Courier and Enquirer* of encouraging an artist to portray him "in various obscene pictures," which could be seen "in the windows of certain bookstores, shops, and lottery-offices" and were "hawked" at the August meeting.[12] This would not have been James Watson Webb's newspaper, one of the expensive Wall Street subscription papers. One possibility is the *Hawk and Buzzard*, edited by John W. Ely, which sometimes advertised itself as the *Evening Star* or the *Courier and Enquirer*. This weekly sheet, sold at taverns and public houses in

New York, focused on the petty vices of its artisanal audience. On occasion it contained sexually provocative woodcuts that to the eye of a McDowall would have been "obscene." If this were the source of the "obscene pictures," then the heart of McDowall's opposition was in the artisanal community of New York, some of the same men who were deeply opposed to Robert Dale Owen and his advocacy of birth control.[13]

Both Owen and McDowall faced men who saw their efforts through the lens of male vernacular sexual culture. In the light of this sexual framework, contraceptive information threatened to give women knowledge that would turn wives and daughters into prostitutes. A sharp division separated the domestic women within a man's home from promiscuous whores outside. From the perspective of male vernacular culture, part of the system of control of a paterfamilias was prostitution. It provided a sexual outlet for all men that protected their own daughters and wives. Prostitution was, as their handbill stated, "A necessary evil in all great cities, particularly in seaports."[14]

McDowall faced another opposition, and this proved beyond his powers. When he presented his *Magdalen Facts* in 1832, he spoke of the effort to silence him from a different quarter. There were those who suggested that "the exposure is indelicate, and deleterious to morals, and should not be made, if true." While these opponents might agree that the cause was just, they "express great sorrow for what they call the injudicious procedure of those who passibly may have meant well, but egregiously erred in the measures they adopted to secure their ends." Although McDowall in this instance did not quote, the language sounds like a paraphrase of his more respectable adversaries, older members of the middle class who, whatever their own sexual practices and economic ties, opposed prostitution rhetorically.[15]

McDowall threatened to expose the men who consorted with prostitutes or who profited by brothel business or real estate. When the young reformer created a weekly newspaper, *McDowall's Journal,* to continue along the lines of the 1831 report, he unleashed a new chorus of criticism. The *Courier* called it an "infamous bawdy chronicle" whose details were calculated to "poison" the imagination of the "virtuous females" among its readers and "make them adepts in all the mysteries of human corruption." The *Commercial Advertiser* declared that "under the pretence of reforming mankind," the journal—"a sort of Directory of Iniquity—a brothel companion," actually "excites the imagination of youth by the most glowing pictures of sensual debaucheries." In 1834 a New York grand jury judged that the journal was "calculated to promote lewdness." The Third Presbytery of New York convicted McDowall of using funds donated to the society illegally, corrupting public morals, and committing other acts "too bad to name."[16]

In opposing McDowall's writings, accusers questioned his motives. They charged that just as his writings were prurient, his efforts were suspect. Was he, as he claimed, a pure-hearted reformer? Or was he, in fact, a man both repelled by and drawn to the world of prostitution, a man skirting the edge? Such questions haunted prostitution reform as it would haunt later efforts to rid the society of obscene materials.

When these questions and condemnation came, McDowall's male supporters dropped him. Under his leadership, tractarians and other male reformers had formed the Magdalen Society in New York City and opened its "House of Refuge." They focused their original efforts on saving souls, hoping to rescue fallen women who were capable of being touched by faith and restored to society. Evangelical women, profoundly moved by Finney's revivals, were drawn in. When the male reformers withdrew, McDowall's female supporters remained loyal and regrouped. Perhaps they had less to lose than the men. Perhaps the business and practice of prostitution touched them more deeply. In 1834 they founded the New York Female Moral Reform Society, committed to a broad agenda of sexual purity. Lydia Andrews Finney, the wife of the revivalist, took the position of directress, and female leadership was in Finneyite hands. The society continued to support McDowall in his missionary work among prostitutes and, after his death in 1836, sent paid workers and volunteers, male and female, into brothels to pray over female boarders and embarrass their customers. With the failure of the House of Refuge to reform prostitutes, the society closed the house in 1836 and redirected its attention to prevention. The society attempted to aid young women to find employment to keep them from being driven to prostitution by want. Members also visited families to offer moral guidance.[17]

Most important for this study, the society developed and published a critique of contemporary sexual mores with their toleration of male lechery. When the Third Presbytery advised that *McDowall's Journal* should cease publishing, the women chose to carry on McDowall's work. In 1835 the New York Female Moral Reform Society took over his journal and issued the *Advocate of Moral Reform* to his list of subscribers. Women now both wrote and edited this twice-monthly paper. As they visited houses of prostitution with McDowall and other missionaries, they reported the stories that the women told them. They took as their motto this passage from Luke 12:2:

For there is nothing covered that shall not be revealed:
Neither hid, that shall not be made known.[18]

By 1837 the paper had 16,500 subscribers, many of whom were members of the society's auxiliary organizations in New England or upstate New York.

The principal intention of these female moral reformers was to change notions of sexual morality. In the language of the following century, they sought to end the double standard. If women fell because of sexual intercourse before or outside marriage, so did men. If fallen women were to be shunned by the morally upright, then so should fallen men. One should not allow the male libertine to enter a respectable parlor. Women should demand of unmarried men the same moral purity—i.e., virginity—that men demand of unmarried women. In an effort to protect their sons from sexual dangers and misdeeds, mothers should teach them the same lessons that they taught their daughters. Included in their concern was the young man come to the city.

The advocates' work taught them that prostitutes did not want to be reformed. Once a woman had taken up the life, she was lost to all entreaties. In acknowledging the failure to uplift fallen women, the advocates made the object of their efforts not the prostitute but the male who engaged her. McDowall had seen him as the harlot's victim; to the women, he was the prime evildoer. The advocates understood that they were engaged in the battle for public opinion. Their journal intended to "call public attention to the vice of licentiousness, and aid in forming such a public sentiment as will banish this vice from the community." When critics stated that they vested too much power in "representing *public opinion* as an engine of such mighty power in accomplishing any work of reform," the advocates retorted, "God does not advance his cause by miracles. It is by the operation of truth on men's minds, leading them to form correct opinions and act upon them." The journal planned to support the work of building auxiliary societies throughout the land. Although men, not women, were the primary source of the problem, men refused to do the work of reform, and thus it fell to women advocates to organize and write. As they presented the journal, the new editors took note of the changes: "We shall take pains to present to our readers the career of licentious men rather than women," with facts to "not serve as a lure, but as a warning." From the start they threatened to expose names. Although cautious in proceeding at first, in time they did so.[19]

Along with stories of the rake in the pages of the *Advocate of Moral*

Reform are tales of the clerk, stories of young men gone wrong. One such story was of the well-born and educated "Henry F———." Deciding on a mercantile life, he became a clerk. He entered into the world of his fellow clerks, who spent all day working in the office of their employer but "each night in visiting the haunts of dissipation, crime and debauchery: dissipating at the Theatre, the Gaming Houses, and the Brothel, their lives and souls away in licentious mirth." Joining them outside working hours, Henry met a beautiful woman with the "semblance of virtue," and she captured him. "Sensual passion and indulgence" led him to alcohol and gambling, the path to ruin. Although his parents and friends urged his return to them and moral-ity, he was lost. "A force like that of the whirlwind had swept across him, and prostrated every moral attribute of his character." Diseased and out of work, he committed suicide.[20]

A male writer to the newspaper, himself a clerk, told readers of the dan-gers of the theater for such as he: "The man who murdered Helen Jewett got his exhalted ideas in this school for *scandal*." Employed on Pearl Street in Mr. Dunham's establishment, this clerk wrote in a manner that viscerally con-veyed the scene of the street. He tried to demonstrate the way that the theater entered into the imagination of the young clerks. When their employers are present, "common decency and common sense will keep their eyes on their books and bills," but not so when they are unsupervised. "Let any observer," he writes, "take a stroll among the retail stores in Broadway, or wholesale stores in Pearl street, between the hours of three and four, when their employers and customers are gone to dinner, and you will there see many of them standing in knots, the quill behind their ears, the bales, the bills, the day-book and ledger, all unstrung, while they are comparing notes about Madam Celeste's dancing, Miss Tree's playing, or Mrs. Flynn's jumping, &c."[21]

If the women who wrote and edited the *Advocate of Moral Reform* com-posed their paper in the basement of 149 Nassau Street, they were in the very neighborhood where the young clerks gathered. While gentlemen may have gambled on Broadway, the younger fellows congregated in establishments on Ann and Fulton Streets or the Bowery. As one of their writers wrote, "Into these are ushered, night after night, scores of the youth of our city, who are tempted to drink, and taught to swear, to lie, and to gamble." These fellows were "apprentices and clerks, and the sons of respectable parents."[22]

From the advocates' perspective, the responsibility for the emerging sporting culture lay directly with employers who refused to be bothered. After a young man from the country secures a job with a merchant, the older man "takes no farther notice of him than to direct his services." Lonely in his boardinghouse, the young clerk begins to talk to fellows around him, and they initiate him into the institutions of their society. Thus he is brought to "the gate of ruin," the brothel. How can this be prevented? The advocates urged that the employer take a kindly interest in his clerks, not as his equals, but as his "dependents and moral beings." He ought to warn them about the dangers they face, give them the means of education, such as access to a library, take them to church, and receive them in his home, where his wife could provide suitable female influence.[23]

It was the advocates' hope that women could reshape the culture. They knew that they had one unquestionable resource: their own children. Mothers needed to be direct with their sons. The advocates printed approvingly the tale of a mother who spoke to her son directly: "She did not hesitate to explain to him the true import of the 7th commandment. She did not *pass over* it, while she explained the rest, but told him plainly what it meant." These reformers believed that by teaching a son about adultery, a mother strengthened him against the temptations that were to come, allowing him to win out over them in his later life.[24]

The advocates faced some of the same criticism as McDowall. Were they, through their publication, giving youths information that might lead to their corruption? Did, as their critics argued, "moral reform efforts tend to debase and corrupt the mind, by the familiarity with vice which they necessarily occasion"? What ought to be the limits of sexual knowledge? These women shared the creed of those writing against masturbation: ignorance, not knowledge, was the danger. "For fear of corrupting the youth, the youth are so much corrupted," was how one writer put it. Advocates tended not to believe in childhood innocence. One woman wrote that after teaching for four years she had learned that "the minds of children are not so pure as many imagine. I have been astonished, O, my heart has bled, to see how familiar the minds of little children were, not only with impure thoughts and words, but with vicious practices."[25]

Many of the words in the *Advocate of Moral Reform* described females, not males, exploring the narratives of the road to ruin or offering advice and warning to young women. Writers gave particular attention to the country girl who, seduced and abandoned, turned to prostitution. In many of the stories they told, class privilege allowed men of higher social standing to gain sexual advantage over the women or girls they pursued through intimidation, the promise of material reward, or the power of prestige. The economic crisis of 1837 heightened the danger that self-employed women faced. How were women thrown out of work to live? Would they be forced into prostitution? "The seducer is already abroad among some of them."[26] The women persisted in the practice begun by McDowall in his journal of publishing letters that identified men (through their initials and locations) who seduced girls or patronized prostitutes. They broadcast their message widely through New England and the "burnt over district" of upstate New York, where they had many auxiliary members.

When the advocates faced race, however, deep prejudice clouded their understanding of the issue of power in sexual relations. As for many in their era, interracial sex was a particular abomination. Thus the villain in this drama tended to be unstable. Although on occasion the journal decried white men preying on black women in the city, the advocates also turned the white man into the quarry of the black Jezebel. For example, in warning Christian parents not to let their sons go south, they wrote about the temptations that youth faced in boardinghouses, where they were visited by loose women. "Many Northern parents have colored grandchildren at the South!"[27]

Insisting on the right to discuss prostitution allowed advocates to break the silence regarding venereal diseases, both a terrible reality in the period and a deep fear among women and men. They criticized newspaper editors for accepting advertisements from those promising cures for what were as yet incurable diseases. In 1837 a writer located venereal disease on foreign shores as an affliction among Greeks and Turks but stated that it was coming to America. A sea captain and his wife and children arrived "tainted . . . with a distemper," the marks of venereal disease visible on their person.[28] Although willing to mention venereal disease, when the advocates reported the death agonies of prostitutes, their illnesses went unnamed.

Advocates offered advice to women negotiating the city. As they advised about risks, they warned women to dress in a way to avoid attracting seducers. They criticized what they saw on New York City streets. Respectable women, they wrote, seemed to wear markers of the loose and abandoned. They appeared on a public way as if they were in a drawing room, wearing ornaments, thin stockings, and dancing shoes and exposing open necks. They dressed "as if on purpose to gratify the passions of men who make it a practice of walking up and down, at least once a day." An author suggested that women should never wear low-necked dresses, asserting that "men will not attack" if they are not given encouragement by a woman.[29]

At the outset of the enterprise, the journal listed the causes behind the

wicked behavior of men and the seduction of women. Men became predators and women their victims because of "want of suitable instruction while
young, the perusal of improper books, plays, &c., that tend to corrupt the
morals, inflame the imagination, and excite the passions; improper amusements, such as balls and theatres; improper associations, and an ignorance of
the wiles of the crafty seducer." All of this set the scene and predisposed the
actors. Thus the advocates agreed with the reform physiologists that the root
of the problem was the sexual culture of the age—the language and images
of conversation, literature, and the theater.[30]

In the issues that followed, the *Advocate of Moral Reform* elaborated. First
and last, they argued, the theater was a particularly dangerous influence. Not
only was it the site of sexual encounters with prostitutes and actresses of
dubious reputation, its representations on the stage were sexually arousing.
Madame Celeste, for example, could be seen dancing "almost *unclothed,* and
throwing herself into attitudes, not only immodest but shameful." Literature also held particular perils. The advocates quoted a minister who warned
about the corruption of the press and the printed page. Could a man respect
"a female familiar with the writings of Byron?" they asked, and then added,
"Almost the whole of our literature is contaminated." In warning young
women to shun indecent books, "such as contain indelicate allusions, double
entendres, sly inuendoes," an author condemned most popular literature,
adding, "How many females can trace their ruin and degradation to the reading of novels and plays?" Reading Frances Wright was a particular danger.
One article told the story of a married woman whose husband, a skeptic in
religion, gave her the "pernicious writings" of Wright. In her husband's
absence, the woman took up with a younger man and bore his illegitimate
child. Divorced now from her husband, who had since remarried, she was
raising the child at the home of her parents. Here was a clear warning against
wrong reading.[31]

Even the games of children were not safe. Blindman's bluff allowed boys
and girls to fondle one another, hide-and-seek put them in dark rooms, in
playing forfeits they kissed. Yet at the same time as they issued such warnings, the advocates were made aware of the danger of the opposite tendency.
One letter writer warned that middle-class reserve was becoming so great
that it turned boys and men away from the parlor. The writer suggested that
men consorted with prostitutes because seeking the company of virtuous
ladies involved "disagreeable and useless formality. It is very often too
starched and reserved and accompanied by repulsive ceremoniousness."

Sexual representation on the stage (note that the two viewers in the
audience are holding the New York *Herald* and *Sober Thoughts*). "Lola
Has Come!" Lithograph, mid–nineteenth century, author's collection.

Wanting a more informal world of men and women in which visiting was
not perceived as courtship, the writer also warned against separate education
for boys and girls. This was, however, an unusual countervoice in a journal
devoted to raising standards of propriety.[32]

In criticizing the world around them, these women were not cut off
from the culture. Their journal reprinted stories from New York City newspapers, such as the *Sun* and the *Transcript,* telling of seduction and rape. In an
unusual admission for the evangelically minded, a writer stated, "We have
long felt that some of the daily penny papers are doing a good work in favor
of moral reform, by their praiseworthy disclosures of vice in their police
report." They criticized, however, the practice in these papers of publishing
the names of women, but not of men.[33]

In discussing the world of prostitution, the female writers of the *Advocate* demonstrated a good deal of knowledge about theaters and brothels in

New York. One article identified the different social groups in the various tiers of the theater, castigating the middle class in the boxes for being willing to associate with the rough men of the pit and the prostitutes and their customers in the gallery. It charged that the theaters allowed harlots to enter without charge "as baits" to attract the young clerks, who buy tickets "even though they receive only salaries enough to pay their board bills." In relating the story of a man from the country who was duped when he came to the city and sought amusement, the *Advocate* printed a report from the *Sun* about the establishment of Mary Cisco, a brothel madam married to Frank Berry, the proprietor of a gambling den. Celebrated as the Duchess de Berri, Cisco loomed large in the imagination of sporting men.[34]

Moreover, when the advocates discussed issues, they revealed their engagement in intellectual subjects of their day. For example, they used the term "amativeness" in the manner of the phrenologists. As they censured America as a sexual hothouse, they employed the language of reform physiology. For example, one advocate spoke out against "double entendres," which she defined as "seemingly decent speeches with double meaning." She stated that it prevailed in some places "to an alarming degree." Although parents regarded it as harmless and men and women both used it, children understood what was being said, and the words led to impure thoughts. The writer continued, "I have been in families where these loose insinuations, and coarse inuendoes were so common, that the presence of respectable company scarcely operated as a restraint upon the unbridled tongues even of the parents!"[35]

As they wrote about the arguments of seducers seeking to convince young virgins to succumb to their desires, the language that they quoted disapprovingly bears some of the marks of Frances Wright and anticipates arguments within the free-love community. For example, the advocates quoted a letter from a young woman writing from upstate New York who gave the reasoning of those attempting to seduce her. She wrote that they had told her that there was no harm in sex outside marriage, for "marriage was nothing but an agreement between two persons" and "God had given them passions, and it was not wrong to indulge them."[36] The teachings of evangelical Protestantism formed the advocates' answer to such a letter. Christianity was for them the only hope of purifying the world. In their pages the advocates discussed ministers' sermons, many approvingly. They agreed with Lyman Beecher that skepticism was a grave danger. Yet they were also critical of men such as Beecher who did not join their cause.

The female moral reformers were accused of the stain of knowledge and of bad associations. Critics forced them to answer the question: Is "knowledge of the nature and statistics of any vice sufficient to enable us to oppose it . . . dangerous to the sensibilities and morals of those concerned in its opposition"? As they faced the dangers to their "refinement and delicacy," they found courage in their deep religious faith and sense of mission. Just as they could enter the sickroom and remain well, so did they go about their work of reform and keep themselves unsullied. They did claim male protection from one source of annoyance, however—the anonymous letters "full of the lowest vulgarity and abuse" that came to their office. They did not read them, letting their male business officer open them to make certain that the female advocates never saw anything "not perfectly proper to be read by ladies." Criticized that females should not engage in such work, they answered, "In great moral questions like this, we *must* claim the privilege of thinking and acting for ourselves."[37]

Neither infallible nor perfect, they admitted that they might have made mistakes for which they could expect some censure: "We may sometimes have been betrayed into what would seem unkind, intemperate, or even indelicate language."[38] Unlike for McDowall, however, censure never came through a court indictment. It may well have been that the advocates' gender shielded them. Or perhaps their language was not as "indelicate" as they imagined, at least in relation to that of others. By the late 1830s and early 1840s, new voices were entering the conversation in print about prostitution in New York City, and they were intentionally much rougher.

8

The Sporting Weeklies and Obscene Libel

One way to look at the many words about sex in and outside New York in the 1830s is to see them in an emerging and multifaceted conversation. Free-thinkers confronted evangelicals, reform physiologists worried about mas-turbation, and moral reformers focused on rakes and harlots. In the late 1830s and early 1840s, a new group of writers joined these contenders. These new-comers were men who came from the theatrical world and penny press, not Princeton and the Protestant ministry. Although on occasion they stated moral objectives reminiscent of John McDowall's, they were open players in the prostitutes' world—clients, lovers, and advocates. As participants in male sporting life, they saw the literate young men around them as opportunities. These writers made no secret of their motives: to sell their words for money. To that end they wrote for sporting men about sexual matters in language known in their day as "racy." Between 1841 and 1843, they created the weekly sporting press.[1]

The *Sunday Flash* began publication in New York in early August 1841. Hawked on the street for six cents, it was a sheet of four folio pages that announced itself as "A weekly journal, devoted to Awful Developments, Dreadful Accidents and Unexpected Exposures; Doings about Town, Doings on the Road, in the Ring and on the Turf; the whole of which will be detailed with all the Horror, Satire, Sagacity, Humeur, Experience, and Fun, neces-sary for the proper treatment of those important subjects." It was brought out by "Scorpion, Startle, and Sly, Editors and Proprietors," pseudonyms of William Joseph Snelling, George Wilkes, and George B. Wooldridge.[2]

Addressed to literate males, who included young clerks in the city, it offered a witty and titillating brew of gossip about New York prostitutes, news of the theatrical world, prizefight intelligence, and clever woodcuts. The weekly spawned imitators—the *Whip,* the *Rake,* and the *Libertine.* Brought to the attention of the courts by libel suits, the *Flash* and its competitors were prosecuted for obscenity under the common law of obscene libel and were driven from the field within two years. Short-lived in their original incarnation, something of their spirit reemerged in many sporting weeklies throughout the country and in the *National Police Gazette,* the long-lived creation of George Wilkes.

The papers of the early 1840s shared an interest in the leisure pursuits of sporting men in the city, both their pleasures and their dangers. An author began a piece describing a prizefight with these telling words, "Knowing your desire to obtain all the important movements in the flash and sporting circles."[3] Characteristically, on their middle and back pages the weeklies carried news of fistic competitions, reviews and notices of theatrical productions, and ads for places of eating and drinking as well as patent medicines. Page 1 was given over to stories and accompanying woodcuts of the exploits of celebrities, and to the lives of felons, some of them many times warmed over. From the outset the weekly featured reports of wrongdoers, usually on the first or second page, and occasionally illustrated. For example, the *Sunday Flash* gave special place to its "Gallery of Rascalities and Notorieties" and had a regular feature, "Ancient Pistols," treating historic or contemporary felons. Threading in between and all around were reports about prostitutes, brothel keepers, and their clients.

As Peter Holmes and Charles Knowlton learned in Massachusetts, courts could interfere with the business of selling words and images about sex. In the small world of New York City in the early 1840s, ideological and personal issues helped bring the editors of the new sporting press into court and shaped the outcomes of their trials. Judges faced a new situation, the explosion of print in the daily penny press and the weekly papers, broadcasting sex as news and contesting the outcomes to trials in their columns. Those involved in the justice system had real questions about how far the press ought to go. What were the press's rights? What were its responsibilities? What limits should be set on its representations of sex?

New York judges and juries worked in a particularly important locale. The city was the site of the movement that ultimately led to federal legislation in 1873 and was the locus of the court that got and sustained federal

SUNDAY FLASH.

VOL. I....NO. 11. | "An Abstract and brief Chronicle of the Time." | PRICE 6 CENTS.

Scorpion, Startle & Sly,   NEW YORK, SUNDAY, OCTOBER 17, 1841.   Editors and Proprietors.

GALLERY OF RASCALITIES AND NOTORIETIES.—No. 2.

"THAT'S A DEM FINE GAL!"

convictions in 1879. Court practices that began at the local level in the trials of the sporting press in 1842 helped shape those of the federal court in 1879. Thus the early cases of the sporting press are not merely interesting narratives, they served as legal precedents shaping what was to come. Finally, one hears in them an oppositional voice. Weak in the beginning, this resistance in the 1840s to the common law of obscene libel began a critical adversarial tradition in the United States that in the twentieth century led to successful challenges to court practices and to federal and state laws dealing with obscenity.

As in many court conflicts, the issues in the early 1840s were not clean and tidy. The first sporting paper emerged out of controversies surrounding the death of the young actress Louisa Missouri, controversies that still swirled around the courtroom when the paper's owners were indicted for obscenity. Involved in the disputes were many issues beyond sexuality,

Two prostitutes in a dance contest, as imagined by a contemporary delineator. "Grand Trial Dance Between Nance Holmes and Suse Bryant, on Long Wharf, Boston," John H. Manning, delineator, Robert H. Elton, publisher. *Whip and Satirist*, 1, no. 27 (June 25, 1842): 1. Courtesy, American Antiquarian Society.

obscenity, suppression, and rights. In the sporting press cases, it mattered to judges and prosecutors where a defendant stood in the theater wars, whether racy speech was connected to disrespect for authority, even whether anti-Semitism was involved. Attending to these specifics will require a detailed narrative of the conflicts surrounding Miss Missouri, but first, the literary precedents of America's first sporting weeklies demand attention.

I

Before the American sporting weeklies there were an English original, a pamphlet about prostitution in New York, gossipy weeklies intended for male artisans in the city, and the *Polyanthos*. American writers had a clear model in the *Town*, begun in London in 1837. Much about the New York weeklies imitated this English paper—regular columns, subject matter, vocabulary, and engraved images on page 1. The London and New York papers took as their central subjects the world of prostitution, public houses, the ring, and theaters. The American version differed, for it could not play against titled birth or in one instance what the *Town* called "the real racy, spicy admixture of aristocratic morality." What took its place in the American sporting press were gossip and invective directed against players in the theatrical world, rival newspapers and their reporters, and ultimately one another.[4]

In 1839 a pamphlet writer, who took the coarse pseudonym "A Butt Ender," published a guide to prostitutes in the city, *Prostitution Exposed*. It pretended to be a moral reform tract, but its real purpose was entertainment and information. It conveyed a basic acceptance of commercial sex, despite occasional moralistic statements. The most significant element of the pamphlet is its tone, what one author has called its *"knowingness—the desire not so much to know, but to be one of those who are in the know, who are wise to the world."* It offered to the male reader paths to navigate the city without being taken or being embarrassed as a greenhorn. Even a fellow who stayed at home or in his boardinghouse could fantasize a sophisticated entry into a brothel parlor. Its printed page allowed him to partake of an imagined identity as a sporting man.[5]

Prior to the *Town* or *Prostitution Exposed*, however, were two interesting papers, New York weeklies sold to men in taverns and public houses. Historians of the New York press have focused attention on the penny dailies, the newcomers on the block that grew to be the big fish. But alongside them were some small fry, largely unstudied but of interest in the emergence of commercial erotic writing in the United States. In the early 1830s, two weeklies were sold at taverns and public houses: the *Hawk and Buzzard* and the *Owl*. Both largely consisted of purported letters written to the paper by indignant New York artisans seeking to expose a wrong, threaten a malefactor, or merely complain.

The papers addressed a male audience, for there were letters about theatergoing, prostitution, and the sexual misdeeds of others. There were occasional complaints against rude whores. Occasionally men of property got rough treatment. At one point, for example, the editor of the *Hawk* wrote that he was arranging a list in alphabetical order of "gentlemen of this city who hire houses and devote a large portion of their time and money to kept mistresses." To personal vilification, these weeklies added gossip about sexual behavior designed to titillate and, most likely, written as blackmail threats. Two unusual articles employed black-dialect humor to attack Frances Wright.[6]

In New York blackface entertainment was emerging as the minstrel show in theaters catering to working-class men. Historian Eric Lott has argued that early white performers of the minstrel were urban northerners of a particular stripe. Bred outside New England, they rejected its emphasis on moral, temperate manhood to create alternative personae in blackface. In their performances at the Chatham and Bowery Theatres, white performers in blackface created sexually expressive characters. Such male portrayals needed female foils capable of playing their game without full agency. The words of Frances Wright and assertions of rights by other women threatened to destabilize this male world of racial and sexual fantasy. In facing this symbolic enemy, the primary weapon was ridicule.[7]

Close to the bright lights of minstrelsy the sporting press came into being. Its writers seldom took on Fanny Wright so directly, and when her name was mentioned it was only to imply that women who read or advocated her ideas were sexually promiscuous.[8] In 1838 George Washington Dixon, a blackface entertainer, joined with a writer, William Joseph Snelling, to create the *Polyanthos,* a short-lived weekly "devoted to Popular Tales, History, Legends and Adventures, Anecdotes, Poetry, Satire, Humour, Sporting, and the Drama." Dixon was the originator of the character Zip Coon, the black urban northern dandy. Born in Richmond, Virginia, around 1801, Dixon began singing "Coal Black Rose" in blackface in 1829 in New York theaters, including the Chatham and the Bowery. In the riots against abolitionists and blacks that broke out in New York in July 1834, it was Dixon who was called in to sing Zip Coon as a way to quell the crowd at the Bowery Theatre. In the years that followed, Dixon tried to reposition himself in the middle class as a writer and editor, but he had neither the character nor the wit to succeed. During this time he was constantly in trouble with the law for petty crimes of theft and forgery and in and out of jail, and his publications hardly met the codes of middle-class respectability.[9]

Dixon had likely known Snelling in Boston, where, a few years earlier, both had been writers down on their luck and in jail. William Joseph Snelling, a writer with claims to a pedigree but a misspent life, was an unlikely ally of the creator of Zip Coon. Born in Boston in 1804, the son of a noted Indian fighter and the founder of Fort Snelling in Minnesota, the younger Snelling's independence of mind could not be tamed at West Point, and he became a trapper and miner. He wrote satirical verse, for which he is best remembered today, and *Tales of the Northwest,* a collection of short stories dealing with Native Americans, highly regarded for its accurate portray-

George Washington Dixon as Zip Coon. Courtesy, Harvard Theatre Collection, The Houghton Library.

als. He returned to the East, took part in the founding of the American Anti-Slavery Society, and became editor of the *New England Galaxy*, a lively weekly of literature and public affairs. In April 1833 he began a campaign against gambling in Boston and found himself the subject of libel indictments. By the mid-1830s, Snelling hit rock bottom and, as he put it, turned to drink out of "utter despair." Condemned to prison in Boston for public drunkenness, he felt his "reputation . . . blasted, . . . pride crushed, . . . hopes extinguished." Snelling left Boston for New York. Talented but wayward, he emerged in the city as coeditor, with Dixon, of the *Polyanthos*. Most likely, Snelling was the weekly's chief writer.[10]

Unlike the *Owl* and the *Hawk and Buzzard*, which focused on the petty vices of their working-class audience, the *Polyanthos* was a more varied publication with literary aspirations. Snelling was an experienced wordsmith with wide-ranging interests. Moreover, the weekly sought to appeal to the middle class. Casting itself somewhat as the upholder of virtue in the mold of the *Advocate of Moral Reform*, the paper took on a wide range of miscreants—elite libertines, the enemies of Dixon and Snelling in the theatrical and writing world, and Madame Restell, the subject of the following chapter. Although Dixon may never have written the material that appeared under his name, he did have to take the fall as revelations of the sexual misdeeds of prominent elite men in the *Polyanthos* mired him in libel suits and again sent him to jail. The *Polyanthos* ceased publication for six months. Dixon resumed his volatile ways and, on November 19, 1841, was charged with publishing an obscene paper.[11]

Ultimately a true villain emerged on the pages of the *Polyanthos*: Thomas S. Hamblin, the actor and owner of the Bowery Theatre. In 1838 Dixon accused him of causing, directly or indirectly, the death of the beautiful young actress Louisa Missouri. Adelina Miller, the ingenue's mother, turned to Dixon and Snelling to tell her story in their weekly. Miller was a well-known madam of a New York brothel.[12] For years Hamblin had provoked public scandal by having open sexual relationships with women he employed in his theater. Hamblin had proven peculiarly dangerous to young women seeking to become protégées, and one had died in childbed in his house three years earlier.[13]

Louisa Missouri had received a fine education that included three years at the Emma Willard School in Troy, one of the great academies for girls. When she decided on the stage, she trained carefully in dance, music, elocution, and drama under New York's best teachers. Her sister Josephine Clifton was a well-regarded actress on the New York stage. When Missouri tried to follow her at age sixteen, Clifton advised her to shun the patronage of Hamblin, who had been a source of embarrassment in her own past. Disregarding her sister's advice, Missouri went to Hamblin for "elocution lessons." In March and April 1838, she made her theatrical debut in Hamblin productions at James W. Wallack's National Theatre. Her mother, determined to protect her, kept her under watch in her house. Using *Herald* reporter William H. Attree as an intermediary, on Sunday, May 27, 1838, the girl turned to the courts for protection against her mother and escaped. It was difficult for Adelina Miller to regain her daughter through the courts because of her well-known occupation as brothel madam, and Nelson Miller, her son and a lawyer, applied for legal custody of his sister. It was denied and given to a police magistrate, widely assumed to be a proxy for Hamblin. Nelson Miller published a statement about Missouri's "abduction" in the *Herald*. Unable to get redress in the courts, he turned to direct action. On Saturday, June 16, he was arrested for threatening Hamblin's life.[14]

Fear about Louisa Missouri's safety was well grounded. While Nelson Miller was in jail, pending bail, his young sister died suddenly in Hamblin's house. A postmortem exonerated Hamblin by determining that she had died of natural causes, and in keeping with its support of Hamblin, the *Herald* released the postmortem in his defense. Hamblin's enemies, however, were neither convinced nor appeased. Adelina Miller believed that her daughter had been poisoned by Louisa Medina, the playwright and author of many of Hamblin's dramas. The outraged mother later gathered a mob at Hamblin's door, causing him to fear for his own life. Nelson Miller could not get a hearing. The *Herald* and other established penny papers refused to print his letter setting out his version. He found a sympathetic organ in the *Polyanthos,* and with that, Dixon and Snelling linked their fate to his.[15]

As the *Polyanthos* took up Nelson and Adelina Miller's cause, Snelling demonstrated that he had a capacity for invective equal to any writer in the penny press. Hamblin went after Dixon, not Snelling, and beat him up. When Dixon was arrested for libel following his exposure of the sexual misconduct of two other elite men, Adelina Miller put up his extraordinarily high bail of $9,000.

The battle over Louisa Missouri was still raging in early August 1841, when Snelling broke with Dixon and joined with George B. Wooldridge and George Wilkes to issue the first *Sunday Flash*. Wooldridge was the young proprietor of the Ellsler Saloon on Broadway, whose business gave him access to gossip and a channel to distribute the weekly. At the time Wilkes was a young man about town with journalistic aspirations. Smart and energetic, Wilkes may have been particularly useful as a representative of the target audience for the publication. This is suggested by his unapologetic response when he was questioned, in November 1842, in a civil court as to how he knew Adelina Miller. Wilkes stated that he had gone to her brothel on more than one occasion. During cross-examination there followed this exchange:

Q[uestion].—What did you go there for?
A[nswer: Wilkes].—I went there for amusement.
Q[uestion].—Did you get your amusement?
A[nswer: Wilkes].—Yes, I got my amusement.[16]

What that civil court case brought out was that Adelina Miller had backed a note to buy a printing press for the *Sunday Flash*.

Snelling and his partners were willing to take support from any source that offered it. They had their own goal. They aimed to present a newspaper offering information about sporting life written with wit rather than censure. Although modeled after the London *Town*, such a paper was an innovation in America. Familiar with the world of theater and minstrelsy, the creators of the sporting press saw a new audience to exploit. Commercial American erotic weeklies as a business were born with American popular culture. Around the Bowery Theatre and the emerging minstrel show were writers— and those who wanted to write—who took as their subject the world of commercial theater, one another, the penny press, games, and prostitution. What these writers understood was that by the early 1840s blackface acts were playing not only to workingmen but also to the young middle-class clerks finding lodging in the neighborhood. Dixon knew the young clerks as part of the audience for his performances. These fellows, unlike many, were literate and oriented to print culture. They enjoyed their freedom after hours and took a devilish pleasure in an association with the "flash" world of sporting men.[17]

Writers of the American sporting press held political beliefs that ranged from Jacksonian to Whig, although all partook of the nativism and racism that were part of the very air they breathed. What they shared, along with their English counterparts, was an edge compounded of economic marginality, the desire for enhanced social status, personal engagement in the world

Young male newspaper readers. Nicolino Calyo, "Reading Room of the Astor House," watercolor and ink, 1840, Mrs. Elon Hooker Acquisition Fund. © Museum of the City of New York.

of saloons and brothels, and hostility to the mores of middle-class respectability. In their weeklies public women constituted an important subject but were of a different sort than Frances Wright—the public women of the "flash" press were prostitutes.

2

The *Sunday Flash* was quickly joined by imitators. After Scorpion, Startle, and Sly split up, Wooldridge went on to publish the *True Flash* with Dixon, and then the *Libertine*, the *Whip and Satirist of New-York and Brooklyn*, and the *Whip*. Snelling left the *Flash* in 1842 and wrote for Wooldridge's *Whip*. Dixon was briefly affiliated with Thaddeus W. Meighan in the *New York Sporting Whip*; Meighan later emerged as the editor of the *Rake*. George G. Scott took over the *Flash* in June 1842 as editor and proprietor, continuing at least until December. The last known issue of these publications is the *New York Sporting Whip* of March 4, 1843.

On its masthead the *Whip and Satirist of New-York and Brooklyn* presented itself to its potential readers as "Devoted to the Sports of the Ring, the Turf, and City Life—such as Sprees, Larks, Crim. Cons, Seductions, Rapes, &c.—not forgetting to keep a watchful eye on all Brothels and their frail inmates." However, typically, it portrayed itself as an agent of reform. Near the masthead is this motto: "Place in every honest hand a WHIP, to Lash the Rascals Naked through the World," allowing moral exposure as defense. It used its regular column "Sketches of Characters" to portray urban types, especially men-about-town and the women they might encounter, under clever engravings, often of a suggestive nature.[18] Evolving into the *Whip* and finally the *New York Sporting Whip,* the weekly kept the same mottoes but grew bolder. In its February 11, 1843, issue of eight pages, it castigated the abortionist Madame Costello and purveyors of obscene prints as its nods to reform. However, in "A Gay Sight" it celebrated a well-known prostitute, Julia Brown. "Princess Julia," in this account, took a sleigh ride with four coworkers, visiting various saloons one evening, playing billiards, and enjoying refreshment. "Then with a merry laugh and a constant waving of handkerchiefs, the reinsman deposited his fair cargo in safety at the mansion of the Princess." A later notice on the same page told of a new prostitute in town: "A STAR.—Bright, brilliant, beautiful—has fallen among us. It is called Miss Sarah Green (a queer name for a planet) and is in the harem of Julia Brown at present." By such commentary the *New York Sporting Whip* confirmed Brown's celebrity status. At the same time, the prostitute Harriet Grandy had a renown of a different sort: "That infamous strumpet Hal Grandy has again been disgracing our city with her conduct. We think it high time the police noticed this woman. She thinks nothing of Promenading Broadway in open day in men's apparel, or of jostling respectable females from the sidewalks. . . . She is the same prostitute who cow-hided in open day a young man, who at the same time shared her affections with a host of lawless fellows. . . . We would give the world to meet her in the street in any other appearance than that of a *she*-male."[19]

The tone of the reports on commercial sex in the sporting press varied somewhat. Like *Prostitution Exposed,* each weekly paper was nominally dedicated to reform, the price that vice pays to virtue. What promised to justify the "moral" intention of the weeklies was exposés, a particular subject of which was the older brothel madam. For example, it wrote of Mrs. Bowen of Church Street, "This hag is of a most repulsive aspect, being fat and filthy." Described as a tyrant to prostitutes under her, she reportedly engaged in girl stealing from places as far away as Poughkeepsie. The author asked rhetorically, Who visits her establishment? "Surely not he who has a single feeling of self-respect." The *Whip* warned that it intended to publish the names of her male clients if they did not stop going there.[20]

While older women came in for repeated abuse, a "frail one" or a "nymph" who was young and beautiful was accorded at the minimum the respect due a victim and at the maximum the admiration due royalty. For example, the *Flash* of July 3, 1842, contained a note about "the beautiful and divine Elizabeth Perkins," about to leave the city and "quit the paths of vice and immorality, and become the wife of a respectable merchant, of Boston." The writer stated, "We hope it is true, as we always had a great regard for the charming Elizabeth." In "Houses of Ill-Fame," a writer gave information from his brothel tour on the Sunday evening preceding. After complimenting the good arrangements of Adelina Miller's establishment, he wrote of Mrs. Brown's on 165 Canal Street, "This house, we believe, is patronized by some very nice young men; the girls seemed well behaved, and order and quiet reigned supreme." Mrs. Ryerson's on 58 Leonard Street got a fuller description: "A party of fashionable bucks sat around a table in the front room, enjoying themselves with wine. . . . This establishment is decorated and furnished in the most costly and magnificent style. We had an agreeable chat with a lively French ballet dancer, and also with the sweet Miss Louisa . . . , the most beautiful frail one Leonard street can boast of." As a writer considered the residents of Julia Brown's establishment, he waxed lyrical: "All the ladies looked charming, and were the true representatives of angels themselves, and seemed as if they had come down from heaven to charm man from this worldly state of misery to that of eternal happiness and pleasure." Of course, a prospectus of the Thursday *Flash* in this same period promised a satirical paper that would stem "social corruption" with a "whip of scorpions" and the declared aim of "exposure and correction of abuses."[21]

The perspective on prostitutes of even a single paper is multiple, representing in part the different interests of writers and, perhaps, individual ambivalences. In the early months of the *Sunday Flash,* for example, the weekly pursued a well-trodden literary path, familiar "seduced-and-abandoned" stories, here presented as "Lives of the Nymphs," or prostitutes. Unlike such narratives in the *Advocate of Moral Reform,* which emphasized victimization, these tales suggestively played with the seduction scenes with hints and winks. For example, the *Sunday Flash* of October 17, 1841, told the story of Amanda Green, a prostitute who boarded at the brothel of Mrs. Shannon on 74 West Broadway. An innocent virgin, she was led on by a man who plied her with wines and food. According to the story, "At the crowing of the cock she was no more a maid." She lived with her lover for a time, but he proved unfaithful. After she fell in with a German man, she was discovered by her mother, "who caught the parties one evening, in *flagrante delicto* in an attic, but enough, the contemplation of their sin is too dreadful to dwell upon." Thrown out, she turned to prostitution.[22]

Despite their content, the sporting weeklies claimed to have moral purposes, especially when faced with criticism. As will be apparent in Chapter 9, they took on the language of outrage and reform in dealing with abortionists. In addition, their words became particularly shrill in dealing with male violators of heterosexual codes, those whom they called sodomites. The *Flash* warned its readers that "the worst and most unnatural of the vices of ancient Athens is extensively practised in modern Gotham" by a score of "habitual sodomites." Several times these men were identified as foreigners—a Frenchman or a Portuguese Jew. The *Whip* conveyed some sense of one writer's anxiety when threatened with what he perceived as enticement: "Fear seizes the mind of the moral man when he is thus accosted and his first impulse is to escape." Both weeklies focused at one point on a particular performer at Palmo's and demanded that he be fired. Occasional letters threatened to expose individual men, including one who enticed the young. Homosexuality must have posed a special threat in this male world that celebrated the sybaritic pleasures of brothel sex.[23]

At an ironic level writers of the sporting weeklies intersected with the world of reform: they appropriated its material to their own different uses. In one example, for instance, a correspondent from Utica, New York, related that a mother who was president of the Moral Reform Society of that city had urged young girls not to lie on feather beds, eat meat, or sit on sofas where the married had sat. She had also advocated that the young receive sex instruction beginning at age ten, giving "all the minutiae attendant upon marriage" followed by a viewing of "practical illustrations." This, the author maintained, led children of the best families to engage in sex relations in barns and woodsheds, even in daylight. By such means the racy press mocked the efforts of sex reformers and educators and turned their work into intentionally salacious material for their weeklies.[24]

Snelling and others, such as Thaddeus Meighan, were clever writers. Needing money, they and the other proprietors of the sporting press put out publications with information and entertainment that they hoped young men would choose to buy. Intermixed with news about prizefights and theatrical productions, they carried neighborhood gossip, much in the manner of the *Owl* and the *Hawk and Buzzard*. For example, the *Whip* had a regular column, "The Whip Wants to Know," offering titillating bits about who had been seen with whom, spicing them up with such queries as "Who is Hal Grandy's lover? Is it sporting Tom?" If it was, it advised, he had better feed his children than "pamper this wretched creature." Like its weekly predecessors, it published letters, supposedly from correspondents with warnings to readers. A writer from Hartford threatened to reveal the name of a dry-goods clerk who took a girl to a public house. Another letter writer warned men riding up Broadway with Mary and Elvira from Julia Brown's establishment to shut the window of the carriage so as not to be visible to those who might recognize them.[25]

The *Whip* boasted a circulation variously of 6,000 to 13,000. (The nineteenth-century chronicler of journalism Frederick Hudson suggested 4,000.)[26] Although no figures can be proved, the weekly attested to its relative prosperity by woodcuts on the first page of each issue, supplied by engraver Robert H. Elton. Despite these signs of fiscal health, however, it seemed constantly in search of funds. Beginning in February 1842, the *Whip* required those who sent in notices designed for their personal benefit to pay a fee of $5.[27] Did it do more? Did the *Whip*—and the other sporting papers—engage in blackmail?

Early and late, the editors were charged with blackmail. Almost a decade after the papers folded, Horace Greeley of the New York *Tribune* testified in England before a parliamentary body, the Select Committee on Newspaper Stamps. He was shown a copy of the *Town* and asked if there were papers like it in the United States. He answered that there were no comparable dailies but that "there are weekly papers got up from time to time, called the *Scorpion*, the *Flash*, the *Whip*, and so on." When he characterized them, it was not as purveyors of erotic material but as organs of blackmail. He stated that their purpose was "to extort money from parties who can be threatened with exposure of immoral practices or for visiting infamous houses."[28] Was Greeley speaking accurately? New York City's district attorney certainly thought so. He marked copies of some sporting papers for possible violations of the law. One issue suggests that an informer told him about likely blackmail. On a copy of the *Flash* are two penned hands drawn by a reader, the index fingers pointing to two obsequious apologies. In the margins beside the hands are the inked words "for Black mail" and "hush money probably paid."[29]

Each weekly faced the accusation of blackmail, and each denied it—but at the same time each accused its rivals of the charge. For example, Snelling reproached Dixon for degrading the *Polyanthos:* "It speedily became a lower kind of Hawk and Bazzard [*sic*], a receptacle of black mail, which, on one occasion, at last, we have known him to receive." After he broke with Snelling and Wilkes, Wooldridge stated that he had originally invested in the paper on the promise that he would get a portion of the profits to come from blackmail. Frequently the compiler of "The Whip Wants to Know" used only initials when chastising men unfaithful to their wives but warned that the *Whip* would publish their full names if the men did not cease their adulterous behavior.[30] Real proof of blackmail came in the *Whip* of February 11, 1843. Amid many letters and statements with threats of exposure, a piece about the dancer Madame Trust stated outright: "Now, the drift of this is that we have on hand a queer, funny, and explicit *exposé* of the doings of a quack who married this *madame*—of her transactions—and of the secret affairs of both. If we can make any black-mail by suppressing it we will. There! We, more daring than Bennett, openly avow that we extort hush-money."[31]

Beyond blackmail, the other charge that the sporting weeklies faced was that they were the parasites or hirelings of brothel madams. This was a constant refrain, taking many different forms. Here there is some clear truth. Although one cannot know whether Wooldridge turned his Ellsler Saloon, as accused, into a house of assignation, as a boy in his teens he had married a prostitute. Adelina Miller provided material support to the *Sunday Flash* and to Snelling individually, when both were in a pinch.[32] At various points Nelson H. Miller either served as a witness in court for Snelling or provided him with bail.

The need for Adelina Miller to tell the story of Louisa Missouri initially powered the sporting weeklies. The first extant copy of these papers, number 6 of the *Sunday Flash,* dated September 12, 1841, carried on the work for Miller that the *Polyanthos* had begun. It called Hamblin's theater "The Slaughter House" or the "Lust Haus." Snelling wrote that Hamblin need not come again to the *Flash* with "flags of truce and proffers of forbearance money." This weekly was not the *Herald,* and "the blood of the murdered Missouri Miller and of mangled Shakspeare [*sic*] still cries to Heaven for vengeance." Snelling avowed that he was preparing a life of Hamblin.[33] When the sketch appeared on October 24 and 31, 1841, Hamblin emerged as a featured subject of the regular column "Gallery of Rascalities and Notorieties." The accompanying engraving had him in one of his important roles,

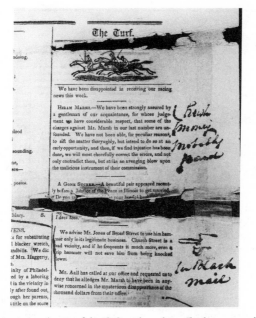

District attorney's copy of the *Flash*, with markings "hush money probably paid" and "for Black mail." *Flash*, 1, no. 14 (November 6, 1841): 3. Courtesy, American Antiquarian Society.

as "Il Jatatore," suggesting that his Satanic evil eye destroyed women and that he was "the Devil in human shape." Against Hamblin, Snelling pulled out all the stops. He chronicled the most notorious extramarital affairs of "The Patriarch of the Slaughter House," with the ensuing children. He labeled Hamblin a sufferer from venereal disease. He underscored any connection Hamblin had with persons of color. He narrated the tale of the battle over Louisa Missouri's custody and its immediate aftermath. In this account Attree emerged as an intermediary, working against the interests of Louisa Missouri's mother and brother. Finally Snelling charged that Medina—a "West Indian creole and a common strumpet"—had poisoned Louisa Missouri and then committed suicide by administering to herself a deadly dose of morphine.[34]

Just as Adelina Miller's causes helped bring the sporting press into being in the United States, they also contributed to its initial undoing. They added fuel to the conflicts surrounding these weeklies that boiled over into New

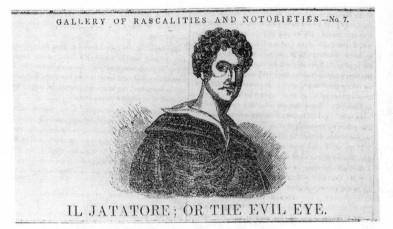

GALLERY OF RASCALITIES AND NOTORIETIES—No. 7.

IL JATATORE; OR THE EVIL EYE.

Thomas S. Hamblin as "Il Jatatore; or the Evil Eye." *Sunday Flash,* 1, no. 12 (October 24, 1841): 1. Courtesy, American Antiquarian Society.

York courts. Progressing from libel involving personal reputations to the common law of obscene libel, the district attorney of New York City moved to suppress New York's first racy papers through the criminal courts.

3

Unlike many trials for obscenity before the Civil War, those of the sporting press left abundant witnesses. The prosecutions and convictions are preserved in the indictment papers of the district attorney and in the minutes of the Court of General Sessions. In addition, the weeklies themselves carried news of the trials, and some of the principals spoke publicly or wrote of their experiences. This rich and dense record allows an unusually close and detailed look. This is fortunate because of the key role that New York played in the larger drama of suppression of obscenity and in the counterassertion of the right of free expression. Critical legal precedents became established in New York state courts, and defendants got significant experience that led to an important tradition of dissent.

Examination of the 1815 Pennsylvania case *Commonwealth v. Sharpless* demonstrated that, in the absence of state statutes, the absorption of the common law of obscene libel into American courts enabled them to move against sexual representations regarded as obscene. Courts relied on Blackstone and Holt for the logic of obscene libel. In the Massachusetts blasphemy trial of Abner Kneeland, the prosecutor additionally used Thomas Starkie's *A Treatise on the Law of Slander and Libel,* second edition, published in 1830. New York in the 1840s had no state statute against obscenity, but common law as interpreted by British commentators was enough.

That there was conflict between English common law and American protection of freedom of expression was apparent in the first American edition of Starkie, published in 1826. Adapted from the previous one-volume English edition, it gave references to American cases and attempted to reconcile Starkie's treatise with the First Amendment and with state constitutions guaranteeing freedom of the press. A detailed footnote in the 1826 edition established the protections provided in each state, including the all-important defense of truth as justification.[35] It is noteworthy, however, that the New York Court of General Sessions relied on the two-volume 1830 British edition with its more extensive practical guidance, which made no mention of constitutional protection.

Starkie followed Blackstone in arguing that, although many elements involved in civil libel suits applied to criminal cases, the logic behind them differed. The state had an interest in protecting its citizens against any libel that threatened its security or might weaken social bonds. These libels included obscene libel, labeled by Starkie as "Publications tending to subvert Morality." He wrote, "It is now fully established, that any immodest and immoral publication, tending to corrupt the mind, and to destroy the love of decency, morality, and good order, is punishable in the temporal courts." Criminal libel was concerned not with the creation of an expression but with its publication. A person might write exactly what he wanted. Only when that writing came into the hands of another did it become a potential criminal act. That a communication be true was no excuse in a criminal libel case, for it did not mitigate the statement's "tendency to provoke and injure."[36] Moreover, in dealing with blasphemy and obscenity, an effort at a truth test led to absurd consequences: "Would proof that indecent transactions have actually occurred, supply any excuse for the public exhibition of them in a print or a pamphlet?" It was always a curious element of obscene libel that the acts depicted or described were not necessarily crimes under the law. Starkie answered this objection: "Although many vicious and immoral acts are not indictable, yet if they tend to the destruction of morality in general, if they do or may affect the mass of society, they become offences of a public nature."[37]

Did a publisher "intend" to do harm? It is at this point that the tricky issues of "malice" and "intention," essential determinants of conviction under English law, come into play. Here Starkie presented that element of English law that bedeviled American defendants charged with obscene publication. "Malice," he stated, needed to be understood "in its legal and technical sense . . . in cases where the act itself is injurious and unlawful, [as] the absence of legal excuse . . . for in the failure of circumstances which justify, excuse, or at least modify the act, a rational being *must*, in law as well as morals, *be taken to contemplate and intend the immediate and natural consequences of his act.*" A madman cannot be held responsible for his acts. Neither can a servant, obeying a master, who delivers a sealed letter without knowledge of its contents. "But where the act is knowingly and intentionally done, it is plain that the mere absence of an actual intention to injure cannot absolve from criminal responsibility."[38]

Starkie allowed no outs. He argued that it went against legal principles to excuse an injurious and illegal act, freely chosen, because a man insisted that he had good motives. As Starkie stated, "The law allows no man to defend himself by saying, 'I did an act, in itself injurious, mischievous, and illegal, but I did it with an excellent intention.' "[39] These words of the law were echoed in American trials dealing with obscenity in the nineteenth and early twentieth centuries.

In criminal libel cases in England, the tasks of the jury were relatively simple and straightforward. The jury was to decide only the facts of the libel and whether the defendant had pursued it with legal malice—"the entire absence of legal excuse." The jury was not to decide the quality of the libel, which was left for the judge to determine, as in cases of crimes such as larceny and forgery: "In ordinary practice, it is, no doubt, for the court [i.e., the judge] to direct the jury, as to the criminal quality of the acts which the evidence tends to prove."[40] In dealing with individual criminal libel and with seditious libel, American law came to modify this by the turn of the nineteenth century, allowing the jury the right to determine the law as well as the facts of the case.[41] In the case of obscene libel, however, the role of the jury would remain in contention.

Starkie offered practical guidance to American courts. For example, in Appendix 24 he gave wording for a standard indictment for obscene libel:

That A.B., late of, &c. being a scandalous and evil disposed person, and not having the fear of God in his heart, but devising, contriving, and intending the morals as well of youth as of divers other liege subjects of our said Lord the King, to debauch and corrupt, and to raise and create in their minds inordinate and lustful desires, on, &c. with force and arms, at, &c. in a certain open and public shop of him the said A.B. there situate, unlawfully, wickedly, maliciously, and scandalously, did publish, sell, and utter to one C.D. a liege subject of our Lord the King, a certain lewd, wicked, scandalous, infamous, and obscene print, on paper, entitled _____, representing, &c. (*as in the print*,) and which said lewd, wicked, scandalous, infamous, and obscene print, on paper, was contained in a certain printed pamphlet, then and there uttered and sold by him the said A.B. to the said C.D. entitled _____, to the manifest corruption and subversion of youth, and other liege subjects of our said Lord the King, in their manners and conversation, in contempt of our said Lord the King and his laws, and against the peace, &c.[42]

These words would become familiar to Americans accused of obscenity. In New York the criminal Court of General Sessions knew its Starkie: as it came to indict the editors of the sporting press for obscenity, it used his model indictment for obscene libel, amending only the references to the English king and his subjects. In this way and others Starkie served as a veritable workbook for American courts, instructing them how they might conduct their cases according to the principles that Blackstone and Holt had laid out.

4

The first skirmish in the war against the sporting press started as a simple criminal libel case and then quickly developed into one of obscene libel. Most criminal indictments for libel involving sexual insults stayed right there. For a district attorney to escalate a charge of criminal libel against an editor and proprietor to a second charge of obscene libel required an additional impetus. In this instance there were both general and specific driving forces. At the base was the highly charged atmosphere of sexual conversation and controversy in New York in 1841, already evident in the words of moral reformers and the sporting press. The specific catalysts were the particular states of mind of the judges and prosecutor.

In its "Gallery of Rascalities and Notorieties" of October 17, 1841, the

Sunday Flash took on Myer Levy. Earlier subjects had been involved in the theater or newspapers and thus were inured to their notoriety. By contrast, Myer Levy was a businessman who could have anticipated no such treatment in a paper. The attack against him came at a time when the *Sunday Flash* carried a number of articles against Jewish business practices, and Levy may have seen the one against him as anti-Semitic. Although the article accused him of making gambling stock transactions and passing counterfeit money, its real intent was to smear Levy with sexual scandal.

"That's a dem fine gal!" was the caption underneath an engraving of a corpulent man labeled "Big Levy." Called at the outset "this walking scarlet sin," Myer Levy was described as a fashionable "dandy." The article linked him to many women and insulted him by calling him the "fancy man" of a well-known prostitute frequently denounced in the publication. It further alleged that, preferring black women, Levy was a "practical amalgamationist." A poem captured the violation of race mixing:

> Black, white or yellow, nothing came amiss;
> "Give me," lewd Levy cried, "a melting kiss."[43]

Caricature of Myer Levy, "That's a Dem Fine Gal!" *Sunday Flash*, 1, no. 11 (October 17, 1841): 1. Courtesy, American Antiquarian Society.

Following a well-established legal path, Myer Levy brought the sheet vilifying him to the attention of the authorities, and the district attorney went to the grand jury of the Court of General Sessions to seek the indictment of its editors—Snelling, Wilkes, and Wooldridge—on a criminal charge of libel. After reviewing the weekly brought by Levy, District Attorney James R. Whiting added a second criminal charge, "Publishing an Obscene Paper," a misdemeanor under the common law of obscene libel.

All of the action took place in the Court of General Sessions of New York. One of several criminal courts in the New York system at this time, General Sessions typically heard important felony trials, such as larceny and counterfeit, whose defendants were indicted by its grand jury. Three judges and two aldermen sat as a panel, although not all might be in attendance on any one day. Its judges were appointed by the state governor. The chief judge, the recorder, held one of the highest-paid offices in the city. At the outset of each monthly session the judges impaneled a grand jury to hear indictments brought by the district attorney and a petit jury to try all the cases brought before them during the session, which normally lasted several weeks. Understanding what impelled Whiting to bring charges of obscene publication against the editors and proprietors of the *Sunday Flash* requires focus on the actors involved in this court drama.

The recorder in 1841–43 was Frederick A. Tallmadge. Much about him can be predicted from his biography, for everything about him suggested a conservative approach to life and law. The son of a Revolutionary War hero and Connecticut representative to the U.S. Congress, Tallmadge lived in the shadow of his father, carrying on his tradition of public service and Christian faith. He served as recorder from 1841 to 1851, broken by two years when he served in the U.S. House of Representatives. Tallmadge is remembered most for his role in suppressing the Astor Place riot of 1849, a time when his military background helped him take command. In 1857, when the metropolitan police force was reorganized, he became its first superintendent. Both during his lifetime and at his death in 1869, Tallmadge was lauded for his integrity and urbanity.[44]

When Tallmadge swore in the grand jury of October 1841, he told the jurors that they had joined for the session an "institution . . . of ancient origin . . . kept up in all countries professing any regard for civil liberty." He then prepared them for what he knew was to come—cases of criminal libel—by attempting to clarify the rationale for libel as a felony. "By the exercise of its legitimate powers," he declared, "the Grand Jury prevented the indulgence of feelings of malignity in the minds of injured persons, by giving them the opportunity" of coming before it and causing the arrest and trial of one who had offended them. At the same time the grand jury "extended the shield of its protective powers to every man" by keeping him from indictment without the consent of twelve jurors.[45]

Tallmadge sat with two associate justices, James Lynch and Mordecai Noah. Little is known about Lynch other than criticism that he was an incompetent benchwarmer. Noah was, by contrast, a well-known and most unusual judge, for his primary career was outside the legal profession. He was a newspaper editor, a playwright, and a partisan in the New York theater wars on Hamblin's side. Heretofore a strong player in Democratic circles in the city, Noah turned briefly to the Whig Party in the 1840s and in 1841 was rewarded with a judgeship. He was perhaps the first Jew to hold such a position in an American criminal court.[46] Noah had thus two known leanings: he held an animus against the Miller family and certain of their supporters as enemies of Hamblin, and he was sensitive to anti-Semitic slurs against Myer Levy.

It is probable that the district attorney knew that Tallmadge and Noah would support him from the bench if he moved against the editors of the *Sunday Flash*, Whiting was an odd choice for chief prosecutor for the city and county of New York when selected by the county court in 1838. A Whig, he came from the world of civil law and banking, not from criminal law.[47] In the fall of 1841, Whiting was operating in particularly difficult circumstances, in an atmosphere highly charged by press vilifications of Madame Restell for causing miscarriages and abortions. As will be discussed in the following chapter, Whiting oversaw the indictment and conviction of Restell in the spring of 1841 and was awaiting Restell's appeal during the initial trials of the sporting press.

After Myer Levy came to him, Whiting collected copies of the sporting papers. He marked them in ways that convey what he saw as potential violations of common law. Snelling was attempting to get Wooldridge indicted for libel after the latter, who had turned state's evidence, published the *True Flash*, filled with invective against his former associates. In the margin of this single-issue paper, Whiting wrote, "Libellous The aff[idavi]t. of W. Snelling must shew what words or name denotes that he is this person alluded to, & an aff[idavi]t. of some witness to prove he is the man referred—J.R.W."[48] In this case Whiting was noting the evidence required if Snelling's accusation were to move forward to an indictment. More common are the penned markings on copies of the sporting papers—such as boxes around articles, lines along the side, underlining, and two slanted lines that serve as check marks—that suggest that the reader, most likely Whiting himself, was searching for potentially libelous or obscene statements.[49]

In late October 1841, the grand jury issued two indictments against Snelling, Wilkes, and Wooldridge as proprietors of the *Sunday Flash*. They were charged with criminal libel and "Publishing an Obscene Paper." As was the practice with the grand jury, when it issued indictments at the end of its term, it offered some general reflections. At the close of the October term, William G. Boggs read for the foreman a presentment to the court on evils to be abated. These included a statement against the Sunday papers and the need for laws to regulate their sale: "The shrill cry of the newsboys pierced to the fireside and the altars of the citizen, and disturbed the quiet, and profaned the sanctity of the Sabbath. It was also a system which destroyed all regard for the Sabbath in the minds of the boys themselves, and was preparing them for a life of vice and crime." Snelling perceived Boggs, the publisher of William Cullen Bryant's Democratic *Evening Post,* as an interested party to the case and as a person influenced by recent ministerial denunciations against the sporting press.[50] Chosen by the city Board of Supervisors— consisting of the mayor, the recorder, and the city's aldermen—the grand jury as a body was hardly synonymous with Boggs. The October group that indicted the three editors was a collection of solid citizens who included, along with the newspaperman, a carter, a hosier, a brush maker, at least one grocer, a bank teller, a gilder, a distiller, a bookseller, two butchers, a hardware dealer, and several merchants.[51]

Snelling called the grand jury the "Star Chamber" in the *Flash,* his renamed weekly, and compared it to the Inquisition. He protested this "iniquitous feature" of the English common law: "Is it not a horrible thing that three innocent men should be accused and judged in private, on the information of such land sharks as this Levy, arrested without know[ing] what they are charged with and sent to prison without a copy of the indictment and without a moment allowed to procure bail or engage counsel." Referring to the spokesman of the grand jury, Snelling intoned, "Mr. Boggs, Mr. Boggs, you and your fellows have brayed a little too loudly and too early this time. Scorpion, Startle & Sly are not news boys and are not to be silenced so easily." In a less high-toned manner, Snelling broadcast anti-Semitic slurs against Levy and accused the grand jury of trying to shut down the *Flash* because its "several sinners and one fornicator" had been threatened with exposure by the *Flash,* a threat that Snelling now insinuated he would make real.[52]

On October 26, following the two indictments, as Snelling sat "quietly smoking his cegar," a policeman arrested him. Wilkes and Wooldridge, also arrested on that day, put up bail, but Snelling, unable to find the money, went to jail. Snelling stated that his bail had been set so high that his friends could not help him, "save two [presumably the Millers], against whose interference I have insuferable [*sic*] objections."[53]

The three men came to trial in January 1842. Judge Noah had opened the January session of the court with a speech to the grand jurors that, according to the *Herald*, seemed more like a state-of-the-union address than the typical opening remarks of an officer of the court. In speaking about the press and libel, Noah echoed Blackstone to state that liberty of the press did not allow the invasion of others' rights. Governments establish laws, he said, to prevent the "rights of reputation" from being "recklessly infringed, or cruelly trampled upon." Although the federal Constitution "allows a citizen to speak, write and print whatever he may think proper," that citizen is nonetheless responsible if he abuses this right. In reflecting on the way that the penny press had taken on bankers and banking practices, Noah told the jurors, "In my long experience, I have never witnessed so great an abuse of the liberty of the press as I have of late in this city." It was the jurors themselves who held the cure, and he promised them that as judge he would support their efforts. "Gentlemen," he stated, the remedy is "in your hands.—When you, as protectors of the public peace, indict the libellers, this Court will not on conviction, shrink from the duty of inflicting the penalty of the law."[54]

The trial of the editors of the *Sunday Flash* was held on January 14, 1842, at the Halls of Justice on Centre Street, known as the Tombs, a building that combined courtrooms and prison. The *Herald* called the chamber "dirty, uncomfortable, and miserably constructed." Arrayed at one end were the judges, "all stuck up on a row like so many hens on a hen-roost." Defendants and their lawyers sat at a semicircular table facing the judges, separated from them by a small, low, round table of reporters.[55] William J. Snelling and George Wilkes stood before the judges, accused of criminal libel and obscene libel. Their former confederate, George B. Wooldridge, had broken with his two partners to turn state's evidence. By testifying against his associates, he was cleared of charges. On the matter of the criminal libel against Levy, both Snelling and Wilkes abandoned their defense and pleaded guilty. Snelling published a letter of apology to Levy in the *Flash* and the *Herald*. On the obscenity charge, however, the two maintained their innocence, and the jury heard the evidence and the arguments of the defendants' lawyers.

The indictment for obscene libel is missing from the files of the district attorney's indictment papers, but according to the New York *Herald* account, "The prosecution stated that they should prove that the sheet contained obscene matter, such as should not be allowed to appear in a public print, and therefore they presumed that it was only necessary to prove who were the actual publishers of the paper." The specific matter isolated as obscene for the court was the article in the *Sunday Flash* of October 17, 1841, on the life of Amanda Green, discussed above. The absence of the district attorney's copy means that the precise passages marked obscene are not known, but a reading of the whole article shows it to be an eroticized "seduced-and-abandoned" narrative. Wooldridge testified that Amanda Green had been the source of the information contained in the article.[56]

The *Herald* paraphrased that Wooldridge, when called to the stand, testified that "he was solicited by George Wilks [*sic*] to take a share in the paper, and that if he would go in with him they would make a good thing of it." He explained that his role for the *Sunday Flash* was "as the collector of items, from which certain articles were written," as, for example, that on Amanda Green's life. He "had turned states [*sic*] evidence to prevent others from getting ahead of him." The district attorney entered a *nolle prosequi,* exempting Wooldridge from further legal action.

The *Herald* added that the defense put on the stand "several persons" to counter Wooldridge's testimony, including one who "stated he would not believe him [Wooldridge] under oath." Though the *Herald* gave no names, this was Nelson H. Miller, Adelina's son. A week after the trial, when Snelling printed in the *Flash*—and challenged—Wooldridge's testimony, Snelling gave full attention to Miller's statement in court. Miller testified that he had known Wooldridge for some time and that he was a "bad character." Miller stated that Wooldridge's actions had been prompted by the desire for revenge against Levy. Had Miller known in advance that Wilkes and Snelling were beginning a connection with Wooldridge, he would "have warned them against such infamy."[57]

The jury retired to deliberate for several hours. Ultimately, one vote for acquittal meant that the jury failed to convict Snelling and Wilkes. The matter did not end, for both men returned to court in April, with Tallmadge, Noah, and Lynch presiding over a different jury. The second time around, Wilkes wanted to ask for a dismissal on the grounds that "the paper had been discontinued, and that he had devoted his time to different pursuits. He therefore thought that the ends of the prosecution had been accomplished."

However, advised by his lawyer, he pled guilty. The jury found Snelling guilty, and he was sent to the Tombs to serve out his sentence.[58]

In the *Whip*, Wooldridge gloated that he had vanquished his sporting press opponents. He must have enjoyed the moment when Snelling joined the *Whip*, not as proprietor and equal but as a writer in his employ. Wooldridge was not satisfied, however, for he had not crushed Adelina Miller. He deliberately set out to ruin her business. In so doing, he ultimately ruined his own.

In his weekly, Wooldridge repeatedly accused Miller and threatened in each issue to station a watch at her house and publish the names of her brothel clients. In one article, he treated Willis G. Thompson, a business associate and friend of Nelson Miller, roughly, stating that Miller, who was staying with Thompson, had taken some steaks from his mother's brothel pantry to Thompson's house. In "The Whip Wants to Know" appeared the question: "How often a notorious liar sleeps at the house of Mr. Thompson, and if Mrs. Thompson knows that her husband visits his house in return." Thompson, like Levy, was a private citizen. Faced with an insult to his wife and himself, Thompson initiated the criminal charge of libel. Once again libel against an editor led to close scrutiny of his paper and his indictment for obscene libel. Several months later Wooldridge was indicted for "publishing an obscene sheet," the July 9, 1842, edition of the *Whip*. The articles named in the second indictment were "The Battery Spy," "The Libertine Dr. B," "Pictures from Fancy No 2," "Poughkeepsee Rakes," and "Seduction—Conviction of the Libertine."[59]

On July 15, another set of indictments was served against the proprietors of the sporting press. The effort was a wholesale one and covered not only the owner of the *Whip*, but also those of the *Rake* and the *Flash*. Obscenity prosecutions involved the publishers of words and images, not their creators. Having lost out in the first round, Snelling was merely a writer for the *Whip* and was not indicted.

Wooldridge insisted that his indictment was a continuation of the old quarrel with Adelina Miller, and he was partially correct. Perhaps to deflect criticism, he also suggested that what probably was the most offending was the following: "A chambermaid is lighting an old gentleman to bed, who, no doubt, becomes heated with love and endeavors to kiss her; in the struggle to obtain it, he manages to straddle the handle of a warming pan which she holds in her hand, and in type is made to say, 'Take care of the warming pan, sir!' " The engraving supplied by Robert H. Elton and copied from the

English weekly the *Town* is indeed suggestive. It shows an older man attempting to seduce a pretty young chambermaid, carrying a warming pan. The stick of the pan is placed so that it looks like an erect penis, and her grasp of the stick can be read as her masturbating him.[60] The articles listed in the indictment have an openly erotic content. For example, "The Battery Spy" describes the prostitutes seen on a visit to the Battery on a Thursday afternoon by "all roués, libertines and sportsmen present . . . [and] suckers, sharps, diners-out, pimps, and drummers with white hats." *Femme de pavé* Mary Smith's costume came in for this praise: it is "rich with simplicity, elegant with neatness," in contrast to that of Harriet Grandy, which is "dirty, slovenly and disgusting as usual."[61]

This indictment, which is in the records, carried traditional language and followed the template in Starkie, modified slightly to fit the conditions of American government. In the case of Wooldridge, the indictment states that the accused, "being a scandalous and evil disposed person and devising, contriving and intending the morals as well of youth as of divers other citizens of the state of New York to debauch injure debase and corrupt and to raise and

"Take care of the Warming-pan, Sir!" Image supplied by Robert H. Elton and copied from the *Town*. *Whip*, 2, no. 3 (July 23, 1842): 1. Courtesy, American Antiquarian Society.

create in their minds inordinate and lustful desires . . . unlawfully, wickedly, maliciously and scandalously did print publish and circulate in the said city of New York and utter a certain lewd wicked and scandalous paper." The indictment listed the specific articles deemed obscene, published "to the manifest corruption of the morals of youth as of divers other citizens . . . in contempt of the people of the state of New York and their laws, to the evil example of all others in the like case offending and against the peace of the People of the State of New York and their dignity."[62]

Wooldridge faced an additional indictment for publishing the *Libertine*, a weekly along the same lines as the *Whip* and at the same address, 31 Ann Street. District Attorney Whiting initially refused to read the offending articles to the court on the grounds that their titles, which mentioned a number of well-known prostitutes, revealed their content. When counsel for Wooldridge insisted that the articles themselves might serve the cause of virtue by pointing out the results of vice, and that if title alone or an isolated passage from the text were the sole guide, then important works of literature could be found obscene, the recorder required the district attorney to read the whole articles. Whiting, who had earlier threatened to resign if so forced, read the works. This aspect of the trial was not repeated. Subsequent district attorneys in future trials did not have to read whole works to the jury.

Recorder Tallmadge charged the jury. He spoke to them of "the blessings of a properly conducted press, and of the evils of an abandoned and profligate press." The jury retired for five minutes and returned a guilty verdict against Wooldridge. Facing other indictments, Wooldridge and his rival editors entered guilty pleas. At their sentencing, each of the primary defendants got prison sentences of sixty days.[63]

5

In their weekly papers, the indicted editors offered their defense. Typically they alleged that the original libel charges had been the result of personal vendettas against them, and they protested their innocence of all wrongdoing. They slammed their opponents, calling them names such as "dirty vagabonds" and "prostitute pimps." And they insisted that their sheets were put forward for moral reformation. They were the advocates of "the oppressed and unfortunate . . . of the people and their pastimes, so long as they are of an innocent nature."[64] In the matter of melodrama, the *Flash* declaimed, "You have chosen your libel ill. . . . At present we bid defiance alike to Jews and negroes, Hell and Hamblin, Farce, Comedy and Tragedy." Snelling, as editor of the *Flash,* fulminated about the wrong of the legal proceedings against him. He sought to put his treatment of prostitutes in a moral light, posing as a reformer: he only exposed the evil that existed, he did not create it. Was his language coarse? Only to his accusers: "Gentlemen; most righteous, virtuous and delicate gentlemen, the dirt of the Flash is all in your own imaginations. You have been looking for naughty words, and it is no wonder that you have found them." To call his writings into question was to threaten the publication of literary works: "Let them punish the publishers of Dean Swift. Let them suppress Byron. . . . Let them present the Bible itself." Snelling seems rather cheeky, given what he had just been publishing, but he was a man who knew his letters. Once a recognized poet, in the years that followed his escapades in New York, Snelling returned to respectability as the successful editor of the Boston *Herald.*[65]

After Wooldridge was found guilty and sentenced to the Tombs, he made a ritualistic promise to reform. The *Whip* did not change; a new editor, now anonymous, promised an even more salacious weekly: "When we happen to see an elegant female promenading Broadway or any other way, we shall, if she pleases our fancy, endeavor to describe her figure and gay dress with all the power of love itself—not caring whether she is frail or fair, for that is not our business. . . . We intend visiting all the first-rate seraglios, and with the pen of truth speak of *things* as we find them—draw out the lovely from their lurking places, and tell the world what flowers are 'wasting their fragrance on the desert air.' " In an article entitled "Our First Walk About Town," the reader was taken on a lighthearted tour of brothels in New York City.[66] Wooldridge himself was to have an eclectic career, surfacing several times in the historical record, most importantly as the initial agent of the Virginia minstrels.[67] He later returned to the newspaper world as the columnist Tom Quick in the New York *Leader.*

James Gordon Bennett, the editor of the *Herald* and a defendant in many libel cases, could hardly come to the defense of fellow journalists imprisoned for obscenity, but he did attempt to put the convictions of Wooldridge and others into perspective. In "The Tweedle-dum and Tweedle-dee in Morals— The Ann Street Licentious Press, and the Wall Street Licentious Press," he questioned why one had been prosecuted in the courts and the other allowed to go free. In doing so, he gave a sense of not only his opposition to banks, but also his view of Ann Street publishers. He saw two classes of "demoralized newspapers" published in New York—one, the business press centered on Wall Street, the other, the "Ann-st. licentious press. . . . One patronizes theft, plunder, and wholesale robberies, through the agencies of banks, loan companies, and all species of incorporated bodies; the other patronizes the same species of plunder by means of faro banks, pool, roulette, hazard, betting, picking pockets, and every other species of robbery." Writing immediately after a prominent pugilist had died in an illegal match, Bennett wrote that while one sanctions death through fights in the ring, the other upholds dueling as an honorable way to resolve a conflict. If the licentious press of Ann Street is jailed, why is that of Wall Street allowed to remain free?[68]

It was George Wilkes who began a line of questioning with the power to challenge court rulings of obscenity. He confronted a legal system that threatened his freedom and his livelihood. When the case of the *Flash* was settled in January 1842, Wilkes was originally given a thirty-day suspended sentence under the condition that he would never write for an obscene publication again. Almost two years later he returned to court. He was working as a reporter for Mike Walsh's *Subterranean* when the radical politician-editor was being tried for libel. When Walsh stood before him, Recorder Tallmadge gave expression to his judgments in ways that reflected back on his handling of the trials of the proprietors of the flash press. He stated to the court that "the licentiousness that had recently presented itself among many of the public journals of this city was more of a curse to the community than a benefit." Not only had journals attacked matters of a public nature, they had "entered the private sanctuary of families, which they have assailed in a manner that calls loudly upon the public authorities to suppress." When the press "attacks individuals and assails private character and relations without justification," it must be condemned.[69]

George Wilkes's presence in the courtroom caused the court to retry him. In this trial he spoke to the court in his own behalf. His testimony gave details of the initial trial for obscenity in 1842. His assertions and the statement by Recorder Tallmadge revealed the extent to which court suppression was really an effort at censorship. As quoted in the *Herald,* Wilkes stated that his counsel "said he had seen the District Attorney, and that as the only object of the prosecution appeared to be to suppress the publication of the sheet, he advised me to go into court, enter a plea of guilty, withdraw from any further connexion with the paper, and further proceedings would be stayed against me." Thus in his April 1842 trial before Recorder Tallmadge and Judge Noah, Wilkes had entered a technical plea of guilty.

Wilkes's statement did not change Tallmadge's decision to penalize Wilkes for violating his suspended sentence. When he communicated this decision in the court, Tallmadge returned to his condemnation of the weeklies that Wilkes had allied himself with. He was moved by "the youth of the accused, his talents." Tallmadge then spoke about "the character of a certain portion of the public press—particularly the penny press—in their personal attacks, harrowing up the feelings of families, and innocent and unoffending persons, and stated in all cases before this Court, parties so offending should be visited with the most severe punishment." Tallmadge sentenced Wilkes to imprisonment in the Tombs for one month, which he said "he hoped would serve not only as a warning to him, but to all others who were concerned in publishing sheets of an infamous and libellous character."[70]

In jail Wilkes kept a journal that he published as *The Mysteries of the Tombs,* using it to argue the case against both his own sentencing and the legal arguments by those such as Holt and Starkie regarding libel and the common law of obscene libel. What particularly galled him were the harsh penalties meted against words that might provoke violence or licentiousness, in the respective cases of libel and obscenity, in contrast to the mild punishments given for deeds such as assault and battery and the total absence of sanctions for sexual relations outside marriage. The "law concerning the sale of obscene books and pictures" seemed to Wilkes particularly illogical. As he put it, obscene materials for purchase "are subject to the same penalties as libel, because they tend to promote licentiousness; while adultery and fornication, the very evils which their prosecution is intended to prevent, go scot free of the law. Is not this supremely absurd? In the latter case particularly, can the proposition stand, that it is criminal to incite to an act, the actual commission of which is innocent by law?" Moreover, sanctions against obscenity were questionable. In the case of the illegal sale of lottery tickets, he said, the law can be applied because it is "a direct violation of an imperative statute." In contrast, "the sale of obscene papers is merely an offence against taste, according to the common law, or in other words, common opinion."[71] When George Wilkes resurfaced in 1845 as the founding editor of the *National Police Gazette,* he had many future opportunities to consider libel and report on obscenity. Later in the century, others would turn to Wilkes's lines of argument as they mounted legal defenses for those accused of obscenity.

6

On the surface, the justice system—with officers grinding away at indict-ments, prosecutions, and convictions—is made to seem impersonal, dispens-ing abstract justice. In the 1840s in New York City, however, nobody was a neutral actor. As judges confronted the new sporting press, they brought many assumptions and concerns to the bench. By and large, they were from the conservative end of the political and cultural spectrum, and the court gave them the power to give public expression to what they understood as community standards. They sought to influence the men of the jury, who had their own opinions on the matter of sexual speech. If judge and jury agreed, judges had the authority to punish. They dealt in the details of spe-cific cases.

What happened in court, however, mattered beyond the specific antago-nists. Courts work by precedent, and some of the precedents set in these cases proved to be strong. The use of the common-law tradition in these tri-als as interpreted by Blackstone, Holt, and Starkie affected future trials, including ones that occurred after state statutes were written and a federal law was in force.

The trials occurred in the early 1840s, and the court decisions probably accorded well with a significant body of public opinion. It was a time when those who agreed with evangelical Christianity saw the sporting weeklies' discussions of prostitutes and their clients as sinful. Those members of the middle class—reading romantic literature and the works of reform physiolo-gists and now linking sexuality to love, the nerves, and heightened emo-tion—saw these same racy discussions as crude. For them the language of vernacular sexual culture contained in the sporting weeklies, linking sex to hot blood, seemed more archaic than satanic. A judge of conservative bent, such as Frederick A. Tallmadge, who perceived the sporting weeklies as "an abandoned and profligate press," one of the "evils" of the city that needed to be curbed, had the power to persuade a jury. This body of artisans and mer-chants, whatever their personal behavior, shared Tallmadge's view that the press should not report the doings of prostitutes, tell stories of seduction and betrayal, or threaten to expose the errant. These men could assume that when they convicted editors of the sporting weeklies, their judgments would be taken as acts done in the public interest.

In the era of Snelling and Wilkes, Recorder Tallmadge's was the domi-nant voice. The 1842 trials of the New York flash weeklies over which Tallmadge presided are part of an important tradition of court supervision of sexually explicit words and images in America. More specifically, the trials point to efforts to criminalize representations presumed to be sexually stimulating to the unattached, literate, urban young men partaking in the city's sporting culture. Sentences against editors and proprietors were intended to deter others from publishing "racy" material and thus act as a means of censorship. What gives these trials greater weight is the precedent they established for the future, especially in the years after the Civil War, when legislation at the state and federal levels redefining obscenity brought increasing numbers of indictments.

In the 1840s, when prosecution for obscenity was haphazard and generally limited to those living on the economic margin, few listened to George Wilkes. Whatever threat judicial decisions posed to freedom of expression and of the press seemed nonexistent or minimal in this period. It was an era when books and pamphlets that middle-class men and women valued as presenting scientific and philosophical discussions of sexual matters—what we have called the third framework—were freely printed and distributed.

Furthermore, during these years—in lectures and in print—the conversation about sexual reform was wide-ranging. Discussion and debate stretching from politics to economics to marriage and the family were carried on without restraint. In a later period, when words about sex came to be more systematically suppressed, Wilkes's arguments had far greater resonance. Courts convicted those who sold books on reform physiology and works advocating sexual reform. With increased suppression, the concerns of writers of the sporting press about what constituted obscenity and what should be the power of the state to regulate sexual speech became part of the opposing tradition.

9

Abortion

Sharp controversy over abortion heated the atmosphere in which the obscenity trials of the sporting press in the early 1840s took place. Both men and women were migrating to the city, spurred by economic need and opportunity, and all faced temptations. Women leaving their home communities were particularly vulnerable, because they could no longer rely on the secret knowledge of women's vernacular sexual culture, including the various means of preventing and terminating pregnancy. This opened the way for the enterprising to advertise abortion services. In what seems like a puzzling contradiction, publications aimed at sporting men opposed abortion with a vengeance.[1]

Beginning in 1841, George Washington Dixon led a campaign in the *Polyanthos* against Madame Restell, New York's most public abortionist. His peers in the sporting press echoed Dixon's hostility, if not his rancor. In 1845, when George Wilkes, "Startle" of the *Flash,* resurfaced as the editor and co-owner of the *National Police Gazette,* he was Restell's sworn enemy. For both Dixon and Wilkes, the level of vituperation against Restell equaled that of Snelling against Hamblin or Wooldridge against Adelina Miller. Essential to understanding this opposition is abortion's roots in the first framework. In this case, vernacular culture was riven by gender.

Aristotle's Master-piece is again a guide. Judging from its locations in western Massachusetts households, the work was a book owned by common people and kept in their houses, hidden from view. Nicknamed the "Granny Book" in Northampton and elsewhere, it purported to be for midwives. Such a man as Jonathan Edwards may have regarded it as a book "unclean to be read" but this phrase needs to be qualified by the words "by men." Edwards never questioned the book's appropriateness for female readers.

Despite its likely male authorship, *Aristotle's Master-piece* contained much of interest to women, including a drawing of a fetus in utero, information on pregnancy and childbirth, and discussion of menstruation. The latter emphasized the need for menstrual regularity, congruent with humoral theory, which sought the balance of fluids in the body. This was the section in which a woman might learn about abortion, for it stated, in guarded language, that a woman might go to her doctor for "a strong enthartical Potion," to restore her monthly flow. Translated, this meant that a woman might seek from a physician a medicine enabling her to abort a fetus. As other historians have demonstrated, ordinary women knew ways of inducing abortion in the early stages of pregnancy and could resort to these means when they did not want to bear a child.[2] These practices can be best understood as part of the secret vernacular culture of women. Although they were deeply disapproved of by Christian authorities, until the nineteenth century they were tolerated under common law.

Much of the important life of women was lived within a community of women. The most dramatic illustration of this is the gathering of women under a midwife to attend one of their own during childbirth; but, less dramatically, many of women's chores were done in one another's company. Laurel Ulrich has likened the way that gender works to a blue-and-white-checkered piece of cloth. Looking at southern Maine in the late eighteenth and early nineteenth century, she delineated squares of shared sociability that blended both blue and white threads, and she also pictured solid squares of white for women and blue for men in which the two sexes, despite living within blended households, partook of separate activities. Extending this metaphor to the mental and emotional realms, it was in the white square of women's separate culture that the secrets of abortion were kept and shared.[3]

Behind these hidden practices lay an understanding by both sexes that human life began not at conception but at quickening, the fetal movements at roughly twenty weeks into a pregnancy. In the eighteenth and early nineteenth centuries, there was no way to determine with certainty if a woman was pregnant. Again, *Aristotle's Master-piece* offered to women a description of some of the important symptoms of pregnancy, such as changes in the breasts. But since no one, neither a woman nor her physician, could be sure, it was reasonable to assume that a woman who missed her menstrual flow was experiencing an "obstruction" of her menses, dangerous in the light of humoral theory. To restore her menses, a woman might take cathartics and purgatives, strong medicines to induce vomiting and evacuation of the bowels. If she needed knowledge or specific herbs or chemicals, she might apply to a woman friend or a midwife, or possibly a physician. Men who treated women were their confidants and were trusted to respect female secrets. In Northampton, for example, the one place where *Aristotle's Master-piece* was displayed openly was in the office of the town physician. If a woman turned to household medical guides, such as William Buchan's *Domestic Medicine,* she could get advice on specific remedies, normally combining a powerful purgative, such as black hellebore, with bleeding to induce a sympathetic reaction in the womb that was believed helpful in flushing out blockages. Other cathartics that might be tried were those known to make a woman violently ill, such as calomel, aloes, extract of juniper berries, snakeroot, or oil of tansy. By the mid–eighteenth century, a woman could easily buy such medications in a store. In 1742 rural Connecticut, acquiring and applying them was understood euphemistically as "taking the trade."[4]

The line between clearing up an obstruction and inducing a miscarriage was a blurred one, and it was important to keep it so. If ingesting "remedies" failed, a woman might seek to dislodge the fetus by injuring herself through falling or blows to the abdomen. If she remained pregnant, a woman might request intervention from her physician. By the early nineteenth century, physicians had the knowledge necessary to terminate pregnancy. Along with pulling out a tooth to incur sympathetic bleeding, a doctor would dilate a woman's cervix to induce contractions to cause a miscarriage or, especially, in the later stages, would rupture the amniotic sac to achieve the same end. In more complicated cases, a physician would intervene surgically to destroy the fetus. When these efforts involved abortion after quickening, they posed problems of medical ethics and conscience. They were violations of common law—abortion after quickening was a misdemeanor—and thus required concealment.[5]

Two important changes altered women's lives in the early nineteenth century. On the one hand, increasing numbers of females were literate, opening to them the world of print. The blue square of men's culture was becoming blended with white. Not only were women readers, they were buyers of books, pamphlets, and newspapers. This meant that printed products once imagined solely for male consumption had to be reimagined for female purchase. One the other hand, as many women in the eighteenth and nineteenth centuries moved away from their families of origin, the white square of women's culture faced disruptions. Some women traveled with their husbands, but some arrived as *femes soles* to earn their bread in cities and towns. They could no longer rely on the oral traditions that had carried women's lore over the generations. They needed to turn to books for information, and books for them were becoming accessible.

There are many works of popular medicine available from the early nineteenth century. Some of them contain information on the reproductive organs and their functions and include instructions for abortion, although often stated through double negatives. Discussions about restoring women to their courses typically carried warnings that specific remedies were to be tried only when a woman knew that she was not pregnant. This was a way of covertly promising that such substances were abortifacients. Such subterfuge was a bow to official culture, which disapproved of all efforts to terminate a pregnancy, even before quickening.

The existence of women's culture and the need for reticence means that there are no reliable ways of learning how many women in the nineteenth century resorted to abortion. While James C. Mohr has written that male physicians believed that only unmarried pregnant women sought abortions in the early nineteenth century and that the practice was not used for family limitation, this may only indicate that the covert culture hidden to nineteenth-century men remained hidden to twentieth-century historians.[6] Unmarried women did not have access to the lore of married women and midwives, and thus they had to turn to their male doctors. By contrast, married women who did not want additional children or who sought fewer children, more widely spaced, could rely, at least in part, on knowledge in the older women's community, knowledge made available perhaps only after the birth of a first child. Their first defense from unwanted conception was nursing an infant, and demographers have linked nursing to the usual spacing of births at two-year intervals. Their second was contraception, as variously understood. Such methods were not foolproof, however, and the third line of defense was likely the purgatives and cathartics discussed above.

It was the disruption of community knowledge that created the grounds for the dissemination of printed information on abortion and for the rise of female abortionists in cities such as New York. The city was a site for both immigration from abroad and migration from the countryside. As many young people came to the city hoping for work and a better life, they separated from their kin. For women, this meant leaving the community of women of their mothers and aunts. Just as mental hospitals took the place of homes in the care of the mentally ill, so abortionists may have emerged to provide commercial services that the women's community had once offered its members. A new need came into being, and entrepreneurial women applied the knowledge they had gained in their households to meet that need.

In New York City, beginning in the late 1830s, there were three female abortionists who openly advertised their trade—Mrs. Bird, Madame Restell, and Madame Costello. Of these practitioners, Madame Restell, the business name of Ann Trow Lohman, was the most famous. In 1831, at age twenty, she had immigrated from England to New York with her husband and baby daughter. Widowed within the year, she supported herself and the child as a seamstress. In 1836 she married a printer at the *New York Herald,* Charles Lohman. A Russian immigrant, Lohman was an avowed freethinker. He frequented the Chatham Street bookstore of Augustus and George W. Matsell, which featured the works of Paine and Jefferson, writers of the French Enlightenment, and local freethinkers Frances Wright and Robert Dale Owen. The Matsell brothers also offered Charles Knowlton's *Fruits of Philosophy* for sale.[7] This freethinking world both accepted the sexual instinct as natural and rejected the traditional notion that nature must take its course in pregnancy. Writing from this perspective, Charles Knowlton explicitly countenanced abortion, suggesting that it was a philosophical mistake to attribute "life" to a fetus in its early stages. Working at the junction of vernacular sexual culture and the early works of reform physiology, the Lohmans could imagine that Ann might successfully coin her knowledge, both traditional and recently acquired, by advertising her services as one who could restore to a woman her monthly courses.

Restell also had the example—and perhaps the training—of her next-door neighbor, Dr. William Evans. He advertised his abortion services in 1838, stating that he could cure both venereal diseases and female complaints, including "suppression and retention of menses." In his practice, Evans was joined by Margaret Dawson, another English immigrant, who had an abortion practice under the name of Mrs. Bird. That Ann Lohman had Evans's support was clear at her first arrest, when Evans put up her bail money.

The Lohmans announced the advent of Madame Restell in the penny press in 1838. They did not use the guarded language of their predecessors but were open and direct. Their first advertisement in the *Sun* of March 18, 1839, is straight out of Robert Owen's *Moral Physiology,* perhaps as cribbed by Knowlton's 1832 *Fruits of Philosophy.* The ad stated, "Is it not but too well

GENERAL VIEW of CHATHAM ST. 1858.
looking down from Chatham Square.

Three views of Chatham Street, the location of the free-thought bookstore of Augustus and George W. Matsell.

Top left: E. Didier, "Auction in Chatham Street," 1843, oil on canvas. © Museum of the City of New York.

Top right: Chatham Square, c. 1858–59. © Museum of the City of New York.

Bottom: Chatham Street view, D. T. Valentine, *Manual of the Corporation of the City of New-York for 1858* (New York: Charles Baker, printer, 1858). Courtesy, American Antiquarian Society.

known that the families of the married often increase beyond the happiness of those who give them birth would dictate? In how many instances does the hard-working father, and more especially the mother, of a poor family, remain slaves throughout their lives, 'urging at the oar of incessant labor, toiling to live, living to toil,' when they might have enjoyed comfort and comparative affluence." The advertisement stated the availability of the services of Mrs. Restell of 160 Greenwich Street, the granddaughter of a "celebrated midwife and female physician," who presumably had the older woman's recipes for family limitation.

It has been argued that Restell's preventative powers were sheer quackery.[8] But they may have instead been the effective spermicides that Knowlton recommended to be added to warm water for the postcoital douche, his preferred method of birth control. It is likely that the female pills Restell advertised were condensed versions of the purgative agents recommended by books of domestic medicine, such as Buchan. At a later point, Restell's pills were subjected to chemical analysis. In one case, they were found to contain ergot and cantharides, known as Spanish fly; in another, oil of tansy and spirits of turpentine. However dangerous to one's health, these were among the ingredients frequently cited in books of domestic medicine as useful for "restoring women's monthly courses." As many women had learned, such cathartic measures could fail. In that case, the Lohmans offered procedures available through physicians: dilation of the cervix, piercing of the amniotic sac, and surgery. Here both Charles and Ann Lohman were practicing without formal training. They were working at a time, however, when medical training was erratic, many alternative systems were in play, and licensing was disputed.

In the first year of Madame Restell's practice, a campaign of vilification began against her that let up only with her death in 1874. Dixon opened the attack in the *Polyanthos* with the charge that Restell's widely advertised preventatives threatened men. Both married and unmarried women could sin without the threat of pregnancy. A man going to sea could no longer count on the "security for the good behaviour" of his wife. A young suitor could no longer know that his beloved had not endured "the sweaty contamination of a hundred palms." In this male imagination, fear of pregnancy seemed to act as a chastity belt that birth control threatened to remove. Dixon called on the police or the grand jury (which he had come to know firsthand) to stop Restell. He gave a menacing reference to lynch law as an alternative and promised to repeat his editorial weekly: "we shall keep this woman's flag, with the death's head, and marrow bones, at her mast head, until she is legally dealt with." In time, a woodcut of Restell as murderess illustrated Dixon's recurring words.[9]

On March 16, 1841, the grand jury acted as Dixon desired, at least in part, and delivered to the court an ex cathedra judgment. Their words gave an odd twist to men's fear of abortion. As the jurors put it, it was the woman who suffered from abortionists, not the man. Her best defense against male predators was her own fear of pregnancy, and this was undercut by the ads of abortionists Restell and Costello. They gave to "the vile seducer" the words of reassurance he needed to enable him to break the resistance of his female "victim." The grand jury suggested that the court seek the passage of a law forbidding abortion advertisements as a "public nuisance." While this did not happen, a man came forward to accuse Restell of performing an abortion on his wife and got the police to take his wife's statement before her death. On March 22, 1841, Restell was arrested for the murder of Ann Maria Purdy.

Physicians and other health practitioners often lost patients through abortion and other invasive procedures. In an era before antisepsis was understood, both women and men were exposed to infection brought on by the use of unsterilized instruments in surgery. The campaign of vilification against Restell and other female abortionists as murderers made them particularly vulnerable, however, when one of their clients died. In 1841, after Mrs. Purdy confessed to her husband on her deathbed that she had sought an abortion, Ann Lohman was indicted for the first time by the Court of General Sessions. She stayed in jail while awaiting trial, because, once informed that any name would be made public, no one was willing to make her bail. A jury declared Lohman guilty, but the case was overturned in the New York Supreme Court on the grounds that the incriminating depositions by the dying Mrs. Purdy were inadmissible evidence.

As the sporting papers emerged, they added their voices to Dixon's. The same issue of the *Sunday Flash* that attacked Myer Levy carried a statement against the *Herald* and the *Sun* for printing Restell's ads. The argument was similar to Dixon's: Restell threatened men by her promises to women. She "openly declares that she will assist them [females] to sin with impunity." The sporting press focused on its regular enemies, the successful penny dailies that accepted Restell's ads. By assisting the abortionist in committing a crime, the papers "ought to be punished as accessories before the fact." When the *Whip* emerged, it initially took Restell's advertisements but quickly thought better. Facing an indictment for obscenity, it turned to attack the hypocrisy of its competitors. As a writer stated, while the *Whip* printed plain speech, other papers satisfied public hunger for salacious material through the subterfuges of "publishing Madame Restell's obscene advertisements, or notices of Saw-dust Graham's nasty pamphlets. How faithfully is the evidence in a case of crim. con. detailed! How feelingly they dwell upon a rape or a seduction!" In this tirade Restell joined an interesting group that included not just penny press police reports but also the writings of reform physiologist Sylvester Graham. By the end of its career the *Whip* was as brutal in its language as had been the *Polyanthos*. In criticizing the *Herald* for its advertisements, the *Whip* stated that Restell "will dip her hands in infant blood, and send the souls of erring parents to the consideration of the devil for five dollars each lick."[10]

George Wilkes took up the campaign against abortion after he emerged from prison in 1843 after serving a month for violating his suspended sentence for obscenity. Jail had enabled him to write *The Mysteries of the Tombs* and had given him an idea. In September 1845, Wilkes and criminal lawyer Enoch E. Camp launched the *National Police Gazette*, a New York weekly "devoted to the interests of criminal police." In the spirit of public service of its British predecessor, it promised to inform the community and give public notice of crooks. Its noble intent was to foil felons whose "success . . . depends mainly . . . upon the public ignorance of their persons and pursuits." To this end it presented "Lives of the Felons," beginning with the tale of Robert Sutton, alias "Bob the Wheeler," a London pugilist whose New York career of forgery had been launched in his beer shop, Darby & Joan, near Chatham Street. The paper promised its readers accurate stories by reporters who were close to the criminal underworld, conversant with its slang, and eager to expose all to the light. From the outset sex crimes and abortion were on its lists of nefarious deeds.[11]

Wilkes learned much of his craft in his apprenticeship on the *Flash*, but his new strategy was safer. By using police records and trial transcripts, he hoped to deflect the libel suits of the earlier weeklies. There was always much writing about sex in the *National Police Gazette*, but it generally came through crime reports, thus avoiding prosecution for obscenity. For example, alongside columns on counterfeits, burglaries, robberies, and pickpockets was one entitled "Seductions, Rape, &c," offering news of sexual crimes and misdemeanors. In its first several issues readers learned about reported rapes and about a woman convicted for bigamy. They read the details of the death of Sarah Decker from oil of tansy, taken to induce abortion at the urging of her lover, Virgil Knapp. With banner headlines came ongoing reports of important trials, such as that of "The Jersey City Murder" of a prominent woman by her husband. In these crime reports there was no need to censor language.[12]

Unlike the sporting weeklies of the early 1840s, the *National Police Gazette* was no fly-by-night operation. Burgess, Stringer & Company served as its general subscription agent. This firm represented a fair sample of the mix of mid-nineteenth-century literature: James Fenimore Cooper, Alexandre Dumas, and Eugène Sue, as well as the "Frenchman" responsible for *Matilda; or the Memoirs of a Young Woman*. As a measure of the *National Police Gazette's* ability to get federal patronage, the crime weekly began publishing a list of deserters from the U.S. Army at the end of each issue. By the middle of its first year, subscriptions reached 23,000, and the weekly bragged that its readers numbered more than a hundred thousand.[13]

In his years at the *National Police Gazette,* Wilkes worked on behalf of many issues, including California development and the transcontinental railroad. And he took up the campaign against Restell and the other abortionists where Dixon had left off. Week after week he wrote against them. Although Wilkes was capable of phrasing many issues in straightforward terms with appeal to reason, when he fought against abortionists his language was as shrill as Dixon's. An important difference, however, was that Dixon had been one of the petty players, while Wilkes was becoming a major one, building a paper with rising circulation and the potential for a national audience. Two months into publication, Wilkes suggested that the mayor needed to establish a watch at the doors of "the slaughter-houses of the murderous abortionists of this city" to expose women clients and thus drive them away. Invective after invective followed, including the charge that Restell and her compatriots were linked to abominable crimes, such as the murder of the cigar girl Mary Rogers, Helen Jewett's successor in the annals of beautiful victims.[14]

The Mary Applegate case gave much new information and ammunition. She testified that when Restell had attended her as a midwife, she had robbed her of her newborn daughter. The dailies printed Applegate's sworn statement to the mayor, which revealed details of the inner workings of Restell's establishment. New Yorkers learned that many women, both unmarried and married, including those imagined to be respectable, went there for abortions. These revelations were worked and reworked by the *National Police*

Gazette until ultimately Restell became the murderess who resorted to infanticide when necessary (the weekly's explanation for the abandoned bodies of newborn babies found on city streets). As patients died, Restell disposed of their bodies or, worse, sold them to dissectors. The weekly called her a trader in human flesh and criticized her wealth, her wardrobe, and her fine house. In its words, Restell was "mistress paramount, in a scheme of practical destruction. . . . In the heart of this metropolis, she holds her bloody empire."[15]

As public opinion began to flare up again, Dixon returned to lead the troops. He had been trying to earn his bread as a professional pedestrian and newspaper writer. In February 1846, after Applegate's statement, he and two other men announced in handbills that they were holding a protest against Restell. Mounting a makeshift platform, Dixon gathered a crowd and threatened mob action if she were not forced to leave the city. At this point George Matsell, once the radical bookseller, was New York City's police chief, and he commanded forty policemen to protect Restell's establishment. Madame Restell responded in both the *Tribune* and the *Herald* with the accusation that Dixon had attempted to blackmail her. She stated, "Again and again have I been applied to by his emissaries for money, and as often have they been refused; and, as a consequence, I have been vilified and abused without stint or measure."[16]

But the larger campaign of vilification was harder to address. Restell may have been successful in responding to the early statements against her. They were essentially ones used against Robert Dale Owen's *Moral Physiology:* that her practice posed a threat to married men by enabling women to commit adultery without fear of pregnancy. To this Restell responded as had Owen: that it wronged women to claim that their virtue rested only upon fear. Other attacks emphasized Restell's wealth and audacious manner, her impunity; they added some fuel to those who opposed her but probably had little effect on those supporting her. The charge that ultimately stuck was that she was a murderer, profiting from the deaths of her victims, unborn children and women who died from botched abortions. Words and pictures demonized her. The *National Police Gazette* carried an image of her of great power. A handsome, unsmiling woman towers above a small flying devil, his fangs biting into the flesh of a tiny baby.[17]

At first it seems odd that one of the creators of the sporting press, George Washington Dixon, led some of the initial charges against Madame Restell and that George Wilkes, who moved from the *Sunday Flash* to the relative legitimacy of the *National Police Gazette,* picked up the spear. Why did men whose lives were led so close to prostitution oppose the work of abortionists? At one level this may have been displacement: those accused of moral wrongdoing turning accuser. At another level it was boundary setting: a newspaperman claims the legitimacy of his writing partially by stating that he has standards, and it is advertisement for abortion, not the affirmation of prostitution, that lies outside the pale. These reasons, however, do not address the heart of the matter.

The sporting press was part of the commercialization of male vernacular culture. Underlying this new breed of publication was an acceptance of male sexuality on the old terms: boys will be boys. That meant that they would seek to satisfy their need for pleasure. Whatever else it did or did not do, the sporting press gave information about games, drink, sex, and places providing a convivial atmosphere for male indulgence. The crime papers that followed in their wake warned of dangers as their ostensible motive but con-

THE FEMALE ABORTIONIST.

"The Female Abortionist," Madame Restell. *National Police Gazette,* 2, no. 27 (March 13, 1847): 208. Courtesy, American Antiquarian Society.

tinued the information, if only in advertisements. This was a world in which only men mattered. Prostitutes could be bought, used, and discarded. Wives, if they existed, were to be ignorant of men's ways; daughters, to be protected from them. That women had a meaningful life apart from male knowledge and control was unthinkable to the sporting press.

Madame Restell and other leading female abortionists commercialized women's vernacular sexual culture and advertised it in the popular penny press. What had long been practiced in private in women's culture was now out in the mixed public one of print. If some men had not known what their wives, mothers, and sisters had been doing to limit childbearing, learning of it in itself would have been shocking. In addition, Charles Lohman's texts, first as advertisements and later as a book of physiology, linked these practices to the freethinkers' avowal of the need for enlightenment and Frances Wright's promise of women's sexual autonomy. This cast real fear into the hearts of sporting men. Above all else, the fight against Restell and other abortionists was a fight against female agency.

If one takes Dixon's words seriously, what an abortionist threatens is male control. In the old vernacular calculus, women, as lusty as men, were the wayward sex. Only fear kept them from promiscuity. The prostitute was living proof of what a woman would become if freed from restraint. If a woman knew how to avoid pregnancy through contraception or abortion, the man who thought he controlled her could be cuckolded. Admittedly, some men might find it convenient to pay for an abortion sought by a paramour who found herself pregnant. Perhaps there should be discreet places where he might take her. But an abortionist who advertised herself openly in the public press was something else. What this allowed was a trip like the one that Mrs. Purdy had made to Madame Restell without her husband's knowledge. News that one such woman had made the journey threatened all men.

Against this threat, the sporting press marshaled its pens. In short order it learned that the way to get attention and to drive home the danger was to stigmatize abortionists as murderers. In the 1840s, the murder was on the body of the woman. Men who sought to reassert control over women were proclaiming themselves as the protectors of womankind. In some of their publications, a devil was a playful figure of fun who invited men to indulge their appetites in mischief. When used with the female image of Madame Restell, the devil became her agent of murder.

Other men took up the campaign against Restell for their own reasons. Key protagonists were the regular or allopathic physicians who attended women. These men were seeking to distance themselves from midwives and from the ranks of irregulars. At a time when medicine was in flux, the doctors forming the American Medical Association attempted to limit the licensing of physicians to those trained along allopathic lines, but they met resistance in many states. Carroll Smith-Rosenberg has argued that male physicians specializing in gynecology found themselves in especially vulnerable positions, challenged on all sides about the propriety of their practice. They drew on the new understanding of reproduction, which determined that the fetus was alive from the point of fertilization and was a being separate from the female carrying it. Opposition to abortion provided an effective tool to separate the allopaths treating women, bound by the Hippocratic oath, from the irregulars willing to countenance abortion.

It also helped secure male doctors' power over their female patients: "The anti-abortion campaign came to assume a central role in the allopath's struggle for professional hegemony." By projecting and demonizing the image of self-indulgent women who chose abortion rather than the responsibilities of motherhood, A.M.A. physicians were able to persuade men of influence and power that abortion constituted a threat to the social order. Women becoming physicians, whether allopathic or irregular, were especially sensitive to the assumption that they were abortionists, and some joined abortion's most severe critics. What is not clear in the case of abortion is the impact on practice as opposed to discourse. Because laws regulating abortion always allowed licensed physicians the discretion to terminate a pregnancy "to save the life of the mother," the new laws may not have altered private medical practice other than to shield it from the public eye.[18]

Medical opponents of abortion actively sought the support of the churches. This came slowly, gaining strength only after the Civil War. As subsequent chapters will show, evangelical Protestants attempted to play a greater role in national life as the century progressed. They found opportunity in legislation intended to regulate the moral realm.

Throughout the early agitation against abortion, Ann Lohman profited and flourished. She dressed well and drove in a carriage drawn by four horses. In time she would move to one of the grandest houses built on New York's Fifth Avenue. Moreover, she had no consciousness of doing wrong. She believed in the value of her work and in the economic gains it offered. If accurate, a report in the *Advocate of Moral Reform* conveys something of her mentality. Members of the Female Moral Reform Society visited her in jail. Ann Lohman refused their religious tract and, pointing to novels in her cell, told them that she had plenty of reading. In defiance, she stated, "I will hear nothing from you—I fear neither God nor man, nor care for heaven or hell!"[19]

In ensuing years, Ann Lohman would be indicted under the 1845 New York law for her work as Madame Restell. It codified and strengthened earlier laws declaring abortion illegal and making anyone administering, prescribing, or advising substances or practices "to procure miscarriage" liable to a jail sentence of up to a year.[20] In 1847 Lohman was convicted under this law and served a year in prison on Blackwells Island. Additionally, the 1845 law ended the open advertisements for abortionists in the *Herald* and the *Sun*. Gone were the paragraphs that justified family limitation. But as a wily printer, Charles Lohman had another strategy: he wrote and published *The Married Woman's Private Medical Companion,* under the name of Dr. A. M. Mauriceau. Ann Lohman's younger brother Joseph Trow came from England to assist the enterprise, and the 1847 copyright was in his name.[21]

The Married Woman's Private Medical Companion was conventional in its treatment of the sexual organs and their functions. It seems that Charles Lohman was as free in taking material on the physiology of sex from British and American authors as he was in taking text from Owen or Knowlton for Restell's advertisements. What provided new copy and new information was the footnotes. Here Charles Lohman advertised Restell's practice. For example, in a footnote on the *baudruche,* known as the "French secret," long used as a defense against getting syphilis from a prostitute, he told how to get condoms by mail order, for $5 a dozen. In a footnote on "Miscarriage or Abortion," he stated that he, as "Professor of the Diseases of Women, has been called upon to effect miscarriages, and in all cases, it has proved perfectly safe[,] recovery following in about three days." The procedure should be performed as early as possible, but it could be done in all cases and was without pain.[22]

What is important is the way that Charles Lohman as Mauriceau muddied the waters. Other authors of physiological texts had hoped for monetary gain from their words. Charles Knowlton, desperate for money, may have been partially moved to write *Fruits of Philosophy* by the hope of success. Frederick Hollick also earned his living as a writer and lecturer. In these cases, there was a mixture of motives: desire to educate a broad public and the need for money, desire for fame, and hope of a paying lecture audience. Charles Lohman, however, tipped the balance. His largely cribbed text served primarily as a marketing tool. It was an advertisement for the business of Madame Restell in book form. Written at a time when his wife was under attack in the press and sold while she was serving a prison sentence on Black-wells Island, the book may have cast doubt in some minds about the larger physiological enterprise.

On September 15, 1847, the grand jury indicted Charles Lohman for pub-lishing an obscene book. Arrested the following day, he made bail. He was never brought to trial.[23] It was often said that Madame Restell had friends in high places who protected her, including the chief of police and erstwhile freethinking bookseller George W. Matsell. Perhaps the real object of Mat-sell's protection was Charles Lohman. In his many years as his wife's business partner and advertising agent and in his new incarnation as author, Lohman—unlike his wife—was never convicted and would die a natural death.

In 1847 Lohman's association with Restell probably served to get him arrested for selling his book, but it was not enough for a conviction. Publica-tions about the body, such as *The Married Woman's Private Medical Companion,* were common in New York, and there were no precedents for treating them as obscene. Three decades later, however, the irregular physician Edward Bliss Foote would be prosecuted and convicted for selling just such a book, though one far more original, offering contraceptive advice, not advertise-ment for abortion. The 1870s were not the 1840s. Convicting Foote required federal law and a federal officer empowered to enforce it.[24]

Future laws would also ban advertisements for abortion. Necessary to understanding their passage is the relation of abortion to female vernacular sexual culture and the role the male sporting press played in vilifying it. With urbanization, the disruption of female networks, and increasing literacy, women's knowledge passed into print, and abortionists moved in to provide services that the women's community had once clandestinely offered its members. Abortion went from a secret, private practice to one performed commercially and advertised in the newspapers. As hidden practices became public, men in sporting culture were alarmed by the specter of female sexual agency. In its campaign of vilification against abortionists, the sporting press found unlikely allies in regular physicians and evangelical Protestants. Their arguments entered into the sexual conversation.

Yet a critical element remains missing from this broad survey of sexual speech in New York. On city streets newsboys who were hawking racy sport-ing weeklies and penny dailies with abortionists' advertisements were offer-ing, more clandestinely, outright erotica. It is to this brisk but furtive trade that this account now turns.

10

Obscenity in the City

The obscenity trials of the New York sporting press are puzzling on one level. Although these weekly publications of the early 1840s were filled with hints, winks, and suggestive passages, their power to arouse did not compare to that of the erotic books and prints sold in the city. Many of these texts were illustrated with sexually explicit, erotically charged engravings, which were also sold and kept separately. Traffic in these materials was well established when, ironically, the federal effort to bar the import of European works actually encouraged American production. New racy works produced in the United States in the nineteenth century found a place among the erotic books that had formed part of an eighteenth-century gentleman's library.[1]

In the case of erotica, the difficulties a historian encounters in finding sources are compounded by the deliberate destruction of material and by secrecy surrounding what has remained. Detective work has yielded five important pieces of data. The first came from an extraordinary series of events that began when George W. Matsell and an alderman made a sweep of booksellers in New York City in August 1842. This ended not only in their arrest but also in indictments that convey a great deal of information on the trade in erotic books and prints in the city. The second emerged from tracking the beginnings of the career of William Haynes in the *National Police Gazette*, starting in 1845. Editor George Wilkes, late of the *Sunday Flash*, proved to have an enduring interest in the crime of obscenity, and so he noted the early arrests of a man who would become a major publisher of erotica. The third is the body of homegrown sensationalist fiction that grew up alongside crime reporting and urban exposés. George Thompson, its most prolific author, skirted the edge of the legally tolerable and, at least at one point, crossed it. The fourth occurred in 1857, when accounts in the papers of another police raid uncovered aspects of the shop of George Ackerman, who printed and sold a wide range of erotic materials. The fifth came after patient searching over several years brought to light important bits of information about Jeremiah Farrell, the only publisher of erotica who conducted his business openly.

I

That a brisk trade in erotic materials existed in New York by August 1842 is revealed in the arrests of eight New York sellers of books and prints. The roundup began when an alderman caught Edward Scofield, a newsboy, vending books he had gotten from Cornelius Ryan, a man who had a book stand on Wall Street near the Customs House. New York streets were filled with newsboys who hawked the penny press and occasionally erotic materials that they technically bought and resold. Scofield gave a deposition stating that "said Books are generally sold to boys who again dispose of them to Strangers and others about the Hotels." Ryan had a tin box under his stand and supplied the boy with *Fanny Hill* and *The Lustful Turk.*[2]

Scofield followed this revelation with a series of depositions. His arrangement with Ryan was similar to that with the booksellers Hiram Cure, William Bradley, James Jones, Charles Huestis, Francis Kerrigan, and John Child. Two of these booksellers were also printers: Huestis, known today for his almanacs and children's books, and Child. In this case both men were indicted for the sale of books. Indictment and trial records reveal that, like Cornelius Ryan, these men typically kept a metal box isolated from their other printed materials. Their indictments demonstrate that in the box resided the primary texts of the erotic canon of their time. According to the indictments, the books in turn went from the metal boxes to newsboys, who sold them in and around the city's hotels. In addition to *Memoirs of a Woman of Pleasure* (or *Fanny Hill*) and *The Lustful Turk* were *Night Thoughts, Rochester, The Curtain Drawn Up, The Cabinet Unlocked, The Confessions of a Young Lady of High Rank, Betty Ireland,* and *Flash Lamp.*

The trail then led in two directions. Following one path, authorities learned that the booksellers were being supplied by the printer Richard Hobbs of Westchester County. After working as a fine printer of novels,

"Newspaper Boy, 'Tribune Sir?'" Street Cries
Occupational Card, n.d. © Museum of the
City of New York.

plays, and short stories in New York City, Hobbs retired to the country to
print the well-known erotica of England and France. The other path led to
the prolific printer of political caricatures Henry R. Robinson. His graphic
work, published between 1836 and 1849, is well known and respected today.

A Whig in an era of political broadsides, Robinson made much of his living fabricating broadside caricatures of Andrew Jackson, Martin Van Buren,
and other leading figures of the day and then selling them in his shop. A
minor artist in his own right, beginning in the late 1830s he printed the
remarkable work of the American caricaturist E. W. Clay, which offered
visual insults to Democratic leaders. Each caricature was copyrighted and
sold separately, either on the street by newsboys or from his store at the front
of his shop at 52 Cortlandt Street. One of his trade cards displays his shop
windows, advertising a range of books and prints.

In his deposition, bookseller William Bradley stated that about two years earlier he had purchased a number of prints from Robinson, who carried "large quantities" of prints in his shop. Others had told Bradley that Robinson not only dealt in prints "but is the getter up and publisher of them." The indictment revealed that, in addition to prints, Robinson sold at his establishment these European erotic texts: *Memoirs of the Life and Voluptuous Adventures of the Celebrated Courtesan Mademoiselle Celestine of Paris Written by Herself, The Amorous History and Adventures of Raymond de B*———, *The Auto-Biography of a Footman,* and what may have been an American one, *The Amorous Songster or Jovial Companion.*

With its Democratic leanings, the New York *Herald* took delight in Robinson's arrest and described the moment in unusual detail. The paper reported that on August 16, 1842, Henry R. Robinson had received an unexpected visit by George W. Matsell and Clarkson Crolius, Jr., in his Cortlandt Street shop. At this point Matsell, earlier encountered as first a manager of the Free Enquirer bookstore and later the possible protector of Ann and Charles Lohman, was at the beginning of his political climb. In 1842 Matsell was the justice of the lower police court in New York City, appointed by the Democrats. Crolius, owner of a pottery firm, was a Whig stalwart and the alderman for the Sixth Ward. The reporter wrote:

> Such a scene was presented to the eyes of modest men as would cause a blush to gleam from the face of brass, engravings, etchings, paintings, lithographic sketches, prints[,] pamphlets, books without number of all sizes and shapes, with every possible characteristic of obscenity and lewdness that could be presented to the eyes or ears, were there disclosed; not even excepting illustrations of all the peculiar passages of scripture, which were done in a peculiarly exquisite style and colored in the most delicate manner. The destruction of the Bastile of Paris and the disclosures that followed with evidences then made apparent, were scarcely more astounding than the opening of this repository of Robinson's.

Perhaps to distract Crolius from his task, or to remind him of the printer's Whig support, Robinson showed him the heads of the national leaders that he portrayed heroically, not in caricature: Clay, Webster, and Adams. But a nod from Democrat stalwart Matsell ("who perhaps had become a little soured because some representations of Little Van, Benton,

&c. were not shown him") put Crolius back on track, and he "ordered Robinson to be sent to the Tombs, together with his collection of obscenity." Bail was set at $2,000.[3]

Robinson's indictment states that he was formally charged with selling obscene prints and books. One witness testified that he had bought eighteen obscene prints from Robinson, who had "a very large quantity of other prints on sale at his establishments . . . in a room partitioned off for that purpose, and others of a less obscene character, though clearly so, publicly exposed in his principal store room where persons were continually passing in and out." In the language of obscenity indictments came the testimony of two additional witnesses. On one occasion, Robinson had sold "six other obscene, filthy, and indecent prints, representing men and women in attitudes, situations, and practices of great and scandalous obscenity, lewdness and indecency." The second account stated that on various occasions, Robinson had had in his possession, with intent to sell, "twenty obscene filthy and indecent prints, representing men and women in attitudes and situations of great and scandalous indecency lewdness and obscenity, and representing men and women with their private parts in most indecent postures and attitudes and representing men and women in the act of carnal copulation in various attitudes and postures." When Robinson was arrested and taken to the Tombs, "Justice Matsell, accompanied by officer Wm H. Stevens & others went to Robinson's Store in Courtland [sic] St. and took there from Several thousand Prints and Books all of an obscene nature."

Three specific prints were named by the indictment. The print referred to as "a standing member of the Abolition Society, giving an example of practical amalgamation," is described as "representing a man in the dress of a member of the society of friends in an obscene, impudent and indecent posture with a negro woman." These words constitute the legal euphemism used for an image of a heterosexual couple engaged in coition. No known copy of this print exists, but other extant prints take up the theme of "amalgamation," the mid-nineteenth-century term for sexual union between the races. E. W. Clay delineated a series, "Practical Amalgamation," engraved by Robinson's chief competitor, John Child, also indicted in 1842. These prints attempted to shock audiences into opposition to anti–slavery reform. In the well-publicized versions available for viewing, whites and blacks are typically shown in polite settings, such as classical musical performances or balls, where, if all the subjects being portrayed were white, the anticipated reac-

PRACTICAL AMALGAMATION (Musical Soirée.)
Published by John Childs, &c.

E. W. Clay, "Practical Amalgamation." Courtesy, American
Antiquarian Society.

tion of the viewer would be positive. In some images black men are leering at
white women or making affectionate gestures toward them.

In these images of race mixing, African-American men consort with,
dance with, and marry white women. The men are typical dandies below the
neck, with tiny, slippered feet, wearing the elegant court dress of European
society with style and grace. Above the neck the black men are often portrayed as hideously ugly in many and varied ways. Such features as jutting
jaws, buckteeth, leering eyes, oddly shaped noses, and hair standing straight
up are intended to make them look repulsive. The black men's faces fit no
mold, unlike those of the white women whom they accompany, who are of a
uniform type, the beautiful and demure middle-class ladies who grace parlor
images. When white men escort or wed black women, the accusation is different. The white men are abolitionists portrayed as typical "philanthro-
pists"—tall, skinny, thin, white-bearded, bespectacled, bloodless, and dressed
in buttoned-up New England or Quaker style. They accompany black

women, who often have full-breasted and wide-hipped bodies, emphasizing their sexual characteristics. Many of the black female faces are grotesque and seem to come out of farcical prints of European peasants or from images of lower primates.

The two other prints by Robinson seized were "Victoria, Studying Her Comfort" and "Queen Victoria and Her Page in Attendance." Attached to them was the normal indictment wording: "Representing a man in an obscene, impudent and indecent posture with a woman." None of the images cited in the indictment can be found in the major collections of Robinson prints. In the Harvard Theatre Collection is a Clay drawing of a bare-breasted woman printed by Robinson, "Madame Lecompte. Principal Danseuse . . . In the Character of the Abbess," of 1837. Below the copyright

"The Prosecuted Picture." E. W. Clay, "Madame Lecompte. Principal Danseuse . . . In the Character of the Abbess," published by Robinson, 1837. Courtesy, Harvard Theatre Collection, The Houghton Library.

line on the bottom are the words: "The Prosecuted Picture." This suggests one reason why erotic prints are missing in the historical record. In 1837 Robinson likely learned that he would be prosecuted if he sought copyright for an erotic image. Sexually explicit materials therefore did not make it into the Library of Congress's collection of prints related to copyright, a major source for historians.[4]

A few images on the bawdy edge that Robinson drew or pulled do exist in libraries. Prior to "the prosecuted picture," Robinson applied for a copyright for an engraving drawn by A. H. Hoffy, purporting to be "a correct likeness & representation" of Helen Jewett, "taken on the spot very shortly after she had become the victim of a foul and barbarous murder and her bedclothes had been set fire to." Like much of the fallout from the Helen Jewett murder, this image plays on the erotic possibilities of the event, here in the death scene itself. The dead Jewett, with a wound to her head, is barebreasted. Her bedclothes are burned tatters. The date of application to the court for the copyright protection, April 18, 1836, was only days after Jewett's death. Quickly moving to coin the Jewett tragedy in a print hawked on the streets, Robinson was clearly on the alert for a way to make money from his engraver's craft. More than a decade later, in some of his own delineations, Robinson took items from the newspaper and gave them an erotic twist. For instance, when James Gordon Bennett's wife traveled abroad in 1847, she wrote travel letters that were published in the *Herald*. Robinson took two of the events she described and created prints that played up their sexualized possibilities. From the titles named in the 1842 indictment, it looks as though Robinson was up to his trick of exploiting the sexual potentials of a historical situation, in this case combining the political caricature for which he was publicly known with explicit representation of sexual acts.[5]

It was one of the odder twists that Democrat Matsell, a former bookseller known to have promoted the works of freethinkers, received possession of Whig Robinson's erotic material. Mistrust was great on all sides. When Robinson sought their return, Matsell "refused to deliver them up." District Attorney James R. Whiting, a Whig, let Matsell know that if Robinson's prints were ever shown in public, Matsell would be indicted. Mike Walsh of the *Subterranean* even accused Matsell of seizing "the obscene and beastly prints" in Robinson's shop that he had once sold to Robinson from his own "infidel bookstore."[6]

With the titles of only the three lost prints of Robinson, there is no way to trace and view the erotic images vended by him and the other sellers. If,

A. H. Hoffy, "A correct likeness & representation" of Helen Jewett, "taken on the spot very shortly after she had become the victim of a foul and barbarous murder and her bed-clothes had been set fire to," published by H. R. Robinson, 1836. Courtesy, American Antiquarian Society.

however, some of the eighteenth- and early-nineteenth-century French engravings in the Kinsey collection were ones sold on the street by these dealers in 1842, they contained explicit and emphatic representations of sexual excitement and varied sexual acts. Some books contain many prints, and these could be separated for distribution. Other prints were sold separately. Explicit images of coition, oral sex, anal sex, females urinating, and females embracing each other seem designed to arouse men and to supply them with a range of titillating visual material intended for varied tastes. In such prints, the genitals of men and women are often highlighted by tinting. Erect penises are rose-colored, as are fulsome female breasts, with deeper rose at the tips and nipples. Ignoring anatomical correctness, the vaginal opening of women is tinted as if it were a separate organ.

In contrast to the seized prints, the books allow a different degree of cer-

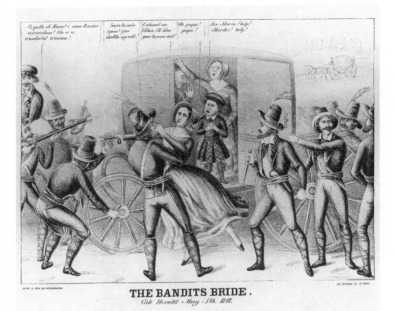

THE BANDITS BRIDE .
Vide Herald . May . 5th. 1847.

Henry R. Robinson, "The Bandits Bride, Vide Herald May 5th,
1847." Courtesy, American Antiquarian Society.

tainty. In documenting the sale by Robinson and others of the books printed
by Hobbs, the language in the indictments is explicit, giving paragraphs of
texts regarded as obscene. These excerpts make it clear that the editions of
the erotic canon in question were not highly expurgated to remove salacious
material. Although there is no way to trace the particular version of *Memoirs
of a Woman of Pleasure* that Peter Holmes sold in Massachusetts in 1818, the
grand jury indictment quoted specific passages of Richard Hobbs's printing
of the book:

> Without more ado, he plants me with my back standing against the
> Wall, and my petticoats up; and coming out with a splitter indeed,
> made it shine and brandished it in my eyes; and going to work with
> an impetuosity and eagerness, bred very likely, by a long fast at sea,
> went to give me a taste of it. I straddled, I humoured my posture
> and did my best in short to buckle to it; I took part of it in, but still

La curiosite
Die Neugierde | The curiosity
La Curiosidad

Lithograph, woman urinating, framed by drawings emphasizing genitalia, untitled, anonymous, A397QB7557.9. The Kinsey Institute for Research in Sex, Gender, and Reproduction.

things did not go to his thorough liking, changing then in a trice his system of battery, he leads me to a table and with a master hand lays my head down on the edge of it, and with the other canting up my petticoats and shift, bares my naked posteriors to his blind and furious guide, it forces its way between them and I feeling pretty sensibly that it was going by the right door and knocking desperately at the wrong one, I told him of it. Pooh (says he) my dear! any port in a storm.

Cleland's humor is not characteristic of the genre, but the passage shares a general attribute of other works in the erotic canon cited in these 1842 indictments. Within an amoral universe in which all sexual postures are possible, a female character describes the beauties of a male's erect penis. In

Lithograph, sexually explicit bucolic rural scene, untitled, anonymous, 97Q.A017.2. The Kinsey Institute for Research in Sex, Gender, and Reproduction.

addition, other selections in the indictment give women's exclamations of their own sexual excitement. For example, one of the characters in *The Cabinet of Venus Unlocked* expands:

> Oh, what rapturous exquisite delight as I took it, when it rushed in and filled the whole deep cavity, where I felt it swell and throb as if it would burst with its exertions within. I strained and struggled with him to the utmost of my strength, and seemed inspired beyond my natural powers in every effort. I screamed with excessive ecstasy, and, oh! God of burning lust! At the last flush and overwhelming flow of bliss that gushed into me from him, my senses were wholly entranced and the whole world of love seemed swallowed up in the heavenly sweet delirium.

These books clearly crossed the line into obscenity in their depiction in print of sexual acts. It is significant that the narrators are frequently women.

The penis is described from their imagined perspective, and they portray their own sexual arousal. If one were to isolate the point of sexual danger in imaginative works in the nineteenth century, it is here. A male erection and a woman's sexual pleasure, fictively described in the female voice (but written by a man), are perceived as incitements to male lust and likely to lead to either sexual intercourse or masturbation. This is what obscenity meant to a district attorney and a grand jury in 1842. The sellers of works in which such elements are found—the erotic canon—constituted the primary target of indictments for obscenity.

In the indictments the eight "vendors of obscene books and prints" were charged with obscene libel or, more familiarly, obscenity, a criminal misdemeanor under common law. With the exception of Robinson, bail was set at $1,000. Their cases, not including Robinson's, were called in January 1843. Typically each received a sentence of thirty days in prison. Out in the wilds of Westchester County, Richard Hobbs was a bit more difficult to secure. New York police officers were dispatched to his house in the town of East Chester. The *Herald,* perhaps embellishing on the known, reported that Hobbs had "an extensive printing office at that place, where nearly all the obscene and infamous books that flood the city are issued from the press." In the paper's portrayal, Hobbs made "an immense fortune in the business, and is a member of the church."[7]

When Hobbs was arrested, his bail was supplied by William Applegate, the New York printer who had recently printed the *Sunday Flash* and then sold his press to Snelling when given Adelina Miller's note. Hobbs did not initially show in court, but he was rearrested and, on January 11, 1843, pled guilty. He was sentenced to prison for sixty days and a fine of $50, but because he had given the police information, his prison sentence was commuted. This sent up a howl in the *Herald* that this "hoary headed debauchee" had gone virtually free. The paper requested that the grand jury of Bedford indict him and cause him to be "punished as he deserves."[8]

Robinson, too, never went to jail, and he was not even fined. His case was delayed until March. The two men who had put up his bail surrendered him to the court, and he was held in jail to await trial. Court documents suggest that he got a dismissal of the case against him. His attorney argued that when Matsell and Crolius had visited him, they had "forcibly entered a back room which was locked and there found a quantity of obscene prints and books of a description similar to those named in the indictment." Robinson's lawyer did not deny that he possessed obscene material, only that there was no proof that he had sold or displayed it: "The public prosecutor is unable to produce a single book or print purchased from or exhibited by defendant." The testimony of William Bradley was insufficient to "constitute a legal publication (without which the indictment can not be sustained)."[9]

Stepping back from these 1842 cases, one thing is immediately apparent. Erotica in this era was normally sequestered. Booksellers had a locked tin box under their stands in which they kept erotic books, some of which they entrusted to newsboys to sell. By one account Robinson had a partition separating the area in which he kept his collection of erotic prints from his principal storeroom. His lawyer stated that Robinson kept his "obscene prints and books" in a locked back room. Thus these materials were never normalized, never brought openly into the world of commerce. One can say that they belonged in male space, but it was not a space for all males. It was for the adult man who asked. Authorities made the arrests after a newsboy broke the silence by his hawking. Perhaps he was stupider than were other newsboys, who knew to wait for an approach or a glance from a potential customer.

If erotica was segregated because it was connected with shame or might be seen by women and children, this factor may have operated indirectly. That is, shame and impropriety may have played into the minds of the sellers not because of their own feelings but because they anticipated that they were the feelings of others willing to act in court against public displays of erotic materials. After all, the booksellers caught in 1842 received sentences of a month in jail. But not the fabricators. Robinson served no time. At issue in the court was not the possession or the printing of obscene material. It was the sale, documented by specific evidence, that constituted the offense convictable under common law.

One more change needs to be noted: indictments for obscenity would never again be so explicit in New York City. In a case being argued in court in the same period, District Attorney Whiting objected strenuously to having to read in court the full articles in the sporting press that the indictments labeled obscene. He may have felt a similar aversion when he read the full indictments of the booksellers that contained libidinous passages, such as those quoted above. From this point on, indictments in the Court of General Sessions of New York suppressed reproduction in the record of the specific materials being charged as obscene. This created yet another layer of silence that prevents historians from discovering the full past.

2

In 1843 George Wilkes, one of the proprietors of the *Sunday Flash,* served a monthlong jail sentence, initially suspended, for obscenity. From then on he had his eye on others brought into court for the same offense. Because of this, his *National Police Gazette* is an excellent source for learning about charges of obscenity in New York City from its founding in 1845. In this weekly newspaper, Wilkes found what he hoped was a legal way to write about crime and sex from police records, but he was always skirting the edge of indictments for libel and obscenity. Perhaps in an effort to distance himself and his new venture from his past in the sporting press, Wilkes sought to guard the boundary by a declared hostility to obscenity. In an early issue, the *National Police Gazette* included this statement: "OBSCENE BOOKS.—We particularly request all persons, who have knowledge of the printing, publishing, stitching, binding, or sale of obscene books in this city, to give us notice, in order that the infamous authors of the numerous publications that flood our country should be exposed to the public authorities."[10]

One typical news item is of particular interest because of the 1842 raid just discussed. In April 1847 the *National Police Gazette* reported that "Officers Doyle and Parison, of the 4th ward, arrested, Saturday, a young man by the name of Edward Thomas Scofield, whom the officer found in the vestibule of the Astor House, offering for sale obscene books." Unable to post bail, Scofield was taken to the Tombs. The newsboy vendor who provoked the 1842 arrests was still at his work as a young man five years later.[11]

This was small stuff compared to another story. Wilkes probably did not know that he had a real scoop in 1846: William Haynes was put on trial. He had sold two items judged obscene, the book *The Curtain Drawn Up* and a print called "Belshazzar's Feast." Found guilty, he was sent to jail for three months. The *National Police Gazette* and the New York courts were to see Haynes a number of times in the next few years. In 1849 the weekly reported that Haynes, working under the alias of Piggot, had sold "obscene books to a young man named James Morrison. Morrison had been arrested before Haynes, for offering the books for sale, and to save himself said that he had purchased the books from Haynes to sell again. Haynes is supposed to be the manufacturer."[12]

Haynes, it turned out, was a publisher who took the erotic canon as his work. It was later said of him that he was a well-educated English surgeon who, after marrying a nobleman's daughter, had been forced by sexual scandal to emigrate. He had come to the United States in the early 1840s and married again. Working in partnership with his American wife, Mary, he first made his mark by publishing John Cleland's *Memoirs of a Woman of Pleasure,* or *Fanny Hill.* With the exception of Cleland's book, such information is not fact but rather the lore that surrounded Haynes's name by the early 1870s.[13]

In 1853 Haynes was indicted by the Court of General Sessions for "Obscene book nuisance." The books named were *The Confessions of a Voluptuous Young Lady of High Rank Illustrated by Numerous Elegant Engravings, Memoirs of a Woman of Pleasure. Wr by Herself—Embellished with Numerous Steel Plate Engravings,* and *La Rose D'Amour,* said to have been translated from Rousseau by Lola Montez. The printer Albert Gurley, also indicted, stated that Haynes had provided him with the plates from which he had printed the books. His list included *Cecile Martin, The Curtain Drawn Up,* and *Fanny Hill.* Albert Gazeley, arrested for selling one of the books, stated that Haynes not only supplied him with the books and plates found in his store on William Street, but also that Haynes "supplies and furnishes other persons and stores with these same kind of books" and that he has been "producing and circulating these most obscene books plates papers and prints for several years."[14]

How did it happen to be that Richard Hobbs, Henry Robinson, and William Haynes saw opportunity in the publishing of erotic prints and books in the 1840s? They were aware of new commercial possibilities. There had been an outpouring of erotic prints from France and England in the revolutionary and postrevolutionary period, much of it politically inspired. Sexual accusation had long been used to delegitimize those in power, such as the monarchy and the clergy, and libertine libels flourished. New opportunities seem to have emerged for erotica in its own right, despite efforts at state censorship, and America was a waiting market. In an effort to stem the traffic in erotic prints, the federal government exercised its power in one of the limited ways it had available, the power to regulate foreign trade. In 1842, in Section 28 of the Tariff Act, Congress prohibited the importation of all "indecent and obscene prints, paintings, lithographs, engravings, and transparencies." Any such matter could be "proceeded against, seized, and forfeited, by due course of law, and the said articles shall be forthwith destroyed." In the public record there is no evidence that the bill elicited discussion or debate.[15]

The provision was immediately put into force, and in the following year in the district court of New York the first case was tried. Attached to nine snuffboxes imported from Germany in three boxes of toys were paintings of

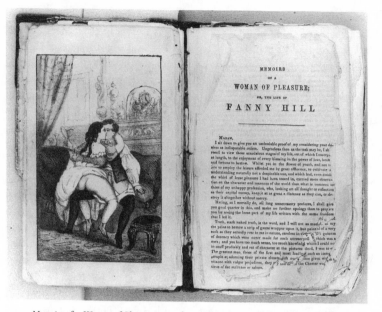

Memoirs of a Woman of Pleasure, 1830, frontispiece and p. 1. The Kinsey Institute for Research in Sex, Gender, and Reproduction.

"an indecent scene or figure of so very obscene a character that they were unfit to be produced in court." One of them, with the offending scene covered by ink, was exhibited to show the way the paintings were attached to the boxes under a false bottom. Without leaving the courtroom, the jury agreed that the entire shipment be confiscated by the government, despite the fact that the importers did not know of the hidden paintings.[16]

The 1842 Tariff Act stimulated publishers in the United States to reproduce European works for the American trade and attracted immigrants for the purpose. International copyrights were not secure in the United States. Moreover, copyright protection did not extend to works that courts judged obscene. There had been some printing and distribution of *Memoirs of a Woman of Pleasure* in the United States earlier in the nineteenth century, but this was a rather modest endeavor compared to Hobbs's and Haynes's activities. After 1842, erotic books printed domestically entered the American market. So much for the unintended outcomes of early federal legislation to regulate American morality.

3

The 1842 Tariff Act also encouraged American writers to produce home-grown works. This development went hand in hand with changes in the organization and technology of printing and new modes of distribution. In these years, publishing and printing were becoming separate enterprises. Publishers took on the financial responsibility for getting a book printed and for marketing and selling it. Printers became responsible for the production of the physical book, increasingly under contract by a publisher. Separated from sale, printing could become industrialized: expensive machinery took the place of men; stereotypes replaced compositors; and steam-powered presses, pressmen. By the late 1840s periodical depots emerged in major cities, blending publishing and selling and serving as points of connection between suppliers of printed materials and readers. The transportation revolution, especially the railroads, allowed increasing concentration of book manufacture in eastern cities, especially New York City. As books began to go down in price, a few found opportunity. Following the lead of their English counterparts, some American printers bought up failing newspapers and, using their format and their ability to take advantage of lower postal rates than books, created story papers and pamphlet novels, typically referred to as paper- or yellow-covered books. Fiction, hitherto reserved for those who could pay $2 a novel—the middle and upper classes—was now available to a mass audience able to pay 6 cents for a story paper or 25 cents for a book.[17]

Some story papers specialized in British works that, unprotected by copyright, could be reprinted cheaply. American writers, reporters, and failed dramatists quickly found that there were rewards, if only modest ones, in writing for the enlarged audience of readers. In a new household industry, women turned their pens to work and produced the sentimental-domestic novel; but some men found consumers with a taste for sensational fiction. Male authors sent their heroes out to sea to encounter pirates and strange beasts and engage in feats of derring-do. Drawing on the penny newspapers that hawked crime and scandal, an urban-based fiction emerged that portrayed sporting life, prostitution, seduction and betrayal, and the contrasts between the rich and the poor.

Drawn by the success of French writer Eugène Sue's *The Mysteries of Paris* and Philadelphian George Lippard's *The Quaker City,* two New York authors took to the presses almost simultaneously. E. Z. C. Judson, who took the pseudonym Ned Buntline, and George G. Foster wrote many books, including two exposés of New York, published in 1849 and 1850. Judson had led a tempestuous life before coming to New York. His *The Mysteries and Miseries of New York* promised that it was "drawn from *life*, heart-sickening, *too-real* life." However, the characters in this poorly written, episodic work of fiction appear taken from well-known literary prototypes: the innocent girl preyed upon, the libertine young man led into evil through gambling. What may have appealed in its time was the effort to place a sensational story in specific sites of New York vice: Julia Brown's brothel, Pat Hisen's saloon, a black dive in the Five Points. Real characters, such as the notorious burglar Bob Sutton, make cameo appearances. There is discussion of "flash patter," the patois of the underworld. Throughout this sensational tale Judson takes the tone of the reformer, enabling the reader to enjoy a voyeuristic look with a good conscience. Following the financial success of this book, Judson established a weekly paper, *Ned Buntline's Own*. In this phase of his career (he reemerged in the 1880s as a chronicler of the Wild West), he took part in the Astor Place riot of 1849 on the side of those opposed to the actor William Charles Macready.[18]

George G. Foster first surfaced with a series of urban sketches in the New York *Tribune* that reached book form in 1849 as *New York in Slices by an Experienced Carver*. The book gave the usual nod to the extent and harm of prostitution, drawing on McDowall's work for numbers, although, unlike the reformer, Foster sympathized with the underpaid working girls for whom prostitution loomed as a continuing temptation. In this book, he labeled as "sporting men" only those experienced gamblers who lured the unwary into their hells. He pictured the young clerks only once: they appear in the oyster cellars, "betting their employers' money with a couple of sharpers at brag, over a bottle of champagne."[19]

In the more polished *New York by Gas-light*, published in 1850, Foster assumes the young clerk's point of view. Adopting the perspective of a young man on the town, he takes the reader to a range of saloons, dance halls, markets, model artist exhibits, brothels, and gambling places, up and down the class ladder. The general tone is typically one of bemusement and gentle titillation, rather than the high moralizing of some of Foster's other writing. Occasionally Foster let down his guard, as when he described the sons of wealth in an upstairs drinking saloon. These "bucks of the blunt, lads of spirit, young men about town, fancy coves" found it "altogether too 'slow' for their use to spend an evening decently at home among virtuous and accomplished women." In what could have been a warning by Beecher, Foster wrote that this saloon was merely a decoy for the whoring and gambling going on in adjacent rooms. "Many a young man, who could not possibly be persuaded into a gambling-house or a brothel, is easily induced to call with his more profligate companions on 'the widow' [tending bar] merely to take a drink and have a little chat." Most of the time, however, a reader could imagine being amused in many of the establishments that Foster described at the upper level of the social ladder.[20]

Not so at the "Five Points," the demarcated hell in Foster's moral geography of New York City. The oyster cellars and saloons here were "for the accommodation of thieves, burglars, low gamblers and vagabonds . . . whose 'pals' are up-stairs carrying on the game of prostitution." All was inverted, as its residents stayed quiet during the day, only to surface at night. According to Foster, Negro men ruled, controlling both property and women. Prostitutes were now the Devil in female form, lost to any possibility of reform. Foster described the low saloons of the Five Points a number of times, perhaps most vividly when he took the New York rube Zerubbabel Green to a cellar where he saw black and white men and women, in various states of undress, dance unrestrainedly to the tunes of a black fiddler. While Foster suggested that he was among the ranks of reformers, his real location was close to that of the sporting press. He was a participant-observer of New York sporting culture who took its haunts as places to describe to a reading and paying audience.[21]

The books by Judson and Foster attained a commercial success that many vied to emulate. One who prevailed was their contemporary George Thompson, perhaps the most prolific sensational author of the 1840s and 1850s. When he wrote *My Life* in 1854, Thompson placed his childhood home near the site of Helen Jewett's murder, Rosina Townsend's brothel. He recalled seeing Helen Jewett out walking with Richard Robinson, "both dressed in the height of fashion, the beautiful Ellen leaning upon the arm of the dashing Dick." He even insisted that he, a boy of thirteen, had been one of the throng who had entered the room after the murder and seen the dead prostitute. His novelistic autobiography has many embellishments, such as his statement about Jewett suggests. Removing them leaves the mundane elements that he was born in New York, became a printer's apprentice as a youth, began to write for periodicals as a young man, tried different cities as he got work as a reporter, and moved to Boston, where he was linked to those in theatrical circles. He clearly wrote very fast, producing two of his fictional offerings during a six-week stint in the Leverett Street jail. His novels, if such they can be called, enable some access into the minds of his readers. Thompson's principal urban subjects were the adventures of "flash-men" and contrasts of wealth and poverty in the city.[22]

Thompson began writing in the early years of the *National Police Gazette.* One of the sources of the crime paper's appeal was the way it introduced readers to the underworld. Thompson followed a similar strategy in his 1848 novel *The House Breaker.* A young gentleman descends to the dives of Five Points and there meets such rough types as Guinea Bill. Thompson's footnotes translated words of "flash" language spoken by the book's characters, and one note explained, "Jonathan Wild was the originator of 'flash' 150 years ago." Thompson also took the reader to Julia Brown's brothel and a party enlivened by young male and female attendants, age twelve to fourteen, who served food and wine in the nude. In language not unlike the moral reformers' but with different intent, Thompson wrote that the wine brought "wild and extravagant desires—mad hopes and reckless thoughts. Passion usurps the throne of Reason, and the mind's proud empire is for a season overthrown." As the partygoers removed their clothing and danced, Thompson abruptly closed the scene. "Stiff, cold, senseless conventional prejudices of society," he stated, prevented him from describing it. The public "flourishes its rattan of Censure above our devoted pate, and talks of 'morality,' and propriety." In addition to this scene, the book contains stock efforts at sexually suggestive description, as for example, in this pen portrait: "Her form was the most seductive, her bust the most distracting, and her eyes the most passionate, that ever graced a woman."[23]

Thompson represented sexual acts of great variety, including, by literary scholar David Reynolds's list, "incest, sadomasochism, homosexuality, group sex, miscegenation, child sex, mass orgies." Thompson showed women impelled by sexual desire, but in his works sex is typically intertwined with violence. The historian Karen Halttunen has written about the way that pain, removed from civilized discourse by nineteenth-century philanthropy, became transgressive and eroticized. In George Thompson's fictional works, the primary force is violence and sadomasochism. The books dwell on the details of violent mutilations and deaths. The final bloody scene of *The House Breaker* is a horrific murder that revenges the death of the hero's sister. Thompson pulled out all stops as he described the burning, piercing, and pouring of hot oil into the ear of the black killer Guinea Bill.[24]

Thompson often attempted to describe his work as nonfiction. In *The*

Countess; or Memoirs of Women of Leisure he contended that the fiction of his time written in the mode of romance was fit only for "cross peevish old maids, and romping school girls." Instead, he promised to put forth "to the sensible mind of man or woman, fact, uncontradictable and solid fact." A year later, in *Venus in Boston,* he wrote that because he believed in "the romance of reality—the details of common, every day life—the secret history of things hidden from the public gaze . . . are fraught with a more powerful and absorbing interest than any extravagant flight of imagination can be, it shall be my aim in the following pages to adhere as closely as possible to truth and reality." Thompson insisted that he based his books on his own wide experience.[25]

Thompson's works followed the path of other writers in his period to describe certain areas of New York, taking the reader, as had Buntline and Foster, up and down through the class system. This became Thompson's stated purpose in *The Mysteries of Bond Street; or The Seraglios of Upper Tendom.* Thompson introduced the reader to characters who moved them through various neighborhoods, especially the high end of the wealthiest New Yorkers and the low of the Five Points. This Thompson novel again salted its tale with violence, sexual titillation, and scenes of opulence. In it Thompson implicitly told readers that the most important emotions are male lust, female revenge, and the desire of both sexes for luxury. All the men of the novel seek to bed the women. The little courtship that exists is only a device by the villainous rake to persuade the virgin that he is not who he really is. Women agree to sexual intercourse not out of desire but to please a lover or because they are hypnotized, drugged, or physically overpowered. Thompson typically described lovemaking in these terms: "the thrilling drama of Venus was enacted, and the sacrifice complete."[26]

What fuels this Thompson drama—and others—is the desire less to consummate the sexual act than to extract revenge after sexual betrayal. Women seek to kill their false paramours; men champion their cause and join with them in the bloody denouements. Along the way, women trade their sexual endowments for men's money and thereby gain a better position from which to enact their deadly punishments. At a time when many voices called for female subordination and piety, these dangerous vixens may have held an allure. David Reynolds has seen George Thompson as a leading exemplar of subversive fiction, which "forged a new irrational style aimed at reproducing the rebellious, savage forces of American culture." Reynolds has given particular attention to Thompson's reformist "unmaking of the social elite . . .

enforced through extreme violence, sexual scenes ranging from the suggestive to the disgustingly perverse, and new variations upon ironic stereotypes such as the reverend rake and the likable criminal." While much of Reynolds's characterization of Thompson's writing holds, an alternative explanation is that he was a cynical author out to coin his words by pushing sexual and violent speech to the limits of what courts allowed. Thompson worked within the unmasking tradition of the sporting press. From this perspective, his use of reform language, like that of the writers of the racy weeklies, was merely a cover.[27]

Thompson gives glimpses into the male fears of his era about women and birth control. When the daughter of a respectable Brooklyn rope maker finds herself pregnant, she travels to Manhattan and asks the proprietress of a house of assignation for the name of a physician "who will shield me from disgrace and keep my secrets." She gets a card from her and goes to the office of the doctor. In return for sexual intercourse with him, she receives a box of pills that he promises will "obliterate all the fruits of her indiscretion" in ten days. She is now in a position to hide from her parents and a future husband evidence that she is not a virgin. Thompson also voices mistrust of the new scientific knowledge of the age. The pill-dispensing doctor, it turns out, had used his arts to rape an innocent country girl. He had gained control of her by promising to teach her the "new sciences of Psychology and animal magnetism." Placing her in a hypnotic trance, he convinced her that he was her lover (the primary male character of the tale). Under the spell, she became, as she later recounted, "a willing sacrifice to the man I loved." When she came to her senses, she felt she was now "a dishonored girl." Believing "that I could not as a true woman yield up heart and hand to a man whom I loved and respected," she agreed to go with the doctor to New York and become his mistress.[28]

She is now started on the road to ruin, a familiar story to nineteenth-century readers. She moves from one paramour to another. She travels the heights: she is one of the many kept women of a rich railroad contractor on Bond Street, a "Sybarite of the nineteenth century, who emulated the Mormons of the Desert, in the heart of the Empire City," and who had every luxury, including the most costly meats and "the most luscious wines." And she plumbs the depths, ultimately reaching the black-and-tan saloons of the Five Points, where she is now "gallus Kate," a ragged, wretched working-class whore. The author checked her in her fall, however. Found by the suitor of her lost youth and installed in decent rooms, she is allowed to become a

Asmodeus figure, detail from masthead, John H. Manning, Del[ineator,] and F. E. Worcester. *Life in Boston and the New England Police Gazette*, 2, no. 28 (April 6, 1850): 1. Courtesy, American Antiquarian Society.

decent, honest working woman. By letting her tell her story in two chapters, Thompson gave readers some titillating glimpses into the spectrum of libertines imagined in New York City.[29]

Thompson also presented to readers the fascinating character of Asmodeus, a fictional devil with origins in the Apocrypha, who had been refashioned in the nineteenth century as a devil-dandy who could reveal urban secrets by taking off roofs of houses to reveal the vices of those dwelling within. Asmodeus appears in a number of American plays and books in this period that dealt with vice at the upper end of society, including *Asmodeus in New York, Asmodeus, or The Iniquities of New York,* and *Revelations of Asmodeus; or Mysteries of Upper Ten-Dom.* Thompson used the character in *New-York Life* and probably took the name as his pseudonym in the initial publication of *Sharps and Flats; or, the Perils of City Life.* Asmodeus—an apt representation of the pleasure of exposure—provides one key to Thompson and other writers who mined the vein of sensationalism. One Thompson publication contains a clever delineation of this devilish figure. Although no one at any social level escaped his notice, Thompson's particular targets of Asmodean exposure were those at the high end, the "upper tendom" and "reverend rakes," hypocritical ministers and reformers who preached piety and restraint amid their lechery.[30]

Thompson was most likely the writer of *Simon the Radical: or, the Cap of Liberty,* a work purported to be by Charles Paul de Kock, a popular French writer. What makes *Simon the Radical* interesting is the way it moves the reader through the class structure from its depths. The book's politics are those of neither the French Revolution nor its opposition, for as the book proceeds, all those around Simon, of both the right and left, act badly. The class anger of the dispossessed, however, drives much of the book. Simon, the hero, is a harassed waiter raised during the course of revolution to become a powerful Jacobin. On the way, Simon trades his clothing for that of a chevalier. Ill, he recovers on the estate of a countess. Ultimately, after the promise of love and sexual union is ended by revelation of his origins, Simon rescues the countess from execution, only to have her shout at him, "A menial! a degraded menial!" At the close, Simon has become a brigand, and here his words suggest Thompson's true position. In 1820, taken prisoner, Simon states why he is a thief: "I was thirsty and I took the means of quenching my thirst from men who get drunk daily upon choice wines." When asked why he, a man with ability, did not engage in useful work, he answers, "You err, monsieur; in order to live, it is not sufficient to have ability; ability now-a-day walks in the mud, while boobies roll past in carriages."[31]

This book and others by Thompson were frequently listed by publishers and sellers alongside works of the erotic canon, but they are clearly of a different stripe. These novels were called "racy" in their day. They are less openly descriptive of sexual acts than the European texts of the erotic canon. They dwell on violent episodes rather than sexual encounters. Perhaps they were written in this manner to avoid obscenity prosecutions. It may well be that in their own time portrayals of acts of revenge were experienced erotically. Written to appeal to sporting men and those who identified with them, at least at the moment of reading, the commercial success of these racy books suggests that they expressed something of the consciousness or fantasy life of their imagined readers.[32] Looking at the wide array of Thompson's fiction, one can see a world in which men seek to get what they can—money, sex, power—without the burdens of religion, ethical values, responsibility, or lasting relationships. The male heroes are limited only by the aggressiveness and capacity for revenge of others.

In the mid-1850s, Thompson was published in New York by Prescott F. Harris, located at 102 Nassau Street. In 1855, to promote his list, Harris began the *Broadway Belle,* a weekly with Thompson as editor. At least at the outset, it served as Thompson's venue, publishing his *The Magic Night Cap* and *The Locket* in serial form and advertising his works as being available at Harris's Nassau Street shop. It used its pages to try to turn Thompson, alias the "Gay Devil," into a minor celebrity. The general tone of the *Broadway Belle* is teasing and mocking. Its name allowed the repeated jest that the weekly itself was a fetching and risqué Broadway beauty, a gay lady stepping out. The *Broadway Belle* blended gossip about prostitutes, coyly written, with gentle satire about prominent New York figures, such as the director of the Five Points Mission and impresario P. T. Barnum. In its first issue the weekly promised that the next would astonish all "by its rich, racy and exciting contents." Its "Ladies' Column" purported (whatever its real nature) to be a forum for ladies of the *pave* to write short notices. As might be anticipated, the authors—Delie, Susie Sumner, Ellen, and Mary—wrote about their lovers, promenading the streets, and the pleasures of both the weekly paper and Thompson's fiction. The text was filled with sex plays. Susie Sumner wrote, for example, that a separate column was a good idea: "It is so much better than to have the ladies scattered promiscuously among the gentlemen. In your 8th number, you were not content with putting Delie next to W., but put her right under him." She added that she wanted to know who Nina was, as did Fred: "Fred says he would like very much to know her, and I'm afraid he uses that word in the scriptural sense of the term."[33]

The *Broadway Belle* advertised Thompson's works—long lists of books with such titles as *Radcliff, or the Adventures of a Libertine, Venus in Boston, Lady's Garter,* and *Bridal Chamber, and Its Mysteries,* as well as *Petite Bunkum, the Yankee Showman,* a life of P. T. Barnum, and works of adventure, such as *Jack Harold and City Crimes.* It also regularly contained a notice entitled "Books That Are Books," a list of books available for sale at Harris's establishment. To Thompson's racy books were added many works of fiction deemed erotic in their day, such as *The History of a Rake* and *Gustavus, the Don Juan of France.* In addition there were books that served to give sexual information: *Aristotle's Complete Works* and *Married Woman's Private Medical Guide.*[34] What this suggests is that whatever their original purpose, these books were purchased as part of the accoutrements of the sporting life. They may have provided information on sex, birth control, or abortion, or they may have had a second life as aids to sexual excitement.

Twice the *Broadway Belle* faced suppression, though of a kind less traceable than that of the sporting press in the early 1840s or the booksellers in 1842. Reports in the weekly about the two incidents and minor notices in daily newspapers provide some information about which printed sexual words were permissible and which forbidden in New York City in the 1850s. Sexually provocative banter, such as that just considered—the staple of the *Broadway Belle* and competitors such as the *Joker, Dandy, Gridiron,* and *Whip*— was clearly acceptable in a New York publication by the 1850s. Fiction that used real names in fantasy situations did not lead to problems. Nor did discussion of prostitution, either as an aspect of urban enjoyment or as a social problem. However, when the January 29, 1855, issue copied an extract about the excessive sexual demands of husbands on wives from a medical book by the phrenological publisher Fowler and Wells, the weekly was called to account. The offending paragraph of "Important to Husbands and Wives" read:

> Speak out, ye weakly nervous wives, now dying by *wretched inches* of these diseases, and say whether your sufferings were not caused mainly, and have not been aggravated to their present painfulness, by the frequency, the fury, the almost *goatishness,* of your husbands' demands? I say fury, because though frequency is bad, yet harshness is worse; nor do husbands always consider how exceedingly tender, and how liable to consequent inflammation and disease, this apparatus. Many a husband has hurried more wives than one, *killed outright,* ignorantly, yet effectually, by the brutality of this passion.[35]

Democrat Fernando Wood had just been elected mayor, and he began a highly publicized campaign to clean up New York by enforcing its laws. He began with saloon openings on Sunday but moved to other seeming violations of social order. On January 29 he had a police officer arrest Thompson and Harris for publishing this article. As part of his reform effort, he established the "Complaint-Book," located in his office, in which citizens could write down accusations against public officials and, more generally, their discontents. Through this Wood learned that "in spite of the arrest of P. F. Harris and G. Thompson, editors and publishers of the *Broadway Belle,* for an indecent article in that production[,] the same is now being sold on Nassau street by half a dozen ragged urchins." This led to Wood's ordering the arrest of the newsboys. After questioning the boys, the police chief ordered that Thompson and Harris pay the boys for the papers they still had in their possession, and the newspaper reporter speculated that the boys would likely be released, "as they were not aware of the offense they were committing."[36]

Thompson reported the matter differently, stating that he had taken the Fowler and Wells book with him to the mayor's office and the complaints had been dismissed. "Our readers can best appreciate the step taken by our worthy Mayor to suppress all publications bearing an immoral tendency, and therefore we shall be very carefully [*sic*] that nothing improper, or any unworthy person is introduced in the *Belle*." The paper bragged that the notoriety had gained it many readers, and it now had a circulation of 117,000. The mayor's summons did lead to Thompson's removal as editor, though not as writer. The paper announced, "We have tried to tame her, and believe her now to be perfectly harmless. . . . We are very sorry Mr. Thompson has been divorced from the *Belle,* but he is with us."[37]

The next violation—"A Nautical Adventure"—faced a mayoral scolding, not police action:

Dear Belle—One pleasant evening in the month of May, between the hours of 10 and 12 o'clock, we were sailing down the *Canal,*

NEW YORK CITY.—POMEROY'S VAN—DISTRIBUTING COPIES OF THE "NEW YORK DEMOCRAT" TO THE NEWSBOYS.—SEE PAGE 75.

The newsboys' life. "Distributing copies of the 'New York Democrat' to the Newsboys." © Museum of the City of New York.

when we spied a neat little *craft* a short distance ahead of us. Soon
after, we saw her put her head to the leeward and sail leisurely up the
river *Mercer;* more fuel was immediately added to our furnace, causing us to sail a little faster, with the determination to explore the
frigate ahead of us, so we also turned to leeward and sailed up the
before mentioned river after the strange craft. In the meantime the
frigate, perceiving that we were following, began to sail considerably
slower, apparently with the intention of permitting us to pass her,
which we had already determined to do. We soon came within
speaking distance, and forthwith commenced to overhaul the craft.
After a short combat, and without much force being used, we
hitched ourselves to the *frigate,* and sailed together up the river. Soon
after we came to a landing, and after a little preparation, we found
ourselves *moored* at the same berth, and seeing the other craft hoist
all her sails, we became excited, and hauling our long tom, which
was already well loaded, we commenced fight with the rival craft,
and after giving her the contents of our long tom she immediately
surrendered.[38]

Mid-nineteenth-century readers would have understood this bit of fun
by Thompson as a verbal play on coitus with a whore. It used names of
streets—Canal and Mercer—known for their prostitutes. It played on the
metaphors of body as ship and penis as cannon, familiar from *Aristotle's
Master-piece.* What offended? Putting such a jest in print in a weekly, perhaps;
but certainly the use in print of the common slang for penis—"long tom."
This time when the mayor called the publication to account, the weekly apologized: "We are very sorry that the article bearing the above head should
have got into the *Belle* last week. Our *innocent* Gay Devil let it slip in during
our absence. . . . We shall be more careful in the future." Although serializa-
tion of George Thompson's *The Locket* continued for a time, he no longer
wrote for the paper. With his exit, the weekly lost its distinctive voice.[39]

Thompson moved on to publish with Gillen and Company, who
financed his new organ, the *Weekly Whip.* Harris continued to print Thompson's books in serial form in the *Broadway Belle,* setting author against former
publisher in a public dispute. Harris wrote that as he owned the copyright to
Thompson's novels, he had the power to print them. Thompson, on the
other hand, insisted that he had the right to his intellectual property. As had
Harris, Gillen and Company advertised on its list Thompson's novels and

other erotic books, including works of physiology. One curious element is that Charles Paul de Kock is listed by Gillen as the author of Thompson's *Venus in Boston,* confirming that at least one publisher passed off Thompson's writing as that of the French novelist.[40]

In racy work meant to appeal to men of his generation, George Thompson wrote in a way clearly different from Cleland and European authors of the erotic canon. Thompson tapped into a vein of writing that emphasized violence with a dash of sex, and this proved to be a powerful force in popular fiction. Aware of the sporting press, he made the prostitute a playful subject in his own weekly. His books were typically sold with the more explicitly erotic works by European authors and could be disguised as those of de Kock. When critics spoke of paper- or yellow-covered fiction in the nineteenth century, they often had George Thompson's work in mind.

4

George Ackerman advertised "Rich, Rare and Racy Reading" in his 1857 weekly *Venus' Miscellany.* He published and sold many of George Thompson's books, along with a few of the familiar European titles and *Aristotle, Illustrated Complete Masterpiece.* In contrast to the sporting weeklies of the 1840s, which specialized in vilification and gossip about prostitutes, *Venus' Miscellany* contained fiction and had much more sexually explicit material. In the May 23, 1857, issue, for example, fictional representations of sexual intercourse occur in four separate items. Ackerman featured stories of high romantic fiction in which European aristocrats and their ladies find their way to wed and bed. In this world of high-flown language, euphemisms abound. In "Inez de Castro; or, the Intrigues of the Court of Isabel of Aragon" by Julia Gaylove, Don Manuel and Inez "soon forgot all but love, every other feeling but that of passion was o'ermastered, and the quick, warm kisses came quick and ardently, . . . the breath of each so co-mingled as to carry a soft electric thrill, and a flow of love from heart to heart, that sent the pulses thrilling, and the warm blood coursing madly through the veins of those two forms." Breasts become "blushing lilies." The word "penis" is not mentioned. Her hand comes "to press with fond and lingering delight, where its lightest touch had caused a thrill of rapture almost to[o] intense to bear. His breast heaves, his breath comes quick and short, he almost writhes under the electric pressure of those taper fingers, yet they are not withdrawn in pity. But ah! the waxen limbs are powerless now, so excessive is the exstacy [*sic*] of bliss which fills her soul, as in retaliation, her lover bathes her in the essence of loves flower." After coition, the two sink "powerless upon the couch."[41]

In the world of *Venus' Miscellany*, all women are desirous and all men are ardent. Women may cry seduction, but they invite the advances. Rape is impossible, for, as one author writing in a woman's voice put it, unless a female's life is threatened or she is insensible, "she holds the scabbard, and the sword cannot be sheathed without her assistance or consent." Although the publication is more serious than comic, the humorous elements play upon sex, offering coy jokes about Queen Victoria and Prince Alfred or double entendres. One paragraph, for example, uses moving day as an extended metaphor for coitus. In three poems about sexual intercourse, each woman is a virgin, and all enjoy the encounter. As with many of the works of the erotic canon, women's passion is the key evoker in a publication likely designed for a male audience.[42]

Whether to arouse or merely amuse, in all cases what is presented is some version of conventional sexual intercourse between a dominant man and an obliging woman. Euphemism abounds: in "My First Lesson in Love" by Trot, an innocent youth relates his first sexual experience. In this case, the woman's pubic hair becomes "mossy beauties of the temple of love" and his penis is his "jewel." However, the discussion of his erection is explicit: "beneath her soft caresses it grew and flourished amazingly, so much so that it fired her tender grasp, and panted with a newly awakened vigor as she fondly stroked its rising shaft." In the two issues of the publication available, only the words are designed to arouse. The woodcuts, which present conventional melodramatic scenes, are not erotic.[43]

Ackerman had a complex business. Using the business name James Ramerio, he published many books, including *Flora Montgomery, The Bridal Chamber and Its Mysteries, Anna Mowbray; or, Tale of the Harem, The Amours of a Quaker; or, The Voluptuary, Venus in Boston, Simon the Radical, The Loves of Byron, Chevalier De Faublas,* and *Aristotle, Illustrated Complete Masterpiece,* among other titles. He sold abortifacients under the name Dr. Ashwell. He took "Jean Rosseau" as the business name for some of his erotic publications and advertised French imports "To the Sporting Fraternity." The material Rosseau offered included French transparent cards, French prints, some of them colored, and books such as *The Adventures and Intrigues of the Duke of Buckingham, Charles the Second, and Earl of Rochester,* "with all their amorous exploits during the 'Merry Monarch's' reign." In addition, Ackerman offered at his shop on 167 William Street French transparent cards and condoms.[44] Informing customers outside New York City that he would send them at the price of $2 a dozen, one of his ads read:

CUNDUMS, CUNDUMS, CUNDUMS.

This great invention is to prevent conception in females, and has been a long time in general use by the French. Its being a cap, or thin transparent skin, that entirely covers a part of the man, and prevents an emission from entering the female, at the same time detracts nothing from the pleasures; and, in fact is, the only safe thing to be relied on.[45]

On September 14, 1857, George Ackerman came before the Court of Special Sessions of Judge Barnabas W. Osborne. Used to try minor offenses, Special Sessions did not require a grand jury indictment or a trial by jury. Ackerman pled guilty to the charge of circulation of an "indecent publication," and Judge Osborne gave him a fine of $50. "The Court, through Judge Osborn, remarked, as this [was] Ackerman's first offense, it was willing to let him off this time with the aforesaid fine. Its object was to make an example of the accused. But on the first repetition of the offense, the District Attorney had assured the Court, the case would be laid before the Grand Jury." The district attorney had been aware of *Venus' Miscellany* since August and had given responsibility to investigate it to a policeman named Walsh. He learned that Ackerman had a mail-order business through the post office, picking up fifty letters three times a day. Working through the postmaster, Walsh learned that the letters were addressed not only to Ackerman but also to James Ramerio, Dr. Ashwell, and Jean Rosseau. Walsh arrested Ackerman in late August, and bail was set at $1,000. This was paid by George A. Ross of Ross & Tousey, news agents. When forced to explain his actions, Ross later stated that he had yielded to Ackerman's entreaties because the two had once been "journeymen mechanics together," but that once he had learned of Ackerman's true business, he had surrendered him to the judge.[46]

After Ackerman was let off with the light fine, Walsh got a search warrant and raided the printing offices of J. G. Wells at 22 and 24 Frankfort Street, responsible for the printing of *Venus' Miscellany*. Although Ackerman escaped, Walsh arrested two boys employed by Wells. Walsh then learned that Ackerman was at 14 Frankfort Street, and he got another search warrant.

This time a *Herald* reporter went with the police and described the scene at Ackerman's establishment on the fifth floor. Ackerman himself had fled, but the counters and floors of its three large rooms were covered with "an immense stock of immoral and profanely illustrated works." The *Herald* reporter estimated that the rooms contained forty thousand volumes. The *Tribune* reduced the amount to several thousand "specimens of yellow-covered literature" in each of two rooms, and in addition "several dozens of volumes of the most obscene and filthy stuff that ever disgraced language, with illustrations to match." These were assumed to be the supplies of Ackerman's mail-order book business. In addition to many stereotype plates there was a large copper plate sent by an engraver: "By announcements made in the columns of the paper it appears that a copy of the engraving struck from this plate was to be given to each subscriber to the paper."

The *Herald* reporter got a look at Ackerman's account books and estimated that *Venus' Miscellany* had a circulation of about 7,000 and that Ackerman had taken in $40,000 in the last year. All the goods were seized and set to be burned. However, one of the persons engaged in business with Ackerman laid claim to the novels of de Kock in the lot, perhaps by the French author, perhaps by George Thompson. Ackerman eluded capture.[47]

5

In the New-York Historical Society are two exemplary books—*American History and Biography, Containing an Epitome of American History* of 1838 and *Echoes from the Gun of 1861: A Book for Boys* of 1864. Published a generation apart, both sought to inspire patriotic feelings. What makes them interesting in the context of this chapter is that both were published by men who were charged with obscenity. The imprint for the first is Charles Lohman, who was later to write as Dr. Mauriceau. In 1838, he had recently married Ann Trow, and in that year she would take the business name Madame Restell. The second book has on the inside of the front board the bookseller's ticket "Frederic A. Brady, Publisher and Bookseller, 22 Ann Street, New York."[48]

In 1858 Brady was brought before General Sessions under the offense of "having obscene publications." On January 15, he sold to John Hackett *The Secret Habits of the Female Sex, The Marriage Bed, or Wedding Secrets,* and *Mary Ann Temple.* A second indictment, on January 23, 1858, suggests that police raided his shop, probably at 12 Ann Street, and found in addition *The Life and Adventures of Silas Shovewell* and *Guide to the Harem*—all works that he "had in

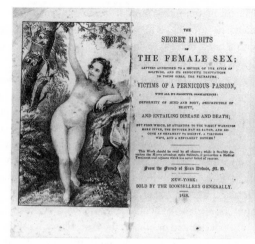

Jean Dubois, *The Secret Habits of the Female Sex,* frontispiece and title page. The Kinsey Institute for Research in Sex, Gender, and Reproduction.

his possession with intent to publish and sell." Brady also used the name Henry S. G. Smith, and in 1857 he applied for a copyright for *The Marriage Bed, or Wedding Secrets,* carrying the long subtitle "revealed by the torch of Hymen being a full explanation of all the Matrimonial duties of both Bride and Bridegroom on the eventful night." Jean Dubois's *Secret Habits of the Female Sex* is an antimasturbation tract giving advice to mothers about how to protect their daughters from the solitary vice. It follows the usual format of such works; however, with its many examples of masturbating girls, it may have seemed a good candidate for male sexual arousal. One edition, published in New York under the imprint "booksellers," had erotic engravings, including a frontal female nude reaching for grapes and two female nudes erotically engaged. Brady also published George Thompson's sensational Greenhorn titles, including *Jack Harold, The Road to Ruin,* and *Grace Willard.*[49]

The two patriotic books reposing in the New-York Historical Society suggest that in the years before the Civil War the lines in New York between the printers and distributors of physiological and erotic material, on the one hand, and those of written works deemed unquestionably legitimate, on the other, were fluid. The best way to see men such as Brady and Lohman is as struggling to get by and looking out for opportunities. One could start small in book manufacturing, tempting men of humble means to rent a press or hire a job printer. The boundaries between printing and publishing could still be porous. With a book in hand, it took only a little stock to get started as either a peddler or the keeper of a bookstall.

As New York grew in the early decades of the nineteenth century, printing presses concentrated in a district at the juncture of Nassau and Ann Streets. In the 1830s one could find a number of struggling enterprises there. Papers such as the *New York Fireman,* Horace Greeley's *New Yorker,* the *Spirit of Seventy-Six,* and the *Libertine* got their start on the street.[50] Although some papers withered within months or a few years, some flourished and required bigger and newer quarters for more powerful presses. As larger newspapers, such as the *Herald,* quit Ann Street, they likely left their heavy equipment behind. Job printers, such as William Applegate, who originally printed the *Sunday Flash,* may have rented or bought these obsolescent presses.

Ann Street's history as a center for the distribution of popular books with an erotic edge goes back at least until 1837, when *A Letter from Richard P. Robinson, as Connected with the Murder of Ellen Jewett* was listed as being sold wholesale at 29 Ann Street. In the 1840s, the *Whip* and the *Libertine* were published at 31 Ann, and the New York *Herald* could refer to "The Ann Street Licentious Press." In this era a printer might seek to distribute his own work through his own bookstore. There were no clear divisions between printing and selling. Printers such as Lohman marketed their wares. Shopkeepers such as Brady sold works that they had printed.

There were many locations for printing and distribution of erotica, to be sure, and one finds in indictments for obscenity the addresses of book and print sellers on Fulton, Cortlandt, and Wall Streets. However, over the decades, small shops selling old and new books and prints concentrated on Ann Street, particularly in the area close to Nassau. For the most part, these dealers did not make erotica a specialty. But in this world of men struggling to get by, erotic texts and illustrations made their way into their batches of books and prints, and they sold them willingly. When they got a plate for engraving erotic prints, they used it and sold the lot that they printed. Some had access to book texts and printed them as well. A few of these men may have been motivated by ideological commitment, seeing themselves as libertine sons of the Enlightenment, but most probably just wanted to survive and were willing to meet the demands of the market. In the process they created in New York a zone where men could find, peruse, and buy printed erotica, an important piece of the gendered and sexual mapping of the mid-nineteenth-century city.[51]

In the 1860s some of Brady's neighbors on Ann Street were Calvin Blanchard, 26 Ann; Dick & Fitzgerald, 18 Ann; and Jeremiah H. Farrell, 15 Ann. A printer and writer, Blanchard was an ideologue who saw himself as following in the liberal tradition of Thomas Paine and the freethinkers. Casting himself as a libertine, he wrote in the 1860s as a votary of pleasure and he published his own works, complete with erotic engravings. The firm of Dick & Fitzgerald was primarily known as a publisher of parlor pastimes, music, and how-to books, but some of these, such as *Anecdotes of Love* by Lola Montez, skirted the edge.[52]

In December 1863 Frederic Brady, then located at 24 Ann Street, went out of business. Jeremiah H. Farrell paid $5,000 for the materials of Brady's shop,

The zone of printed erotica, I. "Birds Eye View of Ann Street from *The City of New York*," detail, executed and published by Galt & Hoy, 111 Liberty Street, New York, 1879. The New York Public Library, Map Division.

inventory, and fixtures. In the sale were printed books, including multiple copies of both *Secret Habits* and *Wedding Secrets*, with both plain and colored plates, and other texts carrying the abbreviated titles of *Beauties, Cloister,* and *Old Man*. Also on the list were the works of Thompson, perhaps some actual novels of Charles Paul de Kock, and many of the books listed in Brady's 1858 indictment. In addition, Farrell got Brady's stereotype plates, which he could use to print more copies.[53]

Two books under Farrell's imprint are Thompson's *Simon the Radical*, under the name Charles Paul de Kock, and *The Amours of Sanfroid and Eulalia, Being the Intrigues and Amours of a Jesuit and a Nun*. The latter is an abridged and translated edition of an eighteenth-century French work of anticlerical fiction. The copy at the Kinsey Library contains hand-colored erotic plates that bear no direct relation to the text and may not have been with the original book. The volume was finely bound in leather stamped with gold. The

The zone of printed erotica, II. "New York Down Town and Bay to the Narrows," Charles Magnus, pictorial lettersheets. © Collection of The New-York Historical Society, negative #74625.

The Amours of Sanfroid and Eulalia, Being the Intrigues and Amours of a Jesuit and a Nun (New York: J. H. Farrell, n.d.), title page. The Kinsey Institute for Research in Sex, Gender, and Reproduction.

handsome, well-made binding was in contrast to the cheap paper and badly printed text, filled with misprints and a misspelling on the title page.[54]

These five episodes are similar to five candles in a dark field, with each lighting up a bit of a vast and dark terrain. Although together they may not reveal the full landscape of erotic printing and publishing in New York City, they convey important elements of the ground. They suggest a lively commerce in erotica, typically sequestered in a locked box or a partitioned room, normally available only to a man who requested it. Such imaginative works tended to portray male erection and female sexual pleasure in ways prosecutors and grand juries perceived as an incitement to male lust, the critical element that defined criminal obscenity before the Civil War. Certain American writers produced sensational works linking sex and violence that were advertised as "racy" and marketed with known European imports of the erotic canon. Sensationalist works in book form did not lead to arrest at this time, but authorities subjected material by their authors published in weekly newspapers to greater scrutiny. A number of New York printers and booksellers met the demand for sexually explicit works, leading to occasional raids on their establishments. Such publishers concentrated their operations in the area around the junction of Ann and Nassau Streets, replete with older presses, making it well known as the primary site in the city where a man could go to examine and buy printed erotica. In 1872, when Anthony Comstock began his first major campaign against materials he regarded as obscene, a reporter directed him to Ann and Nassau Streets. After he learned about the business, Comstock targeted three publishers: Haynes, Ackerman, and Farrell.

PART III

ADDITIONS AND COMPLICATIONS

II

Placing Sex at the Core of Being

The publication of commercial erotica and efforts to police it in New York occurred at a time when social movements were altering the nature of the sexual conversation in the United States. By the 1850s, at the far reaches of reform physiology, a fourth sexual framework emerged that placed sex at the center of life. The impact of this change on American life would be far-reaching and would give new urgency to efforts to regulate obscenity.

Although the concern of this book is with sexual representations in print, not with behavior, in these movements the two cannot be divorced. In the antebellum years state governments were establishing legal codes that replaced the common law, and these typically set forth marriage as a lifelong contract that could, however, be ended by divorce if violated in essentials by husband or wife. Common law shaped the definition of these essentials: a husband was required to support his wife economically; a wife, in turn, had to grant her husband exclusive sexual access. As the nation moved toward a national standard for marriage, many of the ideas and practices of reform and utopian movements were roiling the waters. This chapter examines these movements and the messages they gave to some Americans about sexuality in the three decades before the Civil War.[1]

The Church of Jesus Christ of Latter-Day Saints practiced polygamy beginning in the 1830s and began to advocate it in 1852. John Humphrey Noyes's utopian colony of Perfectionists at Oneida, New York, believed in "complex marriage," where each member of the community was a potential sexual partner of every adolescent and adult of the opposite sex. Moreover, through ideas circulating among advocates of women's rights, some women were coming to have new notions of autonomy and of their bodies. Within the emerging Spiritualist community the concept of spiritual affinity led some people to reject their husbands and wives to take new temporal as well as spiritual lovers. American communities founded on the ideas of French philosopher Charles Fourier attempted to play down his theories of passion, only to see them resurface and become matters of intense debate. On Long Island, Stephen Pearl Andrews's community, Modern Times, carried the Fourierist understanding of "passional affinity" to a new dimension, attracting secular as well as Spiritualist free lovers. Although one cannot trace the origin of the fourth framework to the precise point when it first appeared, one can see it in an early form.

I

Given the discussion in previous chapters, one might assume that alternatives to traditional marriage would arise most easily in the nineteenth century among the freethinkers. Quite the contrary. Two of America's most radical experiments with sexual relations, Mormon settlements and Noyes's community of Bible Communists at Oneida, New York, emerged out of the fires of evangelical religion. Mormonism began in the 1830s near Rochester, New York. Joseph Smith, Jr., declaring that he was a prophet, claimed that he had discovered and translated the Book of Mormon, early Christian texts untainted by Catholicism and the Protestant ministry. As he gathered followers to the Church of Jesus Christ of Latter-Day Saints, he and other elders worked out a way of life that separated them from their neighbors. Like other utopian communities, Mormonism emphasized the authority of the leader, separatism, and economic cooperation. It was, however, more assertive than other groups and more successful in attracting converts. Opposition built against it, and the sect moved its members farther and farther west. In the late 1840s, more than ten thousand Mormons settled in the Great Basin beyond the Rocky Mountains.[2]

For decades plural marriage stood at the center of Mormon faith. Only in 1852 did Mormons openly advocate the practice of polygamy, but revelation about it had come to Smith in 1843. According to Mormon belief, men could ascend spiritually both in life and after death. Elders judged some men to be capable of perfection and ordained them to take more than one wife. Mormon sexuality both contributed to and drew from the larger sexual conversation. In the Mormon view, while others turned to coitus for personal gratification and were therefore guilty of lust, a man with several wives could satisfy his sexual needs, confident that he partook only of perfect manhood. Plural marriage also met the needs of women, as Mormons believed that they experienced less sexual desire and needed protection from sexual intercourse during the long period of pregnancy and lactation. Many Mormon sermons and written texts drew on the literature of reform physiology to argue for the healthfulness and naturalness of polygamy.[3]

The Mormons, however, went far beyond others in their understanding of the power of sex. Not only was sex for procreation divinely decreed, the godhead was a sexual being. As historian Louis Kern has written, Mormons understood God to be "a being of flesh and blood like men . . . susceptible to the same passions and desires." Imagining themselves as the patriarchs of the Old Testament, they assessed their position in the hierarchy by the numbers and strength of their offspring. They judged women by their fertility and submission, men by their virility and control. When elders examined men who aspired to leadership, they looked at their genitalia to be sure that they were physically capable of reproduction. Potency was a critical element of Mormon manhood.[4]

Mormons' distinctive practice of plural marriage was constantly in the minds of Americans by midcentury, a subject of fantasy and the object of denunciation. But because of constant conflict with the larger society, Mormon understandings did not generally enter American conversations about sexuality. This was not true, however, of a smaller, distinctive community located in Oneida, New York. John Humphrey Noyes preached and practiced complex marriage, and his words often resonated in the books and pamphlets of others.

Noyes, the son of a prominent Vermont businessman and member of Congress, experienced religious awakening in the year following his 1831 graduation from Dartmouth and abandoned the study of law. He entered the Theological Seminary at Andover and then transferred to Yale to prepare for the ministry. There, in the midst of revivals, he rediscovered Christian Perfectionism. Once he announced in 1834 that he himself was perfect, Yale requested that he withdraw, and he lost his license to preach. In the years that followed, Noyes searched for an appropriate audience for his radical belief in total freedom from sin. He read widely and drew on a broad range of ideas as he developed his own. An opportune marriage gave him the financial backing he needed, and with his wife he moved back to his family's home in Putney, Vermont. There he gathered a small number of followers who began to practice what they called Bible Communism.[5]

Part of Noyes's creed from the outset was a belief that marriage was incompatible with Perfectionism, but for more than a decade he distinguished between a future state of free love and the current requirement to obey the Decalogue. In 1846 Noyes announced to his disciples that he no longer believed in the necessity of following the Ten Commandments as they applied to marriage. As he revealed his understanding of complex marriage, he linked it to notions of holiness. For those seeking perfection, it was a spiritual duty to free sexual love from exclusiveness and thereby hasten the coming of God's kingdom. Necessary for complex marriage was coitus reservatus, or what Noyes called "male continence." The sexual practice involved male penetration for extended periods without ejaculation. Noyes immediately began to apply his ideas. As news of adulterous sexual liaisons spread, he was arrested on an unrelated charge. Putney neighbors began to talk of mob action, and Noyes fled. In 1848 he established a community in Oneida, New York, with family members who followed.

Soon after settling at Oneida, Noyes put out a pamphlet in the manner of reform physiologists of his day. In it he presented his understanding of sexual intercourse and the practice of male continence. He sought first to make a distinction between "the amative and propagative functions of the sexual organs" and to restore to preeminence the amative function. He wrote that the sexual organs are conductors of urine, semen, and "social magnetism." These three functions are physiologically distinct. Whereas the testicles, like the uterus, are organs of reproduction, the penis and vagina are "the organs of union." The organs of union are concerned primarily with "social magnetism." He wrote, "Sexual intercourse, pure and simple, is the conjunction of the organs of union, and the interchange of magnetic influences, or conversation of spirits, through the medium of that conjunction. The communication from the seminal vessels to the uterus, which constitutes the propagative act, is distinct from, subsequent to, and not necessarily connected with, this intercourse." As part of his argument Noyes argued that ejaculation of semen could happen without sexual intercourse, as in male masturbation.[6]

Noyes had a distinctive understanding of male pleasure. He wrote that for a man, "the pleasure of the act is not produced by contact and interchange of life with the female, but by the action of the seminal fluid on the internal nerves of the male organ. The appetite and that which satisfies it are both within the man." Thus ejaculation is not necessary for a man to receive pleasure. In contrast to withdrawal, which diminishes pleasure, male continence, according to Noyes, "vastly increases that pleasure." It avoids the period after ejaculation of "exhaustion and disgust," which Noyes understood as coming from the natural shame that men feel from the exercise of their sensuality, the shame of Adam and Eve. Coitus reservatus keeps a man on the higher spiritual plane. In contrast to "the process of 'cooling off' which takes place between lovers after marriage and often ends in indifference and disgust, . . . lovers who use their sexual organs simply as the servants of their spiritual natures, abstaining from the propagative act, except when procreation is intended, may enjoy the highest bliss of sexual fellowship for any length of time, without satiety or exhaustion; and thus marriage life may become permanently sweeter than courtship and even the honey-moon."[7]

About female pleasure Noyes was silent. In his hierarchy women were less significant than men, and his book focused on male continence. Elsewhere what the Oneidans expressed were double negatives. Women did not have to submit to the sexual embrace without consent. (However, women in the community did not have the right to remain celibate or practice monogamy.) Women did not have to fear unwanted pregnancy. Yet because many writers on sexual intercourse believed that women needed semen as a balm, its absence under male continence implicitly raised the issue of female sexual satisfaction.

Noyes was as strict as any evangelical in opposing what he regarded as unnatural means of birth control. In 1872 he called them "artificial tricks" or the work of "French inventors." In his descending series of existing means of contraception from most to least harmful, they came after child killing and abortion. Owen's advice, coitus interruptus, he believed was the least objectionable. In 1848, to the charge that coitus reservatus was unnatural, Noyes answered, "The useless expenditure of seed certainly is not natural." God did not make it to be expended except for propagation. But at the same time, God gave to man a "natural instinct" that "demands frequent congress of the sexes, not for propagative, but for social and spiritual purposes." To the charge that the practice was a difficult one, Noyes answered, "Abstinence from masturbation is impossible or difficult, where habit has made it a second nature; and yet no one will say that habitual masturbation is natural." Shifting the moral ground, Noyes insisted that although coitus reservatus was difficult, one trained to purity could attain it. He stated that male continence was a spiritual practice undertaken by men learning to seek "the elevated spiritual pleasures of sexual connection."[8]

Noyes's theory established the ground on which he and his followers built the large and thriving Perfectionist community in Oneida and at other branches. Oneida was often a reference point in the antebellum years, the leading example of an alternative to traditional marriage. Only once was the community threatened, and that resulted from a charge not of unconventional sexual practices but of wife beating by one of the members.[9] Until 1871 the Oneida community was allowed to practice complex marriage undisturbed. A recently published diary by Noyes's niece (and one of his sexual partners) has revealed a sexually active woman's life lived at Oneida at an intense and passionate pitch.[10]

A later era of reformers perceived the Oneidan separation of sexual relations from reproduction and the conscious choice of childbearing as more important than coitus reservatus and the physiological theories behind it. As Noyes put it, the pleasures of amative intercourse were separated from those of the propagative. In what became known as stirpiculture, Noyes and the elders selected those among the flock who would be allowed to join in producing a child. This was compared to the actions of a wise stockbreeder who sought to strengthen his herd. The notion that calculations of animal husbandry might be applied to human beings inspired some Americans, and after the Civil War, a few were willing to claim Noyes as their prophet.

2

The relation of sex and marriage was a question that stirred many Americans in the nineteenth century, not only those in distinctive religious communities. It emerged in the women's rights movement. In her lectures and writing Frances Wright both opened a discussion of sexuality in America and introduced ideas about women's agency and independence. In the years that followed, her voice was largely drowned out by the doctrine of separate spheres being enunciated from the pulpit and in the press, portraying women as the gentler, domestic, more emotional sex.[11]

Thus far this study has looked at notions of separate spheres only as they were reflected in reform physiology. The writings of the phrenologist O. S. Fowler and the irregular physician Frederick Hollick typically expressed this ideology as flattery, applauding women's intuitive and spiritual qualities as necessary counters to the rougher, rational, outward-looking traits of men. Several brilliant women with literary inclinations, such as Margaret Fuller and Lydia Maria Child, accepted some of the positive characteristics attributed to women but refused to yield to the limitations.[12] A few had a different reaction. Angelina and Sarah Grimké, sisters from a slaveholding household in South Carolina, perceived the implied or expressed negatives in separate spheres. They saw that women were expected to cede their independent judgment and be dependent on men, the vine clinging to the male oak tree. In the 1830s, the Grimké sisters began to speak out for women's emancipation.

The seeds of women's rights were nourished in the soil of the many reform movements that flourished in the 1840s. Moved by religious revival, some bold women began to lecture against slavery. Agreeing with William Lloyd Garrison that slavery was a sin, they vowed to sin no more. In New England, conservative ministers opposed women's voices in the churches, using the words of Paul to silence them. Angelina and Sarah Grimké refused to stop their writing and speaking against slavery and asserted their right as children of God to speak openly and publicly. They denied that any man, even a pastor, could interpret God's words for them and began to make an analogy between the subordination of women and that of slaves. While their metaphoric appropriation enabled even independent and privileged women to claim the victimization of black slavery, it also allowed the idea of freedom.[13]

Beginning at Seneca Falls in 1848, women gathered in conventions that issued resolutions and statements. With the exception of specific campaigns to change property laws, most of their work focused on agitation to gather support, often in combination with other reform efforts, such as temperance and abolition. These pioneer women's rights activists were asserting independence and emphasizing female agency. Although they acknowledged their private roles as wives and mothers, they typically downplayed them to focus on the public arena. It was risky for early women's rights reformers to focus on sexual questions, because this meant returning attention to women's bodies. However, as these women sought the freedom of public life, some of them fought a relatively hidden campaign to alter sexual relations.

Such was the work of Elizabeth Cady Stanton. Born in Johnstown, New York, to a prominent lawyer and judge, Elizabeth Cady was educated at the Emma Willard School, where she came under the spell of Charles Finney's revivals. Her brother-in-law, the homeopathic physician Edward Bayard, sought to break religion's hold on her by administering fiction, philosophy, and phrenology. The young Cady emerged as an independent thinker attracted to radical ideas and causes. At the home of her cousin Gerrit Smith, she was exposed to abolition and temperance ideas and learned about conflicts within antislavery circles over women's rights. Disagreement over the appropriate role of women in agitation against slavery was one of the issues that in 1839 split the antislavery forces into radical abolitionists and those turning to the political system. Attending antislavery meetings, she met Henry Stanton, and in 1840 they married and went to the international antislavery convention in London as a honeymoon. There the American female delegates were not seated but forced to observe from the gallery, and Garrison joined them as a sign of solidarity. Sitting in the sequestered space, Elizabeth Cady Stanton met the veteran abolitionist Lucretia Mott and enjoyed important talks with her.[14]

In 1848 Stanton and Mott renewed their friendship in upstate New York and united to call a women's rights convention in Seneca Falls. Writing the Declaration of Sentiments, framed in the language of the Declaration of Independence, they equated men's dominance over women with monarchy and vowed a revolution to gain for women higher education, employment, self-determination, and full citizenship. Over the opposition of Mott, Stanton insisted that the Seneca Falls convention endorse a plank for woman's suffrage. The movement was broad and various. The Declaration of Sentiments listed many wrongs that men had committed against women, including the double standard of morality for men and women. Writing in Amelia Bloomer's temperance paper, the *Lily*, Stanton supported the water cure, advocated women's educational equality, and argued that women, not unlike those in a sultan's harem, must emerge from the false consciousness of luxury and sensualism.

Dress reform was an important way that advocates for women's rights sought to improve women's lot. Amelia Bloomer praised actress Fanny Kemble's controversial new dress, a loose divided skirt. When Elizabeth Cady Stanton's cousin came to Seneca Falls in the winter of 1850–51, she brought with her from a European spa a "turkish trouser" costume, such as Kemble had worn. Bloomer and Stanton tried it out and enjoyed the freedom of movement compatible with modesty that it offered. Its primary virtues were that it eliminated debilitating corsets and removed the weight of approximately twelve pounds of heavy long skirts and petticoats. With an eye toward publicity and a story, Bloomer reported on those adopting the costume in Seneca Falls and elsewhere, offered illustrations in the *Lily*, and invited readers to react. She began to give instructions for sewing the new garment. Circulation soared, and the loose trousers took her name.[15]

Women's rights depicted. "The Age of Brass. Or the Triumph of Woman's Rights," Currier & Ives, New York, 1869. © Collection of The New-York Historical Society, negative #44708.

What happened was instructive. Adoption of the style continued, including the wholesale one by the women of the Oneida community, and its users testified to its comfort and economy. But the Bloomer costume set off a storm of protest and ridicule on both sides of the Atlantic. It became a comic icon of the women's rights movement, a readily identifiable symbol of the danger that the broad changes demanded by its supporters posed. Bloomer girls were seen as smoking cigars and henpecking husbands. It was as if Fanny Wright had returned, now multiplied many times. Women such as Elizabeth Cady Stanton, who had found bloomers comfortable and convenient, felt forced to give them up in order that their message of women's right to full participation in the society could be heard. Memory of the bloomer controversy echoed to remind some supporters of the dangers that women's rights faced when it moved to questions of the body.

For one participant in the movement, however, questions of body and health always predominated. Paulina Wright Davis, an early enthusiast for women's rights, began with physiological reform. Following the practice of Mary Gove, she began to instruct other women about their bodies, using a female mannequin. She helped organize the 1850 National Woman's Rights Convention in Worcester, Massachusetts. In 1853, when her husband served a term in the U.S. House of Representatives as an antislavery Democrat, Davis joined him in Washington and published the *Una,* a monthly paper designed to serve the cause of women. In its career of slightly less than three years, the paper contained news of women's rights conventions, statements in support of women's equality, articles advocating freedom in marriage and the Church, reflective pieces on women and morality, and Davis's considerations of women and their nerves.[16]

Stanton abandoned the bloomer costume but not the larger attitude that it symbolized. As historian Lois Banner has emphasized, she was a radical for women's rights, with an extraordinary, open mind. To the end of her long life she supported women's individuality within and outside marriage, freedom from religious domination, and women's economic and property rights. In the 1850s, she began to voice the need for liberal divorce laws. In 1852 she announced to the Women's State Temperance Society in New York that drunkenness should be a sufficient cause for divorce. Emboldened by that move, Stanton began to seek more venues in which to treat the marriage question. The language she used suggests that she gave a gendered reading to the more conservative physiological writers: "Man in his lust has regulated this whole question of sexual intercourse long enough. Let the mothers of mankind whose prerogative it is to set bounds to his indulgence rouse up."[17]

Other leaders of Stanton's stature agreed with her position in these years but differed on the wisdom of linking marriage and divorce issues with women's rights. In 1856 Stanton wrote a letter to be read to the women's rights convention. "How can she," wrote Stanton of womankind, "endure our present marriage relations by which women's life, health, and happiness are held so cheap that she herself feels that God has given her no charter of rights, no individuality of her own?" It was time for women's rights to address the bondage of marriage so that womankind could see a way of escape from its chains. Words that were conservative in the context of writing about sexuality took on a different meaning within the advocacy of the women's movement. As the early generation of women's rights leaders absorbed physiological reform, it pushed them to reexamine sex and marriage in their quest for full adult independence and autonomy.[18]

3

The kinds of ferment that underlay women's rights provoked some Americans to turn to Europe for guidance. Albert Brisbane studied in Europe and worked with Charles Fourier before the French philosopher's death in 1837. Fourier's plan for a social system was embedded in a broad philosophical program. Rejecting contemporary individualistic and competitive society, which he called Civilization, Fourier projected a future ideal state of Harmony based on cooperation. He imagined a system of communities, what he termed phalanxes or phalansteries, in which all adults would engage in productive work determined by their interests and be rewarded by a complex scheme of remuneration for both labor and capital. The collective would nurture and educate the children. Each phalanx was to assume architectural form in a monumental building combining work, leisure, and living.

In 1840 Brisbane published *The Social Destiny of Man,* offering a version of Fourier designed for American audiences. Understanding the need to communicate Fourierism to a broader public, he purchased space for a column on the front page of Horace Greeley's New York *Tribune* and then established his own journal, *Phalanx.* The failures of the Owenites had taught Brisbane the danger of being connected with irreligion or sexual irregularity. As he sought to adapt communitarian ideas to the American context, Brisbane attempted to make them compatible with religion, private property, and—to at least some degree—domestic life. He emphasized those ideas of Fourier that demonstrated the economic and social value of association and downplayed the larger scheme.

Brisbane pioneered in the creation of American phalansteries, organized as joint-stock companies. He and other American followers of Fourier, meeting in 1844 for the first of their annual conventions, took the name "Association" to describe their movement. Fourier had conceived of communities of 1,620; Brisbane proposed a community of 400 and promoted it by the promise of material abundance. In the main the American phalansteries were small rural settlements, combining agriculture and small-scale manufacture, distinct from other villages in their organization of cooperative labor and communal dwelling houses. From the movement's beginning in 1844 until its demise by 1859, as many as ten thousand Americans were involved in sixty-two Fourierist communities. It has been argued that these communities appealed for two reasons. At a time in which artisanal work was being degraded, the Associations offered workers a means to return to independence. And to those in the middle class uneasy with the rise of class tensions and the pull into domestic privatism, they restored communal life.[19]

The Associationists promised that families could retain their customary structure and relationships within the community, but this proved to be difficult. During the short life of Fourierism in America, the tension between community and family life was unresolved. The North American Phalanx and other actual Association communities typically adapted the structures already existing on the farms they purchased. This often meant that the unmarried shared a large structure but married couples with children lived in separate houses. In places where families were incorporated into the communal dwelling, those women who longed for "the separate fire-side" were discontented. In times of scarcity, conflicts arose over parents' desire to protect their own children. As unattached adults met, fell in love, and married, they often wanted to separate themselves from the community. Each phalanx attempted to resolve the problem of family versus community in its own way.[20]

The growth of Fourierist Associationism in America inevitably led to debates about passion, love, and marriage. Although Brisbane had initially limited treatment of these issues, critics attacked the nascent movement using Fourier's own texts, and Brisbane and others were forced to present and reject elements of the comprehensive scheme. Fourier had brought much of the spirit of Rousseau to utopian dreams. He believed that at the base of human action lay the passions. Society was driven not by reason but by instinct, "the drive given us by nature prior to any reflection." A healthy society accepted the passions as intrinsically good and fostered rather than repressed them.[21]

The uncensored Fourierist project involved the creation of voluntary communities that would gradually lead to the millennial era of Harmony, a state in which the passions would be freed. Much of the imagined change, including that in sexual relations, was projected into the Harmonic future, in which "a 'New Amorous World' . . . would give full scope to human sexual 'attractions' by organizing love in a series of graded 'corporations' ranging from 'vestalic' virginity to complete promiscuity, both heterosexual and homosexual." Brisbane did not bring Fourier's ideas on these subjects to America, and the dominant American effort was first to bypass and then to reject this aspect of Fourierism as "speculative." When questioned, the typical Associationist answer was that changes in sex and marriage were to come only in the future.[22]

But while Brisbane and other Associationists insisted that life in the pha-lansteries was fully compatible with marriage, they nonetheless joined in Fourier's criticism of marriage under contemporary Civilization. The private household trapped women in child care and housework. Women's lack of economic independence forced them into marriages for their support. Men's power in marriage was tyrannical. Sexual relations in marriage were merely "legalized prostitution" or "legalized rape." Under Association, women would be educated and have productive work, housework and child care would be communal, and marriage would thereby be elevated and purified. In 1848, the Fourierite turned Swedenborgian Henry James, father of the novelist, translated Victor Hennequin's *Love in the Phalanstery*. It criticized marriage as the source of prostitution and of deception of all kinds, includ-ing adultery and abortion. Parke Goodwin and other reformers began to argue for more liberal divorce laws.[23]

Fourier's vision began to inspire some American followers to work to bring elements of the future into the present. As the Associations failed in the late 1840s, utopian hopes faltered, and in their wake some American Fourierists edged toward free love. As the most astute writer on American Fourierism has observed, "As long as Fourierism remained a viable commu-nitarian movement, economic cooperation took precedence over the cre-ation of a liberated culture. . . . But the collapse of the phalanxes and the return of prosperity in the late 1840s discredited the economic side of Fouri-erist ideology and favored the psychological. . . . No longer limited to 'Indus-trial Association,' they [the Fourierists] could 'come out' on issues such as sex and marriage."[24]

4

Fourierism began to mix with other religious and social movements, in-cluding Spiritualism, a broad and diffuse religious movement outside the churches. At one level, Spiritualism asserted the eternal life of the soul and focused on communicating with the spirits of those who had died. At another level, it expressed a radical individualism that refused to accept the limitations of existing institutional arrangements.

By the late 1840s, many Spiritualists recognized Andrew Jackson Davis as their philosophical leader. As a young man he had become a healer and a skilled hypnotist. As he began to dictate his revelations of universal harmony, he developed a significant following among Universalists. Davis linked his Harmonial Philosophy to a wide range of reforms. He and many of his followers embraced Fourier's vision, opposition to slavery, alternative medicine, and free love. Davis's insights into the world of spirits were confirmed for many in 1848, when Kate and Margaret Fox announced that they had heard rappings from the dead. First taken up by radical Quakers, these two girls offered demonstrations of their powers to serve as mediums. Spirit circles formed in home parlors to receive communications from the beyond. Sharing a widespread belief that women were the more passive sex, whose nervous organization opened them to stimuli from this world and the next, the circles gathered around young women and girls. Messages from the dead were seen as electric currents; the female mediums, as the receivers.[25]

Women's rights as an organized movement began in Spiritualist homes: in 1848 the table in Seneca Falls on which Elizabeth Cady Stanton and Lucretia Mott wrote the Declaration of Sentiments was one used for rappings from the other world. Although Stanton remained secular and something of a freethinker, the women surrounding her were radical Quakers seeking inspiration and reassurance through mediums.[26] At a time in which anything seemed possible, Spiritualism seemed plausible to some of the mid–nineteenth century's most influential men and women. Two children of Lyman Beecher, Charles and Isabella, became Spiritualists; and Harriet took the movement seriously. Among abolitionists and reformers, William Lloyd Garrison and Sarah and Angelina Grimké joined in efforts to connect to the spirit world. The movement spread beyond white Protestant circles to embrace a wide range of believers. There is no way to verify claims that before the Civil War there were four million Spiritualists; however the movement had wide appeal. It drew on those who, longing for connection with a departed loved one, found comfort and knowledge in spirit circles. Many were ready to reject Calvinist strictures. Others were moving beyond liberal Christianity. To some Spiritualism seemed like a religious form of science: If the power of electricity could be transmitted invisibly, could not the power of spirit follow the same logic?

As Spiritualism grew to be a major force, it had a particular appeal to those questioning slavery and women's place in society. It attracted radicals and led some religious followers to advocate social change. It drew in abolitionists resisting the movement's turn to political antislavery. In particular,

Spiritualists were not to be moved from their commitment to women's emancipation. They continued to imagine the world anew and press for reforms in dress, marriage, and economic rights.[27]

One of the most profound impacts of Spiritualism was on marriage. Spiritualists drew on widely accepted notions that true love was the basis of marriage. Many believed that sexual expression was natural and therefore good. This was normally qualified by insisting that sexual intercourse was natural when it was an expression of love. By lifting it from the realm of the purely carnal, love sanctified sexual intercourse. As Charlotte Beebe Wilbour, a Spiritualist medium, wrote, "All the passions . . . are, in their ideal conception, good and noble, and only become vices when they become warped and contorted by the inadequacy of the corporeal medium through which they attempt to realize themselves in acts."[28]

Many religious faiths posited that the soul was eternal. What Spiritualism added was the belief that the eternal soul was linked forever to its earthly ties. When mothers loved their children and lost them in death, Spiritualism offered the consolation that death was not the end of being but a passage to a different phase. Mothers could remain the guardians of their children in the life beyond. But what about husbands and wives? If spirit life extended beyond death and relationships were sustained, who was to be one's partner for all eternity? Spiritualists believed that there was one person ordained to be a spiritual mate through life and death. In a true marriage based on love, the man and the woman had a special affinity.

But what happened when one realized that a soul mate was not the person to whom one was legally joined? This is the question that cast confusion in Spiritualist ranks as early as 1853, when Mary Fenn Love spoke against marriage and traveled to Indiana to end her own. She became the wife of Spiritualist leader Andrew Jackson Davis and at the 1854 Spiritualist convention spoke against marriage. Although many Spiritualists disagreed, some began to argue that any law that violated the free choice of an individual soul was void. It is here that the Spiritualists entered a realm fraught with controversy. If a marriage was not "true," then the Church or state had no right to ordain or sustain it. At one level, Spiritualism gave individuals the license to dissolve their marriages and seek divorce. At another level, its underlying radical individualism did not recognize the claims of law. A person could simply leave a wrong marriage and unite with a spiritual mate.[29]

More generally, Spiritualism offered a rich and varied critique of marriage from the perspective of women. Women needed economic independence. Without it, many women entered into a loveless marriage as a means of economic support. Spiritualists spoke out against a husband's sexual prerogatives, embedded in common law. Sharing the view of many of the physiologists that there was too much sex in America, some Spiritualists advocated sexual restraint in marriage. Insistence that women had the right to refuse the marital embrace went with Spiritualist belief in the autonomy of the individual. A woman had a right to her own body; thus the decision to have sexual relations was hers as well as her husband's. The link between love and sex gave power to Spiritualists' arguments. If love sanctified sex, the absence of love made it carnal. Husbands and wives who no longer loved each other should not engage in sexual relations even though they were married. A woman who no longer loved her husband had the right to deny him sexual access. Many of those writing about sexuality in the nineteenth century agreed.[30]

Calling on higher authority, Spiritualists gave men and women the right to form new unions that some called free love. As Alfred Cridge wrote in 1856, Spiritualism claimed the "power to dissolve all uncongenial and false relations," allowing its adherents to follow their attractions and form new relations in business and domestic life. "Thus we obtain the elements of Freedom and Love, forming, in combination, Free-love. This then, being the essence of Spiritual progress, Free Love is the doctrine of Spiritualism." Many Spiritualists, however, accepted the concept of freedom more easily than the label "free love." If Spiritualists claimed it, they typically tried to redefine free love as the right to leave a stifling marriage and to love one's soul mate freely.[31]

Only a few Spiritualists insisted that marriage was, like slavery, an oppressive institution, but many accepted the distinction between a true marriage based on spiritual affinity and a false one. With a license to perform weddings in Illinois, Mrs. H. M. F. Brown solemnized an 1865 Spiritualist marriage by contrasting false marriages, which caused all the "heartaches, the suicides, the jealousies, elopements, insanity, drunkenness . . . all the ills and curses that call for prisons, asylums, doctors and preachers," with the true. She told the couple that "wedded hearts had no need of legislation to keep them together, they were bound by natural, by eternal laws." Their hearts were already recognized by Heaven. They joined in a ceremony only for "public recognition" of the established fact.[32]

Some Spiritualists sought more room for personal freedom than the notion of true marriage for life and eternity permitted. They developed a position known as "varietist" that allowed true love to take a sequential course. A very few varietists came to argue for the possibility of multiple, simultaneous love relations.

5

The Fourierist Marx Edgeworth Lazarus published America's first free-love polemic. Lazarus had lived at the utopian colony Brook Farm and the Fourierist North American Phalanx. In the late 1840s, he underwrote Mary Gove's water-cure boardinghouse in New York City and lived there. In 1846 and 1847 he penned articles advocating "perfect liberty to this and every other attraction" as essential to "divine order." His *Passional Hygiene,* published in 1852, attempted to ground human well-being in Fourierist theory. He wrote that although man should be able to live healthily by instinct, in his degenerated state in Civilization, he needs intellect to show him "how to replace himself in conditions where his instincts shall revive and become practically efficient." Like many in his day, Lazarus was concerned with seminal losses, a condition that he called "tabescence." These were the losses that continued in sleep in men even after they had ceased to masturbate or to engage in excessive coitus. In tabescence the body remains "insane after the soul has recovered its sanity." This and other forms of insanity could be cured by the sexual freedom possible under the new order of Harmony.[33]

In 1852, in *Love vs. Marriage,* published by Fowler and Wells, the phrenological publishing house, Lazarus openly espoused free love. Lazarus tried to make a distinction between an ideal and reality: the free-love ideal that he was presenting to change public opinion and the reality of the present, in which a person had to obey the laws of marriage. As Lazarus proceeded, however, his language undercut this intention. He elided into advocacy as he asked, "Are your affinities such as are calculated to unite you only for a season—for a single phase of life and love, ardent but ephemeral, like the contact of electric points?" He then answered, "Accept joyfully this present happiness in each other." Marriage, he suggested, is "putting the police badge on a passion . . . handcuffing a sweet affinity of souls!" If a person is stuck in a marriage that should end, "What need, then, of legal formalities?"[34]

Behind Lazarus's embrace of free love are many elements. He joined the chorus of worry about masturbation and seminal emissions. He grounded his fear in a physiology that saw male seminal losses in heterosexual intercourse as compensated for by the magnetic power imparted by the female.

He believed in the positive benefit of coition. Through sexual relations one can gain, he wrote, "true harmonic equilibrium." If a person is satisfied "in a true-love relation, the organic vigor of the genesic sphere is sustained." This gives ease and perfection to the higher labors of the mind and imparts "a warmer tone of cordiality to all expression of passional affinity in ambition, friendship, or family ties." At least on paper, Lazarus sought variety in ways that suggested his distance from those advocating restraint. He wrote that women appreciated roués, and, perhaps even more surprisingly, he advocated wine and coffee as harmonic aids. Lazarus held his adherence to Fourier in suspension with his sexual notions. Under nineteenth-century Civilization, Lazarus wrote, "marriage converts lovers into owners of personal property, and often renders the most charming love relations at last indifferent or odious by the meannesses, monotony, and exclusiveness of the isolated household, and the arbitrary connection or collision of a thousand impertinences of fortune, interest, domestic cares, and individual tastes and pursuits with the natural tie of love." Women require the economic independence of the phalanstery, freeing them from dependence upon individual men for their support. In the ideal Fourierist phalanx, "a colony with a soil, a government, and social institutions all its own," female independence, economic security, and collective provision for children would allow men and women to move in and out of love relations. They could be monogamous if they chose, or they could enjoy "numerous and varied love relations."[35]

Stephen Pearl Andrews, a reformer and maverick residing in New York, was soon to pick up on all these arguments. By midcentury he had already had a long and diverse career. After working on a diplomatic scheme to free the slaves of the South, he settled in Boston and taught shorthand. There he became attracted to the ideas of Josiah Warren, an Owenite who had earlier left Indiana for New York to join with Frances Wright in publishing the *Free Enquirer.* Warren decided that the fundamental error that Robert Owen had made was the commitment to communal property. Announcing a theory of individual sovereignty, Warren returned to older notions of a just price to check the abuses of competition. He called his principle "Cost the limit of price." Warren's slogan became the bridge that took Andrews to philosophical anarchism and free love.[36]

Andrews moved his family to New York and, making use of his shorthand, became a congressional correspondent in Washington. An invitation by the New York Mechanics' Institute to lecture on "The True Constitution of Government" stimulated him to write *The Science of Society.* Influenced by a reading of Saint-Simon, Proudhon, Fourier, Swedenborg, and Warren, Andrews set forth his version of American anarchism. Andrews declared that the best government was the least government. To this he added Warren's notion that the labor of workers should determine price.

Determined to bring their anarchist principles into being, Andrews and Warren established Modern Times, a utopian settlement on Long Island. The two sought residents among journeymen with skills but no property. More than one hundred invested in the village. In addition to tinsmiths, masons, blacksmiths, and carpenters, the scheme also attracted visionaries, Spiritualists, and reformers. Unlike other such efforts, Modern Times was united by a negative: "We do not believe in Association," Andrews declared. "We are not Communists." Belief in individual sovereignty and the labor theory of value were the community's only tenets. Modern Times began auspiciously, attracting reformers such as Mary Gove and Thomas Low Nichols. It ended, however, fantastically, as the community served as a magnet for enthusiasts of all kinds and eventually dissolved. Andrews himself, who never moved to Modern Times, continued his life in New York virtually unchanged.

The ever-restless Andrews had, however, added free love to his theoretical commitments. As always, he sought a public forum. He tried in 1853 to engage in a literary three-cornered debate in the New York *Tribune* with Horace Greeley and Henry James. Unable to get the two others to take the bait, Andrews published his ideas and theirs as *Love, Marriage, and Divorce, and the Sovereignty of the Individual.* Opposite Greeley's commitment to indissoluble marriage and James's support of freer divorce laws, Andrews stood for free love. In his dry, intellectual presentation, Andrews based his position on individual freedom and self-determination, especially for women, with almost no reference to sexual attraction and passion. Andrews lectured on free love, even carrying the topic to Henry Ward Beecher and his congregation at Plymouth Church in Brooklyn.[37]

The ideas and practices of John Humphrey Noyes, women's rights advocates, Fourierists, Spiritualist free lovers, and Stephen Pearl Andrews do not exhaust the challenges posed to heterosexual monogamous marriage before the Civil War. They do bear a special relation to the sexual conversation, however. Each engaged alternative ideas publicly and explicitly and sought changes in social and sexual arrangements. Working from within physiological reform and extending some of its notions, some participants in these movements began to suggest that sex held special importance. Although many statements were individual expressions, collectively they began to articulate a fourth framework for comprehending sexuality.

What defines this stance as a distinctive sexual framework is the belief that sex lies at the core of being. Sexual expression in heterosexual intercourse becomes the most vital facet of life, as important for women as for men. Its significance for the development of the self underlies the demand for its free play within and outside marriage. To divert or repress sexual urges from their "natural expression" in coitus is harmful to the self. Over time, as this framework develops, sexuality emerges as the critical component of personal identity.[38]

Beyond beginning to articulate this fourth sexual framework, these social movements were important in another way: they raised the threat that printed word might become deed. To evangelical Christians and others concerned with policing the boundary between the permissible and the obscene, these movements intensified anxieties about the power of the word.

THE GREAT REPUBLICAN REFORM PARTY,
Calling on their Candidate.
1856

Social movements as seen from the outside. "The Great Republican Reform Party, Calling on their Candidate," caricature, lithograph, Currier & Ives, New York, 1856. From left to right, each advocate states:

"The first thing we want is a law making the use of Tobacco, Animal food and Lager-beer a Capital Crime—"

"We demand, first of all; the recognition of Woman as the equal of man with a right to Vote and hold Office—"

"An equal division of Property that is what I go in for—"

"Col. I wish to invite you to the next meeting of our Free Love association, where the shackles of marriage are not tolerated & perfect Freedom exist in love matters and you will, be sure to Enjoy yourself, for we are all Freemounters—"

"We look to you Sir to place the power of the Pope on a firm footing in this Country—"

"De Poppylation ob Color comes in first—arter dat, you do wot you pleases—"

"You shall all have what you desire and be sure that the glorious Principles of Popery, Fourierism, Free Love, Womans rights, the Maine Law, & above all the Equality of our Colored bretheren, shall be maintained; If I get into the Presidential Chair."

© Collection of The New-York Historical Society, negative #44725.

12

Blurring the Boundaries

In the years around 1850, as advocates for social change set in play a new sexual framework that put sex at the core of life, their words came at a confusing moment. By midcentury the lines between the acceptable and the obscene were becoming blurred, and important questions came to the fore. What is the distinction between that which is lawful and that which is criminally obscene? When do lecturers gain an audience for scientific knowledge or calls for change, and when, conversely, do they attract patrons who come out of prurient interest? When does published writing about sexual matters slide from reform physiology into erotica? These questions came when some authors were blurring the distinction between scientific discussion about the body and reproduction and commerce in birth control materials and services. Moreover, as the example of Thomas Low Nichols demonstrates, in a time of changing understandings and challenges to traditional marriage, some writing that purported to be reform physiology may have been racy material in another guise.

One way that authorities resolved the question of boundaries is illustrated by the 1855 prosecution of George Thompson and Prescott F. Harris, previously discussed. After the intentionally racy *Broadway Belle* printed the paragraph of a text published by Fowler and Wells complaining of "the frequency, the fury, the almost *goatishness*" of husbands' sexual demands, the mayor had the weekly's editor and proprietor arrested. At that point phrenologist Orson Squires Fowler and his talented brothers and sisters were the entrepreneurs of health reform, and their firm, Fowler and Wells, the leading publisher of books dealing with the body and health. In addition to phrenological works, the press published the books of reform physiologist Russell T. Trall and the philosophical tracts of Marx Edgeworth Lazarus in support of free love.[1]

Although the mayor persisted in watching over the *Broadway Belle,* he did not police the phrenologists, and they continued to thrive. What this incident reveals is that when speaking or writing involved sexual matters in mid-century America, boundaries separating reform discussion and the racy could blur. What appeared to be one kind of work to physiological reformers or women of the middle class could be applied—or read—in a quite different light by someone coming from the sporting culture of urban men. In judgment about writing, context played heavily. It mattered where something was printed, how the work was marketed and sold, and who made up its intended audience.

This affected the way that nineteenth-century physiological reformers went about their work. Unless they enjoyed inherited incomes, patrons, or breadwinning spouses, even the most moral advocates had to make a living. Those who espoused causes, therefore, went out on the lecture circuit, established journals, and wrote books, hoping that they would not be forced to corrupt their high-minded ideas in the bargain. Sylvester Graham lectured, wrote, and published, as did his followers. In time, anticipating a market for physiological wares, alternative presses, such as Fowler and Wells, emerged to print and distribute this material. Complicating the lives of writers and publishers of reform physiology were the ways that some others were moving in to claim their ground.

At its simplest, it was possible for an editor or a publisher of commercial erotica such as Prescott F. Harris, Frederic A. Brady, George Ackerman, and Jeremiah Farrell to advertise a reform tract or book of popular science on the reproductive organs and their functions with the other works on their list. To do so carried the suggestion that a physiological work had been written to titillate or to gain money through appealing to sexual desire. For example, along with long lists of known erotica, Harris sold *Married Woman's Private Medical Guide;* Ackerman, *Aristotle, Illustrated Complete Masterpiece;* and Farrell, Jean Dubois's *Secret Habits of the Female Sex.* Whatever had been their original purposes, when surrounded in advertisements by books of the European erotic canon or the racy novels of George Thompson, a work treating sexuality could be marketed as erotic material that promised male customers sexual stimulation. As a result, it could be difficult to see a clear distinction between intentional erotica and the writings of physiological reformers.

I

In 1846 Frederick Hollick faced the question of boundaries in court. He was indicted by the grand jury in Philadelphia and charged with "a misdemeanor in the nature of a libel, in publishing a 'scandalous' book, The Origin of Life, and also in exhibiting indecent models of the sexual organs at his lectures." According to a newspaper account, the prosecutor remarked to the judge that "he would prove that the book inculcated the doctrine that sexual intercourse was proper, moral and essential to health immediately on attaining puberty, and ought to be encouraged." Hollick's book, The Origin of Life: A Popular Treatise on the Philosophy and Physiology of Reproduction, was first published in 1845. Hollick admitted that he was the author of the book but defended his work on "scientific principles." Released on a technicality, Hollick was indicted a second time. Pending trial, he was prohibited from selling his book in Philadelphia. The judge stated in court that "he had examined the volume, and was of opinion that it was an improper publication, and entirely different from the scientific works adopted as class books by medical students."[2]

The Origin of Life was self-consciously different from medical treatises. By his own account Hollick had written it for the people, not for the profession. Believing that sexual emotion was the strongest feeling and the principal source of human happiness, Hollick was a sexual enthusiast. He did allow that the "ignorant and uncontrolled indulgence" of the sexual instinct "originates more vice, and misery, than all other causes put together," but he normally wrote in a positive vein. In discussing the sexual instinct in 1845, for example, he stated, "A proper gratification of it is, probably, productive of the highest physical enjoyment known, and is also at the foundation of the holiest and dearest moral and social delights." The sex drive needed no apology. "Like the desire for food and exercise, it results directly from a want [i.e., need] of the system; it is part of our nature." Sexual desire is an instinct similar to the hunger and thirst that propel the body to eat and drink. Built into the animal nature of humanity, the sexual appetite is thus natural and benign.[3]

By 1850, when Hollick published The Marriage Guide, he was established in practice in New York City and had T. W. Strong as his publisher. At that

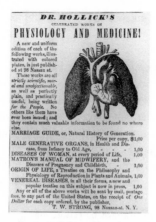

Advertisement for *Dr. Hollick's Celebrated Works on Physiology and Medicine* in *Yankee Notions*, February 1855, p. 320. Courtesy, American Antiquarian Society.

point Strong, whose shop was on 98 Nassau Street, was a leading publisher of comic valentines, almanacs, and children's books, reusing much of the stock of Robert H. Elton. Because Hollick's books had many illustrations, largely anatomical, Strong was in a good position to publish and promote his works.[4]

The Marriage Guide has a great deal of information on human reproduction. Hollick understood the female body as governed by its own laws: "the growth and expulsion of the egg is a process belonging to the female system alone" and is not provoked by sexual intercourse. The sperm can fertilize the ovum if sexual intercourse takes place within a day of expulsion. This means that women can become pregnant without experiencing sexual feeling or even when unconscious and that they can be artificially inseminated via a syringe containing semen. This enabled Hollick to encourage sexual abstinence during a woman's fertile period. The only thing wrong with Hollick's early advocacy of what was later called the rhythm method was that he, like others in his day, thought that the expulsion of the ovum followed menstruation. Understanding that sperm, or what he called "Seminal Animalcules" live for only twenty-six hours after ejaculation and that the ovum takes between two and six days to travel to the uterus, he set a woman's fertile period as between two and ten days after her monthly flow ceased. By this calendar, women were encouraged to have unprotected sexual intercourse on some of their most fertile days.[5]

Hollick was one of those men writing on women's bodies who began to see women as wombs surrounded by flesh and bones. To him the key unlocking female nature was ovulation. As he put it, the "ripening and expulsion of the Egg every month . . . exercises a powerful and peculiar influence over both body and mind, making the Female essentially different to the male in her physical requirements and capabilities, and also in her nervous sympathies." From puberty until menopause, a woman works to produce eggs and, in his eyes, "seems to live chiefly for this purpose." As a result women suffer from "excessive sympathy, sensitiveness, and excitability," as well as female diseases. "The incessant action of the Ovaries keeps the nervous system in a constant state of irritation, and makes all the Organic functions liable to derangement, so that it is impossible for a female to preserve that equanimity of mind, and that evenness of temper and disposition which to individuals of the other sex is a comparatively easy matter." A woman's monthly cycle makes it impossible for her to pursue men's work. Unable to work with male steadiness and strength, she seeks "sympathy and support from some being that she feels is more powerful than herself." Her sexual feeling is periodic and keenest at the time of ovulation. Such notions were becoming well established in the allopathic medical community by the mid–nineteenth century. It is interesting that an irregular physician, radical in many aspects of his thought and practice, held them as well.[6]

Hollick openly considered birth control techniques, justifying all of them as a means of reducing the number of abortions. His opposition to abortion was not moral but medical. To his understanding, "there are *no safe means of procuring Abortion*": all of them endanger a woman's health. Unlike writers primarily interested in selling contraceptives, Hollick was a sober guide to contraceptive techniques. In his mind there were no effortless or certain methods to prevent pregnancy, and he considered the weaknesses of each. Withdrawal he opposed as leading to male "irritation and exhaustion," in a way akin to masturbation. He warned men that it was particularly injurious to try to compress the penis near the scrotum to keep semen from escaping. "Injections," what a later generation would call the douche method, were in his mind not always reliable and required a substance to kill the "seminal animalcules," which, if not chosen properly, could lead to inflammation of the uterus and vagina. Because a woman must immediately remove herself to apply the syringe, the technique is "agitating and injurious," as well as inconvenient. Hollick was one of those who believed that only unobstructed intercourse allowing semen to bathe the vagina and the penis to touch the cervix is fully satisfying to both parties. Thus any barrier device diminished pleasure and threatened to cause sexual excitement in women without total release. On these grounds he warned against the sponge and the condom. That left him with the calendar, known today as the rhythm method, which is vulnerable to female irregularity (and his own timing of ovulation). Women must limit coition to the time of the month in which they least desire it. In birth control, nature and human nature are not in harmony. It is proof that "nature does not favor prevention in any way, but on the contrary favors Reproduction."[7]

Despite the advice, Hollick sold birth control articles. In some copies of the book, there are pages given to advertisements for Hollick's wares, sold and sent through the mails. One could purchase condoms at $9 a package, a steep price in the mid–nineteenth century. Hollick also offered services and sold medicines that place him in a more questionable light. Although he encouraged those coming to New York to locate him by contacting his publisher, he was willing to practice medicine at a distance, allowing correspondents to receive his advice and medicine in the privacy of their homes. He did attempt to get information for a diagnosis, stating that he would inform a potential patient who was unable to visit his office of the ways "by which the necessary examination of the urine, semen, or female ovaries, can be made." He offered a remedy promised to prevent syphilis for $10. The item he highlighted most prominently was "Dr. Hollick's Aphrodisic Remedy," designed to restore sexual desire. He described it as a colorless powder, undetectable and easily portable, intended for those suffering from "impotence, sterility, loss of feeling, and natural torpidity." Hollick sent the powder if the request contained $5 and a letter setting forth the reasons the writer wished to take the remedy.[8]

2

The language of *The Origin of Life* may have offended a Philadelphia judge in 1846, but it was not judged criminally obscene, and after 1846, no court ever indicted Hollick again for obscene libel. *The Origin of Life* was reprinted in many editions in the decades that followed. Hollick was unusual in his long career and wide readership for his many books, works that combined writing about sexual functioning with the sale of his medical ministrations and contraceptives. Others entered the field only once. They had a service or a product to sell, and they needed to market it with words. An earlier chapter examined how Charles Lohman, under the name Dr. A. M. Mauriceau, wrote and published *The Married Woman's Private Medical Companion* in 1847. In this purported medical work, he presented the business of Madame Restell—his wife, Ann Lohman—to a reading public and discussed, if only elliptically, her services as abortionist. He also presented the range of her contraceptive wares available by mail order. Lohman stood at the beginning of writing that blurred the boundaries between scientific writings about the body and reproduction, reform physiology, and the commerce in birth control materials and services.

As contraception became a bigger business in the nineteenth century, it also begot a larger literature. Accompanying the techniques and implements for sale were pamphlets and books setting out the rationale for sexual expression divorced from childbearing. In some cases these written materials were advertisements designed to encourage mail-order purchases. In some cases they were books meant merely for instruction, containing within them all the information necessary for assembling one's own set of contraceptive tools.

The literature written to support birth control countered a belief held by some nineteenth-century writers on health that because nature has the survival of the species as its goal, the end of coition is reproduction. In this view nothing should interfere to prevent nature's goal of procreation from being realized. Beginning with Robert Dale Owen and Charles Knowlton, contraceptive writers needed to oppose this doctrine. Just as the writers on masturbation performed an announcement ritual to justify presenting books and pamphlets that might fall into young hands, so those offering contraceptive advice confronted the question of the natural. Two decades after Knowlton's *Fruits of Philosophy,* an American edition of *The Young Married Lady's Private Medical Guide,* a treatise purportedly by two French physicians, echoed Knowlton but in different language. To the argument that contraception is unnatural, "the authors would reply by inquiring whether Nature also declares it right and proper that our dwellings should remain unprotected from the effects of electricity." If it is right to attach a lightning rod to a house, it is equally so to offer protection through contraception to a woman when pregnancy threatens her life or health or to a young couple who face economic ruin if they have children.[9]

The second issue that writers on contraception addressed was its positive effects. Writing in a tradition that had begun with Owen and Knowlton, they set out the benefits of their techniques to both society and the individual. They insisted on the naturalness and strength of the sexual appetite. By encouraging the young to marry, contraception lessens prostitution. Fewer women will be drawn into the trade, and fewer men will resort to it to satisfy their desires. Contraception also minimizes the need for masturbation. In the words of these writers, men resort to masturbation for the same reason that they turn to prostitutes. Although Knowlton himself found masturbation much exaggerated as an evil, other contraceptive writers deemed that it caused significant injury and insisted that only youthful marriages made possible by contraception could prevent the "solitary vice."[10]

Social betterment was given its due by the contraceptive writers of the 1850s, but it was the benefits to the individual that formed the heart of their arguments. In focusing on the man and woman engaging in the sexual act, these writers made an important contribution to the discussion of sexuality in the mid–nineteenth century. In so doing they are a forceful reminder that in the nineteenth century conflicting perspectives on sexual questions were possible. Many contraceptive writers gave their readers clear information on the physiology of sexual intercourse, focused on the nature of sexual response, and championed sexual pleasure.[11]

Contraception benefits the individual, they argued, because it allows the gratification of the sexual appetite without leading to pregnancy and additional children. Necessary to this reasoning is the belief that sexual desire and sexual expression are not only instinctive, they are essential elements of human well-being. On this point—the importance of sexual desire and the beneficence of sexual pleasure—all contraceptive writers agreed. They disagreed, however, on their specific recommendations for birth control. These recommendations, in turn, derived from differing physiological systems shaping the writers' understanding of the nature of the reproductive organs and their role in physical lovemaking.

One major source of contraceptive information (and misinformation) was medical advice literature that supposedly came from France, as translated by physicians for American lay audiences. "French," to a nineteenth-century American audience, conjured up notions of sensuality that these works attempted to allay with solemn introductory statements. Eugène Becklard's *The Physiologist: An Infallible Guide to Health and Happiness for Both Sexes,* published in 1844, was one of many such books. Its goal was to advertise the Lucina cordial for fostering reproduction and to present a guide (of mixed utility) to methods of contraception, not for sale.

Underlying Becklard's discussion was a belief in the positive elements of desire. "Love," Becklard wrote, "is principally made up of desire; and without desire there would be but little tendency of the sexes for each other's society. Thus nature was compelled to make love a selfish pleasure, to the end of population." He saw it as "mental magnetism," the effect "of a mysterious agency acting on two minds naturally suited to each other, but which have never before come within each other's influence. . . . It is the mutual attraction of two souls, that occasion in each other sensations of ecstasy which they have never before experienced."[12]

Sexual relations are to be understood as the natural result of such attraction. Becklard spent no ink justifying a practice he regarded as completely natural. The reader had only his antagonism to its opposite, abstinence. He wrote, "Persons sworn to chastity grow weak in intellect." Nor did he discuss male or female sexual pleasure; he merely assumed it. In doing so, Becklard weighed in on an ancient question that engaged many nineteenth-century writers on sexuality, including Frederick Hollick. Was it necessary for women to experience sexual excitement to become pregnant? Becklard stated baldly that it was. A woman could become pregnant only if she experienced sexual pleasure. He stated, equally declaratively, a corollary that had an impact on the law: a true rape cannot lead to conception.[13]

A number of American physicians disagreed. Augustus K. Gardner, no friend of contraception, reviewed this question in *The Causes and Curative Treatment of Sterility*, published in 1856. He stated that some sources claimed that at climax, or, as he put it, at the "height of venereal sensation of the part of the female, the mouth of the womb *opens*" to receive semen, enabling her to conceive. He did not disagree on medical grounds. Too little was known about the physiology of women during sexual intercourse to make any scientific judgment. From commonsense observation, however, he believed that the position taken by Becklard and others was false. He knew of raped women becoming pregnant, and he was personally acquainted with passionless women who had large families. Later in his discussion, Gardner, whose concern was not to prevent births but to restore fertility to women unable to conceive, considered the question of sexual unresponsiveness as a cause of female sterility. Here he was more definite, insisting that there is no relation between sexual pleasure and conception. "Frigidity may or may not accompany the act; the result is as independent of sensation, as if it were a chemical transformation that is going on."[14] This is the position taken by most of the contraceptive writers. For quite different reasons they urged women not to rely on the popular belief that they could prevent pregnancy by keeping themselves from experiencing sexual excitement. Sperm acts as sperm on an ovum, irrespective of a woman's emotions and physical arousal.

By the 1850s there were entrepreneurs who, unlike Becklard, were eager to make money by offering the new techniques of contraception for sale. An intriguing element of their business was the campaign that they waged to promote their products in books and pamphlets. Thus many contraceptive writers added their voices. As historian Janet Farrell Brodie has stated, a good number of their arguments were directed at women's health. Of interest here were those of a different nature, arguments that focused on the physiology of sexual intercourse and sexual pleasure. Some statements, such as those of Frederick Hollick, were part of larger works about the human system and its functioning. But other publications were simply marketing tools.[15]

In *Henry's Private Adviser,* for example, Dr. J. Henry of Rossville, Maryland, sought to sell his "Chart of Life," a guide to what is today called the rhythm method of contraception. His sheet advertising this chart, resembling a newspaper, offered a broad justification of birth control. Henry asserted that a man has an "all-powerful instinct . . . demanding gratification, and gratification it must and will have," leaving him with three choices—marriage, prostitution, or masturbation. Marriage is obviously the only rightful, legitimate option: "In its holy bonds a vent is opened for the escape of the animal passions, perfectly according to nature, and conducive to soundness and health, both of body and mind." There is, however, a powerful reason that men do not marry. They do not wish to have children. The author sets out the various techniques of preventing pregnancy, drawing without acknowledgment on Hollick's *The Marriage Guide.* A man can resort to coitus interruptus, described as the biblical practice of Onan, but it does not satisfy a woman. She needs a man's semen to prevent "irritation and exhaustion. In fact, without it, the act is merely a species of masturbation—unsatisfactory and injurious." Coitus interruptus is hurtful to the man because "when emission occurs without the female organs, it is always more incomplete and slower." Sexual relations are insufficient without "the customary warmth and pressure . . . that peculiar influence which the organs of one sex exert upon those of the other."[16]

According to Henry, each existing method of contraception had its negatives, except the one that he offered. The postcoital douche, what Henry called "injections after association," may not remove all semen, and solutions suggested for the douche may harm female sexual desire and cause sterility. Moreover, "the too early separation" required by the woman's having to leave the bed to douche may mean that sexual intercourse is incomplete. This inconvenience and a possible "revulsion of feeling attendant upon the preventive act" may cause distress in both partners, or, as Henry put it, "weakness in the male, and nervous irritation in the female." The insertion of a sponge may also have the same shortcoming. In addition, it may reduce a woman's pleasure because it prevents contact between the penis ("the male organ") and the mouth of the womb. "Now this contact is often necessary for the production of a proper state of excitement, and when it does not occur there is simply an injurious irritation to the female, without any gratification." The sponge can irritate the penis, as well. The condom, Henry argued, did not allow the same gratification as unsheathed sexual intercourse. A technique that men were adopting for birth control—squeezing the penis into the scrotum before ejaculation—was ineffective and posed health risks. And finally, women's belief that "they can avoid being impregnated simply by avoiding all excitement and pleasurable feeling" was a deception with no basis in physiology. Abortion was dangerous. Thus the only solution that protected health and allowed full sexual pleasure was his own calendar with full instructions for the rhythm method, which, for a fee, Henry would send through the mail as a personal letter.[17]

As a way of spreading Hollick's views more broadly, Henry's arguments are significant. Both Hollick and Henry discussed physical and mental health, weakness in men, and irritability in women. They were both concerned with protecting the sensibility of men's and women's sexual organs and about the nature of their sexual response. Even more clearly than Hollick, Henry stated as the objective that both partners fully enjoy sexual intercourse.

Such, also, was the explicit goal of *The Habits of a Well-Organized Married Life,* an 1867 pamphlet put out by the New Jersey firm "Mme. Beach, Putney & Co, Physicians and Importers of and Dealers in French Medicine and Conjugal Goods." The author—"A Married Woman"—repeatedly declared herself to be a physician bringing the knowledge of the women of France to an American audience. The truthfulness of two elements of this assertion— that the author was both a woman and a physician—is as unlikely as it is unprovable, but it need not concern this inquiry. It is the third element, the importation of French knowledge, that is of genuine interest. At midcentury

Americans clearly associated France with both birth control and sensuality. What was negative in one context, however, was positive in another. *Habits* presented the condom as a French invention and linked it to French extravagance, French pleasure in food and drink, and French "amative indulgences."[18]

As did Dr. Henry, Madame Beach surveyed the competition to assert that only her methods were fully acceptable. And as did Henry, she emphasized sexual satisfaction as a primary element. In her treatment of the problems associated with coitus interruptus, she stated that it harms the female, producing "nervous exhaustion and dissatisfaction." Beach continued, "It is important to her that the male pressure be unremitting and natural[,] completing in her the act of copulation, and a healthy reaction of the muscular powers." Beach, too, raised questions about the possible harmful effect of postcoital douche solutions on women's "amativeness." But unlike Henry, she found the rhythm method problematic. Not only are women's menstrual cycles not necessarily regular, the method "confines this intercourse to a term of days when *least* desired by the female, which, of course, is not beneficial to her." She then advertised her particular product, condoms of various kinds and materials—envelopes, safes, and caps—and "The Womb Guard," an early version of the cervical cap, or diaphragm. Its particular advantage was that, once inserted, it was "entirely imperceptible to either party." This was particularly useful to a woman who, "contrary to the wishes of the husband," was seeking to prevent pregnancy.[19]

In addition to supplying contraception, Madame Beach offered advice about sexual problems and treated women suffering from a lack of sexual desire, for a fee. While she seemed to agree in part with the conclusion of certain writers on sex that some women lacked sexual desire, or what she called a "want of amative vigor . . . a want of feeling and enjoyment," she saw this not as a natural state to be accepted but as an unfortunate one to be remedied before it led to later physical or emotional problems. She wrote, "There are thousands of wives thus afflicted, who have no passion whatever for the conjugal embrace, and shun it with dislike. This is owing to a dormant and inactive state of the sexual organs, and by timely aid is easily restored to passionate devotion and enrapture, but by neglect a morbid state ensues, engendering various weaknesses, complaints and disorders." The nature of her cure for women's passionlessness was not disclosed, although from reports it involved a "wash." Printed testimonials from happy husbands suggest that men were readers of Madame Beach's pamphlet and purchasers of her wares. One man wrote that his wife had been fully restored and "has now a natural and firm passion. . . . I can't but feel that it is a new era in her existence, and that no woman is well, who is destitute of natural and positive sexual passions, and a capability for their enjoyment." Another testified that his wife was "a new woman. She has an arduous passion, and no longer that depressed feeling and bearing down on the sexual organs, that rendered her so inactive and passionless. Her spirits are light." But Madame Beach wanted to appeal to respectable women as well and had among her testimonials that of a minister's wife from Maine who regarded Beach's contraceptive company as engaged in "christian work."[20]

Dr. Henry, Madame Beach, and other purveyors of birth control devices and techniques and abortion were at work writing materials that blurred the boundary between commerce in contraceptives and works of physiology. They made it difficult to see Frederick Hollick as different, despite the fact that he was at base a reformer committed to promoting knowledge about the body and health through his words, rather than primarily a seller of goods.[21] But this was hardly the only conundrum. Given the way that many works of physiology were advertised, it seemed possible that some authors were using the cover of science to print racy material. All of this made the conversation about sex in the mid–nineteenth century very confusing.

3

Did certain authors turn to reform physiology in the 1850s as a way to coin the public's interest in sexually stimulating materials and yet remain safe from prosecution for obscenity? Thomas Low Nichols presents that possibility. Nichols traveled from publications close to the sporting press of the 1840s to the physiological tracts of the 1850s. He wed the two discourses by literally marrying one of reform physiology's most prolific writers, Mary Gove. Together they wrote a number of books that blurred the boundaries between reform writing and the erotica that some regarded as obscene.

In the late 1840s, Mary Gove was a major voice in American health reform, the only woman (not working in collaboration with a husband) among a large host of male writers. An earlier chapter considered her work as a lecturer on the body to female audiences and a writer of a physiological guide warning against masturbation. In 1840 she became editor of the *Health Journal and Advocate of Physiological Reform,* a Grahamite monthly. She moved on to water cure and New York City. Finding her a sympathetic spirit, in 1847

Marx Edgeworth Lazarus underwrote the establishment of a water-cure boardinghouse under her supervision at 261 Tenth Street in New York City, where she taught hydropathy. Gove also had a romantic streak and aspirations to live the life of an artist. She wrote fiction published in *Godey's Ladies Book* under the pseudonym "Mary Orme." In 1847 she met Thomas Low Nichols, a man five years her junior.[22]

Little is known of Nichols's origins other than that he was born in 1815 in New Hampshire, had a season at Dartmouth Medical College, and worked as a reporter and newspaperman. At the time of his marriage, Nichols called himself a writer. After marrying Gove, he took the second year of medical school at the University of the City of New York (later New York University), and upon graduation in 1850 wrote "M.D." after his name. With their marriage in 1848 Gove and Nichols began an important collaboration. As a team, they produced a spate of reform writing, fiction, and institution building, most importantly *Esoteric Anthropology* and *Marriage*. Their writings may have influenced fellow Spiritualists. Their presence at the utopian community Modern Times on Long Island helped to define it to outsiders.

In 1855, when Mary Gove and Thomas Low Nichols were working in Cincinnati, part of his past caught up with him, and scandalous rumors circulated in the press. He and his wife were editing *Nichols' Monthly*. To respond to the attack on his reputation, he issued an *Extra,* a broadside addressed to his audience, reviewing his career and declaring that the accusations against him were completely false. He stated that he had begun his career as a teacher and reformer twenty years before with a lecture course, "Phrenology and Human Physiology." He had gone on to work in newspaper writing and had undertaken medical study. His personal vigor and productive work belied the reports of license. He wrote, "Is the life of a *roué* consistent with the industrious labors of a man of science and of letters, and a teacher and healer? Can the man who wastes his time and vigor in debauchery be also a close student, a voluminous and multifarious writer, and attend to his profession and business?" All claims being made about him were false—"scandalous stories spread over the country by the credulous dupes of malignant knaves." His "perfect health" was the "best evidence" of a life well lived. In the antebellum years it seemed quite possible for a person to live one life, give it up, and move on. In the 1850s Nichols was, as he correctly stated, a prolific writer on health and sexuality and a well-known lecturer and reformer. What he was trying to hide was an earlier career close to the sporting press in the milieu of the brothel.[23]

In his memoir *Forty Years of American Life,* Nichols wrote, "Any man can start a paper; a very small capital, or even a little credit, is all that is required. . . . The man who can do nothing else can start a paper, and with reasonable effort, get a support for it." This is what Nichols had attempted to do. At the tender age of nineteen he began a newspaper in the anti-Catholic fury that surrounded the burning of the Ursuline Convent in Charlestown, Massachusetts. In his memoirs he stated that he had gone to New York and gotten a job at the *Herald,* where he had learned to imitate Bennett's style. In 1837 Nichols took himself to Buffalo, New York, and tried the *Buffalonian,* but there he learned something of journalism's risks as well. He was convicted for libel and spent four months in prison. True to his calling, Nichols improved his time in confinement by writing *Journal in Jail,* his first published book. It is an unintentionally revealing document, suggesting an inventive, playful, widely read young man eager for female company and the approbation of the world. By his own statement and that of others, Nichols and George Washington Dixon were friends, most likely from their Boston days.[24]

From Buffalo, Nichols returned to New York City. By September 1841 he was writing for the *Uncle Sam,* where he took on William Joseph Snelling and accused the *Flash* of being a blackmail sheet. In November 1841, as editor of the *Aurora,* Nichols contributed items on social, theatrical, and sporting events in New York. When Nichols made charges of graft, the *Aurora* was threatened with libel, and he was fired. (Walt Whitman took his place.) Nichols then attempted to establish his own two-penny daily, the New York *Arena.* In his April 16, 1842, issue he set up a dialogue with a woman who tells him that his paper is not spicy enough. Nichols demands, "Out with it—you would like something a little more spicy—a dash of double entendre—the cream of a crim. con.—some of those piquant little *morceau* that very elegant people do not object to be amused at." When she replied that she did, Nichols seemingly bowed to chivalry: "He is a poor knight who would refuse to oblige a lady."[25]

In 1841 and 1842 Nichols was the subject of scathing attacks in the sporting press. The *Flash* stated, "After figuring for some years as an unsuccessful editor, lecturer on animal magnetism &c, after contributing to Bennett's Herald and living on his bounty, the writer of the above [Nichols], in debt to everybody, without a rag that he could honestly call his own, became a pensioned hanger one [*sic*] of the Duchess De Berri, at No. 128 Duane Street.— She paid his board, lent him money, filled his belly and covered his back." A week previously, Nichols had planted an article in the *Flash* against Charles Locke, the companion of Mary Cisco, the brothel madam known as the Duchess de Berri. This had led to a physical fight between the two men, and Nichols took to the public prints to claim that Locke had attempted to kill him. This unleashed a stream of invective against Nichols in the sporting press that throughout its short life in the 1840s was never stilled.[26]

In 1843 Nichols published his coyly provocative first novel, *Ellen Ramsay*. Nichols took his hero through a series of unconsummated seduction scenes in New Hampshire and New York City, where the young hero, Edward, a writer very much like Nichols, goes to make his way. Nichols was trying his hand at the sensational writing of his time. In one scene, for example, a married woman who had previously made advances to Edward in New Hampshire, her book of Byron at the ready, is now a brothel prostitute. She shares a room with him prior to his return home to New Hampshire and Ellen. As Nichols focused on Edward's emotions, he wrote, "The hot blood of youth was rushing through his arteries—his unjaded nerves were tingling." Early in the morning, as Edward sees her exposed breast, he begins to kiss her. "Fire was in his veins." As the couple moves once again to consummation, Edward is called to the stagecoach that will take him to the love of his childhood, and thus he escapes temptation one final time. In the strange chapter that followed, Nichols left the fictional mode to argue for the value of marriage, its reality in contrast to the illusions of courtship. In this he countered the moral reformers to contend that the reformed rake makes the best husband.[27]

The Lady in Black, Nichols's short work of fiction published in 1844, takes its title from a woman about town who loomed large in the sporting press in 1842. In January 1842, the *Whip* stated that Nichols was following the mysterious "Lady in Black," seeking to learn her identity, and in the weeks that followed reported numerous sightings and guesses at her name, one of which Nichols adapted in his story. The narrative abounds in cameo appearances by known New Yorkers. Accompanied by her bewhiskered husband and their daughter, Madame Restell appears at the Tivoli Ball and is described by Nichols as "one of the prettiest, and most amiable looking women in the room." Nichols attempted to capture what he saw as an important change in the culture. Austin, a principal character, discusses with a friend attitudes about what is proper. Perhaps overstating it a bit, Austin asserts that it has become fashionable for ladies to go to the theater and see Fanny Elssler or Niblo's Ravel ladies, adding, "They do not faint at a classical picture, nor shriek at the Venus de Medici. Moreover, they read Don Juan, and the novels of Paul De Kock, in the original." When his friend reminds him that there are those who refuse to go to the theater, Austin answers that the high-minded find alternative routes to encounter sexually explicit materials: "They denounce Gustavus, and revel in the obscenities of Maria Monk. They are never seen at Balls, but attend evening meetings and listen to lectures on moral reform and the seventh commandment." As before, Nichols expounded on the subjects of sex and marriage outside the narrative. He stated his fundamental premise that the strongest passion was sex. He argued that variety was good and that, in contrast, indissoluble marriage was a source of great misery. Such topics became important subjects of Nichols's writing about sex during the 1850s.[28]

Thomas Low Nichols met Mary Gove in 1847, when she was separated from her first husband and, by virtue of a kidnapping, had physical, if not legal, custody of an adolescent daughter. She was running her water-cure boardinghouse in New York City. Although alternative health practices had become familiar elements in New England, in New York they carried a differ-ent cachet. As Gove wrote in her autobiographical novel *Mary Lyndon,* "At that day believers in water-cure were considered very radical persons by all, and deemed a little crazed by the staid, allopathic, and conservative people about them." The patients she attracted were all "characters," who brought to her parlors their "literary, artistic, and philosophical friends in the city." Gove was in a position to befriend writers, including Edgar Allan Poe. Her Saturday evenings of conversation, music, and dancing became a literary salon for radical thinkers.

Gove was succeeding in these years in the realm of the useful, but she aspired to the "Art-Life." She wrote that she began to pay particular attention to "the bold words of a most thoughtful man," a writer with a distinctive style and wit expressed in pamphlets, fiction, editorials, and poems. A friend learned that this man was Nichols and introduced him to Gove. She disliked him immediately. She wrote that, despite his handsome looks, graceful fig-ure, and auburn hair, he had "an air of crystalline precision about him" that repelled her. Dressed as a dandy in a white waistcoat "of faultless Parisian fit" and white kid gloves, he made her unusually self-conscious about her own rough-hewn quality and lack of formal manners. Still, Gove was writing fic-tion and sent Nichols a draft of her *Agnes Morris.* Nichols paid her the compli-ment of taking it seriously and encouraging her to develop her characters more fully and at greater length.

A courtship then followed, whose letter trail is embedded in Gove's *Mary*

Lyndon.[29] This was the moment for each lover to reveal secrets to the other, and Gove told Nichols of her past relationships. How much did Nichols tell her? Enough for Gove to characterize him as "one who has wrought in the world's work, who has suffered, and grown strong and worthy." The two married July 29, 1848, in a Swedenborgian ceremony. Gove's letters in *Mary Lyndon* stated that, given the great hardships she had undergone to establish herself economically and professionally as a healer and writer, she could not alter her life's purposes. Instead Nichols joined hers. He completed his medical education and launched his second career as a physician and writer on health. He contributed to the publications that Gove had long written for, such as the *Water-Cure Journal*. With his marriage Nichols found a new medium in which to ply his pen and a new audience to support his writing. As he understood in *Lady in Black*, the world of health reform allowed him freedom to write about sexual matters; and, unlike during his years as a journalist, he did not have to fear prosecution for libel or obscenity.

Moreover, during these years an alternative publishing network was emerging with its own companies and periodicals that were, in turn, linked to newspapers with similar interests that carried their advertisements. Printed material was available by mail or sold in shops. Nichols and Gove established the Reform Bookstore at 65 Walker Street. All these enterprises were further connected through face-to-face encounters. Conventions of the like-minded brought together reformers and the public in major cities and minor towns. In 1853 pioneering physician Elizabeth Blackwell wrote to her sister that "the Nichols set is spreading their detestable doctrines of abortion and prostitution under spiritual and scientific guise—they are placing agents with the advertisements of their books at the doors of the conventions now being held here, worded in the most specious and attractive manner." Blackwell thus revealed more than her own distaste for views different from her own: she gave insight into the ways in which the health reformers marketed their books.[30]

When Nichols put out his early novels, there were no publishers listed on the title pages. He likely had them made up by a job printer. This pattern did not change with *Esoteric Anthropology*, printed in 1854. However, Nichols's *Woman, in All Ages and Nations*, first issued in 1849, was reprinted by Fowler and Wells after Stephen Pearl Andrews chose it as a title in his Library of Social Science. The book that Nichols coauthored with Gove, *Marriage: Its History, Character, and Results; Its Sanctities, and Its Profanities; Its Science and Its Facts*, was reprinted in 1855 by Valentine Nicholson & Company in Cincinnati.

Both imprints indicate an emerging phenomenon—the alliance between authors writing in a reformist genre and commercially viable alternative publishing houses. These companies understood that there was a market for books informing the public about the politics and physiology of sex.

In the three books that Nichols published from 1849 to 1854, he carefully included "M.D." after his name, part of his claim of legitimacy to his new audience. Although Nichols addressed new readers with a new reformist purpose, he revealed positions and a writing style consistent with his earlier writing. From the outset he had asserted that sexual passion was the most powerful force in life and, although often overlaid with romantic notions of love, one of the least governable. But what had been offered initially as "titillating" was now presented as "scientific."

It was also reformist. Gove and Nichols were part of the Fourierist radical circle in New York and considered themselves to be Spiritualists. In *Woman in All Ages and Nations,* Nichols adopted the Fourierist critique of marriage, arguing for women's self-dependence and calling marriage for life "legal prostitution." Nichols also made a distinction, soon to become common among Spiritualists, between the contract of marriage and "true" unions. In his final chapter, he imagined that after Civilization, "the human family would gather in Fourierist 'harmonious association,' where attractions would realize their destinies without social or legal interference." The book was a hastily assembled pastiche. When it was reprinted in 1854, the chapter on marriage carried a note explaining that some paragraphs had come from Lydia Maria Child's book on women. A check revealed that whole pages of Child's text are imbedded in Nichols's work.[31]

Esoteric Anthropology is Nichols's most influential work. He stated that he had composed it to accompany his lectures to students on anatomy and physiology. In the nine years that followed, it went into seven editions. There is no attribution of Gove as collaborator, but her views inform important sections, and the use of the word "we" for women suggests that she wrote parts of the book. Sections of the text that emphasize the naturalness of childbirth and the dire consequences of masturbation are consonant with her earlier writings. Nichols had long been a Grahamite vegetarian, but in his earlier career at the fringes of the sporting press he had joined its digestive messages to sexual hedonism. Mary Gove emphasized the naturalness of sexual functioning but at the outset of her career had subscribed to the larger Graham system designed to cool the sexual appetite. The text of *Esoteric Anthropology* blends all these contradictory elements in an inconsistent mix that allows for multiple readings. Nichols had the dominant hand, for most of the writing is in his easier, more fluid style. And the strongest undertone in the book is Nichols's persistent enthusiasm for sexual expression, put in language more often found in fiction than in works on physiology. He articulated positions that he had taken as early as 1843.

An example at the outset of the section on reproduction signals the reader that Nichols came out of a school different from other writers on physiology. He wrote of generation in lower plants and animals, including flower-producing plants. "It is remarkable," Nichols wrote of the flower, "that the parts of plants devoted to the sexual function, are those we most prize for their beauty and fragrance. . . . The centre of the flower—the home of beauty, and fragrance, and sweetness—is the nuptial couch, the bower of love, sacred to the mysteries of vegetable procreation." Nichols had certainly learned from his years of novel writing. But even when stated in the more prosaic language of skeleton and viscera, digestion and respiration, Nichols repeatedly reminded readers of the God-given naturalness of sexual passion and the intense pleasure of sexual intercourse. As he put it, "There is no action of the body, and no power of the soul, which does not enter into the complicated and beautiful process by which humanity exists, and new beings are created. For the performance of this great function, we have a peculiar power or passion of the soul; a separate organ in the brain; nerves of exquisite sensation, voluntary and involuntary nerves of motion, with their muscular apparatus; and the most complex organs of innervation, circulation, nutrition, and secretion, connected with the system of organic life."[32]

Although many of the physiological ideas that animate *Esoteric Anthropology* were Grahamite commonplaces at the time—the separation of the nerves of organic life and those of animal life, for example—it is an extraordinary book. What sets it apart from all others in the reformist mode is not only Nichols's tone but also the text's detail and its physicality. For example, as Nichols and Gove wrote of the female body and described the uterus, they matter-of-factly stated, "Passing the forefinger up the vagina, its mouth can easily be felt." Accompanying the text is a diagrammatic image of the adult female from the viewpoint of an examining physician: the legs are splayed to reveal each element of female genitalia, and each is labeled. The authors named and clearly described birth control techniques, including the syringe, the sponge, and the condom. Although condemning abortion as a sin against nature, they discussed it plainly and noted various procedures.[33]

They explicitly considered male and female homosexuality in the section on "unnatural manifestations" of the generative passion. In writing about women they stated, "A similar passion of females for each other, and their mutual gratification of each other's desires is called Sapphic love, from Sappho, who has celebrated this not unfrequent perversion in some pretty and passionate verses." Although they strongly disapproved of male homosexual expression, which they called sodomy, they stated that it was "probably less hurtfull than the far more common practice of solitary vice."[34]

Themes in the earlier writings of Gove continued, with masturbation getting full treatment and condemnation. What was unusual was that the book explicitly spelled out the methods that girls and women used to achieve orgasm. In common with many other writers, the Nicholses saw waste of nervous power as the harm in masturbation. In coupled lovemaking, each gives to the other and "there is comparatively but little loss," but in self-sex "there is the simple, artificial, and utterly unnatural excitement of the orgasm, without reciprocity, compensation, or use, the result is only evil."[35]

In key places, Nichols and Gove celebrated the delights of the "sexual embrace" and attempted to describe orgasm. They described sexual arousal's effect on the eye, voice, and manner. They wrote, "A certain warmth and voluptuousness presides over the movements of the body." They emphasized the importance of touch: "A new delight pervades the sense of feeling, which is more than any other the organ of this passion." They concluded in words not far removed from Nichols's popular fiction. "The bolder hands of man wander over the ravishing beauties of woman; he clasps her waist, he presses her soft bosom, and in a tumult of delirious ecstasy, each finds the central point of attraction and of pleasure, which increases until it is completed in the sexual orgasm—the most exquisite enjoyment of which the human senses are capable."[36]

Unlike much of the writing by George Thompson or earlier statements in the sporting press that denied women's agency, Nichols and Gove emphasized female sexual response. Many of their positions are ones that Frances Wright might have taken. They believed that while some women have disturbed amativeness, causing them to have little passion for the sexual embrace, "in a healthy condition, the pleasure of the female is longer continued, more frequently repeated, and more exquisite than that of the male." They, too, supported women's full knowledge of their sexual natures. Yet the shadow of Sylvester Graham still hovered. Seeing monthly ovulation as the guiding element, they asserted that monthly sexual intercourse is ordained by nature. The sex act itself ought to be contained within narrow confines. Male efforts to arouse the female by stimulating her clitoris were dangerous to health: "Where there is already a lack of nervous power, any attempt to force sensation is doubly exhausting. It is even worse in its effects than masturbation. The lives of many women are made wretched by this selfishness or kindness, whichever it may be, of their husbands."[37]

Not only were women limited to monthly sexual relations, they were to refrain from intercourse during pregnancy and lactation. What was a person to do? Here the Graham system came into play, and Nichols and Gove advocated all the usual prescriptions for cooling down the male body. In addition, they suggested friendship and keeping busy. Women faced fewer difficulties not because they had lesser sexual desire but because for them "certain conditions are necessary to the awakening of sexual desire. They must love, and be beloved. Love must begin in the soul as a sentiment, come down into the heart as a passion, before it can descend into the body as a desire. Such a woman will be continent without the least difficulty, so long as she does not love; but when she loves a man, she gives herself to him, soul and body." The notion that a woman might have sexual desire more than once a month or when pregnant or nursing seemed not to occur to the authors.[38]

The real solution for men, however, lay in a direction different from abstinence. Although they were slow to declare it openly, both Mary and Thomas Nichols were moving to support free-love principles. Although this book never used the term "free love," an informal section of the book responding to questions did advocate it. It began with a condemnation of jealousy as an unhealthy condition based on false notions of property, then moved on to consider the possibility of multiple loves and a redefinition of virtue. Because God controls all attraction as basic to the harmony of the world, "No *natural* passion, no *healthy* attraction of any being is wrong." Nichols finally moved on to consider divorce and what a later generation would call "open marriage" in these words: "Thousands of couples live together as friends, who once believed themselves to be married—giving each other freedom and protection."[39]

Another section of the book reflected Mary Gove's different concerns and philosophical underpinnings. While Nichols seemed to be working out the possibility of multiple sexual partners as a solution to the conflict between a man's insistent sexual drive and a woman's periodic one, his wife was still reeling from the stigma of divorce. She (perhaps with Nichols's redrafting) addressed the issue this way: "Marriage, in a higher and purer sense, is the real union of two persons in mutual love; and adultery is, perhaps, best defined as any gratification of mere lust, or the sensual nature, without the sanctification of a true love. According to these definitions, a true marriage may be what the laws call adultery, while the real adultery is an unloving marriage."[40] This redefinition of the word "marriage" to be synonymous with love was becoming part of the arsenal of those Spiritualists who were beginning to advocate free love. Much like abolitionists, opponents of marriage came to see love as wrongly bound by the epiphenomena of the law, particularly in the area relating to property and contracts. Real marriage, they felt, is of the heart, not of the law.

In the openly collaborative book *Marriage: Its History, Character, and Results; Its Sanctities, and Its Profanities; Its Science and Its Facts,* Nichols wrote two parts and Gove, one. Both authors came out explicitly for free love but wrote from two different positions and in two distinct literary styles. Gove restated her insistence that the only basis of marriage is love. Writing autobiographically, she emphasized her suffering in a loveless marriage and the cruelty of her first husband. She imbedded letters written to her by other anguished women and her letters in reply that urged them to leave their husbands and consummate sexual unions with men that they truly loved, bearing their children despite societal censure. Threaded throughout her text is Gove's hostility to allopathic medicine and her belief in the Graham diet and the water cure.

Nichols's sections took up where *Esoteric Anthropology* left off. His long interest in comparative cultures came into play, and he looked at the range of marriage practices over historical time and geographical place. What had in the earlier book been informal questions and answers became chapters in this one, allowing him to articulate his free-love views fully. Nichols was a varietist. He believed that not only can a person have successive loves, he can have many loves at the same time. He argued implicitly that sexual relations with many women were more natural to a man than constancy. He stated that "no instinct or desire of a healthy humanity is sinful, or to be struggled against or subdued." Each person wants to "taste all flavorous delights." A good nineteenth-century man, Nichols put his case on the highest possible ground. Morality for him was not prohibitions but man's "fullest and most harmonious exercise of all his natural faculties, and the complete gratification of all his natural desires." Thus he stated, "It is my right, it is my highest duty, to use every organ, every sense, every faculty which God has given me." Pleasure and happiness are the ends of life. They can be attained only in perfect freedom.[41]

As Nichols worked out some of the practical problems of his position and his commitment to individual sovereignty, he faced the question: Who will raise the children? In opposition to laws granting custody to fathers, Nichols answered that the appropriate parent is the mother. He was a firm supporter of women's rights, emphasizing both freedom from marriage and self-support. When women are "self-sustaining," they can provide for themselves and their children. What was a concession to women's rights, on the one hand, was a denial of male responsibility for children, on the other. Nichols argued that women had a stronger desire for parenthood. As he put it, "This instinct being weaker in man, he is more reckless in the gratification of his passions."[42]

Mary Gove and Thomas Nichols began their own journal, *Nichols' Journal of Health, Water-Cure, and Human Progress,* after editor Russell Trall opposed the direction of their writing and refused to announce *Esoteric Anthropology* in the *Water-Cure Journal.* During their years of writing, Mary Gove and Thomas Nichols attempted a series of short-lived schools, including the American Hydropathic Institute in New York City and Port Chester, New York. They moved to Josiah Warren and Stephen Pearl Andrews's community, Modern Times, and planned Desarrollo adjacent to it. Desarrollo was to be, as their handbill put it, "A School of Life, for the Education of Persons of both Sexes, and all Ages, in Health, Intelligence and Freedom." The foundation was dug, but the building was never built. A scandal, ignited perhaps by Trall, led to the departure of students from the American Hydropathic Institute and economic hard times. Increasingly both Gove and Nichols devoted themselves to writing. After living for two years at Modern Times, in conflict with Josiah Warren, who opposed their insistence on free-love principles and the diversion from his economic aims, they defaulted on their mortgage and left for the West, moving to Cincinnati in 1855. The following year, they founded Memnonia, a community in Yellow Springs, Ohio. Here again they faced the opposition of many neighbors, including the president of Antioch College, Horace Mann.

In 1857 Gove and Nichols announced that they were converting to Catholicism, and in 1861 they emigrated to England with their daughter. They remained abroad for the rest of their lives. Mary Gove and Thomas Nichols were neither the first nor the last American writers advocating greater sexual liberty to reverse course and seek refuge in traditional religion and the Old World. What they left was an ambiguous legacy. At one level they gathered and partially summarized much of the information available in the physiological and reform literatures about sex and reproduction. In their treatment of women's sexual response and homosexuality, they went farther than other writers. As they intertwined free-love advocacy with physiological discussion, they joined the voices articulating the fourth framework, putting sex at the center of life. They wrote both to inform and to earn money, using science to pay the bills. The nature of Nichols's career and writing suggests a further possibility—as he wrote about sex in a way intended to be sexually stimulating, he may have used science as a shield.

Irrespective of his intention, Nichols's unusual position, straddling the worlds of the penny press, fiction, and medicine, led to his creating a literary blend that blurred the boundaries between the physiological and the racy. He did so at a moment when booksellers seeking to attract a wider audience included physiological works in their advertisements of commercial erotica. The marketing of birth control and abortion was also obfuscating the lines between commerce and advice. These developments muddied the waters at the time when social movements placing sex at the center of life were challenging the relation between sex and marriage in word and deed. All of this swirled around those in New York who were thinking about the problem of the young clerk and the dangers he faced in the city.

PART IV

SEXUAL KNOWLEDGE AND OBSCENITY IN NEW YORK AND THE NATION

13

The Y.M.C.A. of New York, the Civil War, and Anthony Comstock

I

Even conservative Christian men in New York were participants in the sexual conversation, if only reactively. By the 1850s physiological reform was in the air. Daily newspapers like the *Tribune* and the *Herald* carried essays on Fourierism and announced Mary Gove's lectures; the court trials of Madame Restell were daily fare. From the pulpit these men heard traditional Christian notions of lust and Satan, which served as lenses to filter and focus information and ideas about sex coming from all sides.

Evangelical Christian merchants from New England or upstate New York could not withdraw from engagement, for they carried a strong sense of community oversight from the region of their birth. They were secure in their own salvation and believed that they could protect their immediate families, but they were profoundly uneasy about their adopted city. Some distributed Bibles and religious tracts. Others concentrated on fighting prostitution, southern slavery, or overindulgence in alcohol. One group took as their specific concern the young men in their employ and the moral quagmires that awaited them in the city.

Evangelical men of business saw challenges to youth at every turn: Was alcohol a necessary part of life for a clerk? Could these young men avoid the lure of prostitution or the ubiquitous printed erotica sold on the street? These Christian merchants saw sporting culture as a threat to their young workers. They joined together to form the Young Men's Christian Association to offer safe havens for "moral" recreation to young clerks surrounded by temptation.[1]

More than a decade earlier the trial of Richard Robinson for the murder of prostitute Helen Jewett had revealed the engagement of young clerks in male sporting culture. Working alongside them, however, were boys and young men of a different nature, committed to a model of restraint and Christian service. Such a boy was Morris Ketchum Jesup, who arrived in New York the year following Robinson's trial. He was born in 1830 into the strict world of Connecticut Congregationalism. In the Panic of 1837 all the advantages that his grandfather's Yale education and social prominence could give him had been wiped away when his father lost his business and died within the year. His mother, responsible for eight children, moved to modest quarters on Bond Street in New York. Morris went to school in anticipation of college, but at age twelve the need to assist his mother caused him to become a very young clerk. He carried an acute awareness of the sharp reversal of his fortunes. To his father's financial ruin and death and his mother's removal to New York must be added the childhood deaths of six of his brothers and sisters from tuberculosis.

He had been named for his father's friend Morris Ketchum, who hired him as a clerk at a salary of $600 a year in the office of Rogers, Ketchum & Grosvenor, a company manufacturing railroad locomotives and cotton-mill machines. Unlike many of the fellows around him, he lived not in a boardinghouse but with his mother. Each day, as he traversed the distance between Bond and Wall Streets on foot, his eyes must have seen much of the commerce available to young clerks in 1842. By young adulthood, Jesup had joined forces with a bookkeeper friend to form Clark & Jesup, a railroad supply firm. He moved with his family to a more reputable neighborhood on Eighth Street. His enterprise became national and branched out to railroad securities. Prosperity came with a special sense of responsibility for others like himself. In 1852, at age twenty-two, he joined with other men of business to form the Young Men's Christian Association of New York, the first American branch of an English organization founded in 1844.[2]

The New York movement was initiated by George H. Petrie, a young importer, who had picked up a tract of the London Young Men's Christian Association at the Crystal Palace exhibition in 1851. The London society was committed to developing the spiritual and mental life of young men working in the business houses of the city. Visits to the association's quarters,

Portrait of Morris K. Jesup, bound with *Fourteenth Annual Report of the Young Men's Christian Association of the City of New York, 1865–66* (New York: The Association, 1866). Kautz Family YMCA Archives.

offering a lounge, library, and classrooms, gave Petrie firsthand knowledge of its work. After he returned to New York and entered his family's importing firm, he called a meeting of friends to discuss forming a New York chapter. They imagined an evangelical Christian organization working outside, but in cooperation with, the city's Protestant churches. The group grew to include important New York ministers, and by April 21, 1852, it had a plan, which it presented a month later to a large gathering at the Mercer Street Presbyterian Church. As its charter and constitution stated, the object of the Y.M.C.A. was "the improvement of the spiritual, mental and social condition of young men."

Reverend Isaac Ferris's speech at Mercer Street on May 28, 1852, stated clearly the founders' sense of the need for the Y.M.C.A. and the purposes it could serve. The young man coming to the city found himself in a "moral Maelstrom" where he confronted "scenes foreign to all former tastes and feelings." In an earlier era such a youth would have lived in his employer's home as a member of the family, but now he boarded with others like himself. Billiards, cards, drink, and other "snares of this wicked city" beckoned. Without the support of home ties, the youth could be persuaded "now by ridicule, and then by persuasion to all manner of indulgences." In this morass the Y.M.C.A. promised the clerk a haven and a group of fellow Christians to help him resist the temptations of the city.

Members of the New York Y.M.C.A. had to be under age forty and regular members of a local evangelical church. Though an organization for young men, it was run by a board of managers, later called directors, for whom there was no age limit. Some young men would move from client to patron as their fortunes rose, staying with the association for life, but most members withdrew when they reached the age limit of forty. The managers immediately found a home for the association in the Stuyvesant Institute on Broadway at Bond Street and opened the doors in September 1852.[3]

Actuated by faith, the Y.M.C.A. effort was both inspired and limited by its expressed goal "to promote evangelical religion." Members were to "seek out young men" moving to New York and try to "bring them under moral and religious influences." Members tried to help them find "suitable boarding places and employment," to make sure that they attended church on Sunday, and to surround them "with christian associates." Overseeing their activities in monthly meetings, the board of managers set up committees in charge of the association's rooms, library, publications, and lecture series. In addition, the board established a committee to compile statistics on the "moral and religious condition of young men in New-York city and its vicinity," their church attendance, and "the number of young men who desecrate the Sabbath."[4]

Three men quickly emerged as important leaders: Morris K. Jesup, William E. Dodge, Jr., and Cephas Brainerd. Dodge, also a very young man, was the wealthy scion and namesake of the leader in the New York Tract Society, considered earlier, who personally met the steamboats and distributed tracts on the wharves. In addition, the elder Dodge had helped found many of the important evangelical organizations of his generation. In the decades ahead, some of those who joined William E. Dodge, Jr., in Y.M.C.A. leadership would bear names such as Stokes and Phelps and, like Dodge, would be sons of Christian businessmen prominent in the evangelical reform causes of previous decades. By contrast, Brainerd, an important lawyer in the Civil War years and a player in Republican circles, had just arrived from Haddam, Connecticut. A lonely young man reading law, he joined the Y.M.C.A. as a member.

In 1854 the Y.M.C.A. moved from its rooms on Broadway to the larger Clinton Hall at Astor Place. Politics, however, cast confusion in the organization's ranks as conflict broke out between those, such as Brainerd, who

Clinton Hall, New York City, date unknown, a place of many uses. Lecturers spoke here to many audiences, and it was an early home of both the phrenological establishment of O. S. Fowler and the Y.M.C.A. of New York. © Museum of the City of New York.

attempted to win the association for John C. Fremont, the first Republican candidate for president, and those fighting to keep party politics outside its walls. In what became known as the "Fremont Incident," mass resignations followed, and the Y.M.C.A. lost Dodge and other men of wealth. With the Panic of 1857 came an ironic expansion of the organization's reach. At the eye of the crisis, the Y.M.C.A. initiated prayer meetings at churches in the financial district, and its numbers swelled to 1,600 members.[5]

Who were the Y.M.C.A.'s youthful members? In a talk later in the century, Dodge reflected on the successes and failures of the association. Underlying both was the fact that the Y.M.C.A. drew in only one group, "the moderately well-to-do class of young businessmen." It did not attract "the great artisan class, the working men." At the outset, Dodge and his fellow directors had imagined the association as a club of young Christian men, offering urban amenities without temptations. What Dodge suggested later was that they attracted the middle-class men they sought.[6]

Such men may have joined for a number of reasons, including the desire for Christian self-expression and service. In addition, in its early years the association offered them both direct and indirect gains. Like the mechanics' institutes and libraries that it partially imitated, the Y.M.C.A. had lectures and books that promised self-culture as well as religious knowledge. There was the fellowship of other young, earnest men, so important in individual biographies. A committee certifying boardinghouses aided young men who wanted to limit temptation and associate only with the religiously inclined. Finally, there was the material help of the Employment Committee, headed by William F. Lee, a prominent merchant. Each morning Lee came to the association rooms, where young men gathered around him as he helped them find jobs. In speaking to a Boston convention, Cephas Brainerd gave the ideal scenario of the New York Y.M.C.A., transposed rhetorically to New England: "When an active brother in the Boston Association takes up a youthful stranger, as he steps upon the docks of your city, and introduces him to its rooms, to its members, to its meetings, to all its privileges, to its holy, purifying influences, to a place of employment where business is conducted according to the rules of a Christian morality, to a quiet and respectable home, to the pastor of a Christian church, to the blessed activities of some mission Sabbath school, and finally, by means of all this, to a place of Christian wealth and large, generous Christian labor . . ."[7]

Underlying this effort were many of the assumptions of the female moral reformers. There was a single standard of sexual morality for males and females. The house of prostitution was the portal to Hell. Spirituous liquor lessened a man's will to resist temptation. Theater and licentious literature aroused his passions and prepared his imagination to accept vice. Unlike females, boys and men could not be sheltered within the home. The need to earn a living sent them to the city, where they were subject to temptations from all sides. All the evils that the moral reformers had decried—theater, gambling, saloons, brothels, licentious literature—awaited the fellows. Against them all, the young clerk must be strong and resist.[8]

What made the Y.M.C.A. distinctive was its focus on the bodies and souls of young men. In these reformers' eyes, male youth face a particularly perilous passage as they traverse the time in life in which "Satan is most vigorously employed." In older men, the passions are cooled, but a young man is fired by "youthful lusts." But it is not simply the lone individual standing against Satan. Surrounding him is a society of young men in the Devil's clutches, encouraging the youth to relent and enjoy himself. They urge him on and make fun of him if he does not. Workplaces and boardinghouses throw boys and young men, the wicked and the pure, together. Impoverished conditions push fellows onto city streets to seek commercial establishments for better air and warmth. Around them unscrupulous men and women of business create appealing places of vice. Everything conspires to lead young men to sin.[9]

Who will help them confront the power of evil? Although many were urging businessmen to take a friendly interest in their employees and even invite them into their homes, no one considered reviving the apprenticeship system or requesting merchants to board their own clerks. The Y.M.C.A. was to stand in their stead. Christian businessmen created a club of fellows able to offer peer pressure of a different sort, rooms that provided a comfortable alternative to the saloon, and a promise of material aid up the ladder of success.

2

With the Civil War all the energy that the Y.M.C.A. put into its effort to protect young clerks shifted into saving the Northern soldiers from their own moral weaknesses. The association helped create the United States Christian Commission, a national organization that sent ministers, Bibles, and tracts along with cooks, soup kitchens, and blankets to the front. Its lending libraries offered proper reading materials to soldiers, drawing attention by contrast to the sensational and erotic materials typically available. The Christian Commission fostered a provision in the Postal Act of 1865 to create a protective shield around the soldier so that he could not receive erotica in the mails. As a result of this wartime experience, the New York Y.M.C.A. had a new belief in the power of legislation at the state and federal level to suppress "obscene literature."

For the leaders of the New York Y.M.C.A., the Civil War was a pivotal moment. These men, no longer young, moved out from the city to work at a national level. Political affairs at the city level had been fraught with frustration, for New York was the center of contested loyalties. Although the men active in the Y.M.C.A. crossed party lines, most were part of the resurgent local elite connected to the Republicans. Before the war they had faced Democrats allied with a national Democratic administration that had long held political power. Some Democratic men of affairs in the city were directly linked to the cotton trade of the South. When the election of Lincoln in 1860 ousted Democrats from Washington, it dashed their hopes for an expanding union based on agriculture and free trade. Although Democrats continued local influence under Mayor Fernando Wood, Fort Sumter ended any possibility of compromise with the slaveholding South. Most New York Democrats supported the Union but without the enthusiasm for war of many Northerners.

The onset of the war found the New York Y.M.C.A. with an abundance of new members but with only a remnant of its leadership. The loss of board members after the "Fremont Incident" meant not only that their ranks were depleted but also that those now in control were intensely engaged in the Union cause. Those who remained active as directors immediately thought of their responsibility to the young soldier. If the clerk faced dangers on New York streets, what about on the battleground and in camp? To Morris Jesup and Cephas Brainerd, the dangers of the Civil War came not only from the weapons of Confederate soldiers, but also from the immoral temptations of the soldiers' life.

The war work of the Y.M.C.A. of New York began spontaneously. As troops answering President Lincoln's call for volunteers moved through New York on April 18, 1861, the artist Vincent Colyer left his studio to pass out tracts to the soldiers and speak to them. A member of the New York Y.M.C.A., Colyer returned the next day with the tracts, joined by others. Their efforts spurred Reverend Stephen H. Tyng to call a meeting of the association's board of directors to discuss the role of the Y.M.C.A. in the war. On May 27, 1861, the New York Y.M.C.A. created an Army Committee.[10]

It immediately published and distributed *The Soldier's Hymn Book,* designed to be carried in the vest pocket. The Army Committee dispatched ministers to hold prayer meetings with soldiers—estimated at more than three hundred meetings in all—and give them hymnbooks and Bibles. The committee held mass meetings to raise money for its religious mission to soldiers. It worked to supply chaplains with religious reading for the troops. After the defeat at Bull Run, Colyer and another New York City Y.M.C.A. member, Frank W. Ballard, went to Washington to minister to the wounded in hospitals and to organize supplies pouring in for their relief. Colyer began to speak of the need for a national ministry.

What motivated the larger Y.M.C.A. effort was concern for the soul of the Union soldier. He was sheltered to a degree by links to home ties. The organization of Civil War soldiers into local volunteer companies with local notables as officers meant that a soldier experienced the war alongside his neighbors, and they were writing home and reporting on him, as he was on them. One can see this in the example of George Kies, a Connecticut lieutenant stationed in Baltimore. In the spring of 1863, he responded to his wife's accusations that he was having an affair with a woman in Philadelphia and that he had told women that he was a widower. Mrs. Kies had learned of her husband's alleged misdeeds from the letters of other soldiers in his company sent to their families in neighboring homes. In another example, David Seibert denied reports his father had received that he had been going with "disreputable women." Letters, visits from home folks, and the talk of soldiers returning home on furlough all served to reinforce local values and local moral codes.[11]

Yet Baltimore and the battlefields were far from home, and not all soldiers imagined themselves returning to the family hearth when the fighting was over. As the war proceeded, fewer soldiers volunteered, and ties between community and unit weakened as towns that needed to meet their quotas paid bounties to nonresidents who enlisted. Moreover, the central mission of

Company G, 7th Regiment, called in to quell the New York draft riots, July 1863, photograph, 1863. © Museum of the City of New York.

a soldier required him to violate the moral codes of civilian life. As historian Reid Mitchell asked, "If a man's duty called upon him to embrace deceit, theft, and murder, is it surprising that he might also fall prey to profanity, tobacco, women, and liquor?" Moralistic soldiers reported home about the many evils they saw about them: drinking, cards, and prostitution.[12]

As an expression of the association's soldierly ideal, the Y.M.C.A. published the letter of Judge E. Rockwood Hoar of Concord, Massachusetts, to his son. Writing to Samuel as he began his military service, the judge counseled his son to lead "as regular and temperate a life as possible," bathe whenever possible, eat moderately, avoid alcohol, and never disgrace himself "by any profaneness, or obscenity." Samuel should be brave and hardworking and obey his officers. "Remember always your home and your friends— those who will welcome your return with pride and joy if you shall come back in virtue and honor; who will cherish your memory if, faithful and true, you have given up your life; but to whom your disgrace would cause a pang sharper than death." To give institutional form to these goals, Cephas Brainerd led the Army Committee of the New York Y.M.C.A. to recruit a regiment of volunteers. The aim of the "Ironsides Regiment" was a corps "of Christian men who would 'preserve their good habits and self-respect as citizens . . . while defending their country as soldiers.' " It required its 750 recruits to have "moral character and habits," be clean, abstain from alcohol, and not swear. This specific notion of the good soldier continued to mold the actions of the Y.M.C.A.'s leaders during the conflict.[13]

In October 1861, with Colyer as the moving force, Jesup and his allies in the Y.M.C.A. of New York sent out a general appeal for a larger ministry to soldiers. The summons stated that "while such numbers of young men are congregated together, surrounded by temptation and danger, an open field of usefulness is presented, vast in extent and interesting beyond expression." The other local branches of the Y.M.C.A. responded to the call, and in November 1861, fifteen associations founded the United States Christian Commission. Although supported by the army committees of the various Y.M.C.A. branches, the Christian Commission became a separate national organization, headed by an executive committee of twelve men. After a hesitant start, the commission organized a volunteer system that sent delegates to hospitals, army bases, ships, and battlefields. Over the course of the war, an estimated five thousand delegates, many of them pastors, ministered to Union troops. They set up tents, held revival meetings, distributed Bibles and hymnbooks, nursed soldiers and wrote letters for them, opened libraries, and operated soup kitchens. In all, it distributed contributions of money and supplies totaling approximately $5.5 million. As George H. Stuart, the Philadelphia philanthropist who served as president, said, "There is a good deal of religion in a warm shirt and a good beefsteak."[14]

As it sought to provide services for the soldier, the Christian Commission competed with the Sanitary Commission for contributions. To the scientific and bureaucratic Sanitary Commission, with its paid agents and coolheaded approach, the Christian Commission seemed too sentimental and personal. Even when it appealed to soldiers' bodies, the Christian Commission also sought to save their souls. Its kitchens and lending libraries were designed with one purpose—to redeem the soldier and bring him to the Lord. A principal strategy of the Christian Commission was to relink the soldiers to home ties. Whenever possible, the commission sent delegates to troops from their communities. A soldier often saw his local minister or neighbor. Delegates were officially instructed to speak to the men "personally and collectively." As a means of converting them or strengthening the converted, delegates were "to encourage them in every right way, discourage every vice, give them information from the people and from home." In the words of the commission's official historian, "Very often such Delegates were 'agents of exchange' between the soldiers and their homes, for letters, photographs, and other mementos of mutual love. . . . Many a reckless soldier, surprised at his own wickedness, but unable to resist the influences which environed him, has been checked in his course, and won to Christ."[15]

In the reports that made their way into the official history, the Christian Commission offered a moral appraisal of Union soldiers very different from other contemporary accounts. Usually specifics about the culture of soldiers are lacking, but here, because of the need to testify to the good that the ministers accomplished, there were frank statements. For example, a minister to the Army of the Potomac described the scene that he entered when he established his station: "The very atmosphere of that fine January morning was reeking with profanity and fetid with vulgarity and obscenity." Armed with books and tracts, he felt overwhelmed by the task. After he built a simple chapel, he watched as it became the living quarters of new recruits and he was able to use it only for evening prayer services. Writing of this period, he stated, "The Holy Spirit and Satan there contended mightily. During the day card-playing, profanity and ribald songs were the order. At evening these gave place to prayer, preaching and praise." A fight broke out after men entered the prayer service and began to pick pockets. The narrative changed

Cover, United States Christian Commission, *Second Annual
Report*, 1863. Kautz Family YMCA Archives.

once the pastor reclaimed the chapel and made it a full-time center for Bible
study and prayer. Only then did he accomplish "daily conversions."[16]

An emerging concern of the Christian Commission was soldiers' reading. Early on, working with the American Bible Society and the American
Tract Society, the commission put religious literature into the men's hands.[17]
Its publication ledgers list the kinds and quantities of books donated to the
soldiers, the expected Bibles and tracts and knapsack books, inspirational
compendia designed for soldiers to carry. Weekly reports listed the reading
matter that each delegate distributed under such categories as "Testam'ts,
Hymns and Psalms, Soldiers' [Book, and] Misc." As the war progressed, the
commission added to these donations purchases of religious weeklies and
secular magazines. An 1862 plan for "each regiment . . . to establish, by subscription its own library" never got off the ground.[18]

What proved successful was the Christian Commission's portable loan
library, sent to four hundred hospitals, army stations, and ships. Reverend

GIVING UP THE BUSINESS.   Page 70.

"Giving Up the Business," Reverend Edward P. Smith, *Incidents of the United States Christian Commission* (Philadelphia: J. B. Lippincott, 1869), opposite p. 70. Kautz Family YMCA Archives.

J. C. Thomas had devised the plan, and he became the commission's Reading Agent for the Army of the Cumberland. He applied these rules for libraries of 75 to 125 books: "None but the best work. None but the best, most suitable and cheapest editions. Secular works, as well as religious. Utility rather than variety." It got publishers to supply books at half price and an express company to provide delivery free of charge. Reports gave its sponsors the reaction they wanted: "The library is having a good effect. It is lessening profanity and intoxication." "Marked improvement in the social life . . . more social purity, less boisterous and rude conduct."[19]

The catalogue of the loan library reveals the choices that the Christian Commission deemed appropriate for young men. With the exception of Harriet Beecher Stowe's *Uncle Tom's Cabin,* there is little recognizable adult fiction, though there are boys' books and compendia of American and British literature that contained approved selections. The loan library offered three copies of the temperance melodrama *Ten Nights in a Bar-Room*. Washington Irving is represented by his nonfictional *Columbus, Washington,* and *Sketch-Book*. There are three copies in English and one in German of Bunyan's *Pilgrim's Progress* (and three English copies of his *Holy War*). Many of the works are religious, such as the three copies of *How to Be Saved*. Many books are historical, including a version of Edward Gibbon's *Rome* and a book titled *Napoleon and His Marshals*. Some books are clearly intended to be useful, for example, Sir Isaac Pitman's *Manual of Phonography*. As might be expected, there are books of counsel, including Henry Ward Beecher's *Lectures to Young Men* and Sylvester Graham's *Lectures on Chastity*.[20]

As the Christian Commission offered soldiers the literature it felt they should read, its leaders became aware of reading the soldiers should avoid. As gifts of books came in, not all were accepted: "Of course all yellow-covered literature, lives of pirates and highwaymen, works against Christ and country, are thrown out as *bad*." Chaplain Thomas told of intercepting a soldier selling such 25-cent novels as *Dick Turpin* and giving him respectable substitutes.[21] But fears for the soldier went beyond sensationalist literature. By its own accounts the Christian Commission learned that publishers and book dealers were sending to soldiers in the army "great numbers" of "obscene books and pictures."

Fearing that printed matter endangered the moral health of Union soldiers, the New York leaders of the Y.M.C.A. began to advocate action. They were aware of Lord Campbell's law of 1857, the successful effort in England to strengthen laws against obscenity. This landmark statute gave English magistrates the power to order police to search, seize, and destroy books and prints deemed to be obscene. Without a statute, U.S. Postmaster General Montgomery Blair reported in 1863 that he had occasionally "excluded from the mails obscene and scandalous printed matter" when he had been shown "its criminal immorality." Morris Jesup, now the treasurer of the New York Christian Commission, traveled to Philadelphia on January 31, 1865, to attend a regular meeting of the Executive Committee of the United States Christian Commission. He came with offers of close cooperation between the New York body and the national commission and a gift of $10,000. He also came with a resolution, as it was euphemistically described in the minutes, "against selling secular Reading matter in the Army." The board referred the resolution to its Committee on Publications.[22]

Within days a provision in the 1865 omnibus post office bill was introduced in the Senate that declared that "no obscene book, pamphlet, picture, print, or other publication of a vulgar and indecent character, shall be admitted into the mails of the United States." As the senator who was managing the bill stated about this provision, "It is said that our mails are made the vehicle for the conveyance of great numbers and quantities of obscene books and pictures, which are sent to the Army, and sent here and there and everywhere, and that it is getting to be a very great evil." In the Senate, real debate ensued only over a part of the provision that seemed to allow postmasters to break the seals of the mail, abrogating one of the sacred elements of the freedom of the mails, and senators were reassured that the papers involved were not sealed. But the part of the proposed measure that allowed postmasters to remove obscene materials before delivery was deleted, as was the clause "All such obscene publications deposited in or received at any post office, or discovered in any mail, shall be seized and destroyed or otherwise disposed of as the Postmaster General shall direct." In 1865, fear of censorship prevented Congress from granting to the federal government the power to search and seize comparable to that of English authorities. The sole power that remained in the post office bill was prosecution after an alleged crime was committed, a power compatible with common law and American court practice. Section 16 of the bill made it a misdemeanor to send obscene material through the mails, punishable by a maximum fine of $500 and up to a year in prison.[23]

Although in itself the 1865 provision had minimal effect, it carried grave import. All earlier federal efforts to bar obscenity had focused on customs laws and the introduction of foreign materials. Section 16 of the 1865 postal bill established for the first time the lawful power of the federal government to regulate the moral content of domestic materials sent through the mails.

The 1865 provision demonstrates the growing importance of the New York Y.M.C.A. in national affairs. Despite this, during the Civil War the city association almost went under. The ranks of board members were already reduced, and the war distracted leaders and took many young members away to serve as soldiers. The draft riots of 1863 provided an additional challenge. Vincent Colyer headed the relief committee established by New York merchants for black sufferers from violence. Cephas Brainerd, then a struggling lawyer in his thirties, volunteered his services to the 1,300 victims.[24] Weakened and buffeted, burdened with a heavy debt and only 151 members, the board of directors of the Y.M.C.A. faced possible dissolution. Fighting to keep the association alive, Brainerd, along with Frank W. Ballard and others, began a series of events to raise spirits and revive support. They believed, as

The riots in New York, I. "Destruction of the Coloured Orphan Asylum," 1863. Wood engraving. The J. Clarence Davies Collection. © Museum of the City of New York.

Ballard put it, in the necessity of a men's club to advance religion in New York—"this suburb of Hell."[25]

The association found Robert Ross McBurney, who became its mainstay. An Irish immigrant, McBurney joined the Y.M.C.A. upon his arrival in New York in 1854 and worked as a clerk. At one time he and Brainerd boarded together. In 1862, at age twenty-five, he became the Y.M.C.A.'s librarian and janitor, at an initial salary of $5 a week. As "general secretary" and a director in the years that followed, McBurney saw the association more from the perspective of its clients than its patrons.[26]

In 1863 Ballard delivered an address designed to stir up the faithful. Many of the themes of "New York City a Mission Field" were familiar to Y.M.C.A. audiences, although in the dark days of the war there were ominous new warnings against foreigners and Catholics. Remarkable in this address was the attention that it gave to New York's trade in "Infidel and Licentious Literature," which Ballard saw as "doing Satan's work with most mischievous energy." In words seldom used since the days of Frances Wright, Ballard spoke out against what he saw as a "press prostituted to the dissemination of

Police repulsing an attack by a mob on the offices of the New York Tribune during the draft riots of 1863. The Tribune's editor, Horace Greeley, recognizing the need for additional men if the North was to win, had come out for the Administration bill, which allowed the wealthy to buy substitutes if drafted. These views are from contemporary sketches in Harper's Weekly

The riots in New York, II. "Police repulsing an attack by a mob on the offices of the New York Tribune during the draft riots of 1863," *Frank Leslie's,* 1863. © Museum of the City of New York.

McBURNEY IN 1870

Robert McBurney, 1870.

positive infidelity by the resurrection of dead and buried systems of skepticism, and the reissue, in attractive form, of those theories respecting religion which have made the names and memories of Voltaire, Hume, Volney and Paine a byword and a reproach." Several additional classes of books came in for his condemnation. Sensational novels, what he called "Yellow Covered Literature," prove the undoing of youth and lead them to the brothel or the hospital. These books "feed the flames of lust, and fan into furious activity the smouldering fires of passion." Crime novels guide young men to prison. Exemplified by "Jack Sheppard," these works confuse virtue and vice and give "details of deception and depravity." Worst of all are the truly licentious—the "obscene books and prints . . . published, imported, and sold along our streets, at our wharves, and in some of our book-stores." These evil works cause "so many of our youth of both sexes [to] fall away into evil courses, and make shipwreck of character and hope." About the trade in such works, Ballard stated, it was perhaps better not to inquire: "The statistics of this prolific source of sin and suffering, could they be collected, would startle and sicken us all; but the attempt to gratify curiosity or gather information, in this direction, would be as dangerous and profitless as the endeavor to scrutinize the cast away rags of a small pox hospital."[27]

Such sentiments as Ballard's underlay the efforts of the New York City Y.M.C.A. to seek a stronger state law dealing with obscene literature at a time in which New York was revamping its codes. The new penal code proposed in 1865 made any person guilty of a misdemeanor who "writes or composes, stereotypes, prints, publishes, sells, distributes, or keeps for sale, or exhibits any obscene or indecent writing" or drawing or picture. Lumped into the act were indecent exposure, model artist exhibitions, the singing of bawdy songs, and advertisements "of any cure, specific or medicine for venereal or other kindred diseases, or for producing or facilitating menstruation, or for producing or facilitating a miscarriage in females." The proposed law authorized those making the arrest to seize the indecent materials and deliver them to a magistrate; the latter was given the power to destroy them. Despite the best efforts of powerful members of the Y.M.C.A., this law was not enacted. Its importance is the indication that it gives of the wishes of its Y.M.C.A. sponsors. Like Lord Campbell's Law in England, it allowed search and seizure, in this case at the state level. And it included a new category within "obscene or indecent"—advertisements for abortion. These two elements are important, for both ultimately became part of subsequent state and federal law.[28]

3

One fellow shows just how difficult life for a moral soldier could be outside the "Ironsides Regiment." In 1864, as a soldier in the 17th Connecticut serving in Florida, twenty-year-old Anthony Comstock kept a diary.[29] The son of Thomas and Polly Comstock, who had a small farm in New Canaan, he had experienced intermittent schooling that had included one year at the village academy and a year of high school in New Britain. Times were hard, and as a youth in his teens, he became a clerk in a country store in Winnebark. As he put it, "Obliged to leave school I started out to take care of myself." Professing his faith, he joined the Congregational Church in nearby Norwalk. Anthony enlisted in the army in December 1863 for a three-year stint, after his older brother, Samuel, a volunteer, died of battle wounds. He was proud that his $300 bounty provided for his brother Chester and two younger sisters.

It was difficult to sustain home ways in the 17th Connecticut. In his hardscrabble New England childhood, Comstock had experienced more privation than temptation, but as a soldier in the Union Army, the ways of the Devil beckoned. His entry into service in early January 1864 was a rude awakening to the ways of men. On the journey, three of the seven traveling with him to the war "pledged themselves to me that they would not swear, drink nor chew tobacco while we were in the army." But when he arrived at camp he was immediately disheartened: "it seems as though I should sink when I heard the air resounding with the oathes of wicked men." Whiskey came with the regular army rations; Comstock poured his out on the ground. Throughout his service he organized prayer meetings and arranged for preachers. Toward the end of the year his work was given official sanction, and he became, while still a soldier, a volunteer agent of the Christian Commission. As agent, he took keepsakes from the sick to forward to those at home and passed out religious reading.[30]

Comstock's writings during his war service suggest that the primary division among male college students of the same era—between fraternity men and future ministers—held among soldiers in the Union Army as well. By refusing to join in the usual dissipations of soldiers and trying to convert them, Comstock set himself apart. No family served as refuge against the pressure of his army peers. He violated the customs of soldiers by his open hostility to their ways, and they retaliated. On January 20, 1864, Comstock noted in his diary, "Have been twitted several times today about being a

Christian." In March, his tentmate threatened to leave his tent because he "worked too hard." Once, when he was unloading a cargo of ration that included whiskey, he reported, "Boys got very drunk, I did not drink a drop: and yet some were going to whip me." By knocking two of them down, he was able to keep going. Sin was situated even in high places. Responsible for the Episcopal church in Saint Augustine in which the troops met, Comstock attempted to close the sanctuary for secular entertainment in the evenings and found himself working in opposition to his officers.

By the end of his first year of military service, the hostility to him had grown worse. He wrote in his diary, "Seems to be a feeling of hatred by some of the boys, constantly falsifying, persecuting, and trying to do me harm." On December 20, after meeting he went up to his room to find "all windows were closed tight, room full of smoke. Bunk ful of rubbish and loaded with broken Benches, Chairs etc. Boys were iniatiating [sic] me." Fortunately for Comstock, the Civil War had almost run its course. In 1865, when the war ended, Comstock returned to Connecticut and was mustered out of his regiment.[31]

Within the next decade, his life would take a number of turns. He had been an inconsequential soldier, and he would become an inconsequential clerk. But events, timing, and his own strength and will would propel him onto the center stage of American life. A young evangelical Christian, he ventured to New York City to earn a living. As he tried to make his way in the city, his attention was drawn to the commercial erotica bought by other clerks. The trade in printed sexual matter was accentuated by the heightened sexual display of the postwar years and the rhetoric of the new sexual framework, which insisted on the primacy of sex. The legions of Satan called.

14

Sex Talk in the Open

Some northerners dreamed that a disciplined and chastened America would emerge from the fires of the Civil War. But those venturing to New York City saw the opposite: a seeming explosion of sensationalism and sexual display. Caught up in this changing world, readers sought help in understanding sexuality and their own sexual natures. New books on phrenology and physiological reform aimed to instruct them. These were now more various and included works that articulated the fourth framework, which placed sex at the core of life, introduced through utopian movements, Spiritualism, and free love. Yet even as readers sought new information, forces of suppression threatened to curtail it. The obscenity conviction of Simon Landis for selling a book of reform physiology was a harbinger of changes to come: changes in law and the courts that would abridge Americans' freedom to publish—and therefore read—works offering sexual knowledge.[1]

I

New York City's population soared to 814,000 in 1860, five times the number in 1825. More than half of the city's population came from abroad, by 1865 making up a majority of its voters. Many immigrants were Democrats, led to the party by the rise of anti-immigrant sentiment in the opposition. The New York draft riots of July 1863 terrified residents and visitors alike. It took federal troops days to quiet the city mobs, which looted houses and stores and murdered eighteen persons.[2]

After Appomattox the city seemed intent on forgetting bloodshed in the Union cause and sacrifice. New York was in full swing. As prosperity followed in the wake of war, businesses that catered to leisure boomed. Male sporting culture permeated larger reaches of the society and appealed to many men once presumed safe in the respectable middle class. Some observers became alarmed as the city's legendary license reached a new level. Commercial sexual display was ever more in evidence, showing its face in the theater, on the streets, and at masked balls.[3]

Theaters vied with one another to offer luxurious surroundings. American theater was part of international show business, and a performer who caused a sensation in Paris or London was certain to be brought to New York. In 1861, Adah Isaacs Menken had opened in *Mazeppa* at New York's Broadway Theatre. By middle-class standards, she had led a shocking life, and her marriage to prizefighter John Heenan had lifted her into the world of sporting life celebrity. In *Mazeppa* Menken played a breeches role that included a bareback ride on a real horse onstage. Dressed in a light-colored body stocking designed to make her appear nude, she was bound and splayed on her back as the horse mounted a ramp. After playing to packed audiences in New York, Menken embarked on a long tour in the West and abroad. When she returned to the role at the Broadway in 1866, she commanded $500 a performance. As the *Spirit of the Times* wrote, "Every gambler, thief, pick-pocket, roué, old blasé man of the world, and would-be flash man of the city was there."[4] The year 1866 also saw *The Black Crook* at Niblo's, one of New York's prestige theaters. It employed a hundred female dancers and was said by a contemporary to be "the first show of its kind on the American stage to make a feature of the diaphiously [*sic*] draped or semi-nude feminine form." Unlike Menken's appearances, however, in its long run *The Black Crook* attracted a significant number of women to the audience, on occasions perhaps almost half. Ellen Strong, the wife of the diarist George Templeton Strong, went with a small theater party to a performance on a Friday evening, after which she gave a supper.[5]

In 1868 the arrival of Lydia Thompson and her theatrical troupe of British blondes challenged respectability even more. Their burlesque performances at Wood's Broadway Theatre titillated and shocked audiences in New York. As Robert Allen put it, "All that had been repressed in the righteous, moral, conservative middle class's conquest of the theater returned in burlesque." After two successful productions at Wood's, in February 1869, Thompson and company opened in *The Forty Thieves* at Niblo's. She was def-

The Black Crook, 1866. Courtesy, Harvard Theatre Collection, The Houghton Library.

initely a hit, and she played for 425 nights. Audiences resonated to her impertinent wit and sexiness. She and her many competitors filled New York stages with "leg-work" burlesques.[6]

Although theaters ended their practice of allowing prostitutes to ply their trade on the third tier, prostitution was visible on the streets and in a new form of entertainment, the concert saloon. Appearing on small stages in drinking places along with variety acts and prizefights, female performers offered public sexualized displays with the promise of private sexual services in balconies or private rooms. The concert saloon blended sexual representation with behavior. Added to the attractions of performers who traded on their sexual allure were waiter girls, known to mix prostitution with table service. Historian Timothy Gilfoyle described Volk's Garden: "Actresses leaned out of the balconies between performances, exposing their breasts and urging men to come up and 'have some fun.'" For those seeking pleasure or just a view of those who did, Harry Hill's saloon offered a heady blend of entertainment and alcohol—"painted chorus girls in tights, minstrel shows, sparring matches, female boxers, suggestive dancing, and the finest liquors"—in a secure establishment free from the threat of attack or arrest. Some of these businesses took the name "theater" or "dime museum" but nonetheless carried a mix of sexual performance, alcohol, and prostitution. What differed among them was the degree of outward decorum demanded by the various proprietors, the price of entry and drink, the welcome extended to diverse racial and ethnic groups, and the nature of the clientele.[7]

New York at midcentury was also the scene of masquerade balls. Brothel madams sponsored some of them; at others, given by leading New York society leaders, prostitutes attended. At the close of the Civil War, these costumed and masked balls became more frequent and extravagant. In the immediate postwar era the French Ball, sponsored by the Cercle Français de l'Harmonie, was "an annual erotically charged masquerade held in a leading public auditorium," the Academy of Music. What delighted or frightened observers was the carnival atmosphere of abandon and the way in which respectable society mixed with the demimonde of prostitutes and sporting men under the cover of costume.[8]

News of New York's sporting world could be found on the pages of the daily press. In addition, in the late 1860s and early 1870s, weekly publications emanating from the city highlighted the racy features of New York sporting life and broadcast them to the broader society. By then George W. Matsell was the editor of the *National Police Gazette*. A familiar figure in this narrative, he had started his career as the co-owner of the successor to Wright and Owen's free-thought bookstore, then moved to the police court and rose to became superintendent of the New York police. Under his direction, the *National Police Gazette* took on a more dramatic look. The technology and style of illustrations meant more exciting visuals emphasizing moments of violence, often linked with sexual crimes from across the nation. The headlines of September 21, 1867, have such titles as "An Appalling Outrage" and "Unprecedented Barbarity—Murder and Mutilation." Some of these reports played on the growing fear of the African-American man. The issue of September 27, 1867, carried the headline "A Negro Ravisher Pulling the Tongue out of his Victim at Brady's Mill, Md." The article reported that the attacker had cooked and eaten part of the tongue of the only daughter of a white mill owner. The melodramatic account of the victim, who was rumored to be dying, played on her innocence and the lost gift of her rare voice. Neighboring pieces in the issue contained other accounts of black violence. Ministerial misdeeds from many sections of the country formed another clear subgroup of articles, and readers learned about men of the cloth who taught masturbation to the young or murdered their wives. New York had its share of features, especially those emphasizing its high and low life. An article in the December 28, 1867, issue, for example, reported on "The Demi-Monde of New York," giving "Alarming Statistics of Vice—Evidence of a Moral Decadence." What followed was the conventional piece discussing the types of New York City brothels and their general locations, décor, and inmates, sorted by social class. The parlor houses at the upper end, for example, contained "handsome young ladies," unlike the basement brothels, whose prostitutes had "pimpled features and blood-shot eyes."⁹

By the late 1860s, the *National Police Gazette* had a competitor in Frank Leslie's weekly, *Days' Doings*. Leslie had several publications appealing to children, *Budget of Fun, Chimney Corner,* and *Boys' & Girls'*. The subtitle of the *Days' Doings* suggests its different emphasis: "Illustrating Current Events of Romance, Police Reports, Important Trials, and Sporting News." Although covering some of the ground of the *National Police Gazette*, the *Days' Doings* primarily promised and delivered salacious gossip about the theatrical world. For example, an 1870 issue developed the story of the "Griffin." Lydia Thompson, the British burlesque entertainer, was pursued by Ellen Griffin, an infatuated fan who frequently dressed as a man. As one columnist put it, "Lydia Thompson is persecuted by a female lover, a red headed fiery Griffin. Our advice is, to clap that Griffin into a lunatic asylum as an erotic maniac." After Griffin assaulted Thompson in her Chicago dressing room, the case went to court, and the weekly reported on the trial, complete with details of the rings given, letters written, and gun toted by the erstwhile lover. More generally, this issue of the *Days' Doings* reveals its relish of any evidence of cross-dressing, female or male, treating each example as one more salacious item for its readers. In "Wearing the Breeches" the weekly described a rescue effort that required the female heroine to wear pants to save a man trapped on a scaffold. Female strength or habits associated with men evoked wide-eyed comment: "There is a girl in Fulton County who speaks four languages, chews and smokes tobacco, plays the most difficult music on the piano, swears, dances superbly and takes whisky 'straight.'" Open to a range of readings, including the possibility of a raised eyebrow or a leer, is this bit of news in the feature "Ripples of Romance": "A correspondent says the prettiest woman in Saratoga is a mulatto girl."¹⁰

As before the Civil War, books were a primary means of informing outsiders of the lights and shadows of New York City. In 1869 George Ellington offered up a rich dish of information and gossip in *The Women of New York.*

He managed to lump together society women, fashionable life and customs, the world of brothels, the demimonde of actresses and showgirls, professional women, women's rights advocates, and charities. In a book that more often titillated than revealed, few distinctions were made between the worlds of society and prostitution. In both women enameled their faces and bound their feet, took drugs, and engaged in sexual affairs. Ellington gave a great deal of information about prostitution and emphasized the pervasiveness of New York's illicit life. "At least two men in three, comprising the wealth and fashion and leisure of the metropolis," Ellington claimed, "devote a certain portion of their time and wealth to some fair one, in regard to whose existence their female relatives are profoundly in the dark."[11]

Even if members of the respectable middle class in New York averted their eyes from papers and books such as Ellington's, it was difficult to shield themselves from the world in which high life consorted with low life. Although he might avoid the burlesque, the masked ball, and the *Days' Doings,* Cephas Brainerd, the epitome of the Christian gentleman, was drawn into the Fisk murder trial as lawyer for the defense. James Fisk, Jr., helped define the age in all its vulgarity. He was the legendary partner of Jay Gould as the two tried to control the Erie Railroad. Fisk was often seen with his mistress, Josie Mansfield. He built the Grand Opera House, one of New York's best theatrical venues. As a colonel in the 9th Regiment, he frequently wore his military uniform, and he courted popularity by extravagant gestures, such as tossing paper money from his carriage. Edward S. Stokes, an antagonist of Fisk's in his financial dealings, also opposed him in love and, on January 2, 1872, killed Fisk on the steps of the Grand Central Hotel in New York. A jury found Ned Stokes guilty of first-degree murder and sentenced him to death. Whatever his financial and personal sins, Ned Stokes was the cousin of James Stokes, a leading player in Y.M.C.A. affairs. Thus, when Cephas Brainerd was called in to organize the Stokes appeal, he accepted the assignment and took pride that he got Ned Stokes's crime reduced to manslaughter and a short jail sentence.[12]

Then there was the matter of Henry Ward Beecher. His actions began to unsettle the respectable middle class as early as 1869, when he performed the deathbed marriage of Abby McFarland and Albert Richardson. In the years immediately after the Civil War, Beecher, the minister of the Plymouth Congregational Church in Brooklyn, New York, was the best-loved preacher in the United States. He was the son of Lyman Beecher and the brother of Har-

Henry Ward Beecher, portrait by Sarony, n.d. © Museum of the City of New York.

riet Beecher Stowe and carried his own credentials as a reformer. With a sonorous voice booming from his ample body, Beecher seemed to speak for his age. In the postwar era, when prosperous white northerners wanted to hear good news from the pulpit rather than the brimstone of his father's evangelical ministry, Beecher preached the gospel of plenty. The wealth of the rich was like the spreading shade of a great chestnut tree, enriching the lives of the entire neighborhood. He also spoke the gospel of love and feeling, warmth exuding from every pore, emotions shaping every relation of life. He drew such huge crowds to his services that the Sunday ferries that plied the water from Manhattan to Brooklyn were affectionately known as "Beecher boats."

On November 25, 1869, Daniel McFarland shot Albert Richardson a second time. Two years previously he had only wounded him after he found him stepping out with his estranged wife, Abby. She moved to Indiana, obtained a divorce, and returned to New York. It was rumored that she planned to marry Richardson. This time McFarland aimed to kill his rival and delivered a mortal wound. Granting Richardson's last wish, Beecher united the dying man in marriage to Abby McFarland. Then Beecher learned that not only did many New Yorkers disapprove of divorce, but also that the state of New York did not recognize Indiana divorces. New York papers fed the flames of the scandal that erupted. When Daniel McFarland was acquitted in the subsequent trial, the jury seemed to have decided that, Beecher to the contrary, a husband and wife ought to be married for life.[13]

By the late 1860s, newspapers had grown to new prominence. The daily press now encompassed a vast industry, and Americans became a nation of daily newspaper readers. By 1860, the New York *Herald* claimed a circulation of 77,000 for the daily paper and 82,000 for the Sunday edition. It was followed by the *Sun,* the *Tribune,* the *Times,* and the *Evening Post,* whose combined daily circulation totaled more than 170,000. News not only traveled quickly but permeated everyday life. Newspaper headlines became larger, and many papers carried engravings on the front page. Some of the most newsworthy items were crimes of passion such as the Fisk or McFarland murders. Because lengthy trials followed investigations and indictments, these murders stayed on the most important pages of the paper for many months. Then as now, sex sold newspapers.[14]

Advertisements brought the commerce of male sporting culture to a wider world. Scanning the *Days' Doings,* for example, one can find, in August 1870, the American Publishing Company offering "Books That Are Books: Racy books that speak right out at less than half price," at 35 cents each or the lot at 75 cents. These books carried the titles *Racy Yarns, Marriage Bed, Wedding Night, Habits of the Female Sex, Gems of Love, Free and Easy, Love's Festival,* and *Kate Percival.* "So wake up, boys," the advertisement admonished.[15]

Offered for sale by Foley & Co. at 75 Nassau Street were "Carte de Visite—Of Beautiful Women for Gentlemen" sold at 25 cents apiece or five for a dollar, along with "Books, French Playing Cards, and Rubber Goods." Dayly and Co. of 19 Ann Street proffered *"The Great Marriage Guide,* 50 cents, containing 300 pages reading matter and fully illustrated," along with cards and rubber goods. A stamp sufficed for its "Catalogue of sporting goods." Several ads promoted *The Ladies Boarding House Directory,* most likely a guide to brothels. H. Cameron and Company sold "Gay French Photographs from Life" and a "Sport's Catalogue." W. Carpenter supplied a microscopic watch charm, containing a "comique" photograph. Such references to France or Paris or a French word or two signaled that material had sexual content. Similar markers were the words "racy," "sporting," "gay," "fancy" (or "phancy"), and "rich."

Sold in the same shops or through the same catalogues that stocked words and pictures were "rubber goods," or contraceptives, and they were

Printing House Square, Park Row, lithograph, n.d. © Museum of the City of New York.

advertised on the same page in the *Days' Doings*. A. Seymour, Dr. Manches, and Dr. Evans offered "French protectors," or rubber goods for gentlemen—condoms. Dr. Julian supplied "Elegant Toilet Articles," imported from France, for men and women. If the rubber goods proved unavailable or ineffective, Doctor Harrison sold his "Female Antidote" for $5, with the promise that it was "the only reliable medicine that ladies can procure" and "is certain to have the desired effect in 24 hours, without any injurious results." He had several competitors on the page. For those seeking organ enlargement, there were purveyors of "mammalian balm" and restorers of "manhood." Advice and elixirs, such as Humphreys' Homeopathic Specific No. 28, were available to men suffering from venereal diseases or the supposed consequences of youthful masturbation. Other ads guaranteed immediate hair growth, curly hair for men and women, and easy divorces, or touted false mustaches, love powders, pocket revolvers, and bartenders' directions for mixing drinks—all the accoutrements of the sporting life that the market could offer in a weekly published in 1870.

Press Room, N. Orr Company, *American Agriculture,* 1869.
© Museum of the City of New York.

2

In the midst of this world of heightened sexual display, sensational newspaper accounts, and ads for sporting life, readers sought guidance. They
needed to understand themselves and their sexual impulses as they faced the
absorbing and difficult questions of intimate life. For more than a generation, phrenology had provided a plausible explanation of the mysteries of life
and love, the relation of mind and body.

Phrenologists located amativeness at the base of the skull, at the link
between the brain and the nervous system. In the 1830s and 1840s, as Orson
Squires Fowler and his brother, Lorenzo Fowler, wrote about love and marriage, amativeness and sex, they were allied with Sylvester Graham and the
water-cure movement and published water-cure books and journals. Their
establishment prospered and included a college, museum, and journal. As
the Fowlers' fear of heightened amativeness lessened over time, they
dropped elements of the Graham system and began to portray sexual desire

in more positive ways. By midcentury, Lorenzo had transferred his practice to London and Orson had left the New York establishment, severing business relations with his brother-in-law Samuel Wells. In the 1860s Orson Fowler devoted himself to phrenological counseling in Boston and writing at his home in Manchester, Massachusetts, and sex was his topic. In 1870, he published his compendium *Creative and Sexual Science*. It is a mammoth work of more than a thousand pages, filled with a mixture of physiology and sentiment on the subjects of human reproduction, sexuality, and love. Fowler sought to reach a wide swath of the middle class and to talk to them about their most intimate concerns and fears.

Throughout his career Fowler had faced opposition to his frank speech. At the outset of this work he addressed those who in the past tried to silence his lectures and writings. He stated that he had been told not to speak "BECAUSE IT IS IMPROPER, immodest, impure, corrupting, and prematurely provokes those passions which should slumber till marriage." He pictured his opponents in this manner: "old-fogy grannies, mostly in sensual breeches, with hands up, eyes bulging, mouths stretched, yelling—'O don't say one world about sexuality, lest you shock public modesty—lest young folk learn something! We'll kill you if you don't hush up.' " As had moral physiologists in the 1840s and 1850s, Fowler replied to his censors that it was not sexual knowledge that was wrong but silence. Terrible sexual problems existed in society, provoking fears about many issues—those who chose not to marry, unhealthy babies, prostitution, and boys and girls "unsexing themselves." These problems needed to be understood and discussed. To his adversaries Fowler issued this challenge: his book "proffers sexual knowledge to old and young, married and single, maidens included, and defies all its opponents to their teeth."[16]

As Fowler established his ground, he used language developed in the decades following Frances Wright's first announcements. The sexual instinct is God-given. The sexual organs are natural, and their laws must be known and obeyed. "All Nature's instincts are God's commands incorporated into us." The family, the critical institution in society, is threatened not by knowledge but by "celibacy, preventions, abortions, sexual degeneracy." At the foundation of a good life is a good sexual constitution. "Improving the sexual origin of all life, improves its entire issues forever! It full, all human interests overflow with bursting capacities and exultant enjoyments: it low, all the springs and rivulets of all things human, throughout all their meanderings, are sluggish."[17]

Fowler stood for a robust sexuality. Expressed in many different ways throughout the long book is his vision of enthusiastic sexual union. At one point he addressed women who see love in spiritual rather than carnal terms. "Poetical maidens," he wrote, "you think your Love is as pure as that of angels, and as far from desire for sexual commerce as earth from Heaven." He stated that they were wrong, that love originates "in sexual action; which creates desire for coition. . . . Love and the sexual organs are to each other precisely what appetite and the digestive organs are to each other." Finally, he asserted, "All loving is cohabiting in spirit; and if completed, in body."[18]

It is woman as passionate participant in sexual intercourse that Fowler embraced: "As the chit of all good seeds predetermines their nature and shape, tap-root and rootlets . . . so cohabitation is the all-predetermining chit of manhood and womanhood, Love and marriage, children and their endowment. . . . Its ends embody all of Nature's sexual ends, and its laws all her male and female laws. Fulfilling its ordinances fulfils, violating them violates, all her sexual commandments. . . . Whenever it is right, all else marital and sexual is right; whilst its imperfection deranges all their other relations."[19]

Men may succeed or fail in their love relations. For women, because their lives are defined by their roles as wives and mothers, all hinges on their success as lovers. "Every female is more or less perfect as such in exact proportion as she is the more or less perfect in this her chit function." Stated in different terms, Fowler intoned, "The perfect woman, wife, and mother reciprocates it perfectly, even though she does nothing else well; while she is no wife, no woman who fails here; however excellent in all other respects."[20]

To the question, What is love? Fowler had an answer that his age could understand: "Throughout all Nature all males and females are mutually drawn to each other by what we will call sexual magnetism, as are the positive and negative electric forces." To Fowler and his readers, magnetism had great explanatory powers, for it provided a scientific basis for powerful invisible forces. The nicknames for falling in love—"smitten, smashed, electrified, enamoured, love-struck, dead-in-love"—indicate love's suddenness and force. All men have the positive, all women the negative charge, but the strength of their "galvanic current" varies, depending upon the degree to which they are "sexed."

In an ideal world men and women would know how to read the signs of the other's sexual nature. However, "in these days of dilapidated sexuality, few know how to read these signs." To aid them, Fowler set out for his readers elements of the sexual presentation of self in voice, walk, body shape, face, complexion, posture, laugh, and smell. He meant this to be a guide to help men and women to select a proper mate. Perhaps relishing his defiant role, Fowler seemed to take delight in frank talk about sexual display and performance, especially in women. For example, as he clarified what men should look for in a woman's posture, he considered the upper body: "Every woman, all women, when in Love with a man, set their shoulders farther back, and chest forward, than usual, and so present and hold them that, if in low dress, they would exhibit their breasts." As he moved to the pelvic area, he considered the mons veneris. "All vigorous females involuntarily carry this pelvic portion at least straight, or more projecting than retiring." This one can see in dances. "Hips rolled back accompany this presentation. The reception of the life-germ must precede its carriage and delivery, and be absolutely provided for; and is in this pubic presentation. Behold its necessity and its provision, in superb mother *having* a large 'mount of Love,' and setting it forward by rolling back their hips, whenever in the life-receiving mood!"[21]

With this work Orson Fowler came full circle. What had begun at the outset of his career as advocacy of sexual restraint, the suppression of "amativeness," was now full celebration. Fowler no longer hedged his inquiry into the reproductive instinct but advocated its regular satisfaction in marriage. His enthusiastic words, however, were mistimed. By the 1870s they seemed out of place to some in his audience. Phrenology was no longer intellectually respectable. The legal climate was shifting. Lacking the legitimacy it had once enjoyed, Fowler's writing began to raise eyebrows. Vulnerable to accusations in 1878 by his business manager of sexual offenses in the conduct of his practice—offenses of representation, not of behavior—Fowler quietly withdrew from the public arena.[22]

3

Those who turned to the literature of physiological reform for guidance found it as varied and unstable as phrenology. An earlier chapter examined the social movements whose advocates began to articulate the fourth sexual framework, one that riveted on the centrality of sex. As Mary Gove and Thomas Low Nichols blurred the boundaries between physiological and racy writings, they popularized some of these notions and brought them to a wider audience. By the 1860s, there were advisers spanning the spectrum from those recommending restriction within marriage to those with enthusiasm for sexual expression. As exemplars, two representatives deserve a brief look. From John Cowan members of the middle class could learn the Graham system, modernized in the language of midcentury. James Ashton, by contrast, offered a guide to sexual pleasure.

In the marriage manual *The Science of a New Life,* John Cowan advised marriage based on clear thinking and a rational love, not what he saw as passing for love, the "mock love, a species of Mesmerism," based on sexual attraction. Cowan discussed the popular understanding of sexual frequency in his chapter "The Law of Continence." He wrote that a man "of overgrown and intensely perverted amativeness" considered the appropriate definition of continence to be "having nightly intercourse with his wife." A man of moderate desires would establish one to three times a week as his definition. He, however, advocated the Graham prescription of limiting sexual intercourse within marriage to either once or twice a month. Although he presented a chapter on the prevention of conception, with instruction on the various techniques of contraception, Cowan advised against all artificial means of birth control. He declared, "The sexual act was intended only for the propagation of the species." He counseled that the only real method is "to refrain from the sexual act," except for the several times during a marriage in which reproduction is the goal.[23]

The knowledge seeker who turned to James Ashton's *The Book of Nature* received a very different sense of sexuality. Ashton asserted his belief in the power and beneficence of sexual attraction. In addition to providing an anatomy lesson and clear information about contraception, Ashton's work offered an anatomical guide to sexual pleasure. Although he discussed the male sexual organs, he gave primary attention to those of the female, focusing on each part in its relation to sexual feeling. He stated the important role of the uterus in strengthening the sensations of the clitoris. Although men are moved most powerfully by sexual desire and women by love, both experience "the ecstatic point of enjoyment . . . the Orgasm." For men, it can be "so intense that all consciousness ceases, and a perfect insensibility to everything around is produced for the moment." Women do not always experience orgasm, "and some females of cold temperament do not know what it is, though they are often excited, and feel a certain degree of pleasure." When women do experience orgasm, it is "often even more intense than in the other sex, causing convulsive motions and involuntary cries." Although a woman "of amative desires" may crave "frequent and repeated intercourse," Ashton believed that an interval of two to three days was most healthful for men. Women can experience more frequent sexual relations "without particular injury," though it might be hard on their nerves.[24]

About only one element did Ashton agree with followers of Graham—the power of sexual intercourse. "Coition, or sexual union, may be compared to a fit of epilepsy, or to an electrical shock. It entirely engages both the mind and the body; we neither hear or see, but the soul is entirely absorbed in the act." Where Grahamites and Ashton disagreed was in judging coitus's healthfulness. To Ashton the effects were salutary: "Sexual intercourse is no doubt beneficial to health in all fully developed persons, and in some females it is actually necessary to preserve their lives." Their differing perspectives were related, at least in part, to the changing nature of therapeutic strategies in medicine. An early generation of doctors feared overstimulation and sought to calm the body through depletion. Thus Graham and his followers were afraid of irritation to the nervous and digestive systems and counseled restricting sexual intercourse even within marriage. The later generation believed that weak organs needed stimulation and braced the body with tonics. In keeping, Ashton saw coition as "a proper stimulant to the nervous system, and . . . a sort of safety-valve when the vital functions are too active." As proof, he gave statistics on the longer lives of married men and women and considered the particular diseases that bedeviled celibate nuns in France.[25]

Within the spectrum of physiological advice the writings of Edward Bliss Foote require a special look. Foote is particularly important because after 1873 he played a central role in the fight against suppression and censorship. What makes him significant in the era around the Civil War is twofold. His understanding of sexuality complemented those medical therapies that emphasized stimulation rather than calming. And he was profoundly influenced by social movements creating elements of the fourth framework, which valued sex as central to human life.

A reader who turned to Foote's *Medical Common Sense,* first published in 1858, received an appreciation of sexual intercourse similar to that of Ashton, but one based on different scientific principles. At the time that he wrote his popular medical work, Foote's primary experience had been in newspaper work, not medicine. Foote was born in 1829 near Cleveland, Ohio, and at age fifteen left school to apprentice to a printer. He came east and worked as a newspaper editor on Long Island. Developing an interest in botanical medicine, he studied privately with a physician. It was at this point that he wrote and published *Medical Common Sense.* Two years later, in 1860, he received a medical degree from Penn Medical University in Philadelphia and opened a medical office in New York. He had a thriving practice, much by correspondence, concentrating on chronic disorders.[26]

Foote applied theories of magnetism and electricity to sexual relations. Both had great explanatory power in the nineteenth century. Electricity, he said, shares with sexual attraction its invisibility and power, and magnetism offers the important principle of the power of opposites to attract. Many writers drew on them as metaphor, but in his treatise Foote saw them as literally at work in coition. He wrote, "No organs of the body, except the brain, are so extensively permeated with nerves or electric conductors, as those embraced by the sexual parts." Electricity is involved in three ways: individual, chemical, and frictional. A man and a woman engaging in sexual intercourse receive satisfaction because during the act their positive and negative charges come into equilibrium. Moreover, they enjoy the balance of his acid and her alkaline natures. And finally, their organs are stimulated and satisfied by friction, much as walking on a carpet produces an electrical spark: "no part of the animal organization is so susceptible to this influence as the glans-penis of the male and the clitoris of the female."[27]

From this understanding came certain corollaries. Marriage must involve attraction and compatibility that are both physical and mental. Unlike many writers, Foote thought about what happened after intercourse took place and full sexual satisfaction was attained. He believed that a couple must be sustained by more than passional love. By his principles, an electrical equilibrium is established after intercourse. The man and woman at that point "are as two positives or two negatives which repel each other." At that moment they require platonic love to be compatible. Foote's theories led him to advocate sexual moderation as a means to the end of greater sexual gratification. "Sexual pleasure depends, in great measure, on the *electrical difference* existing between the parties, and the longer intercourse is abstained from[,] the more unlike will they become electrically, and consequently, greater will be the enjoyment."[28]

From the outset, Foote advocated the use of birth control. He had a particular concern with women's health, and he warned against "quack nostrums, injurious and unreliable 'recipes' " that he feared could cause disease. He opposed Knowlton's postcoital douche as potentially harmful to female organs. To him the use of the withdrawal method was dangerous to both men and women. It was, as he put it, "little better than self-pollution," not because it was immoral but because it produced excitement without the relief of electric impulses. In addition, women do not receive the seminal fluids that bathe the vagina and allay "the irritation which is induced . . . during copulation." There existed reliable "preventatives," appropriate for older, married couples, but Foote questioned the propriety of giving birth control advice to young women, who might otherwise be restrained by the fear of pregnancy. The information he offered was to go only to the married and only when both husband and wife wrote him together. After receiving a letter with both signatures, he would send his "Card for Married People" at a cost of $1.[29]

By the 1863 edition of *Medical Common Sense,* Foote changed his mind about propriety. He now regarded "excessive child-bearing" as "the bane of general society." It is bad for women and for the too-numerous children they bear. Foote added a section called "Preventions" in which he listed two forms of condoms, the womb veil (an early form of the diaphragm) and his own contribution, the "Electro-Magnetic Preventive Machine," based on his discovery that conception cannot take place when "there is too great a disparity between their [the couple's] electrical conditions, in consequence of which the womb is too greatly excited electrically to retain the seed of the male." (Needless to say, this medical advance did not enter the lasting contraceptive repertoire.) When at a later point Foote returned to his earlier approach, the pamphlet in the mail sent upon request, his reasons were no longer propriety but fear of prosecution.[30]

Foote sustained a continuing interest in the social fabric. Beginning in 1870, his *Plain Home Talk About the Human System* offered a greatly expanded version of his basic text in which his political and social concerns assumed a new weight. In this work he added new expository chapters in which he discussed sex, love, and marriage across cultures. He had read many of the works of reform physiology considered in previous chapters of this book, including those coming out of social movements and advocating free love. John Humphrey Noyes gave him ammunition as he reconsidered the value of the "amative or sensual function of the sexual organs" as "separate and distinct from the procreative." In the text Foote revealed that he had not only read Noyes's circular and his community's articles celebrating the health and intelligence of Oneidans, he had gone to observe at first hand the sect's settlement in Wallingford, Connecticut. Foote was also interested in Mormon polygamy, although in this case he read sources on the Latter-Day Saints only by outside observers, not by Mormon writers. The sexual practices of both groups, he wrote, provided matter to ponder for those interested in the

" 'reconstruction' of society." Foote defended free lovers, declaring them neither loose women nor libertines.[31]

The books of Thomas Low Nichols gave Foote many examples of marriage practices outside the monogamic norm of American society. Marriage, for Foote, was no divine institution. Given the variety of practices throughout the world, including bride purchase, he found it absurd to believe that what God had joined together, no man could put asunder. Foote broke into his discussion with "I must laugh; it is too comical for any thing!" At a different level, he regarded belief in the religious base of marriage as an impediment to change. It put "the religious world at war with all attempts on the part of philanthropic physiologists to improve the customs regulating the sexual association of men and women."[32]

Many of the problems that Foote saw in contemporary marriage were also treated by other writers, especially those influenced by Fourier. For example, Foote stated that monogamous marriage heightens selfishness and self-love and makes men treat their wives as possessions. Some of the difficulties with marriage that Foote addressed, however, derived from his particular views and diverged from other texts. For example, the practical need to delay marriage led to a "disregard of Nature's institutes on the part of a very large class, embracing children above the age of puberty." For Foote, this was harmful.[33]

Beginning in 1870, Foote included a section on sexual starvation, the source, he believed, of numerous nervous and blood derangements. Agreeing with Ashton on the healthfulness of sexual intercourse, Foote prescribed it. An earlier chapter examined the guidance given by sexual moralists as a means of viewing the behavior that they saw—the wrongs to be righted. The prescriptions of a sexual enthusiast allow this same trick. Foote was seeing "bloodless debilitated men and women" who pursued moral and mental pursuits at the expense of their bodily needs. He spoke directly to them: "It is necessary that you proceed at once to develop your animal nature." He took women as his main focus, for they were the "greater sufferers from sexual starvation." As he thought about convents, Shaker settlements, and young ladies' seminaries, he worried about their inmates. Virgins in these communities might have seen themselves as innately pure, but Foote undercut their self-regard: "Nothing can be more ridiculous than for a lady to arrogate to herself the possession of more voluntary chastity and virtue than her neighbor, because she feels no sexual desire."[34]

Foote believed that unhealthful disuse of vital organs was the source of

Foote's ironic comment on American marriage. "Clothes of One Size and Pattern for the Million," Edward Bliss Foote, *Plain Home Talk*, 1873, p. 771. Countway Library of Medicine.

contemporary women's lack of sexual passion. Similarly placed, men grow lusty and women desiccated. Men deprived of sexual contact have no way to relieve themselves of accumulated semen, and their sexual desire increases. Women, however, function differently. Foote wrote, "If the unmarried woman does not practise masturbation; if, indeed, she gives no thought to sexual matters whatever, the ova, or germs, nevertheless pass off as fast as they ripen, and do not accumulate in the system." She thus experiences the absence of desire. The result is that "the organs of women, unless they have due exercise, may become as powerless and apathetic, as the arm would if carried in a sling for a period of five or ten years." Because Foote believed that "the sexual appetite is just as natural as the appetite for food," he saw passionlessness as disease; for its cure, he advocated sexual experience.[35]

Foote went beyond stating that sexual expression is a right for women to arguing it to be a duty. Women who do not have sexual intercourse not only hurt themselves, they harm men and society, sending men to concert saloons and prostitutes. His concern was not merely male-centered, however. Foote expressed sympathy for women, some who would never be able to become wives. (Although he does not write about it, the deaths of soldiers in the Civil War meant that in 1870 there was a significant disparity between the sexes, and many women did not marry.) Foote wanted all women, including the single, to enjoy sexual intercourse and bear children if they desired.[36]

Another set of Foote's arguments pointed to the hypocrisy of contemporary statements about monogamous marriage. He stated that urban American men of his day practiced polygamy, visiting prostitutes and maintaining mistresses. Believing that it was wrong to force one form of marriage on the entire society, Foote suggested that the federal government establish a Secretary of Marriage to investigate the various systems and make recommendations for the future. As a start he suggested that the government put into place a "Board of Physiologists well versed in the sciences of temperaments, physiognomy, and phrenology," equally divided between men and women, to examine candidates for marriage and divorce and have the power to grant or refuse their requests.[37] Foote's criticism of monogamous marriage was one of the factors that drew him to a figure about to emerge in New York City, Victoria Woodhull, and lead him to become one of her best-known male supporters.

4

Foote seemed unaware that by his advocacy and his writing he was putting himself at risk of prosecution. There was definitely a change in the air. For the first time since the mid-1840s, a prominent writer of a physiological text faced prosecution. In 1846, Frederick Hollick had waged a successful defense against obscenity charges in the Philadelphia courts. He had established that he was involved in public education and reform, that he was not engaged in an effort to profit from men's desire for erotic printed materials. However, in 1870 a court in Philadelphia again indicted a writer of a physiological book treating sex, and this time the prosecutor got a conviction. Simon S. Landis, an irregular Philadelphia physician, was brought before the Pennsylvania court for publishing *Secrets of Generation*.

In arguing for the defense, Landis's lawyer tried to make an important distinction. The class of "obscene" books was a clear one—in the language of this study, the erotic canon—and he did not attempt to defend it. He argued only that Landis's *Secrets of Generation* did not fit into the category. He stated that *Secrets of Generation* "does not come within the class of publications that the law calls obscene." It is not one of "the Fanny Hill publications which pander to the sensual appetite and injure the rising generation." An obscene book has several characteristics. It is published with bad motives. Landis's book, by contrast, was "published not with malicious views that makes a crime or with the motive of reaching the sensual appetite and causing the public to come forth and buy the book." An obscene book is sold secretly. Landis's book was "not put forth secretly in order to sell the book upon the street without regard to the morals of the community."[38]

The argument here is that a book is "obscene" for two reasons: it is written to appeal to male erotic interests, and it is marketed and sold in a specific way. The lawyer then went on to describe the traffic in obscene material in Philadelphia. Sexually explicit books of fiction did exist on the streets of Philadelphia and were sold without penalty. He continued:

> There is a book, gentlemen, which the law calls obscene; I . . . purchased it since this case was commenced. It was bought at a bookstore on one of the principal streets of Philadelphia, in an aristocratic part of the city, next door to a church, not far from your Honor's home. That book, filled with obscene plates, is a base libel, a miserable, obscene publication which I call upon the District Attorney to suppress. I am told there are more than twenty places in this city, where such books are sold, four of them on Chestnut street. This book was written, not to benefit mankind, but to inflame the passions. It is written and illustrated in the most amorous and lustful style possible, for purposes of gain.

Landis's motive was public enlightenment, not profit. Landis registered his book and sold it openly to adults in conjunction with his medical practice. The law privileges medical and scientific works.[39]

The court accepted the argument that a good deal depended on the circumstances of a work's market and sale. As a counter, the district attorney demonstrated advertisements for *Secrets of Generation* appearing in two sporting periodicals, the *Sharp-Shooter* and *Anti-Fogy*, claiming a circulation of 20,000. To the jury he stated, "No scientific book was ever advertised before in these great staring capitals." These ads made it clear that one did not have to go to Dr. Landis's printing office to buy the book, as had the special agent who served as witness. Any child could purchase it by mail. By advertising in Philadelphia's version of the male sporting press, Landis had clearly breached the boundaries that in the district attorney's mind separated reform physiological works from the erotica that was "obscene."

The judge did not respond to the argument that obscene books were routinely sold on Philadelphia streets. His stated concern was only with the single work. As to the lawyer's argument that a scientific book was privileged, he instructed the jury in a different manner. It is true, he argued, that scientific and medical books are protected from prosecution. But this is when they are confined to their place and time. Instructions to medical students are allowable: "We all know it is necessary to view the human body in all its parts, for diseases of various kinds, by physicians. . . . What then? Why they should be properly treated under proper circumstances. You may do it before a clinic class, you may do it in a private chamber, but nobody would contend, that this thing ought to be brought into a court house and done there, or taken upon the highway, and there expose the human person." Therefore "publications of a character which is strictly scientific, strictly medical, containing illustrations exhibiting the human form, if wantonly exposed in the public markets, and publicly advertised for sale in such a manner as to create a wanton and wicked desire for them . . . would be obscene and libelous." Accepting the objections of the district attorney, the judge allowed no testimony by witnesses as to the scientific veracity of the book. In addition, when "expert" witnesses were asked to comment on whether the marked passages in the book were obscene, the district attorney objected, "That is a question for the jury. I do not suppose there are any experts in obscenity." The judge sustained the objection.[40]

In instructing the jury, the judge turned to the question of the necessity and value of books offering sexual information to the general reader. At this point he posed three arguments against books such as the one before the court. First of all, because "God has implanted within us certain appetites which do not require much knowledge to enable us to exercise," such books were useless. Second, it was harmful to society and to women's health to give instruction to prevent pregnancy. And, third, society had a stake in protecting children in their innocence.[41] These had in essence been the grounds for objecting to Robert Dale Owen's *Moral Physiology* four decades before. But to them were now added what may have proved decisive in Landis's case, the way Landis had blurred the boundary between reform physiology and the products of male sporting culture. Landis had advertised *Secrets of Generation* in the *Sharp-Shooter* and *Anti-Fogy*—in "great staring capitals" he had "publicly advertised [his books] for sale in such a manner as to create a wanton and wicked desire for them"—and thus his book could be declared "obscene and libelous."

In 1870 a Pennsylvania state court in Philadelphia moved the boundary line defining obscenity a critical notch. It marked as "obscene" a book written for the general public about the body and sexual reproduction that was advertised in the sporting press. An earlier chapter considered the way that dealers in erotic materials marketed their wares by adding works of physiology to their lists of books composed largely of the erotic and racy canons. Writers such as Thomas Low Nichols blurred the boundaries between genres. It is almost time to take up the campaign of the Y.M.C.A. of New York against obscene materials and to see how all these factors played. First, however, our attention returns to New York, where a new figure has suddenly entered the scene—Victoria Woodhull.

15

Victoria Woodhull

Victoria Woodhull burst onto the New York scene in the oddest way imagi-
nable for a reformer. In 1869 she and her sister became the first female bro-
kers on the New York Stock Exchange. She then declared herself a candidate
for president of the United States. Whatever else she was or was not, Victoria
Woodhull was a believer in the power of celebrity.

Readers in the early twenty-first century are used to the idea that media
shape the self but tend to regard this as a new phenomenon. In fact, it was
already true in the nineteenth century, when the growth of the daily newspapers reshaped minds and created the conditions for modern celebrity.
Once positive fame had been based on the occupation of high political office
or the doing of heroic deeds, but the celebrity that emerged in the nineteenth
century involved recognition beyond any deeds, or even without deeds. Persons reached iconic status merely because they were well known, because
they were taken up and elevated by the newspapers. In turn, the papers sold
issues on the street in large part because of the fame of those in its pages.
Few made better use of the newspapers than Victoria Woodhull.

Newspapers seized on particular persons as a result of a trial or crime,
such as the Helen Jewett murder in 1836. Once aroused, public interest in the
details of private lives was boundless. The kinds of attention that murder victims received went out to others, such as stage performers, who understood
the power of fame to draw audiences. It may have been the ability to coin

celebrity that caused a woman like Victoria Woodhull to seek it. In her rise and fall she drew in others—Stephen Pearl Andrews, women's rights leaders, Edward Bliss Foote, members of the Beecher family, Spiritualists, and free lovers. She attracted the attention and loathing of Anthony Comstock, the man who in 1872 came to lead Y.M.C.A. forces committed to the battle to suppress obscenity.[1]

Born Victoria Claflin in 1838, in Homer, Ohio, the seventh child of an improvident father and a religious mother, at age fifteen she married Calvin Woodhull, a physician. She began a difficult life that took her to many cities as she tried to support her alcoholic husband and two children. She even had a brief stint on the San Francisco stage. She met with success when she became a Spiritualist magnetic healer and put her hands on Colonel James Harvey Blood, a veteran of the Union Army. In the late 1860s, she arrived in New York with her sister Tennie C. Claflin, Colonel Blood, now her second husband, and a plan. Relying on Tennie's sexual allure, the two sisters allied themselves with Cornelius Vanderbilt, known in the Spiritualist world for his efforts to reach his deceased mother and son. Tennie's sexual liaison and Victoria's access to the spirits and their guidance on matters financial led to Vanderbilt's backing of the brokerage house Woodhull, Claflin & Company. The sisters became the first women on the New York Stock Exchange, and initially their firm was a success.[2]

In May 1870, supported by Vanderbilt, Victoria Woodhull established *Woodhull & Claflin's Weekly*. It was an important newspaper. Woodhull and Blood were attracted to radical ideas in these years of ferment and experimentation, and they allied themselves with Stephen Pearl Andrews. In the years after Modern Times ceased to be a utopian community, Andrews became active in Section 12 of the International Workingmen's Association, created by Karl Marx, while remaining active as a free-love advocate. Woodhull lent her name to a series of Andrews's position papers. Her weekly published his wide-ranging ideas, often under one of the sister's names, news of Section 12, and the first American printing of the English translation of Karl Marx's *Communist Manifesto*. Victoria Woodhull probably wrote few words of the articles she signed or the speeches she delivered, relying on Blood, Andrews, and a host of others. But she represented and defended the ideas and positions printed in the paper under her name and accepted legal accountability for them.[3]

Woodhull was learning from the women's rights movement and offered in return money, inspiration, and hope. As she cast her spell, she wrought

This photograph of Victoria Woodhull by Mathew Brady, c. 1870, captures something of her intensity, as well as, in her shorn tresses, her commitment to new possibilities for women. © Collection of The New-York Historical Society, negative #43574.

chaos in women's rights ranks and became a magnet for opposition to the cause. She entered the movement at a time of confusion and conflict. With the onset of the Civil War, many who had been active in women's rights turned to support of the Union. At the war's close, a serious division arose between those who were willing to accommodate Republican demands that it was the "Negro's Hour" and those who sought a separate path for women's suffrage. In 1869 the women's rights movement split in two. The National Woman Suffrage Association, based in New York City, was headed by the more radical Elizabeth Cady Stanton and Susan B. Anthony. They broke with the Republican Party and cast about for a constituency. Their publication *The Revolution* championed a range of causes, including the labor movement and reform of divorce laws.

At one level Stanton and Anthony were continuing the campaign of broad reform in gender and social relations begun by Frances Wright. Stanton brought to it Wright's commitment of "no secrets," to use historian William Leach's phrase. Believing in exposing life to the open air, Stanton and those in her camp, such as Paulina Wright Davis, championed both the importance of sexual knowledge and the end of hypocrisy. They increasingly came out against traditional notions of marriage and supported new laws to ease divorce. When Daniel McFarland was acquitted for the murder of Albert Richardson, Stanton spoke at a rally in protest. What the jury had reaffirmed, she stated, was a "husband's right of property in his wife" under common law. She compared the New York court's failure to recognize Abby McFarland's Indiana divorce of Daniel to the plight of the fugitive slave. In this light, marriage was slavery; divorce, emancipation.[4]

The American Woman Suffrage Association came into being in protest to the movement of Stanton and Anthony away from the Republicans and into broad reform advocacy. Spearheaded by Lucy Stone and Henry Blackwell, the American sought a more genteel tone, appropriate perhaps to its Boston setting. At the outset it cooperated in seeking passage of Reconstruction amendments that introduced the word "male" into the United States Constitution. As the National pursued a broad agenda that included sexual reform, the American pulled back to focus on the public arena of suffrage and employment. Henry Ward Beecher served as the American's titular head.

In 1869 Woodhull quietly attended the Washington convention of Stanton and Anthony's National Woman Suffrage Association and heard articulated the position that the proposed Sixteenth Amendment, granting women the right to vote, was unnecessary because the Constitution already guaranteed that right to women as citizens. Woodhull immediately made this position her own and returned to Washington in the fall of 1870 as a lobbyist for women's rights. She gained the support of Massachusetts Senator Benjamin Butler, and, under his aegis, she addressed the House Judiciary Committee and presented a memorial in January 1871. Thrilled by what they heard, leaders of the National, present at the hearing and simultaneously in convention again in Washington, had her repeat the address to their meeting. Some of them became Woodhull's first significant allies.

In part Woodhull won the support of women's rights advocates through her great personal charm. Although the Boston wing, led by those determined to make the movement respectable, was impervious, members of the more radical New York wing were drawn to her. When Isabella Beecher Hooker—sister of Catharine Beecher, Harriet Beecher Stowe, and Henry

Ward Beecher—met Woodhull at the 1871 Washington convention, she was immediately smitten. Paulina Wright Davis felt an instant rapport. As Woodhull echoed in speeches and memorials the arguments of women's rights advocates that the United States Constitution already granted women the right to vote, she got the attention of the press. Moreover, she had money to spend on a small, impoverished movement: in 1871 she offered $10,000, and it seemed like a godsend.

In Boston, Lucy Stone was alarmed. In the following months, however, her fears were kept at bay. In May 1871, both the American and the National held their conventions in New York. At the National, Elizabeth Cady Stanton—officially retired from suffrage work—now shared Hooker's enthusiasm for Woodhull. When other New York leaders shunned Woodhull, Stanton placed her on the stage next to herself and beside Lucretia Mott. Woodhull gave a fiery speech, calling for an overthrow of the government if women did not gain suffrage: "We mean treason! We are plotting Revolution." Stanton's embrace of Woodhull proved disastrous for the association, and the National lost members. Woodhull lacked long-term reform credentials and a known past. Those who mistrusted Woodhull formed the New York Central Woman Suffrage Association. The Connecticut Woman Suffrage Association, led by Olympia Brown, severed its ties with the National. Resolutions in Maryland, Pennsylvania, Iowa, and Washington rejected any link to Woodhull.[5]

When Woodhull seized the spotlight in 1871, she initially feared that Isabella Beecher Hooker might snub her. As she walked into a gathering a man said to her, "It would ill become these women, and especially a Beecher, to talk of antecedents or to cast any smirch upon Mrs. Woodhull, for I am reliably assured that Henry Ward Beecher preaches to at least twenty of his mistresses every Sunday." As she got to know suffrage women, several of them, including Davis and Stanton, told her what lay behind those words. Henry Ward Beecher was rumored to have had an adulterous affair with Elizabeth Tilton, one of his congregants and the wife of his coworker and champion, the writer and reformer Theodore Tilton. It should come as no surprise that Tilton was an active supporter of the more radical National Association.[6]

Woodhull kept the secret for more than two and a half years. During this time she remained on high ground as her enterprises—the brokerage business, lecture tours, and weekly newspaper—were prospering. Victoria Woodhull was most of all a celebrity. In this new era in the culture, newspapers and magazines, vying for readers, played on personality, and the "bewitching lady broker" made good copy. Woodhull could hardly object: in this world of fluid opportunity, all her business activities rested upon her fame.

Yet the great undertow of celebrity began to suck her down. Beginning in the spring of 1871, Victoria Woodhull experienced its obverse side—scandal. The sisters had leased a grand house on Murray Hill in New York City. To it they had welcomed not only Colonel Blood but also their parents, Victoria's two children, her alcoholic and ailing first husband, Andrews, and a range of untidy kin. Woodhull's unstable mother lodged a complaint in court against Blood, accusing him of threatening her with violence. Realizing that he had a story, a court reporter for the New York *Herald* took down the testimony, and over subsequent days New York readers learned of the curious marital history and irregular domestic arrangements of Victoria Woodhull. Harriet Beecher Stowe played on her image in the comic novel *My Wife and I,* in the character Audacia Dangyereyes, a jaunty newspaperwoman portrayed as a hussy. Accompanying the taint of notoriety was financial distress as the brokerage company's moves in a risky stock market lost the sisters both fortune and clients. To finance her household and many dependents, Victoria Woodhull turned to the lecture circuit. She worked her mother's court suit to her advantage, bending suggestions of scandal into declarations of right. On November 20, 1871, to an audience of more than three thousand in New York's Steinway Hall, Victoria Woodhull broke through the text prepared by Andrews, "The Principles of Social Freedom," to announce, "Yes, I am a free lover."[7]

This speech, repeated many times on the lecture circuit, turned Woodhull's fame into infamy in conservative circles. She took the free-love position espoused by Spiritualists that romantic love was a union of souls. Marriage exists when two souls "meet and realize that the love elements of their nature are harmonious, and . . . they blend into and make one purpose of life." Sexual relations leading to reproduction are marriage, according to "nature." To be united by nature is to be united by God. Marriage happens when "true, mutual, natural attraction be sufficiently strong to be the dominant power." Unlike most female Spiritualists, who believed in one ordained true union, Woodhull took a "varietist" position, allowing for many lovers. What comes can also leave: "Suppose after this marriage has continued an indefinite time, the *unity* between them departs, could they any more prevent it than they can prevent the love?" Law should have nothing to do with this natural process. "To love is a right *higher* than Constitutions or laws." The state should have nothing to do with love, "since in its *very* nature it is forever independent of both constitutions and laws, and exists—comes and goes—in *spite* of them."[8]

Behind the changes in sexual relations, she asserted, must come the equality that women's rights advocates and Spiritualists were demanding. "Women must rise from their position as *ministers* to the passions of men to be their equals. Their entire system of education must be changed. They must be trained to be *like* men, permanent and independent individualities, and not their mere appendages or adjuncts." Women should control the decision to have children. To prepare for their lives as wives, girls should be given knowledge about their bodies and sexual matters. "I deem it a false and perverse modesty that shuts off discussion, and consequently knowledge upon *these* subjects."[9]

Every word that Woodhull enunciated in this speech was familiar to reform audiences used to talks in which women's rights, Spiritualism, and free love were blended. The written text, supplied by Andrews, used language carefully, employing euphemisms when necessary. As with the works of Spiritualist predecessors, it changed the meaning of common words: love is marriage; a sexual relationship without love is adultery; and sexual intercourse accompanied by loathing is prostitution—"whether it be in the gilded palaces of Fifth avenue or in the lowest purlieus of Greene Street."[10] Despite the fact that these rhetorical devices were often used, in reciting them Woodhull was treading on dangerous ground. Her audiences in New York and elsewhere were not the associations of like-minded souls that one found in the conventions of social movements: they were paying customers who filled a hall to hear a show. Her predecessors on the lecture circuit had spoken abstractly before specialized, homogeneous assemblies, often in out-of-the-way places. She addressed general audiences drawn by her fame. And she—a woman—went beyond universals to claim sexual rights for herself.

A lecturer needs only an audience, but a candidate for president needs a party and a constituency. For her campaign Woodhull turned to her natural allies, the Spiritualists, estimated at four million strong. Like many who believed and practiced Spiritualism, Woodhull had never affiliated with any organization. Theodore Tilton's authorized biography of Woodhull told her story of being guided by spirits, especially Demosthenes. It brought her to the attention of the American Association of Spiritualists, and she was invited to address it in September 1871. She seemed to give hope to a movement that had become demoralized. Filled with enthusiasm by her presence, the group elected Woodhull president.[11]

Advised by Andrews, Woodhull sought the support of workers in Section 12 of the International Workingmen's Association. She broadcast its doctrines in *Woodhull & Claflin's Weekly*. Her lectures now added Andrews's version of Communist beliefs, and she joined in meetings and rallies. Urged by Andrews, Section 12 selected her as its head. Woodhull's titular leadership in American communism was short-lived. She had assumed Andrews's odd combination of anarchic liberalism and economic radicalism, and that did not sit well with the more tightly organized Communist movement as it moved into the post–Civil War period. Woodhull was hardly a worker or an intellectual: by occupation she was a stockbroker and publisher; Cornelius Vanderbilt was her patron; and she lived like a robber baron. Although Woodhull turned against Vanderbilt and other capitalists in her speeches, she did not win the trust of the broader Communist movement. Ultimately the International expelled her as a "pseudo-communist" and all of Section 12 as not being comprised of wage workers.

Support of Woodhull by the women's rights movement also began to falter. In January 1871 Woodhull had been a rich woman who could grab the attention of members of the United States Congress. Her activities had brought to the weakened women's movement the notice of the press that had eluded it since the outset of the Civil War. Some supporters saw Woodhull as a gift that could not be refused. She had won the hearts of the radical women's rights advocates who were Spiritualists, and they would remain with her to the end. She also had the support of Elizabeth Cady Stanton, who had long been the movement's orator and rhetorician, and of Paulina Wright Davis, one of its intellectuals. But by May 1872, Susan B. Anthony, the practical organizer of the New York branch of the movement, began to have her doubts. Woodhull's promised $10,000 had never materialized (though it would be partly delivered in printing services for the 1872 convention). Her scandalous life and her public support of free love were threatening the legitimacy of the National Woman Suffrage Association. At the May 1872 convention, Anthony broke with Stanton, took control of the proceedings, and forced Woodhull off the floor. When all else failed to stop Woodhull's supporters from stealing the convention and turning it into a rally for her presidential bid, Anthony had the lights in the convention hall turned off.

When the Equal Rights Party met the next day, it was without official suffrage support. The delegates, 668 in all, chose Woodhull as their candidate for president. Primarily Spiritualists, their numbers included a revered figure from the past, Robert Dale Owen, alongside the thoroughly up-to-date Belva

Lockwood, who would be the first woman admitted to practice law before the United States Supreme Court. Edward Bliss Foote was among the delegates, as were the former abolitionist turned free lover Ezra Heywood and his radical wife, Angela Tilton Heywood. The party selected Frederick Douglass as Woodhull's running mate, without his permission or knowledge.

But when the gathering was over, Woodhull's political career came to an end. If she had been a reader of Marx, Woodhull would have known that she and her party lacked a material base. Woodhull's strategy of raising money through issuing Equal Rights bonds and then linking her presidential campaign to her business enterprises failed because Equal Rights bond buyers did not materialize. Vilified by Woodhull in her lectures, Cornelius Vanderbilt had finally withdrawn his support of *Woodhull & Claflin's Weekly.* Her two primary business enterprises—the brokerage firm and the weekly—had become sources of debt. Hounded by creditors, Woodhull moved to ever-simpler quarters and ultimately began to live in her office. *Woodhull & Claflin's Weekly* ceased printing.

2

Facing ruin, Woodhull went on the attack, and Henry Ward Beecher was her target. At the meeting of the American Association of Spiritualists in September 1872, she rose to give her presidential valedictory. As she began to speak the words that Stephen Pearl Andrews had prepared on the power of political action, she was, in her words, "seized by one of those overwhelming gusts of inspiration." She began to "pour out into the ears of that assembly . . . the whole story of the Beecher-Tilton scandal in Plymouth Church." When newspapers did not pick up the story, Woodhull had one weapon left—she revived her publication. On October 28, 1872, the November 2 issue of *Woodhull & Claflin's Weekly* hit the newsstands. On page 9 was Victoria Woodhull's full revelation, "The Beecher-Tilton Scandal Case, the Detailed Statement of the Whole Matter."[12]

With her instinct for publicity, Woodhull chose another celebrity, the most prominent minister in the United States, as her target. The "reverend rake" was a familiar figure of American sensational fiction and had long been a bogy for the popular press. Beecher seemed to speak for his age as the expounder of the gospels of love and plenty. For many writers dealing with sexual matters in the era during and immediately following the Civil War, Beecher was a known reference point to be understood and respected by his audience. For example, Edward Bliss Foote, in his 1870 *Plain Talk,* quoted these words that he attributed to Beecher: "A man without his appetites and passions would be like a man pulled up by the roots."[13]

Beecher was identified with the Union cause and Reconstruction, and he allowed his name to be associated with many mid-nineteenth-century reforms, such as temperance. He agreed to head the American Woman Suffrage Association nominally, lending it prestige. In the years between 1872 and 1875, New York and much of America would be riveted to newspaper accounts of the Beecher-Tilton scandal, and the church and court trials that brought its myriad details to light. To many readers, the Beecher story served as a warning about the dangers that romantic love, intense feeling, and sexual desire posed to family, duty, and fidelity. Its telling and retelling in the early 1870s may have raised doubts about what America had become, lending fuel to those seeking to cleanse it of sexual speech.

Elizabeth Richards had joined Plymouth Church and in 1853 married Theodore Tilton there. Theodore became Beecher's protégé and the ghostwriter of many of his articles in the *Independent.* By some accounts, in 1869 Elizabeth Tilton told her husband that she had received more than benedictions from Reverend Beecher and was carrying the preacher's child. As the rumors of the alleged sexual affair began to surface among suffrage friends, Beecher and the Tiltons conspired to protect all their reputations through silence. Relations among them soured, however, and Theodore Tilton threatened to accuse Beecher of alienation of affection. Critical to Beecher's defense was his power to control his image in the press. He had influential congregants eager to believe that he was a man innocent of any wrongdoing. But there were threats out there that even Henry Ward Beecher could not leash. Victoria Woodhull, down on her luck, found it to her advantage to tell the Beecher story through her own weekly newspaper.[14]

At best Woodhull was an unreliable witness in testifying about her own life and those of her contemporaries. Of interest in her account are not her charges against Beecher, which can be neither proved nor disproved, but the ways in which she made them. Her formal arguments were written by Andrews; her more informal statements probably came from her own voice, if not pen.[15] Woodhull attempted to portray her decision to write and publish her exposé as motivated by a cause. The present moment—1872—was a time in which the old form, marriage, was crumbling and the new had not yet taken its place. "Men and women tremble on the brink of the revolution and hesitate to avow their convictions, while yet partly aware of their rights, and urged on by the legitimate impulses of nature, they act upon the new doctrines while they profess obedience to the old." The result was hypocrisy. As a public advocate for free love, Woodhull had spoken out against the slavery of marriage in general. Now the time had come to speak in specifics. She cited William Lloyd Garrison as her precedent: he had denounced not only slavery but slaveholders. Although this had caused individual suffering, this was true of all revolutions. "Is the cost to humanity greater of permitting the standing evil to exist?"[16]

She wanted it to be clear that Beecher's wrongdoing was not in having sexual relations with a woman who was not his wife. Adopting the language of health reformers, she wrote, "With his demanding physical nature, and with the terrible restrictions upon clergymen's lives, imposed by that ignorant public opinion about physiological laws," Beecher had merely sought to satisfy his legitimate sexual desires. His fault was that he believed in free love and lived in accordance with its precepts but refused to speak them openly. "The fault with which I, therefore, charge him, is not infidelity to the old ideas, but unfaithfulness to the new." He failed "to stand shoulder to shoulder with me and others who are endeavoring to hasten a social regeneration which he believes in." For this, Beecher was "a poltroon, a coward and a sneak."[17]

Woodhull's telling of the scandal was most clever. The body of her article was set up as an interview in which she answered the questions of a reporter. As she did so, Woodhull first adopted the perspective of Elizabeth Tilton as the latter had told her story to Paulina Wright Davis:

> Mrs. Tilton spoke freely of a long series of intimate and so-called criminal relations, on her part, with the Rev. Henry Ward Beecher; of the discovery of the facts by Mr. Tilton; of the abuse she had suffered from him in consequence, and of her heart-broken condition. . . . She was, as she stated at the time, recovering [from] the effects of a miscarriage of a child of six months. The miscarriage was induced by the ill-treatment of Mr. Tilton in his rage at the discovery of her criminal intimacy with Mr. Beecher, and, as he believed, the great probability that she was *enciente* [sic] by Mr. Beecher instead of himself.

The intimacy between Mrs. Tilton and Mr. Beecher had lasted for years. Mrs. Tilton's present sorrow was increased by "the knowledge that Mr. Beecher was untrue to her" and by knowledge that her husband "had recently had illicit intercourse, under most extraordinary circumstances, with another person."[18]

The next teller of the tale was Theodore Tilton. Here the drama deepened. To Tilton, the affair was awful not only from "the fact of the intimacy alone, but in addition to that, the terrible orgies—so he said—of which his house had been made the scene, and the boldness with which matters had been carried on in the presence of his children." In this account Tilton had originally learned of the affair from his daughter and then confronted his wife. He became crazed. He tore a portrait of Beecher from the wall. He wrenched Elizabeth's wedding ring from her finger. After the miscarriage, he visited the grave of the fetus and buried the wedding ring, as he put it, "deep into the soil that covered the fruit of my wife's infidelity."[19]

Woodhull cleverly played on her readers' emotions, which had been shaped by the language of romantic literature and religious tracts. She presented her tale to readers with loaded words and conventional moral judgments, because it had supposedly been told by the participants. She let them use phrases such as "criminal intimacy," "illicit intercourse," and "the fruit of my wife's infidelity." Once readers savored the spicy story—the plot of many a sentimental book and stage melodrama rendered in familiar language— Woodhull snapped into a different mode and retorted, "Bah, humbug!" She told the reporter that after Tilton had confided in her, "I ridiculed the *maudlin sentiment* and *mock heroics* and *'dreadful suzz'* he was exhibiting over an event the most natural in the world, and the most intrinsically innocent." It was, in fact, "merely a *bogus sentimentality, pumped* in his imagination, because our sickly religious literature, and Sunday-school morality, and pulpit pharaseeism had humbugged him all his life into the belief that *he ought to feel and act* in this harlequin and absurd way on such an occasion." At this point, the words of Andrews were kicking in, and she compared the discovery of adultery of a spouse to that of a slaveholder's detection of a slave's escape and the charge of "criminal intimacy" with "negro-stealing." Slavery and marriage erred in that both accepted "the barbarous idea of ownership in human beings."[20]

As Woodhull turned from narrative to advocacy, she asserted, probably in Andrews's words, that free love was based on two notions: that the individual is free and that love expressed physically in sexual intercourse is naturally good. Many readers of moral physiology texts would have agreed with these premises. Woodhull continued that, as a result, "the god-implanted human

Left: Theodore Tilton, carte de visite, n.d. © Museum of the City of New York. *Center:* Mrs. Woodhull (Broker), carte de visite, n.d. © Museum of the City of New York. *Right:* Mrs. Elizabeth B. Tilton, carte de visite, n.d. © Museum of the City of New York.

affections cannot, and will not be any longer subordinated to these external, legal restrictions and conventional engagements." This position was controversial but was accepted by many Spiritualists.[21]

When, however, Woodhull explained to Tilton the doctrine of sexual privacy that was the avowed practice at Andrews's utopian experiment Modern Times, she posed a sexual ethic at odds with both Spiritualism and the romantic language of spiritual union. In the light of free-love doctrines, Woodhull explained to Tilton that in a marital relationship this meant "that a true manliness would protect . . . the absolute freedom of the woman who was loved, whether called wife, mistress, or by any other name, and that the true sense of honor in the future will be, not to know even what relations our lovers have with any and all other persons than ourselves." Or, as she put it more succinctly, by free-love tenets, neither Tilton nor Henry Ward Beecher's wife had more right to inquire into their respective spouses' extramarital affair than either had "to know what I ate for breakfast."[22]

If Woodhull believed in the doctrine of sexual privacy, how did she justify making the sexual relationship between Henry Ward Beecher and Elizabeth Tilton the subject of her article? Early in the article Woodhull stated, "I am a prophetess—I am an evangel—I am a Saviour . . . but I, too, come not to bring peace, but a sword." Ideals are the condition of peacetime, but the time was one of war. Just as it had been a paradox throughout history that war was a necessary precondition for peace, "it is the paradox of my position that, believing in the right of privacy and in the perfect right of Mr. Beecher, socially, morally, and divinely, to have sought the embraces of Mrs. Tilton, or of any other woman or women whom he loved and who loved him, and being a promulgator and a public champion of those very rights, I still invade the most secret and sacred affairs of his life, and drag them to the light, and expose him to the opprobrium and villification of the public." Woodhull spoke and wrote, she insisted, to force Beecher to come to her side and publicly stand for free love.[23]

3

How did this all play to an audience in 1872?

The answer begins with some of the known specifics. Victoria Woodhull had some supporters. Several newspapers, fearing abridgment of First Amendment rights, defended her in print. Maverick abolitionist turned free-love advocate Ezra Heywood and his wife, Angela Heywood, consistently defended Woodhull in their monthly *The Word*. They upheld her right to publish the facts of the Beecher scandal (although they questioned its wisdom). They approved of her challenge to the link between marriage and sexual relations and defended her right to state it. *Woodhull & Claflin's Weekly* published personal testimonials of support from across the country. The reformer Martha Coffin Wright, Lucretia Mott's sister, privately voiced her approval. In writing to her daughter Ellen Wright Garrison, Martha Wright echoed the language in which Woodhull argued her case in the weekly: "I think Mrs. Woodhull's notes of warning against the Jesuitism of the Christian Young Men are needed."[24]

Yet some of Woodhull's natural supporters had become alienated by her actions in the preceding year, especially by her threats of exposure and blackmail. In the spring of 1872, she damaged her reputation by printing proof sheets of an article called "Tit for Tat" that she sent to a number of women's rights leaders, threatening to publish it and reveal their sexual histories. Some claimed that she had demanded a payment of $500 (approximately $7,500 in today's dollars) to maintain silence. Woodhull herself, in a public defense of blackmail in her weekly, insisted that she did not seek money with "Tit for Tat," only the silence of those in the suffrage movement who were waging a war of gossip against her. This hardly reassured suffrage leaders threatened with disclosure of their private sexual relations. Male reporters had another reason for fear. The unmasking of Beecher had been coupled with many threats of exposure. The article on Beecher could be seen by newspapermen such as Whitelaw Reid, who were still enjoying elements of male sporting life, as an opening volley of a blackmail campaign against leading New York men, a demonstration of the exposés that Woodhull could write.[25]

Beyond circles close to Woodhull, those in the wider public, some of whom had initially been drawn to her and her arguments for women's rights, had a problem. This broad and up-to-date middle-class public had been educated by lecturers and writers on health to accept the new notions of the relation of mind and body that informed moral physiology. Woodhull's discussions of sex, at their best, represented the new sensibility of the fourth framework, which put sexual passion at the heart of human life and insisted that women as well as men had the right to its free expression. She spoke and wrote at a time when only a small number of people accepted her position. To many her words could easily become confused with either the male vernacular sexual culture, which many members of the enlightened middle class saw as crude, or with the commercial erotica that they opposed.

Moreover, something did not feel quite right. That a minister had committed adultery was one of the staples of nineteenth-century newspaper fare. Victoria Woodhull used words that had been written and printed many times before 1872. But the combination of her celebrity and that of Henry Ward Beecher amplified the power of her text at a moment when an odd thing was happening. In ways that are quite mysterious, America was beginning one of its mood swings, this time away from romantic expressions of passion and high-flown emotion toward a realist appreciation of facts and data. Seeping through the cracks of the older culture were a new mood and a new aesthetic. Some experienced it as a new tough-mindedness. Abjuring sentiment, which now seemed melodramatic, they appreciated cool numbers and detailed facts. It has been suggested that the new mood may have resulted from the Civil War experience itself. Although it was fought far from New York City, it was so brutal, so horrible, that it could be comprehended only by sheer numbers. The wartime Sanitary Commission, given the charge of organizing medical care and supplies for the troops, has been located as an important agent of change. Other explicators, perhaps more technologically minded, have attributed much to the development of photography and the apparent record of reality that it gave. Finally, a more diffuse argument has simply been generational, that sons and daughters reject the aesthetics of their parents. Each of these arguments has a counter: the warm-blooded Christian Commission was equal in power and scope to the Sanitary Commission; the daguerreotype appeared at first to augment sensationalism; generations are hardly self-contained entities. Perhaps an agnostic approach is in order. One may not know why American cultural moods change, but they do nonetheless, causing alternations of hot and cool, of drama and understatement. To those seeking a less emotional, less fervid world, Beecher and Woodhull seemed overheated and, when it came, Woodhull's revelation of Beecher's affair, strangely out of date.

Thus it must have been with confused and conflicted emotions—and perhaps some relief—that the American public learned that on November 2, 1872, as Victoria Woodhull and Tennie C. Claflin were riding in a carriage with three thousand copies of their weekly containing the Beecher-Tilton article, they were arrested by United States marshals for sending "obscene" literature through the mails. The "obscenity" was contained in the issue of *Woodhull & Claflin's Weekly* first distributed on October 28. Unable to get the New York district attorney to prosecute Woodhull for violating state law, Anthony Comstock, using an alias, requested the issue by mail. When it was sent, he had federal marshals arrest Woodhull.

How federal marshals got to Woodhull's carriage is the story the next chapter will tell.

16

The Comstock Law

Before the Civil War, no federal marshal would have been at Victoria Wood-hull's carriage. At that time state governments could indict for common-law crimes, but the federal government could not. Victoria Woodhull's arrest by federal marshals required a federal statute. During the Civil War, acting at the behest of the Christian Commission, led by important New York Y.M.C.A. directors, Congress passed a new section of the post office bill meant to protect the Union troops from obscene books. Under this 1865 law, the mails could not be used to send any "obscene book, pamphlet, picture, print, or other publication of a vulgar and indecent character." Violation was a misdemeanor, with penalties up to a $500 fine and a year in prison. In 1872, Congress codified the postal laws and included a remake of the earlier provision. It was this new law under which Woodhull was arrested.[1]

Arrested but not convicted. It turned out that a tougher statute was needed to secure a conviction in Woodhull's case, and one was gotten between her arrest and trial in June 1873. On March 3, 1873, Congress passed its act for the "Suppression of Trade in, and Circulation of, Obscene Literature and Articles of Immoral Use," introduced and championed by the New York Y.M.C.A. This statute brought about significant change on the federal level, as well as influencing many state laws. Understanding how the 1873 statute came to be requires a return to evangelical Christianity and the New York Y.M.C.A.

I

Historians typically imagine the second half of the nineteenth century as a time when the United States became increasingly secular. Darwinism altered the outlook for many, and a growing industrial economy bolstered emphasis on this world. It is, however, more accurate to see the period as a time of increasing conflict between religious and secular forces, for the era also saw intense efforts to define the nation as Christian. One of the most significant began in a dark moment in 1863 when Northerners feared they might lose the Civil War. A group of Christian men from eleven Protestant denominations gathered in Xenia, Ohio, with an explanation of the national crisis and a plan.

God was angry that the nation had placed itself on a secular foundation, they asserted. Although there was no possibility of establishing a state religion, given the many competing Protestant sects, the nation should rededicate itself to God. These evangelicals believed that the way to confirm the United States as a Christian nation was a constitutional amendment that declared "Almighty God as the source of all authority and power in civil government, the Lord Jesus Christ as the Ruler among the nations, and His Will, revealed in the Holy Scriptures, as of supreme authority." Powerful denominations, including the Presbyterians and Methodists, backed it. This movement to write God into the Constitution attracted strong support among college dignitaries, such as Julius Seelye of Amherst and J. H. McIlvaine of Princeton. The National Reform Association, led by powerful men, came into being to push the amendment. In 1867 the devout Presbyterian layman William Strong was elected president; three years later he was chosen justice of the United States Supreme Court. Several governors served as association vice presidents. Over the next decade, as the association attempted to gather support for the amendment, its spokesmen argued that it did not establish any church but placed "all Christian laws, institutions and usages in our government on an undeniable legal basis." It would thus secure Protestant notions of the Sabbath and marriage and return Bible teaching to the public schools.[2]

Another effort at Christian restoration came from the Young Men's Christian Association of New York, and appropriately it focused on youth in the city. It began in February 1866, when the Y.M.C.A.'s Executive Committee privately circulated a report written by Cephas Brainerd and Robert

McBurney to a thousand "persons of high standing and influence." Entitled "A Memorandum Respecting New-York as a Field for Moral and Christian Effort Among Young Men," the report linked the Y.M.C.A.'s central message to facts and figures drawn from the census, licensing reports, and tax data. The report stated that there were more than 111,000 young men in New York City between the ages of fifteen and thirty. Unlike the youths of an earlier era, these fellows were unsupervised. Once boys and young men who were clerks and apprentices had boarded with their employers and been under their eyes, but those times had passed and "the attention of employers has gradually and unnoticed become diverted from the social and moral interests of young men." Now "the virtuous and the vicious are oftentimes herded together in the same boarding house, room and bed." Their evenings were their own, to be spent in "Billiard Saloons . . . Theaters . . . Gambling Hells . . . Porter Houses and Bar-Rooms" and in "Concert, or 'Pretty Waiter Girl,' Saloons . . . Houses of Prostitution and Assignation." The report put numbers on vice in the city, as each category had its accounting. For example, each year close to $3,640,000 went to 3,417 prostitutes living in 730 brothels.[3]

No figures accompanied one class of agencies "injurious" to youth, the books and papers at newspaper stands that tempted young men into dissolute lives, although some numbers sprinkled the paragraph: "At one place, on a principal thoroughfare, there are openly exposed for sale two vile weekly newspapers, which can be purchased at ten cents a copy, and more than fifty kinds of licentious books, each one illustrated by one or two cuts, at prices ranging from thirty-five to sixty cents, while on each copy there is a catalogue of more than one hundred of the same character." A customer need only demonstrate some interest for the proprietor to show him a catalogue of more expensive items, "more vulgar and atrocious, illustrated with the most obscene cuts. . . . The debasing influence of these publications on young men cannot be over estimated: they are feeders for brothels." Among Y.M.C.A. directors in 1866 there was a clear notion of obscenity in print. It was printed erotica, writing or illustrations, offered for general sale to the public in relatively inexpensive editions and marketed to suggest that it had the power of sexually arousing its readers.[4]

The 1866 memorandum supported a plan to erect a centrally located large building to better serve the young men of the city. This building was to provide not only for the "spiritual, mental, [and] social" well-being of young men, as called for in the original 1852 charter, but also for their "physical condition." These two words, suggested by William E. Dodge, Jr., were included in the new act of incorporation of the Y.M.C.A. taken to Albany by Cephas Brainerd and Charles E. Whitehead.[5]

The memorandum also served as a call to action. After some directors questioned the statement made in it about the ready availability of "vile" weeklies and "licentious books" on New York streets, the board hired Arthur Pember to investigate. According to Cephas Brainerd's later recollection, Pember "collected a great deal of material" and made two presentations to the board. That Pember collected the erotica sold on New York streets is suggested by Brainerd's notes: some members of the board did not believe that such trade existed, but "at a subsequent meeting it was proven by *producing* before the Board some of the things referred to." The board then appointed a committee to confer with the district attorney, "to see whether there was no law by which this traffic might be suppressed." The committee reported that there was no effective law, and the board appointed a committee to draw one up. Although there had continued to be prosecutions under common law for obscenity in the Court of General Sessions in New York after the 1840s, as time went on these had been proportionately fewer and farther between. By the close of the Civil War, twenty states and four territories had criminal statutes against obscenity, and to these men New York seemed to be deficient. Along with the new act of incorporation of the Y.M.C.A., two prominent members of the committee—Brainerd and Whitehead—took a proposed obscenity bill to Albany and applied pressure in its behalf. This effort failed to pass in the New York State legislature, and members of the New York City Y.M.C.A. continued to lobby in Albany.[6]

In 1868 they were successful. H. T. Tarbox, the member of the New York State Assembly responsible for managing the bill through the legislature, told Brainerd in a letter written from Albany at the time of its passage that with only two colleagues in open opposition to the bill, most of those from New York and Kings County "dodged the vote." Tarbox stated, "They did not dare put themselves on record against it." This suggests that the tactic he and other supporters used against opponents of the bill was intimidation. The law as passed was weaker than what the Y.M.C.A. had proposed, and it had suffered from damaging amendments in the association's eyes, but nonetheless the minutes reported, "We still hope it will be sufficiently stringent to stop the circulation of this most fruitful cause of crime and demoralization, especially among young men." The report concluded that, despite the law's weaknesses, "if backed by a proper public opinion, it can accomplish vast good." The Y.M.C.A. appointed a committee to oversee enforcement of the law and, with members Charles E. Whitehead, William F. Lee, and Riley A. Brick acting as "detectives," secured some arrests.[7]

The 1868 New York statute was "an act for the suppression of the trade in and circulation of obscene materials, illustrations, advertisements, and articles of indecent or immoral use, and obscene advertisements of patent medicines." This marked a landmark change from earlier New York efforts to regulate obscenity. Its scope was far more comprehensive than merely the suppression of erotica. In addition to prohibiting the sale or gift (or possession with intent to sell or give away) of erotica or the deposit of it in the mail or other common carrier, the law recast the net to add any "article of indecent or immoral use, or article or medicine for the prevention of conception or procuring of abortion." Following the lead of Ohio, the linking of birth control and abortifacients with erotica had been on the table in New York for some time. A proposed 1865 change in the state's penal code had prohibited the advertisement and sale of products to cure venereal diseases, restore menstruation, and procure miscarriages, along with "obscene exhibitions, books, and prints" and had authorized search and seizure, but the entire code failed to pass the legislature. The successful 1868 effort to which the Y.M.C.A. lent its weight was both specific and comprehensive, and it included the important power of search and seizure. It authorized magistrates to issue warrants allowing officers of the law "to search for, seize and take possession of such obscene and indecent books, papers, articles and things" as mentioned above and give them to the district attorney. If the indicted party was convicted, these materials were to be destroyed.[8]

The 1866 report of the Y.M.C.A. came at a critical moment. It was part of the campaign to resuscitate the New York City association following the Civil War and launch a building program. Brainerd sought to bring back some of the elite who had once defected. He went to William E. Dodge, Jr., and persuaded him that too much was at stake for him to remain away. Dodge took on the presidency at the close of the war, and he and younger men, such as James Stokes and J. Pierpont Morgan, both in their twenties, reinvigorated the association. They worked with Robert R. McBurney, the energetic general secretary responsible for day-to-day operations. In the years that followed, they raised money and planned the Y.M.C.A.'s great building at Fourth Avenue and East Twenty-third Street at a cost of almost $350,000, a great sum in that day. When it opened in 1869, its new gymnasium was a big draw to young men, as were its library and educational programs, foreshadowing the university extension of later decades. Symbolizing

The Y.M.C.A.'s great building at Fourth Avenue and East Twenty-third Street, which opened in 1869.

both old ties and new power, the opening ceremony was attended by Reverend Isaac Ferris, who has spoken at the opening gathering in 1852, and Schuyler Colfax, vice president of the United States.[9]

Within the Y.M.C.A. there had been a long debate between those seeking to release the local association from some of its religious strictures and those intent on retaining them. The New York board of directors had previously opened membership to all young men of "good moral character," but this was reversed in 1869. The national association, at its 1869 meeting in Portland, Maine, passed a resolution requiring Y.M.C.A. members to belong to an evangelical church. Three leaders from the New York City Y.M.C.A.—Dodge, Brainerd, and McBurney—strongly advocated this restoration of the association to its religious origins, a return known within the organization as the "Portland test." Board minutes of the New York City association in 1871 reveal additional efforts by local directors to restore its evangelical mission. Interspersed with urgent appeals for directors to raise money to erase the

Cephas Brainerd.

debt are calls for religious renewal, strict control over outside lecturers, and a ban on use of the hall by clergy who did not profess evangelical Christianity.[10]

It was in this context that in November 1871, on the urgent appeal of James Stokes, Jr., the board returned to the discussion of obscene publications and voted the motion of Robert R. McBurney that "a Committee be appointed to consider the matter of obscene Publications & report to the Board a plan & its probable cost, for overcoming the evil." Morris K. Jesup, who was chairing the meeting, selected Charles E. Whitehead and Cephas Brainerd to return to the work that had engaged them in the 1860s, and added Riley A. Brick. Members gave it the informal name "Committee on Obscene Literature."[11]

The name Cephas Brainerd threads throughout the story of the Y.M.C.A. and its fight against obscenity. By this time Brainerd was a successful New York lawyer, prominent Republican, supporter of the black victims of the draft riots, friend of McBurney, and always a Presbyterian Sunday school leader. He had defended Edward S. Stokes when he appealed his conviction for the murder of James Fisk, Jr. One of the dominant figures in the New York Y.M.C.A., he had begun in 1857 as vice president, served as a director for more than forty-five years, and for twenty-five years been the head of the New York–based board of the United States and Canada, known as the International Committee. For many years, beginning in 1863, Brainerd chaired the rooms and library committee. His contribution was service, not money: almost unique among leaders, his name does not appear on the list of subscribers to the new building.[12]

For Brainerd the written word had special meaning. His son recalled, "Reading was to my father about as essential as breathing." He read for enlightenment and information, and was said to carry a volume of Thoreau with him whenever he traveled. The family read aloud after dinner, and the fiction that engaged them was that of Scott, Cooper, and Dickens. And beginning with $5 given to him by his grandmother for emergencies that he diverted to purchase books, Brainerd became a book collector, ultimately lining the walls of his house and law office with them. He bought through auctions and catalogues and shops dealing in secondhand books. As head of the library committee of the Y.M.C.A., he worked with McBurney to set up its reference library, largely of theological books, designed with Sunday school teachers and ministers in mind. With the opening of the new association building, Brainerd helped develop its large, liberal, and secular library holdings. He wanted young men to be able to enjoy handsome books and fine printing, novels as well as nonfiction, and to allow full access to the library's holdings on Sunday.[13] With his reverence for books, knowledge of the book trade, and commitment to evangelical Christianity, such a man would have been particularly offended by erotic books marketed as sexually arousing to men.

As with all leaders of the Y.M.C.A., young men were his particular concern. He worried about "young men now untouched by Christian influence," the group from which came "our rowdies, drunkards, thieves, and greater criminals." These men read only "yellow covered books and Sunday papers." In contrast, he imagined the young men of the Y.M.C.A., for whom he sought good libraries. Once, as he laid out the basic components of a good secular library for associations across the country, he stated his long-held belief that "young men . . . having real future in them, need books— hunger for books." In 1872 Brainerd voiced some of his deepest fears, including those provoked by Victoria Woodhull and others who were articulating the new sexual understandings of the fourth framework. Brainerd regarded the present as a perilous moment, filled with class conflict and political corruption: "Social theories most startling, striking at the prevailing opinions of civilized society, in regard to marriage and the rights of women, are boldly propounded from the platform and by the press." A new and more wily infidelity was seducing young men to stray from professed

Book buying in a genteel environment. J. W. Orr, "Pioneer Gift Book Store," n.d.
© Museum of the City of New York.

Christianity. Brainerd saw his era as filled with cries for reform, but he
believed that the only true change came from the redeemed heart.[14]

Brainerd gave voice to the vision of the Y.M.C.A. held by his generation
of evangelical supporters. The lay ministry of the Y.M.C.A. had the power to
touch those who were largely beyond the reach of church and clergy, the
young men of the city. These were the fellows who "stand in groups upon
the street-corners; they throng billiard-saloons; they are seen in the bar-
rooms, in the theatres; the cunning politician looks after them." These young
men were a mighty power—"the most tempted, the least cared for, and the
most important class in America." Effecting any reform required that they
first be redeemed. Not only were these young men the drill sergeants for
political parties, they controlled the streets. They were the "young men who
make your streets dangerous, your nights hideous." Many of them who
would never enter a church would come to the rooms of the Y.M.C.A.
There, greeted by "young men like themselves, sharers in their temptations,
and victors over them," they would be led to salvation and in turn become
urban missionaries for the Y.M.C.A. Such a man had just called on Robert

McBurney in the new building of the Y.M.C.A. of New York. He was Anthony Comstock, and it is to him that this narrative now returns.[15]

2

Mustering out in the summer of 1865, Anthony Comstock went home to Connecticut. In his early twenties, he found work as a clerk in New Haven, then briefly as the steward and outdoor superintendent of the Lookout Mountain Educational Institute in Tennessee. When he came back to Connecticut, he was ill and penniless. New York and opportunity beckoned, and, in 1866, with $5 in his pocket lent by a Norwalk banker, he came to the city and roomed in a lodging house on Pearl Street. He got work first as a porter but was quickly promoted to shipping clerk. In 1869 he became a salesman in a dry-goods company. His employer, W. C. Spellman, invited him to worship at the Reformed Church in Brooklyn Heights and interested him in the Bethany Mission in Brooklyn. Comstock joined the Western Branch of the Y.M.C.A. on Varick Street and became close to George R. Graves, its chairman.[16]

By 1871 he was earning $27 a week, largely on commission, a tidy sum in that day. He had saved enough money to put a $500 down payment on a house in Brooklyn and marry. His bride was Margaret Hamilton, ten years his senior and the daughter of an established family down on its luck. He took a job in the notions department of Cochran, McLean and Company on Broadway and Grand at a salary of $500 a year plus commissions. His personal life took on a glow. He was a man destined for domesticity. He delighted in the house he provided for his wife. He enjoyed taking care of her, even to the extent of cooking a Sunday dinner for her and her father. Once, returning home and finding "little Wifey out," he "[f]ound a dress partly done and I finished it on the machine for her and had the bastings almost out before she came. How she laughed." As a salesman of ladies' notions—laces, ribbons, embroideries—he had expert knowledge of women's crafts and seemed to have no hesitancy about doing work traditionally associated with women.[17]

The newly married couple joined the Clinton Avenue Congregational Church in Brooklyn, about six blocks from their house. Here Anthony Comstock came home. The church, located in a prosperous neighborhood, was known as a New England outpost in Brooklyn. William Ives Budington, its minister, had been educated at Yale and Andover Seminary and served the First Church of Charlestown, Massachusetts, prior to his move to New York. During the Civil War, Budington had entered the ranks of the Christian Commission as a delegate.[18] Budington and Comstock shared a New England Protestant understanding of the relation of religion, community, and morality. Comstock later testified to their closeness: Budington "proved not only a pastor but a wise counselor and almost a father to me." Comstock admitted that he had sought Budington's advice day and night. He had never been refused. "Many is the night that I have gone up to his room and by his bedside after he had retired, received comfort and help from him." On Sunday Comstock normally went to church and then taught a Sunday school class for boys. He gathered a group of Christian men and women to hold a Sunday prayer meeting in a jail.[19]

As Comstock's religious work increased, his secular life as a salesman paled. Although earning $1,500 a year, he was now, with his increased responsibilities, in debt. His hopes of rising in the world were not being fulfilled. In his journal he flailed at his inability to get ahead. It was at this moment that violations of the Sabbath laws in Brooklyn appeared to him iniquitous. In June 1871, he wrote in his diary, "Yesterday saw two Liquor saloons open and called Police officer 134 to close them." When the officer refused, Comstock threatened to report him and did. "I am determined to act the part of a good Citizen," he wrote, as he insisted upon the upholding of the law.[20]

He began a campaign against the saloons in his Brooklyn neighborhood. After he complained about them to the Board of Excise, one proprietor, protected by the police, threatened Comstock outside his house. Comstock appealed to Brooklyn's mayor and police chief for help. On their suggestion he got a revolver and brandished it when the saloon keeper attacked him. Comstock again went before the Board of Excise. This time a judge arrested two saloon keepers, and Comstock began to fight them in the courts. H. B. Spelman, a new Brooklyn neighbor whom Comstock admired as "earnest," supported him. Comstock was developing a gift for attaching himself to important people: Mr. and Mrs. Spelman were the parents of John D. Rockefeller's wife. During the days of the trial Comstock had to pass the barroom on foot on his way to Sunday school, going by men loitering "with stones in their hands." One of the saloon keepers died during the trial; the other lost his license.[21]

According to legend, a friend had died three years before. Comstock biographer Charles Trumbull wrote that the friend "had been led astray and corrupted and diseased," language suggesting either venereal disease or the nineteenth-century connection between masturbation, nervous disability, and susceptibility to illness. Comstock laid the blame on Charles Conroy, who had sold his friend erotic materials from a basement in Warren Street. Some years later, Comstock stated that Conroy "was supplying some of the younger clerks" working in Spellman & Co. Comstock bought a book from Conroy and took it to the police captain of the precinct, who, accompanied by Comstock, arrested Conroy and seized his supply of books and pictures.[22]

At the close of Comstock's Sabbatarian court battle, he returned to fight the sale of obscene books. The 1868 New York State law to suppress obscene literature had had little impact on the production or distribution of erotic words and images. Comstock had earlier found the police protecting Brooklyn saloons that were open on Sunday. Now when he tried to have second-hand book dealer William Simpson arrested, the police tipped Simpson off. The Sunday *Mercury,* in a hostile report on the incident, gave Comstock crucial information about the district in the city where erotica could easily be had. If Comstock really wanted to apprehend dealers in obscene materials, he could find "plenty of these men in Ann and Nassau street and elsewhere." Armed with this new intelligence and addresses from advertisements gleaned from the *Mercury,* the *National Police Gazette,* the *Days' Doings,* and *New Varieties,* Comstock joined up with Robert Griffith, a reporter from the New York *Tribune,* and visited the shops. On March 2, 1872, they returned with police, who arrested the owners and employees of two bookstores. A *Tribune* article and editorial praised Comstock's work.[23]

Because businesses that placed ads in the *Days' Doings,* Frank Leslie's sporting weekly, closely match Comstock's notations in his arrest ledger for 1872 and 1873, its ads are particularly useful in determining his understanding of the "obscene." Examined in an earlier chapter, they bear a second glance. The reader may recall that, admonishing its readers, "So wake up, boys," the American Publishing Company offered "Books That Are Books: Racy books . . . at less than half price."[24] Dayly and Co. of 19 Ann Street proffered *The Great Marriage Guide,* as well as cards, rubber goods, and its catalogue.[25] H. Cameron and Company sold "Gay French Photographs from Life" and a "Sport's Catalogue."[26] Commerce in racy literature reinforced a mental connection between published erotic words and images and sexual acts, for sold in the same shops or through the same catalogues that stocked words and pictures were birth control articles called "rubber goods." On the same pages

Book buying on Ann Street near Theatre Alley. Detail: Ann Street, May 3, 1909.
© Museum of the City of New York.

of the *Days' Doings* as "Books That Are Books" are advertisements of three
purveyors of condoms, called "French protectors" or rubber goods for gentlemen.[27] Two providers of substances to induce abortion, Dr. Evans and Dr.
Harrison, also took out ads in the weekly.[28] Comstock went after them all,
seeking convictions under New York State law.

Comstock returned to the shops with police, who made arrests. In the
ensuing trials, he served as a prosecution witness. Increasingly he engaged
in detective work. As he seized old letters and circulars that pointed to the
mail-order side of the business in erotic publications and birth control and
masturbatory articles, he perceived that the distribution system operating
through the mails was more important than sales over the counter. Behind
the sellers of books and images he saw a larger industry—publishers, printers, engravers—and middlemen. As he put it, "I discovered that there was a
systematic business, systematically carried on, the extent of which was simply appalling." He counted 169 titles advertised in circulars that the purveyors
put out. The police were no real help, for they were involved in "levying

blackmail," or taking kickbacks. Comstock began to keep arrest records in a ledger book. It charts his growing knowledge about the production of erotica. In pursuing leads during March 1872, he found men who, if put under enough pressure, were willing to talk and serve as witnesses. Through two men, one who sold plates and another hired to turn them into pictures, Comstock brought into his net John Meeker and his inventory of photographs, as well as "About 250 Negative Plates for printing Ob. Photos. & Stereoscopic pictures."[29]

His biggest quarry during this period was William Haynes, a publisher first arrested for obscenity in 1846. In partnership with his wife, Mary, William Haynes continued publishing erotic books until Comstock got close. In one of Comstock's March 2 raids, he had gotten the arrest of James McDermott, the owner of a small bookstore at 75 Nassau Street. In his remarks, Comstock called McDermott the "confidential man to Haynes" and possessor of one of his steel plates. In the arrest records Comstock related, "In March 1872 E. M. Grandin sent word to Haynes as follows, 'Get out of the way. Comstock is after you. Damn fool wont look at money.' " Grandin, the proprietor of a "sporting goods" emporium that advertised widely, was described by Comstock as the "Confidential Middle Man, between publishers & retailer" who took book orders and money for Haynes and arranged for shipments of his books. On the night Grandin gave his warning, Haynes died. Death did not stop Comstock from putting Haynes into his arrest records: "About 35 years ago he was a prominent Physician in Old Country. Married noblemans daughter. Seduced another. Forced to leave Country about 1840[.] Came to America & married Mary E. present wife. They together published Ob. books since 1842."[30]

Haynes's books were printed in Brooklyn, bound in New York City, and stored in Room 10 of the Atlantic Hotel in Jersey City. Comstock decided to visit Mary Haynes, now a widow, who cursed him but agreed to sell him her capital—"24 Cases Stereotype Plates, 182 to 190 Steel and Copper Plate engravings. (for printing some 20 or 22 different books)"—for $650. Comstock did not have the money. It is at this point that he turned to the Y.M.C.A.[31]

And, of course, it was there—with a New York law on the books and a newly constituted committee of old hands. How much did Comstock know? His own words were "Something seemed to say, 'Appeal to the Young Men's Christian Association.' "[32] Was the "something" Reverend Budington or H. B. Spelman or George R. Graves from the Varick Street Y.M.C.A., all

In contrast to Anthony Comstock's mutton-chopped middle-aged portraits, this photograph reveals him to be a handsome, determined young man. Heywood Broun and Margaret Leech, *Anthony Comstock: Roundsman of the Lord* (New York: Albert & Charles Boni, 1927), opposite p. 78.

well-connected men, telling him where he might go to seek help? Was it, as Brainerd recalled, a police officer at the Tombs, who recommended the association to Comstock because of its success in getting convictions?[33] Or, as a religious clerk with his career in a dry-goods company at a standstill, had he been watching the Y.M.C.A. all along?

Comstock wrote a letter to Robert McBurney to request financial help and brought it by in person. Scribbled in pencil, the letter was, by later accounts, so messy that McBurney asked Comstock to rewrite it before he took it to the association's officers. Before that happened, Morris Jesup, who had just become president of the New York Y.M.C.A., came into McBurney's office. Comstock's original letter was still on his desk. Curious, Jesup asked McBurney about the scrawl, and when he learned its contents he went to see Comstock at Cochran, McLean and Company.

In a letter book of the Y.M.C.A. is a copy of the rewritten letter, addressed to McBurney and dated March 23, 1872, neatly composed in Comstock's hand. In it Comstock recounts his efforts of the previous three weeks to "suppress the Sale and Publication of obscene books pictures &c" through the March 2 arrests of Charles and William Barkley and James McDermott and through the successive arrests of secondhand book dealers Patrick J. Bannon and William Simpson, printer J. Eberley Nichol, and manufacturers D. Hodgman, S. W. Rice, and F. Taturel & Co. In the accounting Comstock makes clear that the "&c" is clearly as important as the books and pictures. At the store of the Brooks brothers, he seized "Rubber Goods of the most (Hellish) obscenity." Taturel & Co. was known as the "Headquarters of all kinds of French goods."

At the establishment of Meeker, Comstock reported that he had seized plates for stereotypes, pictures, cartes de visites, and texts worth $5,000 to $6,000. With some exaggeration he announced that Meeker was "said to own the entire business in this line." He also reported that he had found "where the owners of the Steel Sterotype plates for printing the infernal Books are," and he had been offered them for sale.

Comstock made his request: "Now Sir, my private resources are exhausted. I have borne the costs thus far myself. I have a family to support, and I appeal directly to your Association for whatever may be necessary to complete this work." He wanted neither reimbursement nor a wage for time spent, only the money necessary to buy the plates from Mary Haynes. Although he did not specify what else he needed, he clearly wanted some protection from possible legal costs. As he put it, "I am now threatened by W. F. Howe[,] Tombs shyster, with imprisonment in Ludlow st Jail, on a Civil Suit unless I desist from this work. He is counsel for most of these parties." As Comstock's arrest record narrates, Jesup gave him the funds: "On Apr. through $450—furnished by M. K. Jesup esq Comstock seized stock." In addition, Jesup gave him $150 for his efforts. As he put it, "This was a God send to me. It was unexpected. It was a full answer to my prayer and in a way I dreamt not of."[34]

3

McBurney must have clarified to Comstock that the New York Y.M.C.A. had a band that was ready to hear him, for in the letter book Comstock states that "since commencing this thankless work," he had learned that there was "a Committee in the Y.M. Association" ready to "to suppress this evil." Jesup invited Comstock to a meeting at his house with Y.M.C.A. leaders on May 9, 1872. There Comstock made a dramatic report on his work. He told how he had arrived at Mrs. Haynes's Brooklyn house with the promised funds and found that he had been preceded by a wagon that was at that moment being filled with the printing plates. He jumped onto the wagon and took it to the Y.M.C.A. When he returned to Mrs. Haynes to demand the books, he learned that they were already in a dealer's hands. He got the eleven cases of books delivered to a local express company in his name. He later reported that with Jesup's money he had been able to seize roughly "40,000 books, plates and engravings." Comstock also seized Haynes's account books with customers' names.[35]

Comstock and his audience found each other. He continued his work; they, theirs. On November 18, 1872, the Y.M.C.A. gave Comstock new backing that was strong and unequivocal. The New York board renamed the informally constituted Committee on Obscene Literature the Committee for the Suppression of Vice and elevated it to regular status in the association. On the recommendation of McBurney, the board gave the committee power to raise money for its work and to keep its funds separate from those of the parent organization. Joining the new committee were veterans Whitehead and Brainerd and the powerful Dodge, Jesup, and McBurney. In its discussion of committees, the 1873 annual report of the Y.M.C.A. proudly stated, "The *Committee on the Suppression of Vice* have done much to lessen the traffic in obscene publications and articles of indecent use. The boldness and publicity with which this trade was carried on has been diminished in a marked degree, and the conviction of various publishers and others engaged in this debasing business has been secured."[36] From the perspective of members of the committee, they had begun the battle.[37]

They then hired Comstock to help them fight it. They agreed to pay Comstock for his work as a supplement to his diminished income as a dry-goods salesman. They also promised to pay his expenses. Beginning in 1873 the committee compensated him with a $3,000 salary, double the income he had been receiving at the store. Such a salary allowed him to resign from his job and raised him securely into the ranks of the middle class.[38]

One of Comstock's first major targets was Jeremiah Farrell, a printer at 14 Ann Street. He had purchased the stock of the publisher and bookseller Frederic A. Brady, who had been arrested for obscenity in 1858. In his arrest records for May 1872 Comstock stated that Farrell had "absconded. Received following word from the officer who had warrent, 'Jerry, have warrent for you. If you dont want to be taken get out of the way.' Printed Ob. Books for about 16 years. Published 'Paul de Kocks' works. Reported to have escaped arrest, by blackmail. Died in about 2 weeks after absconding."[39]

As an earlier chapter indicated, Farrell published a wide range of domestic and foreign erotica. Other Farrell books moved over a range of genres, such as medical writing, reform tracts, and travel guides. They included racy books, such as George Thompson's *Simon the Radical,* purportedly by Charles Paul de Kock. Whatever had been their original purposes, when published by Farrell and his competitors, such texts were adapted or marketed as erotic material that promised male customers sexual arousal. By 1872, any published writing, whatever its sources or its author's intentions, that was offered for general sale to the public in a relatively inexpensive edition and marketed to suggest that it had the power of sexually stimulating its readers risked the label "obscene."

Comstock also went after George Ackerman, who in 1857 had published *Venus' Miscellany* and faced a police raid. Although Comstock did not have him arrested, he put Ackerman in his arrest record and noted, "Published about 22–25 years Ob. Books, and manufactured 'French Transparent Cards.' Printed from 18–24 different books. The stock was delivered May 1st, 4th, & 6th by Ackerman in person to Comstock at American Tract Society building. . . . He formerly kept a store in basement 19 Ann. Sold out to Cas. Barkley in 1871. Arrested by Police a number of times. Never convicted. About 100 Plates were seized in 1871 by Police." Comstock's inventory of Ackerman's stock stated that it consisted of "5500 to 6000. Ob. Cards, ½ ton Letter Press, 4000 Pictures, 52 Steel, & 50 Copper plates, 142 woodcuts."[40] In addition, Comstock secured the arrest of William and Charles Barkley, the proprietor of Dayly and Company and his brother, and seized "2000 old letters, and about 2000 Circulars[,] 100 Photographs, and 100 obscene Books." They also got a "Lot of Rubber Goods."[41]

Comstock paid attention from the outset to the trade in what he called "obscene and immoral rubber articles" carried on by those who sold books and pictures. In addition to condoms, materials to prevent conception included the womb veil, an early form of the diaphragm. Rubber goods also included articles for masturbation, such as dildos. To conservative men such as Brainerd, these items of commerce were noxious. Many years later Brainerd recalled that in 1872, when the first seizure had been made, "I attended in court where were a number of young people who were employed in their manufacture, as witnesses, and the boxes were produced which contained some of the articles." The police justice, supposedly inured to such displays, "turned away from the exhibit as if it produced a severe sickness at the stomach."[42] With shops selling printed material and articles for contraception and masturbation and both kinds of matter producing revulsion, it seemed to such men completely natural to label both obscene.

4

When Anthony Comstock saw the attack on a prominent Brooklyn minister in "The Beecher-Tilton Scandal Case" in *Woodhull & Claflin's Weekly*, he was fired to action. He first attempted to get a state court to indict Victoria Woodhull and Tennessee Claflin, but this effort failed. He then requested that the issue of the weekly be sent to him through the mails and turned to federal marshals to arrest the two sisters under the 1872 federal postal code. On November 2, Woodhull and Claflin were arrested by federal marshals and arraigned.

Why did Comstock go after Victoria Woodhull? Contradictory to what was argued at the time, there was nothing sacred to Comstock about Henry Ward Beecher. Although the New York City Y.M.C.A. had often given Beecher a lectern—for example, when the association hosted the meeting that launched the Christian Commission—Comstock's beloved minister William Budington was unsympathetic to Beecher and his version of liberal Christianity, and Comstock himself knew the famous pastor of the Plymouth Street Church only by reputation. What was involved was a strategy on Comstock's part to solidify his position. At the time of Woodhull's arrest the directors of the Y.M.C.A. were considering a plan to augment their backing of him and to put his campaign on a solid financial footing. Given Comstock's mounting ambitions, securing the arrest of Victoria Woodhull—a prominent leader of women's rights and America's most notorious advocate of free love—and thereby gaining immense publicity for his fight must have been very tempting.[43]

Like Woodhull, Comstock had an itch for celebrity. What allowed Comstock to act on his impulse was his conviction that Victoria Woodhull's publication was part of the noxious toxin infecting society. Comstock regarded Woodhull and her sister Tennessee Claflin as "free-lusters" and hated everything they stood for. With the arrest of Woodhull, in addition to erotica and rubber goods, a third type of material, writings on sexual reform and free love, was potentially labeled obscene. This would have an important impact on the future.

How did Comstock come to see Woodhull's words as obscene? In 1871,

Woodhull had ridden the crest of fame as a stockbroker, the editor of *Wood-hull & Claflin's Weekly*, a women's rights spokesperson, and a candidate for president. By November 1872, down on her luck, her enterprises turned sour, she revived her weekly for the purpose of reporting on the Beecher scandal. In the consciousness of a novice vice hunter in 1872, did Victoria Woodhull not cross the threshold into obscenity? Whatever her intentions, she appeared to be writing about sex for a large public audience for money. The elements that unmistakably defined obscenity in the 1860s and 1870s were there: sexu-

"Get Thee Behind Me [Mrs.] Satan" represents Victoria Woodhull as the Devil in female form. Thomas Nast cartoon, *Harper's Weekly*, February 17, 1872, a reproduction from an original in the Amherst College Archives and Special Collections.

ally exciting words offered openly to a broad public for sale. That the author was a beautiful, unconventional woman who drew thousands to her public lectures advocating free love only added to their potential power to incite.

In addition, much about the tone of *Woodhull & Claflin's Weekly* of November 2, 1872, evoked the libertine press of an earlier era. Using almost the same words as the 1840s weeklies the *Whip* and the *Flash*, a preliminary article by Tennie C. Claflin promised to name the names of hypocritical rakes: "We know who they are and what they are, and shall not hesitate to write and publish their history so definitely that all men shall know them." A piece by Woodhull stated that she had five hundred biographies ready to print, a likely reference to the "Mary Bowles" letter, purportedly written by a brothel madam and published in December 1871, that had promised to give Bowles's client books, including five hundred names, to Woodhull. She pledged to reveal more than Eugène Sue's *The Mysteries of Paris* (an 1842 sensational French novel exposing the secrets of the French capital): she promised to name the names of Wall Street bankers, great railroad men, and men of the cloth. She stated that she would tell of the offer of a great sum by a wealthy man to take his damaged daughter off his hands and would reveal a man with a standing application "at all the prominent houses of prostitution for what he terms 'spring chickens,' meaning young girls from twelve to fifteen years of age." A second article in the same issue, telling the story of New York businessman Luther Challis's seduction of a young virgin at a French Ball, led to the arrest for criminal libel of Woodhull's husband, James Harvey Blood, listed as managing editor of the weekly. As in the case of Myer Levy in 1841, Challis was a private citizen, who, unlike a politician, an entertainer, or a minister, had no expectation of being in the public eye. One cannot know what Woodhull's own purposes were, but one can see that her words seemed to fit into a familiar pattern: a representation of titillating sexual matters as reform and the threat to name names. Wittingly or unwittingly, her articles fit the groove etched by the sporting press in the past.[44]

After many legal delays, the obscenity trial for mailing the November 2, 1872, issue of the weekly began in late June 1873. Woodhull had a successful defense, headed by the famed criminal lawyer William F. Howe. He had represented many of those whom Comstock had arrested for selling commercial erotica. Woodhull had wanted her defense to argue on broad free-speech grounds, and Howe and his colleagues did so; but ultimately Howe turned to the technicality that *Woodhull & Claflin's Weekly* was a newspaper. The jury returned a verdict of not guilty after Judge Samuel Blatchford ruled that the prosecution of Woodhull and Claflin under the 1872 federal law could not be maintained because that law did not include newspapers.[45]

5

Woodhull's acquittal reminded Comstock of one of the weakness of the 1872 law, but he had known of many others. Not only did the federal statute not include newspapers, it did not specify that birth control information and appliances and masturbatory materials were "obscene." And it did not allow search and seizure. Americans with their eye on England were aware of Lord Campbell's Law, the 1857 English statute that established the right of police to search for books and other materials and seize copies of those deemed obscene. This was a critical power, for it meant that governmental authorities could go beyond prosecuting sellers of obscene books and prints to suppress their materials.[46]

In discussions of federal obscenity legislation there is missing a critical synapse. The 1865 act had stated that "no obscene book, pamphlet, picture, print, or other publication of a vulgar and indecent character, shall be admitted into the mails of the United States." The 1872 codification of the postal code repeated that statement. At no place was "obscene" or "vulgar and indecent" modified to include rubber goods, information regarding contraception, or advertisements for abortion. Nowhere does the code mention search and seizure. Both would be in the 1873 federal statute. How did they get there?

In 1868 the Y.M.C.A. of New York introduced into the New York State legislature a bill to regulate obscenity. It was under this state law that Comstock went after sellers of erotica and rubber goods in the spring of 1872. The measure included both the explicit prohibition of contraceptives and abortifacients and the power of search and seizure. In both these aspects the 1868 New York State law provided an important model for federal legislation.

Comstock's reflections and writings about his life and work have tended to downplay the Y.M.C.A.'s role. In his recollections, Comstock stated that he urged the committee to work for a stronger federal law to "cover the matters as then advertised on circulars of the dealers in obscene matter" (i.e., birth control literature and products). He recalled that the committee did not unanimously support him: "Certain of the members did not hesitate to ridicule the project."[47] But in fact, it was key members of the committee who championed him and saw a need to broaden his work with a new federal law to strengthen his hand. The model in their minds was the 1868 New York State law, enacted with their support. In winter 1873, in the wake of the jailing of Woodhull and Claflin, Morris Jesup paid for Comstock to travel to Washington as a lobbyist to seek a stiffer obscenity law.

Unquestionably Comstock's work was opposed by some within the association during this period. Publicity that followed his pursuit of Woodhull caused donations to the Y.M.C.A. to decline, and some members of the Committee for the Suppression of Vice turned against his efforts. What was the source of their objection? In Comstock's terms, they wanted a "still hunt" campaign, rather than active pursuit of the quarry. In the 1860s, efforts to seek a tougher state law against obscenity were linked to a desire for willed ignorance and silence about traffic in erotica. As Frank Ballard had put it, efforts to gain information were "as dangerous and profitless as the endeavor to scrutinize the cast away rags of a small pox hospital." The reasons behind this distaste for information and publicity involve both a sense of decorum and a fear of contagion. After McBurney's death, Brainerd went through a trunk of his papers looking for some of the reports of the Committee for the Suppression of Vice. McBurney had his copy of the annual reports of the Y.M.C.A. handsomely bound, but these committee reports were missing. Brainerd wrote, "Why Mr. McBurney did not bind with his Association papers these reports, I cannot understand, except that he was so very scary about having anything of the sort around where young men could get hold of them or learn anything about them." What this suggests is that some of the foot-dragging on the part of leaders of the Y.M.C.A. came from the old fears about youth and knowledge. Publicizing efforts to eradicate obscenity would provide the information needed to find it.[48]

Whatever hesitations some individual directors may have had about Comstock's public presence, as a body the board of the Y.M.C.A. of New York backed his efforts. And its prestige and its members' power were what drove the outcome in Washington. Sustaining Comstock were the authority of the directors of the Y.M.C.A. of New York City and their history of leadership within both the association and the Christian Commission in gaining anti-obscenity legislation at the state and federal levels.[49] With Whitehead and McBurney, Comstock went to work to devise a new federal bill and seek its passage. Sponsored by Representative Clinton L. Merriam, a banker from Locust Grove, New York, Comstock met with members of the House and set up an exhibit of obscene materials to prove his point.

It was a ripe moment, for Congress was distracted by the Crédit Mobilier scandal implicating some leading Republican representatives and Vice President Colfax in a railroad construction investment scheme that lined their own pockets. The legislative branch was also pressed by the need to adjourn before Grant's second inauguration. Comstock, advised and supported by his New York Y.M.C.A. allies, planned a smart campaign. He got Justice William Strong of the United States Supreme Court to draft the bill. Strong had just lost the battle to write "God" into the Constitution. His efforts through the National Reform Association failed after it faced powerful opposition. Justice Strong may have understood the Y.M.C.A. bill against obscenity as a way of accomplishing some of his religious goals in a secular frame. Strong introduced Comstock to William Windom, senator from Minnesota, who took the bill to the floor of the Senate. Sponsored by Norwalk newspaper publisher A. H. Byington, Comstock gained the strong support of Connecticut's wartime governor and current Republican senator, William A. Buckingham, a man in a position to appreciate the wartime sacrifices of the Comstock family. Byington arranged for Comstock to use the room in the Capitol of Vice President Colfax, a warm friend of the New York Y.M.C.A. There Comstock again set up his exhibit of confiscated obscene materials and explained that they were being sent to children in boarding schools. As Comstock wrote in his diary, "I spent an hour or two talking and explaining the extent of the nefarious business and answering questions. Buckingham, [Daniel D.] Pratt, [Adelbert] Ames, [Alexander] Rumsey, [Cornelius] Cole and numerous others were present. All were very much excited, and declared themselves ready to give me any law I might ask for, if it was only within the bounds of the Constitution."[50]

Confusing the legislative process were several alternative anti-obscenity bills that were seeking passage. To draft a consolidated bill, Comstock gained the talents of Benjamin Vaughan Abbott, a man with wide knowledge of legislation. In 1873 Abbott was in the middle of a long and productive career as a compiler of digests of New York and federal laws. Here Comstock's campaign against Woodhull likely stood him in good stead. Abbott's two brothers were Lyman, long associated with Henry Ward Beecher, and Austin, who would write the official report of the Beecher trial that ultimately ensued.[51]

In a coordinated move, backers were inserting a provision in a federal appropriations bill working its way through Congress. In it lay the seeds of Comstock's greatly enlarged future powers. Congress authorized a new position—special agent in the United States Post Office with power to confiscate immoral matter in the mails and arrest those sending it. The office was created with the understanding of the postmaster general that Anthony Comstock himself would fill it.

On his return to New York for court appearances, the Y.M.C.A Committee for the Suppression of Vice passed a resolution in his support. They also resolved that Comstock should not accept the special agent's salary, budgeted in the federal appropriations bill at a generous sum close to $3,500. Comstock agreed to forgo the salary, knowing that his New York backers would make it up. He understood that if a "fat office" (i.e., a paid one) were created, it would ultimately go to a politician. "Give me," he wrote in his diary, "the Authority that such an office confers," and the salary "may go to the winds." If the 1873 provision in the appropriations bill passed, Comstock knew that as special agent of the U.S. Post Office he would have extraordinary power. He could search, seize, and arrest.[52]

During the month of February, as the third session of the Forty-second Congress ground to its end and no progress on the anti-obscenity bill was made, Comstock's days at the Capitol were filled with frustration. The Crédit Mobilier scandal took center stage; Comstock confided his dismay at what he saw to his diary: "Men assailing one another's character while legislation goes begging." However, aided by his powerful legislative allies, Comstock skillfully worked the bill through its complex maneuverings. The most difficult element was an amendment to protect the prosecutions of those indicted under the 1872 law (including Victoria Woodhull). On March 1, the bill was once again laid aside. Jesup and Dodge telegraphed James G. Blaine, the Speaker of the House, to urge action. Just before adjournment, without substantive debate, the bill passed the Senate and House, and President Grant signed it on March 3, 1873.

The 1873 federal act for the "Suppression of Trade in, and Circulation of, Obscene Literature and Articles of Immoral Use" strengthened an established agency of the federal government—the U.S. Postal Service—by giving it vague and broad powers. It made it illegal and punishable to send through the mail six kinds of material: erotica; contraceptive medications or devices; abortifacients; sexual implements, such as those used in masturbation; contraceptive information; and advertisements for contraception, abortion, or sexual implements. In Washington, D.C., and the territories, where the federal government had direct jurisdiction, the act made it a misdemeanor, punishable by fine and imprisonment, to sell, give away, offer to sell or give away, or have in possession with such intent "any obscene or indecent book, pamphlet, paper, advertisement, drawing, lithograph, engraving, wood-cut, daguerreotype, photograph, stereoscopic picture, model, cast, instrument, or other article for indecent or immoral nature, or any article or medicine for the prevention of conception, or for causing abortion." To write, print, or cause to be written or printed "any card, circular, book, pamphlet, advertisement, or notice of any kind" advertising the sale of "said obscene or indecent articles" fell under the same category. The bill gave any district or circuit court judge the power to issue a warrant directing a marshal to "search for, seize, and take possession of any such obscene or indecent books, papers, articles, or things" and allowed those materials to be "condemned and destroyed." Modeling key elements after the New York State law of 1868, the bill has been known from its passage as the Comstock Law.

On March 6, 1873, the day before his twenty-ninth birthday, Comstock received a commission from the postmaster general to serve as special agent of the United States Post Office.

In a simultaneous effort, the Y.M.C.A was working in the New York State legislature to get an act of incorporation for the New York Society for the Suppression of Vice. The decision to seek a separate organization sprang from both negative and positive impulses. Not all Y.M.C.A. leaders approved of Comstock's work and wished to separate it from the association. The circus atmosphere accompanying the Woodhull trial and the criticism in New York newspapers of Comstock's efforts to get the new federal anti-obscenity statute suggested to some that the interests of the Y.M.C.A. were not being served. As Jesup's biographer put it, some felt the association should not support Comstock officially because the matters that he dealt with were "too unpleasant to be touched by persons of sensitive feeling, and that more harm was done by stirring up the pool than by letting it lie." Throughout the momentous year of 1872–73, Comstock reported difficulties with Y.M.C.A. directors in his diary and suggested that some of them hoped to muzzle him. Comstock believed that a separate organization, acting under a state charter, would enable him and his supporters to pursue their goals with greater freedom.[53]

The New York Society for the Suppression of Vice was incorporated on May 16, 1873, and the Y.M.C.A. promptly dissolved its committee. With incorporation came new powers. Although it was financed through private philanthropy, the society was assured of the assistance of the police in New York City and elsewhere in the state "in the enforcement of all laws which now exist or which may hereafter be enacted" for the suppression of obscene literature and articles of immoral use. Along with this, in June 1873 New York

State strengthened its state obscenity law, one of the first of the "little Comstock" laws adopted by forty-five states in the late nineteenth and twentieth centuries. These laws mirrored the language of the first provision of the federal statute, which applied to the District of Columbia and the territories. For more than a year, Comstock had been acting at the state level in a private capacity. Now his work and that of other agents of the S.S.V. were given official sanction.[54]

The state's actions did not remove all resistance by Y.M.C.A. directors to the new organization, however. Their hesitancy may have arisen from fear that Comstock was not a man who was easily controlled. In July 1873, Comstock reported in his diary that he had called on Jesup, who was "glad to see me and was very Cordial. He stands by me. He said he was almost discouraged on account of the jealousies in the Committee. . . . Some of the Committee want to rule, or are afraid to go ahead, and think I make false arrests. Bah!" Although at that point Jesup thought it might be unwise to form the society, by the fall he was ready to go ahead, and he chaired its first meeting, held on November 18.[55]

Although Comstock confided to his diary during the effort to set the bylaws for the society that "only one Man thinks as I do and that is Mr. Jesup," nonetheless a distinguished board assembled at its first meeting. After serving in the chair, Jesup withdrew to an advisory role. Whitehead, who had helped draft the articles, became its first president, supported by Samuel Colgate, Alfred Smith Barnes, and D. H. Cochran as vice presidents, and John Paton as treasurer.[56]

Under the incorporation act, in cases where it brought violations of the law to light, the society had the right to receive half the fines secured. This the society did not want, and the provision was eliminated in the New York State 1873 "little Comstock" law. Thus only the voluntary contributions of society supporters—normally amounting, after the first two lean years, to approximately $10,000 a year—kept Comstock's work going. When the society met for the first time in the fall of 1873, it formally chose Comstock to be its full-time secretary and chief agent.

Until his death in 1915, Anthony Comstock served simultaneously as special agent of the U.S. Post Office and secretary of the New York Society for the Suppression of Vice. Working under state and federal laws that the Y.M.C.A. of New York had helped bring into being, Comstock had the power to arrest those suspected of distributing obscene matter and to search for and seize those materials. The federal law supported publicly as a measure to protect children against erotica included quietly, without discussion, contraceptive information and materials and advertisements for abortion under its ban. As the arrest of Victoria Woodhull demonstrated, it was possible to construe this law as banning printed advocacy of free love. Arrested before the 1873 statute became law, Woodhull got off on a technicality. Free-love proponents arrested after March 3, 1873, however, would not be so lucky.

At this point in the story the federal law is in place and Anthony Comstock has been launched. But a critical piece of the puzzle is still missing: Comstock's motives. Beyond his New England background, religion, ambition, and desire for celebrity, what drove Comstock? The task of divining his intentions is a little more complicated than it looks, for Comstock's words became entwined with those of his backers. It is, however, less important here than in other instances to understand who stated what. Both Comstock and his ghostwriters in the Society for the Suppression of Vice drew from the same well: the notions of the body, health, sexual desire, masturbation, and the power of literature developed by conservative reform physiologists before the Civil War.

17

Comstock's Crusade

Anthony Comstock now had the power of federal office, the backing of federal and state laws, the prestige of the New York Society for the Suppression of Vice, and the influence of members of the Y.M.C.A. of New York behind him. He had personal qualities that steeled him for the work ahead. He had courage and flair and an unconquerable faith. He had an itch for celebrity. In addition, he had an eagerness to publicize his work and express the rationale behind it.

Comstock used the personal dramas of death, street conflict, and suicide to persuade and intimidate. Early in his campaign, Comstock claimed victory in the deaths of the three most important publishers of erotica. William Haynes died just at the point that Comstock was closing in on him. George Ackerman lived long enough to deliver his book stock to Comstock. Only Jeremiah Farrell remained to be indicted, and he died before trial. Comstock portrayed these deaths as conquests and bragged of them in his reports and books. In 1874, book vendor Charles Conroy stabbed Comstock in the head as Comstock was transporting him to jail. Comstock carried the wound proudly as evidence of his valor and added Conroy's two-year prison term for assault on an officer to his list of righteous triumphs.[1]

The most dramatic instance of Comstock's might came in 1878. Comstock visited the office of Madame Restell with the fictional story that he needed birth control for his wife. When Restell supplied him, he arrested her. Her apprehension came at a terrible moment in her life. Her companion, business partner, and husband, Charles Lohman, had died. As she carried on her trade without him, isolated in her grand house, she was afraid and perhaps weary of struggle. On the morning of her court hearing, she slit her throat. Comstock's comment: "A Bloody ending to a bloody life."[2]

Stepping back from these events, reported in the daily papers and in his own writings, Comstock attempted to convey his larger message to the public. He broadcast his words in the reports of the New York Society for the Suppression of Vice and in books that drew substantially on them. Comstock portrayed himself as a crusader. He was in a Christian fight to the death with liberals—infidels and free lovers. He was defending the youth of the country against forces of evil that worked in secret to carry into homes obscene books and pictures inciting lust and leading to masturbation and prostitution. "It is a deadly poison, cast into the fountain of moral purity."[3]

Comstock's words were written to a purpose, or rather two. The society was always trying to raise money. It had wealthy and powerful male backers, but they did not give to the society in anything like the manner that they gave to the Y.M.C.A. For example, in 1876, William E. Dodge, Jr., who presided at the second annual meeting of the Society for the Suppression of Vice, made a contribution of $250, in contrast to the more than $25,000 he had given a decade earlier to help pay for the new Y.M.C.A. building. Morris Ketchum Jesup made no open donation in 1876 but, along with John Paton, advanced money month by month to meet Comstock's expenses, to a total of $1,200. Although generous, the amount stood in contrast to Jesup's gift of $20,000 for the building. Although New York State law allowed Comstock a share of the fines imposed in state courts, he—supported by his backers—refused in order "to avoid all semblance of pecuniary interest in the result of a trial." Their entire work depended on, as the first report put it, the "voluntary contributions of those, who, as public spirited men, have seen the imperative necessity of putting down this abominable traffic." Following a call for contributions was the list of those who had given in the past. Most contributions were in the range of $10 and under. As the report suggested, donors were imagined as male. Sociologist Nicola Beisel's careful analysis of the society's givers in its first twenty years determined that more than 80 percent of them were white men who held "high white collar" positions, "including merchants, businessmen, financiers, and professionals."[4]

In addition to securing funds, the annual reports of the New York Society for the Suppression of Vice attempted to rouse male public opinion. This required the elaboration of a full rationale for suppression of obscenity. Comstock could arrest, but unless he could get judges and juries to convict,

Tract House, as it grew. "The American Tract Society Building—23 Stories High, Nassau and Spruce," n.d. © Museum of the City of New York.

those whom he saw as trafficking in obscenity would soon return to their work. Comstock was often successful at the federal level, the subject of the two chapters that follow. But he frequently faced failure at the level of the New York State courts. It was important for Comstock to claim to have God on his side because the criminal state justice system often was not.

He and the society were troubled by foot-dragging and obstructionism, often on the part of the district attorney. In 1877, Comstock complained that of the forty-seven persons indicted in the last two years, only seventeen had been tried or pled guilty; thus "nearly two-thirds of those whom Grand Juries have believed guilty go from month to month untried and unpunished." Over and again his arrest records state his anger at the district attorney for failure to pursue cases to their conclusion. For example, in 1873 Comstock arrested Frank Leslie for advertisements in the *Days' Doings,* yet, as his remarks state, "This case never called for trial. Fixed in Dist. Attys office." Even if a case came before the grand jury, trial was not ensured. For example, the physician Sarah Chase was twice arrested for distributing birth control materials but not brought to trial. Once a grand jury refused to indict. The annual reports of the New York Society for the Suppression of Vice in the 1870s are filled with vituperation against the state justice system as it operated in New York City.[5]

Outside New York State, the issue was leniency. As a special agent of the U.S. Post Office, Comstock had the power to operate on the national scene. Away from New York, Comstock made a number of forays. Here his success varied depending upon the community and the judge. Even courts that tried and convicted might level low fines or mild sentences. Other federal agents made occasional arrests, but in the early years they did not lead to convic-

The New York State court where many of those accused of obscenity faced trial. "Recorder Hoffman Sentencing Mr. Edward Ketchum in the Court of Sessions, New York, December 30, 1865." *Harper's Weekly,* January 20, 1866, p. 45, a reproduction from an original in the Amherst College Archives and Special Collections.

tions with serious consequences—significant fines or prison sentences—with the exception of those in a few locales. Some fines levied were so small as to mock the statute. In several well-publicized incidents the president of the United States issued pardons to those convicted.[6]

Policing of birth control was a particular failure at both state and federal levels. Neither judges nor juries seemed eager to punish those who sold contraceptive materials. As historian Andrea Tone has demonstrated, even in the home territory of the New York Society for the Suppression of Vice, agents made relatively few arrests of suppliers in the years following 1873, and of those only 62 percent were convicted. Significantly, only a very few went to prison, and these for terms shorter than the maximum allowed by the law. While judges typically permitted the use of decoy letters to entrap those who mailed birth control articles or information, the privacy of sealed materials remained sacrosanct, limiting the ability to inspect packages sent by mail.[7]

Finally, a clear opposition speaking in reasoned arguments coalesced in an effort to alter or overturn the 1873 federal statute and supportive state laws. Comstock had to answer in kind. His words in annual reports and books can be seen as part of a campaign to bring public opinion to his side. This needs to be modified to "male" public opinion: in an era in which only men voted and only men served as judge and jury, the words in question were directly solely at a male audience.[8]

Comstock did not have skill as a writer appropriate to the entire audience he was seeking to reach. In the little that remains today of his unmediated words, he is blunt and to the point. For example, the "Remarks" column in his arrest records contains statements about each person that he brought before the courts, written in his own hand. As he described his encounters with antagonists, he used the colloquial speech of the street. Here are two such entries for 1872:

[Edward. M. Grandin]: The Confidential Middle Man, between publishers & retailer. Has been arrested 2 or three times before & always escaped. A professional Gambler. He shipped 2 trunks to Phila.[,] 1 to Baltimore & a large case of books to Jersey City, of which all were captured. A shrewd villain.

[Charles E. Mackey]: This is one of the worst sneaks in the business. A church member, sunday school teacher, (a class of young ladies) a mason or Od fellow, and yet one of the lowest switches known in the business. He was about publishing a new book, when we seized his stock.[9]

Comstock seemed to enjoy his street-smart language, words like "shrewd villain" and "worst sneaks." In his uncensored writing, Comstock reads, in fact, a good deal like the *National Police Gazette*.

In addition to this voice, Comstock took to the language of numbers, an American impulse heightened by the Civil War. In the first report published by the Committee for the Suppression of Vice of the New York Y.M.C.A., Comstock listed what he had seized and destroyed since March 1872:

> 130,000 lbs. of bound books, mostly 16mo, with from 150 to 300 pages, and from ten to twenty-five cuts of the most improper character.
>
> 4,000 lbs. of the same books in the process of manufacture.
>
> 194,000 bad pictures and photographs.
>
> 6,250 microscopic pictures, knives and rings.
>
> 625 negative photographic plates.
>
> 350 engraved steel and copper plates.
>
> 501 engraved wood cuts and electrotype plates.
>
> 14,200 lbs. stereotype plates, for printing 145 different books.
>
> 20 lithographic stones.
>
> 60,300 articles made of rubber for immoral purposes, and used by both sexes.
>
> 700 lbs. lead molds for manufacturing rubber goods.
>
> 3 establishments for manufacturing rubber goods closed.
>
> 5,500 indecent playing cards.
>
> 3,150 boxes of pills and powders used by abortionists.
>
> 130,275 advertising circulars, catalogues, handbills, and songs.

4,750 newspapers containing improper advertisements, or
other matter.

20,000 letters from various parts of the United States
ordering improper articles.

6,000 names of dealers, as revealed by account books of
publishers.

22,000 names of persons throughout the United States,
catalogued and sold to dealers in bad literature, as
persons likely upon receipt of circulars, etc., to send
orders.

2,050 letters, packages and envelopes, in the hands of
dealers, ready for mailing at the time of their arrest.

To this inventory, Comstock attaches additional explanation: "Of the
bad books there are *thirty-five* different varieties of the more expensive class,
which are sold at prices ranging from $1 to $6. Of the cheap books, sold for 25
to 50 cents, there are *one hundred and nine* varieties."[10]

In these words one can see Comstock the dry-goods clerk, attending to
his stock of notions. The language of the list is cool and restrained. It is
intended to move Comstock's vigilante endeavors to a different level, to lend
gravitas to the enterprise through the authority of accounting. Updated versions of Comstock's list are repeated many times in subsequent annual
reports, presented in ever more formal and detailed formats.

In the first enumeration, categories are jumbled together. Books and
plates are listed with birth control, masturbatory articles, abortion powders,
abortion ads, and playing cards. Interspersed, the words "bad," "improper,"
and "immoral" appear, but they are casual descriptors. The logic is one of
identity. As all the items are in the same class, the order in which they occur
does not matter. The one exception is the final group, which puts together
elements from the business side, the lists of names, the letters of request,
and the letters ready for mailing. This is, for Comstock, the crescendo at the
end, giving emphasis to the wholesale nature of his efforts. He was after the
suppliers.

In the text that followed, as Comstock brought out the business side of
obscenity, he offered some inside dope. "A great part of the business is carried on by means of priced circulars, in which each article is numbered, and

orders are given by reference to these." He fleshed out the numbers by describing individual arrests. "One printer, whose place was seized, has, during the last four years, printed for one dealer, as his own account books are believed to show, not less than one hundred and twenty-five thousand licentious books."[11] At the end of the passage, Comstock enumerated the arrests, convictions, and sentences he had secured. In the society's next report, the data took on a grander title, a table of "Statistics." Here the number of arrests, fines, imprisonments, books seized and destroyed, et cetera, appeared for the period prior to 1874, in 1874, and, as totaled, in three neat columns. Included in this record were the miles traveled by Comstock as he rode the rails in pursuit of his quarry.

To an age that valued fact, Comstock's accounting lists were useful. But clearly they were not enough for the full male audience that he and the society sought to persuade. What was the Society for the Suppression of Vice to do? Lacking direct evidence, historians hazard occasional guesses. The best guess in this instance is that into the breach came the well-educated, experienced rhetoricians of the Y.M.C.A., such as Cephas Brainerd and Frank W. Ballard. They had been brooding over the problem of the young male clerk in the city for many years and had written about it in reports and speeches. In court Comstock admitted that though he wrote a report for 1877, it was revised by another hand before publication. This seems the likely scenario in other years as well.[12]

Comstock claimed many of these words as his own, and he was believed at the time and by historians who followed. In the early 1880s, he published two books, *Frauds Exposed* (1880) and *Traps for the Young* (1883). Both drew substantively on the annual reports of the Society for the Suppression of Vice. Because of the two books in his name, historians have assumed that Comstock was the author in the first instance of the reports. But the words were his only in the sense that he had the authority to use the words of ghostwriters. It is appropriate to think of the reports as serving like paragraphs of speechwriters today, giving those addressing audiences better ways of stating their ideas. Once spoken, such words are the "property" of the speaker and can be reused by him any time. From the early 1870s until his death in 1915, as Comstock stated and restated key themes, he employed the language of his society mentors and ghostwriters in the 1870s, first articulated by them in the annual reports.

This is the explanation for why Comstock speaks in two voices in his books. One keeps the lingo of the dry-goods salesman and tough, savvy man. The language is crude and can, at times, expose the weaknesses of Comstock's education. The other voice sounds like the Y.M.C.A. and the Society for the Suppression of Vice. In this mode, Comstock frames his work in terms of the discourse begun by Sylvester Graham in 1830 and continued by reform physiologists and moral reformers.

In fact, it was the very familiarity of the words attributed to Comstock, not their originality, that gave them their rhetorical power. They repeated the language of the pre–Civil War physiological writers, who had focused on the evils of masturbation and unregulated sexual expression. Underlying Comstock's discourse were the understandings of the way that the mind and body worked of the most conservative pre–Civil War health writers. These assumptions about health and disease were blended with evangelical Christianity and posed as the war between God and Satan. As with the earlier writers, such as Sylvester Graham, Comstock spoke in universals, but he imagined his audience as white men. Although in a later period in his career he would target immigrants as an important danger to the American body politic, in the early phase of his career his central focus generally remained an ethnically undifferentiated people.[13]

As these words expressed the familiar, they restated that the hothouse sexualized culture of the nineteenth century led children and youth into premature sexual behavior. Children should be protected from the dangers of their world. Sexual knowledge causes premature sexual awakening, a state that should be deferred as late as possible. Puberty brings with it new emotions that the Devil is ready to corrupt. While parents seek to protect their children, agents of Satan are at work, spreading disease by tempting youth through erotic images and words, printed and widely distributed.

Just as Lyman Beecher feared Frances Wright, so did Comstock see the danger in the freethinkers of his era. The regime of the God-fearing stood between young people and evil like a firewall. Freethinkers questioned religious faith; some even mocked it. As Comstock put it, the organized freethinkers of his day favored "Blasphemy of the name of the Most High, and the ridiculing of the most sacred things." They stood for "that license which allows appetites and passions to have full sway, which throws off all moral restraint." They were worse than an elephant in a zoo that "broke loose and then opened the cages containing lions and tigers." Only the watchfulness of the keeper protected others. But the freethinker "not only breaks the fastenings which are the only restraints of vice, but he by ridicule and laughter seeks to lull the watchman, Conscience, to sleep" and leave youth unprotected from temptation. In the 1830s Abner Kneeland had been charged with blasphemy for words that incorporated sexualized images. In the 1870s Comstock saw blasphemous words by freethinkers as threatening to weaken the shield against obscenity.[14]

Religion stood hand in hand with marriage as the primary bastions protecting human beings from their own worst selves. The harm of the fourth framework was obvious. Advocates of free love—"free lusters," as Comstock called them—uttered dangerous doctrines. "With them, marriage is bondage; love is lust; celibacy is suicide; while fidelity to marriage vows is a relic of barbarism." They oppose "all restraints which keep boys and girls, young men and maidens pure and chaste, which prevent our homes from being turned into voluntary brothels. . . . Nothing short of turning the whole human family loose to run wild like the beasts of the forest, will satisfy the demands of the leaders and publishers of this literature." With such a sense of the danger of free-love writings, Comstock could elide them with obscenity. They became, in his words, "vile," "foul," the stuff of a "smut-dealer." In this respect, Comstock differed from those opposing obscenity in an earlier era. His predecessors may have hated free-love doctrines, but they tolerated their expression and understood the difference between them and the writings of the sporting press. Marx Edgeworth Lazarus had published his works in the 1850s without fear of legal prosecution.[15]

Comstock's statements are in contrast to those of the pre–Civil War period in two other aspects. Comstock focused on the responsibility of society, not individual parents or young people. Like the New England town writ large, the society must be cleansed so that vulnerable youth can remain sexually innocent. Comstock did the work of God and Christ in trying to rid the culture of all sexually explicit material, and he faced forces of ever-greater strength. Comstock's reports dwell on the growing power of the mails made possible by changes in transportation and the economy. As Comstock's statements put it, "The mails are the great arteries of communication—mighty thoroughfares leading up to all our homes and institutions of learning. The sanctity of the seal is the cloak of security to the villain." The much-vaunted privacy of the mails now becomes what made it so dangerous: "It goes everywhere and is secret." This gave special meaning to his job as special agent in the United States Post Office. With power to confiscate immoral matter in the mails and arrest those sending it, Comstock stood at the center of the

"North Interior View of the New York Post Office," Nassau Street, lithograph by Endicott, 1844. © Museum of the City of New York.

communications system. Using the power of the state and riding the rails, he was the moral crusader to stop agents of Satan from spreading the disease of obscenity that was attacking and destroying the nation's youth.[16]

As physiological writers wrote of the health and disease of the body, they often asserted the need to bring discussion of the body into the cleansing light. Disease provided one of the governing metaphors for Comstock and the Society for the Suppression of Vice. An early report stated that evil men, trafficking in obscene materials, working in stealth in hundreds of schools and thousands of homes, "have succeeded in injecting a virus more destructive to the innocency and purity of youth . . . than can be the most deadly disease to the body." In discussing the campaign against obscenity Comstock and his allies added to "virus" the words "plague," "rats," "deadly poison," and "contagion." Comstock and the society linked darkness with dirt and epidemics. Carriers of disease seek concealment; they "hate the

In this frontispiece to Anthony Comstock, *Frauds Exposed* (New York, 1880), the New York post office is represented as both the receiver and the distributor of obscene matter put through the mail. "Depositing Obscene Books. Rear View of the New York Post Office. Receiving His Mail." Words on the bags at left of center image: "FRAUD, BOGUS, SAWDUST"; on the bags at right: "OBSCENE BOOKS, VILE PAMPHLETS, FRAUD, SAWDUST, LOTTERY."

light." New York was the critical locus as the primary place breeding the plague. The U.S. mails were the dark passage carrying and spreading the contagion. Because of the privacy secured by the seals protecting mail, the post office was the hidden, dark tunnel, and those sending erotic material in the mail were those working in stealth. "The insidious nature of the traffic is one of its most dangerous features. It seeks darkness, it practices concealment, it lives only by deception." In addition to the secrecy of the mails, there was the private nature of the materials received. To Comstock privacy was equated with shame. Receivers of erotica conceal "their guilty acquisitions, and the poison silently spreads through families, schools, and whole villages like an invisible malaria, and hundreds are plague-stricken before the guardians of morals are aware of the danger."[17]

Who is to fight this enemy that prints and sends erotic materials? "Should some fiend attempt to introduce into a city or a nation an incurable disease, infallibly contagious, every citizen would spring to the rescue: the human fiend who shall attempt to infuse a fatal virus into the families and schools of the land must be pursued with a sleepless vigilance, until he is silent within prison walls." It is the task of the Society for the Suppression of Vice and its fearless agent to provide that "sleepless vigilance." The crusader Comstock springs into action.[18]

At a national level the virus of erotica is spread through the mails, but locally it moves in many ways. Here the reports of the society are helpful to the historian in giving sites in New York where erotic materials were sold in the 1870s, conveying a good deal about the trade:

> A man takes his stand on the sidewalk where he displays and sells perfectly proper books and pictures and studies his customers. When he discovers a guileless country youth, or some reckless city lad, whom he judges he may trust, he lures him into an adjoining hallway, exhibits and sells at an enormous price his obscene matter. Another, a sexton of a church, manufactures his licentious photographs in a room separated from the parish school only by folding doors, employs men or boys to sell them on the street as they walk about in crowded thoroughfares. A dealer in jewelry passing among the trade supplies the young men with libidinous microscopic charms. Still others, frequenting the steps of banking houses in Wall and Broad streets, furnish the sons of the wealthy classes with expensive specimens of the highest licentious art. Clerks in book and picture stores eke out their meagre salaries by the clandestine sale of forbidden wares. Newsboys on railroads, porters in steamboats and hotels, boys and young men in schools and colleges, all spread the contagion, and in such stealthy form as oftentimes to escape detection.[19]

In addition to these routes, teachers posed a special danger. In one particular case, a man teaching French in leading schools, including the famed Packard's Seminary, enticed boys around the Y.M.C.A. and Cooper's Institute. He exhibited in secret to his pupils the "vilest books, pictures and articles ever made . . . some . . . brought from France!"[20]

In the physiology and psychology of Comstock and the Society for the Suppression of Vice, there is no middle ground, no possibility of a developmental process by which children learn to control their own appetites and moderate their own behavior. One can see this in the discussions of alcohol in Comstock's writings, which insist that it must be completely banished from the house. Although parents may be able to shield their young from excess within the protected family circle, "this practice of supplying your children with stimulants in the home forms an appetite which outside they will indulge to excess." The danger of alcohol is not only its capacity to destroy health. It weakens the resistance to lust, contributing to youth's destruction by lowering his defenses against debauchery. "Intemperance strikes by means of the appetite, destroying nerve and tissue; natural affection and filial love are drowned; will-power is deadened till it almost fails to act; and it imparts a weakness that renders the victim more open to all other vices." A taste for alcohol must never be cultivated, because it cannot be controlled.[21]

Sexual knowledge is similar to alcohol. Introduce a little, and lust gets out of hand. Boys and girls need to be kept ignorant of sex. Parents make the mistake of keeping light literature in their own libraries and allowing their children to read it. These books, while "not always vicious or criminal," have the power to "pervert the taste of the young and rob the child of a desire for study." Their real harm is that they can "pave the way for that which is worse." From light literature, young people go to newspaper crime stories and the half-dime novels and story papers that do real harm. These inform the young of the evils of the world. They provide scenarios that young boys imitate as they begin lives of crime. Children need to be protected from the popular press—dime novels, boys' and girls' weeklies, sporting journals, the police gazettes—that incite them to lust and crime. They should not have access to scientific information. "There is great danger. This evil is found everywhere. Like the plagues of Egypt it has crept into homes; the mails were formerly literally loaded down with these devil-traps for the young."[22]

Comstock attempted to set out in a logical order the various ways that innocent youths were lured into lives of debauchery, alcoholism, and crime in his book *Traps for the Young*. It did not sort out young people by social class or sex. It put together the temptations in the paths of young clerks, of youthful workers in the Bowery, and of middle- and upper-class children in boarding schools and colleges. The one common characteristic of these young people is that, like the youthful clerks of the 1840s, they were not shielded by parental guardianship.

As the account moved through the list of temptations of nineteenth-century society, it left little unexplored. The theater leads urban boys astray. In Brooklyn a thousand boys go to the theater each night. "Scenes of bloodshed, of domestic infidelity, of atrocities and lewdness that surpass the worst stories, are enacted by painted wretches, whose highest boast is shame, and who seek loud applause by the most ribald jokes." Connected with barrooms and with brothels, theaters are "recruiting stations for hell." Like the moral reformers of the 1830s or Y.M.C.A. ministers of the 1850s and 1860s, this report leaves little to the imagination: "Our youth become inflamed with lust. . . . Often they go directly from these playhouses to the brothel, or if they return home it is to dream over the obscene and cursed spectacles they have witnessed." Such boys become debauchers or customers of prostitutes. They die of venereal disease.[23]

Other, more protected boys with no access to public amusements are destroyed by obscene literature. Introduced to erotic images and words, they sicken and die from masturbatory insanity. "This cursed business of obscene literature works beneath the surface, and like a canker worm, secretly eats out the moral life and purity of our youth, and they droop and fade before their parents' eyes." The curious boy takes a look at a forbidden book sent to him through the mail. He "breaks the seal and lets the monster loose." Tempted by the Devil, the boy takes a second look. "Then a mighty force from within is let loose. Passions that had slumbered or lain dormant are awakened." Once the image is introduced, it "imprints upon the mind of the youth, visions that throughout life curse the man or woman. Like a panorama, the imagination seems to keep this hated thing before the mind, until it wears its way deeper and deeper, plunging the victim into practices that he loathes." Unlike other vices, the secret ones the boy practices cannot be seen by others. Comstock restates the familiar story of the healthy boy who returns from school "with pale cheeks, lustreless and sunken eyes, enervated body, moody, nervous, and irritable—a moral wreck—and the parents mourn 'that the child has studied too hard.' "[24]

It was a well-worn tale told by many writers, beginning with Luther Bell in the 1830s. But now the practice of masturbation is never named, and there is a single, clear cause. What had to an earlier generation of writers been one of the many incitements to masturbation became for Comstock and the Society for the Suppression of Vice its principal explanation: obscene publications that introduce the innocent youth to sexual knowledge. The erotic book "breeds lust. Lust defiles the body, debauches the imagination, corrupts the mind, deadens the will, destroys the memory, sears the conscience, hardens the heart, and damns the soul. It unnerves the arm, and steals away the elastic step."[25]

Comstock's report also follows familiar paths as he discusses the risks to girls. As with his predecessors in the reform literature, Comstock states that the fearful outcome for girls is less masturbation than awakened sexuality, debauchery, and ruin. Despite good parents, girls may have been led to temptation by the actions of an evil nurse or by the wrong children's literature. Contributing to their ruin are contraceptive articles, advertised and sent through the mail, that encourage them to have sex—or, in language familiar to readers since the 1840s, serve as "an incentive to crime to young girls and women." The evil agent can also be abortionists' advertisements sent through the mail. Obscene literature in the hands of girls leads directly to the brothel: it is "the favorite agency of the evil one to recruit these dens. City houses of ill fame, in many instances, are filled with the daughters of country homes."[26]

Seemingly protected daughters of prosperous parents are also threatened by the contraceptive literature and abortionists' advertisements. Girls from Christian homes, sheltered by loving parents who chose good boarding schools for them, become the prey of evil advertisers who send them literature that leads to their downfall. "Circulars of death-dealing articles of a most infamous character" are sent unsolicited to innocent girls, whose names are listed in the school's catalogue or given by corrupt postal clerks. Here the fear, not fully articulated, was that girls would be seduced and abandoned by libertines and led to the abortionist's perilous knife. Comstock reported that a professor at a New England college for women told him of three young women "in one of our most celebrated female colleges, who were ruined by the vile things found in their possession." As with the writers of the earlier antimasturbation literature, young people in schools and colleges are at particular risk. Away from family governance, they are at the mercy of purveyors of obscene material. These evil merchants take advantage of the schools' published lists of students and send materials through the mails to the named students. Young people read and are ruined.[27]

The result of this literary poison, cast into the very fountains of social life, is found everywhere. It is infecting the pure life and heart of our youth. They are becoming weak-minded, vapid, sentimental, lustful, criminal. Parents are mourning over the distaste of their children for all that is sensible and useful. The teacher finds study to be irksome to them; romantic tales, narratives of love, lust, hate, revenge and murder are to their taste. They assimilate what they read, and so down, down our youth go, weaker and weaker in all the *mental* and *moral* elements of true manhood and womanhood.

Corrupt thoughts, desires and aims supplant native innocence. Virtue flies out of the window; vice flies in and takes full possession. We condemn the man who deals out liquid poison to the unhappy drunkard. He stands a nobleman far above the miserable miscreant who supplies the youth with the demoralizing venom contained in many dime novels, flashy periodicals, sporting newspapers and other obscene publications. Let fathers, mothers and teachers watch closely over the pockets, desks and rooms of their children. Be sure that the imagery and seeds of moral death are not in your houses and schools.[28]

All of these words—the emphasis is intentional—were part of the rhetorical package of the nineteenth century that linked the new physiology of the body and its sexual functioning to the need for reform. Sylvester Graham and other critics of the culture saw the era as prematurely sexualizing young people and throwing temptation in their way. He and his followers began with the individual and called for personal control of bodily practices, impulses, and desires. The growth of a youthful society of clerks living independently posed new risks in a dynamic urban economy where commercial services emerged to appeal to them. Alongside boardinghouses came brothels, saloons, gaming houses, and stores catering to their tastes for commercial sex, entertainment, drink, sporting goods, and books. Aware of these developments, early reformers worked largely outside the state. Female moral reformers sought to attack prostitution and sexual license through houses of refuge and a social boycott of licentious men. In New York the Y.M.C.A. offered a counterworld of Christian endeavor and healthful recreation. Both reform efforts drew on the language of reform physiology as it was being absorbed by evangelical religion, its notions of health and disease entwined with the conflict between God and Satan.

Those opposed to printed materials as obscene could turn to the courts, and in some cases their efforts were rewarded with prison sentences and fines that effectively suppressed sexually explicit words and images. The courts acted erratically, however, and often only when moved by political considerations. However, common-law practices developed in state courts before the Civil War proved important to suppression in later generations.

There were some efforts in the antebellum years to get new laws passed. Influenced by the New England tradition of community oversight, moral reformers sought a range of laws to control behavior and limit temptation. Beginning in the 1860s, the Y.M.C.A. of New York fought for state measures against obscene materials. The Civil War opened a new avenue as Congress proved willing to protect soldiers from obscene literature by making it a crime to send it through the mails. And in 1873, the Y.M.C.A. of New York successfully constructed and lobbied for a federal bill to prevent obscene materials, birth control articles, and advertisements for abortion from using the U.S. Postal Service. In addition, the association got the position of special agent and the appointment of Comstock to fill it, elevating their campaign director to a national platform. Whether crudely put or placed within the language of conservative physiology, Comstock's words carried weight.

Comstock's campaign bridged old and new. He and his advisers in the Society for the Suppression of Vice brought a new understanding of the power of the state and an awareness of the dangers of contemporary developments to the rhetoric of evangelical Christianity and physiological reform. Their combined statements blended the new authority of numbers with the arguments of an earlier era. It was a powerful brew that resonated with the era. Although one should not attribute too much might or influence to a single man or organization, undoubtedly Comstock's work and words— buttressed by S.S.V. ghostwriters—contributed to the proliferation of state anti-obscenity statutes that followed the 1873 act of Congress. And in the federal criminal courts that tried cases under the 1873 statute, judges and juries could find in Comstock's crusade clear justification for the suppression of obscenity.

18

Convictions

What Comstock believed and said mattered because behind him was the power of the law. He sought to use words to bolster public opinion to gain convictions, raise contributions for the Society for the Suppression of Vice, and support the new laws. Despite his frustrations and defeats, his crusade brought a major victory. Comstock gained important convictions for word crimes under the 1873 federal statute prohibiting the mailing of obscene materials. His successes were in places that mattered, where legal precedent carried weight.

To inquire into Comstock's triumph requires two chapters and a consideration of the cases of Edward Bliss Foote, Ezra Heywood, and D. M. Bennett. It also requires a return to the common law of obscene libel. An 1879 appellate ruling elevated the common-law practices developed earlier in New York State court cases against obscenity and, to all intents and purposes, declared the Comstock Law constitutional. As these cases were working through the courts, a clear legal opposition coalesced that argued that the Comstock Law was unconstitutional because it violated the First Amendment.

None of the three important cases involve the booksellers of Ann Street. In the 1870s, as in earlier decades, the distributors of outright erotica tended to abscond or face their sentences quietly. They never challenged their sentences through the court system or the pardon process. They were often poor. They were also too marginal or believed themselves too scorned to get a hearing, and, to read the commentary at the time, they were probably right. Most women and many older men of the middle class shared a settled public animus against sporting culture and regarded the erotica associated with it as obscene.

The significant trials involve publishers of material in a different vein, physiological reform and free love. Writers such as Madame Beach and Thomas Low Nichols had blurred the boundaries among physiological, reformist, commercial, and racy texts. The three publishers and writers brought into Comstock's net and discussed here—Edward Bliss Foote, Ezra Heywood, and D. M. Bennett—harked back to an earlier era, however. In many ways they were latter-day versions of Frederick Hollick, Marx Edgeworth Lazarus, and Robert Dale Owen.

I

The 1873 federal act for the "Suppression of Trade in, and Circulation of, Obscene Literature and Articles of Immoral Use," commonly known as the Comstock Law, made obscenity "nonmailable matter." It was a misdemeanor to send through the mails material that treated sexual matters in a manner perceived by a jury to be obscene. If found guilty in court, the sender could be fined and jailed. At its origin, the law was widely understood to target the erotic reading material of sporting life, especially as it was being sent to the young. But the 1873 law did more than bar these printed materials from the mails. What received little notice at the time—until it led to prosecutions—was that the statute greatly expanded the domain of obscenity. Included in nonmailable matter were books and pamphlets written by physicians for a lay audience that discussed the reproductive organs and their functions if they contained birth control information. In the 1873 statute all contraceptive articles were declared obscene, as were advertisements for abortion. Moreover, by judicial decision, some of the reform literature dealing with the marriage relation, divorce, and free love fell under this same onus. Thus publication of texts of physiological reform and works articulating the fourth framework was in jeopardy.

The reach of the statute became visible in 1876. On January 8, 1876, Comstock arrested Edward Bliss Foote, the well-known eclectic physician, who had made a career of treating chronic disorders and writing popular books on physiology. By his own account *Medical Common Sense,* revised in 1860 and 1864, had sold more than 250,000 copies. *Plain Home Talk,* an expanded and retitled version first issued in 1870, sold more than 500,000 copies. In 1872 he

Edward Bliss Foote, frontispiece, *Plain Home Talk*, 1873. Countway
Library of Medicine.

incorporated the Murray Hill Publishing Company, which published *Plain
Home Talk* and *Science in Story,* designed to teach young readers anatomy and
physiology. Murray Hill Publishing was only a name, as Foote made all contracts in his own name and paid all bills. His principal obligations, other than
for his own wants, were for paper and drugs, and they were paid regularly.
The two houses that Foote owned on Lexington Avenue and Twenty-eighth
Street were each worth approximately $30,000, although on both there were
mortgages of approximately half their value. A son, Edward Bond Foote,
who was a regularly trained physician, assisted him in his work.[1]

Foote was legally vulnerable not as the writer of a book but as its distributor. Books caused the arrest of booksellers, not authors. For example, Leander Fox & Son handled James Ashton's *The Book of Nature,* considered in
Chapter 14. Comstock visited the store on Canal Street, wrote a decoy letter
ordering the book, and arrested father and son. In 1879 Samuel Colgate, president of the New York Society for the Suppression of Vice, declared that "we
have yet to have the first report from any responsible and reputable physician, or druggist, or bookseller saying that their practice or business had
been injured through the action of the Society." The key words here are
"responsible and reputable." Newspaper editor D. M. Bennett insisted that
wealthy, regular physicians, druggists, and booksellers were left alone. These

included, according to Bennett, Colgate himself, whose company advertised that "vaseline, charged with four or five grains of salicylic acid, will destroy spermatozoa, without injury to the uterus or vagina." They did not include Foote, an irregular physician whose popularity and success caused allopaths to be jealous.[2]

Edward Bliss Foote believed that persons needed to understand their own bodies, including their sexual organs, and develop healthful ways of living. Though moderate in some of his views on sexual matters, he upheld the necessity and value of sexual intercourse for both men and women. Beginning in the 1858 edition of *Medical Common Sense,* Foote discussed birth control options. In the 1864 edition, he added both his own views on the value of family planning and specific contraceptive recommendations. With *Plain Home Talk,* published beginning in 1870, Foote omitted specific birth control advice in the text but suggested that readers might request his pamphlet. This reticence was countered by outspokenness on another front: the book contained long sections on comparative marriage customs condoning Mormon polygamy and Oneidan group marriage and defending free love.[3]

Foote was a strong advocate of women's expanded rights and worked to increase the number of women physicians. He attended the May 1872 convention of the Equal Rights Party and supported Victoria Woodhull's candidacy for president of the United States. Woodhull's weekly, in turn, commented favorably on his works, including a positive review in 1872 of *Plain Home Talk.* In 1873 Foote paid one-fourth of the fine that Susan B. Anthony incurred for voting.[4]

During Woodhull's arrest and trial Foote was silent. Perhaps he sensed his own vulnerability. He should have. Comstock seems to have taken particular delight in arresting Victoria Woodhull's supporters. In some ways Comstock must have seen replays of the drama of Victoria Woodhull in the trials of her champions, but this time in a court where he could win. Foote's specific offense, as listed in Comstock's arrest records, was "Mailing Obscene pamphlet, and advertisement of obscene pamphlet & article to prevent conception." Comstock's remarks were candid in stating his political animus against Foote, who had opposed the 1872 New York State law and after its passage urged its veto. Comstock wrote that Foote "bitterly opposed the Act of Congress of Mar 3/73. & state laws. . . . He tried to amend law of state through Mr Watts of Assembly & failed."[5]

According to Comstock's remarks, he arrested Foote because in the edition of *Plain Home Talk* then available, Foote "advertised Confidential pamphlet to married. Any one writing for pamphlet he would send a written note to, giving price &c of Womb Veil. He kept his stock up at So. Norwalk Ct. & sent up twice a month to fill orders." The offending pamphlet was *Words in Pearl,* its name derived from the very small type that allowed it to be mailed in a regular letter envelope under seal. The pamphlet provided answers to twenty questions. Foote had tried to be careful not to run afoul of the 1873 federal statute and New York State law. In his own defense, Foote stated that he had never "circulated this pamphlet broad-cast in the thoroughfares or in other ways forced it upon the attention of unwilling readers." While at his trial the prosecution had stressed that the pamphlet was "a dime publication which could be purchased by the youth as well as the adult," his own intention was to keep it small and sealed in an envelope "so that it might only be perused by the enquirer." The freethinking editor D. M. Bennett stated that "the pamphlet was nothing more than advice which is orally given by every well-known practitioner to his inquiring patients." Although Foote's lawyer had advised him that the state would not move against doctors, Foote knew he was vulnerable because he was an irregular physician.[6]

Bail was set at $5,000, and on July 11, 1876, Foote was tried in the federal court of the Southern District of New York under Judge Charles L. Benedict. Foote's lawyer, Thomas Harland, argued for his client on the most narrow grounds. The indictment had not given "a definite description of the pamphlet alleged to have been mailed." The statute had specified "notice," and that clearly did not include a slip of paper giving an answer to a specific question enclosed in a sealed envelope. Judge Benedict answered each objection. He had ruled many times in court that an indictment need not describe the obscene material. "It is neither necessary nor proper to pollute the record by a detailed description of obscene matter." To Benedict, silence in the record was useful for "it prevents the proceedings from being the vehicle of spreading the obscenity before the public." The protection of the seals, long a treasured element of the United States Post Office, could be violated. The U.S. mails should not be "the effectual aid of persons engaged in a nefarious business, by means used to distribute their obscene wares." That a letter was sealed did not protect it from "the criminality of the act." Finally, a letter sent in response to an inquiry was a "notice" just as much as was a printed broadside. Responding more generally to public criticism, Judge Benedict stated that under the current law "medical advice given by a physician in reply to the inquiry of a patient" was not excluded. This was necessary because if all medical men were allowed to send information by the mail, it would be "an easy way of nullifying the law." By stating that "other means of communication may be resorted to by physicians," Benedict conferred privilege on the individual office visit.[7]

Judge Benedict stated at the sentencing that "many persons had called to see him in regard to the case, and he understood many patients might suffer if a sentence of imprisonment was rendered." As a result he suspended sentence on the first count, for which Foote "was liable to ten years' imprisonment." Benedict ordered Foote to pay a fine of $3,500; with lawyer's fees and court costs, Foote estimated that the episode had cost him $5,000. It was often argued by those supporting tougher obscenity laws and enforcement that suppression did not amount to censorship. In Foote's case, as in George Wilkes's before him, it certainly did. Foote's suspended sentence meant that in the years that followed, if he had been found to have violated the law a second time, he could have been sent to jail for ten years without trial.[8]

At one level Foote was silenced: his popular medical books ceased to contain directions for securing contraceptive materials. His 1876 effort to alter state law prohibiting birth control was hamstrung by his arrest and trial. Yet at another level, he became galvanized. He published a spate of books and pamphlets advocating his ideas, including *A Fable of the Spider and the Bees,* an allegory written as a children's tale that directly opposed the Comstock Law. He portrayed Anthony Comstock as a venomous spider in the American garden. Comstock spun a web with the collaboration of sleek, fat bees, the members of Congress. In attempting to keep out commercial erotica, the predatory moths, the spider created a web that caught many useful insects who fertilized the garden and made it fruitful, writers such as himself.[9]

In April 1876 he started his own periodical, *Dr. Foote's Health Monthly,* edited with his son. It combined health news with politics. As others writing on health, birth control, or sex reform were arrested under the obscenity law, Foote publicized their cases. Over and over he argued that laws intended to protect the society from erotica were being misapplied. As he put it in 1876, in words that conveyed middle-class repugnance against sporting literature, "How absurd then to use laws enacted for the suppression of obscene literature in suppressing those physiological and hygienic publications which are calculated to antidote the poison inflicted on the community by prints and pictures which are really and beyond question obscene!" He wrote about reproduction under the language of "stirpiculture," or scientific propagation of human beings, as named by John Humphrey Noyes. He thought about intervening in human reproduction in the ways that those in scientific agriculture were intervening in the animal kingdom, expressing it in this fashion: "Good thorough weeding is in order.—We remove the weeds in gardens which crowd out the vegetables or take the nutritive qualities of the soil from them. We can do some human weeding; not by destroying worthless specimens of the genus homo but by seeing to it that only good and valuable ones are allowed to be born." He imagined finding, as he put it, some "harmless medicament" to prevent human ovulation.[10]

Although Foote was able to afford the heavy penalties imposed by the courts, he knew others were not, and he gave them material aid and lawyers for their defense. He joined with others to create the National Defense Association to work for modification of the laws and defend those unjustly brought before the courts. In the years that followed, he published his monthly, many books and pamphlets, new editions of his guides to health, and retained a thriving medical practice. In 1894 he agreed to run as a candidate for the House of Representatives on the Populist ticket.[11]

What Edward Bliss Foote learned in 1876 was that he could continue to write as a physiological reformer as long as he abided by the new rules. What had been allowed in the 1850s, as contraception became a business, was now forbidden. Writers could discuss the reproductive organs and their functions but could no longer give birth control information in print or sell contraceptive devices openly on the market. Foote adapted, while waging a valiant fight against the new order. He fought the rules directly and openly and defended those who were arrested under them. His own writings after 1876, however, did not place him on the wrong side of the law.

2

Ezra Heywood was a different story. He, too, came out of the 1850s, but, unlike Foote, he never seemed to notice that the world around him had changed. What Comstock tried to teach him (one cannot say that Heywood "learned") was that the language in which sexual reform was waged in the pre–Civil War era was now illegal. On November 2, 1877, Anthony Comstock arrested the veteran reformer Ezra Heywood at a free-love convention in Boston. The charge was sending obscene matter through the mails, a violation of the 1873 federal statute. Heywood had written, printed, and distributed *Cupid's Yokes,* a pamphlet arguing that sexual relations between men and women were subject only to individual self-government and were no business of the state. In addition, he was charged with mailing *Sexual Physiology* by the water-cure reformer R. T. Trall.

A native of Princeton, Massachusetts, the forty-eight-year-old Heywood had been an unconventional radical since his graduation from Brown University in 1856. After a brief stint as a Congregational minister, he became an agent for the Massachusetts Anti-Slavery Society and lectured widely on abolition, following the lead of William Lloyd Garrison. When his pacifism caused him to oppose the Civil War, he lost his following. In 1865, he married Angela Tilton, one of three radical daughters of Lucy Tilton, an anarchist and free-love exponent. Beginning in 1863, Heywood came under the influence of Josiah Warren and came to see capitalism as analogous to slavery. After the war Ezra and Angela Heywood advocated economic and labor reform, anarchism, and free love. In 1871 the two returned to the small Massachusetts town of Princeton and established the Co-operative Publishing Company. They began issuing the monthly reform paper *The Word* in 1872. In May 1872, they traveled to New York City to the Equal Rights Party convention and, like Foote, supported Victoria Woodhull's presidential bid. In addition, Ezra Heywood wrote and published many reform tracts, including *Cupid's Yokes,* first printed in 1876.[12]

To understand Heywood's arrest and its significance, one must turn to *Cupid's Yokes.* What in it was considered obscene by Comstock, the district attorney, the judge, and the jury? Within its turgid prose, the pamphlet's

Ezra Heywood. Courtesy, Princeton (Mass.) Historical Society.

essential line of argument was the anarchist position that the state should have no part in confirming through marriage the love between a man and a woman. It was the responsibility of individuals to regulate their behavior, and any effort of the state to do so interfered with individual rights, destroyed desire ("the magnetic forces which induce unity"), eroded individual virtue, and cast confusion. Love, a blend of "esteem, benevolence, and passional attraction," was a mysterious force that could be destructive or could vanish as unaccountably as it came. Legally sanctified marriage, rather than protecting virtue, sanctioned male sexual coercion and allowed the "reeking licentiousness of marriage beds." The true goal for men and women was the "education of sexual desire and expression, and their subjection to reason." This was undermined by marriage, an institution that confirmed rather than confronted the "savage state" of contemporary society with its linked wrongs: "the lascivious instincts prevalent among men, the destructive courses imposed on women, and the frightful inroads of secret vice on the vitality of youth."[13]

Cupid's Yokes appeared five years after Heywood began *The Word,* his monthly newspaper. Many of the pamphlet's sentences are restatements of positions he had been taking, often in response to specific events, books, or criticism. Thus, threaded throughout Heywood's argument is a range of assertions. Some of the most interesting are statements, perhaps initiated by Angela Heywood, of women's sexual agency and the value for women of sexual experience. These waver in tone. At times, the dominant note is antagonism to male passion; at others, one senses an appreciation of the joys of sexual union. One intriguing element is the statement that monogamous marriage is man's law and that women, "again coming to the front," will create with men "better methods of sexual intercourse and reproduction . . . than exclusive male wisdom has yet invented." A consistent theme is the wrong of celibacy, as in this declaration: "The eye, the arm, or leg perishes by non-use; so without natural vent, exuberant sexual vitality wastes and destroys."[14]

The pamphlet contains a mélange of Heywood's views, including tirades against romantic literature's corrosive impact on real relationships and odd eugenic advice that seemed to remove childbearing from marriage or even love. ("No woman or man should have a second child by his or her marital partner, when there is another person, willing to assume the relation, by whom he or she can have a better child.") Since only sexual knowledge allows for wise choice, an opaque passage appears to argue for sexual experimentation and intimacy, including the practice of men and women routinely sleeping together. One confusing element is that Heywood himself did not equate such familiarities or the phrases "sleep together" or "sexual intercourse" with coitus, which he tended to call by the term "convulsive embraces."[15] His statements suggest that he advocated "male continence," the sexual practice of John Humphrey Noyes's Oneida community, male penetration without ejaculation. In Heywood's eyes, free love restored individual responsibility, including that of continence, and allowed true mutuality between men and women. His ideal was not promiscuity but committed relationships among equals, yokes designed by Cupid, not by the state.[16]

As perplexing as is much of Heywood's prose, a few sentences in *Cupid's Yokes* soar and provide enduring language for advocates of sexual freedom. In arguing that the right of individual judgment should be extended from politics and religion to sex, Heywood stated, "If government cannot justly determine what ticket we shall vote, what church we shall attend, or what books we shall read, by what authority does it watch at key-holes and burst open bed-chamber doors to drag lovers from sacred seclusion? Why should priests and magistrates supervise the sexual organs of citizens any more than the brain and stomach?" Continuing this line of thought, establishing an individual's lawful claim to his or her genital organs, Heywood wrote, "Who but the individual owners can rightly determine when, where and how they shall be used?"[17]

Heywood's words in *Cupid's Yokes* broke no new ground. In the heady days of reform agitation before the Civil War, Heywood's propositions had been the meat and drink of many a proselytizer for sexual reform and free love. To argue that Heywood's positions were well established, however, is not to state that they were generally accepted in the society. By the 1870s, evangelical Christians who had absorbed some of the concerns of the more conservative writers on sexuality and health were on the offensive. Free-love advocates, such as Heywood, now found themselves opposed by Comstock and his supporters. In 1877, Anthony Comstock looked upon Ezra and Angela Heywood with loathing. Comstock's arrest record contained this notation: "Heywood & Wife were holding a Free-love Convention in Nassau Hall Boston at time of arrest. As Comstock went in the Hall a News Dealer 'Gurney' by name was speaking & afterward Mrs Heywood. Both spoke of 'Sexual Intercourse' & used most vile & violent language. Heywood presiding. The Officer sat quietly till Silence was a crime & then arrested H. The audience were principally young men & the addresses were most beastly. H. published free-love books &c."[18]

In *Traps for the Young,* Comstock described attending the 1877 free-love convention. Looking at the audience of about 250 males, "I could see lust in every face." Angela Heywood spoke, delivering "the foulest address I ever heard. She seemed lost to all shame." Comstock noted that her speech delighted her audience. During her address, Ezra Heywood sat on the platform "puffed up with egotism." Disgusted, Comstock went outside for fresh air. He decided to get a policeman to stop the meeting but could find no one. Alone, with no one to aid him, he feared he might fail. "I prayed for strength to do my duty. . . . I knew God was able to help me. Every manly instinct cried out against my cowardly turning my back on this horde of lusters." He went back inside, and his disgust grew so intense that "I could not sit a moment longer." Ezra Heywood left the stage. Comstock moved in and arrested him.[19]

At this distance from the conflict, it is hard to see the source of Comstock's abhorrence in the book itself. *Cupid's Yokes* was not worded in a manner to attract eyes trained to detect "obscenity." The prosecution's copy of the pamphlet marked to bring particularly offensive passages to the attention of the jury does not include the important footnote in which Heywood set out the existing means of birth control.[20] None of these passages contains the vernacular terms that normally served as markers for "obscene" material. For example, the first marked passage states: "Since 'falling in love' is not always ascension, growth, (as it should be), but often degradation; as persons who meet in convulsive embraces may separate in deadly feuds,—sexual love here carrying invigorating peace, there desolating havoc, into domestic life,—intelligent students of sociology will not think the marriage institution a finality, but, rather, a device to be amended, or abolished, as enlightened moral sense may require."[21]

What is in *Cupid's Yokes,* however, are provocative paragraphs of a somewhat different nature. Heywood had taken up the cause of Victoria Woodhull despite his initial questions about her wisdom in attempting to ally Beecher with free love. The meeting at which Heywood was arrested was of the New England Free Love League, an association formed in 1873 to provide a forum for Victoria Woodhull in Boston when she was denied the use of established lecture halls. In *Cupid's Yokes* Heywood discussed the Beecher scandal case, the telling of which had provoked Woodhull's initial arrest in

1872. He denounced the arrests of Woodhull and others in her train. He labeled the 1873 statute the "National Gag Law." He declared Comstock "*a religious monomaniac,* whom the mistaken will of Congress and the lascivious fanaticism of the Young Men's Christian Association have empowered to use the Federal Courts to suppress free inquiry." Comstock was acutely aware of criticism, especially principled criticism. He was particularly sensitive to the attacks on him coming out of his arrest of Victoria Woodhull. From Comstock's perspective, Heywood was engaged in sheer defiance of the will of Congress. If Heywood's words in support of Woodhull and in opposition to Comstock did not cause Heywood's arrest, they certainly helped turn Comstock's attention to him.[22]

However self-referential was Comstock's move against Heywood, the special agent was acting within a context in which he had clear legal precedents. Legal scholars in the twentieth century have made much of the weakness of the legal basis for obscenity prosecutions and convictions under the 1873 Comstock Law.[23] In terms of First Amendment cases argued in the twentieth century, this argument has some merit. But the ground has shifted. In the nineteenth century, prior to Heywood's trial, the First Amendment was largely seen as protecting the rights of the states of the union against the federal government, not of citizens against government intrusion.[24] Moreover, when treating obscenity, the states drew on the traditions of common law derived from England. The traffic in domestic "obscene" materials, that is, those not coming from Europe, was understood before the Civil War as a matter for states (and through them, local communities) to regulate, as falling within the domain of their police powers. When the federal government began to flex its muscles after the Civil War and regulate the internal traffic in "obscene" materials, legal proceedings in federal court remained governed by the traditions well established in state courts, following common law.

The formal charge against Heywood was that in September 1877 he had mailed two obscene publications. Comstock, using the decoy name and address E. Edgewell, in Squam Village, New Jersey, asked for and received Trall's *Sexual Physiology* and Heywood's own *Cupid's Yokes.* Heywood was charged with violating the 1876 revision of the 1873 federal statute for the "Suppression of Trade in, and Circulation of, Obscene Literature and Articles of Immoral Use," which patched up loopholes in the 1873 law by slight changes of wording and the addition of the word "writing" to the list of types of obscene material that could be prohibited from the mails. At Heywood's trial on January 18 and 19, 1878, before Judge Daniel Clark of the U.S.

Circuit Court in Boston, the assistant district attorney sought to prove only two points: "that defendant sent the books through the mails in response to letters, and that the books were of the character indicated in the form of indictment read," that is, obscene.[25]

The federal statute of 1873, now revised, was still relatively new in 1878 and seldom invoked outside the federal courts in the state of New York.[26] What rules were to guide it? Judge Clark followed the precedents established in American state and local courts earlier in the nineteenth century. Despite the fact that he presided over a U.S. federal court dealing with a possible violation of a federal statute, Judge Clark turned to Thomas Starkie, the English writer of legal commentary on the common law of libel and slander for his script.

This explains many of the pronouncements made by Judge Clark. All the issues that the defense wanted to consider—What were Heywood's character and motive? Did physicians and men of sense judge his writings obscene? What constituted obscenity?—were ruled irrelevant. As the *Boston Globe* reported, "The two questions for the Court and jury he [the assistant district attorney] claimed to be, did the defendant mail the works as charged, and were they of an obscene character? He should object to the discussion of other questions, as he judged by the audience present there might be an attempt to discuss the peculiar tenets of the defendant." The eighteen to twenty witnesses gathered to testify to Heywood's character and motive were not allowed. Nor was any effort to discredit Comstock.

Heywood's lawyer was limited as he cross-examined Comstock. He was stopped by the judge when he queried Comstock about his knowledge of obscene books. Defense was not allowed to bring into the court "a very low book as representing the class that the statute was made to prevent the circulation of." The judge declared that "the book in question was to stand or fall by itself, as the law alone was to be taken to show the standing of the book, and the Court recognized no obscene book as a standard of obscenity." Nor would it allow expert testimony from witnesses. The obscenity of the work, the judge declared, "was the very question the jury had to decide and the opinions of other men were not to govern them in their deliberations. Certain medical books, which counsel for defense had proposed to introduce, were also excluded, on the general ground that the questions as to whether other books, having more or less resemblance to these, were obscene or not, could not be passed upon by the jury."

In its closing argument the defense attempted to establish what had been disallowed in the court testimony: that Heywood and his work bore no relation to the typical writer and publisher of materials designed for male erotic stimulation. Counsel stressed Heywood's character and reputation, the moral import of his books, and the importance of freedom of the press. "Being a man of education and of just repute as a reformer, [Heywood] was not likely to be engaged in any business open to the objections alleged in the indictment." He wrote, published, and sent through the mails books "of a useful and moral tendency," works of physiology written in language for the lay reader.

The assistant district attorney, in his close, replied that all the arguments made by Heywood's attorney—"Heywood's character, his reform work, and to defaming Comstock, and to the danger that we should not have a free press and free speech"—were extraneous issues, having "nothing to do with the case." The only matters were whether Heywood had sent the books through the mails and whether or not the books were obscene. As he turned to the books, he "commented upon the effect such pernicious doctrine would be likely to have upon boys and girls at school and others who had not reached the age of mature judgment, and read extracts from them to illustrate his point."

Judge Clark reaffirmed the prosecution's position. He went over the federal statute barring the mailing of obscenity for the jury. He first treated the question of whether Heywood had put the books into the mail either personally or by causing others to act. Then he turned to the trickier issue of what constituted obscenity. Here he, as others before and after him, was reduced to synonyms. "A book is obscene that is offensive to decency. A book is obscene which excites impure or lewd thoughts or is of an immoral tendency. A book is obscene that would incite the practice of impure desires." A book is obscene if any part of it is obscene. Finally, as if he were citing Starkie, the judge stated that Heywood's "honorable" intentions "had nothing to do with it. A man might be opposed to this doctrine maintained by defendant in his book and use the text and pictures in arguing against the doctrine, but he could not be allowed to send the work through the mail." He denied any comparison to other books, for they were not on trial. The jury was not to use themselves as the standard, answering the question as to whether the books would incite impure thoughts in their minds. The issue was not the minds of "men who would be likely to weigh the contents with mature judgment." They were to consider the potential effect of the books "upon the community, upon the home, upon happy children in the home." The judge then "quoted two paragraphs from one of the books, and asked the jury what could be more indecent than those." Although in a U.S. court the jury was to decide the "fact" of obscenity, custom still dictated that the judge could help it make that determination.

When it retired to the jury room for deliberation, the jury received for the first time the two books for perusal. It weighed each separately. In its decision, the jury declared that although Trall's book was not obscene, *Cupid's Yokes* was and that Heywood was guilty for having put it into the mail.

19

Constitutionality and Resistance:
Bennett, Benedict, and Blatchford

The conviction of Ezra Heywood spurred opposition to the Comstock Law on the ground that it violated constitutional freedoms. The lawyers for free-thought publisher D. M. Bennett took the constitutional argument into the courtroom. When they appealed Bennett's conviction, a highly regarded judge confirmed the power of a federal court to enforce the Comstock Law with its broad powers and wide scope. As the 1870s came to a close, Judge Samuel Blatchford established that through regulation of the postal service the federal government could manage the conversation about sexuality that had animated American culture since the late 1820s. At the same time, Bennett's defense elevated the countertradition that posed the important constitutional challenge to the Comstock Law. And just as the court drew on the traditions of the common law, so, too, did defenders of freedom of speech inherit the legacy of opposition to it.

I

Heywood's lawyers mounted an appeal on grounds that the Comstock Law violated the First Amendment's guarantee of freedom of speech. Heywood's appeal was delayed until the Supreme Court rendered a decision in *Ex parte Jackson*. In this landmark 1878 case the Supreme Court ruled that the federal law prohibiting lottery advertisements from the mails was constitutional—as, in passing, was the 1873 statute barring obscenity from the mails—on the grounds that to prevent using the mails for "matter deemed injurious to the public morals" did not violate freedom of the press. As Justice Stephen J. Field stated, "The object of Congress [had] not been to interfere with the freedom of the press, or with any other rights of the people; but to refuse its facilities for the distribution of matter deemed injurious to the public morals." Although what went through the mails was lottery advertisements, not materials determined obscene, this decision was taken to uphold the constitutionality of the Comstock Law. Following *Ex parte Jackson,* the judges denied Heywood an appeal, and he was sentenced to two years in the Dedham jail and a fine of $100.[1]

On August 1, 1878, a group of Heywood's supporters sponsored an indignation meeting, attended by an estimated four to six thousand persons. It brought to the podium of Faneuil Hall an important group of protesters, some of whom would carry the issues far beyond Heywood's arrest. For several of the organizers, the fight for Heywood was a continuation of the struggle for Victoria Woodhull. The indignation meeting was initiated by Benjamin Tucker, one of Woodhull's most fervent supporters a few years before, and he called on those, such as Laura Kendrick, with whom he had been closely allied.[2] Reformers in Heywood's mold, Tucker and Kendrick espoused economic freedom, anarchy, and free love, and their speeches reflected their commitments. But several of those participating in the evening meeting had a different agenda. They were freethinkers who had created the National Defense Association to confront the Comstock Law on different grounds.

When evangelical Christians in the post–Civil War era organized to inscribe the United States as a Christian nation in the Constitution through an amendment, they inspired strong opposition. The liberal Christian Francis E. Abbot led a petition campaign against the amendment. He had helped to found the Free Religious Association and the newspaper the *Index.* Freethinkers created their own organizations and publications to promote rationalism and oppose evangelical Christian influences in government. Large crowds came to hear orator Robert G. Ingersoll, a declared agnostic and nationally respected figure. Although freethinkers could not unite on whether or not there was a God, they did come together to support secularism and to advocate high ethical and moral standards. No reliable numbers are available, but one scholar has estimated that in the late nineteenth century there were roughly thirty to forty thousand freethinkers and about a hundred thousand active sympathizers out of a larger body of perhaps a twelfth of the population who opposed religion. Although free thought claimed important leaders in women's rights, such as Elizabeth Cady Stanton and Matilda Joslyn Gage, men predominated in the movement and often reflected conventional notions of gender roles. Never solidly fused, freethinkers divided along the fault lines of free love and free speech.[3]

In 1876 Abbot and Ingersoll helped found the National Liberal League, committed to making the United States a secular state. It brought together a spectrum of reformers, joining figures from the past, such as Robert Dale Owen and Stephen Pearl Andrews, to those who would be important in the future, such as Edward Bliss Foote, D. M. Bennett, and Thaddeus B. Wakeman. Initially the league joined in the fight for freedom of expression against the Comstock Law, but it quickly divided into two camps. On the one hand, there were those who sought outright repeal of the Comstock Law. On the other, there were those who proposed its modification through a compromise that retained the bar on obscenity yet allowed, somehow, free expression. The National Liberal League circulated a petition against the Comstock Act, urging Congress to repeal or modify it to protect "freedom of the press . . . [and] conscience." While the document did not condone obscenity, it paid attention to the wrongful expansions of the rubric that, in its words, had been made "without the knowledge of your petitioners, and, they believe, without the knowledge of any great number of the citizens of the United States" to include physiological texts and works advocating reform. A federal law to prohibit obscenity was unnecessary because states had effective remedies. Signed by somewhere between fifty and seventy thousand persons, the petition was presented to Congress by Representative Benjamin Butler of Massachusetts in February 1878.

The National Liberal League's petition was taken up in hearing by the House Committee on the Revision of the Laws. Anthony Comstock, supported by Samuel Colgate, an industrialist and leader of the New York Society for the Suppression of Vice, attended the committee meeting. Comstock once again brought his highly charged exhibit of erotica and again appealed for the protection of children in boarding schools. The committee, declaring that "the Post-Office was not established to carry instruments of vice, or obscene writings, indecent pictures, or lewd books," denied the National Liberal League's petition. It never made it to the House floor.[4]

Ingersoll and some of the better-known liberals were clearly frightened that the taint of "obscenity" would harm their cause.[5] They sought to reconcile free speech with barring obscenity, but this proved to be a difficult trick.

In 1878, at the National Liberal League convention in Syracuse, those seeking to modify the law drafted an alternative bill. It allowed the prohibition from the mail (with accompanying fines and imprisonment for offenders) of obscene materials "manifestly designed or mainly tending, to corrupt the morals of youth" but protected any "printed book, argument, essay, treatise, or disquisition, put forth in sincerity and in good faith, and in which no obscene words, phrases, or pictures shall be employed, although its doctrines or sentiments, if carried into practice, would have a bad influence on society or government."[6]

On June 12, 1878, meeting in the office of D. M. Bennett, a less timid group assembled to form the National Defense Association, dedicated to protect those prosecuted under the federal Comstock Law and related state laws. Edward Bliss Foote helped finance the effort. Albert L. Rawson, a leading freethinker, became president; Foote's son Edward Bond Foote, secretary. Although this group assisted the National Liberal League's effort to seek revision or repeal of the Comstock Law, it focused on individuals and their legal battles. The National Defense Association took the lead in circulating a petition for Heywood's release.[7]

At the 1878 indignation meeting to support Heywood, the National Defense Association's voice was held in tension with older approaches. For example, veteran reformer Elizur Wright spoke for those who opposed the fact that "a detective, employed by a bigoted and aggressive religious sect, traps into the mail by a lie . . . a book sold openly, earnestly discussing the most vital question of society." He argued that Heywood had the motives of a reformer and stated the position that "the criminality of words must lie in the intent with which they are used." The judge in Heywood's case, however, was acting from a different script. Arguments such as Wright's against seeming violations of procedure were not effective, for American court practice in dealing with obscenity was rooted in English common law and strengthened by a body of precedent. The specific points being contested had been argued unsuccessfully in American courts at least since the early 1840s. Attempts to combat the Comstock Law along these lines hit a dead end.[8]

What would ultimately be more effective was the newer position taken by attorney Thaddeus B. Wakeman of New York and amplified by the National Defense Association: that the Comstock Law violated the Constitution. A freethinker since religious doubt in his college years at Princeton had turned him away from the ministry, Wakeman had emerged as an important liberal leader. Unlike William F. Howe, who had defended Victoria Woodhull, Wakeman was untainted by a reputation that he defended the disreputable. At the 1878 indignation meeting Wakeman stated the opposition to the Comstock Law on the grounds that Woodhull's defense had initially taken: "The question has become one of constitutional liberty, and freedom of person, speech, and press, as to which a few dirty pamphlets in the mails are as nothing. We are all agreed upon the question of obscenity; no one has a good word for that; but the issue is one of liberty, of constitutional liberty, and upon that we must take sides at once."[9]

Wakeman strengthened his position by rooting his argument in constitutional history. He asserted that as matters had turned to postal powers during the framing of the Constitution, supporters of the federal mails had offered reassurance that establishing post offices and post roads involved no dangerous powers. Furthermore, in the 1836 debate involving abolitionist literature, it had been clearly stated that Congress had no power to regulate the content of the mails. Wakeman invoked the Bill of Rights and its many protections, including the First Amendment. Here he took the position that the Bill of Rights guaranteed the freedoms of citizens against the power of the state, not the freedom of the several states against the power of the federal government. Wakeman then criticized *Ex parte Jackson* as one in a long line of wrong decisions made by the Supreme Court. "The Supreme Court, being always retrograde and conservative, is almost sure to get on the wrong side whenever issues of liberty and progress are presented. They go for the *old*, and *for power*; the people go for the *new*, and *for liberty:* and in such cases they and their government have never failed to reverse the court." The Supreme Court ruling in *Ex parte Jackson* was of the same stripe as the Dred Scott decision, and like the latter, would be reversed.[10]

In making these arguments, Wakeman and others drew a line between the writings they defended and those intended to be sexually arousing. As Wakeman stated above, "We are all agreed upon the question of obscenity; no one has a good word for that." Whatever disagreements the participants in Faneuil Hall had, the speakers to a person felt called upon to denounce the "racy" literature of the time. Even former Woodhull supporters, who wanted a range of medical information and literature against marriage to be available, felt the need to assert the distance between the sexual representations they supported and those intentionally designed to be sexually stimulating. Laura Kendrick put it this way: "Vice, my friends, can never be legislated out of the world: our only remedy is education. When parents teach their children a proper reverence for their physical nature, and instruct them in all the relations growing out of its unfoldment, curiosity will give place to knowledge, and obscene pictures and literature will have no patrons." In the entire meeting not a positive word was voiced for what all agreed was "obscenity"—that is, works of the imagination intended to be sexually arousing. Some speakers sought other means to regulate it, such as state laws that in their minds respected the Constitution. What these speeches make clear is that by the late 1870s no one wanted to be on the wrong side of obscenity. It had become a word that seemed to require repudiation by right-minded citizens.[11]

Heywood's supporters appealed to President Rutherford B. Hayes for a pardon, which he granted in December 1878. This victory was short-lived, however, for D. M. Bennett had been arrested for selling *Cupid's Yokes* in August, and in March 1879 his case came to the United States Circuit Court in New York.

2

Anthony Comstock was lucky in one respect. He could count on one judge in one court, Judge Charles L. Benedict of the criminal court for the Southern District of New York. This proved critical to the development of Comstock's power to suppress sexual representations and to the institutionalization of that power in the U.S. Post Office.

D. M. Bennett was a maverick reformer rather new on the scene. Born De Robigne Mortimer Bennett in upstate New York in 1818, he joined the Shaker community in New Lebanon, where he became a doctor to the society. In 1846 he and another Shaker left the community to marry. Employed variously as a druggist, brick manufacturer, seed collector, and traveling salesman, Bennett moved to New York around 1873 and turned his hand to writing and publishing the *Truth Seeker,* a weekly newspaper dedicated to free thought. Along with the Boston *Investigator,* still extant in the 1870s, the *Truth Seeker* was a leading source of information, both as a paper and as a disseminator of other freethinking materials. Like some other freethinkers, Bennett was an iconoclast with a devilish sense of humor. He published about two hundred freethinking pamphlets and tracts, including a few of his own works.[12]

Bennett came to Comstock's notice as early as 1877, at least in part because of strong statements against Comstock and his methods in the *Truth Seeker.* Comstock visited Bennett at his establishment on 141 Eighth Street and examined his literary wares. At the shop of Bennett's printer Comstock ordered him to "discontinue the printing of the paper under threats" of pros-ecution and arrest. Using a decoy letter, Comstock then requested two of the publications he deemed obscene. When they were sent through the mail, he arrested Bennett. Comstock had confused his sense of blasphemy with the reigning definition of obscenity, as the two books contained only attenuated sexual matter. Although a grand jury indicted Bennett, pressure from Robert G. Ingersoll on the postmaster general and the attorney general got the case dismissed.[13]

Neither Comstock nor Bennett was happy with this outcome. Although he later denied it in court, Comstock vowed to "get even" with Bennett. And Bennett seemed determined to provoke Comstock to arrest him again. At a free-thought convention at Watkins, New York, Bennett had a table with his publications for sale. Next to him was the table of Josephine Tilton, the sister of Angela Tilton Heywood. Bennett helped her out during a break and sold *Cupid's Yokes*. He was promptly arrested for selling obscenity, an offense under state law. Angered by what he believed was a violation of his right of free expression, Bennett announced in his newspaper that he was selling *Cupid's Yokes* by mail. He wrote that although he did not hold the views of Heywood's pamphlet, he believed in "the right of every American citizen to express his views upon marriage and divorce as upon all other subjects" and the right to purchase or sell and read those views. Using the pseudonym G. Brackett, Comstock wrote a letter of appreciation to Bennett and requested a copy of *Cupid's Yokes*. Bennett sent it on November 12, 1878. Comstock had Bennett arrested, this time for violation of the federal statute (now revised) declaring obscene materials to be nonmailable matter. At the trial on March 18, 1879, Judge Charles L. Benedict presided.

Benedict had convicted Edward Bliss Foote in 1876, and Comstock could count on him for convictions and stiff sentences. Born in Newburgh, New York, he had gone to the University of Vermont and made his career in New York City as a member of the bar. Appointed in 1865 by President Lincoln as the first judge of the Eastern District Court of New York, he served until his retirement in 1897. Known as "a Christian and a gentleman," he lived in a "very fine residence" on Staten Island. On the bench he was perceived as "cold and severe," in contrast to his private demeanor, which was said to be warmhearted and open. In testifying to his qualities in the court that yielded high respect, a judicial colleague used the words "virile mind," "sound legal judgment," and "sane and pure mind," all suggestive of a masculine bearing, rationality, and a principled stance unswayed by emotion.[14]

In some of the new federal criminal courts in these years, the first judges had to make determinations in trials arising from new federal statutes. A colleague recalled the difficulty that Benedict faced in these early years on the bench. He had a "duty of deciding a multitude of questions and of interpreting and applying a mass of new statutory provisions, almost without any guiding precedents to aid or fortify his judgment. These questions and the matters connected with them were often of far reaching importance, affecting persons and interests high and low; extending from questionable acts of the lowest to transactions of magnitude by those in high station." What did a judge such as Benedict do? Benedict, it turns out, was most known in the legal world for his admiralty jurisprudence. Attorney Sidney F. Rawson recalled a situation in which Benedict had been presiding over the court. Facing an inexperienced district attorney, Rawson stated to the court "what the rules of practice were in the State courts and that it seemed that they should be assimilated with the rules of the [federal] United States Court." Benedict "carried the idea out and assimilated that practice and made a precedent in that particular case." His approach to obscenity in federal court seems the same, applying known state practice regarding obscenity to the federal court as it dealt with violations of the new federal law.[15]

Benedict presided over the six terms each year of the federal criminal court in New York, and it was in this capacity that he tried the cases falling under the Comstock Law. Although the federal statute was new, New York State courts had experience with obscenity cases going back at least to the 1840s and the trials of the flash press. In these years, despite the lack of legislation, the court had acted, drawing on the common-law tradition of obscene libel. English jurist Thomas Starkie had provided all the directions needed for New York State judges. In addition, Judge Benedict had the precedent of the earlier *Cupid's Yokes* case and the rulings of Judge Daniel Clark of the United States Circuit Court in Boston. Benedict brought all these court practices to the criminal branch of the U.S. Circuit Court in New York.

He did, of course, have choices. It was not foreordained that obscenity law would follow in the grooves of the past, sustaining traditions of English common law. In other areas, such as the economy, federal judges were reinterpreting traditions to innovate in favor of new business enterprises. Benedict could have chosen to follow the lines of law and court practice in the manner that defense lawyers and Bennett's supporters suggested. He did not. In court Benedict could act on his deeply conservative inclinations. Court practices of the past gave him opportunity and justification.

Bennett was ably represented by Abram Wakeman, assisted by his brother Thaddeus B. Wakeman. They argued that Comstock had entrapped Bennett into a violation of the federal statute, because the penalties at the federal level were stronger (and, though Abram Wakeman dared not say it in court, the chance of conviction in Benedict's court was greater). Questions posed to Comstock attempted to demonstrate the extralegal tactics he had used to go after Bennett as part of his acknowledged effort to stamp out the publications of free lovers and freethinkers. Dismissal was sought on narrow procedural grounds, but the case was largely argued on the high ground of the Constitution and free expression and the ambiguities inherent in the designation "obscene." Bennett's case put into the court record the opposition that Thaddeus Wakeman articulated at the 1878 indignation meeting protesting Heywood's conviction.[16]

In its opening the defense stated that the federal statute under which Bennett had been arrested was "unconstitutional," as it stood "in contravention of the fundamental law of the nation." It was "therefore without force and void." Such may have been an unusual tactic at the first rung of the federal judiciary ladder, but Abram Wakeman seemed to know that this case was important. He pointed out to the jury that it was being tried "at the heart, the center of our nation . . . from this great metropolis diverges not only all questions of politics and literature, but also the exposition of justice and of the law in relations to the rights of our citizens."

Wakeman then picked up the line of argument that George Wilkes had stated in the 1840s: the root of the problem was the difficulty in determining the criteria for the crime. Unlike manslaughter or burglary, which can be clearly defined, obscenity cannot. Its determination is a matter of judgment, what Wilkes earlier had called "taste." Determinations about obscenity carry "the greatest possible diversity of opinion . . . people may be honestly divided all through the community." Those educated in different ways differ. "One is a Christian, one is a Liberal, one is a Freethinker, and one is a Freelover. All may have different views upon these matters, depending on circumstances and education."[17]

The reality that the defense faced was that American law had been shaped by the traditions of common law and was still being influenced by English statutes and rulings by English courts. For that reason Wakeman returned to the debate within the House of Lords on Lord Campbell's Law, which authorized search and seizure of obscene materials. When unease had been expressed in Parliament that the proposed law might throw some of the great works of literature into jeopardy, Lord Campbell had stated that he intended his act "to apply exclusively to works written for the single purpose of corrupting the morals of youth and of a nature calculated to shock the feelings of decency in any well-regulated mind." Wakeman upheld Campbell's standard—"minds of intelligence and education and fairness"—not the limited capacity of Anthony Comstock, as the appropriate gauge for obscenity.[18]

How can those in the court know what is truly obscene? Wakeman presented some clear markers. An obscene work is circulated in "a secret, obscure, and covert manner, and not openly." It is bought by youth, "boys, young men, and perhaps girls." Such a work, in Wakeman's words, "excites the amative passions, arouses lascivious and lewd thoughts." In contrast, Heywood's book is designed to appeal to men "of thought and of reflection and not of passion." In the work of transformation going on in society, there are men "who live in advance of the age; they are reformers; they are seeking, discussing, talking, and arguing." Heywood, Wakeman stated, is one of them, and he has written his book for others like himself. *Cupid's Yokes* has to be studied to be understood, and is therefore clearly not obscene. Moreover, the reputation of a book is germane. Dealers and buyers work with established classes of books, such as theological, political, scientific. For them "obscene literature" is a known classification, and *Cupid's Yokes* does not fit into it at all. Again, Wakeman did not build his argument against the existence of "obscenity." He even stated, whether sincerely or not, that the men of the New York Society for the Suppression of Vice have "done hard work, great good, and for which we owe them our sincere and hearty thanks."[19]

What followed was the courtroom ritual dictated by Starkie, in many respects a replay of Heywood's trial. The defense attempted to introduce the question of the author's motive and intent and was stopped by the judge. The defense then turned to the circumstances of the book's sale, its public and open quality, and this, too, was not allowed. When booksellers and book lovers were called by the defense to testify to the book's classification, all of them were silenced by the court. Bennett was allowed to give some of the facts of his life in court but was not allowed to state the length of time he had carried the book, the booksellers to whom he had supplied it, or the clientele to whom he had sold the work. The defense called character witnesses who testified to Bennett's integrity and good nature but were not allowed to speak about the book. Objections from the prosecution canceled out all efforts to establish the nature of Bennett's trade in books, his motives, his state of mind. The defense tried to put on the record a letter by Elizur Wright, signed by a thousand persons (including Bennett), that stated that however they might disagree with the contents of *Cupid's Yokes,* the public had a right to read and possess it; but this element, too, was excluded. The defense tried to read the entire book to the jury, arguing that a passage could be understood only within the context of a work, that a book needed to be judged as a whole. The judge limited reading and discussion solely to the passages marked by the district attorney with these words: "The general scope of the book is not in issue."[20]

The defense turned to establish Comstock's intention and methods. When denied his line of argument, Wakeman explained to the court that it was significant to prove Comstock's animosity because it was he who had initiated the prosecution and provided the facts. "He wrote the letter, and arranged it with the postmasters, and he took it out. . . . The point is to show that he had an animosity toward the defendant in this case." Judge Benedict stopped Wakeman.[21]

In his summation, Wakeman stated that the word "obscene" was used for that "which openly wounds the sense of decency by exciting lust or disgust." "Indecent," in turn, means "the wanton and unnecessary expression in words or exposure in pictures of that which the common sense of decency requires should be kept private or concealed." As he attempted to discuss the book, Judge Benedict interrupted him to remind him of the only matter at issue: "the question is whether those marked passages are obscene or not." What Wakeman was trying to establish was that the meaning of particular words derived from the meaning of the whole. Benedict sought to limit all discussion to the marked words; his assumption was that the words had a fixed and definite meaning that would be clear to the jurors.[22]

Faced with the difficulty of explaining away Heywood's language, Wakeman gave an analogy. If a man sees a beautiful woman in a state of partial undress on the street, "some people looking upon her might feel as did David towards Uriah's wife; there was a disposition aroused which ought to be suppressed." But if one knows that she is insane or ill, "everything is changed." One feels sorrow; "the feeling instantly becomes one of compassion instead of lust." Such, he argued, was the impact of reading many of the passages in Heywood's work. It was in this context that Wakeman put the consideration of Woodhull's treatment of the Beecher case. The district attorney had referred to Heywood's words about Beecher: "While his natural right to commit adultery is unquestionable, his right to lie about it is not so clear."

Wakeman asked if this one sentence should "send my client to the penitentiary for ten years and lay upon him a fine of $5,000 for having mailed a pamphlet having it in." "This New England scientist, explorer, and reformer may take a different view from yours or mine, but he has a right to it. . . . I think, to have all this fuss over a little line and a half like this, on the allegation that it is going to corrupt and upturn the community, usurp the marriage relation, and break down society generally. It is simply absurd." Over and again Wakeman read a passage, objected to its content, but noted that there was nothing in it to cause lust in "well-regulated minds." "We look upon them with disgust, perhaps, because we have not thought of their truth, but that is not the question; it is whether the language actually used tends to excite in you and me or in others libidinous passions."[23]

Many of the marked passages were quotations from the works of other authors. Repeatedly Wakeman asked the jury why this book was held obscene and not the literary works behind the quotes that were the staple of libraries and schools. He raised the specter of growing censorship. "Establish this precedent, and Anthony Comstock may be in your house within twenty-four hours to know whether you have not got a copy of 'Plutarch's Lives.' Or, more in harmony with his mode of procedure, he will write you a private note wishing to borrow a copy of 'Plutarch's Lives.' " Such inquisition, Wakeman insisted, would not be tolerated even in Russia.[24]

About the birth control advice in the book, Wakeman simply chose to ignore the part of the statute that defined it as obscene. He stated instead, "They are matters that have to be talked about; self-knowledge requires it; you can go into your library and take up any book on physiology, and you will find the same sentences and the same doctrines talked about; and it aids you in properly fulfilling the duties and functions of your life. Why should they be objected to here?"

In his summation Wakeman was given full leave to develop the argument for Bennett and the purity of his motives. One of his most powerful arguments was the passage he read from the *Truth Seeker,* giving Bennett's own words in announcing the sale of Heywood's pamphlet: "We do this by virtue of the rights of an American citizen. If we go to prison for it, to prison it is. For every one that falls for selling 'Cupid's Yokes,' ten will rise in his place to sell more. When all the prisons of the country are filled with persons who dare to sell 'Cupid's Yokes,' more can be built. We propose for one to fight the battle out on this line."[25]

When the defense rested its case, the prosecution had its turn. William P.

Fiero, the assistant district attorney, spoke to the jury as a man outraged by Heywood's words. Heywood told him in *Cupid's Yokes* that the wife "married to me by a Christian clergyman, was a prostitute," and that his many children were "but the offspring of a prostituted right." In opposition to Wakeman's learning and that of some of his witnesses, Fiero appealed to the jury's instincts. The definition of obscenity is "nothing but common sense. . . . It is not this learned non-sense." He brought forth the name of Victoria Woodhull as one of Heywood's authorities. "Yes, she stands author for a great many slanders and libels against decent people." He shifted the ground from idea to behavior, using the bridge of the children in boarding school who learned about birth control methods from the book. Fiero insisted that Heywood argued for the right of unmarried couples to sleep together. "If men were to act on the doctrines inculcated here, take any woman they cared for, your wife, your sister, and have children by her, as this book says, what sort of a world would it be?"[26]

Responding to Wakeman's attacks against Comstock, Fiero counterattacked. At the outset, Wakeman had presented witnesses who had portrayed Bennett as law-abiding, hardworking, and long married. The district attorney had undercut the defense by continually reminding jurors of Bennett's blasphemy, asking repeatedly on cross-examination if the character witnesses knew that Bennett was the author of "An Open Letter to Jesus Christ." Now, as he presented his case, Fiero enunciated the line most remembered from the trial: "This case is not entitled 'Anthony Comstock against D. M. Bennett'; this case is not entitled 'The Society for the Suppression of Vice against D. M. Bennett.' Yes, it is; it is the United States against D. M. Bennett, and the United States is one great society for the suppression of vice."[27]

In contrast to the prosecution's appeal to emotion, Judge Benedict spoke as the epitome of reason, but in a way that undercut many of the lines of Wakeman's defense. In language reminiscent of Comstock and the Society for the Suppression of Vice, Benedict stated that the intention of the statute was "to protect the community against the abuse of that powerful engine, the United States mail." He countered the defense argument that questioned Comstock's motives and character: "Most infractions of law are discovered and punished by reason of hostility or enmity on the part of some person in the community against some other person." Benedict stated that a defendant is protected from enemies by the district attorney, who, under the law, takes a complaint and presents it to a grand jury, twenty-three citizens, who determine whether it is a "case proper to be presented to a petit jury." Most of the issues raised by the defense were extraneous. The only duty of the jury is to render a verdict "according to the facts proven. The facts belong to you; the questions of law belong to the Court."[28] The constitutionality of the statute was not in question.

Going to the heart of Wakeman's defense, Judge Benedict proved himself to be a good student of Blackstone and other compilers of the common law. Benedict instructed the jury that no matters of freedom of speech or press were at issue in this case. He affirmed the rights of all to hold and express their views. He warned the jury that any of their opinions on questions of religion or marriage were to have no bearing in court. For the jury to make any decision for or against the defendant because of his beliefs would be to "do injustice to the man, and to the community also." The issue was obscenity, not belief. "Freelovers and Freethinkers have a right to their views, and they may express them, and they may publish them, but they cannot publish them in connection with obscene matter and then send that matter through the mails." The sole issue involved was the use of the mails. "Freedom of the press," he stated, "does not include freedom to use the mails for the purpose of distributing obscene literature, and no right or privilege of the press is infringed by the exclusion of obscene literature from the mails."

Normally a jury must decide on two points of fact. First, did the person knowingly mail the book? In this case, Benedict stated, that fact was proved and not disputed. Benedict put the second point simply: Is the book "obscene, lewd, or lascivious, or of an indecent character"? He justified the court's requirement that the decision be made solely on the marked passages. He explained that if the larger intent of the book could overrule any part, the effect could nullify the law: a person could "write an essay upon the subject of honesty, and fill it with notes containing filthy and obscene stories, and could then pass it through the mails." The words themselves do not have to be of an obscene character to convey even the "most obscene, lewd, and lascivious matter." As Benedict put it, "The question is as to the *idea* which is conveyed in the words that are used, and that idea characterizes the language." Nor does the integrity or intent of the person weigh. He could be a good man and have the belief that "the best way to promote honesty and purity" would be to "bind together all the obscene stories that could be found in a single book" in order to "excite disgust and so to prevent vice." The result could still be obscenity.[29]

Benedict informed the jury that the court alone determined the law. A critical element of that determination was the definition of obscenity. In a statement that would be decisive in this case—and subsequent ones—Benedict redefined obscenity for American courts.[30] Benedict instructed jurors to use this measure: "It is whether the tendency of the matter is to deprave and corrupt the morals of those whose minds are open to such influences and into whose hands a publication of this sort may fall." This standard had two elements. First, it targeted youth, not reasonable men, as the imagined audience. The association with youth was strengthened by Benedict's added clarification: "if it would suggest impure and libidinous thoughts in the young and the inexperienced." Second, it linked sexual representation to sexual acts, under what is known in the law as "bad tendency." Material judged obscene is that which might "deprave and corrupt the morals" of youth and damage the welfare of society. In making his definition Benedict gave to the jury almost word for word the standard established in an English court in 1868, known as the Hicklin test. Benedict stated that the standard "has been often applied; has passed the examination of many courts," but he did not tell the jury he was referring to courts across the Atlantic.[31]

In his judicial practice Benedict followed the familiar scenario for obscenity trials laid down by the English jurist Thomas Starkie and adapted by American courts. This was the script used in Heywood's trial, but Benedict conducted it in temperate, reasoned language and with measured voice. In the context of this script, he placed the Hicklin test, developed in an English court in the mid–nineteenth century, into the American court record.

After the jury found Bennett guilty, Judge Benedict sentenced him to thirteen months in prison. The aging Bennett served out his full term. Despite Robert Ingersoll's appeal to President Hayes and a petition for his release with two hundred thousand signatures, this time there was no presidential pardon.[32]

3

The Bennett case assumed broad significance because on appeal, Judge Samuel Blatchford wrote a landmark decision in *U.S. v. Bennett*. To all intents and purposes, the Blatchford ruling established the constitutionality of the Comstock Law as applied in Benedict's court. The judgment held for fifty years.[33]

Blatchford was Benedict's colleague on the circuit court. He was as close to an aristocrat as American society in the 1870s afforded. A native New Yorker, Blatchford was well schooled before attending and graduating from

Columbia College. He married well into the Boston-Lowell elite. He served many posts with Governor William H. Seward before his appointment as federal district judge by President Grant in 1867. In 1872 he became circuit judge for the Second Judicial District. In this capacity he presided over the trial of Victoria Woodhull and acquitted her on the grounds that the 1872 federal statute did not include newspapers.[34]

In the appellate decision *U.S. v. Bennett,* Blatchford had an opportunity to correct damage he might have caused earlier. In a lengthy, reasoned, and learned decision, Blatchford carefully reviewed the lower-court trial and responded to Abram Wakeman's objections point by point. In doing so, he confirmed Judge Benedict's rulings in all particulars. As had Benedict, Blatchford acted on his conservative instincts and chose to confirm the common-law tradition.

Blatchford stated in his decision that the constitutionality of the revised Comstock Law had been "definitely settled by the decision of the supreme court in *Ex parte Jackson.*" Although the statute excluded lottery materials, not obscene matter, from the mails, "the views of the court apply fully to the present case." As he dealt with specifics, Blatchford cited precedents in both English and American courts. To give one example, he used the case of *Commonwealth v. Holmes* of 1819 and 1821 to establish that it was not necessary to display in the court records an obscene book or picture because this would "require that the public itself should give permanency and notoriety to indecency, in order to punish it." Blatchford affirmed the practice that allowed only isolated, marked passages to be read to the jury. He spent a great deal of time dealing with the meaning of "obscenity" and sanctioned Benedict's definition of "indecent" as meaning "tending to obscenity."

Most important, Blatchford upheld Benedict's use of the "Hicklin test" as the appropriate standard jurors were to use to determine obscenity. As a result, focus was put on vulnerable youth, and the notion of "bad tendency" prevailed. Thus obscenity in American law became "whether the tendency of the matter charged as obscenity is to deprave and corrupt those whose minds are open to such immoral influences, and into whose hands a publication of this sort may fall." Finally, Blatchford restated the common-law principle emphasized by Thomas Starkie that intention inhered in an act: "I hold that, where a man publishes a work manifestly obscene, he must be taken to have had the intention which is implied from that act."[35]

In all this the power of the Anglo-American common-law tradition is evident. The Comstock Law, as administered by the courts, was no simple aberration that could be easily negated in the courts. Behind it stood decisions reaching back to Curl in 1727. Blackstone and Holt had set out a rationale, and Starkie offered a workbook for American courts. The Hicklin test provided a definition of obscenity focusing on youth and "bad tendency." A body of practice and precedent that preceded the federal statute gave conservative judges both opportunity and justification. To this arsenal they now added the Blatchford ruling.

What makes Blatchford's decision important is that it was a U.S. appellate decision by a learned and powerful judge who reviewed the precedents in England and America and determined that a U.S. circuit court judge had acted according to them in a case involving the Comstock Law. The ruling's standing was enhanced when Blatchford was appointed to the United States Supreme Court in 1882. Although the nation's highest court did not review the Comstock Law specifically in the nineteenth century, Blatchford's appellate decision in conjunction with *Ex parte Jackson* carried the necessary weight to govern obscenity law well into the twentieth.[36]

Yet at the same moment, stirred by the Foote, Heywood, and Bennett cases, the countertradition crucial to challenging the application of the Comstock Law was coming into being. Although it never toppled the law as unconstitutional, during the twentieth century it was able to widen the boundaries of speech protected under the First Amendment. Outraged that Heywood's words, like his own, had been confused with obscenity, Edward Bliss Foote wrote, "There ought to be no difficulty in discriminating between publications intended for reformatory purposes and those issued simply for the purpose of pandering to prurient taste. But it looks as if this obscene literature law was to be used for the purpose of knocking out the brains of everyone who don't strictly conform to the established ruts, be they medical, social, or otherwise." In this instance, Comstock's ax had fallen on Bennett, "a hard-working, earnest, able man who has marked out a new road for himself in theology." In the years ahead Foote tried to repair Bennett's life as best he could, corresponding with him in jail, sending him money and supplies, and welcoming him at his release with a reception at Chickering Hall.[37]

More significantly, Foote joined with Thaddeus Wakeman and other liberals in the National Defense Association. When the organization adopted a constitution, it put as its aims that it would investigate "all questionable cases of prosecution" under the Comstock laws, federal and state, and give "sympathy, moral support, and material aid to those who may be unjustly assailed by the enemies of free speech and free press." In what David Rabban has called the "forgotten years," the National Defense Association and its successor, the Free Speech League, founded in the early twentieth century, kept the ideal of freedom of speech alive. In the years before the formation of the American Civil Liberties Union, these two groups defended many persons charged with word crimes under federal and state Comstock laws. It was their broader vision that would ultimately animate the A.C.L.U., when, after initial hesitation, it turned to fight and win key obscenity cases in the twentieth century.[38]

CONCLUSION

20

Conclusion

Is it good to leave on such a note of uplift? Perhaps not. American historians are rightfully wary of history as unfolding progress, and nothing in this book supports such a view. What it does do, however, is something else. I have long felt the inadequacy of historical understanding of America's sexual past. Now I know at least part of the reason why. Many of the sources potentially available to build a more accurate interpretation were rudely suppressed after 1873.

With these sources at least partially recovered, it is possible to reread sex in nineteenth-century America as a complex four-way conversation. American vernacular sexual culture, evangelical Christianity, moral physiology, and a sensibility putting sex at the center of life—each voice had a distinct cultural framework to shape the way it received and conveyed sexual knowledge. These sides in the sexual conversation were unequal in number and influence, but until the 1870s all were legitimate.

There was an exception, however, and that was the realm of the legally obscene. Thus two additional elements entered into the mix of the complex sexual conversation of the nineteenth century. The first was commercial erotica, produced for a largely male audience and purchased as entertainment and sexual stimulant. The second was the legal system, which was willing at times to police and suppress it. Controlled by men, courts interjected themselves into the sexual conversation of the United States, asserting their power to set the ground rules of debate and the authority to prosecute, convict, and imprison. Whatever their own personal practices of private reading, judges and juries in important American courts determined that much of what they deemed printed obscenity, both texts and pictures, should not be allowed in the public arena and acted to suppress it. Drawing on the common law as presented in English manuals, American courts established traditions for cases of obscene libel.

What happened in the 1870s? Why did a federal statute and state laws expand the power of the courts over obscenity? Why did those laws revise the definition of obscene material? The answer is not Victorian consensus. Americans in the 1870s were as divided on sexuality as they ever had been. They now had an additional element of conflict, the fourth sexual framework, which asserted that sex lay at the core of life.

Behind divisions on sexual matters in the nineteenth century were the powerful forces of Christian evangelicalism and religious skepticism. However, stating that these forces were at work throughout the century does not measure their proportions or relative power. Throughout the nineteenth century, the United States experienced growing Christian piety and an accompanying relative loss of power by secularists. The Civil War confirmed this trend. Some evangelical Christians sought to define the nation as Christian and inscribe this identity in the Constitution. While liberals resisted this effort, in the years that followed, as Darwinism began to alter outlooks and a growing industrial economy shifted emphasis to this world, religion fought many battles to retain its hold. Evangelical Christians found arenas of American life in which their voice could dominate. When they turned to the suppression of obscene materials, they found they had a strong ally. Imbedded in the courts were strong traditions and a history of the pursuit of obscenity.

Simultaneously, members of the middle class were increasingly accepting the messages of physiological reform. We have seen that this framework was various: there was no one voice, but a cacophony. However, all those speaking shared a belief in the value of sexual knowledge and, through knowledge, control. As such, the third framework was particularly influenced by those claiming expert knowledge, especially doctors, who often confused their professional interests with the good of the public or the patient. And whatever their differences about the power, frequency, and value of heterosexual coitus, physiological writers from all sides agreed that masturbation was the scourge of the age.

As reform physiology grew in acceptance, vernacular sexuality surrendered much of its cultural power. This first sexual framework never lost out, and it continued to shape sexual practices, but it was pushed to the margins of legitimate discourse. It was transmitted informally by boy culture from generation to generation and was conveyed by institutions such as the barbershop, the police and fire departments, the gang, and the college fraternity. Less visible and thus less easy to trace, vernacular sexuality also informed women. Married women shared knowledge, and sisters, schoolmates, friends, and coworkers in the shop passed down girl culture. In the nineteenth century these gendered vernacular sexualities were imbedded in popular culture, such as the minstrel and the press. They reemerged within the commercial entertainment of the stage (and later screen), the concert saloon transformed into the nightclub, and the affordable worlds of cheap print—tabloids, magazines, and popular literature.

The forces of Christian evangelicalism sought to suppress the commerce in sexual representations originating in vernacular sexual culture—that is clear. They could rely on the powerful tradition in the courts. But they were not satisfied. They sought to broaden the power of the courts. They needed both legislation and public opinion to support it, especially in jury trials. Here they had two tools: commercial erotica and a public that either opposed it or needed to appear to do so.

Commercial erotic writing and prints had been part of the business of many booksellers. However, these works had always been hidden from public view, kept in locked boxes or a separate room or hawked by newsboys on the street. The secret trade in erotica existed in a world that publicly condemned it and, on occasion, prosecuted sellers when they came to light. Almost a half century of writing by physiological reformers convinced the public that erotic publications did wider harm. Prepared by the physiological reformers (and probably by known practice), those pressing for suppression could link printed erotica to masturbation, with all its feared consequences for society.

In the 1870s, there was no one willing to defend publicly the right on any grounds to print, sell, or possess the older works of the erotic canon or even the newer ones labeled "racy." With the passage of the 1873 federal statute Comstock and the Y.M.C.A. linked two powerful forces—organized evangelical Christianity and conservative physiological reform—to the court's pursuit of obscenity through the common law of obscene libel. Their success placed administration of censorship in the U.S. Postal Service, backed by the power of federal courts. At the state level these same forces were generally successful in pushing for passage of expanded state laws against obscenity.

The 1873 federal statute and the accompanying state laws did more than police the secret publications that existed at the edge of male vernacular sexuality. They explicitly defined obscenity to include birth control information and materials and abortion advertisements. At one level, this suppressed the growing commercialization of women's vernacular sexual culture. We cannot understand this development outside the constitutional and political reality that women had no vote, did not serve in legislatures, and were neither judges, jury, nor attorneys in the courts. Yet, of course, it is too simple to see the suppression of contraception and abortion as simply a male plot against women's vernacular sexual culture. Once commercialized, contraception was partially taken over by men and sold in their "sporting goods" establishments. Abortion services could be paid for by men; stories of botched abortions featured libertine men forcing it upon the unwilling victims of their lust.

Traffic in contraceptive information and materials and abortion advertisements may seem to us an uncomplicated story of women's desire to control their own bodies, but at the time, as it entered the public commercial arena, it may have been compromised. Middle-class women may have experienced this traffic as creating new levels of female vulnerability to male exploitation. Such middle-class women may have believed that their personal access to contraception and abortion (and that of their daughters) was protected by a private and privileged relation to physicians and by the black market. They were right, yet they failed to realize that by forcing birth control information and materials out of the public domain, sexual knowledge would be distorted and lost to those without their advantages.

The 1873 federal law extended obscenity to contraception and abortion. In applying it, courts prosecuted some of those whose works lay at the radical edge of physiological reform. Most vulnerable were advocates such as Victoria Woodhull and Ezra Heywood, who were beginning, however messily, to articulate the fourth sexual framework. In the 1870s, these figures were hard to read. They seemed to be continuing the pre–Civil War work of social movements and free-love reform at a time when members of the middle class around them were experiencing a new desire to lower the temperature of rhetoric, to talk the language of fact and numbers. Only from the light of the early twenty-first century is it possible to see what they were about. Although they employed elements of the past, they were not spokesmen of the old, but heralds of the new.

Victoria Woodhull, Edward Bliss Foote, Ezra Heywood, and D. M. Bennett were in the vanguard of a new awareness that placed sex at the center of life. They were legally vulnerable because, at a time when forces seeking to eliminate "obscenity" from the culture became powerful, their words became confused with the bawdy ones of popular culture and commercial erotica. Although in essentials Anthony Comstock and the Y.M.C.A. represented the older Christian position, it was now combined with moral physiology in ways that broadened the appeal of censorship of the obscene to a wider audience educated in the new understandings of sex and health. The power of the Y.M.C.A. and its successful efforts to obtain federal and state legislation conferring police powers on Comstock enabled him to reshape, fundamentally, America's public sexual culture. By 1879 he was triumphant at the start of a long career as the chief watchdog of America's public morals.

A prosecutor at one of Comstock's important early cases stated to the court, "United States is one great society for the suppression of vice." This was not true, any more than that Americans as a whole accepted Victorian notions of morality. The reason the prosecutor's words seemed to characterize the nineteenth century was that much of the opposition to Comstockian restriction was silenced by the courts and forced underground. By winning in critical courts, Comstock was able to suppress for a time materials that might have enabled Americans to understand themselves more fully, including their sexual experiences, desire, and emotions. His victory buried material and required euphemisms. In the process it also hid from the eyes of historians some of the richness and complexity of sexual representations in America's past and obscured the nature of the nineteenth century's complex sexual cultures.

From the hindsight of roughly 130 years, we can see suppression of sexual representation in the 1870s in a new light. Indeed, by the last third of the twentieth century the legal power once assumed by Comstock and the other censors of sexual materials had been curtailed by a powerful combination of advocates for free speech, business seeking the freedom of markets, the desire of many to see vernacular sexuality represented in the media, and arguments about the critical importance of sex. In the 1870s sexual reformers put sexual passion at the heart of life. They started a phase of the conversation about sex that focused on the importance of sexual expression for human well-being. Over time the fourth sexual framework fostered the belief that sexual identity lies at the core of the self, a key understanding of the turn to the twenty-first century. Although Heywood and Bennett were hounded by the courts, their legal defenders challenged the power of the state to regulate sexual speech. Opposing the Comstock Law and state sup-

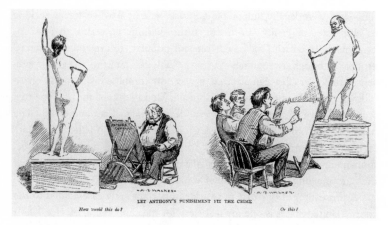

LET ANTHONY'S PUNISHMENT FIT THE CRIME

How would this do?   *Or this?*

By the early twentieth century, Anthony Comstock became a target of humor in so-phisticated circles, but his powerful influence remained. "Let Anthony's Punishment Fit the Crime," *Life*, September 13, 1906, p. 287.

pression, they created a vital countertradition that cherished freedom of speech and upheld the First Amendment. In the twentieth century, their words took on new weight. Linked to pressures by commercial culture to keep markets unfettered, these beliefs in the significance of sex and the First Amendment led to a dramatic weakening of the Comstock Law. By the end of the twentieth century, much of Comstock's effort would be discredited and the boundaries of speech redrawn.

Yet at the beginning of the twenty-first century these issues are hardly resolved. American culture remains profoundly divided over questions of morality and its relation to government. Each day the news presents reports of contemporary clashes over medical research, abortion, pornography, teenage sex education, and censorship of the Internet. New technology and new sources of sexual knowledge bring new threats to freedom of expression. As we read sex in our own times, echoes of America's nineteenth-century battles over sexual knowledge and suppression, one of our first culture wars, still reverberate in our ears.

NOTES

1: *Introduction*

1. Any thought that historians have already dealt a death blow to the Victorian repression hypothesis must confront recent works that keep it alive, such as Charles Grier Sellers, *The Market Revolution: Jacksonian America, 1815–1846* (New York: Oxford University Press, 1991), pp. 237–68. My generation of scholars was introduced to the notion through John S. Haller, Jr., and Robin M. Haller, *The Physician and Sexuality in Victorian America* (Urbana: University of Illinois Press, 1974). Early in research I was fortunate to read a work that helped shape my thinking: Ian Hunter, David Saunders, and Dugald Williamson, *On Pornography: Literature, Sexuality and Obscenity Law* (New York: St. Martin's Press, 1993). The writings of Michel Foucault have been an important part of my intellectual life.

2. I am aware of the complex controversy that surrounds the relation of the physical body, sex, sexuality, and sexual representation, best treated in the preface to Thomas Laqueur, *Making Sex: Body and Gender from the Greeks to Freud* (Cambridge, Mass.: Harvard University Press, 1990). My intention here is to describe and analyze nineteenth-century sexual representations and the political and legal conflicts in which they were enmeshed.

3. Karen Lystra's *Searching the Heart: Women, Men, and Romantic Love in Nineteenth-Century America* (New York: Oxford, 1989); Carl N. Degler, "What Ought to Be and What Was: Women's Sexuality in the Nineteenth Century," *American Historical Review,* 79 (December 1974): 1467–90.

4. Quoted in Roger Thompson, *Unfit for Modest Ears* (Totowa, N.J.: Rowman and Littlefield, 1979), p. 22. Among nineteenth-century American authors revered today, a few dealt powerfully with sex and desire in their writings—one thinks especially of Nathaniel Hawthorne, Herman Melville, Lydia Maria Child, and Walt Whitman. An important subgenre dealt with transgressive sex across the color line. As critical as these writings are to the broader understandings of sexuality in America, they have not been my subject of inquiry. I have examined writing that was subject to suppression by the courts in the belief that debates about what constitutes the "obscene" in any era offer important insights.

2: *Vernacular Sexual Culture, Commercial Erotica, and Obscene Libel*

1. My discussion of *Aristotle's Master-piece* has been shaped by Roy Porter, " 'The Secrets of Generation Display'd': *Aristotle's Master-piece* in Eighteenth-Century England," *Eighteenth Century Life,* 9 (1984–85): 1–16. Unless noted, I have relied for Edwards's inquiry on the narration in Otho T. Beall, Jr., "*Aristotle's Master Piece* in America: A Landmark in the Folklore of Medicine," *William and Mary Quarterly,* 20 (1963): 207–22; and Thomas H. Johnson, "Jonathan Edwards and the 'Young Folks'' Bible," *New England Quarterly,* 5 (1932): 37–54. Roger Thomp-

son, *Unfit for Modest Ears* (Totowa, N.J.: Rowman and Littlefield, 1979), p. 166, suggests that sexual arousal may have been the primary intention of *Aristotle's Master-piece* from the outset, but concludes that, given its content, it was really a book of popular education.

2. The matter was clearly a delicate one, and Edwards made some missteps that would later lead to his removal from the town. From the pulpit he read a list of those he wanted to question, some twenty-two names. In doing so, he failed to separate out those who were serving as direct witnesses, those who were called to provide expert testimony, and those who were accused. Moreover, his effort to keep the proceedings discreet by separating the young male and female testifiers on different floors of the parsonage were foiled when the fellows got a ladder and looked at the young ladies through the chamber window.

3. "Cases of Discipline, apparently in the first church in Northampton" [1744], document 6, Jonathan Edwards manuscripts, Special Collections, Franklin Trask Library, Andover Newton Theology School, Newton, Massachusetts. Edwards's references to the Bible in the two following paragraphs come from this document.

4. "Cases of Discipline, Northampton" [1744], document 9, Jonathan Edwards manuscripts, Andover Newton Theology School.

5. "Cases of Discipline, Northampton" [1744], document 3, Jonathan Edwards manuscripts, Andover Newton Theology School.

6. *Trial of D. M. Bennett in the United States Circuit Court* (New York: The Truth Seeker Office, c. 1879), quote from p. 153. This trial is discussed and documented at length in Chapter 19.

7. Important new work on this and other widely read texts, such as *Onania*, will clarify authorship and their relation to earlier scientific and religious texts; see Thomas Laqueur, *Making Sex: Body and Gender from the Greeks to Freud* (Cambridge, Mass.: Harvard University Press, 1990), p. 68. Charles E. Rosenberg's noting of the persistence of an "older male-oriented behavioral ethos" is one of the few examples of serious treatment of this framework in historical writing; see "Sexuality, Class and Role in 19th-Century America," *American Quarterly,* May 1973, pp. 140–41, quote from p. 140. The term, as J. B. Jackson discusses it, comes from the Latin *verna,* meaning "a slave born in the house of his or her master" and was then applied to ways of life governed by tradition and custom rather than politics and law; see J. B. Jackson, *Discovering the Vernacular Landscape* (New Haven, Conn.: Yale University Press, 1984), pp. 85–86, 149–50. In reference to language, the word relates to dialects as opposed to literary language, the "nonstandard or substandard everyday speech of a country or locality," or the idiom of a particular group; see *American Heritage Dictionary of the English Language,* ed. William Morris (Boston: Houghton Mifflin Company, 1969), p. 1423.

8. Laurel Thatcher Ulrich, *A Midwife's Tale: The Life of Martha Ballard Based on Her Diary, 1785–1812* (New York: Alfred A. Knopf, 1990), pp. 55–58; Herbert Leventhal, *In the Shadow of the Enlightenment: Occultism and Renaissance Science in Eighteenth-Century America* (New York: New York University Press, 1976), p. 192; John S. Haller, Jr., and Robin M. Haller, *The Physician and Sexuality in Victorian America* (Urbana: University of Illinois Press, 1974), pp. 4–5; Anthony Fletcher, *Gender, Sex and Subordination in England, 1500–1800* (New Haven, Conn.: Yale University Press, 1995); Roy Porter and Lesley Hall, *The Facts of Life: The Creation of Sexual Knowledge in Britain, 1650–1950* (New Haven, Conn.: Yale University Press, 1995).

9. Aristotle (pseudonym), *Aristotle's Works Compleated in Four Parts, containing 1. The Compleat Master-piece; 2. His Compleat and Experienced Midwife; 3. His Book of Problems; 4. His Last Legacy* (London: Printed, and Sold by the Booksellers, c. 1741), pp. 12, 23.

10. Ibid., pp. 14–15.

11. Ibid., pp. 13, 17.

12. Laqueur, *Making Sex;* Aristotle (pseudonym), *The Compleat Master-piece,* 1741, pp. 15–16, 22, 18.

13. Aristotle (pseudonym), *His Book of Problems,* 1741, p. 59.

14. Aristotle (pseudonym), *The Compleat Master-piece,* 1741, pp. 39–40.

15. Ibid., p. 38.

16. Ibid., pp. 8–11; quote from p. 10.

17. Aristotle (pseudonym), *His Last Legacy,* 1741, pp. 3, 41, 91, 42, 46. Vern Bullough suggests that this book, condensing material in *Aristotle's Master-piece,* was "clearly intended as a chapbook"; see Vern L. Bullough, "An Early American Sex Manual, or, Aristotle Who?" *Early American Literature,* 7, no. 3 (Winter 1973): 239.

18. Aristotle (pseudonym), *His Book of Problems,* 1741, pp. 53, 55. Bullough, "An Early American Sex Manual," p. 237, states that this book is older than *Aristotle's Master-piece* and is a product of the medieval period.

19. Aristotle (pseudonym), *The Compleat Master-piece,* 1741, p. 21.

20. Ibid., p. 37.

21. Women's vernacular sexual culture is considered in Chapter 9. Much new work has emerged on Sodomite culture in England, especially by Randolph Trumbach; this is being reflected in American work, such as Richard Godbeer, " 'The Cry of Sodom': Discourse, Intercourse, and Desire in Colonial New England," *William and Mary Quarterly,* 52, no. 2 (April 1995): 259–84; Colin L. Talley, "Gender and Male Same-Sex Behavior in British North America in the Seventeenth Century," *Journal of the History of Sexuality,* 6, no. 3 (1996): 385–408.

22. David Foxon, *Libertine Literature in England, 1660–1745* (New Hyde Park, N.Y.: University Books, 1965), pp. 47–51. In this and the following pages I use the word "erotica" to signify writing and visual materials dealing with sexual matters. I eschew the word "pornography" because it is frequently used to denote and stigmatize that which the commentator finds unacceptable.

23. Lynn Hunt, "Obscenity and the Origins of Modernity," in *The Invention of Pornography: Obscenity and the Origins of Modernity, 1500–1800,* ed. Lynn Hunt (New York: Zone Books, 1993), pp. 9–45, quote from p. 11; Peter Wagner, *Eros Revived: Erotica of the Enlightenment in England and America* (London: Secker & Warburg, 1988), pp. 212–14; Thompson, *Unfit for Modest Ears.*

24. Erotic literature is being rediscovered, as two articles in the *Journal of the History of Sexuality* attest: Dorelies Kraakman, "Reading Pornography Anew: A Critical History of Sexual Knowledge for Girls in French Erotic Fiction, 1750–1840," 4, no. 4 (April 1994): 517–48; and Christopher Rivers, "Safe Sex: The Prophylactic Walls of the Cloister in the French Libertine Convent Novel of the Eighteenth Century," 5, no. 3 (January 1995): 381–402. Unlike these authors, however, I continue to see depictions of female desire and woman-woman sexual acts as representations designed for male arousal.

25. For example, Steven Marcus, *The Other Victorians: A Study of Sexuality and Pornography in Mid-Nineteenth-Century England* (New York: Basic Books, 1964), pp. 197–216.

26. One of the more interesting discussions of erotica is found in William H. Epstein, *John Cleland: Images of a Life* (New York: Columbia University Press, 1974), pp. 87–88. Peter Gay offers a witty set of instructions to an author of commercial erotica in *Education of the Senses,* vol. 1, *The Bourgeois Experience: Victoria to Freud* (New York: Oxford University Press, 1984), pp. 370–71. George Ryley Scott, *Into Whose Hands: An Examination of Obscene Libel in its Legal, Sociological and Literary Aspects* (London: Gerald G. Swan, 1945), p. 189; Pepys's diary entry can be found in Thompson, *Unfit for Modest Ears,* p. 22.

27. I am using the word "obscenity" not as a synonym for "pornography" but as a shorthand for the findings of British and American courts. The richly textured language used in cer-

tain works to describe sexual acts and genitalia, in contrast to the repetition of limited curse words, is considered in Lisa Z. Sigel, "Name Your Pleasure: The Transformation of Sexual Language in Nineteenth-Century British Pornography," *Journal of the History of Sexuality,* 9, no. 4 (October 2000): 395–419.

28. Other printers in Massachusetts also used the marbled sheets. In a letter to Marcus A. McCorison, John Alden determined that Munroe and Francis of Boston was the likely printer, after McCorison published *"Memoirs of a Woman of Pleasure* or *Fanny Hill* in New England," *American Book Collector,* 1, no. 3, New Series (May–June 1980): 29–30. All relevant materials, including a copy of John Alden to Marcus A. McCorison, December 8, 1980, and Thomas Evans to Isaiah Thomas, July 29, 1786, discussed below, are gathered in a folder at the American Antiquarian Society, Worcester, Massachusetts.

29. William J. Gilmore, *Reading Becomes a Necessity of Life* (Knoxville: University of Tennessee Press, 1989), pp. 176–78.

30. This is an important theme in the pathbreaking work of David M. Rabban, *Free Speech in Its Forgotten Years* (Cambridge, England: Cambridge University Press, 1997).

31. "The criminal code reflects . . . the moral sense of the community—or, to be more accurate, the moral sense of the people who count, and who speak out, in the community," excluding slaves and women among others; stated in Lawrence M. Friedman, *Crime and Punishment in American History* (New York: Basic Books, 1993), p. 125.

32. Robert Cover, "Violence and the Word," in *Narrative, Violence, and the Law: The Essays of Robert Cover,* ed. Martha Minow, Michael Ryan, and Austin Sarat (Ann Arbor: University of Michigan Press, 1992), p. 203.

33. Morris L. Ernst and Alan U. Schwartz, *Censorship: The Search for the Obscene* (New York: Macmillan Company, 1964). My effort to understand common law in America, especially in the nineteenth century, has been complicated by the relative uninterest in it by recent legal scholars, as attested by Hendrik Hartog, "Distancing Oneself from the Eighteenth Century," in *Law in the American Revolution and the Revolution in the Law,* ed. Hendrick Hartog (New York: New York University Press, 1981), p. 248.

34. For example, this statement in James C. N. Paul and Murray L. Schwartz, *Federal Censorship: Obscenity in the Mail* (New York: Free Press of Glencoe, 1961), p. 11: "There was also common law authority [for suppression of obscenity]. . . . But in the actual cases which had arisen, the courts seemed more concerned with the scandalous behavior of the particular individuals who had been indicted than with the general repression of a particular publication. . . . These were prosecutions, so it was said, for 'breaches of the peace' or for reckless affronts to the rudimentary norms of individual deportment in public places."

35. Ernst and Schwartz, *Censorship: The Search for the Obscene;* C. Thomas Dienes, *Law, Politics, and Birth Control* (Urbana: University of Illinois Press, 1972), offers an effective counter-interpretation, but it has been obscured because it appears to be about birth control, not free speech and obscenity. I draw on both of these sources for the chronology that follows.

36. David Rabban makes a comparable argument for Zechariah Chafee, Jr.; see Rabban, *Free Speech in Its Forgotten Years,* p. 7.

37. Clifton O. Lawhorne, *Defamation and Public Officials: The Evolving Law of Libel* (Carbondale: Southern Illinois University Press, 1971), discussed this same process for the study of seditious libel at the state level. He wrote (p. 52): "There is, however, no systematic body of knowledge concerning these state prosecutions . . . during this period. Reports in the various states concerning criminal law are sketchy; information must be obtained largely from newspapers of the day. The indictments in these state courts were at common law, not statutory law. And the common law that was in force . . . was the common law of England."

38. *Dominus Rex v. Curl,* 2 Stra. 788, reproduced in Edward De Grazia, *Censorship Landmarks* (New York: R. R. Bowker Company, 1969), pp. 3–5.

39. "Wilkes vs. The King," *The English Reports,* vol. 97 (Edinburgh: William Green & Sons, 1909), pp. 123–30, quote from p. 124; Scott, *Into Whose Hands,* pp. 87–89; George Rude, *Wilkes and Liberty: A Social Study of 1763 to 1774* (Oxford: Clarendon Press, 1962), pp. 31–35; Peter Quennell, *Four Portraits: Studies of the Eighteenth Century* (London: Collins, 1945), pp. 207–13; R. W. Postgate, *That Devil Wilkes* (New York: Vanguard Press, 1929), especially pp. 66–68, 71–74, 137–38, 146; *Dictionary of National Biography,* vol. 21 (London: Smith, Elder & Co., 1885–1901), pp. 242–50.

40. William Blackstone, *Of Public Wrongs, Commentaries on the Laws of England,* vol. 4, Facsimile of the First Edition of 1765–69 (Chicago: University of Chicago Press, 1979), pp. 41–42, 64.

41. Ibid., pp. 150–51. I have added italics for emphasis. Rabban, *Free Speech in Its Forgotten Years,* documents the use of "bad tendency" extensively; see especially the discussion on pp. 132–46, 255. I am grateful to David Rabban for pointing this out to me in a communication, January 26, 2000.

42. Blackstone, *Of Public Wrongs,* pp. 151–53. I have added italics for emphasis.

43. Morton J. Horwitz, *The Transformation of American Law, 1780–1860* (Cambridge, Mass.: Harvard University Press, 1977), pp. 4–9; quote from John Randolph, attorney general of Virginia, 1768, p. 7.

44. Francis Ludlow Holt, *The Law of libel; in which is contained a general history of this law in the ancient codes, and of its introduction, and successive alterations, in the law of England* (London: J. Butterworth and Son, 1816), esp. Chapter 3; quotes from pp. 72, 283–84. Blackstone's discussion of the relationship of criminal libel law to freedom of the press contained an important footnote on the history of printing licensing (Blackstone, *Of Public Wrongs,* p. 152, footnote a). Expanding on that note, Holt developed the treatment in an effort to free the law of libel from the onus of the Star Chamber.

45. *Commonwealth of Pennsylvania v. Sharpless,* 2 Serg. & R. 91 (1815), reproduced in De Grazia, *Censorship Landmarks,* pp. 35–40.

46. *Commonwealth v. Peter Holmes,* Supreme Judicial Court for Worcester County, extended Record Book, vol. 5, including records before the Circuit Court of Common Pleas, Archives and Records Preservation, Supreme Judicial Court, Boston, Mass.

47. Gilmore, *Reading Becomes a Necessity of Life,* pp. 130–34; quote from pp. 133, 134.

48. *Commonwealth v. Peter Holmes,* 17 Mass. 336 (1821), reproduced in De Grazia, *Censorship Landmarks,* pp. 40–41.

3: *Free Thought, Sexual Knowledge, and Evangelical Christianity*

1. For Frances Wright's life and career, I have relied on Celia Morris Eckhardt, *Fanny Wright: Rebel in America* (Cambridge, Mass.: Harvard University Press, 1984), and Janet Farrell Brodie, *Contraception and Abortion in 19th-Century America* (Ithaca, N.Y.: Cornell University Press, 1994), pp. 119–25. For Robert Dale Owen, see Richard William Leopold, *Robert Dale Owen: A Biography* (Cambridge, Mass.: Harvard University Press, 1940); Broadus Mitchell, "Robert Dale Owen," *Dictionary of American Biography,* vol. 14 (New York: Charles Scribner's Sons, 1934), pp. 118–20. Brodie has emphasized the contributions of free thought to the diffusion of birth control, pp. 136–43. Much of the detail below has been gleaned from the *Free Enquirer.*

2. Robert Dale Owen, "An Earnest Sowing of Wild Oats," *Atlantic Monthly,* 34 (1874): 73; Horace Traubel, *Conversations with Walt Whitman in Camden,* vol. 2 (New York, 1908–14), pp. 204–6. Whitman was about ten at the time of Wright's lectures.

3. Eckhardt, *Fanny Wright,* p. 191.

4. Jon Butler, *Awash in a Sea of Faith: Christianizing the American People* (Cambridge, Mass.: Harvard University Press, 1990), p. 283; Carroll Smith Rosenberg, *Religion and the Rise of the American City: The New York City Mission Movement, 1812–1870* (Ithaca, N.Y.: Cornell University Press, 1971), pp. 46–48, 70–96.

5. *Free Enquirer,* 2 (January 2, 1830): 80; Eckhardt, *Fanny Wright,* pp. 191, 194; Leopold, *Robert Dale Owen,* pp. 68–71.

6. Bernard A. Weisberger, *They Gathered at the River: The Story of the Great Revivalists and Their Impact upon Religion in America* (Boston: Little, Brown and Company, 1958), pp. 122–26. This was in a city that had only recently seen the end of slavery.

7. Richard B. Stott, *Workers in the Metropolis: Class, Ethnicity, and Youth in Antebellum New York City* (Ithaca, N.Y.: Cornell University Press, 1990), pp. 48–55; David Paul Nord, "The Evangelical Origins of Mass Media in America, 1815–1835," *Journalism Monographs,* 88 (May 1984): 1–30.

8. Stott, *Workers in the Metropolis,* p. 52.

9. For the best statement of women's legal inequalities, see Linda K. Kerber, *No Constitutional Right to Be Ladies: Women and the Obligation of Citizenship* (New York: Hill and Wang, 1998).

10. Brodie, *Contraception and Abortion,* pp. 123–25; Owen, "Earnest Sowing of Wild Oats," pp. 67–78.

11. George S. Rousseau, "Nerves, Spirits, and Fibres: Towards Defining the Origins of Sensibility," *The Blue Guitar,* 2 (1976): 136; G. S. Rousseau, "Nymphomania, Bienville and the Rise of Erotic Sensibility," in *Sexuality in Eighteenth-Century Britain,* ed. Paul-Gabriel Boucé (Manchester, England: Manchester University Press, 1982), p. 109.

12. Much important work has begun to map the European scene, for example, Peter Wagner, *Eros Revived: Erotica of the Enlightenment in England and America* (London: Secker & Warburg), 1988; G. S. Rousseau, and Roy Porter, *Sexual Underworlds of the Enlightenment* (Chapel Hill: University of North Carolina Press, 1988); *Sexuality in Eighteenth-Century Britain,* ed. Paul-Gabriel Boucé (Manchester, England: Manchester University Press, 1982), pp. 95–119; Robert Darnton, *The Literary Underground of the Old Regime* (Cambridge, Mass.: Harvard University Press, 1982); *The Invention of Pornography: Obscenity and the Origins of Modernity, 1500–1800,* ed. Lynn Hunt (New York: Zone Books, 1993), pp. 9–45. Work on eighteenth-century American sexuality awaits a new generation of scholars whose dissertations are just emerging into articles and books.

13. Laurel Thatcher Ulrich, *A Midwife's Tale: The Life of Martha Ballard Based on Her Diary, 1785–1812* (New York: Alfred A. Knopf, 1990), pp. 27–28; Judith Walzer Leavitt, *Brought to Bed: Childrearing in America, 1750–1950* (New York: Oxford University Press, 1986), pp. 39–44. In 1773 William Hunter, a teacher of midwifery to male physicians, wrote *Anatomy of the Gravid Uterus,* a milestone in the scientific understanding of female anatomy. Hunter was the teacher of William Shippen, who brought obstetrical education to America; see Adrian Wilson, *The Making of Man-Midwifery: Childbirth in England, 1660–1770* (Cambridge, Mass.: Harvard University Press, 1995), p. 175, and Leavitt, *Brought to Bed,* p. 264.

14. Eckhardt, *Fanny Wright,* pp. 141–43.

15. Fanny Wright, "Nashoba, Explanatory Notes, &c. Continued," *New-Harmony Gazette,*

17 (February 6, 1828): 132; Eckhardt, *Fanny Wright*, pp. 156–58; Carol A. Kolmerten, *Women in Utopia: The Ideology of Gender in the American Owenite Communities* (Bloomington: Indiana University Press, 1990), p. 126.

16. Wright, "Nashoba, Explanatory Notes, &c. Continued," p. 132.

17. "Reply to the Traducers of the French Reformers of the Year 1789," lecture, Park Theater, January 31, 1829, in Frances Wright, *Course of Popular Lectures* (New York: Free Enquirer, 1829), pp. 227–31, quote from p. 230; Fanny Wright, "On the Nature of Knowledge," in *Life, Letters, and Lectures* (New York: Arno Press, 1972), pp. 20–21.

18. Eckhardt, *Fanny Wright*, pp. 215–20; Sean Wilentz, *Chants Democratic: New York City and the Rise of the American Working Class, 1788–1850* (New York: Oxford University Press, 1984), pp. 176–216.

19. Richard Carlile, *Every Woman's Book, or, What Is Love?* abridged from *The Republican*, 11, no. 18, by Godfrey Higgins (photocopy from Seligmann Collection, Columbia University Library, in Widener Library, Harvard University), p. 6; Robert Dale Owen, *Moral Physiology; or, a Brief and Plain Treatise on the Population Question* (New York: Wright and Owen, 1831), pp. iv, iii.

20. Carlile, *Every Woman's Book*, pp. 4, 3, 15. I have profited by Joel H. Wiener, *Radicalism and Freethought in Nineteenth-Century Britain: The Life of Richard Carlile* (Westport, Conn.: Greenwood Press, 1983), pp. 127–29.

21. Carlile, *Every Woman's Book*, pp. 5, 7–10.

22. After her daughter's birth, Fanny Wright and Philquepal married. She took his family name, d'Arusmont, and remained in France until 1835.

23. Owen, *Moral Physiology*, pp. 13, 16. For a discussion of Owen and this work, see Brodie, *Contraception and Abortion*, pp. 89–94.

24. Owen, *Moral Physiology*, pp. 70, 71.

25. Ibid., pp. iv, 11–12.

26. Ibid., pp. 7–9.

27. Ibid., p. 33.

28. Ibid., p. 42.

29. Ibid., p. 44.

30. Ibid., p. 55.

31. Ibid., pp. 66–67, 61–64 (quote from p. 61), 67. Owen wrote prior to vulcanized rubber.

32. Frances Wright, "Moral Physiology," *Free Enquirer*, 3 (March 5, 1831): 150–51; Leopold, *Robert Dale Owen*, pp. 65–120; Mitchell, "Robert Dale Owen," pp. 118–20.

33. Lyman Beecher, *Lectures on Political Atheism and Kindred Subjects* (Boston: John P. Jewett & Company, 1852), pp. 91–99, quote from p. 92. This is the published text of the lectures that Beecher gave in Park Church, Boston, in November and December 1830.

34. "Bold Tactics," *Free Enquirer*, 2 (January 30, 1830): 112; Beecher, *Lectures on Political Atheism*, pp. 91, 97–99.

35. Beecher, *Lectures on Political Atheism*, pp. 92, 97–99.

36. Keith Thomas, *Man and the Natural World: A History of the Modern Sensibility* (New York: Pantheon Books, 1983), pp. 17–50, quotes from pp. 35, 42.

37. Pierre Hurteau, "Catholic Moral Discourse on Male Sodomy and Masturbation in the Seventeenth and Eighteenth Centuries," *Journal of the History of Sexuality*, 4, no. 1 (July 1993): 1–26.

38. Edmund S. Morgan, "The Puritans and Sex," *New England Quarterly*, 15 (December 1942): 592–93. Thomas A. Foster has reaffirmed Morgan's insistence on Puritans' belief in the importance of sexual pleasure in marriage and has emphasized sexual potency as a critical ele-

ment in Puritan definitions of manhood; see "Deficient Husbands: Manhood, Sexual Incapacity, and Male Marital Sexuality in Seventeenth-Century New England," *William and Mary Quarterly,* 3rd ser., 56, no. 4 (October 1999): 724–44.

39. My understanding of the American Enlightenment and the relationship of America to France and French thought has been shaped by Henry F. May, *The Enlightenment in America* (New York: Oxford University Press, 1976).

40. Timothy Dwight, *Nature and Danger of the Infidel Philosophy,* 1798, as quoted in Chandos Michael Brown, "Mary Wollstonecraft, or, the Female Illuminati: The Campaign Against Women and 'Modern Philosophy' in the Early Republic," *Journal of the Early Republic,* 15, no. 3 (1995): 389–424, quote from p. 396; see also May, *Enlightenment in America,* p. 263. Katherine Binhammer, "The Sex Panic of the 1790s," *Journal of the History of Sexuality,* 6, no. 3 (1996): 409–34, sheds an interesting light on English conservative thinking but sees it as a national movement rather than a political conflict and fails to address the new power of print.

41. Brown, "Mary Wollstonecraft," pp. 401–4, Dwight quoted on p. 401. That Dwight's fears were hardly abstract can be seen in Clare Anna Lyons, "Sex Among the 'Rabble': Gender Transitions in the Age of Revolution, Philadelphia, 1750–1830," Ph.D. dissertation, Yale University, 1996, which documents the varied sexual behaviors and representations in Philadelphia in the late eighteenth and early nineteenth centuries.

42. Lori Ginzberg has written about the way that the invocation of Fanny Wright's very name served the cause of evangelical Christian ministers by associating her freethinking views with sexual license; see " 'The Hearts of Your Readers Will Shudder': Fanny Wright, Infidelity, and American Free Thought," *American Quarterly,* 46, no. 2 (June 1994): 195–226.

43. "Extract of Dr. Beecher's speech at Pittsburgh on the desecration of the Sabbath," *Advocate for Moral Reform,* 2, no. 13 (July 15, 1836): 104.

44. One can see this playing into the second generation as Lyman Beecher's daughter Catharine imagined Fanny Wright "with her great masculine person, her loud voice, her untasteful attire, going about unprotected . . . and standing up with bare faced impudence, to lecture to a public assembly. . . . There she stands, with brazen front and brawny arms, attacking the safeguards of all that is venerable and sacred in religion. . . . I cannot conceive anything in the shape of a woman, more intolerably offensive and disgusting"; see *Letters on the Difficulties of Religion,* 1836, quoted in Jeanne Boydston, Mary Kelley, and Anne Margolis, *The Limits of Sisterhood: The Beecher Sisters on Women's Rights and Woman's Sphere* (Chapel Hill: University of North Carolina Press, 1988), pp. 236–37.

45. "Extract of Dr. Beecher's speech at Pittsburgh," p. 104.

46. Robert Dale Owen, response to William Gibbons, *Free Enquirer,* 2 (February 27, 1830): 141–42.

4: *Blasphemy, Birth Control, and Obscenity*

1. Roderick S. French, "The Trials of Abner Kneeland: A Study in the Rejection of Democratic Secular Humanism," Ph.D. dissertation, George Washington University, 1971 (University Microfilms, 1972), p. 149. Much of the discussion that follows is based on this well-researched thesis. See also Olive Hoogenboom, "Abner Kneeland," *National American Biography,* vol. 12 (New York: Oxford University Press, 1999), pp. 802–3.

2. Samuel P. Putnam, *Four Hundred Years of Freethought* (New York, 1894), pp. 755–56; Richard William Leopold, *Robert Dale Owen: A Biography* (Cambridge, Mass.: Harvard Univer-

sity Press, 1940), p. 70; *Boston Investigator*, 1, no. 1 (April 2, 1831): 1, lists Abner Kneeland as editor.

3. Ben Krapac, "Cogitations of an Infidel," *Boston Investigator*, 3, no. 39 (December 20, 1833): 1; "Tracts! Tracts! Tracts!," ibid., p. 2; Abner Kneeland, "To the Editor of the Trumpet," ibid., p. 3.

4. "The Following Are the Regular Toasts," *Boston Investigator*, 3, no. 45 (January 31, 1834): 3.

5. Leonard W. Levy, ed., *Blasphemy in Massachusetts: Freedom of Conscience and the Abner Knee-land Case, a Documentary Record* (New York: Da Capo Press, 1973); Leonard W. Levy, *Blasphemy: Verbal Defenses Against the Sacred, from Moses to Salman Rushdie* (New York: Alfred A. Knopf, 1993), pp. 400–23; Henry Steele Commager, "The Blasphemy of Abner Kneeland," *New England Quarterly*, 8 (March 1935), pp. 29–41. I have also profited by Joss Marsh, *Word Crimes: Blasphemy, Culture and Literature in Nineteenth-Century England* (Chicago: University of Chicago Press, 1998).

6. *Report of the Arguments of the Attorney of the Commonwealth at the Trials of Abner Kneeland for Blasphemy* (Boston: Beals, Homer & Co., 1834), pp. 13–14, reprinted in Levy, ed., *Blasphemy in Massachusetts*, pp. 189–90.

7. References to Holt and Starkie are in *Arguments of the Attorney*, p. 10, in Levy, ed., *Blasphemy in Massachusetts*, p. 186; Thomas Starkie, *A Treatise on the Law of Slander and Libel*, 2nd ed., vol. 1 (London: J. and W. T. Clarke, 1830), pp. xcviii, xcxix; *Report of the Arguments of the Attorney*, p. 10.

8. *Commonwealth v. Kneeland*, 37 Mass. (1838), 211–25, reprinted in Levy, ed., *Blasphemy in Massachusetts*, pp. 425–39.

9. Levy, ed., *Blasphemy in Massachusetts*, pp. 422–23.

10. "The Late Charles Knowlton, M.D.," *Boston Medical and Surgical Journal*, 45, no. 6 (September 10, 1851): 109–11; and 45, no. 8 (September 24, 1851): 149–57; quotes from no. 8, pp. 156–57, 154; for Knowlton's life, I have relied on Norman E. Himes, "Charles Knowlton," *Dictionary of American Biography*, vol. 10 (New York: Charles Scribner's Sons, 1933), pp. 471–72; James Reed, "Charles Knowlton," *National American Biography*, vol. 12 (New York: Oxford University Press, 1999), pp. 829–30; Janet Farrell Brodie, *Contraception and Abortion in 19th-Century America* (Ithaca, N.Y.: Cornell University Press, 1994), pp. 94–96; and records in the Pocumtuck Valley Memorial Association, Deerfield, Massachusetts.

11. Charles Knowlton, *Elements of Modern Materialism* (Adams, Mass.: printed for the author, 1829); Charles Knowlton, *Two Remarkable Lectures Delivered in Boston, March 31, 1833* (Boston: A. Kneeland, 1833), pp. 8–9. Knowlton's ideas are seen as a precursor of twentieth-century behaviorism.

12. "The Late Charles Knowlton, M.D.," 45, no. 8, pp. 156–57.

13. *Free Enquirer*, 4, no. 28 (May 5, 1832): 224; "Book Store," *Free Enquirer*, 4, no. 30 (May 19, 1832): 240; *Free Enquirer*, 1 (New Series), no. 1 (October 27, 1833): 8.

14. [Charles Knowlton], *Fruits of Philosophy; Or, the Private Companion of Young Married People* (New York, 1832), copyright date: 1831, Rhode Island, copy in Lilly Library, Indiana University, Bloomington, Indiana.

15. Brodie, *Contraception and Abortion*, pp. 97–104; Robert E. Riegel, "The American Father of Birth Control," *New England Quarterly*, 6, no. 3 (1933): 470–90; Norman E. Himes, *Medical History of Contraception* (New York: Gamut Press, 1963), pp. 226–30.

16. [Knowlton], *Fruits of Philosophy*, 1832, pp. 13, 14.

17. Ibid., pp. iv, 71–72. Knowlton's clarity about reproduction and birth control here casts doubt on the applicability of arguments about nineteenth-century American writers on sex in Thomas Laqueur, *Making Sex: Body and Gender from the Greeks to Freud* (Cambridge, Mass.: Har-

vard University Press, 1990). Laqueur's work is helpful in guiding understanding of the European background gathered in *Aristotle's Master-piece;* where it ceases to be useful to U.S. historians is in delineation of the "two-sex" model of the nineteenth century, Chapters 5 and 6.

18. [Knowlton], *Fruits of Philosophy,* 1832, pp. 20, 28.

19. L. S. Everett, *An Exposure of the Principles of the "Free Inquirers"* (Boston: Benjamin B. Mussey, 1831), pp. 34–35.

20. Although riddled with minor errors, Michael Grossberg's discussion in *Governing the Hearth: Law and the Family in Nineteenth-Century America* (Chapel Hill: University of North Carolina Press, 1985), pp. 156–59, is useful.

21. "The Days of Witchcraft Returned," *Boston Investigator,* 2, no. 41 (January 4, 1833): 2.

22. Letter from Dr. Charles Knowlton, *Boston Investigator,* 2, no. 42 (January 11, 1833): 2–3.

23. Ibid.

24. *Boston Investigator,* 2, no. 46 (February 8, 1833): 3; 2, no. 47 (February 15, 1833): 2 (brackets in the original).

25. "Dr. Knowlton's Lecture," *Boston Investigator,* 3, no. 3 (April 12, 1833): 2.

26. "Public Meeting," *Boston Investigator,* 3, no. 4 (April 19, 1833): 3; Card, *Boston Investigator,* 3, no. 3 (April 12, 1833): 3.

27. Charles Knowlton, *Fruits of Philosophy; or the Private Companion of Young Married People,* 2nd ed. (Boston: [Abner Kneeland], 1833).

28. Notice, *Boston Investigator,* 3, no. 3 (April 12, 1833): 3.

29. Himes, "Charles Knowlton," pp. 471–72; Riegel, "American Father of Birth Control," pp. 470–90.

30. Quotes in Knowlton, *Fruits of Philosophy,* 1833, pp. 37, 140.

31. Quotes in ibid., pp. 55–56, 133.

32. Quotes in ibid., pp. 40, 71, 68.

33. Quotes in ibid., pp. 136, 139, 119–20.

34. Charles Knowlton, *A History of the Recent Excitement in Ashfield* (Ashfield, Mass., 1834), p. 16.

35. Ibid., p. 10.

36. Ibid., p. 23.

37. Charles Knowlton, *Fruits of Philosophy, or the Private Companion of Adult People,* 4th ed. (Philadelphia: F. P. Rogers, 1839), pp. 40, 42, 60, iv–v.

38. Ibid., pp. 95–98, quotes from pp. 95, 98.

39. Ibid., pp. 9, 15.

40. Brodie, *Contraception and Abortion,* p. 325, note 142.

41. Italics in original. *Address of Dr. Charles Knowlton, Before the Friends of Mental Liberty at Greenfield, Mass., and Constitution of the United Liberals of Franklin County, Mass.* (Boston: J. P. Mendum, 1845), pp. 10, 16. Copy in Pocumtock Valley Memorial Association, Deerfield, Mass.

42. Although the spermicidal douche is not a reliable method for individual use, it can reduce the birthrate significantly when used by a large population. On the falling birthrate, see Daniel Scott Smith, "Family Limitation, Sexual Control, and Domestic Feminism in Victorian America," in *Clio's Consciousness Raised: New Perspectives on the History of Women,* ed. Mary S. Hartman and Lois Banner (New York: Harper & Row, 1974), pp. 119–36; specific reference to fall in birthrate, p. 123. Norman E. Himes gave Knowlton primary responsibility for population decrease in England where freethinking publishers kept his books in print ("Charles Knowlton's Revolutionary Influence on the English Birth Rate," *New England Journal of Medicine,* 199, no. 10 [September 1928]: 461–63). I recall vividly a summer school class at Columbia University in 1961, when Robert E. Riegel made the point that American copies of Knowlton's work were

so scarce because they had literally been used up as they passed from hand to hand (see Riegel, "American Father of Birth Control").

43. William A. Alcott, *The Physiology of Marriage* (Boston: John P. Jewett & Co., 1856), p. 180.

5: *The Masturbation Scare and the Rise of Reform Physiology*

1. Stuart M. Blumin, *The Emergence of the Middle Class: Social Experience in the American City, 1760–1900* (Cambridge, England: Cambridge University Press, 1989).

2. Biographies provide evidence of the way that Americans absorbed the advice of their era about the body and sexuality, as, for example, Robert H. Abzug's illuminating *Passionate Liberator: Theodore Dwight Weld and the Dilemma of Reform* (New York: Oxford University Press, 1980), especially pp. 208–36. Other evidence comes from diaries, such as *Young Ward's Diary*, ed. Bernhard T. Stern (New York: Putnam, 1935), and from marginalia in the books themselves.

3. Charles E. Rosenberg, "The Therapeutic Revolution: Medicine, Meaning, and Social Change in Nineteenth-Century America," *Perspectives in Biology and Medicine*, 20 (1977): 485–506; Susan E. Cayleff, *Wash and Be Healed: The Water-Cure Movement and Women's Health* (Philadelphia: Temple University Press, 1987), pp. 1–16.

4. John S. Haller, Jr., *American Medicine in Transition, 1840–1910* (Urbana: University of Illinois Press, 1981); Joseph K. Kett, *The Formation of the American Medical Profession: The Role of Institutions, 1780–1860* (New Haven, Conn.: Yale University Press, 1968); John Harley Warner, *The Therapeutic Perspective: Medical Practice, Knowledge, and Identity in America, 1820–1885* (Cambridge, Mass.: Harvard University Press, 1986), passim, quotes from p. 94.

5. Kett, *The Formation of the American Medical Profession*, Chapters 4, 5; John S. Haller, Jr., *Medical Protestants: The Eclectics in American Medicine, 1825–1939* (Carbondale: Southern Illinois University Press, 1994).

6. Madeleine B. Stern, *Heads and Headlines: The Phrenological Fowlers* (Norman: University of Oklahoma Press, 1971), pp. 49–51, 126–27.

7. Martha H. Verbrugge, *Able Bodied Womanhood: Personal Health and Social Change in Nineteenth-Century Boston* (New York: Oxford University Press, 1988), pp. 50–57.

8. Frederick Hollick, *The Origin of Life: A Popular Treatise on the Philosophy and Physiology of Reproduction* (New York: Nafis & Cornish, 1845), pp. vii–viii; Edward B. Foote, *Medical Common Sense; Applied to the Causes, Prevention and Cure of Chronic Diseases and Unhappiness in Marriage* (Boston: Wentworth, Hewes & Co., 1858), p. iii.

9. "Popular Lectures on Tight Lacing," *Boston Medical and Surgical Journal*, 12, no. 21 (July 1, 1835); 337; Augustus K. Gardner, *A History of the Art of Midwifery* (New York: Stringer & Townsend, 1852), pp. 30–31.

10. E. H. Hare, "Masturbatory Insanity: The History of an Idea," *The Journal of Mental Science*, 108, no. 452 (January 1962): 1–25. For the treatment of British medical thought, see Lesley A. Hall, "Forbidden by God, Despised by Men: Masturbation, Medical Warnings, Moral Panic, and Manhood in Great Britain," *Journal of the History of Sexuality*, 2, no. 3 (January 1992): 365–87. The problem of the masturbation scare assumed new importance with Michel Foucault, *The History of Sexuality: An Introduction*, vol. 1. I have used the 1978 translation by Robert Hurley (New York: Vintage Books, 1990). An important addition to the literature on masturbation is *Solitary Pleasures: The Historical, Literary, and Artistic Discourses of Autoeroticism*, ed. Paula Bennett and Vernon A. Rosario II (New York: Routledge, 1995), especially the editors' excellent introduction, pp. 1–17.

11. David Stevenson, "Recording the Unspeakable: Masturbation in the Diary of William Drummond, 1657–1659," *Journal of the History of Sexuality*, 9, no. 3 (July 2000): 223–39; Michael Stolberg, "Self-Pollution, Moral Reform, and the Venereal Trade: Notes on the Sources and Historical Context of *Onania* (1716)," *Journal of the History of Sexuality*, 9, nos. 1 and 2 (January–April 2000): 37–61.

12. H. Tristram Engelhardt, Jr., "The Disease of Masturbation: Values and the Concept of Disease," in *Sickness and Health in America*, pp. 13–14; Alan Hunt has noted the "slippage between medical and moral discourses" in Tissot and other writers on masturbation in the eighteenth and nineteenth centuries ("The Great Masturbation Panic and the Discourses of Moral Regulation in Nineteenth- and Early Twentieth-Century Britain," *Journal of the History of Sexuality*, 8, no. 4 [1998]: 577–78).

13. Sylvester Graham, *A Lecture on Epidemic Diseases Generally, and Particularly the Spasmodic Cholera* (New York: Mahlon Day, 1833), pp. 20, 40.

14. Ibid., p. 49.

15. Sylvester Graham, *A Lecture to Young Men* (Providence: Weeden and Cory, 1834), pp. 16–17, 14.

16. Ibid., p. 16.

17. Ibid., p. 20.

18. Ibid., pp. 16–17. The phrenologist Andrew Boardman recommended succinctly the "avoidance of lascivious books, plays, dances, and associates"; see Andrew Boardman, *A Defence of Phrenology* (New York: Fowler and Wells, 1847), p. 207.

19. Graham, *Lecture to Young Men*, p. 24.

20. Ibid., pp. 26–27, 25.

21. I have read the American edition of S. A. D. Tissot, *A Treatise on the Diseases Produced by Onanism*, trans. from a new edition of the French, by a physician (New York: Collins & Hannay, 1832). Interestingly enough, when the translator apologized for errors, he gave as the excuse that the book had been printed during the cholera epidemic (p. 114). Graham, *Lecture to Young Men*, pp. 40, 42.

22. Graham, *Lecture to Young Men*, pp. 43–46, quote from p. 43. These examples, as others that follow, raise the question of whether the "solitary vice" was really solitary or involved perceived but unnamed homosexual behaviors.

23. Samuel B. Woodward, Superintendent's Report, November 30, 1833, *Reports and Other Documents Relating to the State Lunatic Hospital at Worcester, Mass.* (Boston: Dutton and Wentworth, 1837), p. 52.

24. Samuel B. Woodward, "Insanity, Produced by Masturbation," *Boston Medical and Surgical Journal*, 12, no. 7 (March 25, 1835): 109. Although it is listed in his report as second after intemperance, in this article Woodward states, "No cause is more influential in producing Insanity" and perpetuating it than masturbation (p. 109). While it may well have been that the Swiss physician S. A. D. Tissot brought masturbation to the attention of physicians in his work *L'Onanisme* of 1760, Americans such as Woodward insist that their words are based on their own observations.

25. [Luther V. Bell, M.D.], *An Hour's Conference with Fathers and Sons, in Relation to a Common and Fatal Indulgence of Youth* (Boston: Whipple and Damrell, 1840), pp. 9–12. Bell's insistence that Woodward's writing was crucial, rather than that of Tissot, raises important questions about the transmission and communication of knowledge.

26. S. [Samuel] B. Woodward, M.D., *Hints for the Young* (Boston: G. W. Light, 1856), p. 1; [Bell], *An Hour's Conference*, pp. 14–15.

27. Despite the contested notions of childhood in this era, the desirability of childhood sexual innocence was widely held, even among Calvinists. Perhaps lingering notions of original sin intensified fears about children's susceptibility to sexual initiation.

28. Samuel Gregory, *Facts and Important Information from Distinguished Physicians and Other Sources* (Boston: George Gregory, 1841), pp. 19–20 ["self-abuse" is misspelled "self-abue" in the original]; Mary Sargeant Gove [Nichols], *Solitary Vice: An Address to Parents and Those Who Have the Care of Children* (Portland, Me.: Journal Office, 1839), pp. 9, 13.

29. Gregory, *Facts and Important Information from Distinguished Physicians*, pp. 19–20.

30. [Bell], *An Hour's Conference*, pp. 26–27, 24.

31. Woodward, *Hints for the Young*, pp. 34–35.

32. Ibid., p. 49.

33. [Bell], *An Hour's Conference*, pp. 21–23, 60–61, 62, 65.

34. Ibid., pp. 48–51.

35. Woodward, *Hints for the Young*, pp. 64, 63.

36. Gregory, *Facts and Important Information from Distinguished Physicians*, p. 27; Samuel Gregory, *Facts and Important Information for Young Men, on the Subject of Masturbation; with Its Causes, Prevention, and Cure* (Boston: George Gregory, 1848 [c. 1845]), p. 36. Again, such quotes raise the question, not answered by the sources themselves, of whether or to what extent the fear of masturbation was really a cover for fear of homosexual activity. The best that can be said at this point is that the nineteenth-century concern was with nonprocreative sex. See Vern L. Bullough and Martha Voght, "Homosexuality and Its Confusion with the 'Secret Sin' in Pre-Freudian America," *Journal of the History of Medicine and Allied Sciences*, 28 (April 1973): 143–55.

37. Gove, *Solitary Vice*, p. 13.

38. W [Samuel B. Woodward], "Remarks on Masturbation," *Boston Medical and Surgical Journal*, 12, no. 6 (March 18, 1835): 96; Calvin Cutter, M.D., *The Female Guide: Containing Facts and Information upon the Effects of Masturbation* (West Brookfield, Mass.: Charles A. Mirick, 1844), p. 38; Woodward, *Hints for the Young*, pp. 49–50.

39. William A. Alcott, *The Physiology of Marriage* (Boston: John P. Jewett & Co., 1856), p. 167, p. 51 note.

40. R. T. Trall, *Home Treatment for Sexual Abuses* (New York: Fowler and Wells, 1884 [1858]), pp. 36–37.

41. After drafting this section, I read Alan Hunt, "The Great Masturbation Panic," pp. 575–615, and was struck by the many parallels between my observations and arguments and his, especially his treatment of the "melodramas of self-abuse" and his emphasis on the middle class and its worries about children in school.

42. Cayleff, *Wash and Be Healed*, pp. 1–16; Alcott, *Physiology of Marriage*, pp. v, 18. Robert H. Abzug, *Cosmos Crumbling: American Reform and the Religious Imagination* (New York: Oxford University Press, 1994), understands the moral physiology of Alcott and Graham as constructing a set of bodily practices akin to traditional Judaism's adherence to Mosaic law, pp. 163–82, esp. p. 175.

43. Alcott, *The Physiology of Marriage*, pp. 114–16.

44. Cayleff, *Wash and Be Healed*, pp. 23, 25–26. The discussion of the water-cure movement that follows has been influenced by this provocative and well-researched book.

45. On Mary Gove's early life and career, I rely on John B. Blake, "Mary Sargeant Neal Gove Nichols," *Notable American Women*, vol. 2 (Cambridge, Mass.: The Belknap Press of Harvard University Press, 1971), pp. 627–29; Cayleff, *Wash and Be Healed*, passim; Janet Farrell Brodie, *Contraception and Abortion in 19th-Century America* (Ithaca, N.Y.: Cornell University Press, 1994),

pp. 125–26; and Jean Lara Silver-Isenstadt, "Pure Pleasure: The Shared Life and Work of Mary Gove Nichols and Thomas Low Nichols in American Health Reform," Ph.D. dissertation, University of Pennsylvania, 1997.

46. Gail Bederman kindly gave me the hostile reaction to Mary Gove's lectures in the 1839 New York *Herald;* Mary Sargeant Gove, *Lectures to Ladies on Anatomy and Physiology* (Boston: Saxton & Peirce, 1842), pp. v–vi.

47. Mary S. Gove, *Lectures to Women on Anatomy and Physiology with an Appendix on Water Cure* (New York: Harper & Brothers, 1846), p. 172; Gove, *Lectures to Ladies on Anatomy and Physiology,* pp. 214–15.

48. Gove, *Lectures to Ladies on Anatomy and Physiology,* p. 219.

49. Although the minutes of the Ladies' Physiological Institute of Boston do not document that Gove spoke before it, they do record that Paulina Wright Davis, influenced by Gove, did. (Records of the Meetings of the Ladies' Physiological Institute of Boston & vicinity, January 15, 1851, vol. 3, p. 3, Schlesinger Library, Radcliffe Institute, Cambridge, Mass.). Prior to her second marriage, Paulina Wright was active in abolition circles and petitioned the New York legislature for a married women's property law in the late 1830s. She studied physiology and, after the death of her first husband in 1845, traveled to speak to women in New England and the Middle Atlantic states on physiology and health. Following Gove's practice, she instructed with a female mannequin imported from Paris. Years later, while active in the organized women's rights movement, Paulina Wright Davis wrote its history. She placed Mary Gove in the honor roll of women's rights pioneers, following close behind Frances Wright; see *A History of the National Woman's Rights Movement* (New York: Journeymen Printers' Co-operative Association, 1871), p. 11.

50. Trall, *Home Treatment,* pp. iv, 113 (italics in original omitted).

51. Charles Knowlton, "Gonorrhoea Dormientium," *Boston Medical and Surgical Journal,* 27, no. 1 (August 10, 1842): 11–15.

52. "The Later Charles Knowlton, M.D.," *Boston Medical and Surgical Journal,* 45, no. 6 (September 10, 1851), memoir on pp. 111–20, quote on p. 114.

53. Knowlton, "Gonnorrhoea Dormientium," p. 12.

54. The most unusual of these is the plate in Hollick's *Outlines of Anatomy & Physiology* (Philadelphia: T. B. Peterson, 1847), which allows the reader to lift up leaves to reveal deeper levels of the human body, the most basic being the nervous system. This plate is of a male and has no level for the reproductive organs. Copy in the Huntington Library, San Marino, California.

55. Hollick, *Origin of Life,* pp. 167–68.

56. Ibid., p. 174.

57. Ibid., p. 55.

58. Ibid., pp. 189, 70.

59. O. S. Fowler, *Love and Parentage,* in *Works on Phrenology, Physiology, and Kindred Subjects* (London: J. Watson, 1851), p. 18.

60. Ibid., p. 4.

61. Lorenzo N. Fowler, *Marriage: Its History and Ceremonies . . . ,* 22nd ed. (New York: Fowler and Wells, 1848), p. 137; O. S. Fowler, *Love and Parentage,* pp. 2, 35.

62. O. S. Fowler, *Love and Parentage,* pp. 35, 48; O. S. Fowler, *Matrimony; or Phrenology and Physiology,* in *Works on Phrenology,* p. 31.

63. Trall, *Home Treatment,* p. iv.

64. Boardman, *A Defence of Phrenology,* p. 207.

65. Trall, *Home Treatment,* p. x; Hollick, *Origin of Life,* p. 182.

66. Trall, *Home Treatment*, pp. 46–47.

67. Ibid., p. 45.

6: *New York and the Emergence of Sporting Culture*

1. Patricia Cline Cohen, *The Murder of Helen Jewett: The Life and Death of a Prostitute in Nineteenth-Century New York* (New York: Alfred A. Knopf, 1998).

2. Patricia Cline Cohen, "Unregulated Youth: Masculinity and Murder in the 1830s City," *Radical History Review*, 52 (1992): 33–52; Cohen, "The Helen Jewett Murder: Violence, Gender, and Sexual Licentiousness in Antebellum America," *NWSA Journal*, 2 (1990): 374–80; Cohen, *The Murder of Helen Jewett*; Elliott J. Gorn, *The Manly Art: Bare-Knuckle Prize Fighting in America* (Ithaca, N.Y.: Cornell University Press, 1986); Timothy J. Gilfoyle, *City of Eros: New York City, Prostitution, and the Commercialization of Sex, 1790–1920* (New York: W. W. Norton & Company), pp. 92–116; Philip Howell, "Sex and the City of Bachelors: Sporting Guidebooks and Urban Knowledge in Nineteenth-Century Britain and America," *Ecumene: A Journal of Environment, Culture, Meaning*, 8 (January 2001): 20–50; Amy Gilman Srebnick, *The Mysterious Death of Mary Rogers: Sex and Culture in Nineteenth-Century New York* (New York: Oxford University Press, 1995), pp. 53–54; Howard P. Chudacoff, *The Age of the Bachelor: Creating an American Subculture* (Princeton, N.J.: Princeton University Press, 1999), pp. 32–40.

3. For "flash," see B. F. Tefft, "Pencillings at Pittsburgh," in *The Ladies Repository* (Wesleyan Methodist Church), October 1848, pp. 315–17.

4. *The Oxford English Dictionary*, 2nd ed., vol. 16 (Oxford: Clarendon Press, 1989), p. 315; *Slang and Its Analogues, Past and Present*, compiled and edited by John S. Farmer and W. E. Henley, vol. 5 (London: Routledge & Kegan Paul, 1902), p. 321.

5. Sean Wilentz, *Chants Democratic: New York City and the Rise of the American Working Class, 1788–1850* (New York: Oxford University Press, 1984), p. 109.

6. I have profited from the many lively discussions of the penny press, including James L. Crouthamel, "The Newspaper Revolution in New York, 1830–1860," *New York History*, 45 (April 1964): 91–113; Michael Schudson, *Discovering the News: A Social History of American Newspapers* (New York: Basic Books, 1978), pp. 12–60; Andie Tucher, *Froth and Scum: Truth, Beauty, Goodness, and the Ax Murder in America's First Mass Medium* (Chapel Hill: University of North Carolina Press, 1994); and Steven H. Jaffe, "Unmasking the City: The Rise of the Urban Newspaper Reporter in New York City, 1800–1850," Ph.D. dissertation, Harvard University, 1989. For diffusion, see Richard D. Brown, *Knowledge Is Power: The Diffusion of Information in Early America, 1700–1865* (New York: Oxford University Press, 1989), pp. 218, 230.

7. Tucher, *Froth and Scum*, p. 9; Jaffe, "Unmasking the City," pp. 100, 165.

8. Jaffe, "Unmasking the City," Chapter 3.

9. Tucher, *Froth and Scum*, pp. 19, 14.

10. Ibid., pp. 117–22; Crouthamel, "The Newspaper Revolution in New York," p. 100.

11. Richard B. Stott, *Workers in the Metropolis: Class, Ethnicity, and Youth in Antebellum New York City* (Ithaca, N.Y.: Cornell University Press, 1990), pp. 50–52; Madeleine Stern, "Domesticity and Nostalgia: Dick and Fitzgerald," *Books and Book People in 19th-Century America* (New York: R. R. Bowker Company, 1978), p. 275; Aaron Mendoza, "Some Associations of Old Ann Street, 1720–1920," *Valentine's Manual of Old New York*, no. 4 (New York: Valentine's Manual, 1920), pp. 285–303; for reference to the erotic side, see, e.g., "The Tweedle-dum and Tweedle-dee in Morals—The Ann Street Licentious Press, and the Wall Street Licentious Press," *New York Herald*, September 15, 1842.

12. Peter Buckley, "'The Culture of 'Leg-Work,' " in *The Mythmaking Frame of Mind: Social Imagination and American Culture*, ed. James Gilbert et al. (Belmont, Calif.: Wadsworth Publishing Company, 1993), p. 123.

13. Jaffe, "Unmasking the City," p. 210.

14. Wilentz, *Chants Democratic*, pp. 258–59; quote from p. 257.

15. W. T. Lhamon, Jr., *Raising Cain: Blackface Performance from Jim Crow to Hip Hop* (Cambridge, Mass.: Harvard University Press, 1998), pp. 1–55; Robert C. Toll, *Blacking Up: The Minstrel Show in Nineteenth-Century America* (New York: Oxford University Press, 1974), pp. 27–36, quotes from pp. 34, 36. Beginning in 1843, a blackface performing troop calling itself the Virginia minstrels offered an entire evening of entertainment. Rapidly the minstrel show crystallized into a set sequence that troops of white men performed at the Chatham and Bowery Theatres, both primarily working-class venues, and on tour throughout the country. In the 1850s, New York had ten major minstrel houses. While the minstrel craze swept the nation, it was particularly popular in northern cities, and New York was its central home. Important work on minstrelsy includes *Inside the Minstrel Mask: Readings in Nineteenth-Century Blackface Minstrelsy*, ed. Annemarie Bean et al. (Hanover, N.H.: Wesleyan University Press, University Press of New England, 1996); Ken Emerson, *Doo-dah!: Stephen Foster and the Rise of American Popular Culture* (New York: Simon & Schuster, 1997).

16. Robert C. Allen, *Horrible Prettiness: Burlesque and American Culture* (Chapel Hill: University of North Carolina Press, 1991), pp. 51–58.

17. Lowell M. Limpus, *History of the New York Fire Department* (New York: E. P. Dutton and Company, 1940), p. 169.

18. Gorn, *Manly Art*, quote from p. 134; the entire discussion was helpful, but especially p. 107; Wilentz, *Chants Democratic*, pp. 139, 262.

19. W. J. Rorabaugh, *The Alcoholic Republic* (New York: Oxford University Press, 1979), p. 11; Wilentz, *Chants Democratic*, pp. 53–54, quote from p. 53.

20. Rorabaugh, *Alcoholic Republic*, pp. 149–55, quote from p. 151.

21. Wilentz, *Chants Democratic*, pp. 219–54.

22. Paul O. Weinbaum, *Mobs and Demagogues: The New York Response to Collective Violence in the Early Nineteenth Century* ([Ann Arbor, Mich.]: UMI Research Press, 1979), especially pp. 44–49.

23. Wilentz, *Chants Democratic*, pp. 264–65.

24. Allen, *Horrible Prettiness*, pp. 58–61; Peter Buckley, "To the Opera House: Culture and Society in New York City, 1820–1860," Ph.D. dissertation, State University of New York at Stony Brook, 1984, Chap. 1; Lawrence W. Levine, *Highbrow/Lowbrow: The Emergence of Cultural Hierarchy in America* (Cambridge, Mass.: Harvard University Press, 1988), pp. 63–69.

25. Gilfoyle, *City of Eros*, p. 107.

26. Allan Stanley Horlick, *Country Boys and Merchant Princes: The Social Control of Young Men in New York* (Lewisburg, Pa.: Bucknell University Press, 1975), has written effectively about the young clerk, although his examples are limited to the respectable.

27. An example of such a youth is Henry Pierce, a clerk in a Boston hat store, whose diary is analyzed in Stuart M. Blumin, *The Emergence of the Middle Class: Social Experience in the American City, 1760–1900* (Cambridge, England: Cambridge University Press, 1989), p. 240; Richard D. Brown, *Knowledge Is Power*, pp. 218–44, has written well about the role that reading played in the experience of young men hoping to improve themselves.

28. Karen Halttunen, *Confidence Men and Painted Women: A Study of Middle-Class Culture in America, 1830–1870* (New Haven, Conn.: Yale University Press, 1982), pp. 1–32; Henry Ward

Beecher, *Lectures to Young Men on Various Important Subjects* (New York: M. H. Newman & Co., 1850), pp. 140, 121, 209–10, 214.

29. Beecher, *Lectures to Young Men,* p. 218.

30. Paul E. Johnson, *A Shopkeeper's Millennium: Society and Revivals in Rochester, New York, 1815–1837* (New York: Hill and Wang, 1978), especially pp. 121–23.

7: Moral Reformers

1. "Run, Speak to That Young Man," *Advocate of Moral Reform,* 3, no. 5 (March 1, 1837): 217.

2. Ronald G. Walters, "The Erotic South: Civilization and Sexuality in American Abolitionism," *American Quarterly,* 25, no. 2 (1973): 177–201, quote on p. 183, from the *Liberator,* January 29, 1858; Walters cites similar quotes from the 1830s. This artful piece is one of the most interesting interpretations of moral physiology and its impact on reform movements in the nineteenth century.

3. Maria Monk, *Awful Disclosures of the Hotel Dieu Nunnery* (New York: published by Maria Monk, 1836; facsimile edition, Hamden, Conn.: Archon Books, 1962); Jenny Franchot, *Roads to Rome: The Antebellum Protestant Encounter with Catholicism* (Berkeley: University of California Press, 1994), pp. 135–61. The notorious 1834 burning of the Ursuline convent in Charlestown, Massachusetts, a boarding school for Boston's elite daughters, seems not to have been fueled by these eroticized fears, but by a more general anti-Catholicism and the association of boarding under Catholic auspices with captivity.

4. Timothy J. Gilfoyle, *City of Eros: New York City, Prostitution, and the Commercialization of Sex, 1790–1920* (New York: W. W. Norton & Company, 1992), pp. 29–54; Christine Stansell, *City of Women: Sex and Class in New York, 1789–1860* (New York: Alfred A. Knopf, 1986), pp. 171–92.

5. Gilfoyle, *City of Eros,* pp. 108–12.

6. *The Magdalen Report: First Annual Report of the Executive Committee of the New-York Magdalen Society* (New York: printed for the publishers, 1831), p. 11.

7. Ibid., pp. 19–21, quote from pp. 20, 21.

8. Ibid., p. 7; John D. Stevens, *Sensationalism and the New York Press* (New York: Columbia University Press, 1991), p. 43.

9. *Magdalen Report,* 1831, pp. 8–10, quote from p. 10.

10. Ibid., pp. 7, 8.

11. John R. McDowall, "No. 22, Anti-Magdalen Meeting at Tammany Hall," in *Magdalen Facts* (New York: Printed for the author, 1832), pp. 66–69; McDowall, "No. 27, Genius of Temperance—The City Disgraced," in ibid., pp. 72–73.

12. McDowall, "No. 22," p. 69.

13. See discussion of this weekly, Chapter 8.

14. McDowall, "No. 22," p. 68.

15. McDowall, "To the Public," *Magdalen Facts,* p. v.

16. David S. Reynolds, *Beneath the American Renaissance: The Subversive Imagination in the Age of Emerson and Melville* (New York: Alfred A. Knopf, 1988), pp. 62–63.

17. Carroll Smith Rosenberg, *Religion and the Rise of the American City: The New York Mission Movement, 1812–1870* (Ithaca, N.Y.: Cornell University Press, 1971), pp. 98–113.

18. *Advocate of Moral Reform,* 1, nos. 1 and 2 (February 1835): 1.

19. Ibid.; "Clerical Objections Considered," *Advocate of Moral Reform,* 3, no. 20 (October 15,

1837): 340; "Our Object," 1, nos. 1 and 2 (February 1835): 2; for exposure of names, see, e.g., 3, no. 5 (March 1, 1837): 222, 223.

20. "Story of Henry F———," *Advocate of Moral Reform*, 3, no. 17 (September 1, 1837): 313.

21. "Theatricals" extract from the letter of "the eccentric Grant Thorburn" to editor of New York *Daily Express*, *Advocate of Moral Reform*, 3, no. 14 (July 15, 1837): 291.

22. "Gambling Houses," *Advocate of Moral Reform*, 3, no. 23 (December 1, 1837): 367–68.

23. "City Clerks," *Advocate of Moral Reform*, 2, no. 5 (March 1, 1836): 33.

24. Amicus, letter from New Haven, December 28, 1836, *Advocate of Moral Reform*, 3, no. 2 (January 15, 1837): 199.

25. Rev. W. B. Kirwan, "Character of a Libertine," *Advocate of Moral Reform*, 1, nos. 1 and 2 (February 1835): 3; "Depravity in Infant Schools," 1, no. 9 (September 1835): 69–70.

26. "Distress in Our City," *Advocate of Moral Reform*, 3, no. 10 (May 15, 1837): 260.

27. "A Subject of Thought for Pious Parents," *Advocate of Moral Reform*, 1, no. 12 (December 1835): 91. This is in keeping with the antislavery rhetoric described in Walters, "The Erotic South," pp. 181–83.

28. "For the *Advocate of Moral Reform*," *Advocate of Moral Reform*, 3, no. 1 (January 1, 1837): 187.

29. "Improper Style of Dress for the Street," *Advocate of Moral Reform*, 3, no. 1 (January 1, 1837): 188; "Run, Speak to That Woman," *Advocate of Moral Reform*, 3, no. 4 (February 15, 1837): 209.

30. "Our Object," *Advocate of Moral Reform*, 1, nos. 1 and 2 (February 1835): 2.

31. "Lewdness a National Sin," *Advocate of Moral Reform*, 2, no. 5 (March 1, 1836): 35; "Report of Quarterly Meeting," 3, no. 1 (January 1, 1837): 190; "Run, Speak to That Woman," 3, no. 4 (February 15, 1837): 209; L. B., "Tendency of Fanny Wright's Doctrines," 3, no. 1 (January 1, 1837): 191.

32. "Games and Amusements," *Advocate of Moral Reform*, 3, no. 1 (January 1, 1837): 192; "A Fragment," 3, no. 2 (January 15, 1837): 195.

33. *Advocate of Moral Reform*, 1, no. 11 (November 1835): 87.

34. "The Theatre," *Advocate of Moral Reform*, 3, no. 2 (January 15, 1837): 199; [untitled], 2, no. 1 (January 1836): 4.

35. "Double Entendres," *Advocate of Moral Reform*, 2, no. 19 (October 15, 1836): 151.

36. Adelaide, letter, December 21, 1836, Batavia, N.Y., *Advocate of Moral Reform*, 3, no. 1 (January 1, 1837): 188.

37. Editorial, "Clerical Objections Considered," *Advocate of Moral Reform*, 3, no. 20 (October 15, 1837): 340; Editorial, 2, no. 14 (August 1, 1836): 109; [untitled], 3, no. 7 (April 1, 1837): 238; Editorial, "Clerical Objections Considered," p. 340.

38. Editorial, *Advocate of Moral Reform*, 2, no. 14 (August 1, 1836): 109.

8: *The Sporting Weeklies and Obscene Libel*

1. As I began work on this subject, I learned that Patricia Cline Cohen and Timothy Gilfoyle were also planning articles on the same subject. We each presented our work at the American Studies Association in fall 1999 and hope in the future to collaborate on a book on the New York City sporting press of the early 1840s. I am grateful to both for information and perspectives; Pat Cohen was especially generous in sharing her research finds.

Needing a shorthand to cover the class of materials dealing with sexual matters intended to be sexually exciting and sold to a general public at a cheap price, I have chosen the tag "racy" because of its frequent use at the time. Its derivation is interesting: at least from the seventeenth century, "racy" meant "having a characteristically excellent taste, flavour, or quality," as cider or wine; when applied to speech, "having a characteristic sprightliness, liveliness, or piquancy." It is related to race in that it designates an intensity connected to a species' kind or blood; see *Oxford English Dictionary*, CD-ROM, 2nd ed. (New York, 1992).

2. *Sunday Flash*, 1, no. 6 (September 12, 1841): 1.

3. *Flash*, 1, no. 1 (October 31, 1841): 1.

4. "Characteristic Sketches.—No. V," *Town*, no. 5 (July 1, 1837): 1; Donald J. Gray, "Early Victorian Scandalous Journalism: Renton Nicholson's *The Town* (1837–1842)," in *The Victorian Periodical Press: Samplings and Soundings*, ed. Joanne Shattock and Michael Wolff (Leicester, England: Leicester University Press, 1982), pp. 317–48.

5. Philip Howell, "Sex and the City of Bachelors: Sporting Guidebooks and Urban Knowledge in Nineteenth-Century Britain and America," *Ecumene: A Journal of Environment, Culture, Meaning*, 8 (January 2001): 41.

6. Quote from *Hawk and Buzzard*, 2, no. 18 (July 3, 1830): 3.

7. Robert C. Toll, *Blacking Up: The Minstrel Show in Nineteenth-Century America* (New York: Oxford University Press, 1974), p. 162.

8. "An Incident," *Flash*, 1, no. 7 (July 31, 1842): 1; "The Serving Maiden," *Whip and Satirist of New-York and Brooklyn*, 1, no. 15 (April 2, 1842): 1.

9. *Polyanthos*, 2, no. 5 (July 21, 1838): 1. On Dixon, see Dale Cockrell, *Demons of Disorder: Early Blackface Minstrels and Their World* (Cambridge, England: Cambridge University Press, 1997). On the riots, see Paul O. Weinbaum, *Mobs and Demagogues: The New York Response to Collective Violence in the Early Nineteenth Century* ([Ann Arbor, Mich.]: UMI Research Press, 1979), especially pp. 44–49; Sean Wilentz, *Chants Democratic: New York City and the Rise of the American Working Class, 1788–1850* (New York: Oxford University Press, 1984), pp. 264–65. In May 1835, Dixon started *Dixon's Review* in Lowell; in Boston in early 1836, it was the *Censor and Evening Star* and later that same year the *Bostonian, or Dixon's Saturday Night Express*. The American Antiquarian Society has individual copies of all three papers.

10. Todd G. Willy, "Literary Realism as Anti-Racism: The Case of William Joseph Snelling," *Old Northwest*, 15, no. 3 (1990): 143–61; Allen E. Woodall, "William Joseph Snelling: A Review of His Life and Writings," reprint, *University of Pittsburgh Bulletin*, 29, no. 3 (January 1933): 1–6; William Joseph Snelling, *The Rat-Trap; or Cogitations of a Convict in the House of Correction* (Boston: G. N. Thomson, 1837), pp. 12, 24.

11. I have not been able to find information about Dixon's arrest or trial in the District of Attorney Indictment Papers or the Minutes of the Court of Special Sessions in the New York Municipal Archives.

12. In *Prostitution Exposed; or, a Moral Reform Directory, Laying Bare the Lives, Histories, Residences; Seductions &c. of the Most Celebrated Courtezans and Ladies of Pleasure of the City of New York* (New York, 1839), pp. 5–6, "Mother Miller" receives this description: "In Reed-street, No. 133, a few doors from Hudson St., stands a three story brick house, of respectable appearance; this is occupied by Mrs. Miller, an elderly Cyprian, of about sixty years of age, and about thirteen girls, generally of good appearance and address. She usually dresses in black, with a plaid handkerchief tied round her head to conceal her grey hairs from view. The history of this woman is somewhat singular. She has buried three husbands, two of which she has had children by." After Clifton and Missouri are mentioned, the description continues. "To each of her daughters she gave elegant and classic educations, and kept them free from the lazaar house of crime." She came to her occupation when a husband left her property that was leased to brothels and she learned of the high rents paid. "She is estimated to be worth $100,000. This

being a house of the first class, the price of lodging varies from $10 to $25, according to customer. Champaigne $3. Breakfast Free."

13. Faye E. Dudden, *Women in the American Theatre: Actresses and Audiences, 1790–1870* (New Haven, Conn: Yale University Press, 1994), pp. 64–70.

14. I am indebted here and in many other instances to Patricia Cline Cohen's fine detective work (in this case in getting the roster from the Emma Willard School) and scrutiny of my manuscript. See also *New York Herald,* June 2, 1838, p. 2; "Recorder's Office," *New York Herald,* June 21, 1838, p. 2.

15. The postmortem determined that the cause of death had been "inflammation of the brain," and officials put the word out that Missouri had been a virgin at her death. The examining physicians took the unusual step of stating in their report that "in our opinion, Miss Missouri received from those friends at whose house she died every kindness and attention which her painful situation demanded" ("Miss Missouri," *New York Herald,* June 20, 1838, p. 2). Years later a witness remembered Adelina Miller as "a horrible sight, this old woman, with her long white witch-like hair flying about her face"; see Lester Wallack, *Memories of Fifty Years* (New York: Charles Scribner's Sons, 1889), p. 120.

The earliest extant issue of the *Polyanthos* reprints "The Bowery Theatre," which appeared in the weekly's first number; see *Polyanthos and New-York Visiter,* 1, no. 2 (June 9, 1838): 4. The *Spirit of the Times,* a racing subscription weekly with a regular theatrical column, had long supported Josephine Clifton's career and presented her side of the story sympathetically.

16. "November 12, 1842, Court of Common Pleas Before Judge Inglis," *New York Herald,* July 18, 1842, p. 2.

17. For a discussion of "flash" and "sporting," see Chapter 6.

18. *Whip,* 2, no. 1 (July 9, 1842): 1. Many of the *Whip's* engravings were taken from the *Town.* They carried the name of Robert H. Elton, a master printer in New York City, known for his comic almanacs.

19. *Whip,* 3, no. 3 (February 11, 1843): 6; 2, no. 4 (July 30, 1842): 2. Such comments raise the possibility that Grandy was a biological male.

20. "The Brothel Expose—No. 6," *Whip,* 2, no. 4 (July 30, 1842): 2; by contrast, *Prostitution Exposed,* p. 21, said that Mrs. Bowen "keeps a house of the first class in Leonard st., nearly opposite the National Theatre. The females in her charge are perfectly lady-like, and exquisitely beautiful."

21. *Flash,* 1, no. 3 (July 3, 1842): 3; *Flash,* 1, no. 2 (June 23, 1842): 2 (second ellipsis in original); *Flash,* 1, no. 13 (September 11, 1842): 2; 1, no. 2 (June 23, 1842): 3.

22. "Lives of the Nymphs, No. 11, Amanda Green," *Sunday Flash,* 1, no. 11 (October 17, 1841): 3.

23. "Domestic Communications: A Man-Monster," *Flash,* 1, no. 8 (August 7, 1842), fragment; "The Sodomites," *The Whip and Satirist of New-York and Brooklyn,* 1, no. 5 [*sic*] (January 29, 1842): 2; letter to TWM from "E.Z.," *Weekly Rake,* 1, no. 7 (July 30, 1842): 2. A number of writers, including Howard Chudacoff, have cited an unpublished account of an 1846 police prosecution of two young wage earners "who allegedly had engaged in carnal intercourse while living together in the same boardinghouse room"; see Howard P. Chudacoff, *The Age of the Bachelor: Creating an American Subculture* (Princeton, N.J.: Princeton University Press, 1999), p. 33. Randolph Trumbach has situated the discourse on sodomy in both the emerging homosexual subculture of London and the creation of a new male homosexuality in the eighteenth century; see, e.g., his "Sex, Gender, and Sexual Identity in Modern Culture: Male Sodomy and

Female Prostitution in Enlightenment London," *Journal of the History of Sexuality*, 2, no. 2 (October 1991): 186–203.

24. *Whip*, 2, no. 10 (September 10, 1842): 2.

25. *Whip*, 2, no. 4 (July 30, 1842): 2; *Whip*, 2, no. 10 (September 10, 1842): 1.

26. Frederick Hudson, *Journalism in the United States from 1690 to 1872* (New York: Harper & Brothers, 1872), p. 525. In addition, Hudson gave these circulation figures: *Whip*—4,000; *Flash*—1,500; *Rake*—1,000 (p. 525).

27. "Correspondents," *Whip*, 1, no. 8 (February 12, 1842): 2.

28. Hudson, *Journalism in the United States*, p. 546.

29. *Flash*, 1, no. 14 (November 6, 1841): 3 (copy at the American Antiquarian Society). The informer in this case was not Wooldridge, for beside the ad for his Ellsler Saloon is another pointing hand with this note: "Bawdy House advertised." In regard to blackmail, the sporting press may not have differed substantially from the penny dailies. In two known instances George W. Wisner, the pioneer court reporter of the *Sun*, used threat of publication to extort money, and George Foster made blackmail a general accusation of court reporters; see Steven H. Jaffe, "Unmasking the City: The Rise of the Urban Newspaper Reporter in New York City, 1800–1850," Ph.D. dissertation, Harvard University, 1989, pp. 173–76, 370.

30. "The Passages in the Life of G.W. Dixon, the American Coco La Cour, Negro Dancer and Buffalo Singer," *Flash*, 1, no. 17 (December 18, 1841): 1; *Whip*, 2, no. 4 (July 30, 1842): 2.

31. *New York Sporting Whip*, 3, no. 3 (February 11, 1843): 3.

32. Court testimony in a civil suit between the job printer William Applegate and Adelina Miller shows that when Snelling purchased a printing press from Applegate in November 1841, Adelina Miller backed Snelling's note with her own ("November 12, 1842, Court of Common Pleas Before Judge Inglis," *New York Herald*, July 18, 1842, p. 2).

33. "The Slaughter House," *Sunday Flash*, 1, no. 6 (September 12, 1841): 2.

34. "Thomas S. Hamblin, the Patriarch of the Slaughter House," *Sunday Flash*, 1, no. 12 (October 24, 1841): 1.

35. Thomas Starkie, *A Treatise on the Law of Slander, Libel, Scandalum Magnatum, and False Rumours . . .* , *First American edition, with notes and references to American and the late English Cases* (New York: George Lamson, 1826). A lengthy footnote on p. 569 establishes the state protections. The earliest edition of Starkie, *A Treatise on the Law of Slander*, in the collection of the Harvard University Law School is from 1813.

36. Thomas Starkie, *A Treatise on the Law of Slander and Libel*, 2nd ed., vol. 2 (London: J. and W. T. Clarke, 1830), pp. 155, 16, 248. Many state constitutions, in contrast to English common law, established that truth could be used as justification.

37. Ibid., pp. 255, 158–59.

38. Ibid., p. 240. Italics added.

39. Ibid., p. 241, quote from p. 258.

40. Ibid., pp. 331, 333.

41. I am grateful to David Rabban for pointing this out in a communication, January 26, 2000.

42. Starkie, *Treatise on the Law of Slander and Libel*, 1830, vol. 2, p. 420.

43. "Gallery of Rascalities and Notorieties, No. 6," *Sunday Flash*, 1, no. 11 (October 17, 1841): 1.

44. David McAdam et al., *History of the Bench and Bar of New York*, vol. 1 (New York: New York History Company, 1897), p. 495; *Trial of Hon. Frederick A. Tallmadge* (New York: Baker & Godwin, 1858), p. 64; Obituary, *New York Times*, September 19, 1868, p. 4.

45. "General Sessions," *New York Herald,* September 7, 1841, p. 1; ibid., October 5, 1841, p. 2. This was an era with many libel suits, for in this speech Tallmadge repeated the charge he had given to the September grand jury.

46. Jonathan D. Sarna, *Jacksonian Jew: The Two Worlds of Mordecai Noah* (New York: Holmes & Meier Publishers, 1981), p. 144.

47. Perhaps indulging in a bit of hyperbole, the *Herald* claimed that Whiting's selection as a Whig, defeating the Democratic candidate, had subverted the will of the people; see "District Attorney," "Court of General Sessions," *New York Herald,* June 5, 1838, p. 2.

48. *True Flash,* December 4, 1841, p. 1.

49. *Whip and Satirist,* 1, no. 5 (April 2, 1842). Willis G. Thompson, a business associate of Nelson H. Miller, regarded himself as libeled by George B. Wooldridge; Wooldridge was indicted on the two counts of libel and obscenity. The weeklies that became a part of the court record were rescued by a historian and since 2000 have been in the collection of the American Antiquarian Society.

50. "City Intelligence, Court of Sessions," *New York Tribune,* October 20, 1841, p. 3; quote from "General Sessions," *New York Herald,* October 20, 1841, p. 2. In the October 1841 grand jury list in the *Herald,* Richard E. Mount is named as foreman and William G. Boggs is not listed ("General Sessions," *New York Herald,* October 5, 1841, p. 2). The reports in late October did place Boggs as its spokesman, and Snelling identified him as the foreman. Snelling noted a recent sermon by "Rev. Potts" against the Sunday papers, who may have been Reverend George Potts of the Duane Congregational Church. In its commentary, the *Herald* mentioned a Reverend Hale; see "The Sunday Papers—The Newsboys," *New York Herald,* October 22, 1841, p. 2; "Boggs," *Sunday Flash,* 1, no. 12 (October 24, 1841): 3; "New Lights" *Flash,* 1, no. 1 (October 31, 1841).

51. "General Sessions," *New York Herald,* October 5, 1841, p. 2; "City Intelligence: Court of Sessions," *New York Tribune,* October 5, 1841, p. 3; *Longworth's American Almanac, New-York Register, and City Directory* (New York: Thomas Longworth, 1840); ibid., 1841; *The New York Business Directory, for 1841 and 1842,* 2nd ed. (New York: J. Doggett, Jr., 1841).

52. "Our Indictment," *Flash,* 1, no. 1 (October 30, 1841): 2 (this issue is dated both October 31 and October 30).

53. "Our Indictment," *Flash,* 1, no. 1 (October 30, 1841): 2; "Police," *Evening Post,* October 27, 1841, p. 2; "Mr. Snelling's Letter to Judge Noah," *Flash,* 1, no. 15 (November 20, 1841): 2. Snelling's letter to Noah was dated November 3, 1841.

54. "Curious Proceedings in the Court of Sessions," *New York Herald,* January 4, 1842, p. 2.

55. "Another Curious Scene in the Court of Sessions, in Which Noah, the New Judge in Israel, Figures Largely," *New York Herald,* June 16, 1841, p. 2.

56. "Trial of the Editors of the Sunday Flash," *New York Herald,* January 15, 1842, p. 1.

57. Ibid.; "State's Evidence," *Flash,* 1, no. 18 (January 22, 1842): 2.

58. "Trial of The Sunday Flash," *New York Herald,* January 16, 1842, p. 2; "General Sessions," *New York Herald,* April 20, 1842, p. 2. Nelson H. Miller had put up security for Snelling. No length of Snelling's sentence appeared, but it is likely that he served a month's time.

59. *Whip,* 1, no. 15 (April 2, 1842): 2; *Whip,* 2, no. 2 (July 9, 1842).

60. *Whip,* 2, no. 3 (July 23, 1842): 2, 1; the engraving appeared in the *Whip,* 1, no. 16 (April 9, 1842): 1.

61. *Whip,* 2, no. 1 (July 9, 1842).

62. *The People vs. (28) George B. Wooldridge,* July 14, 1842, District Attorney Indictment Papers, Court of General Sessions, 1790–1879, Reel 211, July 14, 1842, to September 14, 1842, New York City Municipal Archives and Records Center, New York, N.Y.

63. "General Sessions: Trial for Publishing an Obscene Paper," "Another of the Same Kidney," *New York Herald*, September 15, 1842. An exception to the common sentencing was that of a young associate, who was treated much more lightly after his father successfully pled for leniency.

64. "To Our Readers," *Whip*, 2, no. 1 (July 9, 1842).

65. "Our Indictment," *Flash*, 1, no. 14 (November 6, 1841): 2; *Flash*, 1, no. 16 (December 11, 1841).

66. *Whip*, 2, no. 13 (October 1, 1842): 2; 2, no. 15 (October 15, 1842): 2.

67. Wooldridge was instrumental in shaping the minstrel show as a separate evening's entertainment. In January 1843, he heard four blackface musicians play in a room in a Catherine Street boardinghouse. They immediately constituted themselves the "Virginia Minstrels" and performed at the Branch Hotel, a leading sporting house on the Bowery. Unhappy with their contracts, the players agreed to let Wooldridge be their agent, and he accompanied them on a tour in England; see Hans Nathan, *Dan Emmett and the Rise of Early Negro Minstrelsy* (Norman: University of Oklahoma Press, 1962), pp. 116–18, 138.

68. "The Tweedle-dum and Tweedle-dee in Morals—The Ann Street Licentious Press, and the Wall Street Licentious Press," *New York Herald*, September 15, 1842.

69. "General Sessions," report on proceedings of November 10, 1843, *New York Herald*, November 11, 1843, p. 1.

70. "General Sessions," report on proceedings of November 21, 1843, *New York Herald*, November 22, 1843, p. 3.

71. George Wilkes, *The Mysteries of the Tombs; A Journal of Thirty Days Imprisonment in the New York City Prison; for Libel* (New York: Sold at all the booksellers, 1844), pp. 2, 63.

9: Abortion

1. For an understanding of abortion not as rhetoric but as a biological and political process, I have relied on the following works: Janet Farrell Brodie, *Contraception and Abortion in 19th-Century America* (Ithaca, N.Y.: Cornell University Press, 1994); James C. Mohr, *Abortion in America: The Origins and Evolution of National Policy, 1800–1900* (Oxford: Oxford University Press, 1978); Leslie J. Reagan, *When Abortion Was a Crime: Women, Medicine, and Law in the United States, 1867–1973* (Berkeley: University of California Press, 1997); Kristin Luker, *Abortion and the Politics of Motherhood* (Berkeley: University of California Press, 1984), Chapter 2.

2. Aristotle (pseudonym), *Aristotle's Works Compleated in Four Parts, containing 1. The Compleat Master-piece; 2. His Compleat and Experienced Midwife; 3. His Book of Problems; 4. His Last Legacy* (London: Printed, and Sold by the Booksellers, c. 1741), pp. 39–40. For common women's practices, see, for example, Mohr, *Abortion in America*, pp. 6–9.

3. Laurel Thatcher Ulrich, *A Midwife's Tale: The Life of Martha Ballard Based on Her Diary, 1785–1812* (New York: Alfred A. Knopf, 1990), pp. 75–76; Luker, *Abortion*, p. 37. Reagan, *When Abortion Was a Crime*, makes an important distinction between women's silence and women's secrets. Reagan's discussion of the "existence of multiple moralities," p. 22, strengthened my own thinking about the many-sided sexual conversation.

4. Reagan, *When Abortion Was a Crime*, p. 9; Cornelia Hughes Dayton, "Taking the Trade: Abortion and Gender Relations in an Eighteenth-Century New England Village," *William and Mary Quarterly*, 48 (1991): 24–25.

5. Mohr, *Abortion in America*, pp. 6–9, 14.

6. Ibid., pp. 16–18.

7. For Ann Lohman's life and career, I have relied on Clifford Browder, *The Wickedest Woman in New York: Madame Restell, the Abortionist* (Hamden, Conn.: Archon Books, 1988); a specific reference to the Matsell bookstore is on p. 5. For Matsell's advertisement, see *Free Enquirer*, 1 (New Series), no. 1 (October 27, 1833): 8.

8. Browder, *Madame Restell*, pp. 15–16.

9. Ibid., pp. 26–27; Dixon clearly reprinted his original article from set type, for it consistently contains the misspelling "conamination" for "contamination," as, for example, in *Dixon's Polyanthos*, 5, no. 16 (May 1, 1841): 131.

10. "Editorial Depravity," *Sunday Flash*, 1, no. 11 (October 17, 1841): 2; "Morality," *Whip*, 1, no. 20 (May 7, 1842): 2; "Madam Restell the Abortionist," 3, no. 2 (February 4, 1843): 3.

11. "Prospectus," *National Police Gazette*, 1, nos. 1–4 (reprint) (October 16, 1845): 56. Although the best discussion of the *National Police Gazette* is Dan Schiller, *Objectivity and the News: The Public and the Rise of Commercial Journalism* (Philadelphia: University of Pennsylvania Press, 1981), especially pp. 96–124, a more comprehensive study of the weekly is needed.

12. For Sarah Decker, see *National Police Gazette*, 1, no. 5 (October 11, 1845): 59.

13. *National Police Gazette*, 2, no. 2 (September 19, 1846): 14; beginning in 1, no. 35 (April 25, 1846): 288.

14. *National Police Gazette*, 1, no. 12 (November 29, 1845): 115; Amy Gilman Srebnick, *The Mysterious Death of Mary Rogers: Sex and Culture in Nineteenth-Century New York* (New York: Oxford University Press, 1995), pp. 102, 103, 106–7; the boardinghouse that Mary and her mother kept at 126 Nassau Street and its occupants are well described on pp. 14–23, 58.

15. Browder, *Madame Restell*, pp. 58–61; "Restell, the Female Abortionist," *National Police Gazette*, 2, no. 27 (March 13, 1847): 212.

16. Browder, *Madame Restell*, pp. 64–66, quote from p. 66.

17. "The Female Abortionist," *National Police Gazette*, 2, no. 27 (March 13, 1847): 208.

18. Carroll Smith-Rosenberg, "The Abortion Movement," *Disorderly Conduct: Visions of Gender in Victorian America* (New York: Alfred A. Knopf, 1985), pp. 217–44, quote from p. 233; Ellen S. More, *Restoring the Balance: Women Physicians and the Profession of Medicine, 1850–1995* (Cambridge, Mass.: Harvard University Press, 1999), pp. 35–36; Mohr, *Abortion in America*, pp. 182–96; Luker, *Abortion*, p. 36.

19. Browder, *Madame Restell*, quote from p. 39.

20. Mohr, *Abortion in America*, p. 124. Although it could apply to pregnancy before quickening, Mohr states that "in practice the quickening doctrine" was in effect in New York courts into the 1880s.

21. François Mauriceau was the name of a seventeenth-century French obstetrician who wrote on women's anatomy and reproduction; see Thomas Laqueur, *Making Sex: Body and Gender from the Greeks to Freud* (Cambridge, Mass.: Harvard University Press, 1990), pp. 239, 301, note 123.

22. Dr. A. M. Mauriceau, *The Married Woman's Private Medical Companion* (New York, 1850), pp. 144, 169.

23. Browder, *Madame Restell*, pp. 77, 103.

24. For Foote, see Chapters 14 and 18.

10: *Obscenity in the City*

1. My search began with Henry Spencer Ashbee, *Index Librorum Prohibitorum* and successive volumes, which gave me a long list of titles, including many novels of George Thompson.

Steven Marcus, *The Other Victorians: A Study of Sexuality and Pornography in Mid-Nineteenth-Century England* (New York: Basic Books, 1964), and Walter Kendrick, *The Secret Museum: Pornography in Modern Culture* (New York: Viking, 1987) proved useful. The illustration of a George Thompson cover in David S. Reynolds, *Beneath the American Renaissance: The Subversive Imagination in the Age of Emerson and Melville* (New York: Alfred A. Knopf, 1988), fortunately carried the credit "Courtesy AAS" and led me to the American Antiquarian Society. Curators at the AAS have compiled a list of "racy" books and newspapers, many in the library's collection. The Kinsey Library also proved to be an important source of material.

2. Information on Ryan and the other sellers of books and prints is in District Attorney Indictment Papers, Court of General Sessions, 1790–1879, Reel 212, Box 413 (September 28, 1842), New York City Municipal Archives and Records Center, New York, N.Y. This is the primary source for the narrative discussion of Robinson and others caught in the 1842 roundup below. Later quotes in the text, not cited, are from this source.

3. "City Intelligence: More Developments in Wall Street, &c," *New York Herald,* August 18, 1842, p. 2.

4. It is also likely that such material was stolen from New York indictment records at the time or taken later, before they were protected by the Municipal Archives. In addition, suppression by donors or receivers has likely limited gifts to public repositories. The Kinsey Library's collection of erotic engravings contains a significant number of European prints but, as of this writing, lacks homegrown varieties.

5. Here Helen Jewett is called Ellen, as was sometimes the case. Quote from the lithograph, drawn by A. H. Hoffy, published by H. R. Robinson, April 15, 1836, New-York Historical Society, New York, N.Y.; copyright application no. 92, April 18, 1836, Southern District of New York, microfilm, Library of Congress, Washington, D.C.; Henry R. Robinson, "The Lady Correspondent of the New-York Herald on Board the Steamer Visuvius for Genoa" and "The Bandit's Bride," American Antiquarian Society, Worcester, Massachusetts. Few explicitly erotic prints created in the United States remain from the 1830s and 1840s.

6. "City Intelligence," *New York Herald,* September 3, 1842, p. 2; "Morality of the 'Tombs,' " *Subterranean,* 1, no. 21 (December 2, 1843): 165.

7. "City Intelligence: More Developments in Wall Street, &c," *New York Herald,* August 18, 1842, p. 2.

8. "General Sessions," *New York Herald,* January 21, 1843, pp. 1, 2.

9. "City Intelligence: Obscene Print Seller Surrendered," *New York Herald,* March 10, 1843, p. 2; *People v. Henry R. Robinson,* September 28, 1842, Selling Obscene Books, District Attorney Indictment Papers, Reel 212, Box 413, New York City Municipal Archives and Records Center. A useful twentieth-century comparison is Jay A. Gertzman, *Bootleggers and Smuthounds: The Trade in Erotica, 1920–1940* (Philadelphia: University of Pennsylvania Press, 1999).

10. *National Police Gazette,* 1, no. 10 (November 15, 1845): 99.

11. "Selling Obscene Books," *National Police Gazette,* 2, no. 32 (April 17, 1847): 251.

12. General Sessions, July 22, "Trial for Vending Obscene Books, &c.," *National Police Gazette,* 1, no. 46 (July 25, 1846): 388; "Obscene Books," *National Police Gazette,* 4, no. 39 (June 2, 1849): 3.

13. Anthony Comstock, *Frauds Exposed; or How the People Are Deceived and Robbed, and Youth Corrupted* (New York: J. Howard Brown, 1880), p. 388.

14. *People v. William Haynes,* October 18, 1853, Obscene Book Nuisance, District Attorney Indictment Papers, Box 570, Reel 27, New York City Municipal Archives and Records Center. These plates or others like them continued their service. Looking ahead, in 1872 Anthony Comstock, then a young clerk, made his first approach to wealthy businessman Morris Jesup

of the New York Y.M.C.A. with a request for money to buy Haynes's plates, then in the possession of the printer's widow.

15. Iain McCalman, *Radical Underworld: Prophets, Revolutionaries and Pornographers in London, 1725–1840* (Cambridge, England: Cambridge University Press, 1988); "Duties on Imports," Section 28, *Public Statutes at Large of the United States*, vol. 5, ed. Richard Peters (Boston: Little, Brown and Company, 1856), pp. 566–67; James C. N. Paul and Murray L. Schwartz, *Federal Censorship: Obscenity in the Mail* (New York: Free Press of Glencoe, 1961), pp. 248–49, details the authors' efforts to track down the statute's origins.

16. Jane Clapp, *Art Censorship: A Chronology of Proscribed and Prescribed Art* (Metuchen, N.J.: Scarecrow Press, 1972), p. 130.

17. The separation of printing from publishing in Philadelphia is chronicled by Rosaline Remer in *Printers and Men of Capital: Philadelphia Book Publishers in the New Republic* (Philadelphia: University of Pennsylvania Press, 1996). Changes in the economy, technology, and book manufacture and distribution are considered in Michael Denning, *Mechanic Accents: Dime Novels and Working-Class Culture in America* (New York: Verso, 1987), p. 18; Ronald J. Zboray, *A Fictive People: Antebellum Economic Development and the American Reading Public* (New York: Oxford University Press, 1993), pp. 6–14, 34.

18. Peter G. Buckley, "The Case Against Ned Buntline: The 'Words, Signs, and Gestures' of Popular Authorship," *Prospects*, 13 (1988): 249–72; Ned Buntline, *The Mysteries and Miseries of New York: A Story of Real Life* (Dublin: James M'Glashan, 1849).

19. George G. Foster, *New York in Slices by an Experienced Carver* (New York: William H. Graham, 1849), p. 93.

20. George G. Foster, *New York by Gas-light*, ed. Stuart M. Blumin (Berkeley: University of California Press, 1990), pp. 105–6.

21. Ibid., quote from p. 182.

22. Reynolds, *Beneath the American Renaissance*, offered a new way of reading the American canon and, in the process, opened up a wide field of noncanonical writings. George Thompson, *My Life: Or the Adventures of Geo. Thompson* (Boston: Federhen & Co., 1854), quote from p. 7.

23. George Thompson, *The House Breaker* (Boston: W. L. Bradbury, 1848), pp. 6, 20–21, 8.

24. Reynolds, *Beneath the American Renaissance*, p. 223; Karen Halttunen, *Murder Most Foul: The Killer and the American Gothic Imagination* (Cambridge, Mass.: Harvard University Press, 1998), pp. 60–90.

25. George Thompson, *The Countess; or Memoirs of Women of Leisure* (Boston: Berry & Wright, 1849), p. 8; Greenhorn [George Thompson], *Venus in Boston: A Romance of City Life* (New York: Printed for the Publishers, 1850), p. 7.

26. [George Thompson], *The Mysteries of Bond Street; or The Seraglios of Upper Tendom* (New York: n.p., 1857), p. 22.

27. Reynolds, *Beneath the American Renaissance*, p. 183.

28. [Thompson], *The Mysteries of Bond Street*, pp. 17, 22, 27, 29, 29–30.

29. Ibid., pp. 33, 13.

30. The marketing efforts of several of Thompson's publishers give a sense of the way these books may have been connected to potential readers. In the late 1840s, Thompson's Boston publisher, Berry & Wright, created *Life in Boston*, a weekly that serialized Thompson's novels alongside some elements imitative of the New York sporting press. By 1850, it was renamed *Life in Boston and New England Police Gazette*. Its unusually large masthead offered a potpourri of sporting life as imagined by delineator John H. Manning. For Thompson's targets, see Reynolds, *Beneath the American Renaissance*, p. 262.

31. The French author's bibliography does not contain this work. In advertisements a known work by George Thompson is under de Kock's name. The catalogue of the American Antiquarian Society attributes *Simon the Radical* to Thompson. Charles Paul de Kock [George Thompson], *Simon the Radical; or the Cap of Liberty* (New York: J. H. Farrell, 1847?), pp. 32, 102–3.

32. I am grateful to David M. Stewart of National Central University, Taiwan, for conversations about George Thompson and for letting me read his unpublished "Consuming George Thompson."

33. *Broadway Belle, and Mirror of the Times,* 1, no. 1 (January 1, 1855): 4; p. 1 lists George Thompson, editor; P. F. Harris, proprietor; office 102 Nassau St.; "Ladies' Department," ibid., 1, no. 11 (March 12, 1855): 4.

34. For example, "Books that Are Books," *Broadway Belle, and Mirror of the Times,* 1, no. 7 (February 12, 1855): 3.

35. "Important to Husbands and Wives," *Broadway Belle, and Mirror of the Times,* 1, no. 5 (January 29, 1855): 2.

36. "Arrest of an Editor and Newspaper Publisher," *New York Herald,* January 30, 1855, p. 1; Edward K. Spann, *The New Metropolis: New York City, 1840–1857* (New York: Columbia University Press, 1981), pp. 367–72; Donald MacLeod, *Biography of Hon. Fernando Wood* (New York: O. F. Parsons, 1856), pp. 201–2; "The Mayor's Complaint Book: The Police Returns, etc.," *New York Herald,* January 31, 1855, p. 2; "Newsboys in Trouble," *New York Herald,* January 31, 1855, p. 8.

37. "Editor's Chit-chat," *Broadway Belle, and Mirror of the Times,* 1, no. 7 (February 12, 1855): 3.

38. "A Nautical Adventure," *Broadway Belle, and Mirror of the Times,* 1, no. 7 (February 12, 1855): 4.

39. "A Nautical Adventure," *Broadway Belle, and Mirror of the Times,* 1, no. 8 (February 19, 1855): 2.

40. "New Works by Charles Paul De Kock," *Weekly Whip,* 1, no. 1 (February 12, 1855): 4.

41. "Rich, Rare and Racy Reading," *Venus' Miscellany,* 2, no. 2 (May 23, 1857): 2; Julia Gaylove, "Inez de Castro; or, the Intrigues of the Court of Isabel of Aragon," Chapter 6, *Venus' Miscellany,* 2, no. 2 (May 23, 1857): 2 ("lilies" is spelled "lillies" in the original).

42. Bell, "What I Love," *Venus' Miscellany,* 2, no. 2 (May 23, 1857): 2; *Venus' Miscellany,* 2, no. 2 (May 23, 1857): 3.

43. Trot, "My First Lesson in Love," *Venus' Miscellany,* 1, no. 12 (January 31, 1857): 2.

44. "Rich, Rare and Racy Reading," *Venus' Miscellany,* 2, no. 2 (May 23, 1857): 2; advertisement for Rosseau, 2, no. 2 (May 23, 1857): 2, 10; "To the Sporting Fraternity," 1, no. 12 (January 31, 1857): 3.

45. "Cundums, Cundums, Cundums," *Venus' Miscellany,* 2, no. 2 (May 23, 1857): 2.

46. "Special Session," *New York Tribune,* September 14, 1857, p. 8; "Great Seizure of Obscene Literature," *New York Herald,* September 16, 1857, p. 8; *New York Tribune,* September 17, 1857, p. 7.

47. "Great Seizure of Obscene Literature," *New York Herald,* September 16, 1857, p. 8; "A Publishing Establishment Broken Up," *New York Tribune,* September 16, 1857, p. 5; "The Seizure of Obscene Books and Prints," *New York Herald,* September 22, 1857, p. 5.

48. *American History and Biography, Containing an Epitome of American History* (New York: Charles Lohman, 1838); *Echoes from the Gun of 1861: A Book for Boys* (Boston: Loring, 1864).

49. *The People vs. Frederick Brady alias Henry S. C. Smith,* "Having Obscene Publications," filed February 12, 1858, District Attorney Indictment Papers, Court of General Sessions, 1790–1879, Reel 61; copyright application, Henry S. G. Smith, 1857, Folder 13, Box 3, Theodore Albert Schroeder Papers, State Historical Society of Wisconsin, Madison, Wisconsin; Jean

Dubois, *Secret Habits of the Female Sex* (New York: Booksellers, n.d.), copy in Kinsey Library, Bloomington, Indiana.

50. *A Register of Artists, Engravers, Booksellers, Bookbinders, Printers & Publishers in New York City, 1821–42*, compiled by Sidney F. and Elizabeth Stage Huttner (New York: Bibliographical Society of America, 1993).

51. Philip Howell, "Sex and the City of Bachelors: Sporting Guidebooks and Urban Knowledge in Nineteenth-Century Britain and America," *Ecumene: A Journal of Environment, Culture, Meaning*, 8 (January 2001): 20–50, offers many insights into the intersection of urban geography, sex, gender construction, and sexuality.

52. For example, Calvin Blanchard, *Life Among the Nymphs: A New Excursion Through the Empire of Venus* (New York: Calvin Blanchard, 1867). On Blanchard, see L. L. Bernard and Jessie Bernard, *Origins of American Sociology: The Social Science Movement in the United States* (New York: Thomas Y. Crowell Co., 1943), pp. 192–203; Lola Montez, *Anecdotes of Love* (New York: Dick & Fitzgerald, 1858), copy in Kinsey Library.

53. Farrell receipts, 1863, Folder 13, Box, 3, Theodore Albert Schroeder Papers, State Historical Society of Wisconsin, Madison, Wisconsin.

54. *Amours of Sainfroid and Eulalia, Being the Intrigues and Amours of a Jesuit and a Nun* (New York: J. H. Farrell, n.d.); Peter Wagner, *Eros Revived: Erotica of the Enlightenment in England and America* (London: Secker & Warburg, 1988), p. 86.

11: *Placing Sex at the Core of Being*

1. Nancy F. Cott, *Public Vows: A History of Marriage and the Nation* (Cambridge, Mass.: Harvard University Press, 2000), pp. 24–55. This chapter is by no means an exhaustive survey of antebellum social movements but considers only those that particularly affected the sexual conversations that I have studied.

2. Kenneth H. Winn, "The Mormon Region," *Encyclopedia of American Social History*, vol. 2, ed. Mary Kupiec Cayton, Elliott J. Gorn, and Peter W. Williams (New York: Charles Scribner's Sons, 1993), pp. 1089–97.

3. B. Carmon Hardy and Dan Erickson, " 'Regeneration—Now and Evermore!' Mormon Polygamy and the Physical Rehabilitation of Humankind," *Journal of the History of Sexuality*, 10, no. 1 (January 2001): 40–62.

4. Louis J. Kern, *An Ordered Love: Sex Roles and Sexuality in Victorian Utopias—The Shakers, the Mormons, and the Oneida Community* (Chapel Hill: University of North Carolina Press, 1981), pp. 137–89; quote from p. 145; examination from pp. 151–52.

5. My discussion of Noyes and his community is based on Spencer Klaw, *Without Sin: The Life and Death of the Oneida Community* (New York: Allen Lane, 1993). Carl J. Guarneri traces the impact of Fourierism, discussed later in this chapter, on Noyes in "Reconstructing the Antebellum Communitarian Movement: Oneida and Fourierism," *Journal of the Early Republic*, 16, no. 3 (1996): 463–88. Phrenology and reform physiology were other apparent intellectual sources of Noyes's thought.

6. John Humphrey Noyes, 1848 pamphlet, quoted in *Male Continence* (Oneida, N.Y.: Oneida Community, 1872), pp. 11–12.

7. Ibid., p. 14.

8. Ibid., pp. 13–14.

9. In 1851 the district attorney of Oneida County responded to a wife beating, intervened, and called a grand jury. At the inquiry the official inquired into the community's sexual prac-

tices. At the same time the New York *Observer,* a religious weekly, attacked the community, stating that its members lived "in a state of vile concubinage and even worse." Noyes, at that point living in Brooklyn, wrote a statement that the community had forsworn complex marriage. Neighbors petitioned that charges be dropped, one of Noyes's leaders arranged to pay the wife's father a tidy sum, and the threat to the community ended.

10. Robert S. Fogarty, *Desire and Duty at Oneida: Tirzah Miller's Intimate Memoir* (Bloomington: Indiana University Press, 2000). Despite Noyes's rhetorical statements against birth control, Miller relied on the postcoital syringe when one of her sexual partners lost control and ejaculated during lovemaking; pp. 172, 197, note 61.

11. These paragraphs are based on an adult life of reading and research about women's rights that began in college with Eleanor Flexner, *Century of Struggle: The Women's Rights Movement in the United States* (Cambridge, Mass.: The Belknap Press of Harvard University Press, 1959).

12. Carolyn L. Karcher, *The First Woman in the Republic: A Cultural Biography of Lydia Maria Child* (Durham, N.C.: Duke University Press, 1994), points out the many ways in which this fascinating historical figure intersected with the intellectual currents and individual lives of many of the subjects of my study.

13. Karen Sánchez-Eppler, *Touching Liberty: Abolition, Feminism, and the Politics of the Body* (Berkeley: University of California Press, 1993), pp. 18–22.

14. For Stanton I have relied on Lois W. Banner, *Elizabeth Cady Stanton: A Radical for Women's Rights* (Boston: Little, Brown, 1980); Elisabeth Griffith, *In Her Own Right: The Life of Elizabeth Cady Stanton* (New York: Oxford University Press, 1984); Alma Lutz, "Elizabeth Cady Stanton," *Notable American Women,* vol. 3 (Cambridge, Mass.: The Belknap Press of Harvard University Press, 1971), pp. 342–47.

15. Introduction to Amelia Jenks Bloomer, *Hear Me Patiently: The Reform Speeches of Amelia Jenks Bloomer,* ed. Anne C. Coon (Westport, Conn.: Greenwood Press, 1994), pp. 10–13.

16. See especially Paulina Wright Davis, "Woman as Physically Considered," *Una,* February 1, 1853, pp. 8–9, quote from p. 9.

17. Elizabeth Cady Stanton to Susan B. Anthony, March 1, 1852 (previously dated 1853), extracted in *Elizabeth Cady Stanton, Susan B. Anthony, Correspondence, Writings, Speeches,* ed. Ellen Carol DuBois (New York: Schocken Books, 1981), p. 56. Stanton often tried out her rhetoric in her personal correspondence to Anthony.

18. Elizabeth Cady Stanton to Lucy Stone, November 24, 1856, quoted in Griffith, *In Her Own Right,* p. 102. At the 1860 women's rights convention Stanton introduced a set of resolutions on divorce that proved to be deeply controversial and divisive.

19. John C. Spurlock, *Free Love: Marriage and Middle-Class Radicalism in America, 1825–1860* (New York: New York University Press, 1988), p. 59; Carl J. Guarneri, *The Utopian Alternative: Fourierism in Nineteenth-Century America* (Ithaca, N.Y.: Cornell University Press, 1991), pp. 95–96.

20. Guarneri, *The Utopian Alternative,* pp. 198–203.

21. Ibid., pp. 18–19.

22. Ibid., p. 94.

23. Ibid., pp. 142–43; Spurlock, *Free Love,* pp. 59–70.

24. Guarneri, *The Utopian Alternative,* p. 354.

25. Sally Morita, "Unseen (and Unappreciated) Matters: Understanding the Reformative Nature of 19th-Century Spiritualism," *American Studies,* 40, no. 3 (1999): 99–125; Ann Braude, *Radical Spirits: Spiritualism and Women's Rights in Nineteenth-Century America* (Boston: Beacon Press, 1989), pp. 10–31.

26. Braude, *Radical Spirits,* pp. 2, 6, 58–59.

27. Ibid., pp. 56–81, 78.

28. Ibid., quote from p. 120.

29. Spurlock, *Free Love,* pp. 91–98, 143–45.

30. Braude, *Radical Spirits,* pp. 117–35.

31. Ibid., quote from p. 130. One important topic to explore is the impact on fellow Spiritu-alists of the writing of Mary Gove and Thomas Low Nichols, discussed in the following chap-ter. Cridge, for example, was writing in 1856, after publication of *Esoteric Anthropology and Marriage,* and after a 1855 lecture by Thomas, "Free Love: A Doctrine of Spiritualism," pub-lished in 1856; see Jean Lara Silver-Isenstadt, "Pure Pleasure: The Shared Life and Work of Mary Gove Nichols and Thomas Low Nichols in American Health Reform," Ph.D. disserta-tion, University of Pennsylvania, 1997, pp. 293–96.

32. Braude, *Radical Spirits,* quote from p. 132.

33. M. Edgeworth Lazarus, M.D., *Passional Hygiene and Natural Medicine* (New York: Fowler and Wells, 1852), especially pp. 412–13.

34. M. Edgeworth Lazarus, *Love vs. Marriage* (New York: Fowler and Wells, 1852), pp. 56, 57, 59.

35. Ibid., pp. 286, 102; Lazarus is quoted, paraphrased, and discussed in Guarneri, *The Utopian Alternative,* pp. 356–58; Spurlock, *Free Love,* pp. 118–20.

36. For Andrews I rely on Madeleine B. Stern, *The Pantarch: A Biography of Stephen Pearl Andrews* (Austin: University of Texas Press, 1968).

37. *Love, Marriage, and Divorce and the Sovereignty of the Individual: A Discussion by Henry James, Horace Greeley, and Stephen Pearl Andrews,* ed. Stephen Pearl Andrews (New York: Stringer & Townsend, 1853); one interesting element is the heated letter by Mary Gove Nichols written in protest to Greeley's views, but here her opposition to his support of traditional marriage is expressed in terms of the negative, the harm done to wives linked to husbands they hate but forced to endure the marriage bed and male amative excess; see pp. 98–100.

38. One can track the emergence of this understanding in Spurlock, *Free Love;* Hal D. Sears, *The Sex Radicals: Free Love in High Victorian America* (Lawrence: Regents Press of Kansas, 1977); Taylor Stoehr, *Free Love in America: A Documentary History* (New York: AMS Press, 1979).

12: *Blurring the Boundaries*

1. On the Fowlers and phrenology, see Madeleine B. Stern, *Heads and Headlines: The Phrenological Fowlers* (Norman: University of Oklahoma Press, 1971), pp. 49–51, 126–27; Madeleine B. Stern, "Mind and Matter: The Fowler Family," *Books and Book People in 19th-Century America* (New York: R. R. Bowker Company, 1978), pp. 241–56.

2. "Philadelphia Quarter Sessions," *National Police Gazette,* 1, no. 33 (April 25, 1846): 283; "Obscene Book," *National Police Gazette,* 1, no. 34 (May 2, 1846): 290.

3. Frederick Hollick, *The Origin of Life: A Popular Treatise on the Philosophy and Physiology of Reproduction* (New York: Nafis & Cornish, 1845), pp. 167, 166, 171.

4. Janet Farrell Brodie, *Contraception and Abortion in 19th-Century America* (Ithaca, N.Y.: Cornell University Press, 1994), pp. 28, 197–98. Brodie states that Strong also sold aphrodisiacs, contraceptive materials, and cures for venereal diseases.

5. Frederick Hollick, *The Marriage Guide* (New York: T. W. Strong, 1850), pp. 206, 221, 206–13. Hollick does suggest that sexual feeling in women may contribute to pregnancy. "Pleasurable excitement at the time of connexion disposes the organs to more energetic

action . . . makes the Tubes contract more vigorously, and thus causes them to bring the egg down earlier, and probably, also, it may make the womb contract, so as to draw up the semen more completely. In many cases barren females, of a cold temperament, have conceived immediately after having the sexual feeling produced" (p. 222).

6. Ibid., pp. 94–95, 96, 116.

7. Ibid., pp. 334, 324, 340.

8. Ibid., advertising on pp. 30 and 32. At the Countway Medical Library, I examined two copies of the 1850 edition; the advertising pages were only in the copy with the call number HQ56.H65. It is quite possible that an important ingredient in the "Aphrodisic Remedy" was *Cannabis indica*. Hollick not only used an imported product but had grown it and used his own plants. About it Hollick wrote, "It appears to act as a special nervous stimulant, exciting that part of the brain which influences the sexual organs, so that they feel directly an increase of power. It also causes great mental activity, disposes to cheerfulness, and induces a feeling of warmth and comfort over the whole system." It has no negative aftereffects, he claimed. He regarded it as a successful means "of restoring sexual power and desire" (pp. 312–13).

9. P. C. Dunne and A. F. Derbois, *The Young Married Lady's Private Medical Guide*, trans. from the French by F. Harrison Doane (no city: n.p., 1854), p. 248.

10. Writing two decades after Knowlton, Edward Bliss Foote made prevention of prostitution a cornerstone of his argument for contraception. To it he added an important corollary: it is the 100,000 prostitutes in the United States who carry venereal disease to 30,000 men each night, and through them ultimately to their wives. Thus "thousands of virtuous married ladies in our country to-day are suffering with aggravated forms of fluor-albus and annoying humors" carried to them by their husbands from whores with syphilis; Edward B. Foote, *Medical Common Sense; Applied to the Causes, Prevention and Cure of Chronic Diseases and Unhappiness in Marriage* (Boston: Wentworth, Hewes & Co., 1858), p. 66. Knowlton had downplayed the harm that others were ascribing to masturbation, stating merely that, unlike sexual intercourse, the practice might lead to a disquieting state of mind: "the thoughts which attend and follow gratification with females are of a more agreeable cast"; see Charles Knowlton, *Fruits of Philosophy, or, The Private Companion of Adult People*, 4th ed. (Philadelphia: F. P. Rogers, 1839), p. 109. For an example of an advocate of birth control addressing masturbation, see [Dr. J. Henry], *Henry's Private Adviser* (Rossville, Md.: n.p., n.d.), p. 4.

11. Brodie, *Contraception and Abortion*, p. 188.

12. Eugène Becklard, *The Physiologist: An Infallible Guide to Health and Happiness for Both Sexes*, trans. from the French by M. Sherman Wharton, M.D. (Boston: n.p., 1844), pp. 69, 81.

13. Becklard, *The Physiologist*, pp. 34, 27.

14. Augustus K. Gardner, *The Causes and Curative Treatment of Sterility* (New York: De Witt & Davenport, 1856), pp. 48–49, 111–12.

15. Brodie, *Contraception and Abortion*, pp. 180–203. The excellent bibliography of this work led me to many sources in the Countway Medical Library, Boston, Mass.

16. [Henry], *Henry's Private Adviser*, pp. 2, 1.

17. Ibid., p. 1.

18. *The Habits of a Well-Organized Married Life* (New York: Mme. Beach, Putney & Co., 1867), pp. 1, 6.

19. Ibid., pp. 3, 6.

20. Ibid., pp. 5, 10–12.

21. Hollick did, however, sell contraceptives.

22. On Mary Gove's later life and career, I rely on John B. Blake, "Mary Sargeant Neal Gove Nichols," *Notable American Women*, vol. 2 (Cambridge, Mass.: The Belknap Press of Harvard

University Press, 1971), pp. 627–29; Jean Lara Silver-Isenstadt, "Pure Pleasure: The Shared Life and Work of Mary Gove Nichols and Thomas Low Nichols in American Health Reform," Ph.D. dissertation, University of Pennsylvania, 1997; and Brodie, *Contraception and Abortion*, pp. 126–28. Despite the fact that she changed her name when she married Nichols, for clarity's sake I continue to call her Mary Gove.

23. *Nichols' Monthly: Extra*, n.d. but 1854–56, Collection of Charles E. Rosenberg, Cambridge, Massachusetts.

24. Thomas Low Nichols, *Forty Years of American Life* (London: John Maxwell and Company, 1864), p. 324. During this period one of his enemies wrote that Nichols was "an unknown adventurer, who first came to Buffalo under an assumed name, and in the character of a strolling lecturer and ventriloquist!"; *A Vindication of the So Called "Clique"* (Buffalo, 1839), p. 10.

25. *New York Arena*, 1, no. 29 (April 16, 1842): 2.

26. If, as Snelling accused, Nichols joined Dixon in Wooldridge's *True Flash*, this may have been a source of Snelling's efforts at vilification. As we have seen before, not all accusations leveled against rival writers in the sporting press were true, but they were generally not completely false.

27. Thomas Low Nichols, *Ellen Ramsay; or, The Adventures of a Greenhorn, in Town and Country* (New York: For sale by booksellers and periodical agents generally, 1843), pp. 50, 59.

28. Thomas L. Nichols, *The Lady in Black: A Story of New York Life, Morals, and Manners* (New York: Sold by the Principal Booksellers in the United States, 1844), pp. 15, 29; for the exposition, see Chapter 9, "The Morals of Society," especially pp. 20–22.

29. Henry Blackwell treated *Mary Lyndon* as an autobiography and gave the real name of its characters in a letter to Lucy Stone, September 17, 1855. Although Blackwell admired Gove, he wrote of Nichols, "How she can have been so deceived & still continue so deceived by an *artificial* person like her husband is astonishing"; see *Loving Warriors: Selected Letters of Lucy Stone and Henry B. Blackwell, 1853 to 1893* (New York: The Dial Press, 1981), pp. 146–48, quote from p. 146.

30. Brodie, *Contraception and Abortion*, p. 128. Blackwell's own writings on sexuality largely appeared after 1880, although she gave a set of lectures that she published in 1852. Her understandings of sexuality put her firmly as a moderate within the tradition of reform physiology; oddly, her insistence that the woman determine when a couple has sexual intercourse places her in the Nichols camp; see Kate Krug, "Women Ovulate, Men Spermate: Elizabeth Blackwell as a Feminist Physiologist," *Journal of the History of Sexuality*, 7, no. 1 (July 1996): 51–73.

31. Silver-Isenstadt, "Pure Pleasure," pp. 284–96; Carl J. Guarneri, *The Utopian Alternative: Fourierism in Nineteenth-Century America* (Ithaca, N.Y.: Cornell University Press, 1991), p. 356.

32. T. L. Nichols, M.D., *Esoteric Anthropology: A Comprehensive and Confidential Treatise on the Structure, Functions, Passional Attractions and Perversions, True and False Physical and Social Conditions, and the Most Intimate Relations of Men and Women* (New York: Published by the author, at his Reform Bookstore, No. 65 Walker Street, 1854), pp. 129, 127.

33. Ibid., quote from p. 55.

34. Ibid., pp. 201, 202. They also considered bestiality and incest.

35. Ibid., p. 399.

36. Ibid., pp. 152–53.

37. Ibid., pp. 153, 270.

38. Ibid., p. 154.

39. Ibid., p. 215.

40. Ibid., p. 147.

41. T. L. Nichols and Mary S. Gove Nichols, *Marriage: Its History, Character, and Results; Its*

Sanctities, and Its Profanities; Its Science and Its Facts (Cincinnati: Valentine Nicholson & Co., 1854), pp. 317–18.

42. Ibid., p. 307.

13: *The Y.M.C.A. of New York, the Civil War, and Anthony Comstock*

1. Allan Stanley Horlick, *Country Boys and Merchant Princes: The Social Control of Young Men in New York* (Lewisburg, Pa.: Bucknell University Press, 1975), pp. 226–43; Paul Boyer, *Urban Masses and Moral Order in America, 1820–1920* (Cambridge, Mass.: Harvard University Press, 1978), pp. 108–20; C. Howard Hopkins, *History of the Y.M.C.A. in North America* (New York: Association Press, 1951), pp. 15–53.

2. Hopkins, *History of the Y.M.C.A.*, pp. 81–84, 107.

3. Horlick, *Country Boys and Merchant Princes*, pp. 226–43, quotes from pp. 230–31; Terry Donoghue, *An Event on Mercer Street: A Brief History of the Y.M.C.A. of the City of New York* (privately printed, n.d.), pp. 14–23, copy in Kautz Family YMCA Archives, St. Paul, Minnesota.

4. *Constitution of the New-York Young Men's Christian Association* (New York: Theo. H. Gray, Printer, 1852).

5. Hopkins, *History of the Y.M.C.A.*, pp. 81–84, 107; Donoghue, *An Event on Mercer Street,* pp. 26–30.

6. William E. Dodge, Jr., Excerpts from an Address to the 22nd Annual Convention, 1888, p. 2, William E. Dodge, Jr., biographical file, Kautz Family YMCA Archives.

7. "Remarks of Mr. Brainerd," p. 3, William Foster Lee biographical file, Kautz Family YMCA Archives; "Mr. Brainerd's Address," *Proceedings of the Ninth Annual Convention of the Young Men's Christian Association,* Boston, 1864, p. 76.

8. Although stated many times over many years, a good summary presentation is Stephen H. Tyng, Jr., "Timothy's Work," anniversary sermon, May 13, 1866, *Annual Report,* Y.M.C.A. of New York City, 1866, pp. 72–80.

9. Ibid., p. 75.

10. Cephas Brainerd, *The Work of the Army Committee of the New York Young Men's Christian Association, Which Led to the Organization of the United States Christian Commission* (New York: John Medole, printer, 1866), pp. 8–15; Hopkins, *History of the Y.M.C.A.*, pp. 88–89.

11. Reid Mitchell, "The Northern Soldier and His Community," in *Toward a Social History of the American Civil War: Exploratory Essays,* ed. Maris A. Vinovskis (New York: Cambridge University Press, 1990), pp. 78–80, 84, 87.

12. Ibid., pp. 90–91, quote from p. 91; Thomas R. Kemp, "Community and War," in *Toward a Social History of the American Civil War,* pp. 56–57.

13. "Passages from a Letter by Judge E. Rockwood Hoar to His Son, Samuel Hoar, Who Had Just Started for the War," Kautz Family YMCA Archives; Hopkins, *History of the Y.M.C.A.*, p. 84.

14. "Organization of the U.S. Christian Commission," typescript transcription of minutes, Kautz Family YMCA Archives; James H. Moorhead, *American Apocalypse: Yankee Protestants and the Civil War, 1860–1869* (New Haven, Conn.: Yale University Press, 1978), pp. 65–66; R. R. McBurney, *Historial Sketch of the Young Men's Christian Associations* (New York: [Y.M.C.A.], 1886), pp. 40–42.

15. Lemuel Moss, *Annals of the United States Christian Commission* (Philadelphia: J. B. Lippincott & Co., 1868), "Instructions to Delegates," quote from p. 544, Moss quote from p. 565.

16. Reverend Edward P. Smith, *Incidents of the United States Christian Commission* (Philadel-

phia: J. B. Lippincott & Co., 1869), pp. 337–41. The narrator, Reverend J. K. McLean, was minister of the Hollis Congregational Church, Framingham, Massachusetts.

17. The American Bible Society donated half a million Bibles to be distributed by the Christian Commission; see United States Christian Commission, *Second Annual Report, 1863*, p. 25.

18. Publication Ledgers, vol. 3, p. 124, E785, RG 94, National Archives, Washington, D.C; weekly reports of delegates, E755, ibid.; minutes, March 10, 1862, Minutes of the Executive Committee, 1861–1865, p. 4, Box 1, Entry 753, ibid.

19. J. C. Thomas, "Loan Library System," in *United States Christian Commission for the Army and Navy, Third Annual Report, 1864* (Philadelphia, 1865); Moss, *Annals of the United States Christian Commission*, pp. 714–24, quotes from pp. 723, 722.

20. Memorandum, United States Christian Commission, Loan Library Catalogue, Entry 790, RG 94, Entry 790, National Archives, Washington, D.C.

21. J. C. Thomas, "Loan Library System," pp. 49, 51.

22. House Miscellaneous Document 16, 37th Cong., 3rd sess., p. 8; William Adams Brown, *Morris Ketchum Jesup: A Character Sketch* (New York: Charles Scribner's Sons, 1911), pp. 48–49; Minutes of the Executive Committee, 1861–1865, Philadelphia, January 31, 1865, p. 190, RG 94, Entry 753, Box 1, National Archives, Washington, D.C.

23. Senator Jacob Collamer of Vermont, debate in the Senate, February 8, 1865, 38th Cong., 2nd sess. (S. 390), pp. 660–61; James C. N. Paul and Murray L. Schwartz, *Federal Censorship: Obscenity in the Mail* (New York: The Free Press of Glencoe, 1961), pp. 17, 251, 253–55; *Congressional Globe*, 38th Cong., 2nd sess., p. 966; Dorothy Ganfield Fowler, *Unmailable: Congress and the Post Office* (Athens: University of Georgia Press, 1977), pp. 56–57.

24. Jesup, for example, served as treasurer of the New York Christian Commission; see Brown, *Morris Ketchum Jesup*, pp. 48–49. Brainerd pressed claims against the city under the federal Riot Act, which held cities responsible for damages caused by rioters. He argued the case through the court of appeals, and the law was sustained. Brainerd later received "moderate compensation" for this work; see "Biography of Cephas Brainerd" (drafted, at least in part, by E. W. Brainerd; based on autobiographical memoir), typescript, c. 1945, pp. 73–75, 123, copy in Cephas Brainerd Papers, Kautz Family YMCA Archives.

25. Frank W. Ballard to "the Com. on purchase of a house for the Association," February 15, 1864, f. 1864 Committees, Box: Letters, Committee Reports, 1862–64, Historical Material for the YMCA of GNY, Kautz Family YMCA Archives.

26. Hopkins, *History of the Y.M.C.A.*, p. 45.

27. Frank W. Ballard, "New York City a Mission Field," address before Y.M.C.A. of New York, April 27, 1863 (New York: G. A. Witehorne, printer, n.d.), pp. 6–8.

28. *The Penal Code of the State of New York, Reported Complete by the Commissioners of the Code* (Albany: Weed, Parsons & Co., Printers, 1865), pp. 134–36.

29. Heywood Broun and Margaret Leech had access to the diary, which was destroyed in the 1950s, and fragments in their biography *Anthony Comstock: Roundsman of the Lord* (New York: Albert & Charles Boni, 1927) are the only remaining source; see Elizabeth Hovey, "Stamping Out Smut: The Enforcement of Obscenity Laws, 1872–1915," Ph.D. dissertation, Columbia University, 1998, p. 33, note 6; Richard Christian Johnson, "Anthony Comstock: Reform, Vice, and the American Way," Ph.D. dissertation, University of Wisconsin, 1973, p. 5.

30. Broun and Leech, *Anthony Comstock*, pp. 32, 33.

31. Ibid., pp. 45–55; Charles Gallaudet Trumbull, *Anthony Comstock, Fighter* (New York: Fleming H. Revell Company, 1913), pp. 31–42.

14: Sex Talk in the Open

1. For redemptive hopes, see Henry W. Bellows, *The New Man for the New Times: A Sermon Preached in All Souls' Church on a New Year's Day, 1865* (New York: J. Miller, 1865).

2. A concise source for information on New York is Amy Bridges, "Rethinking the Origins of Machine Politics," in *Power, Culture, and Place: Essays on New York City*, ed. John Hull Mollenkopf (New York: Russell Sage Foundation, 1988), pp. 53–73.

3. The sexually open city is described in Timothy J. Gilfoyle, *City of Eros: New York City, Prostitution, and the Commercialization of Sex, 1790–1920* (New York: W. W. Norton, 1992), pp. 224–39.

4. *Spirit of the Times*, May 12, 1866, p. 176; George Wilkes, formerly of the *Sunday Flash* and the *National Police Gazette*, was editor. Faye E. Dudden, *Women in the American Theatre: Actresses & Audiences, 1790–1870* (New Haven, Conn.: Yale University Press, 1994), pp. 157–63.

5. Gilfoyle, *City of Eros*, p. 128 (quote from Mike Norton, New York alderman); Dudden, *Women in the American Theatre*, pp. 149–55; Allen Nevins and Milton Halsey Thomas, eds., *The Diary of George Templeton Strong*, vol. 4 (New York: Macmillan Company, 1953), p. 164.

6. Robert C. Allen, *Horrible Prettiness: Burlesque and American Culture* (Chapel Hill: University of North Carolina Press, 1991), p. 78. One measure of the scale of "legwork" performance is that between 1866 and 1873 there were twenty-three productions of the work of Offenbach and burlesques on it on nine stages; see Peter Buckley, "The Culture of 'Leg-Work,' " in *The Mythmaking Frame of Mind: Social Imagination and American Culture*, ed. James Gilbert et al. (Belmont, Calif.: Wadsworth Publishing Company, 1993), p. 122.

7. Dudden, *Women in the American Theatre*, p. 143; Elliott J. Gorn, *The Manly Art: Bare-Knuckle Prize Fighting in America* (Ithaca, N.Y.: Cornell University Press, 1986), p. 183; Gilfoyle, *City of Eros*, pp. 225–32, quote from p. 225. To the surprise of some observers, some concert saloons attracted middle-class families.

8. Gilfoyle, *City of Eros*, p. 232.

9. Martha Elizabeth Hodes, *White Women, Black Men: Illicit Sex in the Nineteenth-Century South* (New Haven, Conn.: Yale University Press, 1997); *National Police Gazette*, September 28, 1867; "The Demi-Monde of New York," *National Police Gazette*, December 28, 1867, p. 2.

10. "Echoes from the Avant Scene," *The Days' Doings: Illustrating Current Events of Romance, Police Reports, Important Trials, and Sporting News*, 5, no. 117 (August 27, 1870): 195; "The Blond and the Griffin," p. 206; "Unsexed; or, The Man That Married a Man," pp. 202–3; "Wearing the Breeches," p. 205; "Whispers About Women," p. 195; "Ripples of Romance," p. 195.

11. George Ellington, *The Women of New York, or The Under-world of the Great City* (New York: New York Book Company, 1869), p. 166.

12. "Biography of Cephas Brainerd" (drafted, at least in part, by E. W. Brainerd; based on autobiographical memoir), typescript, ca. 1945, pp. 97–111, copy in Cephas Brainerd Papers, Kautz Family YMCA Archives, St. Paul, Minnesota.

13. George Cooper, *Lost Love: A True Story of Passion, Murder, and Justice in Old New York* (New York: Pantheon Books, 1994), pp. 141–44. Octavius Brooks Frothingham also performed the ceremony, but attention was focused on Beecher, the celebrity.

14. For data on New York City newspapers, see Oliver Carlson, *The Man Who Made News: James Gordon Bennett* (New York: Duell, Sloan and Pearce, 1942), p. 300.

15. *Days' Doings*, 5, no. 117 (August 27, 1870): 207, for the advertisements cited here and in the following two paragraphs.

16. O. S. Fowler, *Creative and Sexual Science: Or Manhood, Womanhood, and Their Mutual

Interrelations . . . (Philadelphia, Chicago, St. Louis: National Publishing Company, 1870, 1875), pp. 40, 51.

17. Ibid., pp. 40, 47, 50.

18. Ibid., p. 600.

19. Ibid., p. 601.

20. Ibid., p. 602.

21. Ibid., pp. 194, 213–14.

22. The accusations were of delivering "private lectures to ladies . . . of an immoral character and often grossly obscene in action and speech, and his correspondence and books contained indelicate and unchaste suggestions" and "sustaining the most disreputable relationship with certain female quacks, and . . . writing to them grossly immoral letters, which actually undertook to systematize sexual vice" (Madeleine B. Stern, *Heads and Headlines: The Phrenological Fowlers* [Norman: University of Oklahoma Press, 1941], pp. 241–42). O. S. Fowler died in 1887.

23. John Cowan, M.D., *The Science of a New Life* (New York: Cowan & Company, Publishers, 1869), pp. 46, 115, 112.

24. James Ashton, M.D., *The Book of Nature: Containing Information for Young People Who Think of Getting Married* . . . (New York: Wallis & Ashton, 1861), pp. 34–35.

25. Ibid., pp. 21, 35–37.

26. For Foote's life and career, I have relied on "Edward Bliss Foote," *The National Cyclopaedia of American Biography*, vol. 3 (New York: James T. White & Company, 1893), p. 68; *In Memory of Edward Bliss Foote, M.D.* (New York: Edward Bond Foote, 1907), pp. 9–10; Vincent J. Cirillo, "Edward Bliss Foote: Pioneer American Advocate of Birth Control," *Bulletin of the History of Medicine*, 47, no. 5 (September–October 1973): 475–77; Hal D. Sears, *The Sex Radicals: Free Love in High Victorian America* (Lawrence: Regents Press of Kansas, 1977), pp. 183–98; Janet Farrell Brodie, *Contraception and Abortion in 19th-Century America* (Ithaca, N.Y.: Cornell University Press, 1994), pp. 237–41.

27. Edward B. Foote, *Medical Common Sense; Applied to the Causes, Prevention and Cure of Chronic Diseases and Unhappiness in Marriage* (Boston: Wentworth, Hewes & Company, 1858), pp. 188 [italics deleted], 194–95.

28. Ibid., pp. 202, 246.

29. Ibid., pp. 248, 249, 250, 258.

30. Edward B. Foote, *Medical Common Sense; Applied to the Causes, Prevention and Cure of Chronic Diseases and Unhappiness in Marriage,* rev. and enlarged (New York: published by the author, 1863), pp. 338–39, 378–79.

31. Edward B. Foote, *Plain Home Talk about the Human System* . . . (New York: Murray Hill Publishing Company, 1870), pp. 631, 728, 783.

32. Ibid., pp. 753, 752.

33. Ibid., p. 755.

34. Ibid., pp. 621, 884.

35. Ibid., pp. 881, 884.

36. Ibid., pp. 172, 182, 755, 757.

37. Ibid., pp. 718, 773, 830.

38. *A Full Account of the Trial of Simon M. Landis, M.D. for Uttering and Publishing a Book Entitled "Secrets of Generation"* (Philadelphia: First Progressive Christian Church, 1870), pp. 8–9.

39. Ibid., pp. 38, 9.

40. Ibid., pp. 50, 11–12.

41. Ibid., pp. 49–51.

15: *Victoria Woodhull*

1. Changes in the media that helped create celebrity culture are chronicled in Andie Tucher, *Froth and Scum: Truth, Beauty, Goodness, and the Ax Murder in America's First Mass Medium* (Chapel Hill: University of North Carolina Press, 1994).

2. For Victoria Woodhull, I rely on Lois Beachy Underhill, *The Woman Who Ran for President: The Many Lives of Victoria Woodhull* (Bridgehampton, N.Y.: Bridge Works Publishing Company, 1995); and Mary Gabriel, *Notorious Victoria: The Life of Victoria Woodhull, Uncensored* (Chapel Hill, N.C.: Algonquin Books, 1998). A less reliable treatment is Barbara Goldsmith, *Other Powers: The Age of Suffrage, Spiritualism, and the Scandalous Victoria Woodhull* (New York: Alfred A. Knopf, 1998). These works supersede (but also depend on) the 1920s biography by Emanie Sachs, *The Terrible Siren: Victoria Woodhull* (New York: Harper & Brothers Publishers, 1928).

3. Three male contemporaries—Theodore Tilton, Joseph Treat, and Benjamin Tucker—of Woodhull, representing different judgments of her, agreed that she did not write many of the words attributed to her. Tilton, in his "campaign biography" of Woodhull, presenting her in what both he and she deemed a favorable light, described how she dictated the memorial she presented to Congress to Blood from the spirits: Theodore Tilton, *Victoria C. Woodhull, a Biographical Sketch* (New York: Golden Age, 1871), pp. 28–29. Woodhull herself "wrote" of willingness to use other words when they served her cause and of her "Spirit Guides" in "Lo Here! Lo There!" *Woodhull & Claflin's Weekly*, 10, no. 3 (June 19, 1875): 5–6. On Woodhull's responsibility for the November 2, 1872, issue, see Underhill, *The Woman Who Ran for President*, pp. 220–21.

4. William Leach, *True Love and Perfect Union: The Feminist Reform of Sex and Society* (New York: Basic Books, 1980), pp. 38–63; Norma Basch, *Framing American Divorce: From the Revolutionary Generation to the Victorians* (Berkeley: University of California Press, 1999), pp. 68–69.

5. Andrea Moore Kerr, *Lucy Stone: Speaking Out for Equality* (New Brunswick, N.J.: Rutgers University Press, 1992), pp. 161–65.

6. Quote from Victoria Woodhull, "The Beecher-Tilton Scandal Case," *Woodhull & Claflin's Weekly*, 5, no. 7 (November 2, 1872): 10.

7. *New York Herald*, May 16 and May 17, 1871; Harriet Beecher Stowe, *My Wife and I: or, Harry Henderson's History* (New York: J. B. Ford and Company, 1872); Woodhull, "A Speech on the Principles of Social Freedom." In her able introduction, Madeleine Stern suggests that Woodhull's speeches and writings were generally drafted by both Andrews and Blood; see *Victoria Woodhull Reader*, ed. Madeleine Stern (Weston, Mass.: M & S Press, 1974), p. 5.

8. Woodhull, "Principles of Social Freedom," pp. 13 (posed in the text as a rhetorical question), 15, 16.

9. Ibid., pp. 35, 37.

10. Ibid., p. 17.

11. Ann Braude, *Radical Spirits: Spiritualism and Women's Rights in Nineteenth-Century America* (Boston: Beacon Press, 1989), pp. 169–70. There was opposition to Woodhull within the Spiritualist movement, led by the *Religio-Philosophical Journal;* see Paul A. Carter, *The Spiritual Crisis of the Gilded Age* (DeKalb: Northern Illinois University Press, 1971), p. 104.

12. Woodhull, "The Beecher-Tilton Scandal Case," pp. 9–13.

13. Edward B. Foote, *Plain Home Talk About the Human System . . .* (New York: Murray Hill Publishing Company, 1873), p. 619.

14. On the Beecher-Tilton scandal, the best narrative is Robert Shaplen, *Free Love and Heavenly Sinners* (New York: Alfred A. Knopf, 1954). Important analyses are provided by Altina L.

Waller, *Reverend Beecher and Mrs. Tilton: Sex and Class in Victorian America* (Amherst: University of Massachusetts Press, 1982); Richard Wightman Fox, "Intimacy on Trial: Cultural Meanings of the Beecher-Tilton Affair," in *The Power of Culture: Critical Essays in American History,* ed. Richard Wightman Fox and T. J. Jackson Lears (Chicago: University of Chicago Press, 1993), 103–32; and Richard Wightman Fox, *Trials of Intimacy: Love and Loss in the Beecher-Tilton Scandal* (Chicago: University of Chicago Press, 1999). Fox does not believe there is conclusive evidence that Beecher and Elizabeth Tilton had a sexual affair.

15. Andrews's hand in preparing the article is in the opening and closing arguments. At the 1875 civil trial that Theodore Tilton brought against Henry Ward Beecher, Andrews testified that he had received a draft of the article and had not changed the "recital" or narrative portions: "the introductory part and the close, the literary cast and the philosophic cast of the paper shows my marks, perhaps." On reexamination, he clarified, "I have put a red line around those which I either wrote or recast; the middle portion, which is not so encircled, went as it was brought to me, with the exception of the fact that I may have run my pen through a single line to correct literary style, or something of that kind"; see Theodore Tilton vs. Henry Ward Beecher, *Action for Crim. Con. Tried in the City Court of Brooklyn,* vol. 3 (New York: McDivitt, Campbell, & Company, 1875), pp. 395, 402.

16. Woodhull, "The Beecher-Tilton Scandal Case," p. 5.

17. Ibid., pp. 9–10.

18. Ibid., p. 11.

19. Ibid., p. 13.

20. Ibid., p. 14.

21. Ibid., p. 15; Braude, *Radical Spirits;* John C. Spurlock, *Free Love: Marriage and Middle-Class Radicalism in America, 1825–1860* (New York: New York University Press, 1988), pp. 114–37.

22. Woodhull, "The Beecher-Tilton Scandal Case," pp. 15, 19. This was in keeping with Blood's practice as Woodhull conducted a sexual affair with Benjamin Tucker in the early 1870s, if the latter can be believed (Benjamin R. Tucker to Emanie Sachs, c. 1927, Box 9, Benjamin R. Tucker Collection, New York Public Library, New York).

23. Woodhull, "The Beecher-Tilton Scandal Case," pp. 13, 19.

24. Edward H. G. Clark of Troy, New York, for example, although opposing her views, issued the *Thunderbolt,* defending Woodhull's right to publish as she had; see Martha Coffin Wright to Ellen Wright Garrison, March 12, 1873, Garrison family papers, Sophia Smith Collection, Smith College, Northampton, Mass.

25. Elizabeth Phelps confided to Susan B. Anthony that she had received "Tit for Tat," and mention of it appears in Anthony's letters. Lillie Devereaux Blake's daughter recalled the time in her childhood when her mother had received it. Paulina Wright Davis, one of Woodhull's most ardent supporters, wrote Woodhull a letter of regret from abroad when Davis thought the article had been published; see Goldsmith, *Other Powers,* pp. 316–18, notes 482–83, independently verified. For a full defense of blackmail, see "Magnificent Beats vs. Magnificent Hussies," *Woodhull & Claflin's Weekly,* 4, no. 21 (April 6, 1872): 10, by "One Who Knows."

16: The Comstock Law

1. Register of Arrests for Offenses against postal laws, 1864–1897, p. 246, Bureau of the Chief Inspector, Entry 229, Record Group 28, National Archives, Washington, D.C.

2. Lawrence B. Goodheart, "The Ambiguity of Individualism: The National Liberal League's Challenge to the Comstock Law," in *American Chameleon: Individualism in Trans-*

National Context, ed. Richard O. Curry and Lawrence B. Goodheart (Kent, Ohio: Kent State University Press, 1991), p. 135; Stow Persons, *Free Religion: An American Faith* (New Haven, Conn.: Yale University Press, 1947), pp. 114–17; Jon C. Teaford, "Toward a Christian Nation: Religion, Law and Justice Strong," *Journal of Presbyterian History,* 54 (1976): 428, 430. Strong was also president of the American Tract Society from 1873 to 1895.

3. Ethan T. Colton, Sr., "William E. Dodge, Jr.," p. 10, Dodge biographical file, Kautz Family YMCA Archives, St. Paul, Minnesota; for the role of Brainerd and McBurney, see L. L. Doggett, *Life of Robert R. McBurney* (Cleveland: F. M. Barton, 1902), p. 75. All subsequent historians must be grateful to the abbreviated account in Paul S. Boyer, *Purity in Print: The Vice-Society Movement and Book Censorship in America* (New York: Charles Scribner's Sons, 1968), pp. 1–22.

4. *A Memorandum Respecting New-York as a Field for Moral and Christian Effort Among Young Men* (New York: The Association, 1866), pp. 3–7; Terry Donohue suggests that Frank W. Ballard, chairman of the publishing committee of the New York Y.M.C.A., was the likely author; see Terry Donoghue, *An Event on Mercer Street: A Brief History of the Y.M.C.A. of the City of New York* (privately printed, n.d.), p. 43, copy in Kautz Family YMCA Archives. Cephas Brainerd and Robert McBurney were the authors, according to "The Biography of Cephas Brainerd" (drafted, at least in part, by E. W. Brainerd; based on autobiographical memoir), typescript, c. 1945, p. 194, copy in Cephas Brainerd Papers, Kautz Family YMCA Archives. Lawrence M. Friedman has written of the "Victorian compromise," which criminalized acts when they offended public morality, while tolerating them "in the shadows"; see *Crime and Punishment in American History* (New York: Basic Books, 1993) pp. 127 ff., quote from p. 131.

5. Donoghue, *An Event on Mercer Street,* p. 44.

6. Elizabeth Hovey, "Stamping Out Smut: The Enforcement of Obscenity Laws, 1872–1915," Ph.D. dissertation, Columbia University, 1998, p. 36; Cephas Brainerd, memorandum accompanying letter to J. D. Bowne, March 7, 1885, and notes on "Origin of the Society for the Suppression of Vice," Cephas Brainerd Papers, Kautz Family YMCA Archives; Cephas Brainerd to J. D. Bowne, October 22, 1901, Folder 17, Box 1, Ralph Ginzburg papers, State Historical Society of Wisconsin, Madison, Wisconsin; Heywood Broun and Margaret Leech, *Anthony Comstock, Roundsman of the Lord* (New York: Albert & Charles Boni, 1927), p. 82.

7. H. T. Tarbox to Cephas Brainerd, April 22, 1868, Cephas Brainerd biographical file, Kautz Family YMCA Archives; for Tarbox's role, see *Journal of the Assembly of the State of New York at Their Ninety-First Session, 1868* (Albany: C. Van Benthuysen & Sons, 1868), p. 1104; *Sixteenth Annual Report of the Young Men's Christian Association of the City of New York, 1868* (New York: The Association, 1868); Cephas Brainerd to J. D. Bowne, March 7, 1885, Comstock biographical file, and "Charles Edward Whitehead, Minute Adopted by the Young Men's Christian Association of the City of New York, April, 1903," Whitehead biographical file, Kautz Family YMCA Archives.

8. There are good discussions of this law in James C. Mohr, *Abortion in America: The Origins and Evolution of National Policy, 1800–1900* (Oxford: Oxford University Press, 1978), pp. 215–17; Michael Grossberg, *Governing the Hearth: Law and the Family in Nineteenth-Century America* (Chapel Hill: University of North Carolina Press, 1985), pp. 170–75; Hovey, "Stamping Out Smut," discusses the Ohio law; see pp. 38–39. See also *The Penal Code for the State of New York* (Albany: Weed, Parsons, 1865).

9. Colton, "William E. Dodge, Jr.," pp. 8–9; Donoghue, *An Event on Mercer Street,* pp. 44–45.

10. Donoghue, *An Event on Mercer Street,* p. 48; *Proceedings of the Fourteenth Annual Convention of the Young Men's Christian Association, 1869* (New York: The Association, 1869), p. 101.

11. Minutes of board of directors, beginning January 17, 1870, November 20, 1871, p. 75, Historical Material for the YMCA of GNY, Kautz Family YMCA Archives.

12. Brainerd is discussed fourteen times in the biography of McBurney, who, it turns out, lived in Brainerd's house in the 1860s (Doggett, *Life of Robert R. McBurney,* p. 88); Schedule "A": Subscriptions to the Building Fund [c. 1869], Box: Letters, 1868, Historical Material for the YMCA of GNY, Kautz Family YMCA Archives.

13. "Biography of Cephas Brainerd," pp. 128–30, quote from p. 128, 216–17; for a selection of theological books, see list of books purchased from Robert Carter & Brothers, one half of the price given by the booksellers as a donation (f. 1864 Committees, Box: Letters, Committee Reports, 1862–64, Historical Material for the YMCA of GNY, Kautz Family YMCA Archives).

14. This statement came in a plea for the Y.M.C.A. to staff a mission offering Sunday school training to the young growing up in the rough sections of New York; see "Observations suggested by a recent Plea for City Missions, read twice before the Y.M.C.A. Assn, last Monday eves of June and July 1863," p. 15, Folder 3, Box 1, Cephas Brainard Papers, Kautz Family YMCA Archives; "Biography of Cephas Brainerd," discussion of an 1881 article, pp. 189–94, quote from p. 189; "Address of Cephas Brainerd," *Association Monthly,* 3, no. 11 (November 1872): 181.

15. "Address of Cephas Brainerd," pp. 182, 181–83.

16. "Sketch of Life of Anthony Comstock, taken down stenographically, from his own words, on Friday evening, December 17, 1886, at the Massasoit House, Springfield, Massachusetts by Frank M. Pratt," typescript, p. 5, Comstock biographical file, Kautz Family YMCA Archives.

17. Broun and Leech, *Anthony Comstock,* p. 65.

18. Lemuel Moss, *Annals of the United States Christian Commission* (Philadelphia: J. B. Lippincott & Company, 1868), p. 615. In September 1864, seeking to serve both their congregations and the Union cause, Budington and other Brooklyn ministers had sent a memorial to the national body recommending that it collectively form a mission that would rotate two ministers into service in the field for two-week periods, rather than each serving for the regular six-week stint. The matter was referred to the chair and secretary for action; see Minutes of the Executive Committee, 1861–1865, Philadelphia, September 30, 1864, p. 110, RG 94, Entry 753, Box 1, National Archives, Washington, D.C.

19. "Sketch of Life of Anthony Comstock," p. 5.

20. Broun and Leech, *Anthony Comstock,* pp. 70–72; quote from p. 71.

21. Ibid., pp. 72–73.

22. Charles Gallaudet Trumbull, *Anthony Comstock, Fighter* (New York: Fleming H. Revell Company, 1913), p. 51; "Sketch of Life of Anthony Comstock," p. 2.

23. Letter from Anthony Comstock, January 18, 1873, published in speech of Clinton L. Merriam, House of Representatives, *Congressional Globe,* 42nd Cong., 3rd sess., Appendix, p. 168; "Dealers in Obscene Literature Arrested," *New York Daily Tribune,* March 4, 1872, p. 8; editorial, *New York Daily Tribune,* March 5, 1872, p. 4.

24. It is in the nature of such ads to appear repeatedly; for an example, see *Days' Doings,* August 6, 1870, p. 159. On August 24, 1872, Comstock secured the arrest of Charles E. Mackey, 88 and 90 Centre Street, of the American Publishing Agency; see NYSSV, Arrest Record, Case no. 32, pp. 11–12.

25. *Days' Doings,* August 6, 1870, p. 159; Comstock had William Barkley of 19 Ann Street, the address of Dayly & Co., arrested on March 2, 1872; see NYSSV, Arrest Record, Case no. 3, pp. 3–4.

26. *Days' Doings,* August 13, 1870, p. 175; on August 25, 1872, Comstock got the arrest of

Henry Camp of Cameron & Co., 146 Bleecker Street; see NYSSV, Arrest Record, Case no. 34, pp. 11–12.

27. These were offered by A. Seymour, Dr. Manches, and Dr. Evans, *Days' Doings,* August 6, 1870, p. 159: Comstock went after Lander Fox, Seymour & Co., 369 Canal Street, on January 24, 1873; see NYSSV, Arrest Record, Case no. 48, pp. 15–16; "Manches" was probably Charles Mancher, 635 Broadway, prosecuted March 6, 1872; see NYSSV, Arrest Record, Case no. 9, pp. 5–6.

28. Dr. Evans, *Days' Doings,* August 6, 1870, p. 159; Doctor Harrison, who sold his "Female Antidote," *Days' Doings,* January 22, 1870, p. 15; on August 24, 1872, Comstock went after David Massey, 737 Broadway, who had as an alias "Dr. Harrison"; see NYSSV, Arrest Record, Case no. 33, pp. 11–12.

29. "Sketch of Life of Anthony Comstock," p. 2; NYSSV, Arrest Record, 1872, Case no. 14, pp. 5–6, Library of Congress, Washington, D.C.

30. NYSSV, Arrest Record, n.d., p. 2, Library of Congress.

31. NYSSV, Arrest Record, n.d., p. 2, Library of Congress; re: Grandin, NYSSV, Arrest Record, 1872, Case no. 30, pp. 9–10, ibid.

32. "Sketch of Life of Anthony Comstock," p. 3.

33. Cephas Brainerd to J. D. Bowne, October 22, 1901, Folder 17, Box 1, Ralph Ginzburg papers, State Historical Society of Wisconsin.

34. Anthony Comstock to Mr. R. R. McBurney, March 23, [187]2, copy in Assistant Treasurer Letterbook, 1870–71, pp. 91–93, William W. Alexander, Historical Material for the YMCA of GNY, Kautz Family YMCA Archives; NYSSV, Arrest Record, n.d., p. 2, Library of Congress (all other accounts give the sum as $650); "Sketch of Life of Anthony Comstock," p. 3.

35. Richard Christian Johnson, "Anthony Comstock: Reform, Vice, and the American Way," Ph.D. dissertation, University of Wisconsin, 1973, pp. 58–59; quote from p. 58; "Sketch of Life of Anthony Comstock," p. 3; Anthony Comstock, "The Work of Suppressing Vice," *The Golden Rule,* clipping, undated (c. 1890), p. 204, Kautz Family YMCA Archives.

36. Minutes of board of directors [volume beginning January 17, 1870], November 18, 1872, pp. 105–6, Historical Material for the YMCA of GNY, Kautz Family YMCA Archives; *Twentieth Annual Report of the Young Men's Christian Association of the City of New York,* 1872 (New York: The Association, 1873), p. 5.

37. My understanding of the composition and motivations of the Y.M.C.A. differs from that of Nicola Beisel (*Imperiled Innocents: Anthony Comstock and Family Reproduction in Victorian America* [Princeton, N.J.: Princeton University Press, 1997]) in several respects. New York had many elites in the nineteenth century: post–Civil War Y.M.C.A. leaders came from the evangelical Christian elite, which traced its origins to New England. The concern of these men was not with reproduction of the elite in their own families but with their moral responsibility to the young clerk. By 1872 some of them had been addressing these concerns for twenty years. They were drawing on a tradition of physiological reform that for forty years had been emphasizing the harm of masturbation, the dangers of reading erotic material, and the special risks of children in boarding schools. Nonetheless, I learned a good deal from Beisel's book and benefited from the author's Bourdieuian perspective.

38. Cephas Brainerd, memorandum, accompanying letter to J. D. Bowne, March 7, 1885, and notes on "Origin of the Society for the Suppression of Vice," Cephas Brainerd Papers, Kautz Family YMCA Archives; Johnson, "Anthony Comstock," p. 59.

39. NYSSV, Arrest Record, Case no. 18, pp. 7–8. George Thompson, not de Kock, was likely Comstock's real bête noire.

40. NYSSV, Arrest Record, n.d., p. 2, Library of Congress.

41. NYSSV, Arrest Record, 1872, Case no. 3, pp. 3–4, Library of Congress.

42. Cephas Brainerd to J. D. Bowne, October 22, 1901, Folder 17, Box 1, Ralph Ginzburg papers, State Historical Society of Wisconsin.

43. Anthony Comstock to Mr. R. R. McBurney, March 23, [187]2, copy in Assistant Treasurer Letterbook, 1870–71, W. W. Alexander, Historical Material for the YMCA of GNY, Kautz Family YMCA Archives; minutes of board of directors [volume beginning January 17, 1870], November 18, 1872, pp. 105–6, ibid. This understanding is in contrast to the account in Broun and Leech, *Anthony Comstock*, pp. 84–89, generally cited by others.

44. Tennie C. Claflin, "Beginning of the Battle," *Woodhull & Claflin's Weekly*, 5, no. 7 (November 2, 1872): 2; Victoria Woodhull, "To the Public," ibid., p. 8; "The Philosophy of Modern Hypocrisy—Mr. L. C. Challis the Illustration," ibid.

45. Register of Arrests for Offenses against postal laws, 1864–1897, p. 246, Bureau of the Chief Inspector, Entry 229, Record Group 28, National Archives; "The Charge of Obscenity," *Woodhull & Claflin's Weekly*, 5, no. 11 (February 15, 1873): 9–13.

46. The best discussion of these matters is in the endnotes of Edward de Grazia, *Girls Lean Back Everywhere: The Law of Obscenity and the Assault on Genius* (New York: Random House, 1992), pp. 695–96.

47. "Sketch of Life of Anthony Comstock," p. 4.

48. Frank W. Ballard, "New York City a Mission Field," address before the New York Y.M.C.A., April 27, 1863 (New York: The Association, n.d.), pp. 6–8; Cephas Brainerd to "My dear sir," October 22, 1901, Comstock biographical file, Kautz Family YMCA Archives.

49. C. Thomas Dienes, *Law, Politics, and Birth Control* (Urbana: University of Illinois Press, 1972), pp. 33–34.

50. Persons, *Free Religion*, p. 117; Comstock diary, quoted in Broun and Leech, *Anthony Comstock*, p. 131.

51. The copy of *The Penal Code of the State of New York*, devised in 1865, was given to Harvard's library by Benjamin Vaughan Abbott.

52. Comstock diary, quoted in Broun and Leech, *Anthony Comstock*, p. 137.

53. William Adams Brown, *Morris Ketchum Jesup: A Character Sketch* (New York: Charles Scribner's Sons, 1911), p. 56.

54. Laws of the State of New York, 96th sess. (1873), Chapter 777, pp. 1183–85.

55. Comstock diary, in Broun and Leech, *Anthony Comstock*, p. 153.

56. Whitehead's role is emphasized in "Charles Edward Whitehead," Minute adopted by the Young Men's Christian Association of the City of New York, April 1903, pp. 5–6.

17: *Comstock's Crusade*

1. Ackerman had sold his business at 19 Ann Street to Charles Barkley in 1871. Barkley was sentenced in federal court to a year in prison and $500 fines after Comstock successfully pursued him in March 1872. Ackerman must have felt Comstock's threat; he died the following year; see NYSSV, Arrest Record, Case no. 3, pp. 3–4; Register of Arrests for Offenses against postal laws, 1864–1897, March 2 [1872], p. 214, Bureau of the Chief Inspector, Entry 229, Record Group 28, National Archives, Washington, D.C. Comstock sought Jeremiah Farrell in state court for the sale of "French Bedstead."

2. Clifford Browder, *The Wickedest Woman in New York: Madame Restell, the Abortionist* (Hamden, Conn.: Archon Books, 1988), 158–83; NYSSV, Arrest Record, 1878, Case no. 4, pp. 111–12.

3. Anthony Comstock, *Frauds Exposed; or How the People Are Deceived and Robbed, and Youth Corrupted* (New York: J. Howard Brown, 1880), p. 388.

4. Schedule "A": Subscriptions to the Building Fund [c. 1869], Box: Letters, 1868, Historical Material for the YMCA of GNY, Kautz Family YMCA Archives, St. Paul, Minnesota; cf. *New York Society for the Suppression of Vice, Second Annual Report* (1876), pp. 16, 15; the first report is Committee for the Suppression of Vice, "Improper Books, Prints, etc.," New York, 1874, p. 12 (at the top of the cover are these words: "To be destroyed when read" and "Private and Confidential." A copy in Historical Material for the YMCA of GNY, Kautz Family YMCA Archives, in St. Paul, has the date, in ink, January 28, 1874, the date of the first meeting of the New York Society for the Suppression of Vice); Nicola Beisel, *Imperiled Innocents: Anthony Comstock and Family Reproduction in Victorian America* (Princeton, N.J.: Princeton University Press, 1997), p. 51, chart on p. 50.

5. NYSSV, Arrest Record, Case no. 51, pp. 15–16; NYSSV, Arrest Record, Case no. 18, 1878, pp. 117–18; Andrea Tone, "Black Market Birth Control: Contraceptive Entrepreneurship and Criminality in the Gilded Age," *Journal of American History*, 87, no. 2 (September 2000): 435–36.

6. In addition, other special agents made arrests. I could find only seven obscenity cases in the post office register under the 1865 and 1872 laws before Comstock entered the scene. Beginning with his efforts in spring 1872 the number picked up significantly (Register of Arrests for Offenses against postal laws, 1864–1897).

7. Andrea Tone, *Devices and Desires: A History of Contraceptives in America* (New York: Hill and Wang, 2001), pp. 35–36.

8. Elizabeth Hovey, "Stamping Out Smut: The Enforcement of Obscenity Laws, 1872–1915," Ph.D. dissertation, Columbia University, 1998, pp. 73–78, emphasizes the masculine language of the NYSSV.

9. NYSSV, Arrest Record, 1872, Case no. 30, pp. 9–10, Library of Congress; ibid., Arrest Record, Case no. 32, pp. 11–12.

10. "Improper Books, Prints, etc.," pp. 4–5.

11. Ibid., p. 6.

12. *Trial of D. M. Bennett, in the United States Circuit Court, Judge Charles L. Benedict, Presiding* (New York: Truth Seeker, [1879]), pp. 18–19.

13. This has also been argued by Hovey in "Stamping Out Smut," pp. 9, 14. There are some exceptions to this, such as the 1875 annual report of the NYSSV, and the listing of the countries of origin in early reports.

14. Comstock, *Frauds Exposed*, p. 444; Anthony Comstock, *Traps for the Young* (New York: Funk and Wagnalls, Publishers, 1883), pp. 185–86.

15. Comstock, *Traps for the Young*, pp. 159–60.

16. [Anthony Comstock], *New York Society for the Suppression of Vice, Sixth Annual Report* (1880), pp. 11–12; Comstock, *Frauds Exposed*, p. 391 (italics in the original).

17. [Anthony Comstock], *New York Society for the Suppression of Vice, First Annual Report* (1875), pp. 10–11; *Second Annual Report* (1876), pp. 4, 6, 8, 6; *Third Annual Report* (1877), pp. 6–7.

18. [Anthony Comstock], *New York Society for the Suppression of Vice, Third Annual Report* (1877), p. 9.

19. [Anthony Comstock], *New York Society for the Suppression of Vice, Second Annual Report* (1876), p. 8.

20. [Anthony Comstock], *New York Society for the Suppression of Vice, Third Annual Report* (1877), p. 8.

21. Comstock, *Traps for the Young*, pp. 52, 51.

22. Ibid., pp. 10, 12; Comstock, *Frauds Exposed*, p. 433 (italics in the original). Perhaps as a boy Comstock had been exposed to the *Sketch of the Life and Adventures of Henry Leander Foote*, a Connecticut man who blamed his rape and murder of his cousin and his subsequent murder of his mother on the "licentious novels, and other bad books" he had read as well as his consorting with prostitutes and alcohol (see the discussion of this book, published in New Haven in 1850, in Karen Halttunen, *Murder Most Foul: The Killer and the American Gothic Imagination* [Cambridge, Mass.: Harvard University Press, 1998], pp. 203–6).

23. Comstock, *Traps for the Young*, pp. 46, 49, 50.

24. Comstock, *Frauds Exposed*, p. 389; Comstock, *Traps for the Young*, pp. 135–36; Comstock, *Frauds Exposed*, p. 416; Comstock, *Traps for the Young*, p. 136. Many writers on Comstock have emphasized that he masturbated and felt guilty about it afterward; because this seemed to the age a virtually universal practice, I have not done so. My interests have been less in Comstock's psyche than in how Comstock and his ghostwriters reflected and expressed long-held ideas.

25. Comstock, *Frauds Exposed*, p. 416.

26. Ibid., p. 427; Comstock, *Traps for the Young*, p. 133.

27. Comstock, *Traps for the Young*, p. 134; [Anthony Comstock], *New York Society for the Suppression of Vice, Sixth Annual Report* (1880), p. 9.

28. [Anthony Comstock], *New York Society for the Suppression of Vice, Sixth Annual Report* (1880), p. 11.

18: *Convictions*

1. For sources on Edward Bliss Foote, see Chapter 14, note 26.

2. D. M. Bennett, *An Open Letter to Samuel Colgate* (New York: D. M. Bennett, 1879), pp. 15–16; pp. 11 (Colgate speech), 9 (Colgate ad), and 33 (re: Foote). In Comstock's arrest record, another story is told. In 1873, he seized this inventory of Leander Fox: "1000 R. articles, looner Drgs [?] & various other vile articles. 100 Photo & Stereocopic views. 250 microscopic views. 50 books, 25 Circulars"; see NYSSV, Arrest Record, Case no. 48, pp. 15–16. It is likely that he was the druggist Seymour, who advertised condoms in *Days' Doings* (see Chapter 16).

3. Vincent J. Cirillo, "Edward Foote's Medical Common Sense: An Early American Comment on Birth Control," *Journal of the History of Medicine*, 25, no. 3 (July 1970): 341–45; Wilson Yates, "Birth Control Literature and the Medical Profession in Nineteenth Century America," *Journal of the History of Medicine and Allied Sciences*, 31, no. 1 (January 1976): 50–51.

4. *Woodhull & Claflin's Weekly*, 4, no. 8 (January 6, 1872): 12; Samuel P. Putnam, *Four Hundred Years of Freethought* (New York, 1894), p. 730.

5. Putnam, *Four Hundred Years of Freethought*, pp. 728–29; NYSSV, Arrest Record, 1876, Case no. 1, pp. 63–64.

6. NYSSV, Arrest Record, 1876, Case no. 1, pp. 63–64; Edward B. Foote, Sr., *A Fable of the Spider and the Bees* (New York: National Defense Association, 1881), p. 12; Edward Bliss Foote, "Dr. Knowlton's Book," *Dr. Foote's Health Monthly*, 2, no. 8 (August 1877): 7; D. M. Bennett, *Anthony Comstock: His Career of Cruelty and Crime* (New York: D. M. Bennett, Liberal and Scientific Publishing House, 1878), Case 15, pp. 1036–41.

7. *United States v. Foote*, Case no. 15, 128, 25 Fed. Case, pp. 1140–41.

8. "A Physician Fined $3,500," *New York Times*, July 12, 1876, p. 3.

9. Foote, *A Fable of the Spider and the Bees*.

10. Edward Bliss Foote, "Mr. Bradlaugh and Mrs. Besant Convicted!" *Dr. Foote's Health*

Monthly, 2, no. 8 (August 1877): 4; Foote, "Now Is the Opportune Time," ibid., 2, no. 10 (October 1877): 11–12; Foote, "Causes Limiting Reproduction," ibid., 2, no. 6 (June 1877): 11.

11. In 1881, Foote claimed that *Medical Common Sense* had sold more than 250,000 copies and *Plain Home Talk*, more than 150,000 (Foote, *Fable of the Spider and the Bees*, p. 12); "Forlorn Hope, Glad of It: Dr. Foote, Populist, Will Run for Congress Anyway," *New York Times*, July 8, 1894, p. 9.

12. My discussion of Heywood draws on the important work of several scholars: Sears, *The Sex Radicals*, pp. 153–82; David M. Rabban, *Free Speech in Its Forgotten Years* (Cambridge, England: Cambridge University Press, 1997), pp. 32–36; and especially Martin Henry Blatt, *Free Love and Anarchism: The Biography of Ezra Heywood* (Urbana: University of Illinois Press, 1989) and *The Collected Works of Ezra H. Heywood*, ed. with introductions by Martin Blatt (Weston, Mass.: M & S Press, 1985). Although it treats the years after this study, I have also been influenced by Jesse Battan, " 'The Word Made Flesh': Language, Authority, and Sexual Desire in Late Nineteenth-Century America," *Journal of the History of Sexuality*, 3, no. 2 (October 1992): 223–44.

13. Ezra H. Heywood, *Cupid's Yokes: Or, The Binding Forces of Conjugal Life* (Princeton, Mass.: Co-operative Publishing Company, 1877), quotes from pp. 4, 3, 5, 8, 5.

14. Ibid., pp. 8–9, 13, 6–7, 18.

15. Ibid., pp. 15–16, 17, 19, 3.

16. Heywood seems to advocate Noyes's position when he states the need to keep "intercourse" under control, keeping within "the associative limit, which is highly invigorating, and not to allow themselves to gravitate to the propagative climax" (ibid., p. 20). He also advocates Noyes's approach as the only wise form of birth control (p. 21). As an individualistic anarchist, Heywood abjured the utopian community's communal arrangements, however (p. 15).

17. Ibid., p. 22.

18. NYSSV, Arrest Record, 1877, Case no. 51, pp. 103–4.

19. Anthony Comstock, *Traps for the Young* (New York: Funk and Wagnalls, 1883), pp. 163–65. Comstock had a warrant and had been deputized to make the arrest.

20. Heywood, *Cupid's Yokes*, p. 20, footnote. According to the note on p. 236, Blatt, in *The Collected Works of Ezra H. Heywood*, reprinted the copy that the assistant district attorney marked as obscene to bring to the attention of the jury. It is interesting that Heywood's source is the British publication George Drysdale, *The Elements of Social Science* (1854), rather than an American one.

21. Heywood, *Cupid's Yokes*, p. 3.

22. Both Ezra and Angela Heywood believed Beecher to be "a lecherous hypocrite, a skulking libertine." Such a move, they felt, sullied free love, a principled movement, by allowing it to be linked to the bawdy vernacular. As they wrote, to "suppose free love means what is 'generally understood' regarding it" is like taking a slaveholder's view of antislavery. "It is a lamentable fact that men's natures are so steeped in lewdness they can scarcely discuss love without besmearing it with their foul imaginations" (editorial, *Word*, 3, no. 8 [December 1874]: 2); Heywood, *Cupid's Yokes*, p. 12.

23. See especially Morris L. Ernst and Alan U. Schwartz, *Censorship: The Search for the Obscene* (New York: Macmillan Company, 1964).

24. David Yassky, "Eras of the First Amendment," *Columbia Law Review*, 91 (1991): 1699–1755.

25. R. T. Trall, a hydropathic reformer, represented a more conservative voice within the third framework. He wrote continuously from 1852; his *Sexual Physiology* was first published in

1866. The account of the trial comes from the *Boston Globe*, "The Courts. United States Circuit Court. Before Judge Clark," January 18, 1878, p. 7.

26. Register of Arrests for Offenses against postal laws, 1864–1897, Record Group 28, Entry 229, National Archives, Washington, D.C.

19: *Constitutionality and Resistance: Bennett, Benedict, and Blatchford*

1. *Ex parte Jackson*, 96 U.S. 736 (1977); David M. Rabban, *Free Speech in Its Forgotten Years* (Cambridge, England: Cambridge University Press, 1997), p. 36. Justice Field was one of many post–Civil War jurists who supported greater regulation in the area of morality at the same time that he sought to unfetter the market from regulation.

2. Perhaps parenthetically it is interesting to note that Tucker, in his lengthy letter to Victoria Woodhull's biographer, discussed his sexual affairs with both Woodhull and Kendrick (Benjamin R. Tucker to Emanie Sachs, c. 1927, Benjamin R. Tucker Collection, Box 9, New York Public Library, New York); as Laura Cuppy Smith, Kendrick had been a loyal supporter of Woodhull.

3. In 1876 Ingersoll seconded the nomination of James G. Blaine at the Republican National Convention; see Paul A. Carter, *The Spiritual Crisis of the Gilded Age* (DeKalb: Northern Illinois University Press, 1971), pp. 9–10. On Abbot, see Lawrence B. Goodheart, "The Ambiguity of Individualism: The National Liberal League's Challenge to the Comstock Law," in *American Chameleon: Individualism in Trans-National Context*, ed. Richard O. Curry and Lawrence B. Goodheart (Kent, Ohio: Kent State University Press, 1991), pp. 133–36; Evelyn A. Kirkley, *Rational Mothers and Infidel Gentlemen: Gender and American Atheism, 1865–1915* (Syracuse, N.Y.: Syracuse University Press, 2000), especially pp. 6–19, 100–2; Carter, *Spiritual Crisis*, p. 10.

4. Rabban, *Free Speech*, p. 38; C. Thomas Dienes, *Law, Politics, and Birth Control* (Urbana: University of Illinois Press, 1972), pp. 68–72. Bennett later charged Colgate with violating the law against the advertising of contraceptive materials when his business distributed a pamphlet that promoted Vaseline with the statement that Vaseline, "charged with four or five grains of salicylic acid, will destroy spermatozoa, without injury to the uterus or vagina"; see D. M. Bennett, *An Open Letter to Samuel Colgate* (New York: D. M. Bennett, 1879), p. 9.

5. Conflict over reform versus repeal was so great that Abbot left the league in 1878, Ingersoll in 1880; see Goodheart, "The Ambituity of Individualism," p. 145.

6. Quoted in Anthony Comstock, *Frauds Exposed; or How the People Are Deceived and Robbed, and Youth Corrupted* (New York: J. Howard Brown, 1880), p. 458.

7. Samuel P. Putnam, *Four Hundred Years of Freethought* (New York, 1894), pp. 538–39; Hal D. Sears, *The Sex Radicals: Free Love in High Victorian America* (Lawrence: Regents Press of Kansas, 1977), pp. 199–200.

8. *Proceedings of the Indignation Meeting, Held in Faneuil Hall, Thursday Evening, August 1, 1878, to Protest the Injury Done to the Freedom of the Press by the Conviction and Imprisonment of Ezra H. Heywood* (Boston: Benj. R. Tucker, publisher, 1878), pp. 7, 8.

9. Putnam, *Four Hundred Years of Freethought*, pp. 818–19; *Proceedings of the Indignation Meeting*, pp. 14–15. *Woodhull and Claflin's Weekly*, which printed her full defense ("The Charge of Obscenity," 5, no. 11 [February 15, 1873]), may have played a role in publicizing the constitutional issue.

10. *Proceedings of the Indignation Meeting*, p. 32.

11. Quote from ibid., p. 44. Heywood seems to have had a similar position. In *Cupid's Yokes*

he had written that "the alarming increase of obscene prints and pictures caused both Houses of the U.S. Congress, March 1, 1873, to pass a bill . . . for the suppression of Obscene Literature." He merely saw its cause differently. The market for this increase was caused by the failure of parents and teachers to educate their children appropriately about sex, forcing them to learn about sex "from their own diseased lives and imaginations, and in the filthy by-ways of society." "Where saving truth should have been planted, error has found an unoccupied field, which it has busily sown, and gathers therefrom a prolific harvest" (p. 11).

12. Putnam, *Four Hundred Years of Freethought*, pp. 694–97; Mary O. Bogard, "D. M. Bennett—Shaker Doctor, Druggist, Editor, and Freethinker," *Pharmacy in History*, 29, no. 3 (1987): 125–29; *Trial of D. M. Bennett in the United States Circuit Court* (New York: Truth Seeker Office, c. 1879), p. 49.

13. *Trial of D. M. Bennett*, pp. 16–17, 58; Putnam, *Four Hundred Years of Freethought*, p. 537.

14. All of these characterizations are from *In Memory of Judge C. L. Benedict* (Brooklyn, N.Y., 1901): "Remarks of Honorable Mark D. Wilber," p. 19; "Remarks of Sidney F. Rawson, Esq.," p. 16; "Remarks of Honorable John J. Allen," p. 20; "Remarks of Honorable Edward B. Thomas, District Judge," p. 31.

15. "Remarks of Honorable John J. Allen," ibid., p. 21; "Remarks of Sidney F. Rawson, Esq.," ibid., pp. 17–18.

16. For Bennett's trial, I rely on transcripts in *Trial of D. M. Bennett*.

17. *Trial of D. M. Bennett*, pp. 23–24, 29, 37. Wilkes wrote that in contrast to the sale of lottery tickets, "the sale of obscene papers is merely an offence against taste, according to the common law, or in other words, common opinion" (see Chapter 8).

18. Ibid., pp. 39–40.

19. Ibid., pp. 41–42, 42–43.

20. Ibid., p. 55.

21. Ibid., p. 60.

22. Ibid., pp. 62, 64.

23. Ibid., pp. 82, 83, 84, 109.

24. Ibid., pp. 99–100.

25. Ibid., p. 131.

26. Ibid., pp. 139, 140, 144.

27. Ibid., pp. 128, 135–36.

28. Ibid., pp. 147, 149.

29. Ibid., p. 152 (italics added).

30. One dissenting juror, Alfred A. Valentine, held out for fifteen hours. In a letter to the *New York Herald*, March 24, 1879, Valentine stated that although he wished to "maintain the right of the author, Mr. Heywood, and of those who agree with him, to differ from me," Benedict's definitions ultimately required him to find Bennett guilty. He hoped that on appeal or through new legislation, the law would be changed (letter reprinted in *Trial of D. M. Bennett*, pp. 171–72).

31. *Trial of D. M. Bennett*, pp. 153, 154; The case *Regina v. Hicklin*, 1868, involved an obscenity prosecution under Lord Campbell's Act of 1857; Chief Justice Alexander Cockburn stated that a work was obscene if "the tendency of the matter charged as obscenity is to deprave and corrupt those whose minds are open to such immoral influences and into whose hands a publication of this sort may fall" (*Regina v. Hicklin*, 3 L.R.-Q.B. 360 [1858]).

32. Putnam, *Four Hundred Years of Freethought*, 539.

33. Martin Henry Blatt, *Free Love and Anarchism: The Biography of Ezra Heywood* (Urbana: University of Illinois Press, 1989), p. 119; Rabban, *Free Thought*, pp. 37–38.

34. *Dictionary of American Biography*, vol. 3 (New York: Charles Scribner's Sons, 1928–36), pp. 359–60.

35. *U.S. v. Bennett, Federal Cases Comprising Cases Argued and Determined in the Circuit and District Courts of the United States*, Book 24 (St. Paul: West Publishing Company, 1896), pp. 1093–1107.

36. In the 1890s, the U.S. Supreme Court did review a number of cases dealing with postal laws and obscenity, but these challenged elements of application, not the basic principles of the laws; see Dorothy Ganfield Fowler, *Unmailable: Congress and the Post Office* (Athens: University of Georgia Press, 1977), pp. 76–79. The administration of censorship by the post office prior to 1930 is dealt with in James C. N. Paul and Murray L. Schwartz, *Federal Censorship: Obscenity in the Mail* (New York: Free Press of Glencoe, 1961), pp. 38–49.

37. Edward Bliss Foote, "Everybody Obscene," *Dr. Foote's Health Monthly*, 2, no. 12 (December 1877): 8. Foote's relations with Bennett and his efforts to aid him can be found in the Ralph Ginzburg Papers, State Historical Society of Wisconsin, Madison, Wisconsin.

38. Rabban, *Free Speech*, pp. 64–76.

ACKNOWLEDGMENTS

A book like this requires many teachers. Recently, when I discovered the 1933 article by Robert E. Riegel on Charles Knowlton, I recalled my long-ago delight at his lecture on Knowlton in a summer school class at Columbia in 1961 and realized something of the nature of scholarship's long lineage and collective nature. I have been fortunate in this decade to become interested in sexual knowledge, obscenity, suppression, and free speech at a time when many could guide me. I am particularly grateful to the scholarship of Nicola Beisel, Janet Farrell Brodie, George Buckley, Patricia Cline Cohen, Timothy J. Gilfoyle, Walter Kendrick, David S. Reynolds, Hal D. Sears, Edward De Grazia, David Rabban, Madeleine B. Stern, the trio of Ian Hunter, David Saunders, and Dugald Williamson, and the collective work represented by the *Journal of the History of Sexuality*. Many of the ideas and judgments that inform this book arose out of the extended conversation that Richard Millington and I had as we co-taught the Introduction to American Studies at Smith College and pondered such nineteenth-century works as Susan Warner's *The Wide, Wide World*. I am grateful to Rick for his helpful insights and differing perspective.

As a student at Wellesley College in 1962, I went to what was then the Radcliffe Women's Archives in Byerly Hall to research a junior paper and returned for a senior honors thesis. The archives provided my first job after college graduation in 1963. As a graduate student at Harvard, I spent many hours reading in the Radcliffe Library. The archives changed its name to the Arthur and Elizabeth Schlesinger Library on the History of Women in America and relocated to the former library building. In 1996–97, I had the pleasure of an office at the Schlesinger when I was an Honorary Fellow. It was both an honor and a delight to return again to the Schlesinger in 2000–01 as a Fellow at the Radcliffe Institute for Advanced Study. I want to thank those who wrote letters on my behalf and those who made my year both productive and pleasant. It was a particular pleasure to have as colleagues Virginia Drachman, Regina Kunzel, Ellen More, and Mary Maples Dunn.

For all who enter its reading room, the American Antiquarian Society is a special place. I first ventured there in 1997 to follow some leads and realized that I had come home. Its extraordinary resources, built over its long life, are a historian's dream. In addition, the educational program makes it possible both for many to research there and for fellows and staff to learn from one another. It is a model of what thoughtful care, applied for many decades, can do to build a collection and make it accessible. Its mission is furthered by a staff who remember that research is fun. Everyone, from custodian to president, is interested in history and the process of research. I am grateful to everyone and for the support and honor of the Mellon Fellowship and of membership in the AAS.

Smith College has an extraordinarily generous sabbatical policy that funded three semesters of my research. In addition, I received from the college resources to travel to archives and funds for capable student researchers. Undergraduate research assistants over the years have lightened my load and made it more enjoyable. I am grateful to Erin Blakemore, Carrie Gray,

Acknowledgments

Brook Hopkins, the late Mildred Joyce, and Lori Kauffman of Smith, and Leslie Bradford of Harvard. More recently, I am thankful for the editorial help of new Smith alumna Kimberly Marlowe. Additional support was granted me by the Gilder Lehrman Foundation, for research in New York City at the New-York Historical Society.

A project such as this requires many libraries and archives. First and foremost is the excellent collection of the Smith College Library, supported by the Five College consortium. The efficient staff of the Interlibrary Loan Office brought materials from many other libraries to Northampton. Kenneth Cobb, director of the Municipal Archives of New York City, generously encouraged me to research the District of Attorney Indictment Papers using microfilm reels through Interlibrary Loan. As a fellow at the Schlesinger, I have enjoyed extensive use of the Harvard Library system, especially the incomparable U.S. history collection in Widener and holdings of the Schlesinger, Houghton, Countway, Baker, Theatre Collection, and law school libraries. In addition, I am grateful to the University of Texas at Austin and the Harry Ransom Collection, the Boston Public Library, the University of Southern Illinois at Carbondale, the Huntington Library, the Kinsey Institute at University of Indiana, the Franklin Trask Library of the Andover Newton Theology School, the Library of Congress, the National Archives, the Kautz Family YMCA Archives, the New-York Historical Society, the Museum of the City of New York, the New York Public Library, the Old York Collection of the City University of New York Graduate Center, the Municipal Archives of New York City, and Vassar College Special Collections. I also found useful material in the personal collections of Leo Hershkowitz and Charles Rosenberg.

Once again I was fortunate to have the encouragement and editorial judgments of David Thelen, as I worked out my ideas in article form for "Victoria Woodhull, Anthony Comstock, and Conflict over Sex in the United States in the 1870s," published in the *Journal of American History* in September 2000. I learned a good deal from the criticism of outside readers, especially Anonymous Reader B (who turned out to be Patricia Cline Cohen). I am grateful to the journal and its editor for permission to reprint portions of the article. A number of audiences in the last few years provided me with provocative questions and research guidance, including those at the University of Texas, the Five College Women's Studies Research Center, the Schlesinger Library, the American Studies Association, and the Organization of American Historians.

Supporters along the way deserve special mention. Mary Dunn merits special thanks: it was great not to lose her as a fearless leader. R. C. Binstock first pushed me to examine the materials of sporting life at first hand. Pat Cohen and Gail Bederman were extraordinarily generous in providing research help and stimulating conversation, as were David Stewart and many colleagues at the American Antiquarian Society. Georgia B. Barnhill and Russell Martin at the AAS gave enthusiastic help with their collections. Charles E. Rosenberg was hospitable when I came to examine his library. Leo Hershkowitz was unfailingly generous and kind.

This book owes a particularly heavy debt to family historians Daniel Horowitz and Sarah E. Horowitz, who were willing to listen and confront my early written efforts. I am grateful to the thoughtful and challenging readings given to the first draft by Dan, Lois Banner, Mary Maples Dunn, Desley Deacon, Patricia Cline Cohen, Ellen More, Gail Bederman, and Kimberly Marlowe. I have had the good fortune to have the encouragement and advice of editor Jane N. Garrett and literary agent Nikki Smith. My thanks to all.

INDEX

Page numbers in *italics* refer to illustrations.

Index

Chiswell (Boston bookseller), 19

cholera, 94

Chorier, Nicholas, 32

Christian Commission, *see* United States Christian Commission

Christianity, 26
  common law and, 72–3
  see also specific sects

Christianity, evangelical, 5–8, 299–300, 358–60, 363–9, 413, 439–42
  abortion opposed by, 207, 209
  Christian restoration and, 359–60, 381, 420, 440
  Comstock and, 317, 318, 394, 403
  freethinkers vs., 12, 47–50, 61–73, 86, 159, 420, 452n
  obscenity fought by, 6, 11, 271, 358, 440
  Paine vs., 70
  "Portland test" and, 363–4
  reform physiology and, 14, 93–4, 115, 120
  and sex at the core of being, 252, 253, 318
  technology used by, 49, 128
  tract societies and, 6, 47–50, 145, 146, 148, 150
  see also moral reformers; revivals; Young Men's Christian Association

chronique scandaleuse, 53

Chudacoff, Howard, 464n

Church of Jesus Christ of Latter-Day Saints, *see* Mormons

Circuit Court of Common Pleas, 43

Cisco, Mary (Duchess de Berri), 157, 286–7

Civilization, 261, 263, 267, 268, 290

Civil War, U.S., 12, 13, 317–20, 337–8, 344, 349, 356, 358, 359, 361, 391, 403, 411, 440
  Y.M.C.A. and, 305–8, 314, 315, 477n–8n
  see also Union soldiers

Claflin, Mrs., 343, 347

Claflin, Tennessee (Tennie C.), 343, 347, 357, 376, 378–9, 380

Claflin, Victoria, *see* Woodhull, Victoria

Clark, Daniel, 415–18, 426

Clark & Jesup, 300

Clay, E. W., 212, 214–17, *215*, *216*

Cleland, John, 32–5, 225, 239
  see also Fanny Hill

clerks, 11, 87, 228, 318, 402, 485n
  moral reformers and, 144, 152–3
  sporting culture and, 121–2, 139–43, 168, 299–300

Clifton, Josephine, 166–7, 463n, 464n

clitoris, 27, 81, 114, 293, 332

Cochran, D. H., 384

Cochran, McLean and Company, 367, 372

Cockburn, Alexander, 491n

Cohen, Patricia Cline, 462n, 464n

coitus, *see* sexual intercourse

coitus interruptus, 60–1, 255, 276, 281, 283, 334–5

coitus reservatus, 254–6, 413

Cole, Cornelius, 381

Colfax, Schuyler, 363

Colgate, Samuel, 384, 406, 407, 421

Colyer, Vincent, 306, 308, 313

Commentaries on the Laws of England (Blackstone), 40–1

commerce, 134
  erotica and, 9–11, 19, 25, 32–5, 164, 251, 318, 360–2, 369–71, 404–5, 439, 441, 443
  working-class culture and, 134–40
  see also newspapers; penny journalism; sporting culture; sporting press

Commercial Advertiser, 149

common law, 313, 345, 358, 361, 402, 419, 434–5, 448n
  Christianity and, 72–3
  couverture and, 50–1
  English, 12, 25, 37–42, 177, 183, 422, 426, 440, 448n
  obscene libel and, 12, 37–42, 160, 162, 176–9, 191, 222, 404, 415, 416, 440, 441, 448n
  replaced by legal codes, 251

Commonwealth v. Holmes, 434

Commonwealth v. Sharpless, 176–7

communism, 343, 349
  Bible, 252, 254–5

Communist Manifesto (Marx and Engels), 343

complex marriage, 7, 251, 253, 473n

Comstock, Anthony, 4, 10, 13–15, 248, 367–417, 372, 421, *444*, 484n–5n
  background of, 317, 385
  celebrity of, 376, 385, 390
  in Civil War, 317–18
  crusade of, 386–403, 486n–8n
  domesticity of, 367
  Haynes opposed by, 248, 371, 386, 469n–70n
  language and writing style of, 390–4
  motives of, 385, 431
  and New York Society for the Suppression of Vice, 383–94, 396–8, 400, 403, 404
  religious work of, 367–8
  Sabbatarian court battle of, 368–9
  as special agent of U.S. Post Office, 14, 15, 381–4, 389, 395–6, 403–18
  Woodhull opposed by, 343, 357, 358, 376–80, 407, 414–5, 420, 422–3
  Y.M.C.A. and, 367, 371–4, 379–84, 387, 391–3, 403, 415, 441, 443, 477n–8n

Comstock, Chester, 317

Comstock, Margaret Hamilton, 367

Comstock, Polly, 317

Comstock, Samuel, 317

Index

Index

Index

Index

Gilmore, William, 43–4

Ginzberg, Lori, 452n

Godwin, William, 46, 65

"Gonorrhoea Dormientium" (Knowlton), 112

Gould, Jay, 324

Gove, Mary, 4, 109–11, 260, 267, 288–96, 299, 331, 457n–8n, 474n, 475n–6n
  background of, 109–10, 284–5
  first marriage of, 109, 288, 294
  on masturbation, 7, 101–2, 105, 107, 110
  Nichols's marriage to, 285, 289, 476n

Graham, Sylvester, 4, 6, 7, 86, 92–9, 102, 107–12, 118, 202, 273, 312, 328, 332, 333, 457n
  background of, 94
  Comstock compared with, 394
  diet as viewed by, 94, 95, 96, 103, 107, 108, 111, 290, 294
  Nichols-Gove collaboration affected by, 290–3

Grandin, Edward M., 371, 390

grand juries, 149–50, 181–9, 192, 222, 241, 388, 389, 472n–3n
  abortion and, 200, 201, 209

"Grand Trial Dance Between Nance Holmes and Suse Bryant, on Long Wharf, Boston" (Manning), 162

Grandy, Harriet, 170, 187, 464n

Grant, Ulysses S., 381, 382, 434

Graves, George R., 367, 371–2

Greeley, Horace, 173, 244, 261, 269, 474n

Green, Amanda, 171, 185

Green, Sarah, 170

Gregory, Samuel, 101, 102, 105

Griffin, Ellen, 323

Griffith, Robert, 369

Grimké, Angelina, 257, 264

Grimké, Sarah, 257, 264

Grosvenor, Mason, 82–3

Guarneri, Carl J., 472n

Gurley, Albert, 225

gynecology, 92, 207

Habits of a Well-Organized Married Life, The (Beach), 282–4

Hackett, John, 242

Hall of Science, New York, 44–50, 61, 70, 148

Halttunen, Karen, 230

Hamblin, Thomas S., 166, 174–5, 176, 182

Hamilton, Margaret, see Comstock, Margaret Hamilton

Hannam, Mrs. Eleazar, 20, 23

Harland, Thomas, 408

Harmonial Philosophy, 264

Harmony, 261, 267

Harper's Weekly, 377, 389

Harris, Gillen and Company, 238

Harris, Prescott F., 235–8, 272, 273

Harvard Theatre Collection, 216–17, 216

Hawk and Buzzard, 148–9, 173

Hawthorne, Nathaniel, 445n

Hayes, Rutherford B., 424

Haynes, Mary, 225, 371, 373–4

Haynes, William, 210, 224–6, 248, 371, 386, 469n–70n

H. Cameron and Company, 369

Health Journal and Advocate of Physiological Reform, 284

health reform, 7, 87–91, 94–6, 103, 107–9, 259–60, 272–84, 288, 289, 352, 394

Heenan, John, 320

Hennequin, Victor, 263

Henry, J., 281–4

Henry's Private Adviser (Henry), 281–2

Heywood, Angela Tilton, 350, 355, 411–15, 425, 489n

Heywood, Ezra, 8, 14, 350, 355, 411, 489n, 490n–1n
  Comstock Law and, 404, 405, 410–20, 422, 424, 427, 428, 429, 431, 433, 435

Hicklin test, 433–5

Hisen, Pat, 228

Histoire de Dom B (Latouche), 32

Hoar, E. Rockwood, 308

Hoar, Samuel, 308

Hobbs, Richard, 211, 219–20, 222, 225, 226

Hodgman, D., 373

Hoffy, A. H., 217, 218

Holland, 93

Hollen, Sarah Elizabeth, 110

Hollick, Frederick, 7, 86, 91, 113–15, 120, 125, 208, 256, 274–8, 275, 280, 282, 284, 338, 405, 474n–5n

Holmes, Peter, 43–4, 160, 219

Holt, Francis Ludlow, 41–2, 72, 73, 177, 191, 192, 435

homeopathy, 89

homosexuality, 31, 53, 172, 230, 291–2, 447n, 464n–5n
  female, 291–2
  masturbation and, 456n, 457n

Hone, Philip, 125

Hooker, Isabella Beecher, 264, 345–6

House Breaker, The (Thompson), 230

House of Commons, British, 39

House of Lords, British, 39, 427–8

House of Refuge, 150

House of Representatives, U.S., 61, 260, 345, 380, 382, 421

Howe, William F., 373, 378, 422–3

Hoxie, Joseph, 126

Hudson, Frederick, 173

Huestis, Charles, 211

Index

Index

Index

Index

Index

Index

Index

Index